The Israeli
Legal System

The Israeli Legal System

Marcia Gelpe

EMERITA PROFESSOR OF LAW
WILLIAM MITCHELL COLLEGE OF LAW

CAROLINA ACADEMIC PRESS

Durham, North Carolina

ISBN: 978-1-59460-868-1
Paperback Printing: 978-1-5310-0824-6
LCCN: 2012940584

Carolina Academic Press
700 Kent Street
Durham, North Carolina 27701
Telephone (919) 489-7486
Fax (919) 493-5668
www.cap-press.com

Printed in the United States of America
2017 Printing

*To Eliana Sarah Yonah, Bracha Rivka Yonah,
and Reuben Ziv Gelpe Salamon, my three
Israeli and American grandchildren*

Contents

Preface

This book is about the legal system of the country of Israel. The Israeli legal system would be generally understandable to an American lawyer. This book emphasizes the things that are different. This approach supplies the student with the ability to understand the features of Israeli law that would not otherwise be familiar. It also gives the best grounds for comparative law analysis. Most chapters describe the differences between Israeli and American law and investigate the reasons for and the implications of these differences.

Format of This Book

Presentation

Each chapter (except chapter 2) contains original material. American law students and lawyers are accustomed to learning law by reading legal documents, not just by reading about law, and this book follows that valuable tradition. Original material is typically followed by Comments, designed to aid in understanding the original material and its place in the Israeli legal system. Most chapters also have questions designed to foster thoughtful reflection about the material presented.

Translation and Editing

Primary Israeli legal material is published in Hebrew. Unless otherwise noted, the translations from Hebrew in this book are by the author. Translations are not literal, but are designed to convey the same sense in English that is conveyed by the original Hebrew text. The translation of some statutes and cases has been taken from other sources. Where this has been done, the source of the translation is noted. Translations taken from other sources have been edited by the author of this book for style and to make them more understandable to American students of the law.

In places where full paragraphs of Israeli statutes or regulations have been omitted, the omissions are not indicated by ellipses. The original section numbers are retained. Omissions from cases, except those in the middle of paragraphs, are not indicated. Israeli cases with new legal holdings are typically very long, often more than fifty pages, so the cases have been heavily edited to reduce their length. Footnotes in the original Israeli cases have been omitted. All footnotes in cases that appear in this book have been added by the author and explain terms or historical or other references that are likely to be unfamiliar to the American reader.

A Word about Gender

It is customary in English these days to avoid gender-specific language when a statement is not intended to apply only to people of one sex. Partly because everything in Hebrew is necessarily expressed in either male or female form, and partly because of the customary way Hebrew is written, it is not common to use gender-neutral language in Hebrew. The translations do not use gender-neutral language where doing so would require altering the original in a way that obscures its meaning. No offense is intended.

Spelling and Usage

As a result of the influence of the British rule in the area now covered by Israel, discussed in chapter 2, many English-language Israeli publications adopt British spelling and usage, which is in some respects different from spelling and usage common in the United States. For example, the British spelling is "labour," but the American is "labor." The British write, "He is in hospital," but Americans write, "He is in the hospital." This book adopts American spelling and usage except for documents originally written in English that use British spelling and usage.

Citations and Format

Because citations to Hebrew language materials will not be meaningful to readers of English, most citations within translated cases are omitted without indication of the omissions. Similarly, where a translated case set out in this book includes a quotation from another Israeli case, the quotation may be omitted without indication. Some citations to English language materials are retained to allow the reader to see the types of materials used as sources by the Israeli courts, but where citations are omitted, the omission is not indicated. The format of citations that are given within cases has been changed to conform to Bluebook citation rules. Court cases in Hebrew typically have numbered paragraphs. These are omitted in the cases as presented in this book.

Citations to Israeli statutes do not follow the Bluebook. The Bluebook calls for citation to Laws of the State of Israel (L.S.I.) for statutes. This is a state-published translation of statutes into English. These volumes are not up to date and the translation is not official. The author of this book has translated the statutes to allow, where possible, use of terms familiar to American readers. The L.S.I. translations do not necessarily have this goal. In the few places where the L.S.I. translation is used, the citation to L.S.I. is given. For other statutes, the Bluebook alternative citation is to the official source of original Hebrew Israeli statutes, Sefer HaChokim (Book of Statutes), commonly abbreviated as SH. Citations to SH would in most cases be either inaccurate or cumbersome. Most Israeli statutes are frequently amended and accurate citation to SH would require citations to all the places where amendments appear. In any case, these citations are unlikely to be useful to American readers of English. Therefore, no citation source is given for most Israeli statutes. They are cited by name and year, with the name translated into English.

Reported Israeli court cases are cited to the official reporter. Most unreported cases are available through several commercial subscription services and can easily be located in any one of them by case number and name, which are supplied. Many important Israeli Supreme Court cases are published in English by the Supreme Court. Where such English language translations are available, they are indicated in footnotes.

Students wishing to pursue further research in Israeli law but who do not read Hebrew will have limited access to primary materials. Chapter 3 provides information on accessing official materials available in English. Although accessing primary material in English is difficult, it is much easier to find English-language discussions of Israeli law. A great number of law review articles on various aspects of Israeli law are published in American law journals; some also appear in English-language European journals. Most of these are written by Israeli academics, who are encouraged to publish in English to reach a wider audience than they could reach by publishing in their native language. These articles can be located through the usual means of search for law journal publications.

Acknowledgments

Colleagues at both William Mitchell College of Law in St. Paul, Minnesota, and at Netanya Academic College School of Law in Israel have been enormously helpful in suggesting material and explaining legal issues. At William Mitchell, I have relied on the wise counsel of Professors Jay Erstling, Daniel Kleinberger, Michael Steenson, and Deborah Schmedemann. I received excellent assistance from the research librarians at William Mitchell College of Law. Neal Axton spent many long hours reading over material and helping find and properly cite source material. Jean Boos, Karen Westwood, and Janelle Beitz gave additional essential assistance. The circulation staff, headed by Ayanna Muata, obtained many obscure documents for my use. I am also indebted to Jennifer Miller, the administrative assistant who was patient enough to work with me and to proofread the manuscript; Cal Bonde, who formatted and typed the manuscript; and to Bonnie Claxton, Marissa Dietz, Ochen Kaylan, Erik Levy, James Ristvedt, and Paul Storm, William Mitchell College of Law students who helped with research and review of the manuscript.

In Israel, my colleagues Professor Hadara Bar-Moor, Dr. Barry Feinstein, Dr. Moshe Gelbard, Professor Ruth Plato-Shinar, and Dr. Yuval Sinai helped me identify the main features of their fields of expertise. Vice President and Dean Sinai Deutch brought me to Netanya Academic College and enabled me to work with these outstanding people.

William Mitchell College of Law supported the development of this book by providing generous research grants, funds for research assistants, and, most importantly, a supportive atmosphere. I appreciate the faith President and Dean Eric Janus and former Vice Dean Niels Schaumann have shown in me.

My husband Dennis spent hours reviewing the manuscript and forgiving me for being preoccupied with my work so much of the time. My children, Leah, Rafi, Yaffa, Shawn, Joey, and Rona have been my cheerleaders.

The following publishers graciously provided permission to reproduce excerpts from their copyrighted publications. For those publications originally in Hebrew, they also permitted the author to make minor changes in the translations.

Restatement, Second, Contracts, © 1981 by The American Law Institute. Reproduced with permission. All rights reserved.

Restatement Third, Torts: Liability for Physical and Emotional Harm, © 2010 by The American Law Institute. Reprinted with permission. All rights reserved.

Excerpts from English translations of opinions of the Supreme Court of Israel in the following cases: Academic Center of Law and Business, Human Rights Division v. Minister of Finance, Adalah Legal Centre for Arab Minority Rights in Israel v. Minister of Defense, Adalah Legal Center for Arab Minority Rights in Israel v. Minister of Religious Affairs, Anonymous v. Tel-Aviv-Jaffa Regional Rabbinical Court, Beit Sourik Village Council v. Government of Israel, Bishara v. Attorney General, Design 22 — Shark Deluxe Furniture, Ltd. v. Rozenzweig, Dobrin v. Israel Prison Service, El Al Israel Airlines Ltd. v. Danielowitz, Estate of Ettinger v. Company for the Reconstruction and Development of the Jewish Quarter, Luzon v. Government of Israel, Nahmani v. Nahmani, Schnitzer v. Chief Military Censor, Solodkin v. Mayor of Tiberias, and United Mizrahi Bank v. Migdal Communal Village: The Supreme Court of the State of Israel. Reprinted with permission. All rights reserved.

The Israeli Legal System

Part One

Introduction

Chapter 1

Why Study Israeli Law?

This book is about the law of the country called the State of Israel, or, simply, Israel.

Israeli law is a fascinating legal subject. Israeli law has developed quite recently, since the founding of the state in 1948, but has roots in several very old legal systems. Some Israeli law is derived from British law, some from Ottoman law, and some imported from other countries. In addition, certain areas of Israeli law derive from religious law, both Jewish law[1] and Islamic law. Israeli law also has many very new and modern features, which reflect the once socialist and now increasingly capitalist nature of the state. All of this fits together in an interesting and sometimes surprising manner. For example, although people of different religions cannot marry each other in Israel, if they marry outside of the country, their marriage is recognized for most purposes under Israeli law. The limitation on intermarriage within Israel stems from Ottoman law, later adopted by the British under the British Mandate,[2] and still later adopted by Israel. Under this system, the religious authorities have exclusive power to perform marriages, and none of the recognized religious authorities will marry two people of different religions. Mixed marriages entered into outside of the borders of Israel are accepted as valid marriages under Israeli law. This is based on Israeli adoption of the doctrine of comity of nations, under which one country recognizes legal acts of another nation. Thus, if a Jew and a Muslim wish to marry, they must leave the country, most often by taking a short flight to Cyprus, and marry there. They will then be treated as husband and wife under Israeli law.

This book provides an opportunity to study all these aspects of Israeli law. The material presented is based on the proposition that the legal system of any country reflects the history of the country, the nature of its society, and its basic values. Israeli law provides a particularly good forum for American law students to examine the influence of these factors on legal development. Both the United States and Israel were born from entities governed largely by British law, but law has developed in the two countries in different historical and social contexts. Therefore the study of Israeli law gives Americans an opportunity to observe how history and societal values influence the content of the law. In Israel, the historical influence on the law is obvious in the mix of sources of law. It also explains other features of Israeli law, such as the strange situation described above under which the religious authorities have exclusive control over marriage. The socialist attitude of the founders of the state is reflected in the strong legal protections given

---

1. The distinction between Israeli law, as law of the State of Israel, and Jewish law, as law of the Jews, is discussed in chapter 12.

2. The term British Mandate describes the British rule from 1917 until 1948. It is discussed in chapter 2.

to workers. The influence of the nature of the society is seen, for example, in the Israeli law on surrogacy, which derives from the high value the society puts on children and family life.

There are several justifications for studying Israeli law. One is that it is so interesting. This is not dry material, concentrated on the intricacies of a complex code. The Israeli legal system is full of surprises for the American student of the law.

The study of Israeli law can also be utilitarian. Lawyers are often deeply involved in the many business transactions between Israeli and American businesses. Israeli products are sold in the United States and American products are sold in Israel. One hundred and forty-five Israeli companies are listed on the NASDAQ.[3] The list includes giants such as Teva, one of the largest generic pharmaceutical companies in the world; and Check Point Software Technologies, a leading company in internet security. Furthermore, major American companies have significant presence in Israel. These include well-known firms such as Intel (whose Pentium and Centrino chips and dual-core processing were developed in Israel), Microsoft, and 3M. In addition, Israel has a vigorous start-up sector, with 3000 such operations reported in 2010, a number that exceeds that for all of Europe and is close to that in the United States.[4] American companies have shown a good deal of interest in Israeli start-ups, acquiring many of them.[5] Even when the Israeli side of a transaction is handled by Israeli lawyers, an American lawyer with some background in Israeli law and legal culture is in a much better position to represent the American clients in business deals between companies in one country and purchasers in the other.

Study of Israeli law is also valuable as an exercise in comparative law. The United States and Israel have much in common. By observing differences in the legal systems of the two countries, Americans can learn a lot about alternative ways of handling legal issues that arise within the American legal system. This identification of alternatives should lead an American lawyer to ask why the American system uses the mechanisms it does, what justifies or explains the differences in the law of the two countries, whether the American way of handling a legal issue is the best way, and what can be learned for improving the American system.

Finally many people read about Israel in the news or hear about the country in other media reports. Others know about Israel because of their religious backgrounds. Both types of exposure make people curious about the country, and learning about its law is a good way of learning about the country.

This book is about the domestic law of Israel. It does not cover the law of the Arab-Israeli conflict, which is mainly one of politics, not law. To the extent that law does apply, it is mainly international law, although some Israeli law is also relevant. A considerable amount of easily-accessible published material addresses the legal issues of that dispute.

And now, before we begin, here is a quick taste of Israeli law. This is an uncharacteristically brief case, decided in the Supreme Court of Israel. This short and rather quirky case illustrates a number of features of Israeli law that are covered in this book.

---

3. Listed by Globes, the leading Israeli financial newspaper, on November 30, 2009, http://www.globes.co.il/news/home.aspx?fid=3670&indexid=12.

4. Daniel Doron, Opinion, *Crony Capitalism in Israel*, WALL ST. J., Oct. 9–10, 2010, at A13.

5. On Israeli start-ups in general, see DAN SENOR & SAUL SINGER, STARTUP NATION: THE STORY OF ISRAEL'S ECONOMIC MIRACLE (2009).

Israeli Case

Avni v. State of Israel

In the Supreme Court of Israel, Sitting as the High Court of Justice
HCJ 6167/09 (Nov. 18, 2009)

Justice E. Rubenstein:

The Petitioner asks that after his death he not be buried but that instead his body be given to animals to provide them with food. He turned to us after he submitted a will with such a provision to the Ministry of Justice and was informed by the ministry that the will would violate the laws of the state. The reason the Petitioner gives for what he proposes is that he, like everyone else, is destined "to live and thrive at the expense of animals and plants and, when it comes time to die, I should serve as food for the same animals and plants that sustained my life."

The Respondent is of the opinion that what the Petitioner proposes would be at odds with the public interest in not having the corpse of a person being thrown out as food for animals, would violate the standard of human dignity, and would cause environmental pollution.

We have no grounds for granting the petition. For any person to be granted such a wish — which is different, for example, from a person's dedicating his body to science, with eventual burial (governed by section 5(a) of the Anatomy and Pathology Law, 5713-1953) — conflicts with both the public good and value of human dignity. Even if the Petitioner relinquishes his own claim to dignity, he cannot relinquish the claim of others to dignity, which will be adversely affected by an act involving debasement and environmental degradation. We need not consider what would happen if many people turned to us with the same request, how this would affect the environment and what kinds of problems would result. In the Bible the prophet Jeremiah spoke of a terrible vision, as part of a curse, "and the carcass of man shall fall silently upon the fields and shall be like the sheaf that is left behind by the reaper, and there is no one to collect it." (Jeremiah 9:21). In Israeli law, the dignity of man is not limited to respecting the last will of the deceased, but also entails respecting the dignity of the living and their sensibilities (see *Additional Consideration HCJ 3299/93 Vickselbaum v. Minister of Defense*, 49(2) PD 195, 200–01, Justice S. Levine).

Justice Procaccia in *HCJ 52/06 Alecksa Corp. v. Weisenthal Center* (unpublished) described the normative foundation for the subject of burial and observed that, "a line of legislative actions protects the dignity of the deceased by protecting the integrity of the body after death, and by providing for an obligatory dignified burial." See also section 8(2) of the Public Health Ordinance, 1940, requiring burial within 48 hours.

In addition, Dr. Michael Vigoda, the head of the area of Jewish law in the Ministry of Justice, who has investigated the normative issues in the case, wrote, "It is strange that there is no Israeli law that requires burial of the dead or some other treatment of dead bodies" (except the Law on Military Cemeteries, 5910-1950, that in section 4(a) requires burial of soldiers). The author notes that a private bill on the subject was presented (by Knesset member E. Yishai) (Proposed Law on the Obligation to Provide Burials, 2005).... According to Dr. Vigoda, the Public Health Ordinance does not explicitly require burial, although in my opinion it is possible to find support for such a requirement in section 8(2) of that law, and also in requirement for removal of nuisances in environmental laws, such as the Law for Prevention of Nuisances, 5721-1961 (see, for example, section 3 which provides, "No one shall cause a substantial or unreasonable odor from any source, if it harms, or be likely to harm, a person found in the area or passing by;" and see also section 4 on the subject of air pollution.)

It is clear that what the Petitioner requests, even if he were to renounce his claim to his own dignity, would harm the dignity of others who would be exposed to this spectacle and to the accompanying health hazard. This does not even address the interests of his family members, whose view of the request is not before us.

Jewish law and tradition recognize a *requirement* of burial; see Rambam,[6] Judges, Mourning 4: 1–4; Shulchan Aruch, Yoreh De'ah[7] Mourning, 348: 2–3: "Do not listen to the person who asks not to be buried," "even if someone has no money and directed that he not be buried, we do not follow his request." See also Professor N. Rakover, *The Dignity of Creation is Great: Human Dignity as a Supreme Value*, 91–92, who cites the statement of Rabbi Meir of Rothenburg[8] (Responsa[9] of the Maharam of Rothenburg, 5526) who said, "The scholars felt that they should give honor to the dead even if against a person's will, even if the person did not want it for himself," and, "We do not listen to the command of a person who says we should write degrading things about him on his gravestone." As Dr. Vigoda states (on p.4), "Judaism strongly objects to cremation ... which is defined as a disgrace to the dead, a degradation and an insult to the dignity of man, such that there is no force to the last will of the person who asks to be cremated." If cremation is forbidden, it is even more clear, that the more objectionable action of throwing a body into a field is forbidden.

In light of all of these reasons, we cannot grant the petition. We wish the petitioner a long life.

Comments

The case is a petition against a decision of a state agency. In this case, the petitioner asked the Court to invalidate the Ministry of Justice's decision that it would not allow the enforcement of the petitioner's proposed will after his death. The petitioner was able to bring his case against the state straight to the Supreme Court of Israel. Therefore this is not an appeal from a lower court, but rather a case of original court jurisdiction. This unusual feature of Israeli law is discussed in chapter 5. The Supreme Court *sat as* the High Court of Justice. This is discussed in the same chapter. The Court based its decision on its conception of public good and of human dignity, on statutes, and on case precedent. "Human dignity" is a constitutional right in Israeli law and is discussed in chapter 8. The

---

6. Rambam was an eminent Jewish scholar and philosopher who lived in the twelfth century in Spain and Egypt. The name "Rambam" is an acronym for his full name, Rabbi Moses ben (son of) Maimon. One of his famous works is the Mishneh Torah ("Repetition of the Torah"), which is a code of Jewish law, and the reference here is to one section of that work.

7. The term Yoreh De'ah ("Teacher of Knowledge") is used to refer to two different, related and major works of Jewish law. The first Yoreh De'ah is part of a larger compilation of Jewish law called the Arba'ah Turim ("The Four Rows"). It was written by Rabbi Jacob ben Asher, who worked in the thirteenth and fourteenth centuries, C.E., first in Germany and later in Spain. (Jews, and Israelis, customarily use the term C.E., "Common Era," rather than A.D., "Anno Domini," ("the year of our lord"). See chapter 2.) A later work, also called Yoreh De'ah, is part of the compilation of laws called the Shulchan Aruch ("The Set Table"), written by Rabbi Joseph Karo in the sixteenth century in Safed, a city now in Israel.

8. Rabbi Meir of Rothenburg worked in thirteenth century Germany.

9. Responsa is a type of literature in Jewish law made up of questions and responses. See chapter 12.

types of statutes are discussed in chapter 3; the role of precedent, in chapter 5. The judges who decided the case also examined the Jewish law on the issue before them. Jewish law and its status in the Israeli legal system are discussed in chapters 12, along with Shari'a (Islamic law) and the law of other religious communities in Israel.

The case shows the difference between Israeli law (state law) and religious law. The Court based its decision on sources of state law familiar to American lawyers: the public interest, constitutional law, statutory law, and case law. The analysis was less structured, perhaps, than the analysis you might expect from an American court, but it referred to the same sorts of sources. The reference to Jewish law and to the Bible was added, but was not necessary to the decision. Jewish law is not state law for the issue of disposal of corpses. Religious law does serve as Israeli state law, but only for specific limited subjects (mainly marriage and divorce) and only when Israeli state statutes provide that religious law controls. In such cases, laws of several different religions come into play. All of this is discussed in chapter 12.

Three justices decided this case. Fifteen justices now serve on the Supreme Court, but the Court commonly sits in panels of three. See chapter 5. Often each justice writes a separate opinion, but in this case, all three justices agreed to the opinion presented above. The panel in this case reflects the diversity in the Court: one was a Jewish man, one was a Jewish woman, and one was an Arab man. Of the fifteen justices on the Court, four are women (including the Associate Chief Justice) and one is an Arab. The makeup of Israeli society is discussed in chapter 2.

In the opinion, there are citations to both the Public Health Ordinance, 1940, and to the Law for Prevention of Nuisances, 5721-1961, as well as discussion of other Laws. Both *ordinances* and *laws* are statutes. The former originated during the period of the British Mandate from 1917 to 1948; a statute called a law is original Israeli legislation. Laws use the common Israeli method of dating, giving both the date on the Jewish calendar and the corresponding common date. The calendar is described in chapter 2.

Chapter 2

Geography, History, and Society

Because a country's laws are so heavily influenced by its history, societal structure, culture, economy, and geography, we begin with a survey of these matters. History has a heavy influence on law. In the United States, the historical tie with England explains why we have the common law system and not a civil law system. The history of slavery in the United States also explains the heavy emphasis on equal protection law. In Israel, history similarly explains the origin of many laws, although because the history is so extraordinarily complex, the connection is complex and the result often very complicated. Societal structure also has an effect on law. In the United States, for example, the particular religious nature of American society has made abortion a major issue not only in the political realm but also in law. Israelis, by contrast, are for the most part uninterested in the issue of abortion. Some groups practice it and some do not, but the law surrounding the issue is not significant. Culture also has its claim. The American culture of individualism, personal independence, and fear of tyranny has strong effects on the constitutional separation of powers doctrine, designed to limit governmental power, and also on the social welfare system. Furthermore, Americans by culture pay a lot of attention to their government, and so they are deeply concerned about legal and governmental arrangements. Israelis have a deeper sense of communal interdependence and mutual responsibility, and this strongly influenced governmental arrangements, at least until the recent wave of free-market capitalism. Another influence on a country's laws is the wealth of the country. A wealthy country will be able to afford more social services and will anchor their provision in the legal regime. Finally, geography and climate play a role. A water-rich area will not need the kind of laws about allocating and saving water that are essential in a water-poor area. For example, the traditional system of riparian water rights in the water-rich eastern United States was not adopted in the more arid west, which developed a system of prior appropriation.

In the material below, geography is considered first. Begin by finding Israel on a map.

A. Geography and Climate

Israel is located at the eastern end of the Mediterranean Sea, at the southwest corner of Asia and bordering on Africa. Lebanon is on its border to the north, the Mediterranean Sea and Egypt to the west, the Gulf of Eilat (a branch of the Red Sea, and also known as the Gulf of Aqaba) to the south, and Syria and Jordan to the east. Part of the western border touches Gaza and much of the eastern border touches on areas under partial or complete control of the Palestinian Authority.

The capital of the country is Jerusalem, located in the Judean hills, just east of the center of the country from east to west and about centrally located from north to south.

Israel is about 8522 square miles in area; this includes two lakes, both of which are well known: the Sea of Galilee and the Dead Sea.[1] Israel is roughly the size of New Jersey, the fourth smallest of the US states. Israel is long and narrow: it is 290 miles long, 85 miles wide at its widest point, and 9 miles wide at its narrow waist, from the sea at Netanya to the Palestinian Authority city of Tulkarm.

Both the Sea of Galilee and the Dead Sea are below sea level. The Dead Sea surface, at 1385 feet below sea level, is the lowest point on the surface of the earth. Fed by the Jordan River and nearby springs, it has no natural outlet. Evaporation of water leaves behind the salts, causing it to have a salinity level substantially higher than that of the ocean.

Israel has a fertile but narrow coastal plain. The central inland areas are hilly, as is the north. Part of the northern portion of the country is forested. The southern part of the country is occupied by a large desert, the Negev. The Jordan River Valley runs along a portion of the eastern border. This valley runs along the Afro-Syrian rift, which runs from the Syrian-Turkish border in the north to the Zambezi River in Mozambique in Africa.

Approximately half the land is semi-arid. Annual precipitation, which falls almost exclusively from November to April, is 20–30 inches in the north and only one inch in the south. The humidity is high on the coast but very low in the hills and Jordan River Valley.

B. History

1. Dates

In the brief history that follows, dates are given in the format typically used in Israel. *BCE* (Before the Common Era) is used rather than *BC* (Before Christ), and *CE* (Common Era) is used in place of *AD* (Anno Domini—In the Year of Our Lord). For obvious reasons, a Jewish state does not measure time in terms of Jesus Christ, but neither does it divorce itself from the common measurement of time. Thus, the terms indicated here are used.

Many Israelis see their history as beginning with the residence of Abraham and his descendants in the area now included in the State of Israel. This very long view of history might seem strange, and even irrelevant, to many Americans, but that may be a product to the relative brevity of history of the current rulers in the United States. (Of course, Native Americans, or American Indians, have a long history in the area that is now the United States.) In fact, even many non-religious Israelis read the Bible as history.

Abraham and his family came to the area in about the seventeenth century BCE. After a period of slavery in Egypt, in the thirteenth and twelfth centuries BCE the ancestors of the Jewish people returned to the area now covered by Israel, as well as some of the areas presently occupied by its neighbors. The story of the successes and failures of their effort to capture the land is told in the Biblical books of Joshua and Judges. The first Jewish

---

1. Although both of these bodies of water are called "seas," they are both lakes. The name of each in Hebrew is quite different from the common English name. Israelis call the freshwater Sea of Galilee by its biblical name, "The Kinneret." This name may derive from the shape of the lake; *kinnor* is a Hebrew word for harp or lyre, and that is the shape of this body of water. The Hebrew name for the Dead Sea translates as the Salt Sea, an accurate description of this body of water.

monarchy began with the kingship of Saul in about 1020 BCE. Jerusalem became the capital of the kingdom under his successors, King David and King Solomon. King Solomon built the First Temple in Jerusalem, which was the center of Jewish worship. In about 930 BCE, the kingdom split into two parts, Israel in the north and Judah, which included Jerusalem, in the south. Assyria captured Israel in about 720 BCE and exiled the population. Babylonia captured Judah in 586 BCE, also exiling much of the local Jewish population. The period from the time of Solomon until the 586 BCE exile is commonly called the First Temple Period by Jewish sources. The Jewish population of the northern kingdom disappeared and is commonly referred to as the *ten lost tribes*. The leadership of the Jewish population of the southern kingdom was sent to Babylonia, located between the Tigris and the Euphrates rivers, in an area within present-day Iraq.

Jewish quasi-sovereignty was reestablished about 50 years later, under supervision of the Persian Empire, which had defeated the Babylonians. Jews were allowed to return to Judea from Babylonia and to reestablish a capital in Jerusalem. The Temple in Jerusalem was soon rebuilt. As the great powers in the area vied with each other for power, local rulers continued to run local affairs under the oversight of the Persians, later under Alexander the Great, and still later under the Ptolemaic and the Seleucid Greeks. Beginning in 142 BCE, Jewish rebels defeated the increasingly oppressive Greek regime and established an independent Jewish monarchy. This lasted until the conquest by the Romans under Pompey in 63 BCE. In 66–73 CE and again in 132–135 CE, the local Jewish community conducted an unsuccessful revolt against Rome. Rome destroyed the seat of Jewish power and of Jewish worship, exiled the Jews from the area of Jerusalem, and sold many captured Jews as slaves. The period between the return from Babylonia and the defeat by Rome is commonly called the Second Temple Period by Jewish sources.

Thereafter, the center of Jewish life moved away from the Jerusalem area to the north of the country. Although Jews continued for several centuries to form the majority of residents of the Roman-administered Palestine, eventually the population dwindled, suffering first from heavy taxation and later from anti-Jewish legislation of the Christian Byzantine rule.[2] At the same time, there was a very large Jewish community in Babylonia, which eventually became the pre-eminent Jewish community in the world. Later, Jews spread throughout the Middle East and the Mediterranean basin, and still later established communities in various parts of Europe.

Meanwhile, the Roman rule (63–313 CE) in the area that is now Israel was followed by Byzantine rule (313–636 CE), Arab rule (636 CE–1099 CE), Crusader domination (1099–1291 CE), Mamluk rule (1291–1516 CE),[3] and then conquest by the Ottoman Empire (1517 CE). In 1917, the Ottoman Empire, allied with Central Powers in World War I, lost the area when defeated near the end of the war. The British took over, with their administration confirmed by a British Mandate from the League of Nations in 1922. The Mandate covered not only most of the area that is now Israel, but also those areas now

---

2. Gedaliah Alon, The Jews in Their Land in the Talmudic Age (70–640 C.E.) (Gershon Levi trans., Harvard Univ. Press 1989).

3. The Mamluks were descendants of military slaves in Egypt who overthrew the rulers of Egypt and ruled in their place. The Mamluks gained control of much of the Middle East, stopped the advance of the Mongols, and remained in power until defeated by the Ottomans. *See generally* Rene Grousset, The Empire of the Steppes: A History of Central Asia 364–65, 446 (Naomi Walford, trans.,1970); David Nicolle, The Mamluks 1250–1517 (Men-at-Arms) 5–6 (1993); John Masson Smith, Jr., *Ayn Jalut: Mamluk Success or Mongol Failure?*, 44 Harvard Journal of Asiatic Studies 307 (1984) (comparing Mamluk and Mongol battle tactics and describing how the Mamluks stopped the Mongol advanced into Africa).

subject to the Palestinian Authority and the modern Hashemite Kingdom of Jordan. British administration under the Mandate lasted until 1948; it was first under the League of Nations and later under the United Nations.

Beginning in the thirteenth century, Jews from other parts of the world began returning to the land of Israel as their historic homeland. The rate of return increased significantly in 1882 and continued in waves during the last years of Ottoman rule and the period of the Mandate. Many of these Jewish returnees were idealists, dedicated to resurrecting a Jewish nation. The *Zionist* movement, established in the late nineteenth century, advocated the return of Jews to the land of Israel and the establishment of a Jewish state there. Others Jews came because they were fleeing persecution in Europe. Few were religious Jews; the resettlement of the land was initially a secular endeavor carried out by people identifying with the Jewish nation but not observant of the Jewish religion. Both the Jewish and, to a lesser extent, the Arab population of the area increased. In 1947, in response to increasing violence from both the Jewish and the Arab local populations, the British indicated they wanted to leave the area and the United Nations voted to partition the area of the Mandate between a Jewish state and an Arab state. The local Jewish authorities accepted partition, but the local and foreign Arab authorities rejected it. When the British left in 1948, the Jewish authorities declared the establishment of the State of Israel. War ensued between Israel on one side and the local Arab population and five Arab nations (Egypt, Iraq, Jordan, Lebanon, and Syria) on the other. This led to a 1949 armistice, under which the borders of Israel were more extensive than they would have been under the proposed UN partition. This armistice line is often referred to as the *green line*.[4]

2. Terminology

Most people today have heard the term *Israel* and *Palestine*. Let us explore where these terms came from in light of the history set out above.

In the Bible, Jacob, grandson of Abraham, is also called Israel, and the people that grew from and associated with his family are called *the Children of Israel*. After the Israelite conquest described in the book of Joshua, the area came to be referred to as the *land of Israel*. Later, after the Kingdom of Solomon was split into two parts, the northern kingdom used the name Israel. (This area later came to be known as Samaria, while the southern kingdom was called Judea.) When the modern state was founded, the name of Israel was chosen due to its connections to the Jewish past.

The term Palestine probably derives from the term the Greeks used in the twelfth century BCE to refer to the land of the Philistines on the southern coast of modern Israel. The Romans later used it in the second century CE to refer to a different area, the southern portion of the Roman province of Syria. After defeating the Jews in 135 CE and banishing them from Jerusalem, the Roman changed the name of the city of Jerusalem to the Latinized Aelia Capitolina and the names of the districts formerly inhabited by the Jews from Judea and Samaria to Palestine. That name was later attached to the southern military district of Syrian province ruled by the Umayyad caliphate, one of the early Islamic regimes. Later, the name Palestine was attached to one of the British mandatory areas. At that time, it first described both the area covered by present-day Israel and the West Bank and also the area now included in Jordan. *Transjordan* was soon split off as an Arab emirate to be

---

4. This term derives from the fact that the line was drawn in green ink on the maps used during the armistice negotiations. Israelis refer to the line by a Hebrew term meaning "the seam line."

ruled by Abdallah, a son of sharif Husayn; this area eventually became the modern Jordan. The name Palestine was retained for the area that remained under British administration.[5]

C. Population, Ethnic Identity, Religion

The population of Israel as of April 2010 was 7,587,000.[6] The population is growing rapidly, with a 1.9 percent growth rate in the year from the end of 2009 to the end of 2010.[7] In addition, the population is relatively young, with 28 percent under the age of 15 and only 9.7 percent above the age of 64.[8] By comparison, in the United States, 21.4 percent of the population is under the age of 15 and 12.4 percent is above the age of 64.[9]

The Israeli population at the end of 2010 comprised 75.4 percent Jews. 20.5 percent Arabs (including several groups, described below), and 4.1 percent "other."[10] The category of "other" is comprised mostly of immigrants from the former Soviet Union who are not officially recognized as Jews but who identify with the Jewish community.[11]

Almost all of the Arab population is Muslim, mainly Sunni Muslims. The Arab population includes small groups of Christians and of Bedouin. The latter are also Muslims, but are ethnically distinct from the remainder of the Arab population. Most live in the Negev in the south of the country, although significant numbers also live in the north and elsewhere. The Bedouin were once a nomadic people, many of whom crossed areas now defined by modern political borders. Today, many of the Israeli Bedouin live a more settled life, but some cling to at least some aspects of a nomadic lifestyle.

Christians comprise only 2 percent of the Israeli population, and these are mostly Greek Orthodox Arabs, although there are some Armenian Christians and small communities representing other churches and ethnic groups. About 1.7 percent of the people living in Israel are Druze. The Druze are an Arabic speaking people who have their own religion and culture. They live mostly in the north. The Circassians, a separate and small ethnic group, live in two villages in the north. They are non-Arab Muslims. Finally there are other small distinct groups in the population, including Maronite Christians, Samaritans, and the African Hebrew Israelites (Black Hebrews). The Bahai World Center is in

---

5. See Bernard Lewis, The Middle East: A Brief History of the Last 2,000 Years 31, 195, 341, & 343 (1995).

6. The data on the population comes from various publications of the Israeli Central Bureau of Statistics (CBS). The CBS conducts a census every ten years, on the anniversary of the foundation of the State in 1948. Therefore the most recent census was in 2008. In addition, the CBS publishes more limited data each on Independence Day and the Jewish New Year. The data are available at the CBS website, in Hebrew, at http://www.cbs.gov.il/reader. A more limited selection of data is found at the CBS English language website, http://www.cbs.gov.il/reader/?MIval=cw_usr_view_Folder&ID=141.

7. Calculated from Central Bureau of Statistics, Statistical Abstract of Israel 2011, Table 2.1, *available at* http://www.cbs.gov.il/reader/shnaton/templ_shnaton.html?num_tab=st02_10x&CYear=2011.

8. Calculated from *id.* at Table 2.10.

9. US Department of Commerce, Profiles of General Demographic Characteristics 2000 (2001).

10. Calculated from Statistical Abstract of Israel 2011, *supra* note 7, at Table 2.1.

11. Israeli citizenship law, discussed in chapter 13, allows any person who is a Jew or who has one Jewish grandparent to enter the country and automatically become a citizen. Large numbers of Jews lived in the Soviet Union and many intermarried. Many non-Jewish descendants of these intermarried Jews have become Israeli citizens.

Israel, in the city of Haifa, but few Bahai other than volunteers at the Center live in the country.

The divisions in the population in Israel are sometimes hard for Americans to understand. In the United States, Jews are seen largely as a religious group. This is not the way most Jews in Israel see themselves, nor is it the way many Jews even outside of Israel have seen themselves for much of their history. Jews see themselves as a national group with a shared history, as an ethnic group with a shared culture (despite the cultural differences between Jews who lived in various places outside of Israel), and as a people with a shared identity. This is difficult to explain in terms familiar to Americans due to the difficulty of transposing the cultural assumptions of one country to discussions about another. Thus, the custom of grouping the Israeli population into two main groups, Jews and Arabs, does not merely make a distinction between people of different religious identities, but rather a distinction between two peoples. Arab Israelis also see themselves to some extent as having among themselves a shared identity that does not depend on ethnic, national, or religious lines, as those terms are traditionally understood in the West. Furthermore, Arab identity is built partly on the clan, which is a concept largely unfamiliar to many American readers.

As a result of an extraordinarily high level of immigration, discussed below, the population of Israel is very diverse. The major fault line of diversity is different from that in the United States. Americans tend to think of diversity along racial lines, especially as African-American, white, Hispanic, and Asian-American. Israelis do not think of diversity in these terms. The phrase *African-Israeli* would not be used; indeed, most of the African Israelis come from the Arab countries of North Africa and are not black. With its significant Ethiopian population, Israel has some degree of racial diversity in American terms, but the main fault line is between Arabs and Jews.

The major groupings within the Israeli Jewish community are *Sephardim*, *Mizrahim*, and *Ashkenazim*. Sephardim are Jews derived from the large and influential Jewish community that lived in Spain and Portugal before the expulsions from the two countries in 1492 and 1497, respectively. The Jews from these communities moved to other countries, especially, but not only, those in the Mediterranean basin. Mizrahim are descendants of the Jewish communities that existed for centuries in the countries of the Middle East, North Africa, and the Caucuses, but, technically, not including those who later arrived in the same destinations after their expulsion from Spain. The terms Sephardim and Mizrahim are sometimes used interchangeably, and there are significant similarities and overlaps between the communities. Ashkenazim are Jews who came from communities living mainly in northern and eastern Europe. In addition, there are smaller Jewish groups that belong to none of these three, including the Italian Jews and Yemenite Jews.

Jews came to Israel from many parts of the world and brought with them their own languages, cultures, and culinary traditions. Jews from northern Africa and Iraq arrived in Israel with Arabic as one of their native languages. Yemenite Jews came with families that consisted of one husband and more than one wife, an arrangement allowed in Yemen. Amharic-speaking Jews arrived from small villages in remote areas of Ethiopia. The number of Russian-speaking Jews who immigrated to Israel from areas of the former Soviet Union was so large that a common joke was, "What is second most common language in Israel? Hebrew!" These same immigrants had a well-developed cultural tradition, leading to the comment that Russian musicians brought with them not only their instruments, but also their audiences. The Russian immigrants were also characterized by a high degree of secularism, resulting from decades of forced suppression of religion. The differences between these communities are fading as their children mingle and intermarry.

While many Americans who visit Israel have contact with Americans living there, in fact the American presence is quite small. Americans make up less than three percent of the Israeli population.[12]

The groupings in the Jewish community are also defined along lines of religious observance. The religious groups are different from those familiar in the American setting. Israeli Jews are usually grouped as secular, traditional, national religious, and Ultra-Orthodox. The groups Americans would call Conservative or Reform are very small. While many American immigrants belong to these later two communities, they do not have a large presence in Israeli Jewish life. Secular Jews are typically not religiously observant, but see themselves as having a Jewish identity. Traditional Jews are typically Sephardic Jews, those whose families arrived from Arab countries, who may strictly observe some Jewish religious practices but not observe others. National religious Jews are religiously observant but also fully integrated into the fabric of modern life, combining in their lives secular learning and all sorts of work with Jewish religious practice. Ultra-Orthodox Jews tend to live in separate enclaves and limit their engagement with modernity. The Ultra-Orthodox community is itself composed of many sects that differ in their world view. These differences may seem minor from the outside, but can be crucially important to those within the system. Ultra-Orthodox Jews are often pictured in photographs of Israel because many of the men dress in long black coats, large fur hats, and side-curls, looking attractively exotic to visitors to the country.

The divisions set out here are not clear-cut in practice. Thus, for example, most secular Jews engage in some degree of Jewish practice, such as having Jewish weddings and Jewish ritual circumcision of their sons, and fasting on the Jewish Day of Atonement (Yom Kippur).[13] In addition, because the secular, traditional and national religious learn in the same institutions of higher education, serve in the same army units, and work in the same workplaces, they have regular contact with each other. Furthermore, many Israeli families have members who belong to more than one of the religious groupings, so the contact among the groups is closer than it might otherwise be.

D. Residence Patterns

Most of Israel's population lives in very crowded conditions. The overall population density in 2010 exceeded 850 persons per square mile. The actual population density is exacerbated by the fact that the hilly, forested north and the southern part of the desert are only sparsely populated. As a result, the population density of the coastal strip is

---

12. The figure given is an estimate based on data found in CENTRAL BUREAU OF STATISTICS, STATISTICAL ABSTRACT OF ISRAEL 2011, Table 2.24, *available at* http://www.cbs.gov.il/reader/shnaton/templ_shnaton_e.html?num_tab=st02_24x&CYear=2011. According to this table, those who were born in North American or Oceania or whose fathers were born in North American or Oceania comprise just under 2.7 percent of the Jewish population. It is likely that the percentage in the non-Jewish population is smaller. Furthermore the statistic given includes immigrants from Canada, Australia and New Zealand. Taking both of these factors into account, it is likely that the percentage of Israelis who are also citizens of the United States is closer to two percent.

13. *See* SHLOMIT LEVY, HANNA LEVINSON, & ELIHU KATZ, BELIEFS, OBSERVANCES, AND VALUES AMONG ISRAELI JEWS 2000 (2002), *available at* http://www.idi.org.il/sites/english/PublicationsCatalog/Documents/PortraitofIsraeliJewry.pdf.

among the highest of any place on earth. By comparison, the overall population density in the United States in 2000 was about 80 persons per square mile.[14]

Ninety-two percent of Israelis live in or around cities, with the capital, Jerusalem, and the Mediterranean coastal city, Tel Aviv-Jaffa, being the largest and most well-known outside of the country. Five percent of the population lives in collective or cooperative style rural communities, either in a *kibbutz* or in a *moshav*. The remainder of the population lives in other types of rural settlements. The American type of solitary farm is practically unknown.

The kibbutz is a collective community. All property is owned communally and members work either on the kibbutz or off it, but all earnings are contributed to the common pool. Use of property is allocated among members by communal decision. Some of today's kibbutzim (the plural of kibbutz) allocate payments to members based on their earnings. Nearly 270 kibbutzim are found in Israel. The moshav is a cooperative community. Each member of a moshav may own his or her house and land, but certain services are provided collectively. The property arrangements of the kibbutz and the moshav are discussed further in chapter 17.

The Arab and Jewish populations mix in some settings, such as institutions of higher education, hospitals, and some other workplaces, but they live largely in separate communities. The Supreme Court has ruled that this separation cannot be imposed by law, but that has not ended the separation in fact.[15] While some mixed residential areas exist, for the most part separation is maintained by individual preference, social convention, and societal pressure. Even in the large cities that have both Jewish and Arab populations, including Jerusalem, Tel Aviv-Jaffa, and Haifa, most local neighborhoods are almost exclusively either Jewish or Arab. Druze, Bedouin, and Circassians also tend to live in separate communities.

E. Immigration

Israel sees herself as the successor to the Jewish regimes of the past, as well as a place of refuge for Jews persecuted in other countries. Jewish immigration is viewed as the return of the Jewish people to their historic homeland. The term used in Israel for the return of Jews is *aliyah*, which means *going up*. Jews who move to Israel are thought to be going up to a higher spiritual plain in returning to their natural home.

Israel has a very high rate of immigration. Between the founding of the state in 1948 and 2006, 3,012,298 immigrants arrived in Israel. The largest number arrived during two periods: the years immediately following the founding of the state and in the 1990s. The earlier group of immigrants included large numbers from Iraq, Yemen, Libya, Morocco, and other Arab countries, as well as immigrants from Romania and Poland who had survived the Holocaust. The immigrants in the 1990s were mainly from the Soviet Union and, after its fall, the areas of the former Soviet Union, and

---

14. US CENSUS BUREAU, STATE AND COUNTRY QUICK FACTS (April 22, 2010), *available at* http://quickfacts.census.gov/qfd/states/00000.html (last visited Aug. 4, 2010).

15. HCJ 6698/95 *Ka'adan v. Israel Lands Authority* 44(1) PD 258 [2000].

also from Ethiopia. Over the years, immigrants have come from other areas as well. Altogether, immigrants have arrived from more than one hundred different countries, including places as diverse as Afghanistan, Argentina, Australia, India, Myanmar, the United States, and Zimbabwe. While most of the immigrants have been Jews arriving legally under the Law of Return, see chapter 13, the first decade of the twenty first century saw a substantial number of illegal non-Jewish immigrants from Eritrea, Sudan and various countries in central Africa, some of whom were refugees from wars in their home countries.

As of April 2010, 70 percent of Israelis were native born and 30 percent had arrived as immigrants. Of the native born, many had parents who had arrived as immigrants.[16] By comparison, people who were foreign born comprised 11 percent of the US population in 2000.[17] While Israel's level of immigration is the result of a deep commitment to accept all Jews as citizens, it has economic and social implications of staggering dimensions. For example, when more than a million immigrants arrived in the 1990s, mostly from the areas of the Soviet Union, Israel was hard pressed to provide work and housing for all its new people. Virtually all immigrants arrive without substantial knowledge of Hebrew, so the country must provide language training and some degree of support for people until they gain sufficient language skills to allow absorption into the economy. Differing cultural traditions of the immigrant groups cause social friction between them. More significantly, some immigrants bring cultural traditions that are inconsistent with the Israeli way of life established at the time of their immigration. This has two results, both of which occur to some degree: the immigrants change, and Israeli society changes in response to the immigrants' pressure.

F. Languages

Hebrew and Arabic are the official languages of the country. Hebrew is the original language of the Bible, and it continued to be used in Jewish prayer and Jewish texts. Its use as a modern language was revived at the beginning of the twentieth century. Arabic is an official language because of the presence of a large Arabic-speaking minority. English is a required subject in both elementary and high schools and in institutions of higher education. It is spoken extensively in areas frequented by tourists and used in international business dealings. In addition, many of the country's recent immigrants speak Russian, Amharic (an Ethiopian language), French, and Spanish. Former generations of Jewish immigrants spoke Arabic, Romanian, German, Yiddish, Ladino, Polish, and a variety of other languages, and these are still used in some circles today.

Education in the Arab sector is in Arabic, although Hebrew is taught as a second language. In the Jewish sector, Israel has had none of the debate about bi-lingual education in the schools that has been so prominent in the United States. With a highly diverse population, Israelis, including generally new immigrant Israelis, see it as essential that everyone has a common language, and that common language is Hebrew. Hebrew is also

---

16. Central Bureau of Statistics, Press Release, 62nd Independence Day—7,587,000 Residents in the State of Israel (Apr. 18, 2010), *available at* http://www.cbs.gov.il/reader/newhodaot/hodaa_template.html?hodaa=201011074.

17. QUICK FACTS, *supra* note 14.

essential to service in the army, so the army has programs to improve the Hebrew of young immigrants who have reached the age of army service.

G. The Draft

Israel has a nearly universal military draft, and this has played a significant social role in Israeli society. Both men and women are drafted at age 18, with some exceptions discussed below. Homosexuals serve like everyone else. Men serve on active duty for three years; women, for two, except that women in combat units and those in forces requiring a lengthy period of training also serve for three years. Most men, and some women, must continue their service with reserve duty until age 40, with women leaving earlier and officers, later. Reserve duty consists of service for a period of up to a month each year; in addition, reserve soldiers are usually called up to serve in times of war.

The military fulfills a number of important functions other than defense of the country. Because the service obligation is so broad, it provides an opportunity for young Israelis to meet and become close to people from different geographic, cultural, and socio-economic backgrounds. Israelis in military service typically form strong bonds with people whom they would not otherwise encounter. Furthermore, the Israeli Defense Forces have programs to provide education to soldiers who have had education problems prior to their draft, to teach all soldiers about Israeli history and culture, and to provide social assistance to soldiers in need. Military training also provides both leadership and technical skills that are important in civilian life. Israeli businesses seek out these sorts of skills and value the abilities of military veterans. Because of all of these activities, military service strengthens Israeli society in ways that exceed the main security function.

Three groups have not been subject to military service: Arabs, religious women, and Ultra-Orthodox men. The exception for Arabs is based on two considerations: security concerns about the loyalty of the Arab population, some of whom side with Arabs that Israel fights in its wars, and sensitivity to asking people to fight against those whom they may consider as part of their own ethnic group. The exception for Arabs does not apply to Druze; neither does it apply to the non-Arab Circassians, who are also Muslims. Furthermore, Arabs may volunteer for service, and by tradition many Bedouin do so. Recent proposals to expand the draft to Arab citizens of Israel have been opposed by the Arab political parties and have not been enacted over their opposition.

Women whose religious beliefs would be violated by service in close proximity with men are also exempt from the draft. Nonetheless many religiously observant Jewish women do serve, and many of those who do not serve in the military volunteer instead for National Service, in which they work in hospitals, schools, and other social-service institutions and receive the same minimal pay as soldiers.

The exemption for Ultra-Orthodox Jewish men was highly controversial and terminated on August 1, 2012. As of this writing, the Government reported that it was working on arrangements to draft Ultra-Orthodox men in a manner that would meet their religious needs. In the early years of the state, the exemption applied to a small number of men engaged in full-time study and was justified by the need to restore the tradition of studying Jewish texts, which had been nearly wiped out in Europe by the Holocaust. With the growth of the Ultra-Orthodox population in Israel, attributed mainly to a very high birth rate in this sector, the exemption came to apply to about 60,000 men. The appropriateness of this exemption became a major issue among those who are not Ultra-Orthodox. The exemption has also had a significantly adverse economic effect on the country. This is discussed in the next section on the economy.

H. Economy

Between 1948 and 1977, the government of Israel was led by the Labor party, which advanced socialist economic policies. The thirty years of socialist rule has had an enduring effect on the legal landscape and on the mindset of Israelis. Since 1977, the government has sometimes been in the hands of parties with a distinctly non-socialist point of view, sometimes in the hands of centrist parties, and sometimes in the hands of somewhat socialist-oriented parties. During the non-socialist periods, the economy has undergone a significant degree of privatization.

Israel today has a vibrant, modern economy. In 2010, it was accepted as a member of the Organization for Economic Co-operation and Development (OECD).

Israel is home to a vigorous high-tech sector. The country has been called *The Start-up Nation*, due to the prevalence of start-ups, predominantly in high tech.[18] A great deal of familiar computer hardware and software was developed in Israel, including dual-core processing for computer processors and the internet chat program ICQ. Israel exports pharmaceuticals, non-pharmaceutical chemicals, communications and scientific equipment, electronic equipment, medical technology, cut diamonds (the raw diamonds are imported), and computer components. Israel also has a significant agricultural sector. Drip-irrigation systems are another important Israeli product and export.

On the ownership side, Israel's economy is highly concentrated, with about twenty business groups controlling about half of the market.[19]

Wages are low as compared with the United States. As of February 2010, the average monthly gross wage for a worker in Israel was about $2,190 per month, or an annual wage of $26,280. The average annual wage in the United States in 2009 was $43,460.[20] On the average, Israelis live in smaller living quarters than Americans and have fewer cars.

The unemployment rate is lower than in the United States.[21] In both countries, unemployment figures consider only those who had no work at all and were looking for work. They do not take into account those who are not looking for work. This omission

---

18. Dan Senor & Saul Singer, Start-up Nation: The Story of Israel's Economic Miracle (2009).

19. Summary of the Address by the Governor of the Bank of Israel, Professor Stanley Fischer, to the 18th Caesarea Economic Policy Planning Forum, Nazareth, Israel (June 16, 2010), *available at* http://www.bankisrael.gov.il/deptdata/neumim/neum357e.htm.

20. News Release, Bureau of Labor Statistics, The Employment Situation—May 2010, tbl.B-3 (June 4, 2010) *available at* http://www.stat-usa.gov/stemplate.nsf/validate?OpenAgent&dbID=online.nsf&filekey=emp.pdf.

21. In the first five months of 2010, unemployment dropped from 7.1 to 6.5 percent. Central Bureau of Statistics, Press Release, May 2010 Preliminary Trend Data of the Unemployment Rate from the Labour Force Survey (July 19, 2010) (in Hebrew). The comparable figures for the United States are 9.7 to 9.5 percent. Bureau of Labor Statistics, Labor Force Statistics from the Current Population Survey (Aug. 6, 2010), *available at* http://data.bls.gov/PDQ/servlet/SurveyOutput-Servlet?data_tool=latest_numbers&series_id=LNS14000000.

is particularly significant in Israel because two large groups of the population by tradition do not work, and so are not looking for work.[22] If all those not looking for work are considered, the rate of non-employment is very high.[23]

About 55 to 60 percent of the Ultra-Orthodox men do not participate in the labor force.[24] Ultra-Orthodox men have a tradition of studying full-time in special institutions devoted to study of Jewish texts. The tradition is reinforced by the rules surrounding the draft. Ultra-Orthodox men get an exemption from the draft only if they are engaged in full-time study in such institutions, or if they teach full-time. In a community that does not value military service but values study of Jewish texts, the draft rules act as an added incentive for men to remain full-time in such study and not to look for work, at least until they are too old to be drafted.

Among Arab women, labor force participation is only 21 percent.[25] This compares with a labor force participation of just over 60 percent by non-Ultra-Orthodox, non-Arab women.[26] Among Arab women, participation is much stronger among modern Arab women than among traditional ones, with traditional Arab women essentially not participating in the workforce. This pattern is similar to that found in Muslim countries, which suggests that the reasons are cultural.[27]

The non-participation of both of these groups in the labor force has a strong influence on their economic condition. For most Israelis, it takes two wage earners to support a family. In fact, poverty is virtually absent in families with two wage earners. The absence of persons of one gender within a community from the labor force condemns that community to poverty.

Both Ultra-Orthodox Jews and Arabs tend to have larger families than the rest of the population. In addition, Arab men who participate in the work force have higher unemployment rates and lower salaries than Jews. It is not surprising, then, that both Ultra-Orthodox Jews and Arabs also have a substantially higher poverty rate than the rest of the population. About 60 percent of the Ultra-Orthodox Jews live in poverty, as do about 50 percent of Arabs.[28] For the remainder of the population, the poverty rate is much lower, similar to the OECD average.[29]

---

22. Stanley Fischer, Governor of the Bank of Israel, Address at the Third Annual Jewish-Arab Business Conference (November 13, 2007), http://www.bankisrael.gov.il/deptdata/neumim/neum250e.htm.

23. Taub Center for Social Policy Studies in Israel, E-Bulletin: Unemployment vs. Non-employment in Israel (May 27, 2010), http://taubcenter.org.il/index.php/e-bulletin/unemployment-versus-non-employment-in-israel-2/lang/en/.

24. Press Release, Samuel Neaman Institute, Survey: The Employment Rate of Ultra-Orthodox Men Increased by 28% Within a Decade (August 2012) (in Hebrew). The problem of Ultra-Orthodox male employment may be even worse than this statistic indicates. Unemployment is probably higher in younger adult men, who are most likely to be engaged in full-time studies. Furthermore there are debates as to whether the employment rate is as high as reported in this source.

25. Central Bureau of Statistics, Arab Population Aged 15 and Over, by Civilian Labour Force Characteristics, Type of Locality of Residence, District, and Sub-district of Residence, Religion and Sex, Labour Force Surveys 2008, Table 8.1.

26. Organization for Economic Co-operation and Development, *OECD Reviews of Labour Market and Social Policies: Israel* 59 (2010).

27. Eran Yashiv & Nitxa Kasir, Bank of Israel, Research Division, Arab Israelis: Patterns of Labor Force Participation 44 (2009).

28. *OECD Reviews: Israel*, supra note 26, at 58. Organization for Economic Co-operation and Development, *OECD Reviews of Labour Market and Social Policies: Israel* 58 (2010).

29. *Id.* at 58–59.

Twenty-three percent of Israelis over the age of 14 have academic degrees. This should be evaluated in light of the fact that some institutions of post-high school learning in Israel grant certificates, and not academic degrees. The United States measures higher education degrees for those over 18, and the rate is 27 percent.[30] Given the difference in the measurement techniques, it appears that Israeli meets or exceeds the American standard.

The currency of Israel is the new Israeli shekel (NIS). In 2011, on average the NIS was worth about $0.28; in other words, there were about NIS 3.6 per dollar. The value of the shekel against the dollar fluctuates and can be quite different from this amount at other times.

I. Education

Education is mandatory through twelfth grade. The state runs three streams of schools: state schools, Arab schools, and state religious schools.

The state schools are open to everyone. Almost all the students are secular or traditional Jewish students. The language of instruction is Hebrew, and students learn a required curriculum including the usual subjects. The state religious schools are for religiously observant Jews, but are not used by the Ultra-Orthodox. Classes are taught in Hebrew. The curriculum is the same as in the state schools, but a substantial course of study of Jewish religious topics is added. Students learn Bible, Jewish law, Jewish religious practice, and also Jewish texts. Most Arab Israelis study in state sponsored Arab schools. The language of instruction is Arabic, and the curriculum is partly the same as in the Hebrew-speaking schools and partly different. These schools are underfunded by comparison to the state and the state religious schools. The Druze have schools of their own within the Arab school system. Ultra-Orthodox Jews study in a fourth stream of schools. Although some receive state support, they are not run by the state and do not teach the standard curriculum, but rather a curriculum that consists almost entirely of religious studies. Lessons may be in Hebrew or, in some schools that serve students from sects that reserve Hebrew to be used only as a language of prayer, in Yiddish.

J. Calendar

Israel follows the same calendar as is used in the United States. Dates are written in the same format that is common throughout Europe and much of the world: day, month, year. This is different from the American custom of writing the month first. Thus, 9.11.01 is November 9, 2001, and not September 11, 2001. In addition, Israel uses the Jewish calendar. Statutes and many official documents carry both the date in the Jewish calendar and the common date. Thus, the main statute dealing with water issues is called The Water Law, 5719-1959. The number 5719 denotes the Jewish year.

The week is arranged differently in Israel than in the United States. The work week begins on Sunday and continues through Thursday. On Friday, some people work but many

---

30. US Census Bureau, Current Population Survey: 2009 Social and Economic Supplement tbl.1 (2010), *available at* http://www.census.gov/population/socdemo/education/cps2009/Table1-01.xls.

have the day off. It is a day of rest for Muslims. Saturday is the main day off; it is the Jew-ish Sabbath. The main national holidays are the Jewish holidays, and almost everyone gets off work on these days. In addition, accommodations are made for non-Jews to observe their religious holidays. Christian holidays are observed by the Christian population and by visitors, but because the number of Christians in Israel is so small, even Christmas is likely to go unnoticed by most of the non-Christian population. There is greater general awareness of the Muslim holidays.

The dates of the Jewish holidays follow the Jewish calendar and do not fall on the same date in the American calendar each year. That is, the Jewish holidays fall on the same date each year in the Jewish calendar, but this does not correspond to the same date in the common calendar. The Jewish calendar is a solar-lunar calendar. The months are lunar in length, with the first of each month falling on the new moon. A purely lunar calendar would not follow the solar year, so that different holidays would fall at different seasons each year. Because many of the Jewish holidays are agricultural in na-ture, this would be problematic. A holiday celebrating the time of the spring harvest would be celebrated in many years at a season other than spring, and the fall harvest holiday would also often occur out of season. To compensate for this, there are peri-odic leap years, in which an entire month is added to the calendar. The added month ensures that holidays occur at about the proper time of the solar year. As a result, spring holidays always occur sometime in spring, although a holiday, such as Passover, may be in March in some years, in early April in some, and in middle April in others. This is similar to the way Easter occurs on different dates in different years in the United States.

The Muslim calendar is purely lunar, with twelve lunar months to the Muslim year. Each month is 29 or 30 days long, so that the length of the year is about 354.4 days. As a re-sult, holidays which are designated to fall on a given day in the Muslim calendar, move from season to season. For example, the fast of Ramadan begins each year ten or eleven days earlier on the common calendar than it began the year before. Over a period of years, Ramadan occurs successively in the fall, the summer, the spring, and then the winter.

Chapter 3

The Israeli Government

A. Nature of a Parliamentary System

Israel has a parliamentary system of government. Parliamentary systems differ from presidential systems, such as that in the United States, in the degree of linkage between the legislative and the executive branches. A parliamentary system lacks the high degree of separation of the legislative and executive branches of government that is typical of a presidential system. In a parliamentary system, the people vote for the members of the parliament, or legislative branch. The members of parliament then choose the Government,[1] which serves as the executive branch. The tenure of the Government may be terminated by a no-confidence vote in the parliament. The parliament can vote no confidence in the Government because it disagrees with one or more of its decisions; it need not find any misbehavior in the Government, although that may also be the basis for a vote of no confidence. The head of the Government, typically called the prime minister, sits in the legislature. The office of head of Government is separate from that of the head of state, who is the official representative of the country. The latter job is filled by a different official, who typically fulfills ceremonial duties but has few real powers.

By contrast, in a typical presidential system, not only the legislature but also the head of the executive branch (the president) is elected by the people. The head of the executive branch serves for a set term and is not subject to a vote of no confidence. The legislature may have the power to remove the head of the executive branch for misbehavior, but it could not do so simply because it disagreed with executive decisions. The head of the executive branch does not sit in the legislature. No separate position exists for the head of state; the president is both the head of Government and the head of state.

There are many variations on these themes of governmental structure. For example, several countries have semi-presidential systems. This is found in France where citizens directly elect the president, who has real power. In such systems, either the president or the legislature appoints the head of Government, and the head of Government is subject to a legislative vote of no confidence.[2]

---

1. In a parliamentary system, the term *government* can refer to either the government as a whole or the executive authority. In order to clarify the distinction between these two uses of the word in this book, government with a small *g* refers to the government as a whole, while Government with a capital *G* refers to the executive authority. Thus, the Government is one part of the government.

2. On the various forms of parliamentary government and the differences between them and presidential government, see Richard Albert, *Presidential Values in Parliamentary Democracies*, 8 Int'l J. Const. L. 207 (2010).

Israel's governmental system is set out in a series of laws: Basic Law: The Knesset; Basic Law: The Government; Basic Law: The President of the State; Basic Law: The Judiciary; and Basic Law: The State Comptroller. The essential sections of these laws are examined in the remainder of this chapter, except for the law on the judiciary, which is covered in chapter 5.

B. The Knesset (Parliament)

Israeli Statute

Basic Law: The Knesset

1. Identity

The Knesset is the parliament of the state.

2. Location

The seat of the Knesset is Jerusalem.

3. Composition

The Knesset upon its election shall have one hundred and twenty members.

4. Electoral System

The Knesset shall be elected in general, national, direct, equal, secret, and proportional elections, under the terms of the Knesset Elections Law; this section may not be changed except by a majority of the members of the Knesset.

5. The Right to Vote

Every Israeli citizen of the age of eighteen years or older is entitled to vote in Knesset elections unless a court has denied that right under law.

5A. The Right to Submit a List of Candidates

A list of candidates may be submitted only by a political party.

6. The Right to Be Elected

Any Israeli citizen who is of the age of twenty one or older on the day of submission of the list of candidates that includes that person's name has the right to be elected to the Knesset.

8. Term of Office

The term of office of the Knesset shall be four years from the date of its election.

17. Immunity of Members of the Knesset

Members of the Knesset have immunity; details shall be set out in a statute.

24. Quorum

The Knesset may hold debates and make decisions with any number of members participating unless otherwise provided by law.

25. Majority

Except as otherwise provided by law, the Knesset shall make decisions by a majority of the votes of those participating in the voting, without counting those who abstain as participating in the voting.

Comment

As indicated in this statute, the name of the Israeli parliament is the *Knesset*. The word Knesset means *assembly*. The name has a historical connection. An institution called *The Men of the Great Assembly* (in Hebrew: Anshei Ha*Knesset* HaGedolah), a body of religious leaders and other learned men, operated during a portion of the Second Temple period, fulfilling a religious and legal role in the Jewish community. The Great Assembly had 120 members and so does the modern Knesset.

The powers of the Knesset are not specified in the Basic Law given here. A different law, the Transition Law, 5709-1949, which is set out in the next chapter, states that the "legislature" of Israel is the Knesset. The Hebrew term for *legislature* means literally *the body that enacts laws*. Thus, the Knesset has the power to enact statutes, but is not limited to statutes on specified matters. In this way, the Knesset is unlike the United States Congress, which is limited to the powers set out in Article I of the Constitution.

Israel has no complete written constitution, such as that of the United States and of most other countries. The Knesset enacts two types of statutes: regular statutes and statutes called *Basic Laws*. It is easy to tell from the name of the law whether it is a regular statute or a Basic Law. A regular statute has the date as part of the name of the statute. The Law for Prevention of Nuisances, 5721-1961, referred to in the case in Chapter 1, is an example. A Basic Law includes the term "Basic Law:" as part of its name and is given without a date. There are twelve Basic Laws:

Basic Law: The Knesset

Basic Law: The Government

Basic Law: The President of the State

Basic Law: The Judiciary

Basic Law: The State Comptroller

Basic Law: Israel Lands

Basic Law: The State Economy

Basic Law: The Army

Basic Law: Jerusalem, the Capital of Israel

Basic Law: The State Budget

Basic Law: Freedom of Occupation

Basic Law: Human Dignity and Freedom[3]

The first five of these deal with the structure of the main institutions of the government. The last two deal with individual rights. As we shall see in chapter 8 on constitutional law, at least some of these Basic Laws are considered by the courts to be of constitutional status. Thus, under the case law, the Knesset has the power to enact a constitution as well as regular statutes.

Israel has a unicameral parliament. This is a feature it shares with only a small number of other countries. In 1994, it was reported that there were eight other unicameral countries, most of them, like Israel, relatively small. They were Denmark, Finland, Greece,

---

3. By convention, the term Basic Law is always capitalized.

Luxembourg, New Zealand, Portugal, Sweden, and Turkey.[4] In the United States, by contrast, one house of the legislature represents the people based on population, with each seat representing approximately the same number of people, and the other represents the states, with each state getting the same number of votes. Israel has no state or district government of any inherent powers.

Sections 24 and 25 of the Basic Law: The Knesset control how the Knesset enacts laws, both regular statutes and Basic Laws. Section 24 provides that there is no minimum number for a quorum. In other words, the Knesset can conduct business if only three of its 120 members are present. Under section 25, only a majority of those voting is needed to enact a law. Therefore most laws can be enacted by a vote of two members in favor and one against the law. A few provisions of laws are *entrenched*. These laws include provisions stating that they can be changed only by a larger majority. For example, section 4 of the Basic Law: The Knesset is an entrenched provision. It provides that it can be changed only by the vote of a majority of all the members of the Knesset.

Elections for the Knesset are national; there are no elections by district. The electoral system is based on a system of party lists. Each party submits a list of candidates for the Knesset. A party list typically consists of 120 names, enough to fill all Knesset seats. A party list is ordered from the first choice to the 120th choice. In the elections, citizens vote for a party and not for individual candidates. Each party then gets a percentage of the seats in the Knesset that is equal to its percentage of the popular vote. If a party gets 25 percent of the popular vote, the first 30 candidates on its list (25 percent of 120 = 30) become members of the Knesset. This is the meaning of "proportional" elections in section 4 of the statute set out above.

A party needs to obtain at least 2 percent of the popular vote to get a seat in the Knesset. In the February 2009 elections, 33 political parties participated in the elections and 12 received a sufficient number of votes to gain seats in the Knesset. Twenty-one parties failed to receive the required minimum percentage of the vote. Of the 12 parties elected, three are fairly centrist (one right of center, one left of center, and one in the center, although different people have different views on how to characterize these parties); two represent the far left; one represents the far right; three represent different Jewish religious groups; one is on the right and represents mainly Russian immigrants; and two are Arab parties (although Arabs can, and do, run on the lists of the other parties and other parties have Arab members in the Knesset).

The proportional system of elections is based on a philosophy of giving legislative representation to all political views that are held by more than a small number of Israeli citizens. The variety of representation provides a voice in the Knesset to groups with many different interests, but it also makes governance of the country almost unmanageable. In the last election, no party had more than 23 percent of the vote. The Knesset comprises many parties and obtaining a majority on any matter is difficult. This problem is more fully examined in the next section.

All Israeli citizens 18 and older are eligible to vote in national elections. Voting participation tends to be high. Israel greatly restricts absentee voting. Only state representatives who

---

4. GIOVANNI SARTORI, COMPARATIVE CONSTITUTIONAL ENGINEERING: AN INQUIRY INTO STRUCTURES, INCENTIVES AND OUTCOMES 183 (1994). In addition, Iceland and Norway elect one legislature, but it then splits into two separate groups. *Id.*

are out of the country on official duty can vote via absentee ballot. The restrictions on absentee voting prevent the large number of Israelis who have left the country and are permanently living elsewhere from participating in elections. This is justified on the grounds that elections in Israel typically revolve around issues crucial to the existence of the state, to the dangers of military service, and to the difficulties of living under terrorism and military attack. The widespread feeling is that those who do not share the dangers in their everyday life should not have a voice in elections that can affect those who do. The side effect is that the large number of young Israelis traveling outside of the country on post-army trips and those abroad for business or pleasure cannot vote.

Section 17 of the Basic Law: The Knesset grants members very broad immunity that extends to all matters; immunity is not limited to actions relating to performance of the official role of the Knesset member. The following excerpts discuss the reasons for this broad immunity law:

Israeli Case

Bishara v. Attorney General
HCJ 11225/03 60(4) PD 287 [2006][5]

Justice E. Hayut:

Immunity is intended to ensure that a member of the Knesset can properly discharge his duties and represent the public that elected him by giving free and full expression to his opinions and outlooks, without concern or fear that this may result in a criminal conviction or a personal pecuniary liability in a civil proceeding. Chief Justice Agranat explained the importance and purposes of the immunity granted to members of the Knesset when he said:

> Before us we have a privilege of supreme constitutional importance, in that it is intended to guarantee that members of the legislative house of the state have freedom of opinion, expression and debate, so that they can discharge their duties, as such, without feeling fear or trepidation and without being concerned that they may have to answer for this to any person or authority; *for the whole nation has a clear essential interest in the realization of this right,* so that it does not suffer a major or minor violation by anyone; without it the democratic process cannot exist effectively and it will become valueless.

Thus we see that the independence of members of the Knesset is essential for the proper functioning of a democracy. In discussing this rationale that underlies substantive immunity, Chief Justice Shamgar said:

> A member of the Knesset, who cannot express himself without concern for the legal consequences of his remarks, cannot discharge his duty to the voter. The representatives of the people ... have the task of conducting the political debate. The freedom of political debate requires that no restriction is placed upon the ability and right of free expression of the elected representatives.

An additional central purpose that can be identified in the historical development of parliamentary immunity concerns the desire to preserve the separation of powers and to

---

5. The English translation is based on that on the website of the Supreme Court of Israel, http://elyon1.court.gov.il/files_eng/03/250/112/v08/03112250.v08.htm (last visited March 10, 2011).

protect the proper activity of the legislature so that the executive authority does not intervene in it.

There are various models of parliamentary immunity around the world. There are legal systems that give a member of parliament substantive immunity while limiting it only to the activity that is done in the parliament building itself (the United States, England, Canada, Australia, Germany and Holland). Other countries (France, Italy and Spain) do not attribute any importance to the place where the activity protected by immunity is carried out and the immunity extends both to activity carried out inside parliament and to activity outside it, provided that there is a connection functionally related by subject matter between the activity and the duties of the member of parliament. Some countries give a member of parliament immunity only for a vote or expressing an opinion and a few give immunity also for an act.

The Israeli legislature adopted a broad model of substantive immunity, which is regulated in section 1 of the Immunity Law, according to which:

1. Immunity in carrying out duties

(a) A member of the Knesset shall not have criminal or civil liability, and he shall be immune from any legal action, for a vote or for expressing an opinion orally or in writing, or for an act that he carried out — in the Knesset or outside it — if the vote, expressing the opinion or the act were in the course of carrying out his duties, or for the purpose of carrying out his duties, as a member of the Knesset.

From this we see that the substantive immunity of members of the Knesset extends also to acts and not merely to a vote or opinion, and it includes the activity of the member of the Knesset whether it is carried out inside the Knesset or outside it, provided that there is a functional connection between this activity and his position as a member of the Knesset. This substantive immunity cannot be lifted (section 13(a) of the law) and it continues even after the member of the Knesset leaves office (section 1(c) of the law). Alongside the substantive immunity, the Immunity Law further provides a procedural immunity. The procedural immunity, as distinct from the substantive immunity, protects a member of the Knesset from being indicted in criminal proceedings for actions that were not in the course of carrying out his duties or for the purpose of carrying out his duties as a member of the Knesset. This immunity is provided in section 4 of the Immunity Law and it applies to offences that were committed while a member of the Knesset holds office and also to offences that were committed before a member of the Knesset held office, unless the Knesset decides to lift the immunity. Lifting procedural immunity is done by means of the process set out in section 13 of the law and subject to the conditions set out therein. The Immunity Law further includes specific provisions concerning the immunity of members of the Knesset from searches, eavesdropping and arrest.

Chief Justice A. Barak:

As my colleague says, substantive immunity is intended, first and foremost, "to ensure that a member of the Knesset can properly discharge his duties and represent the public that elected him by giving free and full expression to his opinions and outlooks, without concern or fear." This immunity was not given to members of the Knesset for their own benefit. It is not a sovereign privilege that the member of the Knesset enjoys by virtue of his exalted position. Substantive immunity is given to members of the Knesset in order to guarantee essential public interests. *First*, this immunity is essential in order to guarantee the right of all citizens to full and effective political representation. Substantive immunity protects the right of all citizens to have their opinions and outlooks heard, through their elected representatives, in the various frameworks of public debate in general and in parliament in particular. This protection is essential mainly for citizens who are members of minority groups in society. In this sense, substantive immunity also furthers civil equality, in that it protects even the right of members of minority groups in society to full and effective political representation, and it protects them by protecting the member of the Knesset, who represents their interests and their opinions, against the power of the majority. *Second*, substantive immunity is essential in order to guarantee a free marketplace of ideas and opinions. Here too this immunity is especially important when we are speaking of opinions and ideas that are offensive or outrageous, and it is especially required for elected representatives who express opinions that are regarded by most of the public as such. Indeed, "freedom of expression is also the freedom to express dangerous, offensive and perverse opinions, from which the public recoils and which the public hates." *Third*, following from the aforesaid, substantive immunity is essential in order to guarantee the democratic character of the government. Thus we see, as my colleague says, the purposes underlying substantive immunity are of different kinds. They are intended to protect basic political freedoms. They are intended to allow the proper functioning of the legislature. They express a desire to ensure the independence and the freedom of action of members of the Knesset. They are intended to strengthen democracy.

Comment

As the case states, the law distinguishes between substantive immunity, which is extensive and cannot be lifted, and procedural immunity. The former applies broadly to actions connected to Knesset duties; the latter applies to other actions.

Question

1. What are the disadvantages associated with immunity for members of the legislature?

A great deal of information on Knesset activities is available to the Israeli public on the Knesset website. The main website, in Hebrew, has background information on the Knesset, its history, and its activities, as well as current information such as proposed laws before the Knesset. The English version of the website, found at http://www.knesset.gov.il/main/eng/home.asp, has the background information but does not include proposed laws. There are also Arabic and Russian versions of the website.

C. The Government

Israeli Statute

Basic Law: The Government

1. Identity

The Government is the executive branch of the state.

2. Location

The seat of the Government is Jerusalem.

3. Confidence of the Knesset in the Government

The Government serves based on authority derived from the confidence of the Knesset.

4. Responsibility

The Government has shared responsibility to the Knesset, and a minister is responsible to the prime minister for the tasks as to which he was appointed.

5. Composition of the Government

(a) The Government is composed of the prime minister and the other ministers.

(b) The prime minister shall be a member of the Knesset; any other minister may be a person who is not a member of the Knesset.

(c) A minister shall be appointed to be responsible for a ministry, but can be a minister without portfolio.[6]

(d) A minister who is a member of the Knesset may serve as acting prime minister.

(e) A minister may serve as a deputy prime minister.

7. Assignment of the Task of Forming a Government

(a) When a new Government is to be constituted, the president of the state, after consultation with representatives of the parties serving in the Knesset, shall assign the task of forming a Government to one of the members of the Knesset who has agreed to do so.

13. Formation of the Government

(a) When the president of the state has assigned the task of forming a Government to a member of the Knesset, he shall notify the Chairperson of the Knesset and the Chairperson shall notify the Knesset.

(b) When a member of the Knesset has formed a Government, he[7] shall notify the president of the state and the Chairperson of the Knesset, and the Chairperson shall notify the Knesset and shall set a date for a session for the purpose of constituting a Government.

---

6. A minister without portfolio is a person who is part of the government, with the privileges of a minister, and who joins the other ministers in meetings of the Government, but who is not in charge of a ministry.

7. Although the Hebrew uses the male gender, in fact Israel had a female prime minister, Golda Meir, from 1969 to 1974. Another woman, Tsippi Livni, was head of the party that received the largest number of votes in the 2009 elections, but failed to attract enough parties as coalition partners to allow her to form a coalition under her leadership.

(c) The member of the Knesset who formed the Government shall be the prime minister.

(d) Once formed, the Government should be presented to the Knesset. It shall provide an outline of its policies, a list of the members included in the Government, and the division of jobs among the ministers. It shall request an expression of confidence. The Government is constituted after the Knesset has expressed confidence in it, and at that time, the ministers shall assume office.

28. Expression of No Confidence in the Government

(a) The Knesset may adopt an expression of no confidence in the Government.

(b) An expression of no confidence in the Government shall be in the form of a vote of the majority of the members of the Knesset to ask the president of the state to assign the task of forming a Government to a named Knesset member who has agreed in writing.

(c) If the Knesset voted no confidence in the Government, the Government is treated as though it had resigned from the time of the decision; within two days, the president shall assign the task of forming a Government to the Knesset member named in the vote.

32. Residual Powers of the Government

The Government may, in the name of the state, undertake all acts, subject to law, that are not assigned to another branch of government.

Comment

As is clear from the provisions set out above, the person asked to form a Government will, if successful, become the prime minister. A Government is formed only when it gains a vote of confidence from the majority of the members of the Knesset. Notice that this requires a vote of a majority of members, and not just a vote of a majority of those voting (such as is needed for most laws). Given the fact that in recent years the Knesset comprises a large number of parties, none of which has close to 50 percent of the seats, the formation of a Government requires formation of a coalition consisting of several parties that together hold at least sixty-one seats. Usually there are a number of different possible combinations that will serve this purpose. In order to form a Government, the person hoping to be prime minister must negotiate with all the parties he or she wishes to bring into the Government.

Usually the two largest parties will not agree to form a Government together. In most cases, the head of one is asked to form a Government and the head of the other hopes that the first one will fail. This will force the president to ask the head of the other large party to try to form a Government. As a result, the person forming the Government must rely on bringing in many of the smaller parties. Negotiations with the smaller parties to convince them to join the Government are extensive and complex. The smaller parties are in a position to demand a price for joining the coalition. Negotiations usually center on general issues of policy, on assignment of ministerial positions to the leaders of a party's list, and on enactment of laws that advance specific policies that serve a party's constituency.

The negotiations have two important effects on the composition of the Government. First, the ministerial jobs are usually doled out on the basis of political heft and not on the basis of substantive expertise. The head of a party with a relatively large number of seats in the Knesset can insist on being appointed as head of one of the important ministries, and can also demand other ministries for the people high on that party's list. Thus, the minister of foreign affairs is rarely appointed to that position due to expertise on dealing with delicate negotiations with other countries. It is more likely a person will be appointed to such a prestigious post in order to get the appointee, and the appointee's party, to agree to join the coalition. The importance of ministries depends partly on the visibility of the position as ministerial head, so that the appointed minister can use the position to stay in the public eye and thus have a better chance of remaining as the head of the party and of garnering more votes in the next election. Importance may also depend on the budget commanded.

The second effect of the negotiations over formation of the Government under the Israeli system is to give small parties a stronger voice than they would otherwise have. This is because those small parties are needed to give the new Government a majority in the Knesset. The price for getting a small party to join the coalition may be high, even if the party represents only a small number of voters.

Considerable public concern about the content and effects of coalition agreements led to the following litigation, in which the Supreme Court had to decide whether publication of the agreements was required:

Israeli Case

Shalit v. Peres

HC 1601/90, 44(3) PD 353 [1990]

Chief Justice M. Shamgar:

The dispute in the case before us revolves around only one question: whether the Knesset parties that join in coalition agreements prior to establishment of the Government must publish these agreements.

The political agreement, as found in the coalition arrangements among the parties in the Knesset, is part of the process for establishing the Government. In a great measure, it is the result of the structure of our government and of our system of elections.

The Government is established by power of the confidence of the Knesset. When it is time to establish a new Government, after elections or as a result of an expression of no confidence in the Government, and the member of the Knesset assigned the task of forming a Government succeeds in doing so, the Government stands before the Knesset to receive its vote of confidence. At this time, it announces an outline of its policies. For a number of reasons, among them the system of elections that operates under Section 4 of the Basic Law: The Knesset and the number of parties in the Knesset at all times, from the first Knesset onwards, it has generally been necessary for a number of parties to enter an agreement to support the establishment of the new Government. We have never had a Government composed of only one party.

The result of this need for cooperation among several parties is the formation of one or more agreements between Knesset parties. These agreements relate to basic policies and to the composition of the Government and the areas in which it will take action.

The coalition agreement is therefore an accepted instrument in Israel ... functioning as a tool for setting out matters such as who will hold what position in the Government.

Such an agreement belongs to the area of public law. An agreement that is in the area of public law ... is not necessarily governed by the general law of contracts, but this does not prevent all judicial supervision over its terms.... These agreements are made by people holding public office, who were entrusted by the voters to manage the systems of legislation and government. They are not to be used to further private or personal interests.

The public nature of the agreements under discussion has direct implications on two matters: (1) the standards that should apply to how they are made and how they are treated, and (2) the role of the Court in regard to these agreements.

The democratic process depends on the open exposure of the problems facing the state and on free exchange of ideas on these problems. The link between the elector and the elected is not as intensive as they are during the period of elections, but the elections do not sever the perpetual connection between the public and those it elected. The political process is at all times subject to observation by the general public, so that it can express its opinion and draw conclusions as to the present operations of government and as to what should be done in the future. Public awareness and free expression of opinion on what occurs in the governmental sphere are an integral part of the structure of the democratic regime. The democratic regime is built upon the continued public exposure to information on what is happening in public life. Withholding of information is justified only for exceptional reasons of state security or foreign relations or out of fear of interfering with an important public matter.

A public agreement must be designed to serve the public good, it should observe the legal rules requiring fairness, and it should be calculated to prevent corruption. All of this is important if the public is to have trust in the system of government. The agreement provides a basis on which a person can formulate ideas about what should be done in the future. Moreover, everything said here about the public applies also as to a Member of the Knesset, who must express his opinion on the matter of confidence in the Government, either in the situation covered by Section 15 of the Basic Law: The Government, or in the course of fulfilling his parliamentary duties.

It is impossible for public trust to be based on hidden information [except in unusual situations in which secrecy is justified]. It is accepted that normally, it is best to have open publication, available to the voting public and to the members of the Knesset, of information on governmental arrangements and the activities of the elected officials, so the public can see, can know, and can form judgments.

Public access to information is not just a result of the right to know, but also the result of the right to supervise.

This analysis also provides the answer to the second question posed above: the role of the Court on this matter. In the absence of judicial supervision, there is no efficient manner for reviewing and enforcing the obligations that arise from public law. Observance of the norms of public law in general and supervision by the courts are intertwined.

[It is claimed] that Section 15 of the Basic Law: The Government creates a negative implication; by addressing publication of the outline of the policies of the Government, with no reference to coalition agreements, it implies that the latter need not be published.[8] I do not accept this interpretation. We should not understand Section 15 to mean that there are no additional obligations of a public nature that derive from the democratic nature of our regime. Provision of open information on the agreements is not only an integral part of our basic conceptual vision, as indicated above, but also part of the positive democratic commandments,[9] that must be performed. Section 15 addresses only those ac-

---

8. The same requirement that was in Section 15 at the time of *Shalit v. Peres* has now been recodified in section 13 (d) of the current Basic Law: The Government, reproduced above.

9. The term "positive commandment" comes from traditional Jewish interpretation of the Bible as containing both positive commandments, relating to things a person must do, and negative commandments, relating to things a person must not do. For example, "Honor your father and your mother" is a positive commandment. "Do not murder" is a negative commandment.

tions that relate to the act of presenting the Government and is not intended to address everything related to the procedures for parliamentary actions that occur prior to presentation of the Government. The evidence of this is the fact that coalition agreements have been put before the Knesset ever since the seventh Knesset,[10] without any relation to the matter in Section 15 of the above law.

The attorney for the Labor Party is of the opinion … that it would be better if the matter of publication of agreements were left to treatment by statute.

We agree that the matter is appropriate for legislative treatment. In fact, under the present constitutional law, it would better to have matters treated by statute, rather than left to clarification of constitutional concepts in case law alone.

Nonetheless the matter having been brought before us by the petitioners, we do not see that it is proper to leave the issue in a state of disarray, without relating to it at all. As long as there are no statutes on the matter, it is appropriate for the Court, exercising judicial supervision within the borders set for it in Section 15 of the Basic Law: The Judiciary,[11] and on the basis of the underlying constitutional principles, which are part of our law, to address the matter and determine the rules that will apply in the absence of statute.

It is our opinion that it is appropriate to publish agreements among parties, between parties and members of the Knesset, and among members of the Knesset, that deal with activities of the legislative or of the executive branch, and that were entered into as part of the process of formation of the Government.

In our opinion, it does not matter whether the agreements in question were entered into as part of successful formation of a Government or as part of an unsuccessful attempt to form a Government.

The timing of publication should properly be no later than the intended time of presentation of the Government before the Knesset, as set out in Section 15 of the Basic Law: the Government.

Justice A. Barak:

I agree with the decision of my colleague, Chief Justice Shamgar. Because of the importance of the matter, I would like to add a number of comments relating to the legal source of the obligation to publish political agreements before the vote of confidence and the role of the Court in imposing that obligation. I am addressing the matter of a political agreement as to the vote of confidence, made between parties or between members of the Knesset. Such an agreement may be between parties and members of the Knesset to vote in favor of a vote of confidence in the Government (a *coalition agreement*), or between parties and members of the Knesset to vote no confidence in the Government or to refrain from voting (an *opposition agreement*).

The Source of the Obligation

Israel is a parliamentary democracy. The people elect parties or lists, whose candidates are elected as Members of the Knesset. "The Knesset is the parliament of the state." (Section 1, the Basic Law: The Knesset). The Knesset has the legislative authority, both constitutive and regular. It establishes the Government and can bring it down. "The Government is the executive branch of the state." (Section 1, the Basic Law: The Government). The Gov-

---

10. It is common to refer to the first Knesset, the second Knesset, etc., the same way that, in the United States, we refer to the 112th Congress, which was the Congress that began serving in January, 2011. As of the same date, the 18th Knesset was sitting in Israel.

11. This provision is set out in chapter 5.

ernment serves based on the confidence of the Knesset. The Knesset and the Government are two organs of the state, and together with the courts they constitute the three central branches of the state, with mutual checks and balances in relationship to each other.

At the foundation of this system of government stands the citizens' right to elect the legislature, through a system of lists or parties.... The political parties are the constitutional instrument through which the political will of the citizens is expressed. As a result of the system of elections, we have a multi-party government. This system of governance is based on formation of ruling coalitions. The coalition agreement thereby becomes an essential political-legal tool, which in our constitutional system has great importance in functioning of the political process. It is natural that citizens, whose votes determined the composition of the Knesset, should be aware of the content of these agreements. Just as citizens need to know the platforms of the parties, they need to know the content of the political agreements that often deviate from or add something to the political platforms. The political struggle between the parties requires that citizens have information on both topics and personalities connected to political actions.... It is only on the basis of this information that the public can decide how to vote on election day, and only on the basis of this information can people freely exchange opinions in the period between elections.

The obligation to reveal the contents of political agreements is essential not only to allow the citizen to form political opinions. There is another immediate need, related to the process of forming the Government. The Government is established from the time when the Knesset votes its confidence in the Government (Section 15, Basic Law: the Government). The Members of the Knesset who participate in the vote must know what obligations have been undertaken by those who formed the Government. If the purpose of the political agreement is to control future action, it is necessary that the agreement's influence on the future be known to the Members of the Knesset who vote in favor of forming the Government. From the response of the attorney general we have learned that in practice, the coalition agreements are presented to the Knesset before the vote of confidence.

The obligation of revealing agreements has another aspect. The fact that the parties to an agreement know that it will be publically available and subject to open review affects the content of the agreement. It has been rightly said that sunshine is the best disinfectant and electric light the most effective policeman (see Chapter 5, Louis Brandeis, *Other People's Money* (1914)). Therefore the exposure of public agreements will influence the legality of their contents. It will allow public review and will increase the public faith in the governmental authorities and strengthen the structure of the regime and the government.

Now I want to turn to another source of the obligation to reveal the agreements.... Parliamentary parties and Members of the Knesset who sign a political agreement do not act for themselves. They serve as trustees of the public.... A number of obligations derive from the position of trust, [including] the obligation of revealing information.

[Another source of the obligation to reveal information is the public's right to know.]

Justice E. Goldberg:

None of the parties to this case denied that this Court has authority to hold that publication of coalition and opposition agreements is required.

I agree with the legal principles upon which my esteemed colleagues based the obligation of revealing the documents. I have doubts, though, as to whether we should intervene in this case in light of the fact that all the parties are willing to publish their agreements voluntarily, but not because such publication is obligatory. The natural branch for determining the framework and content of a constitutive matter of the first degree, such as that involved in this case, is the legislature and not the courts. In my opinion, even if a standard for public law is missing, we are not always responsible to develop one by judicial legislation in place of leaving the matter to legislation of the Knesset. My agreement to join the decision of my colleagues is based on the fact that, if the present matter is left in complete disarray until enactment of legislation, and if publication is left to the good will of those involved in such agreements, we will not have prevented the chance of an injury to the fabric of our public life, with all the implications this would carry.

Therefore I join in the decision of my colleagues.

Comment

While the Basic Law: The Government does not refer to coalition or opposition agreements, all three justices who participated in the *Shalit v. Peres* case saw them as essential to the Israeli system of government. Justice Barak says they are "an essential political-legal tool, which in our constitutional system has great importance in functioning of the political process." Justice Goldberg refers to them as a "constitutive matter of the first degree." The justices recognize that, given the large number of Israeli political parties, without the coalition agreements, it would be impossible to form a Government. They thus raise the agreements to constitutional status; that is, they see the agreements as relating to how one branch of government is constituted.

Israeli political parties, like American political parties, publicize their platforms prior to elections. In fact, because voters in Israel vote for party lists and not for individuals, the party platforms are more important than are party platforms in the United States. An individual candidate in the United States can deviate from the party line; it is much harder for an Israeli candidate, who must run on the party list, to do so. A candidate who does not adhere to the party line will not be on the party list for the next election. Furthermore, because the votes are for the party, an elected Member of the Knesset who opposes a party position betrays those who voted for the party.

On the other hand, parties sometimes enter coalition agreements that are not fully consistent with the party's platform. This happens when some sort of compromise is needed to form a Government. Again, because of the strength of the party in the Israeli system, it is hard for Members of the Knesset to deviate from a coalition agreement entered into by their party.

The political parties involved in *Shalit v. Peres* were willing to publish their agreements on a voluntary basis, but opposed the imposition of a legal requirement to publish the agreements. The Court was unwilling to accept mere voluntary publication. In such a circumstance an American court would probably not decide the case for lack of a case or controversy. The Israeli Court was not deterred by the fact that its decision would have no effect on whether the agreements involved in the present case would be published. As we shall see throughout this book, it is common for Israeli courts to rule on matters when American courts would not. Israeli courts see themselves as active players in making the system of government work. This approach is evident in Justice Goldberg's determination that judicial intervention is necessary because "if the matter is left in complete disarray until enactment of legislation, and if publication is left to the good will of those involved in such agreements, we will not have prevented the chance of an injury to the fabric of our public life, with all the implications this would carry."

Shortly after deciding *Shalit v. Peres*, the Supreme Court considered a challenge to the substance of a coalition agreement. In a case that ran more than a hundred pages, H.C. 1635/90, *Cherchevsky v. Prime Minister*, PD 48 (1) 749 (1991), Justice Menachem Alon held the content of such agreements could be reviewed only to determine whether they violated any recognized law. Justice Aharon Barak held that coalition agreements are reviewable on the same grounds that apply to review of any action of a branch of the Government; in other words, they were subject to review on administrative law grounds. In Israel, this means a court could decide whether such agreements were reasonable and fair. Justice Barak's opinion in the matter is particularly important because he later became the Chief Justice of the Court.

Questions

2. Given the importance of and publicity given to party platforms in Israel, why is publication of the coalition agreements, and opposition agreements, important?

3. What are the advantages of Justice Alon's position on judicial review of the content of coalition agreements? What are the advantages of Justice Barak's view?

———————

After formation of a Government, maintenance of the coalition remains a central problem. Usually only those parties that are within the coalition vote in the Knesset for the initial acceptance of the Government and vote with the Government on subsequent major votes of no confidence. In order to remain in office after approval of the Government, the prime minister must ward off votes of no confidence. Any one of the coalition parties can threaten to jump sides and join in a vote of no confidence against the Government. If the Government coalition is small, comprising parties representing only 61 or just over 61 votes, the threat of any party to leave the coalition is significant. This leads to a situation in which the Government of Israel is in a constant state of crisis, and the prime minister must devote much time and political capital to the task of keeping the coalition together. For example, the demand of a coalition party for more housing starts in areas where its constituents live requires immediate attention. In this way, the demands of any coalition party must be taken seriously. This is true even where the party represents only a small portion of the electorate. As a result, the exaggerated influence of the small parties continues even after formation of the Government.

The Israeli system of proportional representation, with a large number of parties, is vastly different from the American two-party winner-takes-all system. In theory, the Israeli system gives a stronger voice to minority points of view. It does not depend only on constitutional protection of minorities, but instead gives them a direct voice in the political process. On the other hand, as should now be clear, the Israeli system comes at a considerable price to governmental stability. There have been many proposals for reforming the system. One proposed reform is to increase the percentage of the popular vote a party needs in order to get a seat in the Knesset. This would decrease the number of small parties represented. Another proposal is to allow the electorate to vote for individual candidates for some of the Knesset seats. This would reduce the power of the parties. So far, no substantial reforms have been adopted.

During one brief period, the law allowed direct election of the prime minister. Each voter got two votes: one for an individual to be prime minister and the second for a party's Knesset list. It turned out that this increased the power of the small parties. Under the system where all votes are for parties, the head of the party that gets the most votes is usually asked to form the Government.[12] Therefore a person preferring that the head of one of the larger parties become the prime minister will tend to vote for that person's party. With direct election of the prime minister, a voter could combine a vote for one candidate for prime minister with a vote for a small party's list. The vote for the small party did not decrease the chance that the person at the head of a large party would get to form the Government. This led to the Knesset having an even larger number of parties. When this effect became apparent, the law was changed back to the original system of requiring someone elected on a party list to form a Government.

The number of ministries varies from time to time; as of mid-February 2011, there were thirty ministries. Not infrequently, a ministry is created to accommodate a party that demands a ministerial post for one of its members as a price for entering the Government. As a result, in addition to the main ministries, such as Foreign Affairs, Defense, Finance, Interior and Justice, there are ministries of a more peculiar nature such as the Ministry of Pensioner Affairs and the Ministry of Improvement of Government Services. Some ministries reflect interests peculiar to Israeli society, such as the Ministry of Immigration Absorption, the Ministry for Home Front Defense,[13] and the Ministry of Religious Services.

Section 4 of the Basic Law: The Government provides that the Government has "shared responsibility." Section 5 provides, "The Government is composed of the prime minister and the other ministers." The effect of these two sections, taken together, is that the Government can thwart the proposed action of a single minister to which a majority of other ministers object. Thus, when the minister of environmental protection wants to enact a regulation that will reduce pollution but may adversely affect some sector of the economy, enactment of the regulation can be stopped by the united opposition of the minister of industry, trade and labor, the minister of finance, and their allies if they hold a majority of cabinet votes. Since all ministers, who comprise the Government, have a shared responsibility for the position taken by any individual minister, all ministers get a voice in what any individual minister wants to do. In theory, this system makes sense in that it requires coordination of all interests before the Government can act. In practice, it makes it difficult for weaker ministries to take actions. This matter is further explored in chapter 9 on administrative law.

A good deal of detailed information on the Government is available at the website of the Government of Israel. This site is in Hebrew. An English language version, available at http://www.gov.il/FirstGov/English, is not as extensive, and is designed partly to meet the needs of tourists and English speaking immigrants and migrant workers. Links to English language websites of the various Governmental ministries can be found at http://www.gov.il/firstGov/topNavEng/Engoffices/EngMinistries. The Government also maintains Arabic versions of its websites. In addition, each Ministry has a multi-lingual website.

---

12. This is not always the case. Sometimes, it appears that the head of the party that got the most votes will not be able to form a majority coalition because most of the votes went to parties on the opposite side of the political spectrum. Therefore the head of the party with the second largest number of votes, but with the greatest number of potential coalition allies, will be asked to form a government.

13. The position of minister of home front defense was created in January 2011. It is not clear whether there is a ministry or just a minister.

D. The Attorney General

The attorney general is an executive official with an important role in the legal system. The attorney general provides legal advice to the Government[14] and also functions as the state's chief prosecutor. In the latter role, the attorney general has the authority to decide which cases should be prosecuted. In a number of cases, the attorney general has had to decide whether to prosecute high governmental officials. Frequently these officials are the same people to whom the office of the attorney general must provide legal advice. This creates a troublesome conflict of interest, which has been the subject of considerable discussion in Israel. The matter is especially important because, in a few cases, the prosecution of prominent high governmental officials has had a significant effect on the Israeli legal landscape.

In the United States, the head of the Department of Justice is called the attorney general. In Israel, the situation is different. The minister of justice and the attorney general are two different people. The minister of justice appoints the attorney general from among candidates recommended by a public committee.

E. The President

The president is the head of state, but not the head of the Government. The president has two significant powers: (1) selection of the person who will try to form a new Government and (2) granting pardons and reducing sentences of criminal offenders. Other than this, the powers of the president are largely ceremonial. The president is chosen by vote of the majority of the members of the Knesset and serves for seven years.

The president has a website but, as of this writing, it is still under development and available only in Hebrew. The site is found at http://www.president.gov.il. By the time you read this, you may find that this site includes a link to an English language site.

F. The Courts

The courts are covered in detail in chapter 5. The Israeli judicial system has an extensive website in Hebrew. The English version, at http://elyon1.court.gov.il/eng/home/index.html, contains information on the courts, but very few court decisions because very few have been officially translated into English. The website also has an Arabic version.

---

14. Because of this function, the Hebrew term for the office is "Legal Advisor to the Government."

G. The State Comptroller

The office of the State Comptroller is established in the Basic Law: The State Comptroller, but most of the duties of this office are set out in a regular statute, the State Comptroller Law (Consolidated Version), 5718-1958. The state comptroller has two main duties. The first is to perform an audit of all public authorities. The second is to serve as an ombudsman for public complaints. The state comptroller is appointed to a term of seven years by the Knesset and reports to it. This is a respected position in the state, and the Comptroller and staff are usually seen as highly professional and divorced from all politics. Several prominent retired judges have served as state comptrollers.

The institutions and persons subject to audit by the comptroller include all ministries in the Government, all local governmental authorities, all other governmental institutions, all government companies, all organizations in which the government participates in management, all organizations and institutions directly or indirectly supported by the government, all workers' unions, and all persons holding governmental property. The scope of the audit is very broad. It is described in the applicable statute in this way:

Israeli Statute

State Comptroller Law
(Consolidated Version), 5718-1958

10. Scope of Audit

(a) Within the framework of the job, the Comptroller shall examine, to the extent necessary—

(1)

(a) Whether all funds were spent in a lawful manner and for the intended purpose;

(b) Whether income received was lawfully received;

(c) Whether all expenditures are adequately documented;

(d) Whether all actions undertaken in relation to the matter under audit were undertaken in accordance with the law and by the person authorized to undertake such actions;

(e) Whether the accounting, balancing of accounts, review of funds and of property and the system of management of documents are efficient;

(f) Whether the funds were handled and property maintained in an acceptable manner;

(g) Whether the funds and property on hand correspond to that in the records.

Comment

The Comptroller, aided by a staff, prepares an annual report. In each year, the report may emphasize different aspects of each ministry's work. Although the report is formally issued to the Knesset, it is released to the public and extensive excerpts are published in the major newspapers.

In the ombudsman function, the Comptroller receives and investigates complaints from members of the public about the functioning of most of the institutions subject to audit. In this capacity, the Comptroller receives about 6000–7000 complaints a year. About 35 percent are found to be justified.[15] This does not mean that 35 percent of public decisions are wrong, but that 35 percent of those someone complains about to the Comptroller are wrong.

The Comptroller's website in English is at http://www.mevaker.gov.il/serve/site/english/index.asp. The Hebrew version has much more extensive information on reports and complaints. There is also an Arabic version.

H. Local Governments

Israel has a highly-centralized government; all of the institutions described above are national institutions. In addition, local and regional governmental authorities operate throughout the country. These are units of the national government and are established by laws enacted by the Knesset. A local government in Israel is typically the government of a city or a smaller urban unit. A regional government typically covers several small towns and moshavs and kibbutzes. Unlike American states, Israeli local and regional governments are not inherent units of governmental power. The national government does not need the agreement of the local and regional governments to act, nor do the local or regional governments have any formal role in constituting the Knesset.

Local and regional governmental authorities have only those powers granted to them in the national laws. Those powers include the power to enact local ordinances that apply within the jurisdiction of the local or regional government, but only on subjects permitted in the national laws. For example, education is controlled much more on the national level, with local levels administering the educational system but the basic requirements being set by national laws. Furthermore, part of the budget of the local and regional authorities comes from the national government. Local and regional governments also get a substantial portion of their budgets from local property taxes, but their power to set the level of those taxes is limited by national law. The role of the local and regional governments is probably strongest in the field of planning, and there have been recent moves to strengthen local and regional government independence in such matters, but national supervision remains. Local and regional governments in Israel are not the major players that local and state governments are in the United States.

Local and regional governments vary considerably in population and character. Some have very diverse populations. Others have almost exclusively Arab, or Bedouin, or Druze, or Jewish Ultra-Orthodox populations. Some have large numbers of recent immigrants; others have few. Some are located on the Mediterranean and others are in the hill country of the Galilee or in the very dry desert regions in southern Israel. Some cities have mainly wealthy populations, some have a large number of very poor people, and some are home to varied economic groups.

Local government elections are held separately from national elections. In cities, the local residents elect both a mayor and a city council. Elections for mayor are direct; people vote for a specific candidate. Elections for the city council, like national elections for the Knesset, are by party lists, although local parties may be different from those that

---

15. Website of the State Comptroller and Ombudsman, http://www.mevaker.gov.il/serve/site/english/eombuds-intro.asp.

compete in national elections. One interesting feature of local election law in Israel is that all residents, including those who are not citizens, can vote in local elections. Only citizens vote in national elections.

Many local governments have websites in Hebrew and Arabic, and some of them have extensive English language versions, including those of Jerusalem and Tel Aviv:

Jerusalem: http://www.jerusalem.muni.il/jer_main/defaultnew.asp?lng=2

Tel Aviv: http://www.tel-aviv.gov.il/english/

Question

4. In what ways is power more concentrated in the Israeli system of government than in the US system?

Part Two

The Legal System

Chapter 4

Legal History

This survey of Israel's legal history serves two purposes. First, it helps understand parts of the current law. The law in effect in Israel today is influenced by legal history, although the degree of that influence decreases as time passes and Israel produces more of its own law. Second, it provides us with an opportunity to see how a country is established in the modern world and how its legal system comes into being.

A. The Ottoman Period: 1517 to 1917

The area now within the boundaries of Israel was part of the Palestine region of the Ottoman Empire from 1517, when the Ottoman sultan defeated the Mamluks, until 1917, when British forces entered the region during World War I. The Ottoman legal system changed during the course of the long Ottoman rule, with the most significant changes for our purposes occurring in the mid-nineteenth century. The changes were driven by the growing importance of industry and commerce and the growing secularization of the Empire.

This period saw the enactment of the *Majalla*, an extensive code based on the principles of Islamic law according to the Hanafi School.[1] The *Majalla*, while based on Islamic law, was designed to be useful to the non-Muslim judges sitting on the benches of the civil courts in some parts of the Ottoman Empire. The *Majalla* covered many substantive areas of civil law, such as contracts, tort, labor, and property law, and also included provisions on procedure and evidence. It omitted other topics, the most important of which were those associated with personal status, including marriage, wills, and inheritance. The law on these topics was left to the religious authorities.

While the *Majalla* itself no longer has the force of law in Israel,[2] some of the legal rules in the *Majalla* have been adopted in Israeli statutes even though they differ from the rules of the generally more influential English law. Most provisions of the *Majalla*, however, do not have a sustaining effect on Israeli law; they applied to a society, a way of thinking, and a time that is not represented in the modern Israeli state. For example, the *Majalla* has provisions only on certain types of contracts; it lacks general contract law. It seems that the law on which the *Majalla* was based allowed enforcement of agreements in specified commercial settings, but lacked a general concept that all agreements should be enforced.

---

1. The Hanafi School is one of the four major schools of jurisprudence of Islamic law for Sunni Muslims.
2. The Repeal of Majalla Law, 5744-1984, makes this explicit. It provides an exception for the Shari'a Courts, which are the Islamic courts functioning as state institutions in areas of personal status issues for Muslims. See chapter 12.

The limited approach to contract law is inappropriate for modern commercial society, which needs general contract rules. As another example, the *Majalla* provided tort remedies for damage to property, but not for personal injury (perhaps on the assessment that determination of the proper measure of monetary compensation for personal injury is not feasible or not appropriate).[3]

Ottoman law, enacted in the period from the mid-1800s until the defeat of the Ottoman Empire, derived in part from the *Majalla*, but also included a number of codes derived from various European sources of law. It is likely that French law was highly influential, although records are not always clear on the sources of various sections of the codes or on why changes were made.[4] The Ottomans were also legal innovators. The Ottoman Land Law of 1858 was different from other laws in that it apparently did not derive from either European law or the *Majalla*, but was developed independently.[5]

B. The British Period: 1917 to 1948

British rule began in 1917 with the British defeat of the Ottomans and was legally sanctioned by the international community in 1922 with the decision of the League of Nations to establish the British Mandate for Palestine.[6] The Mandate covered the areas now included in Israel, the West Bank, and Jordan. After World War I, it became necessary to decide how to govern territories captured from Germany and the Ottoman Empire. Rather than allowing them to become colonies of the conquering countries, it was decided to set up a system for each area to be administered by one of the Allied powers under international supervision. The League of Nations functioned as the supervising body. The British Mandate over Palestine was only one of several Mandates set up in this way: others included, in the Middle East, the British Mandate over Iraq and the French Mandate over Lebanon and Syria; in Africa, the British Mandate over Tanganyika and the Belgian mandate over Ruanda-Urundi; and elsewhere, the Australian Mandate over New Guinea. For the Middle East mandates, at least, it was expected that the areas subject to mandate administration would eventually become independent countries.

Shortly after the League of Nations established the British Mandate, the British adopted the following law:

British Law

The Palestine Order in Council
Palestine Order in Council (1922)

WHEREAS the Principal Allied Powers have agreed, for the purpose of giving effect to the provisions of Article 22 of the Covenant of the League of Nations, to entrust to a Mandatory selected by the said Powers the administration of the territory of Palestine,

---

3. *See* Daniel Friedman, *The Effect of Foreign Law on the Law of Israel: Remnants of the Ottoman Period*, 10 Isr. L. Rev. 192, 198 (1975).

4. Friedman, *supra* note 3, at 198–99.

5. *Id.* at 201.

6. Recall the explanation of the use of the term *Palestine* in chapter 2.

which formerly belonged to the Turkish Empire, within such boundaries as may be fixed by them;

And whereas the Principal Allied Powers have also agreed that the Mandatory should be responsible for putting into effect the declaration originally made on November 2, 1917, by the Government of His Britannic Majesty, and adopted by the said Powers, in favour of the establishment in Palestine of a national home for the Jewish people, it being clearly understood that nothing should be done which might prejudice the civil and religious rights of existing non-Jewish communities in Palestine, or the rights and political status enjoyed by Jews in any other country;

And whereas the Principal Allied Powers have selected His Majesty as the Mandatory for Palestine;

And whereas, by treaty, capitulation, grant, usage, sufferance and other lawful means, His Majesty has power and jurisdiction within Palestine;

NOW, THEREFORE, His Majesty, by virtue and in exercise of the powers in this behalf by the Foreign Jurisdiction Act, 1890, or otherwise, in His Majesty vested, is pleased, by and with the advice of His Privy Council, to order, and it is hereby ordered, as follows:—

Part I

1. Title

This Order may be cited as "The Palestinian Order in Council, 1922."

46. Law to be applied

The jurisdiction of the Civil Courts shall be exercised in conformity with the Ottoman Law in force in Palestine on November 1st, 1914, and such later Ottoman Laws as have been or may be declared to be in force by Public Notice, and such Orders in Council, ordinances and regulations as are in force in Palestine at the date of the commencement of this Order, or may hereafter be applied or enacted; and subject thereto and so far as the same shall not extend or apply, shall be exercised in conformity with the substance of the common law, and the doctrines of equity in force in England, and with the powers vested in and according to the procedure and practice observed by or before Courts of Justice and Justices of the Peace in England, according to their respective jurisdictions and authorities at that date, save in so far as the said powers, procedure and practice may have been or may hereafter be modified, amended or replaced by any other provisions. Provided always that the said common law and doctrines of equity shall be in force in Palestine so far only as the circumstances of Palestine and its inhabitants and the limits of His Majesty's jurisdiction permit and subject to such qualification as local circumstances render necessary.

Comment

Section 46 of The Palestinian Order in Council had several notable effects. It left existing Ottoman law in force at the beginning of the British rule so that the Mandate immediately had an effective legal system already familiar to its residents. Additionally it allowed replacement of Ottoman law by new law, so that the fragmented and dated Ottoman law could be modernized with law enacted by the British. Moreover English common law and the doctrines of equity, neither of which were part of Ottoman law, were given effect. This moved Israel into the common law tradition, and that tradition continues to influence, although not fully to define, Israeli case law. The influence of the common law in Israel is explored further in chapter 5.

The new British statutes came from two sources: (1) statutes in effect in England and (2) statutes used by the British in other areas subject to British rule, such as Cyprus and Australia. In these cases, the statutes covered matters which were left to judicial development through the common law in England and on which there were no comparable English statutes. Apparently the Mandatory administration thought it better to confine the discretion of the courts operating in Palestine by spelling out the rules of law in statutes.[7] Statutes from both sources have had enduring influence on Israeli law after the establishment of the state.

English common law precedents were to be used in interpreting both types of British statutes. This requirement was set out in section 46 of the Palestine Order in Council. It was also implicit in statutes drawn from their English counterparts, which were subject to interpretation by the courts in England. Furthermore, statutes designed specifically for the colonies and for the Mandate typically had explicit provisions requiring interpretation in accord with English law.

The British also set up a court system, partially modeled on its Ottoman predecessor and partially on the English legal system, with three levels of courts of general jurisdiction: the magistrates' courts, the district courts, and a Supreme Court. The Supreme Court would also sit as the High Court of Justice to hear petitions against decisions of administrative officials. In other words, the Supreme Court would sit in one capacity on most cases and in another capacity, following different rules, on administrative law cases. Supreme Court decisions could be appealed to the English Privy Council, which sat in England.[8] Lower level courts were staffed largely by Arab and Jewish local residents; but the Supreme Court had mostly British judges, and the panel of Supreme Court judges sitting on major matters had to include at least one British judge.[9]

After World War II, the League of Nations Mandate System was replaced by the United Nations Trusteeship, under which British rule in Palestine continued until 1948.

C. The State of Israel: 1948 to Present

Six legal documents were crucial to the establishment of the State of Israel and to the ordering of the democratic legal system of the new state. These are:

1. United Nations General Assembly Resolution 181 (II); Future Government of Palestine (November 29, 1947).

2. Israel's Declaration of the Establishment of the State of Israel, May 14, 1948.

3. The Law and Administration Ordinance, 1948.

4. Constituent Assembly (Transition) Ordinance, 1949.

5. The Transition Law, 5709-1949.

6. The Law on Foundations of Law, 1980.

---

7. ARIEL BEN-NUN, THE LAW OF THE STATE OF ISRAEL 17–19 (1992).

8. Government of Palestine: Ordinances, Regulations, Rules, Orders and Notices 1–6 (1924).

9. SHIMON SHETREET, JUSTICE IN ISRAEL: A STUDY OF THE ISRAELI JUDICIARY 50 (1994); Eli M. Salzberger, *Judicial Appointments and Promotions in Israel: Constitution, Law, and Politics*, in AP-POINTING JUDGES IN AN AGE OF JUDICIAL POWER: CRITICAL PERSPECTIVES FROM AROUND THE WORLD 241, 244 (Kate Malleson & Peter H. Russell eds., 2006).

The first of these documents, commonly referred to as UN Resolution 181, provided for the termination of the British Mandate for Palestine and the establishment, in its place, of an Arab state, a Jewish state, and an internationalized City of Jerusalem. The content of the Resolution reflects the political concerns regarding the division of the Mandate territory.

UN Resolution

United Nations General Assembly Resolution 181 (II)

Future Government of Palestine
Resolution Adopted on the Report of the Ad Hoc *Committee on the Palestinian Question, G.A. Res. 181(II), UN Doc. A/RES/181(II) (Nov. 29, 1947) (Part A: Future of Palestine)*[10]

PLAN OF PARTITION WITH ECONOMIC UNION

PART I

Future Constitution and Government of Palestine

A. TERMINATION OF MANDATE, PARTITION AND INDEPENDENCE

1. The Mandate for Palestine shall terminate as soon as possible but in any case not later than 1 August 1948.

2. The armed forces of the mandatory Power shall be progressively withdrawn from Palestine, the withdrawal to be completed as soon as possible but in any case not later than 1 August 1948.

The mandatory Power shall advise the Commission, as far in advance as possible, of its intention to terminate the Mandate and to evacuate each area.

The mandatory Power shall use its best endeavours to ensure than an area situated in the territory of the Jewish State, including a seaport and hinterland adequate to provide facilities for a substantial immigration, shall be evacuated at the earliest possible date and in any event not later than 1 February 1948.

3. Independent Arab and Jewish States and the Special International Regime for the City of Jerusalem, set forth in part III of this plan, shall come into existence in Palestine two months after the evacuation of the armed forces of the mandatory Power has been completed but in any case not later than 1 October 1948. The boundaries of the Arab State, the Jewish State, and the City of Jerusalem shall be as described in parts II and III below.

4. The period between the adoption by the General Assembly of its recommendation on the question of Palestine and the establishment of the independence of the Arab and Jewish States shall be a transitional period.

B. STEPS PREPARATORY TO INDEPENDENCE

4. The Commission [established by the United Nations], after consultation with the democratic parties and other public organizations of The Arab and Jewish States, shall select and establish in each State as rapidly as possible a Provisional Council of Govern-

---

10. This is a very long document. The portion presented here relates to the legal arrangements for the establishment of the State of Israel. Portions on economic and political arrangements are omitted.

ment. The activities of both the Arab and Jewish Provisional Councils of Government shall be carried out under the general direction of the Commission.

If by 1 April 1948 a Provisional Council of Government cannot be selected for either of the States, or, if selected, cannot carry out its functions, the Commission shall communicate that fact to the Security Council for such action with respect to that State as the Security Council may deem proper, and to the Secretary-General for communication to the Members of the United Nations.

9. The Provisional Council of Government of each State shall, not later than two months after the withdrawal of the armed forces of the mandatory Power, hold elections to the Constituent Assembly which shall be conducted on democratic lines ...

10. The Constituent Assembly of each State shall draft a democratic constitution for its State and choose a provisional government to succeed the Provisional Council of Government appointed by the Commission. The constitutions of the States shall embody chapters 1 and 2 of the Declaration provided for in section C below and include inter alia provisions for:

(a) Establishing in each State a legislative body elected by universal suffrage and by secret ballot on the basis of proportional representation, and an executive body responsible to the legislature;

(b) Settling all international disputes in which the State may be involved by peaceful means in such a manner that international peace and security, and justice, are not endangered;

(c) Accepting the obligation of the State to refrain in its international relations from the threat or use of force against the territorial integrity of political independence of any State, or in any other manner inconsistent with the purposes of the United Nations;

(d) Guaranteeing to all persons equal and non-discriminatory rights in civil, political, economic and religious matters and the enjoyment of human rights and fundamental freedoms, including freedom of religion, language, speech and publication, education, assembly and association;

(e) Preserving freedom of transit and visit for all residents and citizens of the other State in Palestine and the City of Jerusalem, subject to considerations of national security, provided that each State shall control residence within its borders.

C. DECLARATION

A declaration shall be made to the United Nations by the provisional government of each proposed State before independence. It shall contain inter alia the following clauses:

General Provision

The stipulations contained in the declaration are recognized as fundamental laws of the State and no law, regulation or official action shall conflict or interfere with these stipulations, nor shall any law, regulation or official action prevail over them.

Chapter 1
Holy Places, religious buildings and sites

1. Existing rights in respect of Holy Places and religious buildings or sites shall not be denied or impaired.

2. In so far as Holy Places are concerned, the liberty of access, visit and transit shall be guaranteed, in conformity with existing rights, to all residents and citizens of the other

State and of the City of Jerusalem, as well as to aliens, without distinction as to nationality, subject to requirements of national security, public order and decorum.

Similarly freedom of worship shall be guaranteed in conformity with existing rights, subject to the maintenance of public order and decorum.

3. Holy Places and religious buildings or sites shall be preserved. No act shall be permitted which may in any way impair their sacred character. If at any time it appears to the Government that any particular Holy Place, religious building or site is in need of urgent repair, the Government may call upon the community or communities concerned to carry out such repair. The Government may carry it out itself at the expense of the community or communities concerned if no action is taken within a reasonable time.

4. No taxation shall be levied in respect of any Holy Place, religious building or site which was exempt from taxation on the date of the creation of the State.

No change in the incidence of such taxation shall be made which would either discriminate between the owners or occupiers of Holy Places, religious buildings or sites, or would place such owners or occupiers in a position less favourable in relation to the general incidence of taxation than existed at the time of the adoption of the Assembly's recommendations.

5. The Governor of the City of Jerusalem shall have the right to determine whether the provisions of the Constitution of the State in relation to Holy Places, religious buildings and sites within the borders of the State and the religious rights appertaining thereto, are being properly applied and respected, and to make decisions on the basis of existing rights in cases of disputes which may arise between the different religious communities or the rites of a religious community with respect to such places, buildings and sites. He shall receive full co-operation and such privileges and immunities as are necessary for the exercise of his functions in the State.

Chapter 2
Religious and minority Rights

1. Freedom of conscience and the free exercise of all forms of worship, subject only to the maintenance of public order and morals, shall be ensured to all.

2. No discrimination of any kind shall be made between the inhabitants on the ground of race, religion, language or sex.

3. All persons within the jurisdiction of the State shall be entitled to equal protection of the laws.

4. The family law and personal status of the various minorities and their religious interests, including endowments, shall be respected.

5. Except as may be required for the maintenance of public order and good government, no measure shall be taken to obstruct or interfere with the enterprise of religious or charitable bodies of all faiths or to discriminate against any representative or member of these bodies on the ground of his religion or nationality.

6. The State shall ensure adequate primary and secondary education for the Arab and Jewish minority, respectively, in its own language and its cultural traditions.

The right of each community to maintain its own schools for the education of its own members in its own language, while conforming to such educational requirements of a general nature as the State may impose, shall not be denied or impaired. Foreign educational establishments shall continue their activity on the basis of their existing rights.

7. No restriction shall be imposed on the free use by any citizen of the State of any language in private intercourse, in commerce, in religion, in the Press or in publications of any kind, or at public meetings.

8. No expropriation of land owned by an Arab in the Jewish State ([or] by a Jew in the Arab State) shall be allowed except for public purposes. In all cases of expropriation full compensation as fixed by the Supreme Court shall be paid previous to dispossession.

Chapter 3
Citizenship, international conventions and financial obligations

1. Citizenship. Palestinian citizens residing in Palestine outside the City of Jerusalem, as well as Arabs and Jews who, not holding Palestinian citizenship, reside in Palestine outside the City of Jerusalem shall, upon the recognition of independence, become citizens of the State in which they are resident and enjoy full civil and political rights. Persons over the age of eighteen years may opt, within one year from the date of recognition of independence of the State in which they reside, for citizenship of the other State, providing that no Arab residing in the area of the proposed Arab State shall have the right to opt for citizenship in the proposed Jewish State and no Jew residing in the proposed Jewish State shall have the right to opt for citizenship in the proposed Arab State. The exercise of this right of option will be taken to include the wives and children under eighteen years of age of persons so opting.

Arabs residing in the area of the proposed Jewish State and Jews residing in the area of the proposed Arab State who have signed a notice of intention to opt for citizenship of the other State shall be eligible to vote in the elections to the Constituent Assembly of that State, but not in the elections to the Constituent Assembly of the State in which they reside.

Comment

The division of territory between a Jewish and an Arab state, with the internationalization of Jerusalem, gave neither the Jewish community nor the Arab community all it wanted. Although the areas with the greatest Jewish population would have been allocated to the Jewish state, and those with the greatest Arab population to the Arab state, both of the states would have had discontinuous territory. Neither state would have included Jerusalem. Nonetheless the Jewish community celebrated in the streets and agreed to accept the partition plan, although the local Arab community and surrounding Arab states rejected it.[11]

UN resolution gave the British until August 1, 1948, to terminate the Mandate, but Great Britain, worn out by the fighting between the Arabs and the Jews and the opposition to the Mandatory regime, decided to terminate its rule on May 15, 1948. One day earlier, the Jewish People's Council met and declared the establishment of the State of Israel to be effective upon the British withdrawal. The Jewish People's Council, also known as the Jewish National Council, was the main institution established by the Jewish community during the period of the British Mandate to govern the Jewish community and

---

11. The legal aspects of the Jewish acceptance and Arab rejection are discussed in the first six articles in a Symposium, The Middle East Crisis: Test of International Law, 33 LAW & CONTEMPORARY PROBLEMS 1, 5–109 (1968). *See also* SUZIE NAVOT, THE CONSTITUTIONAL LAW OF ISRAEL 20 (2007).

conduct communal affairs. The written declaration issued by this body set out the legal basis for the provisional government that was to set up the permanent government of the state. It also met many of the requirements set out in the UN Resolution for establishment of the Jewish state, but it did not address them all.

Israeli Document

Declaration of the Establishment of the State of Israel, 5708-1948

1 LSI 3 (1948)[12]

ERETZ-ISRAEL [(Hebrew)—the Land of Israel, Palestine] was the birthplace of the Jewish people. Here their spiritual, religious and political identity was shaped. Here they first attained to statehood, created cultural values of national and universal significance and gave to the world the eternal Book of Books.

After being forcibly exiled from their land, the people kept faith with it throughout their Dispersion and never ceased to pray and hope for their return to it and for the restoration in it of their political freedom.

Impelled by this historic and traditional attachment, Jews strove in every successive generation to re-establish themselves in their ancient homeland. In recent decades they returned in their masses. Pioneers, ma'pilim [(Hebrew)—immigrants coming to Eretz-Israel in defiance of restrictive British legislation] and defenders, they made deserts bloom, revived the Hebrew language, built villages and towns, and created a thriving community controlling its own economy and culture, loving peace but knowing how to defend itself, bringing the blessings of progress to all the country's inhabitants, and aspiring towards independent nationhood.

In the year 5657 (1897), at the summons of the spiritual father of the Jewish State, Theodore Herzl, the First Zionist Congress convened and proclaimed the right of the Jewish people to national rebirth in its own country.

This right was recognized in the *Balfour Declaration* of the 2nd November, 1917, and re-affirmed in the *Mandate of the League of Nations* which, in particular, gave international sanction to the historic connection between the Jewish people and Eretz-Israel and to the right of the Jewish people to rebuild its National Home.

The catastrophe which recently befell the Jewish people—the massacre of millions of Jews in Europe—was another clear demonstration of the urgency of solving the problem of its homelessness by re-establishing in Eretz-Israel the Jewish State, which would open the gates of the homeland wide to every Jew and confer upon the Jewish people the status of a fully privileged member of the comity of nations.

Survivors of the Nazi holocaust in Europe, as well as Jews from other parts of the world, continued to migrate to Eretz-Israel, undaunted by difficulties, restrictions and dangers, and never ceased to assert their right to a life of dignity, freedom and honest toil in their national homeland.

---

12. The English translation presented in Laws of the State of Israel (LSI) is the official translation. The use of capital letters in part of the document is the way this is presented in the official translation. Hebrew does not have capital letters, so they are not used in the original.

In the Second World War, the Jewish community of this country contributed its full share to the struggle of the freedom- and peace-loving nations against the forces of Nazi wickedness and, by the blood of its soldiers and its war effort, gained the right to be reckoned among the peoples who founded the United Nations.

On the 29th November, 1947, the United Nations General Assembly passed a resolution calling for the establishment of a Jewish State in Eretz-Israel; the General Assembly required the inhabitants of Eretz-Israel to take such steps as were necessary on their part for the implementation of that resolution. This recognition by the United Nations of the right of the Jewish people to establish their State is irrevocable.

This right is the natural right of the Jewish people to be masters of their own fate, like all other nations, in their own sovereign State.

ACCORDINGLY WE, MEMBERS OF THE PEOPLE'S COUNCIL, REPRESENTATIVES OF THE JEWISH COMMUNITY OF ERETZ-ISRAEL AND OF THE ZIONIST MOVEMENT, ARE HERE ASSEMBLED ON THE DAY OF THE TERMINATION OF THE BRITISH MANDATE OVER ERETZ-ISRAEL AND, BY VIRTUE OF OUR NATURAL AND HISTORIC RIGHT AND ON THE STRENGTH OF THE RESOLUTION OF THE UNITED NATIONS GENERAL ASSEMBLY, HEREBY DECLARE THE ESTABLISHMENT OF A JEWISH STATE IN ERETZ-ISRAEL, TO BE KNOWN AS THE STATE OF ISRAEL.

WE DECLARE that, with effect from the moment of the termination of the Mandate being tonight, the eve of Sabbath, the 6th Iyar, 5708 (15th May, 1948), until the establishment of the elected, regular authorities of the State in accordance with the Constitution which shall be adopted by the Elected Constituent Assembly not later than the 1st October 1948, the People's Council shall act as a Provisional Council of State, and its executive organ, the People's Administration, shall be the Provisional Government of the Jewish State, to be called "Israel."

THE STATE OF ISRAEL will be open for Jewish immigration and for the Ingathering of the Exiles;[13] it will foster the development of the country for the benefit of all its inhabitants; it will be based on freedom, justice and peace as envisaged by the prophets of Israel; it will ensure complete equality of social and political rights to all its inhabitants irrespective of religion, race or sex; it will guarantee freedom of religion, conscience, language, education and culture; it will safeguard the Holy Places of all religions; and it will be faithful to the principles of the Charter of the United Nations.

THE STATE OF ISRAEL is prepared to cooperate with the agencies and representatives of the United Nations in implementing the resolution of the General Assembly of the 29th November, 1947, and will take steps to bring about the economic union of the whole of Eretz-Israel.

WE APPEAL to the United Nations to assist the Jewish people in the building-up of its State and to receive the State of Israel into the comity of nations.

WE APPEAL—in the very midst of the onslaught launched against us now for months— to the Arab inhabitants of the State of Israel to preserve peace and participate in the up-

---

13. The term *ingathering of exiles* refers to the return of Jews to the land from which they were exiled at the destruction of the first and second temples. This is discussed in chapter 2 in the section on history.

building of the State on the basis of full and equal citizenship and due representation in all its provisional and permanent institutions.

WE EXTEND our hand to all neighbouring states and their peoples in an offer of peace and good neighbourliness, and appeal to them to establish bonds of cooperation and mutual help with the sovereign Jewish people settled in its own land. The State of Israel is prepared to do its share in a common effort for the advancement of the entire Middle East.

Comment

This declaration bases the right of the Jewish people to a state on Jewish history and on the "natural right of the Jewish people to be masters of their own fate, like all other nations, in their own sovereign State." It refers to the UN resolution as recognizing that right, but not as the source of that right.

The declaration also contains provisions setting out legal principles that were later incorporated into Israeli law, sometimes by common law development by judges who cited the declaration as a source of law and sometimes by legislative action. Later legislation also dealt with some of the requirements of the UN resolution that were not addressed in the declaration.

Questions

1. Look at the Declaration of Independence of the Thirteen United States of America, which is readily available online. Compare what the colonies saw as the source of their authority to declare the establishment of their own government, free of rule by Great Britain, with what the Israelis saw as the source of their authority to establish their own rule.

2. What legal principles do you find set out in the Israeli Declaration of Independence?

———————

The declaration also provided a mechanism for the establishment of a legal system. Because a democratic regime was envisioned, the declaration provided for elections to a Constituent Assembly. It was explicitly assumed that the Constituent Assembly would adopt a constitution, which would provide the permanent legal framework for the state. Of course, elections could not be held immediately. A date three-and-a-half months later was chosen for these elections. In the meantime, the new state would need some sort of governing structure. The situation was different from that in the United States, where functioning state governments carried out the everyday tasks of governing while the national government was established. Under the terms of the Israeli Declaration, the People's Council became the Provisional Council of State, the legislative branch of the interim regime. The People's Administration, which became the Provisional Government of the Jewish State, would be the executive branch. Once the constitution was written, these two institutions would be replaced by new institutions elected according to the provisions of the yet-to-be-written constitution.

The Provisional Council of State immediately took the essential step of establishing a system of law. It was important to have functioning laws so that life could continue as normally as possible. People needed to be able to conduct business while the government was organizing itself. Likewise, people needed to be able to marry, criminal prosecutions had to continue, etc. Therefore the following statute was enacted by the Provisional Council of State on May 19, 1948, to set up the structure of the provisional government and provide for continuity of the existing regime of legal rules.

Israeli Statute

Law and Administration Ordinance, 1948

Under the authority granted to the Provisional Council of State by the Declaration of the Establishment of the State of Israel of the 5th Iyar, 5708 (May 14, 1948) and by the proclamation issued on that date, the Provision Council of State hereby enacts the following:

Chapter One: The Administration

1. The Provisional Council of State.

(a) The Provisional Council of State comprises the persons whose names are set out in the appendix to this ordinance.

2. The Provisional Government.

(a) The Provisional Government comprises the persons whose names are set out in the appendix to this ordinance.

(b) The Provisional Government shall act in accordance with the policy set by the Provisional Council of State, shall implement its decisions, and shall present it with a report on its activities.

(c) The Provisional Government shall select one of its members to be prime minister and shall prescribe the functions of each of its members. A member of the Provisional Government shall be called minister.

(d) The Provisional Government may grant some of its powers to the prime minister and to any of the ministers, insofar as it is not inconsistent with any of the ordinances of the Provisional Council of State.

Chapter Three: Legislation

7. Ordinances.

The Provisional Council of State is the legislative authority. Laws shall be called ordinances.

Chapter Four: The Law

11. Existing Law

The law which existed in the Land of Israel on the 5th Iyar, 5708 (May 14, 1948) shall remain in force, insofar as it is consistent with this ordinance and with the other laws which may be enacted by the Provisional Council of State or under its authority, and with such modifications as may result from the establishment of the state and its authorities.

12. Termination of Dependence on Britain

(a) Any privilege granted by law to the British Crown, British officials, or British subjects is hereby declared to be null and void.

(b) Any provision in the law requiring approval or consent of any of the secretaries of state of the King of Britain or requiring taking an action in accordance with his instructions is hereby declared to be null and void.

(c) Any power assigned by the law to judges, officers, or members of the police by virtue of their being British, is now assigned to judges, officers, or members of the police who hold the same office or rank in the state of Israel.

15. Further Adaptations in Law

(a) Every appearance of the term "Palestine (Land of Israel)" in a law shall henceforth be read as "Israel."

(b) Every provision in the law requiring the use of the English language is void.

Chapter Five: Law Courts

17. Law Courts

So long as no new law concerning law courts has been enacted, the law courts existing in the territory of the state shall continue to function within the framework of the powers granted them by law.

Comment

This ordinance, unlike the declaration, is a purely legal document. While the Declaration of Independence declared that the Provisional Council of State should act as the legislative body and the Provisional Government as the executive body, this ordinance provided not just a declaration that this should be so, but legal authority for these two bodies. It provided a full legal basis for the interim legislature, the Provisional Council of State, and the interim executive authority, the Provisional Government. The ordinance also provided that, for the most part, existing legal rules would remain in effect until changed. The Provisional Council of State separately enacted the Courts (Transitional Provisions) Ordinance that set up a revised and simplified system of law courts.

The declaration, issued on May 15, 1948, contemplated that elections for the Constituent Assembly would be almost immediate. Due to the difficulty of organizing an electoral mechanism during the 1948 war against the Palestinians and the Arab nations, the elections were delayed until January 1949.

The Provisional Council of State was composed of a named group of members and was not democratically elected. On January 14, 1949, just eleven days before the date set for the elections for the Constituent Assembly, the Provisional Council of State enacted another ordinance that would put the legislative power into the hands of a democratically elected body. Departing from the original idea expressed in the declaration that the Provisional Council of State would serve as the legislature until a constitution was written, the ordinance provided that the Constituent Assembly, while writing the constitution, would also exercise the legislative power.

Israeli Statute

Constituent Assembly (Transition) Ordinance 1949

1. The Provisional Council of State shall continue to serve until the Constituent Assembly of the State of Israel is convened; upon the convening of the Constituent Assembly, the Provisional Council of State shall be dissolved and shall cease to exist.

3. The Constituent Assembly shall have all the powers granted by law to the Provisional Council of State, so long as the Constituent Assembly does not make a different decision on the matter.

Comment

Once the elections occurred, the newly elected Constituent Assembly did not write a constitution. The reasons are explored in chapter 8. Accepting its legislative function, the Constituent Assembly transformed itself into the first Knesset, the parliamentary body that still functions. The transition was given legal basis in the following statute:

Israeli Statute

Transition Law, 5709-1949

1. Designation of the Legislature and its Members

The legislature of the State of Israel shall be called "the Knesset." The Constituent Assembly shall be called "the First Knesset." A delegate to the Constituent Assembly shall be called "a Member of the Knesset."

2. Statutes

A legislative enactment of the Knesset shall be called a "law."

Comment

This chain of events gave Israel a working democratic legal system with a legislature that could revise the existing laws and enact new ones. Other provisions in the Transition Law established the presidency and the Government; these have since been superseded by other laws.

Recall that by virtue of section 11 of the Law and Administration Ordinance, the law of the British Mandate that was in effect at the end of the British rule remained in effect, unless it was repugnant to the new laws of the nascent state. Over time, the Knesset revised the law, replacing the remnants of Ottoman law that remained in force throughout the period of the Mandate and modifying or replacing much of the British law as well. Nonetheless the influence of the British law has been enduring, especially in areas of public law.

The major issue that arose as to the British law was whether courts should refer to English common law in deciding cases. Although Section 46 of the Palestinian Order in Council and several ordinances from the British period required such reference, Israeli courts were understandably reluctant to behave as though bound by the decisions of a court of another country. After several cases dealing with the issue and an amendment to the Law and Administration Ordinance, 1972, the matter was settled in a 1980 statute which unequivocally cut the ties to the English common law as binding precedent for Israeli decisions. It provides that Israeli courts do not need to rely on English precedent, even when interpreting statutes that originated during the period of the Mandate.

Israeli Statute

Law on Foundations of Law, 5740-1980

1. Sources of Interstitial Law

When a court encounters a question that must be decided and cannot find an answer in a statute or regulation, case law, or by way of analogy, it shall decide based on the principles of freedom, justice, equity, and peace of the heritage of Israel.

2. Revocation of Section 46 of the Palestine Order in Council and Preservation of Laws

(a) Section 46 of the Palestine Order in Council, 1922–1940, is revoked.

(b) Nothing in subsection (a) shall nullify any law that has been absorbed into Israeli law prior to the effective date of this statute.

Comment

Israel now had its own democratic government and its full independence in developing its law. The remainder of this book examines those laws.

D. Terminology

Statutes that were enacted during the period of the British Mandate and retained in Israeli law kept their original title, but were translated into Hebrew. They are called *ordinances*. Ordinances from the Mandatory period should not be confused with laws of local government. In the United States, we usually refer to legislative acts of local government as ordinances. The comparable Hebrew term for local governmental legislation is *accessory law*, although that term is so odd in English that it is also translated as *ordinance*. Ordinances, in the sense of statutes from the British period, use only the common date as part of their title, rather than both a Jewish calendar date and a common date. An ordinance designated as "(New Version)" has an official Hebrew text and may differ from the original British law due to amendments and additions enacted by the Knesset. An ordinance designated as "(Consolidated Version)" is one which replaces (consolidates) several different prior ordinances into one statute. Statutes enacted by the Provisional Government of Israel in the early days of the state are also called ordinances. Statutes enacted by the Knesset that are original and not just an alteration of an ordinance have the word *law* in their title. Most Israeli statutes in force today are laws, but some important ordinances remain.

Chapter 5

Character of Legal System and Court Structure

A. Type of Legal System

Legal systems are often characterized as either common law or civil law. The latter is also sometimes referred to as continental law, because the civil law characterizes the countries of the European continent. Common law systems derive from the English system of law and are found in the countries that were once part of the British Empire. The common law gives prominence to judge-made law developed by courts in adjudicating cases, with the precedential value of the decisions creating binding legal doctrine. Of course, modern common law countries also have extensive statutory law, but they have not entirely displaced the importance of case-by-case adjudication. Legal analysis in a common law system employs a good deal of the type of inductive thinking taught extensively in American law schools.

Most common law courts are generalist, hearing both civil and criminal matters, and, within the civil sphere, a wide variety of types of cases. While in a common law system specific matters may be handled by specialized courts, their decisions are almost always subject to review by a higher generalist court. For example, decisions of state family courts are subject to review in the general jurisdiction courts of the state, and decisions of the Article I bankruptcy court in the federal system are subject to review in federal district courts.[1] In addition, if constitutionality of statutes and administrative actions is subject to judicial review, such review is typically done in generalist courts. In the United States, any court of general jurisdiction can consider constitutional questions. Appellate review in common law systems is usually de novo as to the law, but highly deferential as to determinations of fact. Judges are chosen from among practicing lawyers and legal academics, and usually have a substantial career in practice, teaching, or both before their appointment to the bench.

Discourse in judicial opinions in common law courts tends to be reasoned, with full examination of alternative arguments and detailed discussion of case law precedent. Much of the reasoning is inductive, deriving general rules from the specific holdings of prior cases. Furthermore, in examining precedent, judges distinguish the holding from dicta. They usually carefully consider whether case law precedent made in one set of facts should be applied to another set of facts. It is not unusual for judges to use policy analysis to help resolve new legal questions.

---

1. In some jurisdictions, parties may elect instead to have review heard by a Bankruptcy Appeal Panel. 28 USC § 158 (2010).

The civil law system, which originated in Roman law, is used in the countries of the European continent as well as the countries of Latin America and some other locations. Not all civil law systems are alike, and although they have important shared characteristics, they also have significant differences. The major emphasis is on legal codes, and decisions in specific cases are derived more from the code than from case precedent. The job of the judge is to apply the code to a controversy. Many of the codes include a statement of general principles, which are to guide in their application. Legal thinking tends toward the deductive, going from the general principles to the result in a case. Great importance is placed on scholarly analysis, which often proceeds at the theoretical level. Scholarly opinion or statements of legal principals may be cited as a source of law, something rarely seen in the common law as practiced in the United States.

A civil law system is usually characterized by multiple court systems, with one generalist and several specialist courts. Germany, for example, has four sets of specialist courts, one each for administrative law matters, social welfare cases, labor law, and tax law. Each set has both courts of original jurisdiction and appellate courts, and decisions of the highest specialist court are not appealable to any generalist court. Review of the constitutionality of statutes is typically assigned to a separate high-level constitutional court. The generalist court hears all cases not within the jurisdiction of one of the specialist courts. Within each set of courts, appellate review is de novo. The highest appellate court is usually a large body, comprising many judges who sit in different divisions. For example, the Federal Supreme Court of Germany (Bundesgerichtshof) has 127 judges[2] and the Supreme Court of France (Cour de Cassation), the highest general jurisdiction court in France, has 189 judges.[3] Judges are lawyers who have chosen a career in the judiciary, usually shortly after completing their university studies in law, and serve as judges throughout their careers.

The reasoning in cases is more formal and deductive than in common law cases. The reader accustomed to the rhetoric of the common law will find that civil law cases use a more abstract analysis.

The division between common law and civil law systems is not complete. In the modern world, some common law systems are taking on specific characteristics of civil law, and some civil law systems have integrated common law features into their operations. Still, we often characterize systems by their predominant characteristics. Thus, Great Britain is considered to be a common law jurisdiction and Germany a civil law jurisdiction.

Israel has a mixed system of law.[4] This means that it has some features of the common law and some features of the civil law. For example, the structure of the courts and court procedure, described in the rest of this chapter, is very much like that in common law countries. Judges have authority to make law, and that authority derives from the common law legal tradition and not from express statutory authorization.[5] On the other hand, Israel has encoded much of its law in statutes, and is in the process of transforming the extensive statutory private law, now found in a large number of separate statutes, into a comprehensive code (The Codex) embodying rules that apply broadly, in more than one

---

2. The Federal Court of Justice 13 (2010) *available at:* http://www.bundesgerichtshof.de/Shared-Docs/Downloads/EN/BGH/brochure.pdf?__blob=publicationFile.

3. About the Court 5 (2010) *available at:*
http://www.courdecassation.fr/IMG/File/About%20the%20court_mars09.pdf.

4. Other mixed law jurisdictions include South Africa, Sri Lanka, Malta, the Provence of Quebec in Canada, and the state of Louisiana in the United States.

5. Aharon Barak, *The Tradition and Culture of the Israeli Legal System,* in EUROPEAN LEGAL TRADITIONS AND ISRAEL 473, 476–77 (Alfredo Mordechai Rabello ed., 1994).

specific area of law.[6] This type of codification and use of overarching legal principles is typical of civil law systems. Public law generally has more of the characteristics of the common law system, and private law generally more of the civil law characteristics.

The common law aspects of the Israeli legal system derive from the legal system Israel inherited from the British with the termination of the British Mandate. The civil law aspects have a more complex origin. The civil law of the Ottoman Empire, which reflected in good measure the French legal system, might be suspected as a source, but it does not have much continuing influence. As described in chapter 4, most of this law was displaced by English common law during the British Mandate. More influential is the fact that many of the influential jurists in both the Ministry of Justice and academia during the early years of the state had been trained on the European continent, particularly in Germany. As these people helped shape the legal system of the newly independent state, they left the marks of their civil law orientation.[7] In many areas of private law, the common law or civil law that existed at the founding of the state was replaced by civil codes, many of them drawn from German law. Today, most Israeli jurists receive their initial law degrees from Israeli institutions, and many who receive advanced degrees from outside of the country study in the United States. Despite this change, Israeli authorities continue to look to European countries as sources of legal concepts. Perhaps this is because most Israelis are from families that immigrated to Israel from European, North African, and Middle Eastern countries that were not part of the common law system, and more particularly because the governing elite for many years were from families that came from Europe.[8]

Israeli law is not just a mixed system, but a distinctive system. For example, some of the codified law is based on the inherited common law, making it different from the common law in its reliance on a broad code and different from the civil law in the content of the code.

The distinctive nature of the Israeli system is even more prominent in case law. Israeli cases examine scholarly legal literature to a much greater extent than do American common law cases, but it is not clear that the degree of reliance placed on scholarly opinion equals that typical of civil law adjudication. Israeli case law discussions show qualities characteristic of neither the common law nor the civil law system. One Israeli scholar described opinions in many modern Israeli cases in this manner:

> They focus far more on abstract concepts and pseudo-scientific terms (many of them coined by judges); they discard the mode of pragmatism, reasoned persuasion, and induction in favour of analytic deduction from almost axiomatic principles leading to ineluctable truths; they replace the tone of ambivalence with that of almost oracular pronouncement. In such decisions, cases are cited

---

6. A description of the proposed code is found at Pablo Lerner & Alfredo Mordechai Rabello, *The (Re)codification of Israeli Private Law: Support for, and Criticism of, the Israeli Draft Civil Law Code*, 59 Am. J. Comp. L. 763 (2011).

7. Celia Fasserstein Fassberg, *Language and Style in a Mixed System*, 78 Tul. L. Rev. 151, 157, n.16 (2003). The irony of Israel, as a Jewish state, adopting some features of the legal system of Germany, at whose hands Jews suffered such horrors in World War II, has not gone unremarked. *Id.* Nonetheless Israelis still look to German law as a model in some areas where the law itself seems an appropriate model.

8. A discussion of the mixed Israeli legal system is found at Nir Kedar, *Law, Culture and Civil Codification in a Mixed Legal System*, 22 No. 2 Can. J.L. & Soc'y 177 (2007). The relationship between the culture of a society and its legal system is discussed in Oscar G. Chase, *American "Exceptionalism" and Comparative Procedure*, 50 Am. J. Comp. L. 277 (2002).

less for their holding and facts and more for what was said in them; the problem of distinguishing cases is barely mentioned, as is the distinction between ratio decidendi and obiter dicta; and judges frequently choose to cite themselves.[9]

Professor Aharon Barak, former long-serving and influential chief justice of the Israeli Supreme Court described the analysis by Israeli judges as follows:

> The common law jurist distances himself from generalizations, and focuses on concrete judicial decisions. The Israeli jurist does not fully share this way of thinking. It would seem that many Israeli jurists, both from the generation educated largely on the Continent and those educated in Israel, think in more abstract terms. They generally derive specific rules of law from the general principle of good faith; develop concrete duties from the general concept of the duty of care in torts; and base the rules of proper behavior for the individual and government on the general principle of reasonableness.[10]

This Israeli approach leaves a lot of power in the hands of the judge. Unlike the common law judge, the Israeli judge is not bound by the narrow facts of a case in formulating a rule. On the other hand, unlike a civil law judge, the Israeli jurist is not bound by the terms of a fairly detailed civil code. Furthermore, as discussed in the next section, the rulings of an Israeli judge create precedent, and this gives Israeli case law decisions much greater importance and impact than case law has in a civil law system without precedent or with a limited concept of precedent. An Israeli judge reasoning deductively from concepts as broad as *good faith*, *the duty of care*, or *reasonableness*, has broad discretion and an active role in fashioning the result in a case. Israeli judges, especially Israeli Supreme Court judges, are very powerful actors in the Israeli legal system. For the Supreme Court, this power is extended by the large number of cases the court decides each year, a subject discussed later in this chapter.

In the treatment of specific areas of Israeli law, this book strives to distinguish among those that reflect a common law approach, those that reflect a civil law approach, and those that reflect a distinctively Israeli approach. Students should also watch for the distinctive characteristics of Israeli court opinions described above.

Beyond the common law-civil law divide are a number of legal systems that do not fit into either mold and are not mixed systems. They are, rather, different systems. These are the religious law systems, and several of them operate in Israel. The most prominent are the Jewish law system and the Islamic law system, both discussed in chapter 12. These are very old legal systems and are like neither common law nor civil law in form.

The influence of Jewish law on the Israeli legal system has been limited, and the question arises as to why this is so. Several contributing factors may be at work. The state was founded and at first populated largely by secular Jews who saw themselves as members of the Jewish people but who did not feel themselves bound by Jewish religious doctrine or Jewish law. In addition, in 1948 the need was strong for adoption of a legal system that could function im-

---

9. Fassberg, *supra* note 7 at 168 (2003).

10. Barak, *supra* note 5 at 480. Another observer of Israeli law takes a different view and opines that "Israeli courts exhibit an aversion, characteristic of English judicial practice, to abstract-methodical construction of decisions." ARIEL BIN-NUN, THE LAW OF THE STATE OF ISRAEL: AN INTRODUCTION (1992). Perhaps this was an accurate description of the method of judicial analysis in the earlier years of the state, but the mode of judicial analysis of the last twenty years seems to depart from that described by Bin-Nun. See Eli M. Salzberger, *Judicial Appointments and Promotions in Israel: Constitution, Law, and Politics, in* APPOINTING JUDGES IN AN AGE OF JUDICIAL POWER: CRITICAL PERSPECTIVES FROM AROUND THE WORLD 241, 242 (Kate Malleson & Peter H. Russell eds., 2006).

mediately and the time available for modifying it from that inherited from the British was limited due to the ongoing war. Few of the judges in the courts were well trained in Jewish law, and this situation has continued.[11] More recently, the hesitancy to impose concepts of Jewish law on the substantial minority of non-Jews in the country is also a contributing factor. So is the concern about increasing the power of the more radically conservative wing of the Jewish religious establishment, which is now in control of many of the national Jewish institutions as well as the Jewish courts. Today, most Israelis prefer to be governed by a legal system similar to that of most modern Western democracies and not by religious law.

Jewish law is a very old legal system that can, in substantial measure, adapt to meet the needs of society at different periods. But in most periods and places in the past two thousand years, Jewish communities had only limited capacity to govern their own affairs, so the development of Jewish law may have been adversely affected on matters on which the community was not self-governing. Importantly Jewish communities were not in charge of affairs of state, and law on this subject is essential in modern Israel. Furthermore, the development of Jewish law in the decades immediately preceding the founding of Israel was impeded by the destruction of the Jewish communities of Europe in the Holocaust, including some of the communities with the most prominent establishments associated with Jewish law. Therefore it was not clear whether Jewish law could be relied upon to govern a vibrant, modern state and economy.

An interesting development in this regard has been the establishment of the Center for Application of Jewish Law in the School of Law at the Netanya Academic College. When requested to do so by a judge, the center supplies a written memo on the position of Jewish law on an issue before the judge.

B. Stare Decisis, Precedent and Obiter Dictum

Israeli Statute

Basic Law: The Judiciary

20. Case Law

(a) Case law laid down by one court shall guide any lower court.

(b) Case law laid down by the Supreme Court obligates all lower courts, but not the Supreme Court.

Comment

The Basic Law: The Judiciary provides that Israeli law follows the system of stare decisis, or binding precedent, only to a limited extent. Under the statute, the decision of a district court (an intermediate level court) must be used as a guide by a magistrates' court (the lowest level court). Decisions of the Supreme Court bind all courts except the Supreme Court itself.

The rule that decisions of the Supreme Court are neither guides to the Supreme Court nor binding on that court is significant, especially because the Supreme Court sits in panels on most

---

11. *See* Fassberg, *supra* note 7 at 156, n. 15.

cases. Thus, a panel on one case need not even consider the decision of another panel on a similar case. In practice, Supreme Court judges often consider earlier opinions, but they do not always do so. They may use earlier opinions to bolster conclusions they reach independent of those opinions. This makes precedent much less of a constraint on the Supreme Court of Israel than it is on the Supreme Court of the United States.

On the other hand, dicta of the Supreme Court are in fact taken very seriously by lower courts. It is clear that the Supreme Court intends to make law through dicta. It writes dicta freely and uses dicta to address very weighty matters. There is no doubt that it means for other courts to follow that dicta.

In the following case, several justices of the Israeli Supreme Court discuss the propriety of setting out major legal rules in dicta. The case involved significant issues of constitutional law, but the Court's ruling on those issues did not affect the outcome of the case. Therefore it was dicta. In the excerpt below, four justices set out their justifications for deciding the constitutional issues in dicta, rather than leaving those issues for decision in another case. The fifth justice objected to their approach to the matter.

Israeli Case

United Mizrahi Bank v. Migdal Communal Village
CA 6821/93, 49(4) PD 221[1995]

[Shortly after enactment of the Basic Law: Human Dignity and Freedom, the Knesset enacted an amendment to a different, regular statute on the subject of debts. The amendment, referred to as *the Gal Law* after its author, was part of an effort to rehabilitate the agricultural sector of the economy, which had become saddled with a very high debt load during a period of economic crisis. The law established a special body with authority to revise the terms of certain agricultural debts. United Mizrahi Bank sued to collect on outstanding debts. The district court held that these debts were covered by the Gal Law and the bank could not collect on them until they had been reviewed by the special body established under that statute. The bank appealed to the Supreme Court, claiming that the debts could not be restructured under the Gal Law because the Gal Law was unconstitutional under the new Basic Law: Human Dignity and Freedom. The case was heard before an expanded panel of nine justices, which signaled the perceived importance of the case.

This decision recognized the Basic Law: Human Dignity and Freedom as a constitutional law provision and stated that statutes conflicting with it were invalid.

It was a hard question whether the Basic Law, itself a statute enacted by the Knesset, was of constitutional status. The substantive issue of the status of the Basic Law is discussed in chapter 8 on constitutional law. For now, it is sufficient to understand that this was a difficult and important issue that had not been resolved prior to this case.

Eight of nine justices sitting on the case agreed that the Basic Law was of constitutional status. The justices also addressed the question of whether the Gal Law conflicted with the Basic Law; if it did, the Gal Law was invalid. All nine justices agreed that there was no conflict. Therefore the Gal Law was valid whether or not the Basic Law was of constitutional status.

The result raised the question of why the justices decided the constitutional issue. There was no need to reach the question of the constitutional status of the Basic Law.

The justices could have ruled that, even if the Basic Law were of constitutional status, the Gal Law was valid and the appellants would prevail. Why did they not do this? Several of the nine opinions addressed this question. The relevant portions of the opinions are presented here.]

Former Chief Justice M. Shamgar:

In summary: The amendment to the statute is constitutional. For this reason, I see no place for holding the amending statute as invalid.

Our analysis has been lengthy. The main reason has been the need to try to chart the lines that will serve us in the future in determining the constitutionality of statutes under the Basic Law: Human Dignity and Freedom.

In this connection, it is appropriate to mention that in countries with a constitutional tradition longer than ours, it is customary to examine constitutional claims carefully and with restraint. Special rules have been designed that are to be considered by a court that is asked to invalidate a statute based on its unconstitutionality. Justice Brandeis addressed this issue extensively in the case of *Ashwander v. Tennessee Valley Authority*, 297 U.S. 288 (1936). *Ashwander* dealt with the acquisition from Alabama Power Company of facilities, lands, and electricity in bulk by the Tennessee Valley Authority. Some of the shareholders in the Alabama company sued to invalidate the contract on the grounds, among others, that it exceeded the constitutional powers of the federal government.

Justice Brandeis considered the rules requiring restraint in examining constitutional claims in stating:

> Considerations of propriety, as well as long-established practice, demand that we refrain from passing upon the constitutionality of an act of Congress unless obliged to do so in the proper performance of our judicial function, when the question is raised by a party whose interests entitle him to raise it. *Blair v. United States*, 250 U.S. 273, 279 (1919). *Ashwander* at 341.

> The Court has frequently called attention to the "great gravity and delicacy" of its function in passing upon the validity of an act of Congress. *Ashwander* at 346.

He continued by setting out a list of guidelines (*id.* at 482), based on a diverse assortment of precedents, and these may also serve us as food for thought, although we should consider independently whether they are appropriate for our use. These are the guidelines set out by Justice Brandeis at 346–349:

1. The Court will not pass upon the constitutionality of legislation in a friendly, non-adversary, proceeding, declining because to decide such questions is legitimate only in the last resort, and as a necessity in the determination of real, earnest, and vital controversy between individuals. It never was the thought that, by means of a friendly suit, a party beaten in the legislature could transfer to the courts an inquiry as to the constitutionality of the legislative act.

2. The Court will not … decide questions of a constitutional nature unless absolutely necessary to a decision of the case.

3. The Court will not formulate a rule of constitutional law broader than is required by the precise facts to which it is to be applied.

4. The Court will not pass upon a constitutional question although properly presented by the record, if there is also present some other ground upon which the case may be disposed of. This rule has found most varied application. Thus, if a case can be decided on either of two grounds, one involving a constitutional

question, the other a question of statutory construction or general law, the Court will decide only the latter.

5. The Court will not pass upon the validity of a statute upon complaint of one who fails to show that he is injured by its operation.

6. The Court will not pass upon the constitutionality of a statute at the instance of one who has availed himself of its benefits.

7. When the validity of an act of the Congress is drawn in question, and even if a serious doubt of constitutionality is raised, it is a cardinal principle that this Court will first ascertain whether a construction of the statute is fairly possible by which the question may be avoided.

As to the fifth point above, the concept of the right of standing has been recently been broadened in Israel, in England, and in the United States [citing Israeli and English sources].

It is appropriate for us to note and consider the approach set out in these guidelines and the principles they entail, because the accumulated experience in other places with the same issues we face here can assist us. We do not desist from examining comparative law on any legal topic, and this is a laudatory approach.

In our case, the appellant raised an alternative claim that "even if the court should decide that the statutory amendment is valid and applies to this case, then even according to the statute in its amended form, the amendment should not be applied to the respondents." [According to the appellant's claim, the court could decide that the statutory amendment did not make a person in the appellant's position liable on the debt at issue. The court rejected this claim on the grounds that such a reading of the statutory amendment would violate the objective of the amending statute.]

Justice Zamir:

The special nature of constitutional law requires that this court take a special approach to deciding constitutional issues. This supports the importance of the rules that Chief Justice Shamgar sets out, following the scheme of Justice Brandeis, for determining when there is a need to decide constitutional issues. Among other things, Chief Justice Shamgar sets out that, "The court will not consider a constitutional issue unless doing so is absolutely necessary for deciding the case," and that, "The court will not formulate a rule of constitutional law that is broader than necessary in order to decide on the concrete facts before it, to which the rule will be applied." I agree with these rules. In this spirit, I prefer to leave to another time various issues of constitutional law discussed in this case.

Nevertheless I cannot ignore the fact that the dispute over these issues is already an open one, and that various opinions on them are being expressed in this case. These opinions, even those presented only as dicta, are likely to influence the development of the legal rules. In such a situation, the weight of support for one opinion or another is important. Therefore I think I should express my own opinion at least in a clear, summary fashion, on two questions.

First, on the question of the source of the authority of the Knesset to restrict its own power.... I believe that this authority is based on the Knesset's status as a constituent assembly.

Second, [even if the Basic Law is of a constitutional nature, the Gal Law is not invalid].

Justice M. Cheshin:

I agree with my colleagues Chief Justice Shamgar and Chief Justice Barak. The statutory amendment meets the tests set out in Basic Law: Human Dignity and Freedom and there is no need to discuss statutory or constitutional barriers to its validity.

One topic that my colleagues addressed at length, and on which they had differing opinions, is the authority of the Knesset to enact a set constitution for the state.

The disagreements among us on the matter of the constituent authority of the Knesset and its sovereignty all constitute obiter dicta. We have no disagreements as to the outcome of the case before us. So why should I make a nuisance of myself by adding my own long dictum to those of my colleagues. I shall begin by giving my justifications for doing so.

First, in my opinion, the question of the authority of the Knesset to limit itself (in a constitution or in a statute) is the most important question arising from this case. It is ten times more important than all the other questions presented.

Moreover as I see it, from the founding of this court until today, no question has come before us that is as important as the question of the constituent authority of the Knesset to enact a constitution for Israel, or whether it must be enacted as a complete constitution rather than piecemeal. Of course, even now the question has not been put directly before us.

The question of whether there is a constitution and the question of the authority to enact a constitution are tied to the basic issue of the nature of the Israeli legal system. We have a strong interest in any question that stands at the foundation of the Israeli legal system. When we stand before so lofty an issue, it is hard for us not to say anything about it.

Second, and this is the most important point: some day the Knesset may enact a law, or a Basic Law on a constitutional type of topic, and will say in it that it may be changed only by a majority of seventy or of eighty members of the Knesset (or by ninety or a hundred) [out of 120 members]. What will be the rule of law regarding such a provision? Will it be effective and binding as written, such that the Knesset will not be able to change the law, or the Basic Law, except by the special majority that is set out? Or should we say that a provision that limits the power of the Knesset to enact laws in the future is of no effect in that it limits the power of the Knesset to enact a law through the same means that are used to enact the limited law? My colleague, Chief Justice Barak, would give full effect to such a limitation with no conditions, as long as it appeared in a Basic Law, finding that such an enactment derived from the constituent authority of the Knesset. [Justice Cheshin continues to explain his disagreement with Chief Justice Barak on the question of whether a statute can limit legislative acts in the future.]

Justice E. Matza:

I shall relate briefly to only these of the important topics as to which several of my esteemed colleagues expressed differing opinions. First, I want to emphasize that the appeals before us do not require us to reach a decision on any of these three constitutional law topics. My brief remarks are intended to emphasize my support of one of the possible approaches to each of the three topics.

Justice G. Bach:

Some of my colleagues have addressed in great detail issues that need not be addressed in order to reach a decision on these appeals. Apparently they did so because of their perception of the great importance of this case from the perspective of legal, constitutional and judicial history of the State of Israel. This court has been asked for the first time to decide whether to hold invalid a statute enacted by the Knesset because that statute is inconsistent with the Basic Law: Human Dignity and Freedom and to decide whether such a law is unconstitutional.

Several of my colleagues stated in their opinions that it is unnecessary to reach a decision on these issues and that they are therefore ready to leave their consideration to another day. Despite this, they have clarified their positions on these matters and led others to expound their differing positions on the same matters. This leads to the natural desire of those judges who would have been glad to leave these topics unexamined in this case to clarify their positions even further.

The truth is that the issues involved are fascinating. They speak to both the heart and to the mind. They involve questions of both general and constitutional law, as well as issues of governmental structure, public policy, and philosophy. The temptation to engage in detailed examination of these problems is great. Nevertheless I have decided to resist this temptation and to limit my comments to those topics that seem essential to our decision in these specific cases.

I agree with the position agreed to by my esteemed colleagues ... with which the majority of the justices on this panel also agree. According to this position, the Knesset is authorized to enact both regular statutes and special Basic Laws that constitute an Israeli constitution. Through this latter type of law, the Knesset is authorized to restrict its own authority and of the Knesset in the future to amend those same constitutional Basic Law or to enact legislation that conflicts with them. This restriction is expressed in procedural terms; it requires a special, enlarged majority to invalidate or amend those laws. It is also done in substantive terms by conditioning amendment of such Basic Laws on meeting certain substantive conditions.

I see no need in these appeals to take a position on the important and interesting question ... of whether the Knesset, in enacting Basic Laws of a constitutional nature, relies on its inherent authority, which it has by virtue of being the highest legislative body in the state, as Chief Justice Shamgar proposes, or whether the Knesset enacted those Basic Laws relying on its special, separate authority wearing the "hat" of its constitutive authority, as Chief Justice Barak proposes.

[The opinion continues with a lengthy analysis of why Justice Bach agrees that the Basic Laws involved in this case have the status of constitutional law.]

Comments

Former Chief Justice Shamgar remarked that the decision was long. There were nine opinions, one from each justice sitting on the case, stretching over 338 pages. This method of decision-making has its own implications for the rule of stare decisis. Although judges may agree as to the outcome, they may present different rationales to support that outcome. Separate opinions that disagree on rationale make it difficult to determine the legal rule that is binding. Furthermore, the mere length of the opinions makes it difficult for lawyers and judges to read the cases carefully and determine the content of the legal rules set out in them.

The five excerpts from different opinions all gave lip service to the concept that the court should not decide constitutional questions unless necessary to the resolution of a case before the court, and four recognized that the constitutional rulings in this case were unnecessary to support the result. In other words, four justices explicitly recognize that the constitutional rulings were obiter dicta. (Israelis refer to such unnecessary rulings as *obiter*, while Americans call them *dicta*.) So why did the justices decide the constitutional issues anyway?

First, examine the rationale of Chief Justice Shamgar. He sets out Justice Brandeis' guidelines for avoiding unnecessary constitutional questions and considers whether guideline number four applies in this case. He determines that the case cannot be decided on statutory interpretation grounds. That is correct, but it is insufficient to meet all of Brandeis' guidelines. Chief Justice Shamgar does not consider whether any of the other guidelines apply. The second guideline does apply. It provides, "The court will not consider a constitutional issue unless doing so is absolutely necessary for deciding the case." Since the constitutional issue had no effect on the outcome of the case, its consideration was unnecessary.

Now look at the other four opinions. Justices Zamir, Cheshin, Matza, and Bach all recognize that decisions on at least some of the constitutional issues in the case are unnecessary. Nonetheless they all state openly that they will give their opinions on these matters because they think it is important to do so. What makes the constitutional issue so important? Justice Zamir explains: The opinions on the constitutional questions will be treated as rules of law in later cases, and he wants to influence the content of those rules. What is interesting is his perception that the opinions, which he acknowledges are dicta, will be treated as the source of legal rules. Under Israeli practice, his perception is correct. Israeli case law usually follows statements of legal rules in opinions of the Supreme Court without regard to, and without even paying attention to, whether those rules are necessary to the holding of the case in which they are set out or whether they are dicta. The result is that the Supreme Court justices do not usually refrain from writing extensive dicta in their opinions, and what they write is often crucially important to the development of the law. Rules developed in dicta are treated just like outcome-determinative rules set out in case law.

This is just what happened in the case set out above. Later cases and literature regard this case as part of a *constitutional revolution* and as establishing the legal rules that (1) Basic Laws are constitutional laws and (2) courts can hold invalid regular statutes, even later statutes, that conflict with these Basic Laws. These legal rules and how they have been applied in later cases are discussed in chapter 8 on Constitutional Law. For now, the point is that these very important rules were set out in dicta and were nonetheless accepted as valid and binding.

Contrast the method of analysis in this case to that in *Marbury v. Madison*, 5 U.S. (1 Cranch) 137 (1803), the American case that established the principle that courts can review the constitutionality of statutes. In *Marbury*, Chief Justice Marshall considered jurisdiction, the issue that raised a constitutional question, last and not, as would normally be the case, first. The opinion is constructed so as to show that the Supreme Court had no choice but to reach the constitutional issue. It may be claimed that the Court's decisions on the other issues of the case were wrong, but still the structure of the decision is far different from the structure in *Migdal*. Chief Justice Marshall writing in *Marbury* reveals an understanding that the constitutional aspect of the decision would be recognized only if necessary. The justices in *Migdal* understood that the constitutional aspects of their decision would be accepted even if they themselves knew it was totally unnecessary. Furthermore, the constitutional holding in *Marbury*, that the courts can review the validity of statutes under the provisions of a document called a constitution, is much more narrowly drawn than the holding in *Migdal*. *Migdal* allows courts to conduct judicial review under Basic Laws that are not otherwise denominated as a constitution and that were enacted through normal legislative processes.

This tendency of the Supreme Court to speak in precedent-setting dicta is not limited to the constitutional sphere.[12] A court willing to make law in dicta in the essential constitutional area does not hesitate to do so in other less crucial matters.

Question

1. What are the advantages and the disadvantages of the type of broad dicta found in the *Migdal* case?

C. Structure of the Courts: Courts of General Jurisdiction

The regular courts of general jurisdiction in Israel comprise three levels: the magistrates' courts, the district courts, and the Supreme Court. There are twenty-nine magistrates' courts of general jurisdiction, six district courts, and one Supreme Court.

Israeli Statute

Basic Law: The Judiciary

15. The Supreme Court

(a) The Supreme Court shall sit in Jerusalem.

(b) The Supreme Court shall hear appeals of decisions of the district court and other rulings of the district courts.

(c) The Supreme Court shall also sit as the High Court of Justice; in this capacity it shall hear matters as to which it finds it necessary to provide a remedy in the interest of justice and that are not in the jurisdiction of another court.

(d) Without detracting from the general instruction of subsection (c), the Supreme Court, sitting as the High Court of Justice, has jurisdiction—

(1) to issue orders to free persons who have been illegally detained or incarcerated;

(2) to issue orders or negative injunctions to state agencies, to local governments, to their sub-units, to their employees, and to other persons filling public positions under law, requiring them to act or to refrain from acting in lawful fulfillment of their positions; and if they were unlawfully elected or appointed, to refrain from acting;

(3) to issue orders to courts of general jurisdiction and to courts of limited jurisdiction and to other bodies and people with judicial or quasi-judicial authority under law, except for [regular general jurisdiction law] courts otherwise treated under this law and except for religious courts, to hear or not to hear a specific matter, or to de-

---

12. See Marcia Gelpe, *Constraints on Supreme Court Authority in Israel and the United States: Phenomenal Cosmic Powers; Itty Bitty Living Space*, 13 EMORY INT'L L. REV. 493, 537–38 (1999).

sist from further consideration of a matter, to quash the completed consideration of a matter or a decision in a matter that was unlawfully issued;

(4) to issue orders to religious courts to consider a matter within their jurisdiction or to desist from considering or continuing the consideration of a matter not within their jurisdiction; except that the High Court of Justice will not be required to respond under this subsection if the petitioner did not raise the question of the jurisdiction of the religious court the first time it could have been raised; and if the petitioner could not reasonably have raised the issue of jurisdiction until after the decision of the religious court, the High Court of Justice may quash a hearing that already unlawfully occurred or a decision that was already unlawfully rendered by the religious court in excess of its jurisdiction.

(e) Further jurisdiction of the Supreme Court shall be set in statute.

16. Other Courts

The establishment, jurisdiction, place of sitting, and areas of venue for district courts, magistrates' courts, and other courts shall be determined by statute.

17. Appeal

Appeal of right may be taken from the decision of a court of initial jurisdiction, except for decisions of the Supreme Court.

Israeli Statute

Courts Law (Consolidated Version), 5744-1984
Part 1: The Supreme Court

25. Number of Justices

The Supreme Court shall have the number of justices that is set by decision of the Knesset.

Part 2: District Courts

40. Jurisdiction

A district court shall hear the following matters:

(1) Every civil or criminal matter that is not in the jurisdiction of the magistrates' court ... ;

(1)(a) An administrative petition, administrative appeal, and administrative complaint, under the Administrative Courts Law, 5760-2000;

(2) Every matter that is not in the exclusive jurisdiction of a court of limited jurisdiction ... ;

(3) Appeals of decisions and other rulings of magistrates' courts.

41. Appeal

(a) Decisions of a district court in matters in which it sat as the court of original jurisdiction can be appealed to the Supreme Court.

Part 3: Magistrates' Courts

51. Jurisdiction

(a) A magistrates' court shall hear the following matters:

(1)(a) Crimes for which the punishment is just a fine or incarceration for a period of no more than seven years [subject to several enumerated exceptions that may be tried before a district court];

(b) [Certain crimes that are normally tried before the district court may be tried before a magistrates' court upon choice of the state's attorney, with the limitation that the court may not impose a sentence of more than seven years];

(2) Civil complaints, except those involving real property, if the amount of the claim or value of the claim is not greater than NIS 2,500,000 [about $70,000] at the time of the filing of the complaint ... ;

(3) Complaints related to possession or use of real property or division of real property or division of use, including complaints that also relate to possession or use of personal property, whatever the value of the complaint.

52. Appeal

(a) Decisions of a magistrates' court can be appealed to a district court.

Comment

The Supreme Court usually sits in panels of three, although the chief justice may decide that a case will come before a panel of five or more justices. The number of justices must always be uneven.[13] In the district courts, a panel of three judges sits on serious criminal cases, appeals from decisions of the magistrates' courts, and any other matter that the chief judge of the court decides should be heard by a panel of three. Other cases are heard by a single judge. These include less serious crimes and civil cases in the original jurisdiction of the district courts. Cases in the magistrates' courts are heard by a single judge unless the chief judge of the court decides it should be heard by three judges.

To allow a comparison of the method of operation of the Israel Supreme Court and the US Supreme Court, consider the following material:

US Constitution

Article III

Section 2.

In all cases affecting ambassadors, other public ministers and consuls, and those in which a state shall be a party, the Supreme Court shall have original jurisdiction. In all the other cases before mentioned, the Supreme Court shall have appellate jurisdiction, both as to law and fact, with such exceptions, and under such regulations as the Congress shall make.

---

13. The Courts Law (Consolidated Version), 5744-1984, Section 26. A panel of three that has begun to consider an issue can also decide that the panel should be expanded. A single justice may determine technical matters, such as requests for intermediate orders.

US Statute

Original Jurisdiction [of the Supreme Court]
28 U.S.C. § 1251

Original Jurisdiction

(a) The Supreme Court shall have original and exclusive jurisdiction of all controversies between two or more states.

(b) The Supreme Court shall have original but not exclusive jurisdiction of:

(1) All actions or proceedings to which ambassadors, other public ministers, consuls, or vice consuls of foreign states are parties;

(2) All controversies between the United States and a state;

(3) All actions or proceedings by a state against the citizens of another state or against aliens.

Comments

The Israeli Supreme Court is strikingly different from the US Supreme Court in several ways. Although there are presently fifteen justices on the Israel Supreme Court, the practice of sitting in panels of three for most cases allows the court to hear many more cases than does the United States Supreme Court, which sits as a full panel of nine justices. The Israeli Supreme Court closed 4736 cases in 2010.[14] By comparison, the typical docket of the US Supreme Court is between eighty and ninety cases a year.[15]

Israel's Supreme Court has much less control over its docket than does the US Supreme Court. Under Israeli law, all cases get one appeal of right. Because many civil and criminal cases must be heard in the first instance in the district courts, the Israeli Supreme Court is required to decide appeals from these cases. In addition, the Israeli Supreme Court has discretionary jurisdiction over whether to hear appeals from cases that began in the magistrates' court and were already appealed to the district court. It is customary that only one justice decides whether the court will exercise such jurisdiction, but writes an explanation if the decision is not to hear the case.

The Israeli Supreme Court also sits as a court of first instance on a significant number of cases. Pursuant to the authority granted in The Basic Law: The Judiciary, section 15(d)(2), it hears many petitions for review of decisions of administrative agencies as part of its task sitting as the High Court of Justice. Prior to the enactment of the Administrative Courts Law, 5760-2000, almost all petitions to review administrative agency decisions were heard directly by the Supreme Court sitting in this capacity. The 2000 statute granted jurisdiction over many of the more routine administrative law cases to the district courts, thus withdrawing original jurisdiction from the Supreme Court by virtue of section 15(c). That section allows the Supreme Court to sit as the court of first

---

14. Court's Administration, The Court System in Israel, Semi-Annual Report: 1.7.09–31.12.09 (February 7, 2010), chapter 9 (in Hebrew) available at http://elyon1.court.gov.il/heb/haba/dochot/doc/7-12_2009.pdf. [The dates covered in the report are July 1, 2009 to December 31, 2009. This report, although semi-annual, also includes information for the prior half year.]

15. Craig S. Lerner & Nelson Lund, *Judicial Duty and the Supreme Court's Cult of Celebrity*, 78 Geo. Wash. L. Rev. 1255, 1268 (2010).

instance only for cases that are not in the jurisdiction of other courts. The Administrative Courts Law put these cases in the jurisdiction of other courts. Still, many important types of cases are not covered by the Administrative Courts Law, and the Supreme Court remains the court of original jurisdiction for these cases.

The practice of the Supreme Court sitting as the court of first instance on administrative law cases was instituted by the British during the period of the Mandate. In England, review of administrative agency decisions was in the High Court of Justice, but this was not the highest court of the country. During the period of the British Mandate, the convention of hearing petitions for review of administrative agency decisions in the High Court of Justice was adopted, but in the area of the Mandate, unlike in England, it was the Supreme Court that sat as the High Court of Justice. That means that the cases were heard by justices of the Supreme Court, sitting where they normally sat, but functioning under special High Court of Justice procedural rules. The agencies being reviewed by the High Court of Justice were staffed by British dignitaries and workers, and the ruling British apparently did not want their work reviewed by lower courts, where the majority of the judges were locals. The Supreme Court, in contrast, had a majority of English justices.[16] Therefore it appeared to be a more favorable location for review of the decisions of the British administrators.

Of course, Israel was free to change this arrangement after the establishment of the state. After May 1948, administrators were all Israeli and so were Supreme Court justices. The British were no longer involved. Nevertheless the practice of locating review of administrative decisions in the Supreme Court, sitting as the High Court of Justice, was maintained. For many years, it was a mark of great pride that the common citizen, claiming injury by decision of a governmental agency, had access to the Supreme Court. Furthermore, Supreme Court review was seen as a more effective way of controlling the potentially overreaching agencies and preventing them from harming the individual and the public by arbitrary decisions. As a result, with the growth of the population, the work burden on the Supreme Court grew intolerable. Because many of the cases did not raise particularly novel or difficult legal issues, the Supreme Court developed a number of doctrines that allowed it to avoid deciding some types of administrative review petitions and to refer some petitions to the lower courts. Eventually the Knesset stepped in with the Administrative Courts Law, 5760-2000, to organize and extend the process that the Supreme Court had begun in developing these doctrines. Even after the enactment of the 2000 statute, though, a significant number of cases were unaffected by that law and remained in the original jurisdiction of the Supreme Court. In 2009, the Supreme Court disposed of 1,845 cases presented to the High Court of Justice.[17]

In the United States, by contrast, the Supreme Court has almost complete discretionary control over its appellate docket and rarely sits as a court of first instance. Nearly all cases have first been heard by another court and come to the Supreme Court through writ of certiorari, and the court has broad discretion whether to grant *cert*. Furthermore, the Court rarely explains its decision on petitions for certiorari.

Law in the United States distinguishes between the original jurisdiction of the Supreme Court, when the Court may hear a case as the court of first instance, and the original and exclusive jurisdiction of the Supreme Court, when the Court must sit as the court of

---

16. Itzhak Zamir, *Administrative Law*, in Itzhak Zamir & Allen Zysblat, Public Law in Israel 18, 39 (1996).

17. Court's Administration, The Court System in Israel, Semi-Annual Report, *supra* note 14.

first instance. The US Constitution, Article II, Section 2 defines the original jurisdiction of the Supreme Court, but 28 U.S.C. § 1251 provides that most of that jurisdiction is not exclusive. This mean that original jurisdiction can and has been assigned to lower federal courts as well. Where the Supreme Court's jurisdiction is not exclusive, the Court rarely accepts original jurisdiction.[18] Moreover the Court interprets restrictively its original and exclusive jurisdiction as set out in 28 U.S.C. § 1251(b), further reducing the number of cases the Court hears as a court of first instance.[19] Even for a case that the Court interprets as falling within its original and exclusive jurisdiction, the Supreme Court usually appoints a special master to hear the case, establish the facts, and propose a decision. In essence, then, the Supreme Court decides the case on the basis of review of the decision of the special master.

Another difference between Israel's Supreme Court and the US Supreme Court is in the way opinions are written. Israel's court follows the English tradition of each judge writing a separate opinion. In the United States, each justice sometimes writes a separate opinion, but this is less common than in Israel. Prior to Justice John Marshall, well known as the author of *Marbury v. Madison*,[20] the US Supreme Court also followed the English tradition with each justice writing a separate opinion in each case. Justice Marshall established the practice of issuing a single opinion of the court reflecting the view of the majority.[21]

As discussed in the section on stare decisis, the Israeli practice can make it quite challenging to determine the legal rule of a case. It also creates less pressure for the justices to agree on a legal rule that supports the outcome of the case. The tendency of Israeli opinions to contain lengthy examinations of legal theory and to look more like scholarly discourses on a range of issues than like practical analysis oriented narrowly to the facts of a case exacerbates this problem. (It is probably not irrelevant that arguably the most prominent justice on the Israeli Supreme Court, former Chief Justice Aharon Barak, a noted author of many opinions of the scholarly mode, came out of academia.) This method of opinion writing, and the large number of Supreme Court cases, also makes it harder for lawyers to keep up with Supreme Court opinions and puts a significant burden on law students trying to learn the law.

Undoubtedly the Israeli method of case writing has countervailing advantages. In a young country, it aids in development of the law. This is especially true because, as discussed above, dicta are regarded so seriously. The treatment of dicta as precedent also makes less critical the need to identify the narrow rule of the case, although it does not solve the problem of knowing which justices' dicta matter when they conflict.

D. Structure of Supreme Court Opinions

Most decisions of the Supreme Court, and sometimes the decisions of lower courts, follow a pattern. The first opinion in the case usually begins with a description of the facts, a review of decisions of lower courts on the case (if any), and a statement of the legal issues. It will then review the claims of the two sides. After that, for major cases raising

---

18. *E.g.*, Illinois v. City of Milwaukee, 406 U.S. 91 (1972).

19. *E.g.*, *id.*

20. 5 U.S. (1 Cranch) 137 (1803).

21. Thomas G. Walker & Lee Epstein, Supreme Court of the United States: An Introduction 16 (1993).

new issues, the justice typically writes a long theoretical analysis of the issues. This analysis often includes reference to decisions and literature in other countries and to Israeli literature on the issues raised in the case. This section of the opinion will include conclusions on theoretical issues, without application to the facts. Finally the opinion will include a section labeled "From the General to the Particular," in which the conclusions of the theoretical analysis are applied to the facts of the case. This style of reasoning is deductive rather than inductive.

Opinions of other justices follow a more abbreviated pattern. An opinion may say, "I agree with Justice X." Or it may state agreement except as to a specific issue, followed by a theoretical and then applied analysis of that issue. For a very important case, each justice may write a separate long theoretical analysis followed by a brief section on application of theory to the facts, as was done in the *Migdal* case, parts of which are set out above. At the end, the opinion will give the outcome and which opinion, if any, has garnered a majority. The first opinion in the case is not necessarily that of the majority.

Because many important Israeli cases are very long, few are set out in full in this book. What is included is only part of the decision. For most cases, the theoretical analysis of the majority opinion is provided, or, more typically, a heavily edited selection from that analysis. Where there is no majority opinion, you will usually read the opinion that proved to be the most influential on the development of the law. This is the opinion that set out the analysis that was generally accepted by lower courts or cited in later Supreme Court opinions (not as precedent, but as influential analysis), or accepted in the literature.

E. Appointment of Judges

Israeli Statute

Basic Law: The Judiciary

4. Appointment of Judges

(a) A judge will be appointed by the president of the state in accordance with the selection of the Committee for Selection of Judges.

(b) The committee shall have nine members: the Chief Justice of the Supreme Court, two other justices of the Supreme Court selected by their fellow justices, the minister of justice and another minister as determined by the Government, two members of the Knesset chosen by the Knesset, and two representatives of the bar association selected by the National Council of the association. The minister of justice shall be the chairperson of the committee.

Israeli Statute

Courts Law (Consolidated Version) 5744-1984

6. Committee for Selection of Judges

These directives apply as to the Committee for Selection of Judges under Section 4 of the Basic Law: The Judiciary (hereinafter the committee):

(1) The Knesset shall choose in secret elections two members of the Knesset who shall serve as members of the committee; they shall serve as long as they are members of the Knesset.

(2) The National Council of the Bar Association shall choose its members in secret elections; they shall serve for a period of three years;

(3) Two justices of the Supreme Court shall serve for a period of three years;

(4) The composition of the committee shall be published in Reshumot [the official publication of the government of Israel, comparable to the Federal Register in the United States].

6a. Committee Votes

A member of the committee shall vote according to that person's own judgment, and shall not be obligated to follow the decisions of the institution which selected him for the committee.

7. Committee Functioning

(a) If the minister of justice determines that a judge should be appointed, the minister shall publish a notice to this effect in Reshumot and shall convene the committee.

(b) The following are entitled to propose candidates:

(1) The minister of justice;

(2) The Chief Justice of the Supreme Court;

(3) Three members of the committee who agree on a proposal.

(c)

(1) The recommendation of the committee to appoint a judge shall be based on the decision of a majority of the members who participated in the vote;

(2) Despite what is set out in subsection (1), the recommendation of the committee to appoint a justice to the Supreme Court shall be based on the decision of at least seven members of the committee; if fewer than nine participated in the vote, the vote shall be based on the decision of the majority of the participants, but not less the number of participants minus two.

Comments

The role of the president in appointment of judges is purely formal. The real selection is done by the Committee for Selection of Judges. This committee selects both Supreme Court justices and judges of the lower courts of general jurisdiction. The Hebrew term for *judges* includes both.

As set out in the Basic Law, the Chief Justice of the Supreme Court always sits on the committee. The other two members of the Supreme Court who sit on the committee serve terms of three years. After the three years, two new representatives of the court are selected. The selection is traditionally on the basis of seniority.[22]

The Israeli system for selecting judges is radically different from the American system. Many praise the Israeli system because it is gives political actors only a minor role in ju-

---

22. Malvina Halberstam, *Judicial Review, A Comparative Perspective: Israel, Canada, and the United States*, 31 CARDOZO L. REV. 2393, 2397 (2010).

dicial selection.[23] This is thought to increase the independence of the judiciary. Furthermore, Supreme Court justices and members of the bar, who are all legal professionals, hold five of the nine seats on the committee. This is thought to increase the professional influence in selection of judges and provide more qualified judges.[24]

Some find the Israeli system objectionable because it leads to the Supreme Court being too isolated. The selection process is so isolated from the political system that justices have no contact with changes in public opinion. Judges sometimes make decisions after consideration of social values. This is especially true in Israel. The very influential former Chief Justice of the Israeli Supreme Court, Aharon Barak, has written extensively on the role of the judge in making the law function for society. For example, he wrote, "The role of a judge in a supreme court is to help bridge the gap between the needs of society and law without allowing the legal system to degenerate or collapse into anarchy. The judge must ensure stability with change, and change with stability."[25] It can be asked how the Israeli Supreme Court, being so far divorced from the political arena, can know enough about the "needs of society" to allow it to perform the function set out. Chief Justice Barak recognizes the limits of judicial knowledge of the society when he writes, "One cannot bridge the gap between society and law without having reliable information about society. The court does not always have information about social facts that might justify a change in the law.... The court may, in developing the common law in its legal system, impose a new duty of care in torts. But it cannot, for example, impose taxes or establish a licensing regime."[26] Yet, as will be clear in the remaining chapters of this book, while this recognition of limits may lead to Israel's Supreme Court to desist from levying taxes, it does not lead the Supreme Court to shy away from issuing opinions of huge social impact, especially in areas of the public law.

Another objection to the method of selection of judges in Israel is that it reduces the checks and balances.[27] The Israeli system may keep the judicial branch separate from the other branches, but it interferes with the checks and balances that keep the system of separated powers working and restrains the power of each individual branch.

Others observe that the system leads to the ideology of the court being self-perpetuating. Until a recent amendment to the Courts Law, only a majority vote of the committee for the Selection of Judges was needed to appoint a Supreme Court justice. It has been a longstanding tradition that the committee does not recommend a candidate for the Supreme Court if the choice is not acceptable to the representatives of the Court who sit on the committee.[28] This tradition may result from respect for the court, or from the fact that the members of the bar on the committee will not vote against the wishes of the Supreme Court justices before whom they may need to appear. For this reason, Israelis refer to their system of judicial selection as *a friend brings a friend*. More specifically, it has been observed that the committee will never vote for a new justice who does not agree

---

23. *See, e.g., id.* (remarks of Justice Elyakim Rubinstein).

24. Salzberger, *supra* note 10 at 248–50.

25. Aharon Barak, *Foreword: A Judge on Judging: The Role of a Supreme Court in a Democracy*, 116 Harv. L. Rev. 16, 29 (2002).

26. *Id.* at 33.

27. Richard Posner raises the checks and balances problem as to the practically unlimited power of the Israeli Supreme Court in general. Richard Posner, *Enlightened Despot*, The New Republic, April 23, 2007, at 53.

28. Allen Zysblat, *The System of Government*, in Itzhak Zamir & Allen Zysblat, Public Law in Israel 1, 15 (1996).

with the ideology of the sitting justices.[29] Furthermore, the Chief Justice has traditionally been selected on the basis of seniority.[30] This also contributes to the ideological continuity observed by some in the Court's opinions.

A 2008 amendment changed the vote for appointment of a Supreme Court justice to seven, if all committee members vote. The amended form of the statute is set out above. It is not clear whether this change will ameliorate the perceived problems. It gives the Supreme Court justices, as a bloc, veto power on appointing new justices, but it also gives a veto power to any three other members of the committee. Arguably this will lead Supreme Court justices to be more willing to compromise on the selection of new justices.[31]

A justice of the Supreme Court or judge of another court is entitled to serve until the mandatory retirement age of 70 unless subject to disciplinary action. See Basic Law: the Judiciary, section 7, and the Courts Law (Consolidated Version) 5744-1984, section 13. This guaranteed tenure is also intended to contribute to the independence of the judiciary.

Israelis vigorously criticize their own judicial selection system, but have thus far failed to agree on a substantial change to the system. Most want to stay away from the American system, which they see as an undignified political circus.

Question

2. Is the Israeli system of selecting judges, especially for justices of the Supreme Court, superior to the US system?

F. Extra-Judicial Statements of Judges

Israeli judges have been involved in development of legislation. It has been reported that judges in general, and the chief justice of the Supreme Court in particular, took part in development of the two Basic Laws enacted in 1992 that formed the basis of what is commonly called *the constitutional revolution* in Israel. They were also involved in the important 1994 amendment of the same laws. Justice Aharon Barak, then assistant chief justice of the Supreme Court and soon thereafter the chief justice, wrote a long letter to the Chairman of the Knesset Committee on the Constitution, Statutes, and Law about a proposed amendment to one of the Basic Laws. His suggestions about changing the language of the proposed amendment were apparently accepted.[32] Justice Barak wrote that he was taking a professional, rather than a political, stand. Shortly after this, Chief Justice Barak was involved in interpreting that Basic Law. This is not an isolated instance of

---

29. *See* comments of Professor Daniel Friedman, former Israeli minister of justice, in Halberstam, *supra* note 22 at 2406.

30. Comments of Michael Eitan, minister of improvement of government services and member of the Knesset, in Halberstam, *supra* note 22 at 2399.

31. *See* comment of Professor Daniel Friedman, former Israeli minister of justice, in Halberstam, *supra* note 22 at 2398 n.9.

32. The full text of the letter and a report of what happened in its wake appears at Aharon Barak, *Al Ha'tikunim B'chok Yasod: Chofesh Ha'eesuk* [*On the Amendments to the Basic Law: Freedom of Occupation*], 2 MISHPAT U'MIMSHAL [LAW AND GOVERNMENT] 545 (1995) (Hebrew). *See also* Ruth Gavison, *The Israeli Constitutional Process: Legislative Ambivalence and Judicial Resolute Drive* 18 n.58 (The Hebrew Univ. of Jerusalem Center for the Study of Rationality, Discussion Paper No. 380, 2005), http://ratio.huji.ac.il/dp/dp380.pdf or http://ideas.repec.org/p/huj/dispap/dp380.html.

Justice Barak's participation in legislative debates. He also spoke about the meaning of the decisions recognizing the Basic Laws as constitutional laws before a Knesset committee[33] and took a strong, and possibly outcome-determinative, position before the Knesset against establishment of a constitutional court.[34] In another instance, he stated publicly that the Knesset should enact additional Basic Laws.[35]

The Supreme Court in Israel participates in legislative matters in another way. It is not unusual for the Court to recommend steps the Knesset should take in enacting or amending statutes. The Knesset is typically sensitive to such input. The Court also recommends actions to administrative agencies. Such recommendations may be made in obiter dicta in written opinions, or in dialogue with representatives of the Government during court hearings.[36]

Despite Justice Barak's position that his comments on the legislation are purely professional, the participation of a sitting judge in legislative considerations raises the question of the propriety of a judge taking part in formulating a law that the same judge is likely to be later asked to interpret. Similarly comments of the Court on matters before the legislature or the administrative agencies raise issues of whether the Court is fulfilling its proper role. These comments are likely to be taken as more than the comments of an unrelated professional. Judicial participation in the legislative process interferes with separation of powers. Furthermore, it raises concerns about the impartiality of judges when they hear cases and suggests that the judge sitting on a case may have already have a firm position on a question presented.

In the United States, the practice is different. The Code of Conduct for United States Judges allows federal judges to appear before legislative bodies,[37] but it also requires that judges act "in a manner that promotes the public confidence in the integrity and impartiality of the judiciary."[38] The practice is that justices of the Supreme Court and other federal judges refrain from legislative appearances. As one scholar put it, "[The] unofficial addresses [of judges] by tradition are confined to subjects other than those before their courts, and are ordinarily given before a bar association or at commencement exercises. No press conferences, no committee hearings, no stump speeches, no *Face the Nation*."[39] Judges get involved in legislation only in matters that relate directly to administration of the courts.[40] A proposal to allow American judges broader participation in legislative processes has been subject to substantial criticism.[41]

---

33. Gavison, *supra* note 32, at 16 n.52.

34. See *id.* at 17 and at 26 n.78.

35. Nina Gilbert, *Supreme Court President Tells the Knesset: Expand Basic Laws*, JERUSALEM POST, Dec. 9, 1998, at 4.

36. SHIMON SHETREET, JUSTICE IN ISRAEL: A STUDY OF THE ISRAELI JUDICIARY 187–88 (1994); comments of Professor Daniel Friedman, former Israeli minister of justice, in Halberstam, *supra* note 22 at 2316–17.

37. CODE OF CONDUCT FOR UNITED STATES JUDGES, Canon 4A(2) (2009).

38. *Id.*, Canon 2A.

39. Geoffrey C. Hazard, Jr., *Law Reforming in the Anti-Poverty Effort*, 37 UNIV. CHI. L. REV. 242, 250 (1970).

40. See Neal Kumar Katyal, *Judges as Advicegivers*, 50 STAN. L. REV. 1709, 1815–16 (1998). Professor Katyal argues that judges actually have taken broader political roles and should do so. Judge and Professor Abner Mikva strongly disagrees. Abner J. Mikva, *Why Judges Should Not Be Advice Givers: A Response to Professor Neal Katyal*, 50 STAN. L. REV. 1825 (1998).

41. The proposal is found in ROBERT A. KATZMANN, COURTS AND CONGRESS (1997), at 68, 97–8. Criticism is found in Toni M. Fine, *Dialogues between Coordinate Branches and Stories of Their Failings*, reviewing ROBERT A. KATZMANN, COURTS AND CONGRESS (1997) and LOUIS FISHER, THE POLITICS OF SHARED POWER: CONGRESS AND THE EXECUTIVE (1998).

G. Power of the Supreme Court

As the sections on appointments and on extrajudicial statements of judges suggest, the Supreme Court of Israel is a very powerful body. The Court decided that laws enacted by the Knesset through the regular legislative process constitute a constitution, and it allocated to itself the power of judicial review of other statutes for consistency with these constitutional laws; it invalidates administrative agency actions if they are inconsistent with rights that are not protected by constitutional statutes but identified as basic rights by the court; it reviews actions of the Knesset for compliance with principles of administrative law; it reviews actions of the Israeli military during a period of armed conflict with a close degree of scrutiny; and it has allocated to itself nearly unbridled discretion to recognize standing of a person before the Court and to determine whether a dispute is justiciable. All of these types of decisions are examined in greater detail in the remaining chapters of this book.

The extensive power of the Supreme Court derives not only from the breadth of its authority, but also from the lack of constraints on its exercise of that authority. The absence of some constraints has already been discussed. The Court is not bound to follow its own precedent. Without a firm distinction between holding and dicta, the Court is free to address issues as it sees fit, without being bound to the issues raised by a case before it. This allows the Court to address whatever it sees as the important issues of the day, even if no case directly raises those issues. With each justice writing a separate opinion, there is little pressure to moderate the contents of an opinion in order to gain acquiescence of a majority. Because there are no set rules on standing or justiciability, neither doctrine prevents the Court from considering theoretical cases. Finally as we have seen, some justices participate directly in the political process, rather than speaking only when operating in the judicial setting.[42]

Whether the power of the Supreme Court should be restrained is the subject of a sometimes sharp debate within Israel.[43] The debate is conducted both in the popular press, in academia, and in the Knesset. On the one side, the power of the Supreme Court is seen as allowing it to defend both democracy and human rights in a strong and meaningful manner. Furthermore, given the constraints on the functioning of the Israeli parliament and the executive branch, stemming at least in part from the multitude of political parties and the way the coalition system functions, the Court is seen as the best functioning branch of government. As a result, representatives of a segment of the public disgruntled with the inaction of the Knesset or the Government on some important public issue often turn to the Supreme Court and ask it to address the issue, even if that issue is in large measure political. On the other side lies the danger of having the Court operate without effective checks and balances. Judicial consideration of political matters also endangers the system of separation of powers and threatens to place the decision on political issues in the hands of a body that has no formalized tie to the people and is divorced from all political actors.

Part of the debate centers on the nature of the democratic regime. For those who see the main characteristic of democracy in the strong protection of individual rights, the Court seems on the right track.[44] To those for whom the key characteristic of democ-

---

42. *See* Gelpe, *supra* note 12 at 530–56.

43. *See* the views of various Israelis who participated in the discussions recorded in Halberstam, *supra* note 22 at 2397.

44. In fact, there are those who assert that the purpose of the courts is to advance a specific ideology: that of adherence to liberal and democratic values. See Salzberger, *supra* note 10 at 251–53.

racy lies in a structure of government that protects people from tyranny exercised by any part of government, the concentration of power in the hands of the Court is deeply troublesome.

H. Structure of the Courts:
Courts of Limited Jurisdiction

In addition to the courts of general jurisdiction, Israel has a number of courts of limited jurisdiction. These courts have jurisdiction conferred on them by statute and usually operate under procedural rules different from those that apply in courts of general jurisdiction.[45]

A number of courts of limited jurisdiction operate parallel to the magistrates' courts. These include the family law courts, courts on local government matters, juvenile courts, and traffic courts. Some of these courts are separate institutions. Some operate within the framework of a magistrates' court; that is, a judge from the magistrates' court sits on the matters of the court of limited jurisdiction. The procedures in these courts are sometimes tailored to their subject matter. For example, when a magistrate's court is sitting as a family law court, it is allowed to close the proceedings, something that is strictly limited in normal procedures for the magistrate's courts. Decisions of these limited jurisdiction courts are treated as decisions of a magistrates' court for purposes of appeal. This means that mandatory appeal is to the district courts. Small claims courts also exist under a slightly different regime: procedures are simplified and there is no appeal as of right.

The administrative court is a court of limited jurisdiction that operates within the framework of the district courts. Each district court is authorized to sit as the administrative court on actions for review of agency actions. Special rules on administrative law cases apply when the district court is sitting in this capacity. Most decisions are subject to appeal as of right to the Supreme Court.

In addition, Israel has a number of court *systems* of limited jurisdictions. Among these are the labor courts, the rabbinical courts (Jewish law courts), the Shari'a courts (Islamic law courts), and the military courts. These systems typically have two levels of courts, with appeals from decisions of the lower level to the court of the higher level within the same system. Decisions of the highest level courts within each system are subject to review by the Supreme Court, but not by way of appeal. Instead, they are reviewed by petition for review to the Supreme Court sitting as the High Court of Justice. The rules for review are the same as the rules for review of decisions of an administrative agency.

Some of the courts systems of limited jurisdiction have authority to hear cases in certain areas of criminal law. Criminal law decisions of the highest court in one of these systems may be appealed to the Supreme Court by way of a criminal appeal, where the standards of review are different from those for petitions for review by the High Court of Justice.

---

45. In Hebrew, different terms are used for courts of general jurisdiction and for courts of limited jurisdiction. Both of those terms are translated here as *courts* because that word is closest to how these bodies function. Some of the English language literature on Israeli law refers to courts of limited jurisdiction as *tribunals*. *See, e.g.,* Zysblat, *supra* note 28 at 11 (1996). In the text above, the term tribunal is reserved for quasi-judicial bodies operating within administrative agencies.

I. Administrative Tribunals

In addition to courts operating as separate institutions, Israel has numerous tribunals that operate within administrative agencies or in connection with the workings of a specific agency. These are not to be confused with the administrative court, described in the previous section, which is a regular court that has limited jurisdiction, functioning within the district courts. The administrative tribunals include a wide range of bodies. For example, one is the Appeals Committee under the Law on Disabled Ex-Servicemen Who Served in the War Against the Nazis, 5714-1954. This statute authorized payments of compensation to Israelis who were injured in World War II forces that fought against the Nazis.[46] An applicant who is denied compensation or who thinks the amount granted is too low can appeal to the committee, which is composed of a judge, a doctor, and one other person. This appeals committee is an administrative tribunal.

Another example of an administrative tribunal is the Water Court, established under the Water Law, 5719-1959,[47] that deals with a variety of disputes arising under the statute. For example, the governmental agency responsible for preserving water may enter private property to protect water resources. A person whose property was harmed by such an action is entitled to compensation. Complaints over inadequate compensation are heard by the Water Court, composed of one judge and two public representatives. The law also requires that a person engaged in certain activities that involve water, such as desalinization of sea water, obtain a license. A person denied a license may appeal the denial to the Water Court. Although the statute uses the term *Water Court* for this body, the context shows that it is an administrative tribunal and not a regular court.

Generally decisions of an administrative tribunal are appealable to a court, although different arrangements on the details of the appeal are provided in different laws.

The rules that apply to the operation of some administrative tribunals, including the two described in the previous paragraph, are set out in the Law on Administrative Tribunals, 5752-1992. Other administrative tribunals are governed by requirements in the statute establishing the specific tribunal or by those imposed by the head of the agency in which the tribunal is located.

---

46. Section 3. This law is important because not only did many Israelis who lived under the British Mandate join the war against the Nazis, but also many people fought during World War II in the armed forces of countries where they then lived and later immigrated to Israel.

47. Section 140.

Chapter 6

Procedure

A. The Adversary System

Common law systems usually employ the adversary system of court procedure. In the adversary system, the parties and their attorneys each bring their own view of the facts and the law before the court, and the case is shaped largely by their contrasting claims. Each side submits documents and calls witnesses, including expert witnesses, and the trier of fact is limited to this information in deciding which side will prevail. The adversary system puts heavy emphasis on procedural fairness and is founded on the underlying theory that the truth, or at least the truth as far as the trial is concerned, will emerge from the contrasting claims. The role of the judge is largely that of a referee charged with ensuring that the parties abide by the rules in presenting their cases.

Civil law courts typically employ an inquisitorial system of court procedure. In the inquisitorial system, the judge is tasked with discovering the truth. Of course, the parties each bring their claims before the judge. The judge may take an active role in discovering what really happened, rather than rely solely on documents submitted by the parties, testimony elicited by them, and experts brought by them, as in the adversarial system.[1] The judge may seek out relevant documents, question witnesses, and call expert witnesses for the court. The judge, and not the parties, controls the order of consideration of issues, allowing the judge to first address the issues most likely to be determinative of the outcome of the case, although again, the degree of this control is subject to dispute. The judge is more than a referee, although the extent to which the judge functions in an active capacity varies from country to country.[2]

Although it is generally agreed that the adversary system and the inquisitorial system are distinguishable, the differences are not absolute. Furthermore, modern developments reflect a tendency toward convergence of the two systems. For example, in complex multi-party litigation in common law courts, the judge takes a more active role in case management than is traditional in the common law system. Another example is found in the fact that some civil law systems assign significant roles to the parties in presentation of material.

---

1. In the US federal courts, the court has authority under Rule 706 of the Federal Rules of Evidence to call its own expert witnesses, but rarely exercises this authority.

2. *Compare* John H. Langbein, *The German Advantage in Civil Procedure*, 52 U. Chi. L. Rev. 823 (1985) (alleging that the judge has extensive responsibility for ferreting out the facts), *with* Ronald J. Allen et al., *The German Advantage in Civil Procedure: A Plea for More Details and Fewer Generalities in Comparative Scholarship*, 82 Nw. U.L. Rev. 705 (1988) (alleging that the judge's role is much more limited).

Israel employs an adversary system of justice, inherited from the British although, as demonstrated here, some features of Israeli law deviate from the pure adversarial model, conferring greater authority on the judge than would normally be expected in adversarial justice. Consistent with this, Israel has never had jury trials, even though they have at some time been a feature of most adversarial systems.

Israeli Statute

The Law of Contracts
(General Provisions), 5733-1973

12. Good Faith in Negotiation

(a) In negotiations leading up to the formation of a contract, a person must act in the customary manner and in good faith.

(b) A party that did not act in the customary manner and not in good faith must pay the other party damages for the injury caused him due to the negotiations or due to the formation of the contract, and the provisions of sections 10, 13 and 14 of The Law of Contracts (Remedies for Breach of Contract), 5731-1970, subject to any necessary changes.

39. Good Faith in Performance

A person should act in the customary manner and in good faith in performing the obligations that derive from the contract; and this applies also to effecting rights that derive from the contract.

61. Applicability

(b) The requirements of this law shall apply, to the extent appropriate and with the necessary changes, to all legal actions that are not contracts and to obligations that do not derive from contracts.

Comments

We will examine the statutory provisions presented here further in chapter 15 on Contracts. For now, we can note that these provisions impose a duty to act in good faith and that this duty applies not only to a person negotiating a contract or performing the obligations derived from a contract, but also, according to the language of Section 61(b), more broadly to "all legal actions ... and to obligations."

One Israeli scholar, who regularly writes about civil procedure, suggests that application of the doctrine of good faith to civil procedure transfers some of the power to shape the form of litigation from the parties to the judge and reduces the degree to which Israeli civil procedure operates under the traditional rules of the adversary system.[3] For example, it would let the judge decide whether claims of one party would be considered without waiting for objections by the other party. If, in the opinion of the judge, the claim was not made in good faith, it can be excluded.

---

3. See David Schwartz, *T'Chulah shel Ekron Tom Ha-lev B'Seder Ha-din Ha-ezrachi* [*Application of the Principle of Good Faith in Civil Procedure*], 11 Iyunei Mishpat 295 (1998) (Hebrew).

Question

1. In what other ways might application of the doctrine of good faith transfer power from the parties to the judge and alter the traditional rules of the adversary system? Is this a good thing and should it be adopted in the United States?

B. Absence of Juries

The most prominent difference between court procedure in Israel and in the United States is that there are no juries in Israel. Israeli courts use juries in neither civil nor criminal trials. The absence of juries may seem surprising, given the fact that the court system in Israel is heavily based on the British system instituted during the British Mandate, and, of course, juries were then used in England. Nonetheless the British did not utilize juries in the courts they established in Mandatory Palestine. It has been posited that the British did not import their jury system out of concern that Jews on juries would render inappropriate decisions against Arabs and that Arabs would render inappropriate decisions against Jews.[4] Another explanation is that the British desired to keep all trials in the hands of professional judges, who were appointed through a mechanism set up by the British administration.[5]

When the State of Israel was established, the court system established by the British was retained. Thus, history explains why juries did not participate in trials at the time of the founding of the state. It does not explain why this condition continued. Israeli law has changed in many ways from that inherited from the Mandatory authorities. Why has this feature not changed? Several answers have been given. It may be that Israelis who considered whether juries should be instituted were aware that the use of juries was subject to significant criticism in England during the 1950s, the period shortly after the establishment of Israel.[6] Perhaps the nature of Israeli society makes juries impractical. It would be difficult to find twelve people who have no connection to each other or to one of the parties. Israelis usually have widespread connections with people all over the country. Families are large and close-knit. Strong connections are formed during the years of compulsory and reserve army service, and reserve military service lasts, for men, until they are in their mid-40s. The small size of the country makes it easy to maintain contacts with people who live in different locations. Additionally it has been suggested that it would be hard for twelve Israelis to agree on anything.[7] While this proposition may seem tongue-in-cheek to an American reader, in fact Israeli society is a very disputatious one in which independence of opinion is highly valued. Furthermore, Israeli society has subgroups that disagree on fundamental issues. It might be hard to get agreement on anything from a jury composed of radical secularists, Ultra-Orthodox Jews, conservative Druze, na-

---

4. Ori Strausman, *The King Has No Clothes or the Jury Rules in the Israeli Court*, 13 TEL AVIV U.L. REV. 175, 207 (1988) (in Hebrew).

5. Eli M. Salzberger, *Judicial Appointments and Promotions in Israel: Constitution, Law, and Politics*, *in* APPOINTING JUDGES IN AN AGE OF JUDICIAL POWER: CRITICAL PERSPECTIVES FROM AROUND THE WORLD 241, 244 (Kate Malleson & Peter H. Russell, eds., 2006).

6. *See* C. Bentel, *Integration of the Citizen in the Judicial Authority*, 13 HAPRAKLIT 299, 300–01 (5721-1961).

7. *See* Amnon Straschnov, *The Judicial System in Israel*, 34 TULSA L.J. 527, 528 (1999).

tional religious Zionists, and Arab Muslims. All these groups work successfully side by side in many settings, such as Israeli hospitals and governmental offices, but agreement on value-laden litigation issues might be especially difficult.

The absence of juries is not as unusual as it may seem. Criminal juries are found in only about a quarter of the world's countries.[8] In those countries, they are often restricted to the most serious crimes. Even in common law countries, restricted use of criminal juries is not unusual, and they are totally absent in other places in addition to Israel. In Canada and Spain, juries are regularly impaneled for some categories of offenses. In Australia and New Zealand, criminal juries are available for at least some offenses, but rarely used. In France, Italy, and Germany, a mixed panel of judges and lay jurors deliberates on serious crimes. Singapore, Malaysia, Zimbabwe, the Philippines, and South Africa have no juries for any criminal cases.

Civil juries are unknown in most countries, and those that have them typically use them to a very limited extent. The use of juries in civil cases is extremely limited in England. While juries were established in many parts of the British Empire, they have been abolished or restricted in many of these areas, sometimes before they achieved independence and sometimes afterwards. Today, civil juries have been abolished in India, Singapore, South Africa, and Zimbabwe, and the use of civil juries in Australia and New Zealand is even more limited than in England. Juries are used in civil cases in some, but not all, Canadian provinces. Civil juries were never introduced into the Philippines, despite the fact that other aspects of American civil procedure were imposed by the United States after it gained control in 1898. This situation is an interesting parallel to that in Israel, where the ruling foreign power did not import the jury system into the area it controlled. Civil law countries generally do not have civil juries; this includes the countries of the European continent.

In the United States, juries are available in federal criminal cases under the Sixth Amendment and in state criminal cases under the Sixth and Fourteenth Amendments.[9] Thus, as a matter of federal constitutional law, juries are available in both federal and state courts for criminal cases. The legal basis for juries in civil cases is different. The Seventh Amendment to the US Constitution makes a jury available in federal courts for cases like those that were known at common law. The Seventh Amendment does not apply to the states, and availability of civil juries in state proceedings depends on state constitutional and statutory law. Furthermore, it has been reported that most civil cases are not tried before juries but rather are settled or tried before a judge.[10] Of course, the availability of the jury may affect the substance of settlements.

In light of the limited use of juries in other countries, the real question may not be why Israel does not have juries, but why the United States does. Of course, the Constitution and state laws mandate juries in many cases, but we could ask why this has not been changed or more restrictively interpreted. After all, the original job of the jury, as it was conceived of in England not long after the Norman Conquest, was to provide a panel of witnesses to the event at stake in a trial. The modern use of the jury as the neu-

---

8. As of 2008, jury trials of some type were available for at least some criminal cases in fifty-one of the one hundred and ninety-two states that are members of the United Nations. See Ryan Y. Park, *The Globalizing Jury Trial: Lessons and Insights from Korea*, 58 Am. J. Comp. L. 525, 527 (2010).

9. *See* Duncan v. State of Louisiana, 391 U.S. 145 (1968).

10. *See* Geoffrey C. Hazard, Jr., *Two Valuable Treatises on Civil Procedure*, 37 N.Y.U.J. Int'l L. & Pol. 611, 620 (2005) (reviewing Neil Andrews, English Civil Procedure: Fundamentals of the New Civil Justice System (2003) and Peter L. Murray & Rolf Sturner, German Civil Justice (2004)).

tral trier of fact dependent on evidence presented by the parties in a trial has been called a "historical mutation."[11] The persistence of the American devotion to the jury has been attributed to American values of egalitarianism, populism, and anti-statism.[12] While all of these characteristics are shared by Israelis to a significant degree, Israelis show no significant interest in juries. In the end, the answer may be that jury trials are deeply embedded in the American experience, but not in Israeli usage.

In some countries that have no juries, another method is provided for popular participation in the administration of justice. Cases are decided by a panel comprising both lay people and professional judges. The lay members of the panel may or may not have expertise in the subject matter of the case. Israel does not have lay judges of this sort in regular courts of general jurisdiction, but lay judges sit in labor courts and in other courts of limited jurisdiction.

Question

2. One of the values of studying foreign law is that it leads us to see different ways of doing things and to question why American law is the way it is. The foregoing discussion calls into question one of the accepted norms of American law: that it is best to have jury trials. What do you see as the advantages of having jury trials? The disadvantages?

C. Civil Procedure: Attorney's Fees and Costs

Israeli Case

Kinneret Quarries (Limited Partnership) v. Local Planning Commission, Upper Nazareth
CA 2617/00 60(1) PD 600 [2005]

Registrar Y. Marzel,[13]

[Two cases raising a similar question had previously been decided by the registrar. In the first case, Kinneret Quarries sought a permit to operate a quarry on a certain plot of land. The local government refused a permit and Kinneret Quarries sued. A court order was issued preventing any quarrying operation on the land in question. Later, Kinneret Quarries brought a separate action claiming that the local government and other Respondents were themselves operating a quarry on the site and seeking a decree of contempt of court against them for violating the prior court order. After some time, having discovered that the activity on the site did not involve quarrying operations, but rather

---

11. The quotation is from George P. Fletcher, *The Deliberators*, N.Y. Times Book Review, Dec. 11, 1994 (reviewing Jeffrey Abramson, WE THE JURY: THE JURY SYSTEM AND THE IDEAL OF DEMOCRACY (1994)).

12. *See* Oscar G. Chase, *American "Exceptionalism" and Comparative Procedure*, 50 AM. J. COMP. L. 277, 288–292 (2002).

13. The registrar of a court is an official appointed by the chief justice who has power to make decisions for the court in statutorily specified types of cases. The basis of the registrar's authority in this case in explained within the opinion.

work to prepare for construction of a military base, Kinneret Quarries moved to dismiss its action against the local government. The local government agreed to the dismissal, but asked that Kinneret be made to pay its litigation costs. The registrar agreed to this request.

In the second case, an import firm filed a petition challenging the refusal of several governmental agencies to grant it a license for the year 2005 to import dried milk. The governmental agencies first said they would not grant a license, but then decided to reconsider the matter. After reconsideration, the agencies again stated they would not grant a license in the future, but agreed to grant an import license for the year 2005. Because the import firm obtained the license for the year requested, it asked to withdraw the petition. At the same time, it asked that the governmental agencies be ordered to reimburse its costs in bringing the petition. The registrar agreed to this request.]

The Question in Dispute

The factual and legal circumstances in the two matters before us are different, but they have one legal question in common: In light of the fact that it was decided to impose costs, including attorney's fees, (hereinafter costs) on one party, what is the appropriate measure for determining the amount of these costs? The dispute is essentially over whether the costs should be the actual costs, that is to say the costs that were actually paid by the other party (or that it is obligated to pay), or if there is another appropriate measure, such as reasonable costs or minimal costs.

The Normative Framework

In civil proceedings, the power to impose an obligation to pay costs is granted, along with other powers, to the Registrar of the Court (Law on Courts (Consolidated Version), 5744-1984, § 99), and the relevant rules are set out in several provisions of the Rules of Civil Procedure, 5784-1984 (hereinafter the Rules). These provisions also apply in proceedings before the High Court of Justice (see Rules for Procedure in the High Court of Justice, 5744-1984, rule 20(b)). The fundamental provision in the matter under discussion is set out in rule 511(a) of the Rules, under which, "at the end of the hearing on any matter, the court or the registrar determining the matter shall decide whether or not to obligate one party to pay the attorney's fees and legal costs of the other party." According to the rules, costs may be imposed in one of two main ways: one is by explicitly determining the amount of the costs; and the other is by determining that one party must pay costs, without determining the amount. For those cases in which the amount of the costs is determined, rule 511(b) adds, "If the court or registrar decides to impose costs on one party, the decision-maker has discretion to determine the amount, subject to the provisions of rule 512." Rule 512, entitled "Determination of the Amount of Costs," provides,

(a) If the court or the registrar sets the amount of the costs, it may set the amount of the attorney's fees and the court costs, each separately and without itemization, and, as long as the requirements of subsection (b) are met, the amount of the attorney's fees shall not be less than the minimum amount set as attorney's fees under the Rules of the Bar Association (Minimum Fees), 5737-1977 . . . , except if a court decides, for specific reasons that shall be given in writing, on a lower amount.

(b) In issuing an order imposing costs and in setting the amount, a court or the registrar shall consider, among other matters, the value of the remedy in the dispute between the parties and the value of the remedy provided in the decision, and also it may consider the manner in which the parties conducted the case.

As already stated, a court may decide to impose costs on one party without setting out the precise amount. Rule 513 deals with such a case, providing,

> If the court or the registrar imposes costs without determining the amount, then the amount shall be the total of the following amounts, unless the court or the registrar determined otherwise:
>
> (1) Court fees, costs of preparing the court record, its copying, the costs of issuing a court document…, witness fees, payment for doctors and other experts, their fees for travel and housing within Israel, and all other costs legally incurred in relationship to the complaint, as shall be set by the chief secretary of the court according the material in the file, without need for a request and without the presence of the parties;
>
> (2) Other legal costs, as set by the registrar in response to a written or oral request after the parties have had an opportunity for a hearing, on condition that the court is of the opinion that such legal costs were reasonable and necessary for conduct of the case.

These rules grant the court discretion as to whether to impose costs and also in setting the amount of the costs. A close examination of the rules set out above shows that this discretion is not sufficiently limited. When a court imposes costs and sets their amount under rule 512, a minimum threshold is set, but the court can deviate even from this. That minimum is the minimum attorney's fees as set out in the Rules of the Bar Association (Minimum Fees), 5737-1977…. Other than this, the language of the rules does not set out the appropriate measure for setting the costs. Of course, rule 512(b) sets out criteria that may act as a guide for the court is setting the amount of costs, including the value of the remedy and the conduct of the parties. Except for this, it is not clear how the amount is to be set. This lack of clarity is relevant not only to cases in which the court sets the amount of the costs. While rule 513(1) sets out a list of cost components that were paid by one of the parties, such as fees, payments to experts, etc., the rules do not set out how the rest of the legal costs, including the attorney's fees, should be measured, other than stating that a party shall be obligated to pay them if the court "is of the opinion that such legal costs were reasonable and necessary for conduct of the case." The language of the rules does not specify what is meant by reasonable or when it should be determined that a certain cost, including attorney's fees paid by a party, were necessary for conduct of the case. In order to provide the necessary clarification, we must examine carefully the purposes and the principles that form the basis for imposing costs as part of the decision. We now turn to this issue.

The Obligation to Pay Legal Costs

Legal proceedings cost a great deal of money. The cost of the proceedings includes those costs associated with using the courts. In most cases, the party who brings the case pays a fee to the court. Of course this fee, which is paid into the state treasury, is just part of the cost of using the judicial system. It does not represent the actual cost of the proceeding. Given this situation, there are countries in which, as a matter of principle, the losing party is obligated to pay the state a substantial amount in costs. This is the situation, for example, under Swiss law (W.J. Habscheid, *Droit Judiciare Privé Suisse* 295 (2nd ed. 1981) at p. 295) and in German law (P.L. Murray, R. Stürner, *German Civil Justice* 341 (2004)). But this is not the issue raised in these cases, and it will not be investigated further. The question in the present cases is related to the costs of the parties and not to the costs of the court. Clearly legal proceedings involve great costs for the parties, both the litigation costs and the attorney's fees that they incur. Who must pay these costs?

Different legal systems have different answers to this basic question. In most systems, the rule is that the loser must pay the costs of the winner. This is the rule in Israel, and also in England (N. Andrews, *English Civil Procedure: Fundamentals of the New Civil Justice System* 825 (2003)). This is the rule in other countries as well, such as Italy (M. Capelletti & J.M. Perillo, *Civil Procedure in Italy* 247 (2005)), in Germany (P.L. Murray & R. Stürner, *German Civil Justice* 341 (2004)), in Sweden (R.B. Ginsburg & A. Burzelius, *Civil Procedure in Sweden* 367–68 (1965); B. Lindell, *"Sweden" in International Encyclopedia of Laws—Civil Procedure* 163 (Deventer, R. Blanpain & P. Lemmens eds., 1994)), in Canada (B.A. Crane & H.S. Brown, *Supreme Court of Canada Practice* 83 (1996)), and in Australia (B.C. Crains, *Australian Civil Procedure* 486 (3rd ed. 1992)). But even though this approach is widespread, it is not the only approach. In the United States, in general, but subject to a number of exceptions, there is another system, under which each party pays its own costs whether it wins or loses the case (see G.C. Hazard & M. Taruffo, *American Civil Procedure: An Introduction* 96 (1993)). This is also the basic approach in Jewish Law. Each system has its advantages and disadvantages, and no system is free of criticism (see also N. Rickman, *The Economics of Cost-Shifting Rules, in Reform of Civil Procedure: Essays on "Access to Justice"* 327 (A.A.S. Zuckerman & R. Cranston eds. 1995)).

Measure of Legal Costs

The law in Israel has always been that, as a matter of principle, the loser bears the costs of the winner. This is the rule known as *costs follow the outcome*. We shall examine closely this rule, which is not disputed in the current case, to determine what stands behind it. This examination will reveal that the principle that the loser pays the costs of the winner does not necessarily tell us how to determine the amount of the costs. It is not clear whether the rule refers to costs actually incurred, to reasonable costs, to minimal costs, or to costs imposed as a punishment. We still must face the question: When a party is obligated to pay the costs of the other party, what is the measure of this obligation?

One way of answering this question is to derive the measure of the costs from the underlying legal nature of the obligation to pay costs. For example, it is possible to see the obligation to pay costs as a tort (ex delicto) or quasi-tort obligation. Chief Justice Barak took this approach when he wrote, "The right to obtain costs is provided to the winner under the law of torts. A person who conducts legal proceedings against another, where it becomes evident that a reasonable person would not have done so, violates the protected interests of the other party. Sometimes such an action meets the requirements of a malicious prosecution. Sometimes it meets the requirements of a cause of action in negligence. The court's imposition of legal costs is therefore a shortcut that allows efficient effectuation of the right to damages." If so, the obligation to pay costs is in the nature of a tort remedy, so that the amount must be that which will return the situation to what it was before commission of the tort. The amount of the costs, therefore, subject to the obligation to minimize the damages, is the actual costs, that is, the costs that were actually incurred by the winning party. But this approach is not free from problems. The main one is the fact that in most cases, it cannot be shown that the suit was filed maliciously so as to constitute malicious prosecution, or that it was conducted in a negligent manner. In essence, the loss does not flow from the fact that there was anything wrong or unjustified in the proceedings.

There are also difficulties in basing the obligation to pay costs on a theory of punishment. The obligation to pay costs is not a punishment to be inflicted on the loser because it brought a dispute before a court. Clearly the amount of the costs is not penal, in that the loser must pay the amounts actually incurred. It is not for nothing that it has been ruled that "the obligation to pay costs is not intended to punish the losing side in a case," and that a court lacks authority to impose costs as punishment. The obligation to pay costs is of a unique nature. It has been correctly observed that the authority to obligate a party to pay costs, an authority that derives from the Rules (ex lege), is a *hybrid* obligation. It is not a clear tort obligation and it is not a penal obligation. It is an obligation that derives from a law giving discretion to the court. Therefore we cannot derive the amount of the costs from the nature of the obligation.

The Purpose of Imposing Costs of One Party on the Other Party

Therefore we must derive the answer to the question of what principle to use in setting the amount of the costs from the purpose of imposing costs. The imposition of costs is based on several goals. Several fundamental values are involved. One value is assuring the right of access to the courts. There is no longer any dispute that this is a basic individual right. It is also related to the interest of the public as a whole in the rule of law and in enforcement of the law. The question of whether a party can withstand the costs of a legal proceeding, like the question of whether a party can withstand the costs of the opposing party, has implications for the right of access to the courts and on the ability to realize this right. We must refrain from excessively deterring the parties from realizing their rights. The second value is found in protecting the individual's property rights. Requiring a party to pay the costs of a legal proceeding can be considered as a denial of that person's property rights, whether we mean that the winning party must pay its own legal costs, or that the loser must pay the legal costs of the winner. The third value is that of equality between the parties to a case. In light of the substantial monetary costs of legal proceedings, any rule regarding costs has different effects on parties of different economic means. Thus, for example, imposing on one party the costs of the opposing party has a much greater influence on a person of limited means than on a person of substantial means. But the rule that each side pays its own costs also has a differential effect on parties of different economic means. Therefore the question arises of whether imposition of costs is an interference with the right to equality or furthers equality. Finally imposition of legal costs is related to administration of the resources of the legal system, because it is possible to claim that the way courts impose legal costs influences the number of cases considered in the courts, on the substance of these decisions, and on the way the parties conduct the cases. It may deter frivolous cases and burdensome methods of presenting cases.

Full Costs (Actual Costs) or Partial Costs

Different balances between the various rights and interests I have described can lead to different approaches to the question of the measure of costs that should be imposed on the losing party. As a matter of principle, it seems that there are two main approaches: one is the approach of actual costs. Under this approach, a party who was involved in a case and lost must pay the actual costs of the other party, without regard to how great they are. This includes the full costs of the trial, including the attorney's fees of the winning party, whatever they are. This approach is apparently based on a sense of justice, under which it is unjustified for the winner to suffer any monetary loss. This approach has some degree of effect of deterring the litigants in certain cases from bringing frivolous actions and wasting valuable judicial time. It protects the constitutional property rights of the winning party. Its goal is to prevent a situation in which it does not pay to enforce a right, which protects the rule of law. But this approach also has disadvantages. Imposition of full costs on the loser may discriminate against a party who lacks sufficient economic means and deter that party from bringing a lawsuit. Such a party may fear being made to pay the very high costs of a wealthy opponent. Moreover, there is a concern that imposing actual costs will cause an unnecessary appreciation of legal costs.... On this grounds, the English law, under which imposition of all actual costs is allowed and is usually imposed (indemnity costs), has been subject to criticism. According to the critique, the costs of legal proceedings and the other costs imposed are too high, and reform limiting the amount of costs is needed.

Another approach to the question of the proper measure of costs is that, although the losing side in a case must pay the costs of the winning side, the loser is not obligated to pay the full costs actually incurred, but rather some lower amount. Underlying this approach is the desire to avoid excessively deterring one side by providing some degree of equality between the two sides. This approach gives considerable weight to the right of access to the courts. It also prevents the winning side, or the winner's attorney, from gaining a financial benefit from the other side having to pay unnecessary costs. It prevents a legal case from becoming a gamble. Of course this approach also involves not insubstantial difficulties. There is a certain degree of injustice in the fact that the winning side will not be compensated for all legal expenses. This is an infringement of the winner's property rights. The rule of law and enforcement of the law may be negatively affected. Imposition of partial costs creates an incentive for bringing lawsuits, and it may encourage frivolous proceedings or inappropriate conduct of trials. It creates a measure of uncertainty such that a party to a case cannot know what measure of costs to expect if he wins, and he cannot decide what steps are economically justified.

Then what is the proper approach? As a matter of principle, we should begin from the assumption that the winning side should be able to recover full legal costs; that is, the amount the winner actually paid or is obligated to pay. But this is just a starting point. It is not the final decision, because the person sitting in judgment must examine the amount of costs requested and check whether they are reasonable, proportional, and necessary, considering all the facts of the matter. The amount actually paid for attorney's fees and for legal costs is relevant, but it is not the only relevant factor. Costs of a case are not a prize or a bonus paid to the winner, but rather a return of appropriate and necessary costs incurred in the proceeding. Therefore it is unnecessary to cover any actual cost that was not necessary to the conduct of the case, and each side should be careful of its expenses. The costs should be proportional to the type of proceeding so that excessive costs are not imposed on the loser and so that the winner is encouraged to conduct the case in an appropriate manner. Therefore imposition of costs and attorney's fees is based on objective exercise of discretion in each individual case.

A number of justifications underlay this approach, under which actual costs are imposed to the extent they are reasonable, necessary, and proportional: First, in my opinion, this type of rule takes elements from each of the approaches, and it realizes the advantages of each while reducing the disadvantages of each. Using the actual costs as a starting point provides justice to the winning side in the case, protects that side's property interests, and to some degree, encourages conduct of cases in an efficient manner. At the same time, making payment of actual costs subject to the requirements of necessity, reasonableness, and proportionality, all in light of the circumstances of the specific case, prevents a situation in which costs imposed will be so high as to excessively deter the parties and create inequality between them. Making legal proceedings too costly interferes with the right of access to justice. Second, although the language of the Rules does not set out the measure of costs that are to be imposed, both section 512 and section 513 set out a basis for determining that costs imposed do not always have to cover the full costs.

Comments

Although the issue in this case is how costs should be measured when imposed on the losing side in civil litigation, the case also presents a thorough analysis of the reasons for imposing costs on the losing party. As the case indicates, the Israeli rule imposing costs on the loser is consistent with the rule in England and in many other countries. The court examines many reasons for adopting this rule, but none of them is fully satisfying.

It is important to note that any justification for imposing costs on the winner should work whether the winner is the plaintiff or the defendant in the suit. Otherwise, we need different justifications for making plaintiffs pay costs and for making defendants pay costs. With this principle in mind, let us examine the justifications offered by the decision:

Tort theory: As the decision states, the bringing and conduct of the lawsuit does not usually constitute a tort. The decision stated, "A person who conducts legal proceedings against another, where it becomes evident that a reasonable person would not have done so, violates the protected interests of the other party." This is what happened in the first of the cases involved here, where Kinneret Quarries brought a lawsuit before fully checking the facts of what was happening on the site in dispute, but this is not the typical situation. The lawsuit in the second case clearly was not tortious. The claim was so reasonable that the governmental agencies agreed to reconsider their position and to grant the license requested, if only for one year. Presumably most lawsuits are based on claims that are reasonable, even if they are not always successful. Furthermore, defending against a lawsuit in which there is a reasonable defense is not tortious. Therefore the tort theory justifies granting of costs in only a small percentage of lawsuits.

Punishment: The decision rightly rejects the idea that costs are a penal measure. In most cases, nothing warrants punishment for bringing a lawsuit. The obligation to pay costs applies to all lawsuits, not to those in which something suggests a problem in bringing, or defending, the suit. Furthermore, punishing the filing of even unjustified lawsuits might have a chilling effect on the filing of justified claims.

Assuring access to justice: Israeli courts in other cases have recognized a right of access to justice. The origin of this right is not entirely clear. In any case, it is hard to see how the rule on costs ensures access to justice. A person who has a justified claim will be more likely to bring a lawsuit if that person is confident that the other side will lose and will have to pay costs and attorney's fees. But what is the influence on a person who is convinced of the rightness of his or her claim, but who thinks the case may be lost because courts are sometimes quirky? That person may be deterred from bringing a lawsuit out of worry that costs will be imposed. Isn't this an interference with that person's access to justice? The philosophy behind the access to justice argument assumes a high degree of confidence in the rightness and predictability of judicial outcomes.

Property rights: The decision says that making the prevailing party pay its own costs would interfere with the winner's constitutional property rights. In other words, there is an unconstitutional interference in property rights in (1) the actions of the plaintiff in bringing an unjustified lawsuit and forcing the defendant to pay costs or (2) the actions of a defendant in defending against a justified lawsuit brought by the plaintiff and thus forcing the plaintiff to incur costs. It is true that Israeli law provides a constitutional protection of property rights. The above analysis, though, seems to assume that there is a constitutional protection against private interference with property rights and not just against interference by the government. After all, the decision to bring or to defend against a lawsuit is a private decision (unless the government is a party to the litigation). Indeed, in some cases, constitutional rights in Israel stand as protection from private interference, but it is not so simple to assume that this would be the case as to the property right that is injured by having to pay the other side's litigation costs. The property theory justification requires discussion of whether property rights stand against private interference, a discussion absent from the case.

Equality: As the decision notes, it is hard to say whether the Israeli rule promotes or inhibits equality between litigants.

Efficient administration of justice: The decision states that the loser pays rule deters frivolous cases and poor case presentation. Presumably the argument is that if you bring a frivolous case, or conduct your case poorly, you will lose and will have to pay your attorney and the other side's attorney as well. Of course even without a loser pays rule, we might think that the requirement to pay your own attorney's fees would discourage frivolous litigation. Furthermore, the requirement to pay the other side's costs applies even when the lawsuit is neither frivolous nor poorly presented.

In summary, none of the arguments are fully convincing. Yet much of the world does make a loser in a lawsuit pay the winner's costs and attorney's fees.

The situation in the United States is different. In the United States, the matter is usually analyzed in terms of attorney's fees, which typically are much higher than other costs. The usual rule in federal litigation is that each party pays its own litigation costs and attorney's fees. Congress has enacted many exceptions to this rule in statutes that allow awards of costs and attorney's fees in specific cases, and courts have established rules allowing award of attorney's fees in a small number of specific circumstances.[14] The same *American rule* is followed in all US states except for Alaska.[15]

The history of the American rule seems to lie in the history of the struggle over the level of attorney's fees. In pre-revolutionary America, the English rule applied and the loser paid the prevailing party's attorney's fees. The level of fees was regulated and enforced by the courts that made the attorney's fees awards. Attorneys in the United States were more independent than the bar in England, though, and moved to charging fees higher than allowed by the original regulation and charging these fees directly to the client. Neither courts nor legislatures halted this development. As attorneys gained the ability to charge substantial fees directly to their clients, they became uninterested in obtaining low, regulated fees through a court award. Over time, the American rule developed mainly out of attorneys' disinterest in continuing the English rule. The American rule was further supported by the willingness of business clients to pay for the best attorneys and by the general notion of freedom of contract in American law.[16]

In the United States, in those types of cases in which fee awards are allowed, courts determine the amount of the award by beginning with a *lodestar* figure. This is a calculation of the number of hours worked times a reasonable hourly rate in the community where the lawyers did the work. The court has discretion to adjust this amount. A court

---

14. *See* Pennsylvania v. Delaware Valley Citizens' Council for Clean Air, 478 U.S. 546, 561, (1986); Alyeska Pipeline Serv. Co. v. Wilderness Soc'y, 421 U.S. 240, 247 (1975).

15. Monzingo v. Alaska Air Group, Inc., 112 P.3d 655, 665 (2005).

16. *See* John Leubsdorf, *Toward a History of the American Rule on Attorney Fee Recovery*, 47 L. & Contemp. Probs. 9 (1984).

may exclude hours not reasonably expended or improperly documented, enhance the award due to expertise of an attorney or the complexity of the issues (although this is rare), and allow less than the lodestar amount if an attorney achieved only partial success in the lawsuit. In addition, the prevailing party in an American case may receive costs such as fees paid to expert witnesses.

Notice the review of the legal rules in other countries in the *Kinneret Quarries* case. Israeli courts often engage in examination of foreign rules. Although in this case, the registrar looked at the law in many continental countries, the Israeli Supreme Court more often looks at English and American sources than at continental sources.[17]

The Israeli Supreme Court probably developed a habit of looking to the laws of other countries early in Israeli history when there were not many Israeli precedents. It was natural to examine English authorities for two reasons: First, until 1980, Article 46 of the Palestinian Order of Council remained in effect in Israel, and directed that courts look to the common law and doctrines of equity in English law to deal with issues not otherwise covered by existing law. The Law on Foundations of Law, discussed in chapter 4, abolished Article 46 as part of Israeli law. Second, many Israeli laws derived from English laws, so it was natural to look at English law in interpreting them, even after the enactment of the Law on Foundations of Law removed the binding effect of English precedent.

Furthermore, many prominent Israeli judges and lawyers in the early days of the state were educated in European countries. Even of those educated in Israel, many knew languages other than Hebrew because they, or their parents, were immigrants. Today, a large number of Israeli-trained lawyers are fluent in English. They have ready access to English language foreign law materials. Another factor that may explain the resort to foreign material is the fact that the Israeli Supreme Court has a very popular program for unpaid foreign law clerks, who supply the judges with perspectives of foreign law on issues before the Court.[18] These positions are considered very prestigious and are sought by graduates of leading foreign (to Israel) law schools. Finally the consideration of foreign law may be a way for a small, relatively young country to gain legitimacy.

Questions

3. Which is better: the Israeli rule imposing costs on losers or the American rule that, in most cases, each side pays its own costs? What justifies the American rule? Do you think the fact that legal costs are generally lower in Israel than in the United States affects the adoption of different rules?

4. How does the Israeli approach to setting the amount of costs and attorney's fees differ from the US approach in cases in which attorney's fees are allowed? What justifies the difference in approach?

5. Would you expect a court in the United States to examine foreign law the way the Israeli Supreme Court does? Why or why not?

---

17. *See* Binyamin Blum, Note, *Doctrines Without Borders: The "New" Israeli Exclusionary Rule and the Dangers of Legal Transplantation*, 60 Stan. L. Rev. 2131, 2154 (2008).

18. *See* State of Israel, the Judicial Authority, http://elyon1.court.gov.il/eng/Clerking_opportunities/index.html.

D. Criminal Procedure

Israeli criminal procedure is based on the system used during the British Mandate, which, in turn, was derived from the English system.

1. Reviewability of Decision to Prosecute

Israeli Statute

Criminal Procedure Law
(Consolidated Version), 5742-1982

62. Prosecution

If the prosecutor who receives the investigative material determines that the evidence is sufficient to convict the accused, he shall prosecute the case, unless he is of the opinion that it is not in the public interest to do so.

Israeli Case

Ganor v. Attorney General
HCJ 935/89 44(2) PD 485 [1990]

Justice A. Barak:

[In 1983, the share prices of the publically traded stock of all but one of the major Israeli banks fell dramatically. The share prices of these banks had been artificially inflated by bank practices. Bankers, who also served as investment advisors, had advised customers to purchase shares in their own banks and provided loans to allow customers to make such purchases. When, in response to other economic factors, investors began to sell bank shares, the government intervened at significant cost, purchased the bank shares and became the major owner of the banks.[19] After investigation of the practices of the banks and the head bankers during the time leading up to this crisis, the attorney general decided not to indict them because the prosecution would not be in the public interest. Based on this determination, the attorney general found it unnecessary to determine whether the evidence was sufficient to support an indictment.

Several Petitioners sought judicial review of the attorney general's decision not to prosecute. Justice Aharon Barak reviewed the decision of the attorney general and found that it violated the rules of administrative law. Israeli administrative law requires that an administrative decision be reasonable. Under Israeli law, this requires an administrative authority to properly balance the arguments for a decision and those against a decision. Justice Barak found that the attorney general's decision that prosecution would not be in the public interest was unreasonable for failure to give sufficient weight to the value the public would derive from the prosecution. This part of the decision is set out and discussed

---

19. For further information on the events leading up to the crisis, see Ehud Ofer, Note, *Glass-Steagall: The American Nightmare that Became the Israeli Dream*, 9 FORDHAM J. CORP. & FIN. L. 527 (2004).

in chapter 9. Justice Barak then turned to the question of whether the Court could review the decision of the attorney general at all.]

Scope of Intervention of the High Court of Justice

We have concluded that the attorney general's decision was not reasonable. Unreasonableness is not based on a minor deviation from the proper balancing of various factors, but on a substantial deviation that reaches to the very heart of the matter, such that the attorney general's final conclusion must be completely rejected as totally unreasonable. We have here a serious deviation from the proper balancing of factors. This invalidates the attorney general's decision and justifies the intervention of this Court. Indeed, the Supreme Court has in the past taken the position that such extreme unreasonableness justifies the intervention of the High Court of Justice. At first the scope of this Court's intervention was limited to cases in which it was claimed that the decision of the attorney general was not made in good faith. Over time, the scope of review was broadened to include claims of arbitrariness, claims that the attorney general failed to take into account some relevant factor in reaching a decision, and claims that irrelevant factors were considered.

[We see from dicta in prior cases that all judges who have addressed the matter] agree that extreme unreasonableness, which goes to the heart of the matter, justifies intervention by this Court. It is just such a defect in the decision of the attorney general that we see in the case before us. Therefore we not only have authority to intervene, but as the defenders of the rule of law, we must do so.

The rules on intervention of the Court in decisions of the attorney general are based on three basic assumptions. One is that the attorney general has broad discretion as to the decision whether to prosecute a suspect. This means that he may choose freely among various legally permissible outcomes. As we have seen, this free choice depends on, among other things, giving the proper weight to various factors that must be considered in reaching the decision as to whether the prosecution is "in the public interest." In determining how to balance the various factors, the attorney general has a lot of maneuvering room. The weight given to various considerations is to be based on an evaluation of the physical and normative situation and on the outlook of the attorney general. It is natural that different attorney generals would give different weights to the various factors that go into determining where the public interest lies. As long as the weight given to various factors serves the objectives of the law, the ultimate decision is legally permissible. Therefore different attorney generals may come to different decisions as to when the public interest is served, and they may all be legally permissible. In such cases, the High Court of Justice will not intervene. The reason for non-intervention is not that the decision of the attorney general has special immunity from judicial review, but because the decision is legally permissible and there is no reason for the Court's intervention. Of course, the High Court of Justice may be of the opinion that, were the original decision whether to prosecute in its hands, it would make a decision different from that of the attorney general. In such a case, the Court might characterize the decision of the attorney general as erroneous, but that does not mean that it is a legally impermissible decision. The Court does not put itself into the position of the attorney general. It is not a super-attorney general. It examines the legality of the decision, not its wisdom.

The second basic assumption ... is that this Court will intervene when the attorney general chooses an option that is not only erroneous but also legally invalid. It is this Court's opinion that ... there is congruence between those claims that invalidate the decision of the attorney general and those claims that justify intervention by this Court. If a claim would not lead to holding invalid the decision of the attorney general, then the claim does not raise a justification for this Court's intervention. On the other hand, if there is a claim that would lead to invalidating the decision of the attorney general, there is also a justification for the High Court of Justice's intervention. The attorney general has not been granted a special immunity from review by the High Court of Justice. The Court will not tolerate a situation in which a reason to hold the decision of the attorney general invalid may exist, but this Court will withhold judicial review. Such immunity, if it existed, would violate the rule of law. We have recognized such immunity from judicial review only in special circumstances, in which the governmental body with immunity is the legislature itself. We have also recognized immunity in other extraordinary situations in which we categorized the matter as non-justiciable. The matter of the attorney general does not fall within any of these situations. The decisions of the attorney general are justiciable, and he is not part of the legislative branch. He has extensive governmental powers.... Judicial supervision is essential to assure proper exercise of the attorney general's authorities, just as it is essential to assure proper exercise of all governmental authorities.

The conclusion to which these two assumptions lead is that the key question is not the scope of intervention of the Court, but rather the validity of the decision of the attorney general. The real question is not the cause of intervention by the Court, but the cause for invalidating the decision. The issue is not the authority of the Court, but the authority of the attorney general. The question is not the Court's exercise of its discretion, but the discretion of the attorney general. Therefore the scope of intervention by the Court is the scope of the illegality of the attorney general's decision.

The decisive question is what types of administrative law claims show an invalid exercise of discretion by the attorney general. Are there claims that can be made against *regular* exercise of discretion by an agency but that do not apply to the exercise of discretion by the attorney general? Examination of Supreme Court case law shows that there is no special law that applies to the attorney general. To the contrary, the goal of this Court in all its decisions on administrative exercise of discretion is to maintain consistency as to the types of claims that invalidate an administrative exercise of discretion. We do not recognize that certain officers are immune. The claims that lead to invalidation of an administrative action apply to all authorities in the executive branch. Thus, the same claims as to defects in the exercise of discretion by any governmental authority generally apply to the exercise of discretion by the attorney general. This brings us to the third assumption on which this Court's case law is based: equal application of the rules of administrative law as to what is required in exercise of administrative discretion. Just as any administrative exercise of discretion is invalid if based on consideration of irrelevant facts, if it involves improper discrimination, if it is not based on fairness and good faith, so to as to the exercise of discretion by the attorney general. Just as any administrative exercise of discretion is invalid if it is done in an extremely unreasonable manner, so to as to exercise of discretion by the attorney general. I accept the position that the exercise of discretion by the attorney general is not invalid if it is only slightly unreasonable. In order to invalidate the exercise of discretion by the attorney general, it is necessary to find substantial or extreme unreasonableness. My conclusion is not based on any special immunity of the attorney general. No exercise of discretion by a governmental authority is invalid due to slight unreasonableness; a determination of substantial unreasonableness is needed.

Based on this view, I find that in the case before us, intervention in the decision of the attorney general is appropriate. This decision is not just slightly unreasonable. The decision is substantially unreasonable and is therefore invalid under the rules of administrative law.[20] When a decision is suffers from a substantial defect, we have authority to declare its invalidity and to annul the decision.

We return the matter to the attorney general to determine whether there is sufficient evidence to indict the bankers and the banks.

Comments

Notice that the Court first found that the decision of the attorney general was invalid under the standards of administrative law review and then reached the question of whether the Court should review the attorney general's decision at all. We would expect an American court to treat the questions in the opposite order: to first determine whether judicial review is appropriate and then, if it is, to review the decision. The Israeli Court was less concerned with the separation of powers issues that affect the question of when a court should review an administrative decision and more concerned with maintaining the rule of law. In other words, the Israeli Court's primary concern was in seeing that an illegal decision by the attorney general, as chief prosecutor, not be allowed to stand.

Justice Barak examines the justifications for allowing full judicial review of the decision of the attorney general not to prosecute, but does not examine the reasons that might be given for not providing judicial review in such a case. Those reasons are prominent in the radically different American law on the matter. Under US case law, the government has broad discretion to decide who to prosecute. The courts do not interfere with the exercise of that discretion unless it is shown that the government is involved in selective prosecution that violates the equal protection clause of the Constitution.[21] The Supreme Court of the United States explained the reasons for allowing the prosecutor broad, almost unreviewed discretion as follows:

> This broad discretion rests largely on the recognition that the decision to prosecute is particularly ill-suited to judicial review. Such factors as the strength of the case, the prosecution's general deterrence value, the government's enforcement priorities, and the case's relationship to the government's overall enforcement plan are not readily susceptible to the kind of analysis the courts are competent to undertake. Judicial supervision in this area, moreover, entails systemic costs of particular concern. Examining the basis of a prosecution delays the criminal proceeding, threatens to chill law enforcement by subjecting the prosecutor's motives and decisionmaking to outside inquiry, and may undermine prosecutorial effectiveness by revealing the government's enforcement policy. All of these are substantial concerns that make the courts properly hesitant to examine the decision whether to prosecute.[22]

In another case, the Supreme Court had a similar approach when faced with the question of whether under the Administrative Procedure Act a court would review an agency's decision to initiate enforcement action:

> This Court has recognized on several occasions over many years that an agency's decision not to prosecute or enforce, whether through civil or criminal process,

---

20. Under the rules of administrative law, the courts do not hold invalid administrative agency decisions that are slightly unreasonable; the decision must be substantially unreasonable to be declared invalid.

21. *See* Wayte v. United States, 470 U.S. 598, 607–10 (1985).

22. *Id.* at 607–08.

is a decision generally committed to an agency's absolute discretion.... This recognition of the existence of discretion is attributable in no small part to the general unsuitability for judicial review of agency decisions to refuse enforcement.

The reasons for this general unsuitability are many. First, an agency decision not to enforce often involves a complicated balancing of a number of factors which are peculiarly within its expertise. Thus, the agency must not only assess whether a violation has occurred, but whether agency resources are best spent on this violation or another, whether the agency is likely to succeed if it acts, whether the particular enforcement action requested best fits the agency's overall policies, and, indeed, whether the agency has enough resources to undertake the action at all. An agency generally cannot act against each technical violation of the statute it is charged with enforcing. The agency is far better equipped than the courts to deal with the many variables involved in the proper ordering of its priorities. Similar concerns animate the principles of administrative law that courts generally will defer to an agency's construction of the statute it is charged with implementing, and to the procedures it adopts for implementing that statute.

In addition to these administrative concerns, we note that when an agency refuses to act it generally does not exercise its *coercive* power over an individual's liberty or property rights, and thus does not infringe upon areas that courts often are called upon to protect. Similarly when an agency *does* act to enforce, that action itself provides a focus for judicial review, inasmuch as the agency must have exercised its power in some manner. The action at least can be reviewed to determine whether the agency exceeded its statutory powers.... Finally we recognize that an agency's refusal to institute proceedings shares to some extent the characteristics of the decision of a prosecutor in the Executive Branch not to indict—a decision which has long been regarded as the special province of the Executive Branch, inasmuch as it is the Executive who is charged by the Constitution to "take Care that the Laws be faithfully executed." US Const., art. II, § 3.[23]

In these excerpts, we see that the reasons that American courts do not review the decision whether to prosecute are concern over (1) the court's competency to review the prosecutor's decision, (2) the effect of judicial review at an initial stage on the criminal process as a whole, and (3) separation of powers constraints. Those concerns did not bother the Israeli Court that, as stated previously, was focused exclusively on the need to maintain the rule of law.

The *Ganor* case leaves a great deal of discretion in the hands of the Court. Under the rule of the case, the Court may review all decisions of the attorney general to determine if they are reasonable; that is, to determine if the appropriate weight was given to various factors in deciding where the public interest lies. The question of what weight is appropriate is one not subject to a clear, rule-bound answer. Therefore the Court has a significant degree of discretion in determining whether the attorney general's weighing of various factors was appropriate. This discretion is somewhat limited by the need to find *substantial* unreasonableness, but it is far from eliminated. Thus, while the opinion gives great emphasis to maintaining the rule of law, it in effect leaves in the hands of the Court considerable discretion to determine just what the law is in a specific case.

The decision in the *Ganor* case is not hard to understand from a political point of view. The bank shares crises was a major event with a significant effect on all Israelis. As a result of the affair, the Israeli currency was devalued by 23 percent. Purchase of the bank

---

23. Heckler v. Chaney, 470 U.S. 821, 831–32 (1985).

stocks cost the government $7 billion. Even before *Ganor*, most of the head bankers had resigned from their positions. After the case, most had to pay fines and some were sentenced to prison.

Under American law, prosecutorial discretion can be confined by a specific statute, and, if it is, courts will enforce those confines. The Israeli Court based its decision on a statute that confined the attorney general's discretion. Still, the Israeli statute could have been read to give the attorney general broad discretion to determine the public good. The Court rejected such a reading.

Questions

6. Under the rationale of *Ganor*, is the decision of the attorney general not to prosecute always reviewable or sometimes reviewable? If sometimes, when?

7. If a decision not to prosecute is reviewable, is a decision to prosecute also reviewable?

2. Private Criminal Prosecutions

Israeli law allows private criminal prosecutions for some, but not all, criminal violations. The following material investigates the reasons for, the limits on, and the wisdom of this arrangement.

Israeli Statute

The Criminal Procedure Law
(Consolidated Version), 5742-1982

11. The State as Prosecutor

In a criminal proceeding, the state is to make the accusation of a crime, and is to be represented by a public prosecutor who will conduct the proceedings.

68. Private Criminal Complaint

Despite what is provided in section 11, in the matters listed in the Second Appendix to this statute, an individual can file a criminal complaint in court.[24]

69. Private Criminal Complaint

A private criminal complaint may not be filed against a public servant based on an act done in fulfilling that person's job, unless the attorney general agrees to the filing of the complaint.

70. The Law Applying to a Private Criminal Complaint

The provisions of this law that apply to an indictment by a public authority apply also to a private criminal complaint, with such changes as are necessary. In each place where the statute uses the term indictment, it shall be understood to include a private criminal

---

24. A *complaint* as used in this statute is not like a private complaint to the police, asking the police to investigate the commission of a crime. This is a complaint to a court and constitutes the filing of a criminal action. As the following provisions of the statute make clear, it is the private action equivalent of an indictment.

complaint. In all places where it uses the term prosecutor, it shall be understood to include a private criminal complainant, if there is no other meaning to be drawn from the context.

71. The Prosecution in a Private Criminal Action

When a private criminal complaint is filed, the court shall transmit a copy of the complaint to the district prosecutor. The action shall be prosecuted, despite the provisions of section 11, by the private criminal complainant or that person's representative, unless, within fifteen days of receiving the copy of the complaint, the district prosecutor notifies the court that a state prosecutor will prosecute the case.

72. Replacement of Prosecutor

If a notification is submitted under section 71, an indictment by the public prosecutor shall replace the private criminal complaint.

73. Arrangements Regarding the Private Criminal Prosecution

If the court determines that the private criminal complainant is not capable of conducting the proceedings in court, or that he is conducting the proceedings in an inappropriate manner, the court may stop the proceedings until the private criminal complainant appoints an attorney to prosecute the case.

Israeli Case

Israel Law Center v. The Attorney General
HCJ 4957/08 (Oct. 17, 2010)

[The facts of the case are based on activities conducted on the Temple Mount. The Temple Mount is an area in Jerusalem that is holy in Judaism as the site of the binding of Isaac (Genesis 22:1–14) and as the site of the First and Second Temples, and holy in Islam as the site associated with Mohammed's journey to Jerusalem and ascent to Heaven. At present, under Israeli law, the Temple Mount is administered by the Waqf [pronounced Walkf], an Islamic trust, but security is in the hands of the Israeli police. The golden-domed Dome of the Rock, a Muslim shrine, and the Al-Aksa Mosque,[25] which has huge prayer halls, are the most prominent structures now located on the Temple Mount. Both Muslims and Jews have access to the Temple Mount, but Jews are not allowed to pray openly there. Jewish prayer services are held at the Western Wall, below the Mount. This is a retaining wall that holds up the western side of the Temple Mount.]

Justice A. Procaccia:

The subject of this petition is the request by the Israel Law Center and 159 citizens to order the Respondent, the attorney general, to reverse his decision to prevent criminal proceedings under the private criminal complaint that the Petitioner filed in the magistrate's court in Jerusalem. This would allow the Petitioners to pursue their complaint.

The Background of the Petition

The Petitioner is a public-interest organization that works to achieve various goals both in Israel and abroad. The organization, and 159 individuals, submitted the private criminal complaint in the magistrate's court in Jerusalem. According to the complaint, the

---

25. Although the building containing these prayer halls is commonly called the Al-Aksa Mosque, that term is sometimes used by Muslims to refer to the entire area of the Temple Mount.

Islamic Waqf and six of its senior representatives are accused of committing the crimes of malicious damaging of property under section 194 (a) of the Criminal Offenses Law, 5737-1977,[26] destruction of property under Section 196,[27] and causing a public disturbance under section 452.[28] Under the authority granted to him in section 231(a) of the Criminal Procedure Law (Consolidated Version), 5742-1982, the attorney general decided to prevent criminal proceedings under this private complaint. This petition seeks judicial review of the decision of the attorney general.

The Main Points of the Petition

As claimed in the petition, everyone agrees that the Temple Mount is a holy place to Jews. Since the beginning of the existence of the Jewish nation, the Temple Mount has been a symbol of its unique religion and of its national independence. Both in Israel and in the rest of the world, the Temple Mount is understood as the special area with the greatest importance to the Jewish people. Even though the Temple Mount is part of the area of the State of Israel, and even though Israeli law applies to that area, the Governments of Israel decided, it is claimed, to allow it to be internally administered by the Muslim Waqf, although security in the area is provided by the Israeli Police. It is claimed that in 1987 those people conducting the business of the Muslim Waqf began to carry out various projects on the Temple Mount that damaged the Jewish holy artifacts. The Waqf has denied that in the past that Jewish temples stood on the Temple Mount. The works the Waqf carried out on the Temple Mount over the years caused the destruction and ruin of items of special value that are found on the site. This was possible because the authorities responsible for enforcing the law desisted from enforcement.

The petition details a list of various works that the Waqf undertook on the Temple Mount since 1987, including excavations carried out in 2007 using heaving equipment, without significant supervision from the authorities. These excavations were justified on the grounds that they were related to the installation of the infrastructure for providing electricity to the Al-Aksa Mosque.... According to the petitions, the excavations conducted in recent years, and especially those in August and September of 2007, caused a great deal of damage to the antiquities on the Temple Mount, and greatly impinged on the importance of the area in terms of Jewish values and history, and on the religious and national sensibilities of Jews worldwide. The Petitioners claim that the Waqf acted in a calculated malicious manner designed to deny the sovereignty of Israel over the Temple Mount, and to damage the attachment of the Jewish people to this holy place, and that its activities rise to the level of criminal violations. They claim that Israeli authorities responsible for law enforcement have not acted to prevent these criminal acts, and so have violated their duty to enforce the law as it applies to the Temple Mount.

According to the Petitioners, because the law is not being enforced, they filed their private criminal complaint.

The attorney general decided to use his authority under section 231 of the Criminal Procedure Law to prevent judicial consideration of the private complaint.

---

26. This section provides, "A person who maliciously and illegally destroys or damages property is subject to imprisonment of three years."

27. This section provides, "A person who writes, draws, or carves on the property of someone else in an illegal manner, or who illegally posts on such property any writing or sign, is subject to imprisonment of a year."

28. This section provides, "A person who causes an uproar or disturbance in a public place, without reasonable cause and in a manner likely to disturb the residents or to cause a disturbance of the peace, is subject to imprisonment for three months."

Position of the Respondents

The Respondents claim that the decision of the attorney general to prevent consideration of the private complaint was a proper legal decision, based on considerations of the public interest. The matter involves issues that are publically, religiously, and politically of great sensitivity. The attorney general has broad discretion in matters of law enforcement, and especially as to enforcement in the area of the Temple Mount, in light of these sensitivities. The matter should not be left to be treated by a private party.

As to the excavations in 2007, ... it is claimed that they received all necessary permits.

The Nature of the Private Criminal Complaint

The basic principles of the Israeli system of justice provide that the state has the responsibility for enforcement of the criminal law and for prosecuting violators. Under section 11 of the Criminal Procedure Law, the state is prosecutor in criminal cases, and is represented by the office of the public prosecutor, who conducts the case in the name of the state.

The laws of criminal offense are a collection of norms that delineate the line between what is forbidden and what is permitted, and these are based on the public interest. A criminal violation is a deviation from the standard of proper behavior as it is set out in the law. The criminal act injures the public and all of society. Therefore punishment of the criminal is a matter for the society as a whole, and not just for the victim who was injured by the crime. In this way, the criminal process effectuates the sovereign responsibility to maintain the social order. Even if the person injured by the crime is a specific individual, the criminal process is thought of as addressing the relationship between the violator and the public, and not that between the violator and the victim.

These principles are subject to a recognized exception: the private criminal prosecution, as it is dealt with in sections 68 to 73 of the Criminal Procedure Law. Within the framework of this exception, a private party can initiate and conduct a criminal proceeding against someone, under appropriate circumstances and subject to certain conditions. This exception is based mainly on the assumption that there is a class of matters which are essentially disputes between the person causing the harm and the person suffering the harm. As to these matters, it is appropriate to grant the private person standing to conduct the criminal proceeding where the state has not done so.

The list of offenses subject to private criminal prosecution is a closed list. Most are listed in the second appendix to the Criminal Procedure Law, but some are specified in other statutes. An examination of the crimes included in the list shows that most such crimes are of a predominantly private nature, involving a dispute between two individuals. In addition, there are some crimes of a public nature, characterized by the fact that the private person is injured by the action of some public authority, and is allowed to proceed against that authority.

The types of crimes that fall into the category of predominantly private crimes include trespass, simple assault, causation of damage to property, interfering with intellectual property rights, etc. Crimes of a more general nature [where the violation is by a public authority] that are subject to private criminal prosecution are found, for example, in the elections laws. Other crimes of a public nature that allow private criminal prosecution are violations of the Law on Protection of Privacy, 5741-1981; laws on environmental matters in the Law for Prevention of Nuisances, 5721-1961, Law on Maintenance of Cleanliness, 5744-1984, the Water Law, 5719-1959; and others. What characterizes these statutes is that, despite their public nature, the individual has a special interest in their enforcement, and they do not always get a high priority in the enforcement activities of the public agencies.

In summary, it appears that the institution of the private criminal prosecution is designed to provide a solution to a specific and defined type of criminal matters that relate to the interactions between two individuals. These cases overlap with the civil law but also constitute violations of criminal norms. Due to the nature of such offenses, despite their classification as crimes, the public authorities are likely not to see a particular public interest in prosecuting them. Therefore, the legislature has allowed the individual the option of conducting the criminal prosecution in place of the state doing so. Even though the private criminal prosecution is conducted by an individual, it is a criminal proceeding and should reflect and serve the public interest. The state can get involved and undertake the conduct of the prosecution, in place of the private prosecutor. If the public prosecutor finds that the public interest would so be served, the state can also prevent the proceeding from going forward.

Protection from Misuse of Private Prosecutions

The institution of the private prosecution has both advantages and disadvantages. The main advantages are that it grants the individual status in the criminal process, recognizes the interest of the individual in prosecuting the criminal, and allows application of the law in cases in which the public prosecutor refrained from bringing an action. In this way, the private prosecution is likely to contribute to effectuation of the goal of enforcing the law. On the other hand, the main disadvantages are that the private prosecution is not subject to the protections provided when the state prosecutes a case, such as that prior to prosecution there will be a sufficient investigation of the case, sufficient evidence will be collected prior to the indictment, and that the accused will be provided with all evidence against him. Moreover the private prosecution might be pursued simply out of a desire for revenge, or to harass the defendant, or might be futile, wasting the time of the legal system. In light of these problems, the law sees fit to provide the means to be sure that the private prosecution will not be improperly pursued.

First, the filing of a private complaint against a public servant for an act done in fulfilling his job requires the agreement of the attorney general ... (section 69 of the Criminal Procedure Law). Second, notice of the filing of a private complaint must be provided to the district prosecutor. The district prosecutor can choose to prosecute the case if the public interest justifies prosecution by the state (section 71 of the Criminal Procedure Law). Third, the court has authority to interfere in the prosecution of a private criminal proceeding if it becomes clear that the case is being conducted in a manner that constitutes harassment, or that the private complainant is not capable of properly conducting the case (section 73 of the Criminal Procedure Law). Fourth, based on his general responsibility for the criminal process, the attorney general has authority to prevent the prosecution of a case, including that of a private criminal prosecution (section 231 of the Criminal Procedure Law).

Improper use of the private criminal complaint can take different forms. It can serve as a means for a plaintiff to avenge himself on a defendant, or of harassing a public servant; it can be used by an individual without a sufficient factual basis for making a claim; and it can be used by an individual in a matter that is clearly public in its nature and is not appropriate for determination in the framework of a criminal proceeding.... In this latter type of case, the attorney general has broad discretion to decide to stop the proceeding.... The factors that the attorney general may consider in deciding what to do are varied: it may be necessary to consider the unique nature of each particular matter, the priorities of enforcement, timing of the prosecution, location of the violation, the resources required for enforcement, and alternative means of dealing with the problem. Consideration of all of these factors must be done in light of the public interest in maintaining social order during the period involved.

Application to the Specific Case

The Petitioners' filing of a private criminal complaint against the Waqf and its representatives is subject to two substantial deficiencies that led the attorney general to prevent the proceedings. The first deficiency is that private criminal complaint is not in any way connected to a private dispute, but rather involves a matter that is clearly public in nature, affecting all of society. The second deficiency is that it entails enforcement of the law in the area of the Temple Mount, an area involving public and political issues of extreme and unique sensitivity. This requires that policy regarding the area be determined by a public authority and not be left in private hands, to be determined by a private criminal proceeding.

In light of the facts of this case, the decision of the attorney general to prevent the private criminal proceedings was reasonable and appropriate.

Comment

The case involves an unusual use of the private criminal prosecution. More often, private criminal actions are brought for very different sorts of problems. For example, they have been used to prosecute violations of the environmental laws, particularly where the entity violating the law is a local government or other governmental unit and there are political barriers to enforcement by the state, or where governmental resources are insufficient to allow full public enforcement of the law.

Compare the *Ganor* case to the *Israel Law Center* case. In *Ganor*, the Court reversed the decision of the attorney general not to prosecute a case. In the *Israel Law Center*, the Court upheld a decision of the attorney general not to allow a private prosecution. Are the two cases inconsistent? Arguably they are not. In *Ganor* the Court found clearly unreasonable the attorney general's decision that the public interest required that the case not be prosecuted. In other words, the Court found it unquestionable that the public interest would require prosecution. In the *Israel Law Center* the Court agreed with the attorney general that the public interest required that the case not be prosecuted. In other words, both cases turned on a review of the reasonableness of the attorney general's decision. But the underlying question is what made one decision unreasonable and the other reasonable. Is it that the judges disagreed with the attorney general's underlying decision in *Ganor* but agreed in the *Israel Law Center*? Perhaps it was that the judges knew that courts have the tools to determine the issues in prosecution of the banks and the bankers, but thought they lack the tools to sort out who should be allowed to do what on the Temple Mount. Viewed in this light, the question is whether the issue in the *Israel Law Center* is justiciable. A matter is nonjusticiable if it is not appropriate for a court to decide the issue. As we shall see in chapter 9, Israeli courts are hesitant to find any issue nonjusticiable. This decision was then perhaps an alternative way of reaching the same result as would be reached had the Court decided that the entire question of whether to prosecute the Waqf was non-justiciable.

In the United States, private criminal prosecution is not generally allowed, although some states provide for some degree of private involvement in limited types of cases.[29]

---

29. *See* Roger A. Fairfax, *Delegation of Criminal Prosecution Function to Private Actors*, 43 U.C. Davis L. Rev. 411, 421–24 (2009).

Question

8. Under the rule set out in the *Israel Law Center* case, would the attorney general have a free hand in preventing the private criminal proceedings against a local government's sewage treatment plant that was violating treatment standards set out in law and releasing polluted effluent to a stream? Assume that the action was brought by a private nongovernmental organization (NGO) devoted to protecting the environment, that the statute violated allowed private criminal prosecutions of violators, that the NGO had qualified lawyers on its staff, and that standing would not be a problem.

3. Exclusionary Rule

The Israeli Supreme Court has several times examined the question of whether illegally obtained evidence should be excluded in a criminal trial. In 1978, it held that a court could decide what weight to give illegally obtained evidence, and could even give it zero weight, but could not exclude it. This was the law until the decision in the following case, which made illegally obtained evidence excludable in some cases.

Israeli Case

Issacharov v. Chief Military Prosecutor
CrimA 5121/98 61(1) PD 461 [2006][30]

[Rafael Issacharov, a soldier in the Israel Defense Forces (IDF), was arrested for being absent without leave. On entering military prison, he was searched and found to be hiding marijuana in his clothes. An interrogation followed in which he was not warned that he had a right to an attorney. During the interrogation, Issacharov admitted to possession and use of marijuana, and provided a urine sample that showed the prior use of drugs. Afterwards, he was told he had a right to an attorney. The issue before the Court was whether the admission and the evidence from the urine sample should be excluded because they were obtained prior to informing Issacharov of his right to an attorney.]

Justice D. Beinisch:[31]

[The opinion considers whether there is a constitutional right to consult an attorney and to be informed of such a right before interrogation and search. It concludes that it is not clear in Israeli law whether there is such a right.]

Having considered all aspects of the matter, I have come to the conclusion that in the case before us, there is no need to reach a decision on the encompassing and complex matter of the constitutional status of the rights of criminal suspects, detainees, and defendants, even though it seems that under our case law, the right to consult with an attorney is a constitutional right. Nonetheless even if the right of a detained person to consult with an attorney is not of constitutional status, and I see no need to express an opinion on whether it is, the importance and centrality of such a right in our legal sys-

---

30. This case is also available in English on the website of the Supreme Court of Israel, http://elyon1.court.gov.il/files_eng/98/210/051/n21/98051210.n21.htm. The translation in the text is not from this source.

31. Three months after this decision was rendered, Justice Dorit Beinisch became the Chief Justice of the Israeli Supreme Court.

tem is indisputable.... In consideration of this, the lack of notice of the right to consult with an attorney can, in certain circumstances, lead to the exclusion of an accused's admission of guilt made at the time of the investigation. The normative basis for doing this, and the circumstances that require exclusion of evidence, are covered in our discussion.

Section 12 of the Evidence Ordinance—Free and Willing Admission

For decades, Section 12 of the Evidence Ordinance was the controlling law on the question of admissibility of an admission made during investigation of an accused. It provides:

12. Admission

(a) The testimony of admission of an accused that he committed an offense is admissible only if the prosecutor supplies testimony on the circumstances under which the admission was made and the court determines that the admission was given freely and willingly.

Section 477 of the Military Justice Law is similar:

477. Admission of an Accused as Evidence

A military court will not admit the admission of an accused as evidence unless it is convinced that it was given by the *good will* of the accused. (The italics are not in the original. D.B.)

The parties agree that test of *good will* in Section 477 of the Military Justice Law means the same thing as the test of *freely and willingly* in Section 12 of the Evidence Ordinance. Even though our discussion will revolve around the interpretation of Section 12 of the Evidence Ordinance, our conclusions will also be valid as to Section 477 of the Military Justice Law.

[The opinion then reviewed the case law under Section 12 of the Evidence Ordinance and found that an accused's admission could be given freely and willingly even if given without being informed of the right to first consult with counsel, and if it was so given, it would be admitted at trial.]

Section 478 of the Military Justice Law sets out an interpretation similar to that set out in the case law [on Section 12 of the Evidence Ordinance] in this language:

478. Admission by the Good Will of the Accused

The fact that an accused admission was obtained in a manner inconsistent with the requirements of Section 266 to 272 (including the obligation to warn the accused of the right to remain silent during the investigation—D.B.), does not prevent the court from determining that the admission was made by the good will of the accused.

The requirements of Section 478 of the Military Justice Law are like the judicial interpretation given to Section 12 of the Evidence Ordinance, according to which the fact that an admission of guilt was made without notice of the right to remain silent or the right to consult with an attorney does not by itself require exclusion of the admission of guilt, and the treatment of the matter depends on the facts of the specific case.

[Section 12 of the Evidence Ordinance is designed to protect an individual's autonomy. Therefore, evidence illegally obtained must be excluded only when the nature of the illegal act creates a serious interference with the free choice and autonomy of the person under investigation. We need to develop through case law a judicial rule for determining when such evidence should be excluded and when not.]

In the past, our case law on the issue of admissibility was based on the objective of effectuating the search for the truth and on fighting criminal activity, without examining how the evidence was obtained. We now need to engage in a flexible balancing that gives greater consideration to the duty to protect the rights of the accursed and to the fairness of the criminal process. The appropriate balance among all the competing values and interest in this matter leads us to the doctrine of discretionary exclusion, under which the court will have discretion to determine the admissibility of illegally obtained evidence based on the circumstances of the specific case and based on standards set out here.

The adoption of the doctrine of exclusion of illegally obtained evidence and setting the scope and standards for the exercise of such a doctrine is a matter that is appropriately handled by legislation. Nonetheless ... our law of evidence has been largely developed in case law, in the absence of prohibitory legislation, this Court bears the obligation of adjusting the rule it set out in the past to the changing legal norms.... The time is ripe to adopt a common law doctrine that allows, in the appropriate circumstances, exclusion of illegally obtained evidence.

Models of the Doctrine of Exclusion of Illegally Obtained Evidence—Comparative Law

(a) The Exclusionary Rule as Practiced in the United States

The exclusionary rule in the United States is based mainly on exclusion of evidence obtained in violation of the Fourth Amendment to the Constitution, on the matter of search and seizure; the Fifth Amendment, on the matter of protection against self-incrimination and the right to a fair trial; and on the Sixth Amendment, on the right to be represented by an attorney. The cases of the Supreme Court of the United States accept the approach that says that the exclusionary rule is designed mainly to attain an educational and deterrent goal, to prevent the future use of investigative tools in the future that violate the constitutional rights of the accused suspect.... The goal of deterrence and education has been the dominant influence on the design of the American exclusionary rule. It led to the development of the *fruits of the poisonous tree* theory. Under this theory, the court excludes not only evidence directly obtained by violation of the constitutional right of the accused, but also all other evidence obtained directly or indirectly through the information revealed by the original excluded evidence. This applies even if there is no doubt as to the reliability of the evidence. This theory is meant mainly to deter investigators from making use of improper investigative methods in the future, by completely excluding evidence found through illegal means.

The theoretical model on which the exclusionary rule in the United States is based is the *corrective model*. Exclusion of evidence is a remedy for the violation of the constitutional right of the accused that occurred at the time of obtaining the evidence. Exclusion of the evidence is designed, therefore, to provide a remedy for a violation that occurred in the past, and is not designed to prevent a future violation of a protected value or right. From the beginning, the American exclusionary rule was extensive in its reach, and left little discretion in the hands of the court to decide whether to exclude evidence unconstitutionally obtained. Still, in reaction to critiques leveled over the years at the inflexibility of the exclusionary rule, the federal Supreme Court recognized exceptions to the rule that ameliorated the sweeping scope of the rule. It should also be emphasized that the inflexibility of the American exclusionary rule had a far-reaching erosive effect on the enforcement of the law, the war against crime, and the exposure of truth. Due to this social impact, the rule has been criticized both within and outside of the United States.

(b) The Exclusionary Doctrine as Practiced in Canada, England, South Africa and Australia[32]

Other common law countries, among them Canada, England, Australia, and South Africa, adopted a more discretionary and moderate exclusionary doctrine, based a different conceptual model from that used in the United States.

Section 24(2) of the Canadian Charter of 1982 provides:

24. Enforcement

(2) Where, in proceedings under subsection (1), a court concludes that evidence was obtained in a manner that infringed or denied any rights or freedoms guaranteed by this Charter, the evidence shall be excluded if it is established that, having regard to all circumstances, the admission of it in the proceedings would bring the administration of justice into disrepute.

As to England, the doctrine that applies to exclusion of evidence illegally obtained is set out in section 78(1) of PACE (Police and Criminal Evidence Act 1984), which is a regular statute of Parliament. Section 78(1) provides:

78. Exclusion of unfair evidence

(1) In any proceedings the court may refuse to allow evidence on which the prosecution proposes to rely to be given if it appears to the court that, having regard to all the circumstances, including the circumstances in which the evidence was obtained, the admission of the evidence would have such an adverse effect on the fairness of the proceedings that the court ought not to admit it.

The Constitution of South Africa of 1996 also deals explicitly with exclusion of illegally obtained evidence, in this language:

35. Arrested, detained and accused persons

(5) Evidence obtained in a manner that violates any right in the Bill of Rights must be excluded if the admission of that evidence would render the trial unfair or otherwise be detrimental to the administration of justice.

Like the exclusionary doctrine of England and Canada, Section 35(5) of the Constitution of South Africa provides a discretionary doctrine that allows a court to exercise discretion as to whether to exclude evidence. The theoretical model on which this is based is not to provide a remedy for a violation of a primary constitutional right, but rather prevention of future violations of protected values—fairness of process and protecting the justice system from harm—due to the admission of the evidence in a court (the *preventative model*).

Adoption by the Court of the Exclusionary Doctrine for our Legal System—Guiding Principles

Between the two conceptual models we have described, it seems that the preventative model is the one appropriate for our legal system. Under this model, the goal of exclusion of evidence is to prevent future harm from admission of such evidence, and not a corrective remedy due to the primary injury to the accused, which injury was completed at the time of obtaining the evidence. Rejection of the corrective model rests on several justifications. *First*,

---

32. The portion of the decision examining Australian law is omitted here.

the corrective model as practiced in the United States is based on providing a remedy for violation of a *constitutional* right at the time of obtaining the evidence. At present, our legal system lacks a full and inclusive constitutional bill of human rights.... The question of the constitutional status of the rights of those under investigation, of suspects, and of the accused in a criminal procedure has not been fully and completely determined.... *Second*, conceptually it is doubtful whether excluding illegally obtained evidence really provides a remedy for the already completed injury in a protected right of the accused. Take for example the case of an illegal search. The violation of the right to privacy and to property occurred at the time of the search. Whether evidence was discovered during the search or not does not add or detract from the degree of violation of the right.... *Third*, there are those who claim that the corrective model leads to impermissible discrimination among those investigated. This occurs because under this model, a remedy is provided only to the person investigated who was later indicted and against whom the evidence was presented. *Fourth*, there are other remedies—criminal, disciplinary, tort, and perhaps even statutory—for the violation of a protected right of the person under investigation. In consideration of the existence of such alternative remedies, and in light of the societal cost of exclusion of evidence that can aid in the discovery of what really happened, it is doubtful whether adoption of the corrective model is justified.

Most of these difficulties do not arise in connection with the preventative model, under which exclusion serves as a remedy designed to prevent future violation of the protected value. Except for the American system, all common law countries which we considered adopted the preventative model and base their exclusionary rules on that model.

As to the degree of flexibility of the discretionary exclusionary doctrine, the attorney for the appellant, the bar association, and the public defender's office all support adoption of the discretionary doctrine that grants the court discretion as to whether to exclude illegally obtained evidence in light of the circumstances of the specific case. In addition, there are many reasons for adopting this doctrine. As indicated above, the question of whether to exclude illegally obtained evidence requires a balancing between defending the rights of the accused and protecting the fairness and integrity of the criminal process on the one side and the opposing values and interests, including the value of determining the truth, the war on crime, and protecting the public peace and the rights of the victims of crime.

The Common Law Exclusionary Doctrine—Its Nature and Extent

Considering the conclusions we have reached up to this point in our discussion, we can formulate the exclusionary doctrine we are adopting in this way:

On the matter of admissibility of evidence, we have always begun with the presumption that evidence that is relevant is admissible at trial. Nonetheless the court has discretion to exclude evidence in a criminal proceeding if it determines that the evidence was illegally obtained and that its admission at trial will cause a substantial violation of the accused's right to a fair trial to a degree that exceeds the limitation clause.[33]

---

33. In Israel, the constitutional provisions that protect individual rights include a limitation clause. This clause sets out the conditions under which it is permissible to infringe on the constitutional right. Generally the limitation clause requires that the infringement be sufficiently important and the degree of infringement be sufficiently minimized. The limitation clause is discussed more thoroughly in chapter 8 on constitutional law. Justice Beinisch, up to this point, has not established that a constitutional right is violated when evidence is improperly obtained. Nonetheless she uses a concept from constitutional law to determine whether evidence so obtained should be excluded from trial. This demonstrates a constitutional approach to the issue of the exclusionary rule, without building a firm foundation to show that a constitutional approach is appropriate. This approach is discussed in the comments after the case.

Exclusion of evidence in a criminal proceeding due to the manner in which it was obtained depends on the presence of both of the following conditions. One is that the evidence was illegally obtained. The second is that admission of the evidence at trial will cause a substantial injury to the accused's right to a fair trial.... Let us emphasize that, consistent with the preventative model that we have adopted, exclusion of the evidence is designed to prevent an illegal violation of the right to a fair trial due to the admission of the evidence, a violation that is distinct and separate from the initial violation that occurred at the time of obtaining the evidence.

Standard for Exercising Judicial Discretion within the Framework of the Exclusionary Doctrine

In order to decide whether to exclude evidence under this doctrine, the court must consider a range of factors, and they may depend on the facts of the specific case. As will be explained below, there are three main groupings of considerations that are relevant to the question of when to admit illegally obtained evidence that will substantially violate the accused's right to a fair trial in a manner not permitted under the limitation clause. We emphasize that we are not providing a fixed and unchangeable list of the considerations, but rather providing guidelines for exercise of the court's discretion.

(a) The Nature and Seriousness of the Illegality in Obtaining the Evidence

As described above, the first consideration in applying the judicial doctrine for exclusion of illegally obtained evidence, that is, evidence obtained in an unlawful or unfair manner or in a way that illegally violates a protected right of the person under investigation, revolves around the improper behavior of the investigative authority. In this connection, the following factors should be considered:

First, what is the nature and seriousness of the illegal or unfair behavior involved in obtaining the evidence?

Second, it is appropriate to consider whether the investigating authorities used the inappropriate investigative techniques intentionally and with malice or in good faith.

Third, the court should consider whether in the matter before it, there are mitigating circumstances that take away from the seriousness of the illegal actions in obtaining the evidence. This would be the case, for example, if the illegal actions were intended to prevent the accused from concealing or destroying crucial evidence, ... or when the illegal action derived from an urgent need to protect the public safety.

Fourth, it is necessary to consider how easy it would have been to obtain the evidence by legal means.

Finally the court should consider whether the evidence could have been revealed or obtained by the law enforcement authorities without using the impermissible investigative means.

(b) The Degree to Which the Illegal Investigative Means Influenced the Evidence Obtained

The second relevant group of considerations for exercising judicial discretion under the judicial exclusionary rule relates to the influence of the illegal or unfair investigative means on the evidence obtained. In this regard, two related questions should be considered: First, to what extent did the illegal investigative mans affect the credibility of the evidence and its value as proof? ... Second, was the evidence obtained for reasons independent of the illegal means?

(c) The Social Cost Versus the Social Benefit Associated with Exclusion of Evidence

The third group of considerations that are relevant to deciding on the admissibility of illegally obtained evidence relate to the effect that exclusion will have on the accomplishment of justice in the broadest sense. The essential question that arises in this connection is whether the social price associated with excluding the evidence is greater than the benefit that flows from doing so. The main parameters are the importance of the evidence in proving guilt, and the type and seriousness of the crime of which the defendant is accused.

As indicated previously, the list of considerations given above is not intended to be a closed list. It provides guidance as to the type of facts and situations that may influence a court's exercise of discretion in applying the judicial exclusionary doctrine.

Comments

Justice Beinisch's opinion in the case was ninety pages long. Much of it is omitted here. Nine justices sat on the case. The assignment of such a large bench indicates that this case was seen as raising a very important matter. Six justices simply wrote that they agreed with Justice Beinisch's opinion; one wrote a brief opinion but essentially agreed with the reasoning, and one dissented. This is a high level of agreement for the Court.

a. Applicability of Opinion

The *Issacharov* case involved a criminal proceeding in a military court, where the applicable procedural rules are different from those in a criminal trial in a regular court. Nonetheless in discussing the exclusionary doctrine, Justice Beinisch's opinion emphasizes the similarity between the rules that apply in a military court and the parallel rules that applies in a regular court. The opinion states that Rule 477 of the Military Justice Law, which applies in military courts, means the same thing as section 12 of the Evidence Ordinance, which applies in regular courts. Furthermore, in a portion omitted here, the opinion undertakes a long analysis of the interpretation of section 12, reaching the conclusion that it means the same thing as rule 478 of the Military Justice Law. None of this discussion of the Evidence Ordinance was necessary to resolution of the case. Why, then, was it undertaken? A decision that related only to the rules of the military courts would not have the far-reaching implications that a decision on the general law of evidence has. Apparently the justices wanted to be sure that their announcement of the power of a judge to exclude evidence, and the requirement that it be excluded in some cases, was understood to apply generally. The opinion is careful to show that whatever it says about the military proceedings also applies to proceedings in regular courts.

b. Constitutional Analysis

The full opinion includes a long discussion of whether Israeli law provides a constitutional right to consult with an attorney before being questioned or searched. Under the constitutional law theories we shall examine in chapter 8, it is not clear whether such rights are constitutionally protected in Israel. Furthermore, the extent of statutory protection of such rights is questionable. The opinion assumes that there is some sort of right to a fair trial, founded either on a constitutional right or on a right recognized under prior case law. This is arguably different from rights relating to how evidence is obtained. By basing the exclusionary rule on the need to protect the right to a fair trial, Justice Beinisch avoids having to decide whether there is a constitutional right to consult with an attorney prior to being questioned or searched.

To the extent that the right to a fair trial is a constitutional right, it can only be infringed for a purpose that meets the requirements of a *limitation clause*. A limitation clause is found in two Israeli statutes and delineates the circumstances under which constitutional rights can be limited. The limitation clause also specifies that any limit on a constitutional right can be no greater than is needed. Israeli case law provides that the limitation clause applies also to basic rights even if they do not reach the level of constitutional rights. All of this is discussed in chapter 8.

The Court holds that the Israeli exclusionary rule is designed to protect the right to a fair trial. Admission of illegally obtained evidence at trial impinges on this right. Therefore such evidence can be admitted only when its admission meets the requirements of the limitation clause. The discussion of how the judicial exclusionary doctrine with its discretionary rule should operate is designed to outline how courts can decide when admission falls within the limitation clause and when it does not.

All of this seems like convoluted reasoning and it is. Such reasoning is the product of the uncertainties of Israeli constitutional law and the tendency of the Israeli Supreme Court to examine many legal issues by applying constitutional law doctrine. This tendency is probably designed to extend the development of Israeli constitutional law. As we shall see in the chapter on constitutional law, the legislature has taken only very small steps in establishing constitutional law in Israel, and the Court has filled in and developed constitutional law through case law.

c. Foreign Law and the Justification for Adopting an Exclusionary Rule

In the discussion of the *Kinneret Quarries* case, we noted the tendency of the Israeli Court to look at foreign law. Here we see another example of this tendency. Justice Beinisch's decision in the *Issacharov* case includes an extensive examination of the exclusionary rule in several common law jurisdictions, including the law of the United States. The opinion also shows a danger that lies in examining foreign law: the failure to understand or characterize it correctly. The opinion first says, "The goal of deterrence and education has been the dominant influence on the design of the American exclusionary rule." In the next paragraph, it says, "The theoretical model on which the exclusionary rule in the United States is based is the corrective model." The corrective model means that the exclusion of evidence is a remedy for a violation of law that occurred in the past. Since the opinion sets up the deterrent or preventative model as different from the corrective model, these statements are contradictory.

Many American decisions and commentators emphasize the deterrent function of the exclusionary rule. Case law repeatedly relates to the deterrent function of the rule, giving it great prominence in the justification for excluding otherwise probative evidence.[34] Similarly commentators recognize the importance of the deterrent function. "The general purposes usually asserted for the exclusionary rule [are] to vindicate the right that the unlawful police conduct infringed, to avoid compromising the integrity of the trial court, ... and to deter similar unlawful conduct in the future...."[35] In this regard, the American exclusionary rule is forward looking.

Another problem with using foreign law is failure to see how the law in another country fits in with features of the foreign law that are not examined. While the opinion relates

---

34. *See, e.g.,* United States v. Leon, 468 U.S. 897, 906–10 (1984); Hudson v. Michigan, 547 U.S. 586, 596 (2006); Herring v. U.S., 555 U.S. 135, 141 (2009).

35. Lloyd L. Weinreb, *The Exclusionary Rule Redux—Again,* 37 FORDHAM URB. L.J. 873, 880 (2010). *See also* Donald A. Dripps, *The "New" Exclusionary Rule Debate: From "Still Preoccupied with 1985" to "Virtual Deterrence,"* 37 FORDHAM URB. L.J. 743 (2010).

to the differences between the constitutional law framework in Israel and in the United States, it does not relate to an important difference in procedural frameworks. The United States has juries in criminal trials. Arguably one objective of excluding illegally obtained evidence is to keep information out of the hands of non-expert jurors, who will not be able to ignore evidence once they learn about it. The dynamic of dealing with evidence is arguably different when there is no jury. Under the American approach, exclusion of illegally obtained evidence may still be justified to deter police misconduct, correct a constitutional violation, or for other reasons. The question of whether these goals would or should prevail in a non-jury setting at least requires discussion.

d. Discretionary Versus Absolute Exclusionary Rule

The Court opted for a discretionary exclusionary rule. A judge could exclude improperly obtained evidence but was not required to do so. The Court discusses at some length the factors which a judge should consider in deciding whether to exclude evidence in a specific case, listing at least nine factors which are relevant to that decision.

Questions

9. Given that there are no juries, does Israel need an exclusionary rule at all?

10. What are the advantages and disadvantages of the Israeli exclusionary rule as compared to the more absolute American rule?

Chapter 7

The Legal Profession

A. Legal Education

Lawyers in Israel must obtain an academic degree, but it is an undergraduate degree and not a graduate degree as in the United States. Legal studies are undergraduate studies in most countries of the world; the American system is unusual. In Israel, academic studies in law are for seven semesters, or three-and-a-half years. Although legal education is undergraduate, the students in Israel are typically the same age, or older than, American law students. Most high school graduates cannot begin their law studies until they complete their military service, which, as described in chapter 2, is almost universal and lasts at least two years for women or three years for men. In fact, the delay before beginning law studies is usually longer than this. Many young people spend a year of added study or public service after high school. Army service is longer than the minimum for anyone who becomes an officer. Officers are selected from the ranks of enlisted soldiers, and many of the brightest become officers. This is the same group of people that are most likely to go to law school. In addition, after the difficult army service, most young Israelis take off several years to work and travel. The mountains of South America and the country of India are favorite destinations for stays that are often a year in length. Finally, admission to a university law school requires very high scores on an exam, and young people usually take off several months to prepare for it. Thus, it is usual for a student to begin law studies five to seven years after completion of high school.

Two types of institutions provide legal education in Israel. There are four law schools that are affiliated with Israeli universities. All universities in Israel are traditional research institutions and are publically supported. In addition, there are six private law schools. At least some of these are also research institutions, but they receive no public funding. Tuition is about $2,500 a year at a public university and almost $7,000 a year at a private institution. The tuition amounts seem low in comparison to the cost of American legal education, but it is important to remember that Israeli incomes are lower than American incomes, that Israeli law students are older and are usually not supported by their parents, and that there is no extensive system of government-supported loans as in the United States. Therefore almost all students work a significant number of hours while they are in school.

The university law schools are usually considered the most prestigious, and therefore the most desirable, for both students and faculty. This is partly because of their connections with the larger universities, their firm identities as research institutions, their long traditions, and their significantly lower tuition levels. Therefore they are more selective in student admission. The private law schools are relatively young, and some are making great strides to build their reputations while serving a broader student base. They have the reputation of providing more individualized attention to their students.

Until the opening of the relatively-new private law schools, access to legal education was very limited. Admission required very high grades on high school exams and also on the standard college entrance test taken by all Israeli applicants to institutions of higher education. The private law schools do not admit all candidates, but have opened up the access to legal education. One significant impact has been that greater numbers of students from families where the parents did not have a higher education, of immigrants, Arabs, Ultra-Orthodox Jews, and those who live far from the urban centers where the universities are located are now studying law and becoming lawyers. Today, the majority of new lawyers are graduates of these private law schools.

Students usually take seven or eight courses a semester, the equivalent of about 20 credits a semester. This is a heavier load than in the typical American law school. Most courses require some written work during the semester in addition to a final exam. The exam system is quite different from that in the United States. Students get two or three opportunities to take each exam. This began as a way of accommodating student reserve soldiers who were called up to active duty during exam periods, but spread to give all students two opportunities to be tested in each subject. Grading is usually lower than in American law schools.

The legal classroom depends heavily on the formal lectures. In this way, it resembles the traditional formal European classroom more than the easy give-and-take typical in American law classes. In recent years, there have been significant efforts to diversify the teaching methods with introduction of more student questions and some use of the problem method, but an American-trained lawyer would still find the Israeli classroom markedly different from that in the United States. For the most part, instructors lecture and students write down everything that is said. Clinics have been introduced into Israeli legal education, but they are not a central or extensive part of the curriculum. Cost is a significant factor limiting growth of clinics in law schools.

In the past, the Israeli law school saw itself as part of the tradition of scientific investigation that is central to academic institutions and not as the bridge between academia and the practicing bar. That view is changing somewhat, but it still predominates. For example, students in Israeli law schools write short research papers in most courses.

Israeli law schools have law journals, but most differ from those associated with American law schools in two ways. First, the articles, like legal studies, tend to be more theoretical and less practical in orientation. Second, while the journals may be staffed partly by students, many are run by faculty members. Articles must undergo peer review by law faculty members before publication.

Some Israeli lawyers continue their studies beyond their initial degrees and receive masters degrees or doctorates in law, in either Israeli or foreign institutions. Many study in the United States. Those with doctorates may take positions in academia, but many work as practicing lawyers, with the advanced degree providing an advantage in the job market.

University law faculties are traditionally more inbred than is common in United States law schools, with many faculty members having earned their law degrees at the same institution where they teach. Israeli law faculty generally must also have a doctoral level degree (Ph.D., S.J.D., etc.), and many have these also from their own institution, although the trend today is to go to the United States, England, Canada, or elsewhere for the doctoral degree. It may be that the fact that people teach where they studied leads to a narrowing of focus, but, on the other hand, Israeli academics tend to travel widely, teaching and participating in conferences in the United States and other countries. All Israeli academics are at least bi-lingual, with many fluent in more than two languages.

Questions

1. What do you see as the advantages of the relatively formalistic Israeli method of teaching law largely through lectures, and what do you see as the advantages of the American method that you have experienced?

2. In what ways does difference between the situations of the Israeli and American law student justify the use of a more structured, formal method of education in Israel?

B. The Bar

Israel has about 46,000 lawyers, and the number of lawyers per capita is among the highest in the world.[1] The *lawyerization* of Israel is a relatively recent phenomenon, occurring over the past twenty years, when legal education became more broadly available. About 60 percent of the lawyers are male, but of the new lawyers, a slight majority is female.[2] Most practice in small law offices. The largest law firms are not nearly as large as those in the United States, but that may change. Until recently, a statute limited the number of partners in a law firm to fifty; but that limitation was removed in 2010.

Israel has a unified bar. The Israel Bar Association is established by a law, the Bar Association Law, 5721-1961, which sets out the powers of the association. The association sets and enforces the ethical rules for lawyers, manages the internship system that applies to all law school graduates before they can take the bar exam, and runs the examinations for entrance to the bar. All lawyers must be members of the Israel Bar Association, and only lawyers may engage in the practice of law.

The rules on admission to the bar require graduates of Israeli law schools to complete a year of internship with an experienced attorney or a judge. After completion of the internship, the law graduate must pass a written and oral examination in order to be admitted to the bar. Graduates of foreign law schools, including those in the United States, must usually fulfill the same requirements, but must also pass six to nine additional written exams on substantive areas of Israeli law and, in addition, a Hebrew proficiency exam.

The bar association has enacted rules on numerous matters, including an ethical code for lawyers, a minimal fee schedule, and supervision of legal interns. One of the more interesting rules is that on court attire.

---

1. Israel Bar Association, General Information, Oct. 4, 2010, http://www.israelbar.org.il/english_inner.asp?pgId=103336&catId=372.

2. Mark Schon, *Mispar Orchei Ha'din B'Yisrael L'see Chadash: K-46 Elef (The Number of Lawyers in Israel Reaches a New High: About 46 Thousand)*, Calcalist, June 9, 2010, http://www.calcalist.co.il/local/articles/0,7340,L-3407419,00.html.

Israeli Rules

Bar Association Rules (Court Attire), 5766-2005
1 R.F. 5737, 1719[3]

By virtue of the powers vested in it pursuant to Section 109(7) of the Bar Association Law, 5721-1961, the National Council of the Bar Association hereby enacts these rules:

1. Male Attorneys Court Attire

The attorneys' court attire is: a white collared shirt and long or short sleeves, tie, trousers and jacket, all in black or navy blue, and dark closed shoes.

2. Female Attorneys Court Attire

The court attire for female attorneys is: white collared shirt, long or short sleeves, black or navy colored trousers or skirt and black or navy jacket, or black dress with long or short sleeves with a white collar and dark colored shoes.

3. Duty to Wear Robe

In addition to the provisions in Sections 1 and 2 the court attire in the Supreme Court, district court, national labor court and special courts will also include a black robe, an example of which is found at the Bar's offices in Jerusalem.

4. No Duty to Wear Jacket

During the period between April 1 and through until November 30 of each year, an attorney need not wear a jacket.

Comment

It is interesting that in a country as informal as Israel, lawyers must wear robes in court. This is a requirement that comes from England. Also notice that Rule 4 takes into account the hot climate of the long Israeli summer, exempting lawyers from suffering in jackets during this period.

C. NGOs Operating in the Legal Sphere

Several non-governmental organizations (NGOs)[4] are important players in the making and implementation of law. Of these, several litigate regularly before the courts, especially before the Supreme Court sitting as the High Court of Justice, and in this way they have helped to shape the Israeli legal landscape. Among the more prominent NGOs that work in the legal field are Adalah—The Legal Center for Arab Minority Rights in Israel, the Association for Civil Rights in Israel, the Israel Religious Action Center, the Israel Union for Environmental Defense, and the Movement for Quality Government in Israel. All have English language websites that can be found by simple internet searches.

---

3. The English translation is that provided by the Bar Association and is found at http://www.is-raelbar.org.il/uploadFiles/Bar_Association_Rules_(Court_Attire)_english_nov_2008.pdf.
4. A non-governmental organization is what is commonly called a public interest group in the United States.

Part Three

Public Law

Chapter 8

Constitutional Law

A. Initial Absence of a Written Constitution

When Israel was established in 1948, it had no written constitution. This is hardly surprising; the country was plunged into a war for its existence immediately upon its founding and its leaders were concerned with matters more pressing than constitution writing. More remarkable is that once the war was over and the business of nation building undertaken, these same leaders succeeded in creating a flourishing nation but still did not produce a written constitution.

Numerous reasons can be given as to why no unified constitution was written in the early years of the state. The British, who ruled the area before the establishment of the state, had no written constitution, so there was no existing tradition of constitutional law based on a written document. Also, the founders of the state were divided over whether the legal system of the new state should be based on Jewish law, be totally secular, or be secular with some Jewish law influence. Furthermore, they disagreed on whether the new state should be socialist or not. Some thought a constitution important in order to establish a regime of protected individual rights; others saw this as an undesirable, anti-majoritarian, undemocratic move.

This strong majoritarian position may seem strange to American students of the law, who are familiar with the protections provided by the Bill of Rights and other constitutional amendments, but it was indeed a serious consideration. In addition, some powerful voices in Israel opposed a constitution because it would give too much power to minorities, a particular problem in a country where many members of the largest minority group, the resident Arabs, had fought against establishment of the state. There was also a peculiarly Israeli objection to writing a constitution in the early years of the state. One of the foundational concepts of the State of Israel is the *ingathering of exiles*. This is the notion that Israel is the homeland of the Jewish people from which they were exiled in 70 CE, and that all Jews are welcome, and encouraged, to return to live there. The Jewish return to the land was severely limited by British policy before 1948, but a significant influx was expected soon after that. Therefore it was argued that the people present in the state in its very first years would soon represent only a minority of the inhabitants. It would not be fair for them to establish a constitution under which the large number of expected immigrants would have to live. This argument had added force because those expected immigrants were considered returnees rather than immigrants. Indeed, Israel has seen a huge influx of immigrants, with the population growing from 800,000 in 1948 to nearly 7.5 million in 2009 and much of this increase coming from immigration.

In the years after 1948, some of the reasons that prevented constitution-writing remained in force, and other barriers to constitution-writing arose. The continuing security threat to the state's existence is a significant barrier. It poses a dilemma that Israelis have not solved: they could either enact a constitution with strong rights provisions and endanger the existence of the state when perpetrators of terror claim protection under such rights, or enact a constitution with weak provisions on rights and provide inadequate protection to peaceful members of Israeli society. Since the Six Day War in 1967, Israelis have disagreed even as to what the boundaries of their state should be, so it is hard to write a constitution without knowing what areas will be subject to its provisions. Struggles over religious issues have increased, and it is widely perceived that constitutional provisions on religion would affect the resolution of these issues, but Israelis disagree on what that effect should be. All of these divisions are deep and they touch on basic principles. Unable to resolve these issues, Israelis have not formulated a complete constitutional document.

B. Development of Constitutional Law through Supreme Court Decisions

The absence of a complete written constitution has not meant the absence of constitutional law. The Knesset, in the latter part of the 1950s, began to enact Basic Laws which set out some of the institutions of the state. These enactments were piecemeal and did not fully define the relationships between the various institutions. The Supreme Court stepped into the void, holding that the Israeli system of government was founded on such basic principles as separation of powers and checks and balances. Until 1992, the Basic Laws did not provide for individual rights. In this area, also, the Supreme Court acted by identifying basic values and deriving from them a variety of individual rights. The following excerpt describes this process.

Law Review Article

Marcia Gelpe, Constraints on Supreme Court Authority in Israel and the United States: Phenomenal Cosmic Powers; Itty Bitty Living Space
13 Emory Int'l L. Rev. 493, 506–08 (1999)[1]

A. Judicial Identification of Basic Values and Individual Rights

1. Basic Values Not Founded in Basic Laws

Before 1992, Israel had no Basic Laws defining individual human rights. During this period, the Israeli Supreme Court identified numerous individual rights that it found worthy of special protection. The Court called these rights *basic values* or *principles of the constitutional structure of our country*. The Court found such norms in various sources: Israel's Declaration of Independence, the United Nations' Universal Declaration of Human Rights, the democratic nature of the state, the inherent nature of man, considerations of justice and decency, "the legacy of all advanced and enlightened states", and "the demo-

---

1. Citations omitted.

cratic freedom-loving character of our state." These rights so identified include the following: gender equality, equality on the basis of nationality, presumption of innocence, freedom of association, freedom of movement, freedom of expression, privacy, dignity of man, freedom of property, integrity of the body, judicial integrity, freedom to strike, freedom of demonstration, freedom of conscience, and freedom of occupation. The Israeli Supreme Court created, or recognized, these values and rights through a process that American jurists might call constitutional common law. The Court itself referred to such rights as those "not recorded in texts." Similarly the Court, through case law, established the principles of separation of powers and checks and balances.

The Israeli Supreme Court not only developed the norm that such basic values exist, but also developed the principle that statutes should be interpreted to avoid impairing these values. The Court reads statutes in such a way as not to violate the rights it has recognized. The Court also uses the values when reviewing the validity of administrative actions. Administrative actions that violate the basic values are held invalid, either directly or on the presumption that the legislature did not intend to authorize the administrative agency to violate such a value. Under this approach, administrative actions may violate basic values only if the administrative authority to take such action is clearly and unequivocally grounded in a statute. Again, the Court developed this approach without explicit statutory authority. The approach is inherent in the Court's understanding of the meaning of a basic value.

This process of identifying rights and principles, then using them to interpret statutes and to review administrative actions, increased the power of the Court over other governmental institutions.

Comment

The case set out below is an example of the type of analysis leading to development of basic rights through Supreme Court decision.

Israeli Case

Schnitzer v. Chief Military Censor
HCJ 680/88, 42(4) PD 617 [1989][2]

Justice A. Barak:

What is the authority of the Military Censor, acting pursuant to the Defense (Emergency) Regulations, 1945, to bar publication of a newspaper article that criticizes the functioning of the head of the Agency for Intelligence and Special Duties (the Mossad), while noting that the occasion for such criticism is his impending replacement—that is the question which is at the center of the petition before us.

The Petition

[A daily newspaper, *Ha-ir* (The City), prepared an article criticizing the outgoing head of the Mossad. The article was submitted to the chief military censor, as required by the Defense Emergency Regulations. The chief military censor refused to allow publication of portions of the article, stating that publication would prejudice state security. The newspaper sued, and the Supreme Court considered whether the censorship was lawful.]

---

2. This translation is based on that on the English language website of the Supreme Court, at http://elyon1.court.gov.il/files_eng/88/800/006/Z01/88006800.z01.pdf.

The Normative Framework

The military censorship exists by virtue of the Defense (Emergency) Regulations — henceforth the Defense Regulations. Chapter 8 of these regulations deals with censorship. Regulation 87 (1) provides that:

> The censor may by order prohibit generally or specially the publishing of matters the publishing of which, in his opinion, would be, or be likely to be or become, prejudicial to the defense of Palestine or to the public safety or to public order.

The censor is also empowered to demand that material be submitted for censorship before publication (regulation 97). Publication of material whose publication was banned is an offense against the Defense Regulations. The censor was appointed by the high commissioner [during the period of the British Mandate], whose powers have now been assigned to the minister of defense. The censor is an army officer, and censorship pursuant to chapter 8 of the Defense Regulations is performed within the framework of the army. Hence the term *military censor*.

The First Question: Circumstances in Which Publication May be Prohibited.

The Defense Regulations were enacted by the high commissioner pursuant to the powers vested in him by Article 6 of the Palestine Order-in-Council (Defense), of 1937. These regulations are, therefore, part of the Mandatory legislation. However, pursuant to section 11 of the Law and Administration Ordinance, 1948, they became part of Israeli law. This change from Mandatory law to Israeli law was not a purely technical matter. A change in the framework brings in its wake, by the nature of things, a change in content. Section 11 of the Law and Administration Ordinance provides that the law which existed in Palestine on May 15, 1948, remains in force subject to "such modifications as may result from the establishment of the state and its authorities."

A colonial regime was replaced by political independence. Autocratic rule was replaced by democracy, which is the government of the people, based on representation, operating according to the will of the majority, but upholding the rights of the individual. This change, in the natural course of events, brings in its wake a new approach to law and to judicature.

One of the changes that may result from the establishment of the state and its authorities is the manner of interpreting Mandatory legislation.

This change in the interpretation of Mandatory law is twofold. First, Mandatory legislation is not interpreted according to the rules of interpretation current during Mandatory times, but according to the rules of interpretation followed in Israel. Second, legislation is interpreted against the background of the basic principles of the legal system. Mandatory legislation will not be interpreted against the background of the basic principles of the system of law that prevailed during the Mandate, but against the background of the basic principles of the system of law that operates in Israel.

The basic principles can be learned from different sources, one of the most important of which is the Declaration of Independence, "which constitutes a legal charter that expresses the nation's values."

The Declaration of Independence is not the only source from which one can learn about the basic values of the state. For example, the Supreme Court refers from time to time to the "basic principles of equality, freedom, and justice, which are the legacy of all advanced and enlightened states" and to "basic rights which are not recorded in texts, but emanate directly from the character of our state as democratic and freedom-loving."

The Defense Regulations were enacted by a colonial legislature and not by a democratic one.... The interpretation of the Defense Regulations must necessarily differ in Israel from that given to them during the Mandate.

What are the basic values which shape the interpretation of the Defense Regulations? First and foremost are security considerations, which spread their influence across the entire scope of the regulations. The realization of this interest concerning the defense of the state and public safety and order is the main purpose of the regulations and they must be interpreted against the background of this purpose.... Alongside considerations of security (in their broad sense) there are other values, in the light of which every enactment in a democratic society must be interpreted, and which the Defense Regulations affect. Thus, for example, the Defense Regulations deal with the military courts. It is only natural in this context that the value of judicial integrity must be taken into account. The Defense Regulations contain provisions pertaining to crimes, punishments and detention prior to conviction. In this context, account must be taken, among other things, of the individual's right to personal freedom and the presumption of innocence. Another chapter of the Defense Regulations deals with unlawful associations. In this context account must be taken, of course, of the basic right to freedom of association. Yet another chapter of the Defense Regulations deals with orders restricting the freedom of movement. In this context it is only natural that the right to freedom of movement will be taken into account. Defense Regulations which provide for military censorship prejudice, first and foremost, the right to freedom of expression. Censorship of publications prejudices privacy. The broad authority to search (censorship of travelers) prejudices privacy, the dignity of man, and the integrity of property and person. This list of basic values which are adversely affected by the Defense Regulations is by no means complete or comprehensive. It only serves to show how broad a range of values are promoted by the Defense Regulations (defense, public safety and order) and are prejudiced by them (judicial integrity, personal freedom, freedom of association, freedom of movement, freedom of expression, privacy, dignity of man, and integrity of property and person).

In interpreting the Defense Regulations account must be taken of both the basic values which are their raison d'Ître and also the basic values which every legislative act in a democratic country must be assumed to intend to promote. Sometimes all these values lead to the same result. But sometimes they may clash with one another.... In all such cases a court must strike a balance between the conflicting values.

In the petition before us, the value of state security clashes with the values of freedom of expression and the public's right to be informed. These conflicting values are basic to our legal system. The state cannot exist without security. Nor can the social consensus upon which the state is built. So, too, individual freedoms which the state is supposed to promote cannot exist. This explains the centrality of security in the general complex of values in the legal system. Without freedom of expression, truth cannot be disclosed, the individual cannot fulfill himself and the democratic regime, which is based on the exchange of opinions, cannot continue to exist. The free exchange of information, opinions and points of view is essential to the existence of a democratic regime, which is based on the rule of the people, by the people, for the people. Without freedom of expression, democracy loses its soul. On more than one occasion this Court has noted "the close connection that exists between the principle of freedom of expression and debate and the proper functioning of the democratic process." It noted therefore that "freedom of expression is a condition precedent for the existence of democracy and its proper functioning." Freedom of expression thus has a special status. It secures the existence of a democratic regime which, in turn, secures the existence of other basic rights.

How is the Clash Between the Security of the State and Freedom of Expression to be Resolved?

The proper balance between state security and freedom of expression seeks to protect state security, but because of the importance of the basic right to freedom of expression, it seeks to limit the harm to this value as much as possible. It is permissible to infringe on freedom of expression only when absolutely necessary in order to preserve the value of state security.

To summarize: the Mandatory Defense Regulations must be interpreted against the background of Israel's values. In interpreting them one must balance state security and public safety and order against freedom of expression. This balance means that freedom of expression can be restrained, as a last resort, only when there is a near certainty of substantial danger to state security and public order.

[Justice Barak determined that the military censor had not shown a near certainty of substantial danger to state security, so the prohibition of publication of the criticism of the former head of the Mossad was not lawful.]

Comment

Notice that this case uses "basic values" to hold invalid an administrative decision, not to invalidate legislation. The military censor has the status of an administrative agency. The administrative action here was the military censor's decision to prohibit publication of the criticism of the former head of the Mossad.

Questions

1. The opinion discussed numerous basic values. List them.

2. The central basic value in this case is the freedom of expression. Did the opinion find that freedom of expression is based on a document? If so, what document? If not, on what was it based?

3. What are the sources of other basic rights discussed by the opinion?

4. Compare the source of basic rights in this case with the way the US Supreme Court identifies basic rights.

C. Basic Laws

As explained in chapter 4 on legal history, less than a year after declaration of the State of Israel, elections were held for a Constituent Assembly, which had the power to adopt a constitution for the new state.[3] The Constituent Assembly immediately turned itself into the First Knesset. The First Knesset, in turn, adopted a resolution, the *Harrari Resolution*, named for the Knesset member who sponsored it, which provided,

> The First Knesset charges the Committee on the Constitution, Legislation, and Law to prepare a recommended constitution for the state. The constitution should be comprised of individual chapters, in a manner that allows each to be a Basic

---

3. The name was derived from the term *constitute*. This assembly had the authority to constitute, or establish, the structure of the state.

Law standing on its own. The chapters will be brought before the Knesset, as the committee completes its work, and all the chapters together shall form a constitution for the state.[4]

Beginning in 1958, the Knesset enacted a series of Basic Laws. Ten deal mainly, but not exclusively, with the structure of the state and its principle institutions: they are entitled Basic Law: The Knesset; The Government; President of the State; The Judiciary; The State Comptroller; Israel Lands [on administration of the more than 90 percent of the land owned by the state]; The State Economy; The Army; Jerusalem, Capital of Israel; and The State Budget. Two deal with individual rights: Basic Law: Human Dignity and Freedom and Basic Law: Freedom of Occupation. These two, which are discussed extensively in the remainder of this chapter, are set out here:

Israeli Statute

Basic Law: Human Dignity and Freedom

1. Basic Principles

Basic rights in Israel are founded upon recognition of the value of the individual, the sanctity of human life, and the principle that a person is free; these rights shall be honored in the spirit of the principles set forth in the Declaration of the Establishment of the State of Israel.

1a. Purpose

The purpose of this Basic Law is to protect human dignity and freedom in order to secure in a Basic Law the values of the State of Israel as a Jewish and democratic state.

2. Preservation of Life, Body, and Dignity

There shall be no infringement on the life, body, or dignity of any person.

3. Protection of Property

There shall be no infringement of the property of a person.

4. Protection of Life, Body, and Dignity

Every person is entitled to protection of life, body, and dignity.

5. Personal Liberty

There shall be no withholding or limitation of the liberty of a person by imprisonment, arrest, extradition or otherwise.

6. Leaving and Entering Israel

(a) Every person is free to leave Israel.

(b) Every Israeli citizen who is abroad has the right to enter Israel.

7. Privacy

(a) Every person is entitled to privacy and to intimacy.

(b) There shall be no entry into the private premises of a person without the person's consent.

---

4. Harrari Resolution, DK (1950) 1743.

(c) No search shall be conducted on a person's private premises, body, or personal possessions.

(d) There shall be no infringement on the confidentiality of a person's conversation, writings, or records.

8. Infringement[5] of Rights

There shall be no infringement of rights under this Basic Law except by a law befitting the values of the State of Israel, enacted for a proper purpose, and to an extent no greater than is required, or by legal requirement enacted under express authorization in such law.

9. Reservation Regarding Security Forces

There shall be no restriction of rights under this Basic Law of persons serving in the Israel Defense Forces, the Israel Police, the Prisons Service and other state security organizations, nor shall such rights be subject to conditions, except as provided by law and to an extent no greater than is required by the character and nature of the service.

10. Validity of Laws

This Basic Law shall not affect the validity of any law [statute, ordinance, or administrative rule or determination] in force prior to the commencement of the Basic Law.

11. Application

All governmental authorities must respect the rights under this Basic Law.

Israeli Statute

Basic Law: Freedom of Occupation

1. Basic Principles

Basic rights in Israel are founded upon recognition of the value of the individual, the sanctity of human life, and the principle that a person is free; these rights shall be honored in the spirit of the principles set forth in the Declaration of the Establishment of the State of Israel.

2. Purpose

The purpose of this Basic Law is to protect the freedom of occupation in order to secure in a Basic Law the values of the State of Israel as a Jewish and democratic state.

3. Freedom of Occupation

Every citizen or resident has is entitled to engage in any occupation, profession, or trade.

4. Infringement of Freedom of Occupation

There shall be no infringement of the freedom of occupation except by a law befitting the values of the State of Israel, enacted for a proper purpose, and to an extent no greater than is required, or by legal requirement enacted under express authorization in such law.

---

5. Many translations use the term *violation*, rather than *infringement*. The same is true in section 4 of Basic Law: Freedom of Occupation. The word *infringement* more correctly conveys the meaning of the provisions, and that term is inserted here and used in all material translated by the author.

5. Application

All governmental authorities must respect the freedom of occupation of all citizens and residents.

7. Entrenchment

This Basic Law shall not be changed except by a Basic Law passed by a majority of the members of the Knesset.

8. Validity of a Nonconforming Law

(a) A provision of a law that infringes on the freedom of occupation shall be valid, even if it does not meet the requirements of section 4, if it is found in a law passed by a majority of the members of the Knesset that states expressly that it shall be of effect, notwithstanding the provisions of this Basic Law; the validity of such a law shall terminate four years from its entering into force, unless a shorter duration is been stated therein.

Comment

These two Basic Laws raise a number of essential legal questions. First, what is the status of the rights set out in these laws? Both Basic Laws use the language of "rights," and we tend to think about rights as having constitutional status. Do these laws have constitutional status? Indeed, do all Basic Laws have the status of constitutional law? Second, what rights are included within the scope of the rights set out in these laws? For example, section 2 of the Basic Law: Human Dignity and Freedom protects the dignity of a person. What is included within the scope of this protection? Third, how absolute are the rights? They are expressed in absolute terms. For example, section 5 of the Basic Law: Human Dignity and Freedom provides, "There shall be no withholding or limitation of the liberty of a person by imprisonment...." Common sense tells us that it cannot mean that all imprisonment is abolished in Israel and that all criminals are free to roam the streets. How does the law limit these apparently absolute rights?

These three sets of questions are examined in the three sections that follow.

D. Constitutional Status of Basic Laws

Under the Harrari Resolution, the Basic Laws were to form chapters of a constitution. It was not clear whether the Basic Laws were to have the status of regular statutes until unified in a constitution, or whether they were to have constitutional status from the time of their enactment. The Harrari Resolution seemed to contemplate that they would have some status different from that of regular laws because they were to be given the special title of *Basic Law*. Yet they were enacted under the same procedures as were used for regular statutes, requiring only a majority vote of those present and with no quorum requirement. For example, the Basic Law: Human Dignity and Freedom was enacted by a vote of 32 in favor, 21 against, and one abstention, and the Basic Law: Freedom of Occupation by a vote of 23 in favor, with no votes against and no abstentions. The Knesset has 120 members, only a minority of members voted in favor of each law. Furthermore, all Basic Laws were enacted by Knessets subsequent to the First Knesset. Although the First Knesset received the constituent authority of the Constituent Assembly, it was not clear whether, and how, this authority passed to later Knessets. These issues were not considered extensively by the Supreme Court until after the enactment of two Basic Laws that address not the structure of government but individual rights.

Section 7 of the Basic Law: Freedom of Occupation is an *entrenchment* clause, or supermajority clause, limiting the way the law can be amended or repealed. An American lawyer would immediately question why this provision is binding. The usual rule in American law is that a later statute can amend or repeal an early one. This rule protects the democratic nature of the Congress; one congress cannot tie the hands of a congress later elected by and charged with effectuating the will of the people. The only exception is that a statute may not alter the Constitution. The Constitution provides a special mechanism for its own amendment which does not include amendment by congressional statute, and this provision is binding on Congress because of the higher normative status of the Constitution. So the question is how the Knesset, by an act of simple legislation, can bind the hands of a later Knesset. This would be possible only if the Basic Law's entrenchment provision had some special status.

Some other Basic Laws have entrenchment clauses. For example, the Basic Law: The Government is entrenched, and in the Basic Law: The Knesset, section 4, The Electoral System, is entrenched, but the rest of the law is not. None of the provisions in the Basic Law: Human Dignity and Freedom are entrenched, and most of the other Basic Laws are also not entrenched. In addition, one regular statute has an entrenchment provision.

American law has nothing comparable to entrenchment clauses. The nearest analogy is the provision in article 5 the US Constitution requiring a special procedure for amending the Constitution. That is different, however, in that the Constitution itself was adopted by a special procedure. Entrenchment provisions in Israeli law can be adopted by regular legislative procedures, but they require special procedures for their amendment.

Section 8 of the Basic Law: Human Dignity and Freedom and section 4 of the Basic Law: Freedom of Occupation are virtually identical. They are commonly called *limitation clauses*. Both set out the circumstances under which a right guaranteed by the Basic Law may be infringed. Such limitation clauses are found in these two Basic Laws, but not in the others. As we shall see below, the Court has interpreted these clauses to impose a set of detailed requirements. For now, we need only understand that the limitation clause raises the same problem as does an entrenchment provision. A limitation clause purports to limit the power of a later Knesset to alter a right set out in a law enacted by an earlier Knesset. It allows a later Knesset to limit the rights provided in these Basic Laws only if the law of the later Knesset meets the requirements of the limitation clause. Again, this raises the question of the power of one Knesset to limit the power of a later Knesset. An entrenchment clause imposes a procedural limitation on the power of the later Knesset, while a limitation clause imposes a substantive limitation. We can surmise that this would be possible only if the Basic Law had some status different from that of a regular law.

The Supreme Court had skirted the issue of the legal status of the Basic Laws until after the enactment of the two Basic Laws on individual rights, when it addressed the matter head on, although only in dicta. We examined this in chapter 5. In the case that follows, the Court considered whether the Basic Law: Human Dignity and Freedom had a special, constitutional status. If it did, then the entrenchment provision and limitation clause could be valid. Additionally by implication, the entrenchment provisions and limitation clauses in other Basic Laws would be valid. Furthermore, a regular law that conflicted with the Basic Law would be invalid.

Brief selections from this case are set out in chapter 5. The facts were given in that chapter and are repeated here.

Israeli Case

United Mizrahi Bank v. Migdal Communal Village
CA 6821/93, 49(4) PD 221 [1995][6]

[Shortly after enactment of the Basic Law: Human Dignity and Freedom, the Knesset enacted an amendment to a different, regular statute on the subject of debts. The amendment, referred to as *the Gal Law* after its author, was part of an effort to rehabilitate the agricultural sector of the economy which had become saddled with a very high debt load during a period of economic crisis. The law established a special body with authority to cancel or change the terms of certain agricultural debts. United Mizrahi Bank and other creditors, who stood to lose the ability to collect on outstanding debts owed to them, petitioned the district court to hold the Gal Law invalid because it violated their property rights. The district court held that section 3 of the Basic Law: Human Dignity and Freedom protected the creditors' property rights in the outstanding debt, that the Gal Law infringed on these rights, and that, as a result, the Gal Law was invalid. The Supreme Court reviewed this decision. The case was heard before an expanded panel of nine justices, which signaled the perceived importance of the case.]

Chief Justice A. Barak:

In March 1992, the Knesset enacted Basic Law: Freedom of Occupation and Basic Law: Human Dignity and Liberty. The enactment of these two Basic Laws effected a substantive change in the status of human rights under Israeli law. Such rights became constitutionally protected and were accorded supra-legislative constitutional status. They cannot be changed by *regular* legislation. A regular law cannot infringe a protected human right unless the constitutional requirements set forth in the Basic Law have been met. The failure of a regular law to meet those requirements renders it unconstitutional. Such a law is constitutionally flawed and the Court may declare it void.

Israel is a constitutional democracy. We have now joined the community of democratic countries (among them the United States, Canada, Germany, Italy, and South Africa) with constitutional bills of rights. We have become part of the human rights revolution that characterizes the second half of the twentieth century. The lessons of World War II, and at their center the Holocaust of the Jewish people, as well as the suppression of human rights in totalitarian states, have raised the issue of human rights to the top of the world agenda. International accords on human rights have been reached. Israel has acceded to them. International tribunals have been established to address issues of human rights. The new constitutions include extensive sections treating of human rights — particularly at the head of those constitutions and in their unique entrenchment provisions. Judicial

---

6. This translation is based on that on the website of the Supreme Court, at http://elyon1.court.gov.il/files_eng/93/210/068/z01/93068210.z01.htm. The English translation of the full case runs 330 pages, of which Justice Barak's opinion occupies 113 pages. The portion presented here, while long, has been severely edited.

review of the constitutionality of laws infringing human rights has become the norm in most countries. This revolution has not passed us by. We joined it in March 1992.

A. The Constitutional Revolution in Human Rights

The constitutional revolution occurred in the Knesset in March 1992. The Knesset endowed the State of Israel with a constitutional bill of rights.

B. The Constitutional Framework

1) The Source of the Knesset's Authority to Enact a Constitution for Israel

a) The Doctrine of Constituent Authority

The opening question is, of course, whether the Knesset is endowed with the authority to enact a constitution for Israel (constituent authority) and, if so, what is the source of this authority.

It seems to me that the most appropriate view is that the Knesset is endowed with constituent authority. This power derives from the central constitutional fact that the Knesset was given the authority to enact a constitution for Israel. The Knesset does not create this authority for itself. It is not granted to the Knesset by a Basic Law or by any other law enacted by the Knesset. In order to frame a constitution, which will be placed above the law in the normative hierarchy, there must be an Archimedean foothold located outside the constitution or the law, which provides the Knesset with the authority to adopt a constitution. The constitution cannot create the authority by which it will be created. Statute cannot create a constitution to which statutes will be subject.... This foothold must come from the people, whose will is supreme. Thus, the doctrine of the Knesset's constituent authority is based upon the principle that this authority derives from the sovereign, i.e., the people. Constituent authority endows the Knesset with the power to enact a constitution for Israel (as embodied in the Basic Laws). This authority endows the Knesset with the power to enact regular laws as well as to act in other ways (for example, to supervise the Government). Indeed, the Knesset wears a number of "hats" or "crowns," among them the crown of constituent authority—under which the constitution is adopted (by enactment of the Basic Laws)—and the crown of legislative authority, under which legislation is adopted. Three legal models may illustrate this view. Each model stands alone as a basis for the doctrine of constituent authority. That all lead to the same conclusion lends that conclusion greater weight. I will begin with a brief introduction to each of the three models. I will then present the constitutional facts that sustain the models.

b) Presentation of the Three Models

(1) Constituent Authority Derives from the Basic Norm

The first model is based upon the importance of constitutional continuity. Under this model, the basic norm for Israel is that the Provisional Council of State is the supreme authority of the State of Israel. The Provisional Council of State declared in the Declaration of Independence that a constitution would be drawn up "by the elected Constituent Assembly." In addition, the Provisional Council of State declared itself the legislative body (in the Law and Administration Ordinance, 5708-1948).

The Constituent Assembly was elected (on January 25, 1949), and with its establishment the Provisional Council of State was dissolved. Its powers passed to the Constituent Assembly (Transition) Law, 5709-1949. The Constituent Assembly therefore had two main powers: constituent authority and legislative authority. The same entity was given two functions, two *crowns* or *hats* as it were: one constituent (to adopt a constitution), and the other legislative (to enact regular legislation). This arrangement, in which constituent and legislative authority are granted to the same entity, is widely accepted. The Constituent Assembly provided (in the Transition Law) that "the legislature of the State of Israel will be known as the 'Knesset.' The Constituent Assembly will be known as the 'First Knesset.' The delegates will be known as 'Members of Knesset.'" (section 1). The First Knesset (i.e., the Constituent Assembly) devoted considerable time to debating the matter of the constitution. These debates concluded with a compromise decision (the Harrari Decision), according to which:

> The First Knesset charges the Constitution, Law and Justice Committee with the preparation of a proposed constitution for the state. The constitution will be composed of chapters, with each chapter comprising a Basic Law unto itself. The chapters will be brought before the Knesset if and when the committee completes its work and all the chapters together will constitute the constitution for the state.

Before it dispersed, the First Knesset provided that all of its powers would pass to subsequent Knessets (Second Knesset (Transition) Law, 5711-1951). To avoid doubt, it was emphasized that this transfer would also include all powers of the Constituent Assembly (see section 9).[7] The Second Knesset dealt with the preparation of Basic Law: The Knesset but did not succeed in adopting that law. Only the Third Knesset succeeded in adopting the Basic Law: The Knesset, which was the first Basic Law. Since then, Basic Laws have been enacted by the various Knessets. From this brief survey, the first model concludes that the constituent authority of the Constituent Assembly has rested continuously in the hands of the Knesset.

(2) Constituent Authority Derives from the Rule of Recognition

The second model supporting the Knesset's constituent authority is not based upon constitutional continuity. Rather, this model examines the constitutional structure as it exists at any given time. It is based upon the thesis of Professor Hart. Professor Hart distinguishes between primary and secondary norms. Secondary norms determine how the primary norms are created, how they may be changed and how disputes concerning them may be resolved. Among the secondary norms the *rule of recognition* occupies a preeminent position (*see* H.L.A. Hart, *The Concept of Law* 100 (2d ed. 1994)). This rule determines how primary norms are created as well as their relative status—which is a superior norm and which is subordinate. The rule of recognition is determined by a court, which does not make this determination at its own whim. Rather, it reflects the views of the community as to the way in which norms (including constitutional norms) are created. Under this model, one may determine that the rule of recognition of the State of Israel is that the Knesset is endowed with both constituent and legislative authority.... The basic understanding of today's Israeli community—expressing our entire national experience—is our national consciousness that the Knesset is the body authorized to enact a constitution for Israel. This consciousness originated before the establishment of the state, and in the preparations for the framing of a constitution. This consciousness was crystallized in the Declaration of Independence. It took on real form in the elections for the Constituent Assembly. It was consolidated in the socio-legal understanding that the Knesset is endowed with constituent authority. It became part of our political culture. Based on these factors the Justices of the Supreme Court determine today that according to the rule of recognition of the State of Israel, the Knesset was given constituent and legislative authority; that the Knesset is authorized, in using its constituent authority, to limit its

---

7. This section provided, "From the time of assembly of the Second Knesset, each place where a statute relates to the Constituent Assembly or the First Knesset shall be read as though it related to the Second Knesset, if no other intention is evident from the context."

regular legislative authority; and that the constituent acts of the Knesset stand above its legislative acts. The historic journey—upon which the first model of constitutional continuity is based—is an important factor in the second model [Hart's model] as well. Constitutionality and the constitution are not merely formal instruments. They are not mere law. They are the product of the national experience, of society, education, and culture. They reflect the national experience. Our national experience, in today's comprehensive view, leads to the conclusion that the Knesset has the authority to enact the constitution.

(3) Constituent Authority is the Best Interpretation of Social and Legal History

The third model for the constituent authority of the Knesset is also an empirical model. It seeks the best interpretation of the entire social and legal history of a given system at a given time. This is Professor Dworkin's model (*see* Ronald Dworkin, *Law's Empire*, (1986); Ronald Dworkin, *A Bill of Rights for Britain* (1990)). Under this model, one may conclude that a given body (such as the parliament) is empowered to enact the constitution for a country if that conclusion is the best interpretation of the body of social and legal history of that country. In applying this model to Israel, it appears that the interpretation that best fits the entirety of Israel's social and legal history since its establishment is that the Knesset is empowered to enact a constitution for Israel. This conclusion is based upon the same factors as those underlying the first and second models. Thus the best interpretation of our constitutional history is not that the Knesset wasted its time by spending over forty years preparing a constitution; the best interpretation of our constitutional history is not that some of the entrenched provisions of the Basic Laws are unenforceable; the best interpretation of our constitutional history is not that the various judicial decisions dealing with the Basic Laws miss their mark. On the contrary: in interpreting our legal and social history, its ways and its traditions, as that history presents itself today— against the background of the Declaration of Independence, the establishment of the Constituent Assembly, the Harrari Decision, the election campaigns in which the stated goal of the parties was the adoption of a constitution, the enactment of twelve Basic Laws that include entrenchment and limitation clauses, judicial precedent and the reaction of the Knesset thereto, and the position of the legal community—the inescapable conclusion is that the most fitting interpretation of our history is that the Knesset is endowed with constituent authority.

c) The Constitutional Data Underlying the Three Models

(1) Survey of the Constitutional Data

I open with those factors that evidence constitutional continuity. These factors are particularly important in the context of the first model, which sees constituent authority as derived from the basic norm. Of course they serve the other two models as well. I then move to the Knesset's perception of itself. This is also an empirical factor that provides the basis for the Court's conclusion according to each of the three models. From there I will focus on the understanding of scholars and commentators. This factor is an important one, for it presents the view of the Israeli legal community as to the Knesset's authority to enact a constitution for Israel. This is important in all three models, particularly the second and third. Finally I will discuss the judicial case law of the Supreme Court. Two Supreme Court decisions have adopted the doctrine of constituent authority in its entirety. In the context of these constitutional factors, I will discuss the body of judicial precedent, which implicitly recognizes the normative supremacy of the Basic Laws. I will complete this analysis with a number of conclusions that are common to all three models and which arise from these objective data.

(2) Constitutional Continuity

May 15, 1948 is the point of departure for the view that the Knesset has constituent authority. On that day the State of Israel was established. The basic norm of the state—its superior norm, which is not itself part of the body of positive law, but provides a basis for the other legal norms of the state—is that the Provisional Council of State is the supreme legislative institution of the state.

The Provisional Council of State decreed in the Declaration of Independence that a constitution would be enacted by the Constituent Assembly, which in turn would be elected no later than October 1, 1948. It thus gave expression to the Resolution of the General Assembly of the United Nations of 28 November 1947, according to which "the constituent assembly of each state will enact a democratic constitution for its respective state." As stated in Israel's Declaration of Independence:

> We hereby declare that as of the termination of the Mandate at midnight, this night of the 14th and 15th May, 1948, and until the setting up of the duly elected bodies of the state in accordance with a constitution, to be drawn up by a Constituent Assembly not later than the first day of October, 1948, the present National Council shall act as the provisional administration, and shall constitute the Provisional Government of the Jewish State, which shall be known as "Israel."

The Provisional Council of State published the proclamation and enacted the Law and Administration Ordinance, 5708-1948. This statute provided, inter alia, that "the Provisional Council of State is the legislative authority" (section 7(a)). The Provisional Council of State similarly enacted the Constituent Assembly Elections Ordinance.... The accepted view then was that the assembly would prepare and draft a constitution for Israel.

The Constituent Assembly was elected on January 25, 1949. As stated in the Declaration of Independence, its role was to draft a new constitution for the state. According to the original plan, and as envisioned by the declaration, upon its election the Constituent Assembly was to have existed simultaneously with the Provisional Council of State. These two were to have been separate entities, each with its own composition and its own function. The Provisional Council of State was to have continued to exist in its role as legislative body. Its role was to enact the laws of the new state as they were needed. As evidenced by its name, this was to have been a provisional entity, which was to have been replaced by the "duly elected bodies of the state in accordance with a Constitution" (Israel's Declaration of Independence). The Constituent Assembly, whose only role was to enact a constitution for the state, was meant to operate alongside the Provisional Council. The Provisional Council of State was not elected by all the citizens and its composition was set by the Law and Administration Ordinance. The Constituent Assembly was chosen by a general election in which all the members of the Israeli community participated. In fact, the parallel existence of both of these bodies was not long lasting, for with the establishment of the Constituent Assembly, the Provisional Council of State was dissolved.

> According to the declaration, the tenure of the Council of State was to have ended on October 1, 1948. From that day, at the latest, the activities of the elected and regular authorities were to have commenced in accordance with the Constitution, which was to have been adopted in the meantime by the Constituent Assembly. However, the specified date passed without the adoption of a Constitution and without the establishment of regular, elected governmental bodies. According to the Declaration of Independence, the Provisional Council of State and the Provisional Government were to have continued to function not only until the election of the Constituent Assembly, but until the establishment of new gov-

ernmental bodies in accordance with the new constitution. The role of the Constituent Assembly was limited to the preparation and adoption of the constitution, and the task of regular legislation was to have remained in the hands of the Provisional Council of State until after the Constituent Assembly completed its work. Until that time, the two entities were to have existed in tandem and the Provisional Government was to have continued to function until after the election of a parliament in accordance with the new Constitution. This plan was tied to the cut-off date of October 1, 1948; all phases were intended to have been implemented within only four months (between May 15, 1948 and October 1, 1948). The drafters of the declaration cannot be criticized for this plan. They signed the declaration before enemy aircraft appeared in the skies over Tel Aviv (albeit only one day earlier), before seven nations invaded the state, and they could not have foreseen the events of the next few months. In retrospect, in light of the events that took place following the establishment of the state, it is clear that the original plan could not have been implemented. The existence of the Provisional Council of State could no longer be reconciled with the simultaneous existence of the Constituent Assembly. It was therefore necessary to impose upon the Constituent Assembly all of the functions of the Council of State. Aharon Barak & Tena Shefnitz, eds., *Sefer Uri Yadin* 80 (1990).

The next stage in constitutional continuity was the enactment of the Transition Law, 5709-1949. This was the most important piece of legislation enacted by the Knesset (now acting as both the constituent and legislative authority). This statute provided that "the legislative body of the State of Israel will be known as the 'Knesset.' The Constituent Assembly will be known as the 'First Knesset.' A delegate to the Constituent Assembly will be known as a 'Member of Knesset'" (section 1). It also provided that an enactment by the Knesset would be denoted "law" (section 2). The Transition Law, 1949 did not affect the dual authority of the Constituent Assembly (now the First Knesset). Indeed the First Knesset engaged in lengthy debates on the subject of the constitution. No claim was made that the First Knesset was not empowered to do so. All agreed that the Knesset, as the Constituent Assembly, was authorized to enact a constitution for the state. The ensuing debate dealt with whether the Knesset was required to enact a constitution, and with the proposed content of the constitution.

The First Knesset (i.e., the Constituent Assembly) concluded this debate with a compromise decision adopted on June 13, 1950. This decision was initiated by Member of the Knesset Harrari and is therefore called the Harrari Decision, which provides as follows:

> The First Knesset charges the Constitution, Law and Justice Committee with the preparation of a proposed constitution for the state. The constitution will be composed of chapters, with each chapter constituting a Basic Law unto itself. The chapters will be brought before the Knesset if and when the committee completes its work and all the chapters together will constitute the constitution for the state.

This was a compromise decision. It left several options open. Although it accepted the principles that there would be a formal constitution and that the idea of a constitution would not be abandoned, it also adopted the position that the constitution would not be enacted immediately as one discrete document, but rather chapter by chapter, over the course of time, which would certainly extend beyond the term of the First Knesset. Nevertheless after this decision no one disputed the Knesset's authority to enact a constitution for Israel. The Harrari Decision was not intended to negate the Knesset's authority to enact a constitution and, as a decision of the Knesset, it could not negate this authority. Thus, the significance of the Harrari Decision was, as it stated, that the Constitutional Committee would prepare a constitution for the state in installments. It was clear to all that this would not be an immediate procedure. It was clear to all that it would not be completed by the First Knesset.

During the term of the First Knesset—i.e., the Constituent Assembly—no constituent action was undertaken. The Knesset had to enact a special law to decide upon its dissolution. In so doing, the Knesset was aware that it had not only regular legislative powers, but also constituent powers. It sought to ensure that all powers with which it was invested would pass to subsequent Knessets as well. This act seems superfluous to me. The powers given to the Knesset were given to every Knesset. As the central organ of the state, the Knesset endures forever. There is no need for special provisions as to the Knesset's continuity other than those dealing with issues of secondary character (such as the continuity of draft laws). The reference to the *First Knesset* and the *Second Knesset* and so on is only theoretical and reflects the first steps of the Israeli parliamentary system. In principle, a change in the composition of the Knesset cannot be considered a change in the Knesset. The Knesset is one body; elections and changes in the members of the Knesset do not require a formal passing of authority from one body to the next. Apparently this matter had not yet been clarified in the early days of the state and therefore—purely for caution's sake—the Second Knesset (Transition) Law was enacted in 1951. That law provided for continuity between the end of the First Knesset's term and the beginning of the Second Knesset's term (section 1). Thus, "the Second Knesset and its members will have all the powers, rights and obligations as the First Knesset and its members" (section 5). It provided further that the Second Knesset would act in accordance with the charter, decisions, precedent and procedures of the First Knesset (section 6). Moreover it provided explicitly in section 9 that, "Wherever in any law reference is made to the Constituent Assembly or the First Knesset, such reference shall, from the day of the convening of the Second Knesset, be deemed to refer to the Second Knesset, unless the context requires a different meaning."

Thus it was provided that "this law will also apply, with the necessary changes, to the Third and any subsequent Knesset, so long as the Knesset does not adopt a contrary law dealing with this matter" (section 10).

The First Knesset—which was also the Constituent Assembly elected for the express purpose of drafting the constitution—was dissolved. The Second Knesset was elected. Was the Second Knesset also invested with constituent authority, empowering it to enact a constitution for Israel? This is not a simple question. Had it been brought before the Supreme Court at the beginning of the Second Knesset's term, the matter could have been decided either way. On the one hand, it could have been argued that constituent authority was given to the Knesset, to every Knesset, regardless of its composition. The Constituent Assembly itself provided in the Second Knesset (Transition) Law that each Knesset is empowered with constituent authority. This edict of the Constituent Assembly must be heeded. It is not appropriate for the Court to declare that the Constituent Assembly itself deviated from its own authority in such a central matter. Similarly it could have been claimed that the Harrari Decision—which was adopted by the Constituent Assembly—determined that the constitution was to have been enacted chapter by chapter; clearly this process would not have been completed during the term of the First Knesset. Constitutional continuity must be recognized in order to give effect to this decision of the Knesset. On the other hand, it could have been contended that the Constituent Assembly derived its authority from the people—and therefore with the dispersal of the Constituent Assembly it was necessary to turn again to the people for its reelection. The Constituent

Assembly was not authorized to transfer its authority. Thus it might have been argued that the Harrari Decision required that the powers of the First Knesset could only have been transferred to the Second Knesset by Basic Law and not by regular law.

Had I been asked to decide this constitutional question at the beginning of the Second Knesset's term, I would have asked the following question: What are the underlying beliefs of the Israeli community at this time as to the enactment of a constitution and the power of the Knesset to adopt a constitution for Israel? I would have inquired as to the best interpretation of the legal and social history in the matter of the constitutional undertaking with the convening of the Second Knesset. In this context I would have examined the flow of constitutional continuity from the Declaration of Independence. Similarly I would have asked whether the party platforms in the elections for the Second Knesset dealt with the continuation of the constitutional undertaking and with the continuation of the Knesset's activities in endowing Israel with a constitution. An affirmative answer to these questions would have enabled me to determine even then that, despite strong assertions to the contrary, the Second Knesset was endowed with constituent authority, whether because of constitutional continuity..., or because it had become generally recognized that the Knesset was invested with constituent authority (Hart's model), or because that was the best interpretation of the legal practices of the Israeli community at that time (Dworkin's model).

I have now undertaken this examination. For example, I have studied the election platforms of all the political parties that participated in the elections for the Second Knesset. Most of the platforms include statements regarding the constitution and its implementation. Often this is a central issue.

It follows that there can be no doubt that the issues of the constitution and the Basic Laws were on the national agenda, were discussed in the elections, and were the subject of clear positions taken by the various parties. It is true that the matter of the constitution and the Basic Laws was not the only subject on the national agenda. But that is of no account. It is enough that the question was brought to the attention of the voter, who gave his opinion on the question of the constitution. If in the next Knesset election a constitution for the state were presented, and the people demanded, by electing the various parties, in light of their various platforms, to either approve or disapprove the constitution—would anyone contend that the people did not thereby express its will as to the constitution? The determining factor is clearly the understanding of the community and consequently the understanding of the Court. Such an understanding existed in the elections for the Second and subsequent Knessets. There is therefore no reason to negate constitutional continuity, and to deny the Second Knesset—on the basis of the arguments that we have brought—the authority to enact a constitution for Israel. Accordingly with the convening of the Second Knesset (on December 22, 1952), the new Government presented its outline plan. The first clause of the outline—before any other clause, including the clause referring to "the concern for the security of the state and the ingathering of exiles"—provides that "with the series of the Basic Laws that will form the basic constitution of Israel, the democratic government of the state will be strengthened and secured." This is followed by a long list of subparagraphs, constituting approximately half of the outline, as to the content of the future constitution.

The question of the constitutional continuity of the Knesset's power to enact a constitution did not come before the Supreme Court in 1951, with the convening of the Second Knesset. We do not have a judicial determination of this matter. The constitutional question arises before us today, in 1995 during the term of the Thirteenth Knesset. I have no doubt that our decision today must be unequivocal: constitutional continuity was not interrupted. The Second Knesset was given the powers of the Constituent Assembly. Any other conclusion is inconsistent with our national experience. Forty-four years have passed since the Second Knesset was convened. The matter of the constitution has appeared on the agenda and has been included in all the campaigns for each of the many elections that have been held since then. During all those years the Knesset continued in the constitutional undertaking and has enacted eleven Basic Laws; it has continued to see itself as authorized to enact a constitution for Israel; it has continued to entrench the clauses of the Basic Laws against infringement by regular legislation. During all those years teachers and scholars of law have continued to see the Knesset as the authority empowered to enact a constitution for Israel. They have raised generations of students and teachers of law who, in their turn, see the Knesset as empowered with both constituent and legislative authority.

In the intervening years the Supreme Court has ruled that the entrenchment provisions of the Basic Laws have constitutional power and may invalidate contrary provisions of regular legislation. In my opinion, these facts lead to the inescapable conclusion that constitutional continuity persists. By general recognition, the Knesset—the Second Knesset and each subsequent Knesset—is authorized to enact a constitution for Israel. Today's Knesset has constituent authority. The Knesset has two hats: the hat of constituent authority and the hat of legislative authority.

My position relies, therefore, on all of the factors that attest to a continuous constitutional history, beginning with the convening of the Second Knesset. I will continue with a description of [the Knesset's understanding of its constituent authority, which supports] my conclusion that according to the rule of recognition of the Israeli legal system, our Knesset—every Knesset—is endowed with constituent authority. That is the best interpretation of the entirety of our legal and social history.

(3) The Knesset's Perception of Itself as Invested with Constituent Authority

As to the Knesset's understanding of its constituent authority, I will mention five points. First, in every Knesset election the matter of the constitution was included as part of the party platforms. I verified this as to the passage from First to Second Knesset. [A cited article notes] that in the elections for the Eighth Knesset most of the parties promised to work towards enactment of a constitution or Basic Laws as to human rights. I did not check the party platforms for other Knesset elections. It seems that this is a well-founded assumption, inasmuch as the matter of the constitution in general, and human rights in particular, found a central place in the party platforms. This is very significant. It indicates that recognition of the Knesset's constituent authority was an item on the national agenda, was debated in the political forum, and was determined by means of election results. When the Knesset dealt with the matter of the constitution and enacted the various Basic Laws, it drew its power from the people. The Basic Laws were not enacted without the people's knowledge.

Second, in four instances the Supreme Court invalidated regular legislation that conflicted with entrenched provisions of the Basic Law: The Knesset.[8] In accordance with

---

8. The first of the cases the opinion refers to was HCJ 98/69 *Bergman v. Minister of Finance* 23(1) P.D. 693 [1969], translated in 8 SELECTED JUDGMENTS OF THE SUPREME COURT OF ISRAEL 13 (1969–88). It presented issues similar to those involved in the other cases. In *Bergman*, the Supreme Court considered a challenge to a law on financing political parties. The law provided public financing only to parties represented in the previous Knesset, thus treating new parties differently from parties that already had seats. This arrangement was invalid because it contradicted an entrenched provision of an earlier Basic Law requiring equality in elections. The Court did not undertake a substantial analysis of whether it had power to hold invalid the public financing law. It addressed this issue only indirectly because it had not been argued by the state. The justices deciding the case warned that it did not constitute a full consideration of this important issue. *Id.* at 696. The opinion was only five pages long.

those decisions the Knesset subsequently revised its regular legislation to conform to the entrenched provisions of the Basic Law. We are therefore presented with a new aspect of the Knesset's understanding of the matter. The Knesset, in exercising its legislative authority, understood well that it was bound by limitations it had imposed in accordance with its constituent authority. Third, all of the entrenchment provisions were enacted within the framework of the Basic Laws, in the context of the constitutional process. Only in one case has a formal entrenchment provision been included in a regular law. This is in section 3 of the Protection of Investments by the Israeli Public in Financial Assets Law, 5744-1984. That section provides that "this law may not be changed nor may the appendix be revised unless by a majority of the members of the Knesset." It should be noted that during the debate on the first reading of this proposed law a number of members of the Knesset expressed the view that this self-limitation was not binding since it was not included in a Basic Law.

All this is evidence for the widely held understanding of the Knesset that it is endowed with both constituent and legislative authority, and that the enactment of a constitution is the realization of the Knesset's constituent authority. In the context of this authority a supra-legislative constitutional norm may be created.

Fourth, in the first years after establishment of the state there were many references to the Constituent Assembly, the Declaration of Independence, and the Harrari Decision. With the passage of time—and changes in the composition of the Knesset—the rhetoric changed. This is natural. A generation goes, and a generation comes, but the national memory did not change. The connection to the past was not severed. The Knesset continued to see itself as the heir of the Constituent Assembly, and as endowed with constituent authority.

Fifth, it is clear from the Declaration of Independence that the role (and authority) of the Constituent Assembly was to enact a constitution ("in accordance with a constitution, to be drawn up by a Constituent Assembly"). The intention underlying this provision was that a formal constitution would be adopted, in other words, that "the form of these norms would differ from that of other norms, particularly that of 'regular' laws. This difference in form is expressed as a difference in the identity of the institution creating the norm ('constituent institution' as opposed to 'legislature') or at least in the process of its creation."

(4) The Understanding of Writers and Commentators

I will now discuss the views of writers and commentators.... From the understanding of writers and commentators one may learn about the basic approach of the Israeli legal community to constituent authority. Clearly this does not constitute decisive proof. Nonetheless, it is important evidence which, when seen together with other factors— the objective facts as to constitutional continuity, the political debates before the elections, the Knesset's understanding of itself, the legal precedent and the Knesset's reaction thereto—grounds the foundation upon which the Court may and should determine that the Knesset—every Knesset—is endowed with constituent authority; that by the principles of Israeli law, the Knesset—every Knesset—is empowered to enact a constitution for Israel; that this is the most appropriate interpretation of the social and political history of Israel.

Most of Israel's scholars have viewed and continue to view the Knesset as endowed with constituent authority and therefore authorized to enact a constitution for Israel. It is true that in the past some disputed this position.... These views were debated, analyzed and rejected. They remain the minority position. Since the end of the 1950s (with the enactment of the Basic Law: The Knesset) ... the recurrent theme in Israeli constitutional literature has been that the Knesset has constituent authority, and that it is therefore authorized to adopt a constitution that will limit the Knesset in its role as legislature. Generations of law students have been inculcated with this view since the 1960s. [The opinion here examines numerous articles.]

(5) Judicial Precedent of the Supreme Court

The Court has recognized the Knesset's power to *entrench* the Basic Laws against change or infringement. Otherwise, we cannot explain the invalidation of four regular laws for violating the principle of election parity set forth in the Basic Law: The Knesset, when these invalidations stemmed from the failure of those laws to meet a formal requirement (the special majority) set forth in section 4 of the Basic Law. It is true that in these decisions (except for the *Laor Movement* case) the Court did not employ the rhetoric of constituent authority.[9] We cannot conclude from these decisions that this specific doctrine was before the Court at that time. However, it is clear that the Court recognized the normative primacy of the entrenched Basic Laws. This primacy is certainly consistent—and as I will explain, only consistent—with the constituent authority of a Knesset empowered to enact a constitution for the state.

Comments

Chief Justice Barak's opinion first attacks the problem that would seem obvious to American lawyers: How could the Knesset, an ordinary legislative body, enact a law that is of constitutional quality? In the American system, the Constitution was prepared by a special body, the Constitutional Convention, comprised of delegates of twelve of the thirteen states (Rhode Island declined to send a delegate) that constituted the Confederation, the national government that preceded our current government. Once the Constitution was formulated, it was referred to the states for ratification. The newly drafted Constitution set out that it would come into force upon ratification by nine states. US Const. art. VII. In other words, the Constitution was prepared by a body different from the ordinary legislature and was voted into force by a procedure different from the procedure for enacting ordinary legislation.

Chief Justice Barak shows that there are various theories of constitutional authority, and that not all of them require that the constitution-making body be separate from the ordinary legislature. The American system is not the only possible system.

Of course, a showing that in theory a legislature can enact a constitution does not mean that the Israeli legislature can do so. Chief Justice Barak next sets out to show that the Knesset in Israel had authority to enact laws of constitutional quality. His opinion begins with the clear authority of the Constituent Assembly to enact a constitution and shows that this authority was passed to the First Knesset and then to each successive Knesset. Because the authority was not passed through any explicit document, the opinion must not only set

---

9. Again, Chief Justice Barak is referring to a series of decisions in which the Court considered the validity of a statute that violated an entrenched provision, where the violating statute was not passed by an absolute majority. In none of these cases did the majority opinion consider the normative status of the entrenched law. In the *Laor Movement* case, Chief Justice Barak's own opinion raised the issue, but it was a minority opinion. The majority opinion, written by Assistant Chief Justice Menachem Alon, assumed that an entrenchment provision was valid. The majority opinion considered only whether the later law actually violated the entrenchment provision. *Migdal* is the first case to directly address the issue of the status of Basic Laws.

out a theory of how it passed, but also bolster this theory with additional evidence. The additional evidence is found in three places: (1) the Knesset's understanding of its own constituent authority, (2) the opinions of legal experts who hold that the Knesset has constituent authority, and (3) Supreme Court precedent recognizing this authority. Based on some of the Knesset's past actions, Chief Justice Barak's opinion also concludes that the Knesset used this constituent authority in enacting the Basic Laws on human rights.

Six of the nine justices who sat on this case agreed with Chief Justice Barak's analysis of the source of the Knesset's authority to enact laws of constitutional status. Thus, the same body had authority to enact regular laws and authority to enact a constitution. This is commonly called the two hats approach.

Chief Justice Emeritus Meir Shamgar came to the same conclusion as Chief Justice Barak, but he reached it through a different analysis. According to Chief Justice Emeritus Shamgar's approach, the Knesset has unlimited sovereignty and can use it to enact either regular legislation or constitutional law. In enacting the Basic Laws on human rights, it exercised its constitutional law authority.

Justice Mishael Cheshin alone disagreed with the view that the Knesset could enact constitutional law. A number of scholars also challenge the validity of the majority's analysis. Here is an excerpt from Justice Cheshin's 98-page concurring opinion:[10]

Israeli Case

United Mizrahi Bank v. Migdal Communal Village
CA 6821/93, 49(4) PD 221 [1995][11]

Justice M. Cheshin:

Firstly did the Constituent Assembly of the First Knesset have the authority to frame a constitution for Israel, and secondly, assuming that it had such power, was this power transferred to all subsequent Knessets?

Regarding the Establishment of the "Constituent Assembly"

The establishment of a Jewish state in the Land of Israel—the State of Israel—was declared on the fifth of Iyar 5708, May 14, 1948.... The second subsection [of the Declaration of Independence], which relates directly to the matter currently before us, provides as follows:

> WE DECLARE that, with effect from the moment of the termination of the Mandate being tonight, the eve of Sabbath, the 6th Iyar, 5708 (May 15, 1948), until the establishment of the elected, regular authorities of the state in accordance with the Constitution which shall be adopted by the elected Constituent Assembly no later than the 1st of October 1948, the People's Council shall act as the Provisional Council of State, and its executive organ, the People's Administration, shall be the Provisional Government of the Jewish State, to be called "Israel."

---

10. Justice Cheshin concurred in the result, that the Gal Law was valid, but not in the determination that the Basic Law was of constitutional status. Because he thought the Basic Law was not constitutional, it was no barrier to the validity of the Gal Law.

11. This translation is based on that on the website of the Supreme Court, at http://elyon1.court.gov.il/files_eng/93/210/068/z01/93068210.z01.htm. Justice Cheshin's opinion, like that of Chief Justice Barak, is severely edited for length.

This portion of the declaration informs us of a number of matters pertaining to the central institutions of the state, all of them at the pinnacle of the state's norms. Our current concern is with the "elected Constituent Assembly," mentioned in the declaration. Taking a closer look, we discern that this was an interim, short lived entity, with a single purpose of framing a constitution that would include (among other things, apparently) instructions for the election and establishment of "elected, regular authorities of the state." The Provisional Council of State, and the Provisional Government (previously called: the "People's Council and the People's Administration") were to continue functioning as the central institutions of the state, and the Constituent Assembly was supposed to function parallel to them in the fulfillment of its one and only task: the establishment of a constitution, within a short period of time, measured in terms of just a few months. The constitution would be written (and the Constituent Assembly would disperse); elections for the "elected regular authorities" would be conducted thereunder, and the elected regular authorities would be established. Only then were the Council of State and the Provisional Government to stop functioning, and all powers would be vested in those elected regular authorities.

For our purposes, the following two issues are of primary significance: First, the exclusive devotion of the Constituent Assembly to its task, and second, the termination of the activities of the Constituent Assembly within the short, prescribed period.

Thus, (normatively) two bodies were created: the Provisional Council of State as the legislative authority, and along with it, the Constituent Assembly, which had yet to be established—as the body meant to draft the state's constitution.

A constituent assembly as per the instructions and the definition of the Declaration of the Establishment of the State never actually materialized. On January 14, 1949, eleven days before the elections to the Constituent Assembly, the Provisional Council of State published the Constituent Assembly (Transition) Ordinance, and in section 3 of the Ordinance it enacted the following powers of the Constituent Assembly:

Powers of the Constituent Assembly

The Constituent Assembly shall, so long as it does not itself otherwise decide, have all the powers vested by law in the Provisional Council of State.

The Constituent Assembly (Transition) Ordinance introduced a change: The Constituent Assembly was no longer intended exclusively to frame the state constitution. From now on, it was also to hold the powers of the Provisional Council of State, i.e., it was to fulfill the legislative role. The Constituent Assembly was charged with two tasks: the task of writing a constitution for the state and the task of enacting laws—one body wearing two crowns.

Elections were accordingly held, but the Constituent Assembly, at least under that name, was short-lived. On February 14, 1949 the Constituent Assembly convened for the first time, and two days later—on February 16, 1949—the Transition Law was enacted. Section 1 of that law terminated the use of the designation *Constituent Assembly*:

1. Designation of the Legislature and its members

The legislative body of the State of Israel shall be called the Knesset. The Constituent Assembly shall be called "The First Knesset." A delegate to the Constituent Assembly shall be called "a member of Knesset."

The Knesset as Possessor of Constituent Authority; the Entrenchment of Statutes

The issue before us is whether the current Knesset possesses constituent authority, i.e., the authority to frame a formal constitution for Israel. To that end, a distinction must be drawn between the question of the Knesset's authority to exercise the powers of a constituent assembly, i.e., the power to enact a constitution, and the question of the Knesset's authority to enact entrenched laws. These powers are not identical, and one power cannot necessarily be inferred from the other. In fact, constituent authority to enact a constitution may, in principle, include the power to enact entrenched constitutional laws, and quite possibly this is its essence. However, the same inference cannot be made in the other direction. In other words, authority to enact entrenched laws does not per se indicate the Knesset's authority as a constituent authority. The Knesset may acquire the authority to enact entrenched laws, but still be lacking in constituent authority. As we will explain below in detail, this in fact is our view. The Knesset is empowered to enact entrenched laws—within certain limits—but it lacks the power of a constituent authority.

Thus we must differentiate between the two, and we will maintain this distinction throughout. As mentioned, our current concern is not with the authority of the Knesset to enact entrenched laws. Our current concern is solely with the question of whether the Knesset was vested with constituent authority to enact a constitution.

Has the Continuity of the Authority of the Constituent Assembly been Maintained from the First Knesset to the Knessets that Followed?

The Constituent Assembly (First Knesset) possessed the authority of a constituent assembly, namely, authority to frame a constitution. The question is whether it transferred that authority to the Second Knesset.... The Constituent Assembly changed its name to the First Knesset ... and towards the end of its term it enacted the Second Knesset (Transition) Law. Section 5 of the latter provided as follows:

5. The Powers etc. of the Second Knesset and its Members

The Second Knesset and its members shall have all the powers, rights, and duties which the First Knesset and its members had.

Whereas the provisions of this law referred exclusively to the transfer of authority from the First Knesset to the Second Knesset, section 10 of the same law established a general norm with respect to transfer of powers:

10. Application

This law shall also apply mutatis mutandis to the transition to the Third and any subsequent Knesset, so long as the Knesset does not pass any other law concerning the matters dealt with by this law.

Supporters of the two-crown doctrine claim as follows: The Constituent Assembly was vested with authority to frame a formal constitution for Israel, and that is not disputed. Following that, these statutory provisions were adopted, each at its own time and place, which transferred that authority from one Knesset to the next, until the current Knesset. The legislative crown, and with it the constituent crown, were passed down, as if from father to son, so that today's Knesset wears the legislative crown together with the crown worn by the constituent authority about 50 years ago. Is that indeed the case?

The question remains: Which powers could the Constituent Assembly and all the past and future Knessets transfer to one another? After all, we all agree that a person can transfer only such authority that he is permitted and authorized to transfer; and if the transferor is not permitted and authorized to transfer, then his intention to transfer is simply of no consequence.

Indeed, in my view, when the Constituent Assembly—which was the First Knesset— dispersed without having framed a constitution for Israel, the Knesset's right to draft a constitution as established by the Declaration of the Establishment of the State, expired. The continuity that was maintained by the transition provisions quoted above relates solely to matters of legislation, and not to constitutional issues.

We should recall that the same Constituent Assembly—as established by the People's Council in the Declaration of Independence—was meant to complete its task of writing the constitution within a few months. It was to write it and then disperse. Hence, the Constituent Assembly was singular, exceptional and unique. Knowing this, we also know that the task of the Constituent Assembly to write a constitution was a specific, one-time mission. The authority of the Constituent Assembly to write a constitution could not be viewed as a property right, transferable at its owner's will. It was a kind of trust that the People's Council entrusted to the hands of the Constituent Authority, and a trust—as is known—is not transferable from person to person at the trustee's behest. Indeed, in going to the polls to elect a Constituent Assembly—as dictated by the Constituent Assembly (Elections) Ordinance—the nation was meant to have elected a Constituent Assembly whose function it was to frame a constitution for Israel. Concededly the Constituent Assembly was also supposed to possess regular legislative powers. However these powers existed independently, while its primary function remained as it was, in accordance with the decision of one whose very existence embodies the basic norm. On the face of it, it would seem therefore that the Constituent Assembly was not empowered to transfer its constituent authority to another.

A basic legal principle, rooted in common sense, is that agency cannot be transferred. An agent cannot appoint another agent.... When I repose my trust in someone, such trust by its very essence, is not transferable. In the absence of the principal's authorization, an agent is not permitted to appoint another person to perform the agency.... So it was with the Constituent Assembly that could not transfer to the Second Knesset the authority that originated in the personal trust reposed in it by the electorate.

I ascribe tremendous importance to the election for the Constituent Assembly. When the voters went to the polls to elect the Constituent Assembly, their purpose was to elect, by law, a body that would grant Israel its constitution. Even were we to say that the issue of a constitution was raised by political parties in various Knesset elections, nevertheless, the election for the Constituent Assembly was different from all of the later elections for the Knesset, because only in that election was the constitutional question put to the voters by force of law. The Constituent Assembly was created for the express purpose of writing the constitution, and voters therefore knew that they were electing a body that would be drafting a constitution. This feature distinguishes the Constituent Assembly, setting it aside from all subsequent Knessets.

We all know that in the elections to the Second Knesset and to all the subsequent Knessets, the universally discussed issues were peace and security, adopting an aggressive or moderate policy, the social gap and integration, social welfare and the standard of living. The issue of the constitution assumed modest and unassuming proportions, hovering on the peripheries of the operative programs, even if it featured prominently in the party platforms, and it is doubtful whether the voters seriously considered the issue. As such, nothing can be inferred from the mandate ostensibly given by the people to the Second Knesset and to those following it to enact a constitution. While that is true in general, it is even more so the case considering that certain parties totally omitted the constitutional issue from their platforms, and others expressed their opposition to a constitution for Israel. The division of opinions was so great that it is almost impossible to draw a conclusion that the Knesset elections following the First Knesset were for the purpose of framing a constitution.

The Harrari Resolution

My colleagues view the Harrari Resolution as one of the important links in what they view as an unbroken chain that began with the authority of the Constituent Assembly to enact a constitution, and ends (for the time being) with the authority of the current Knesset to enact a constitution. I cannot accept their view. Firstly it should be remembered that the Harrari Resolution was only a resolution, and we find it difficult to anchor the authority to frame a constitution in nothing more than a Knesset resolution. Secondly reading the Knesset proceedings teaches us that the Harrari Resolution is open to a variety of interpretations, and that each Knesset member relied on it to prove the argument that he found most politically convenient.

The most that can be inferred from the Harrari Resolution is that in place of one integrated constitution, the Knesset would be enacting Basic Laws, and that when the time comes, all of the Basic Laws would be consolidated under one roof.

The Knesset has changed Basic Laws by means of regular legislation. In other words, the Knesset did not see the Basic Laws as possessing unique status as constitutional laws, changeable only by force of other constitutional laws.

My colleague, Chief Justice Barak purports to buttress the doctrine conferring constituent authority upon the Knesset by relying on the writings of writers and scholars, and by asserting that the vast majority of the Israeli legal community shares this view. I do not think that this claim substantiates the doctrine of constituent authority.

First of all, not all of the writers and scholars are of the same view. Not all of them concur with the two-crown theory.

Furthermore, it is hard to avoid the impression that supporters of the two-crown doctrine, or at least some of them, have confused matters of legal agenda with matters of law, and the ideal law with the real law. And so, in their desire for an Israeli constitution that will protect the individual against governmental power, they seek ways of anchoring such a constitution in the existing law. My heart is with them. I too would like to see an Israeli constitution that defines the rights of the individual, and the sooner the better. But I think that first and foremost it is necessary to find a true, certain anchor for such a constitution in the existing law. We must remember that a constitution means the invalidation of Knesset statutes that conflict with the constitution.

Neither have I found any basis for the Knesset's constituent authority in the case law of the Supreme Court. In fact, the Court acknowledged the Knesset's authority to entrench laws against change, as well as the Court's authority to invalidate laws that violate the provisions of an entrenched law.... I wholeheartedly concur with the Court's ruling, and in the second part of my judgment I have attempted to provide it with a legal foundation.

However, needless to say, nothing in this case law compels recognition of the Knesset's constituent authority. On the contrary, apart from an obiter dictum of my colleague Justice Barak, the Supreme Court did not even hint at constituent authority as the basis for its decisions in any of those cases.

A clear distinction must be drawn between the Knesset's constituent authority to adopt a constitution for the state, and its authority to entrench laws. They are not one and the same. We, too, believe that the Knesset possesses the power to entrench laws (subject to certain limitations), but concurrently, we think that the Knesset lacks constituent authority.

The Knesset's Authority to Enact Entrenched Laws

[Does the Knesset] have the authority to legislate entrenched laws? A law states expressly that it can be neither varied nor violated except by a majority of the members of Knesset. Is such entrenchment valid?

Section 19 of Basic Law: The Knesset provides that "The Knesset shall itself prescribe its procedure." ... [T]he issues of quorum and voting both concern the organizational procedures that the Knesset establishes in order to enable it to function, and the procedure by which it adorns itself before it adorns others.

Section 24 of Basic Law: The Knesset specifically provides that, "The Knesset shall hold debates and pass decisions whatever the number of members present." The rule stipulating the lack of a quorum requirement is binding as long as it is not changed.

Section 25 of Basic Law: The Knesset provides that, "Save as otherwise provided by law, the Knesset shall pass its decisions by a majority of those participating in the voting — those abstaining not being reckoned as participating — and the voting procedure shall be prescribed by the articles."

These are the voting rules followed in the Knesset by force of Basic Law: The Knesset. Knesset decisions are adopted on the basis of the democratic principle of majority rule, and Knesset members who were absent or abstained from voting are not included in the counting of the votes.

However, nothing compels us to adopt this specific provision.... In comparison with the majority provision appearing in section 25 of Basic Law: The Knesset, the requirement of a 61 vote majority for the passage of a decision may be classified as a requirement for a special majority.... When the Knesset prescribes that a particular statute can be repealed, changed or infringed only by a majority of 61 Knesset members, it does not limit its authority, nor does it curtail its legislative power. All that it does is give direct expression to the majority rule dictated by the democratic principle.... I would further add, incidentally, that the establishment of a special majority must be specifically anchored in law, primarily because of the statutory provision regarding the formation of a majority in section 25 of Basic Law: The Knesset.... We are unaware of any legal obstacle to the Knesset's adoption of any law with entrenchment by 61, and we see nothing legally unique in that kind of law.

Comment:

Justice Cheshin's opinion reveals the problems with the legal grounds for the momentous ruling in *Migdal* that the Knesset has the authority to enact a constitution. Justice Cheshin deals with the problem of the entrenchment provisions by finding these to be within the Knesset's power to set its own procedural rules. A law passed without observance of the procedural rules of a legislature is not a valid law.

Whatever the constituent authority of the Knesset, there are those who take issue with the assertion that the Knesset meant to exercise this authority when it enacted the two Basic Laws on human rights. Consider the following statement by Michael Eitan, a lawyer by training who has been a member of the Knesset since 1984:

I was in the Knesset in 1992. I clashed with the Chairman of the Constitution, Law and Justice Committee when he brought the law to the final reading and I can testify personally that the word *constitution* was not mentioned by anyone of the members of the Knesset. Ninety-five percent of them never thought that they had a constitutional power. It's the first time I hear that a country can get a constitution retroactively. At the time of the legislation, the members of the Knesset did not know that they were adopting a constitution for the State of Israel, nor did anyone else. How do I know? In the newspapers the day after the enactment of the law, no one mentioned it. It came to our knowledge that we made the constitution a few months later, when Barak said the words I quoted, in a speech and later in an article. But, no one contemplated it at the time the law was enacted.[12]

Questions

5. Justice Barak writes about the "constitutional revolution" that occurred in 1992 with the enactment of Basic Law: Human Dignity and Freedom and Basic Law: Freedom of Occupation. According to his analysis, the Knesset always had constituent authority and exercised it whenever it enacted a Basic Law. What, then, was the nature of the constitutional revolution of 1992?

6. Which position do you find more convincing, that of Chief Justice Barak or that of Justice Cheshin, and why? Consider the following points: the authority of the Knesset to enact a constitution, whether Basic Laws are constitutional laws, the reason that an entrenched provision is binding, and the question of whether entrenched provisions prove that Basic Laws are constitutional laws.

E. The Rights in the Basic Laws

1. Explicit Rights

Some of the rights protected in the Basic Law: Human Dignity and Freedom are familiar to Americans. Section 5 protects a right to personal liberty, and section 3 protects the right to property. These are rights which are protected by the due process clauses of the Fifth and Fourteenth Amendments to the United States Constitution. The rights set out in the Israeli law are phrased in absolute terms, but section 8 on Infringement of Rights limits the absolute character of all rights.

Other rights are different from those recognized in American constitutional law. The right to privacy in section 7 is parallel to, but broader than, the right to privacy recognized as inherent in the Amendments to the US Constitution. The right in section 6 on leaving and entering Israel has no parallel in the US Constitution, but it is understandable given Israeli sensitivity to the fact that, even in recent history, Jews have experienced persecution and vast numbers have been killed in countries they were not allowed to leave.

The right covered in the Basic Law: Freedom of Occupation is unlike any constitutional right recognized in the United States, but it is similar to rights recognized elsewhere. For example, the European Union Charter of Fundamental Rights includes the following provision:

---

12. Statement of Michael Eitan in Malvina Halberstam, *Judicial Review, A Comparative Perspective: Israel, Canada, and the United States*, 31 CARDOZO L. REV. 2393, 2422 (2010).

European Law

European Union Charter of Fundamental Rights
200 O.J. (C 364) 1

Art. 15. Freedom to Choose an Occupation and Right to Engage in Work

Definition

1. Everyone has the right to engage in work and to pursue a freely chosen or accepted occupation.

Comment

The freedom of occupation in Israel has been interpreted to include the freedom of a person to choose a line of work, freedom of competition of the firm (the right to be free of restrictions not imposed on competitors), and freedom from governmental regulation. Under this last component, regulation by government is permitted only to the extent that it meets the limitation clause, but most regulation does meet the requirements of that clause.

Question

7. Other rights familiar to Americans are not covered explicitly in the two Basic Laws. What rights found in the US Constitution, including its amendments, do not appear as explicit rights in the two Israeli Basic Laws?

2. Implicit Rights: Individual Rights

One of the persistent issues in Israeli constitutional law is whether rights not explicit in these Basic Laws are implicitly included, or whether they are omitted. The Supreme Court has interpreted the Basic Laws to include some rights not explicitly set out in them. For example, in *Issacharov v. Chief Military Prosecutor,*[13] the Supreme Court ruled that the right of a person to be free from a search by the government is included in the rights to privacy and to property.

The question of whether the Basic Law: Human Dignity and Freedom protects the right to equality has been an enduring and difficult one. Some aspects of the right to equality were recognized by case law prior to the enactment of this Basic Law. Therefore it is possible to argue that, because the right to equality is seen as such an important right in these cases, it must have been included in the Basic Law. But it could also be argued that, because it is such a prominent right under Israeli case law, the exclusion of explicit mention of a right to equality in the Basic Law must have been intentional, and that the Knesset did not agree that it should be treated as a basic right.

Some aspects of equality are seen as presenting especially thorny issues in Israel. Equality of Arabs and Jews is seen as closely related to security issues because at least some of the Arab communities identified in the past with enemies of the state, and there are those who are concerned that this is still true for some Arab citizens of Israel. The issue of gender equal-

---

13. CrimA 5121/98 Issacharov v. Chief Military Prosecutor 61(1) PD 461 [2006] (discussed in chapter 6).

ity is complicated by the connection to the outlooks and internal legal systems of the major religious communities. Under traditional views in both Judaism and Islam, men and women are treated differently. Legal recognition of gender equality is seen by some as endangering protection of freedom of religion and could also be a political threat to a Government that depended on the Jewish Ultra-Orthodox parties to maintain its parliamentary majority.

At first, the courts continued to treat the right to equality as a right protected by case law, without holding that it was incorporated into the Basic Laws. Under this approach, courts could not hold that legislation that impinged on equality was invalid. Invalidation of legislation can be done only if the legislation violates a constitutional right, so as long as a court did not hold that there was a constitutional right to equality in the Basic Law, it could not strike down legislation for violating the right to equality. It could narrowly interpret legislation that had the potential to adversely affect equality so as to prevent it from having such an adverse effect, but where the legislation made explicit distinctions between two groups, a court could do nothing.

This changed in two cases in which the Supreme Court recognized that the right to equality had constitutional status and was protected by the Basic Laws.

Israeli Case

Movement for Quality Government in Israel v. Knesset
HCJ 6427/02, 61(1) PD 619 [2006]

[Israel has nearly universal obligatory military service. The Deferment of Service Law for Yeshiva Students Engaged in Full Time Yeshiva Studies, 5762-2002 (hereinafter the Deferment of Service Law) allows young men who engage in full-time yeshiva[14] studies to be exempted from such service. The statute also allows these men to leave full-time studies and perform reduced military service. The Petitioner brought an action challenging the validity of this statute, claiming it violates the right to equality of all those who are subject to the mandatory draft. The Court agreed that the law creates inequality between those required to serve and those exempted from service. It then considered whether this violation of equality constitutes an infringement of a right protected by the Basic Law: Human Dignity and Freedom.]

Chief Justice A. Barak:

Is Equality Included in "Human Dignity"?

Is the equality that is violated by the Deferment of Service Law part of the human dignity of a person that is based in the Basic Law: Human Dignity and Freedom? Does the discrimination perpetrated by the Deferment of Service Law impinge on the human dignity of those who are drafted into military service? We must find the answer to this question by determining the objective of the Basic Law: Human Dignity and Freedom in general and of its provisions on the right to human dignity in particular. This determination depends on the answers to two questions: First, what is the nature of the right to human dignity and what are the limits of its reach? Second, does the type of impingement on equality that is caused by the Deferment of Service Law fall within the scope of the right to human dignity? We shall start with the first of these questions.

---

14. A *yeshiva*, as used in this context, is a post-high school institute for learning traditional Jewish texts. Jewish law values study of these texts, independent of any utilitarian goal for such learning.

The term "human dignity" in the Basic Law: Human Dignity and Freedom is not an expression of policy or of ideals.... The provision on human dignity in the Basic Law established a new normative reality.... Human dignity is an independent right that stands on its own feet. It exists alongside other human rights.... The right to human dignity imposes on all governmental authorities the negative obligation not to infringe on human dignity and the positive obligation to protect it.

What is the scope of human dignity as a human right? ... The scope of the concept of human dignity depends on its objective. This requires consideration of, among other factors, the structure of the Basic Law, its history, case interpretations of the term, its relationship to other Basic Laws, and comparative law. The concept of human dignity has its roots in Judaism. The concept has been developed in philosophical thought in general and in the writings of Kant in particular. Moreover, we must remember that it is our task to understand the concept of human dignity against the background of the existing Israeli social reality and Israel's basic values.

The legal literature suggests three possible models of the scope of the right to human dignity. The first is the narrow model. According to it, human dignity protects only against clear violations of dignity connected to the humanity of the individual.... These are physical and mental violations, humiliation and slander, etc. that cause real harm to the core values of human dignity. The second model, opposite to the first, is the broad model. According to it, human dignity is the basis for all human rights and includes them all. The third model is the intermediate model. Under it, human dignity is not limited to impingements on its core values, nor does it cover every possible human right. It includes only those rights that are closely related to human dignity in practice, whether to the core values or to those that are more marginal.

What is the best approach? This has not yet been determined by the case law.

I think the intermediate model offers the best approach for analyzing the relationship between equality and human dignity as a constitutional right. I think we should not adopt the narrow model for three reasons: First, case law already has language suggesting that the intermediate model is best.... Second, the Declaration of the Establishment of the State of Israel provides that Israel "will ensure complete equality of social and political rights to all its inhabitants irrespective of religion, race or sex." These words, even if they are not a direct source of a constitutional right to equality (a matter in dispute that I leave to later consideration), certainly should influence us to interpret the right to human dignity to include some aspects of equality. Indeed, section 1 of the Basic Law: Human Dignity and Freedom provides explicitly that the basic rights of a person in Israel "shall be upheld in the spirit of the principles set forth in the Declaration of the Establishment of the State of Israel." Third, the proper approach to human dignity, which puts at its center the autonomy of the individual's will, freedom of choice, physical and emotional integrity, and the sum total of the individual's humanity, justifies including within the scope of human dignity those aspects of equality that assure the maintenance of these values.

As my colleague Justice Levi points out in his opinion in this case, "A person who finds out that his choices are not given the same weight as those of another person, when there is no rational reason to prefer the preferences of the other person, feels that no one pays attention to him except when his choices serve the interests of others, and feels injured by choices made without rational basis, without doubt that person feels a loss to his dignity." This analysis leads to rejection of the broad model. Human dignity as described by Justice Levi does not include all aspects of equality. "Even someone who holds that the right to equality is part of the right to human dignity does not necessarily hold that every impingement on equality is an infringement of human dignity."

Under the intermediate model, the way that the Deferment of Service Law impinges on equality constitutes a violation of human dignity. The law violates those rights and values that are the essence of human dignity, in the sense that this term recognizes the importance of individual autonomy, freedom of choice, and freedom of action for the person who is created free. The law violates the rights and values that must be protected in order to realize the human dignity of every person in the majority that is obligated to do military service. While most members of society are obligated to do full military service, which sometimes endangers that which is of greatest value to us, yeshiva students have the possibility of being released from this service. This situation violates the most basic concept of equality among members of society. It violates the status of a person who is obligated to perform military service as an equal among equals, based on the social group to which the person belongs, his religious beliefs, and his way of life. It constitutes a serious violation of equality as to basic societal rights and obligations. It leads to discrimination.... The obligation to serve in the military impinges on a whole list of basic freedoms of the person doing the service. This is true of obligatory service in any army and is especially true of service in the Israel Defense Forces. Such service is often connected to endangerment of the most basic right of an individual: the right to life and bodily integrity.... A person is ready to give his life to protect his homeland. He expects no return for this. He only expects that others will do the same.

Comment

In this case, the Court recognized that the right to human dignity in the Basic Law: Human Dignity and Freedom includes a right to equality, but not as to all matters. It includes the right to equality so far as the right is closely related to human dignity in practice. This seems to require a case by case analysis of equality claims to see whether the equal rights violation in each case is sufficiently severe in practice that it will be seen as closely connected with human dignity.

The unequal treatment of draftees under the Deferment of Service Law violated human dignity because it exposed them to a life threatening situation. Protection of life and bodily integrity, the Court held, is central to human dignity. The opinion leaves open the question of whether other types of infringements of equality are infringements of human dignity.

In a portion of the opinion not included here, the Court found that the Deferment of Service Law was not unconstitutional even though it did infringe on the basic right to human dignity of the draftees. Israeli law allows infringements on rights found in Basic Laws if the infringing law meets certain requirements. These requirements are explained later in this chapter. The Deferment of Service Law reduced the scope of deferments for yeshiva students from what it had been previously by providing incentives and opportunities for yeshiva students to serve for at least a shortened period of time in the armed services. The Court, recognizing that a law forcing all yeshiva students to do full military service would be hard, if not impossible, to implement, accepted the Knesset's position that it was best to move by degrees toward fuller military service and that this statute did as much as could be done at the present time. Under these circumstances, the statute met the requirements for a law that is allowed to infringe on a right protected by a Basic Law. Six years later, in HCJ 2698/07 *Ressler v. Knesset of Israel* (Feb. 21, 2012), the Supreme Court held that, in light of the failure of the same law to reach its goal, the law was unconstitutional because it violated the constitutional principle of proportionality (discussed later in this chapter).

In a case decided three days after *Movement for Quality Government*, the Court revisited the issue of equality as a basic right protected by the Basic Law.[15] The case dealt with family reunification where one spouse was an Israeli and the other was a Palestinian living in the territories that are held by Israel but are not within the area of the state. In general, Palestinians living in the territories who are not Israeli citizens are not allowed to live in Israel. An exception had been made for Palestinians married to Israelis; they had been allowed to live in Israel under the framework of family reunification. In reaction to terrorist attacks, the Knesset enacted, and then renewed, a temporary law that prohibited Palestinian men aged 14 to 35 and women aged 14 to 25 living in the territories from entering Israel for family reunification. The reason given was that a number of terrorist attacks had been planned or perpetrated by Palestinians from the territories living with their Israeli spouses in Israel. Most of the judges noted that the only Israelis affected by this law were Israeli Arabs, since they were the only Israelis that in fact married Palestinians from the territories. Therefore the law resulted in inequality between Israeli Arabs, who could not always have their foreign spouses join them, and Israeli Jews, who could. Six of the eleven justices on the case found that this inequality violated the right to human dignity in the Basic Law, but did not give a detailed analysis of why this is so. These six justices also found that the law violated a constitutional right to family life, a separate right they found to be included in the scope of human dignity. Two justices found that the law violated only the right to family life, but not the right to equality. Three found it did not violate a human right at all, noting that in most countries, the rights of foreign spouses to live in a country are statutory but not constitutional. Of the eight justices who found a violation of a constitutional right, only five found that the violation was not justified. The majority ruled that even if there was an infringement, it was justified by security considerations and the law was therefore valid.

3. Implicit Rights: Social Rights

Chief Justice Barak makes a statement in his opinion in *Movement for Quality Government* that the government has a "positive obligation" to protect those rights included in the Basic Law: Human Dignity and Freedom. The government's positive obligation does not arise in the case because the question is the constitutionality of a statute that violates the government's negative obligation not to infringe on human dignity. The question of the government's positive obligation usually does not arise when addressing individual rights. For example, as to freedom of expression, the government may not prevent a person from expressing a political opinion, but that does not mean the government has an obligation to provide a platform for expressing such opinions. The government's positive obligation is clearer when it comes to social rights. A social right is the right to have the government provide some goods or service, such as the right to health care, the right to education, the right to housing, and the right to be employed.

---

15. HCJ 7052/03 Adalah Legal Center for Arab Minority Rights in Israel v. Minister of Interior, (Feb. 14, 2006). The case is available in English at the English language website of the Supreme Court, at http://elyon1.court.gov.il/files_eng/03/520/070/a47/03070520.a47.htm.

In the following case, the Supreme Court had to determine whether a right to health care is included in the Basic Law: Human Dignity and Freedom.

Israeli Case

Luzon v. Government of Israel
HCJ 3071/05 (July 28, 2008)[16]

Chief Justice D. Beinisch:

[Under the National Health Insurance Law, 5754-1994, any resident of Israel can join one of the health funds. Health fund members receive for free, or at a heavily subsidized cost, a range of goods and services, including medications, in the health services basket. A professional committee meets periodically to decide what medications to include in the health services basket. The decision is based on a ranking of the medications based in part on their importance. The Petitioners suffered from various forms of cancer, and their doctors prescribed medications not in the basket. The Petitioners argued that failure to subsidize the cost of their medications violated their constitutional rights.]

The Constitutional Status of the Right to Health

The Petitioners asserted that the committee ranked the new medications and technologies in a manner that violated their constitutional right to health, thereby contravening the conditions of the reservations clause. The Petitioners conceded that the right to health is not explicitly prescribed in the basic legislation, but claimed that it derives from the right to life and bodily integrity as well as from the right to human dignity, both of which are anchored in Basic Law: Human Dignity and Liberty.

This petition is concerned with the right to health care, and more precisely with the right to receive publicly funded medical and medicinal treatment. Inarguably the right to medical treatment is not explicitly mentioned in the framework of the Basic Laws concerning human rights. As is known, the attempts to enact basic legislation that would confer explicit constitutional status on social rights, including the right to health and medical treatment, have thus far failed.... Taking this into consideration, the question of the degree to which the right to medical treatment enjoys constitutional status in our legal system is far from simple. This is especially the case in relation to the *affirmative* aspect of the right, which imposes upon the state a positive duty to act, the essence of which is responsibility for the public funding of health services in Israel.

The view has been expressed in our case-law that "a person without access to elementary medical treatment is a person whose human dignity has been violated." It has also been determined that "the social right to the provision of *basic* health services can be anchored in the right to bodily integrity under section 4 of the Basic Law."

It emerges from the case-law of this Court that the constitutional rights enumerated in Basic Law: Human Dignity and Liberty are likely to include various aspects from the areas of welfare and social security, including health care. However, our case law has yet to consider directly the question of which basic health services are included within the parameters of the constitutional rights enumerated in the Basic Law, and whether a constitutional right to health services that extends beyond the basic level required for human existence

---

16. This translation is based on that on the website of the Supreme Court, at http://elyon1.court.gov.il/files_eng/05/710/030/n12/05030710.n12.htm.

in society should be read into these constitutional rights. This dilemma is reflected in the pleadings of the parties in the case before us. The centrality of health to the maintenance of decent human existence, to the welfare of the individual, and to his ability to realize all other human rights is undisputed. Where medicinal treatment with any particular potential for saving, prolonging or improving the patient's quality of life is concerned, significant weight should be assigned to the value of the sanctity of life, the integrity of body and soul, and human dignity, all of which are central values with constitutional standing in our legal system. Regarding the receipt of publicly-funded medical treatment, the legislation of the State of Israel is characterized by a commitment to a public health system grounded in the principle of mutual responsibility and concern for the society's indigent, as indicated by the provisions of the National Health Insurance Law.

Yet recognition of a right to public health services in the present context means imposing a positive duty on the state, the main substance of which is responsibility for public funding of medical-medicinal treatment. Naturally the issue of the constitutional scope of that right involves general distributive questions that derive from the nature of the socio-economic regime governing a society and the scope of public resources at the state's disposal. Indeed, the human rights recognized in our system, which are generally referred to as *civil and political rights*, also impose upon the state positive duties of protecting the realization of a right, and not just negative duties of not violating the right. Quite often the state's duty to protect the realization of civil and political rights also includes a positive duty that involves the allocation of substantial resources. Even so, it seems that the right to publicly funded health services, like other rights connoted as *social-economic rights*, has a dominantly positive character that arouses greater concern for questions of policy on social resource distribution, in accordance with the determination of a national scale of priorities.

Since its earliest days, the accepted view of this Court has been that the Court should be wary of intervening in the formulation of overall economic policy and in the determination of national priorities; the general rule is that the executive and the legislative branches shoulder the public and national responsibility for the state economy. Bearing this in mind, and in the absence of an explicit anchoring of social rights in basic legislation, the question that arises is to what extent can judicial-interpretative tools be used to construe the rights enumerated in Basic Law: Human Dignity and Liberty as including a right with a correlative duty to provide public healthcare services on a larger scale than that of the minimum requirements for decent human existence in a society.

The right to health has indeed gained recognition in various international conventions, and it is included in the constitutions of a number of states around the world. Nevertheless the delineation of the internal scope of the right and the extent to which it is protected remain vague, and they are characterized by a cautious approach that considers the budgetary capabilities of each state and the principle of the progressive realization of the right. For example, in 1946 the Constitution of the World Health Organization (WHO) recognized the basic right to health, but the scope of this right is defined as "the highest *attainable* standard of health".... As for the Universal Declaration of Human Rights of 1948: this convention entrenches a number of social human rights, including the right to a decent standard of living which includes aspects of the right to health and to medical treatment. At the same time, the preamble to the declaration states that these rights are to be realized by "progressive measures."

The constitutions of many states, including Canada and the United States, do not confer explicit constitutional status upon the right to health. The constitutional law of these states protects only limited aspects of this right. In contrast, section 27 of the South African Constitution confers explicit constitutional status upon the right of access to medical treatment. However, the South African Constitution adds that the state must take *reasonable* legislative and other measures, *within its available resources*, to achieve *the progressive realization* of each of these rights.... It should be noted that the constitutions of India and Holland expressly entrench the right to promote public health, but this right is not enforceable by the judiciary and it is only a type of fundamental principle that is intended to guide the actions of the executive and the legislative authorities.

[Prior to the decision in the case, the medications requested by all but one of the Petitioners were added to the health basket. As a result, these petitions became moot. The remaining petition] is directed against the non-inclusion of Erbitux in the publicly-funded health services basket. Erbitux is an innovative medicine for the treatment of colon cancer.... There is no consensus regarding the effectiveness of this medication in the saving or even the prolonging of life; the research data from studies of this medication are still disputed, and the medication is expensive. I therefore lean towards the view that this particular medication, and other similarly experimental innovative medications, would not fall within the rubric of the *basic* health services required for minimal human existence in society. Indeed for patients suffering from life-threatening illnesses, any medication that offers some chance to save or at least to prolong their lives, even if only for a short time, is of critical, inestimable value. At the same time, from a broad social perspective and given the limitations of the public resources, I doubt whether the demand for public funding for these innovative medications is part of the hard kernel of constitutional rights enumerated in the Basic Law.

Furthermore, even according to an exegetical approach that extends the constitutional scope of the right to human dignity beyond the level of the basic minimum in the area of welfare and social security, it would appear that only in extreme and exceptional circumstances would the state be constitutionally obligated to fund a specific medication, one of many in respect of which applications are submitted for public funding.... Courts the world over refrain from ruling that the lack of public funding for a concrete medical treatment amounts to a violation of the patient's constitutional right. (For exceptional circumstances in which it was ruled that a violation of a constitutional right had been proved, *see and compare, Minister of Health v. Treatment Action Campaign* 2002 (10) BCLR 1033 (CC). In that case, the South African Supreme Court obligated the government to enable the distribution of medicinal treatment designed to prevent the transmission of the AIDS from mothers to their children, under circumstances in which the medicine was provided *free of charge* to the government by the manufacturer.) Considering all that is stated here, it would appear that in the Petitioners' case it has not been proven that a constitutional right has been violated.

Comment

The case also held that the Petitioner had no right under the Israeli health statutes to receive the requested drug.

Social rights are not usually included in the rubric of constitutional rights in the United States. Statutes create entitlement to certain rights to education, housing, and environmental protection, but so far, the US Constitution has not been interpreted as including rights of this sort. Some state constitutions include some such rights. As Justice Beinisch's opinion indicates, outside of the United States, there is much more extensive discussion of constitutional social rights. As this opinion strongly suggestions, some social rights are likely to be included in the Israeli Basic Laws through judicial interpretation, but the extent will be limited.

4. Summary

It is now clear that rights that were recognized by case law prior to the enactment of the two Basic Laws on individual rights in 1992 persist in one of three forms. Some are incorporated explicitly into the Basic Laws. Courts have found that others are implicitly included in one of the Basic Laws. Still others are not included in the Basic Laws either explicitly or implicitly but continue to exist by virtue of their judicial recognition. In the future, case law may decide that they are included in the Basic Laws. While it could be argued that the intent of the Knesset in enacting the Basic Laws was to define what rights exist and to exclude others, the courts have rejected this position. Chief Justice Barak wrote, in regard to a right to a suitable degree of environmental quality, "I agree that such rights as were recognized in the past, or may be recognized in the future, exist. We should not conclude from the fact that some rights were anchored in the Basic Law: Human Dignity and Freedom a negative implication as to the existence of legal rights outside of the Basic Law." HCJ 4128/02 *Israel Union for Environmental Defense v. Prime Minister of Israel* 58(3) PD 503 [2004].

Rights not included in the Basic Laws remain important. Courts try to interpret statutes and decisions of administrative agencies in a way that does not infringe on either included or non-included rights. As is discussed in the next chapter, courts may also hold administrative decisions invalid for failure to protect either included or non-included rights. The main functional difference between rights included in the Basic Laws and those founded only on case law is that courts will sometimes hold a statute invalid for infringing on an included right, but not for infringing on a non-included right.

5. Who Must Honor Basic Rights?

Some of the rights under Israel's Basic Laws have been held to limit private, as well as public, action that infringes on those rights. The law in this area is still developing and it is not yet clear how extensive the application of rights against private action will be. In contrast, constitutional rights under the US Constitution are generally valid only against government action. For example, the First Amendment provides, "Congress shall make no law respecting an establishment of religion, or prohibiting the free exercise thereof; or abridging the freedom of speech, or of the press; or the right of the people peaceably to assemble, and to petition the government for a redress of grievances." Through the doctrine of incorporation under the due process clause of the Fourteenth Amendment, states also may not interfere with some federal constitutional rights. In addition, some of the post-Civil War amendments directly limit what states may do. But the usual American concept of rights is that they do not stand against purely private actions.

F. Limitations on Basic Rights

Recall that the rights enunciated in Basic Law: Human Dignity and Freedom and Basic Law: Freedom of Occupation are phrased in absolute terms. It is not possible that rights are in fact so absolute. Society must sometimes limit a person's freedom (consider incarceration for a crime), a person's rights regarding property and freedom of occupation (consider environmental regulations dictating how a factory may be operated), etc. Under Israeli law, this problem is handled by the limitation clauses, found in section 8 of the Basic Law: Human Dignity and Freedom and section 4 of the Basic Law: Freedom of Occupation. The limitation clauses provide that a regular law may infringe on a protected basic right if the infringing law meets the requirements of the limitation clause. These requirements are substantive. They relate not to the way the infringing law was enacted, but rather to the content of the infringing law. We return to Chief Justice Barak's opinion in *Migdal* to read his interpretation of the limitation clauses, an interpretation that has been, as we shall see from later cases, accepted as definitive.

This portion of Chief Justice Barak's opinion not only interprets the substantive requirements of the limitation clause, but also determines that courts will perform judicial review of statutes to determine whether they comply with those requirements. A statute that infringes on a protected basic right but complies with the limitation clause is constitutional. One that infringes on a protected basic right but does not comply is not. The courts determine whether the infringing statute complies with the limitation clause.

Israeli Case

United Mizrahi Bank v. Migdal Communal Village
CA 6821/93, 49(4) PD 221 [1995][17]

Chief Justice A. Barak:

The Limitation Clause

a) The Importance of the Clause and the Relativity of the Human Right

The limitation clause (section 8) of the Basic Law: Human Dignity and Liberty is a key ingredient in the protection of human rights. It delineates the limits of the right and the limitations upon the legislature. The role of the limitation is two-fold. It protects human rights and licenses their infringement, at one and the same time. It expresses the notion of the relativity of human rights. It reflects the basic outlook that human rights exist in a social context that maintains them. It mirrors the underlying view that human rights do not view the individual as an island, but as part of a society with national goals. It is the product of the recognition that while basic human rights must be realized, the national framework must be protected as well. It is intended to permit infringement of human rights in order to maintain the social framework that itself protects human rights.... The limitation clause provides the foundation for the constitutional balance between private and public, individual and community. It reflects the viewpoint that alongside human rights there are human obligations; that the normative world is not only one of rights

---

17. This translation is based on that on the website of the Supreme Court, at http://elyon1.court.gov.il/files_eng/93/210/068/z01/93068210.z01.htm.

but also of obligations; that alongside each right of a human being stands his duty to the community.

b) The Elements of the Limitation Clause

The limitation clause provides four cumulative tests that determine the constitutionality of a law that violates a constitutional human right. The four tests are as follows:

    (a) the infringement is made by law or in accordance with law and by means of an express authorization;

    (b) the infringing law must be consistent with the values of the State of Israel;

    (c) the infringing law must be intended for a proper purpose;

    (d) the law may infringe the human right to an extent no greater than is required.

In the future, the Supreme Court will be required to define each of these tests. Thus, for example, the requirement [of the first test] that the violation be by law or according to law reflects the principle of legality.... The second test refers to the values of Israel as a Jewish state (in the context of both Jewish tradition and Zionism) and as a democratic state. Indeed, we are different from other nations. We are not only a democratic state but also a Jewish state. The Basic Law is intended to "establish in a Basic Law the values of the State of Israel as a Jewish and democratic state" (section 1A). One of the important innovations of the Basic Law is its provision that "the purpose of the Basic Law is to protect human dignity and liberty in order to establish in a Basic Law the values of the State of Israel as a Jewish and democratic state" (section 1). Those values were thereby given constitutional supra-legislative status. The meaning of the values of the state as a Jewish and democratic state, and a solution to the clash between those values, will certainly occupy us greatly in the future.

"A Proper Purpose"

The third element of the limitation clause requires that the purpose be fitting. This element, too, raises significant difficulties, which we may reserve for future consideration. In essence, a purpose is fitting if it serves an important social objective regarding human rights. Thus, legislation intended to protect human rights is certainly intended for a proper purpose. Legislation intended to serve general social goals, such as welfare policies or protection of the public interest is fitting as well. In American constitutional law, distinctions are drawn among the various human rights in determining whether a purpose is worthy. The courts there have created different levels of constitutional scrutiny. Thus, for example, when the injury is to freedom of movement, freedom of expression or racial equality, the highest level of scrutiny applies. In such cases, a purpose will be deemed fitting if it is intended to fulfill a compelling state interest or a pressing public necessity or a substantial state interest. When the harm is gender or age-based discrimination, an intermediate level of scrutiny applies. In such cases the purpose will be deemed fitting if it serves an important governmental objective. The third and lowest level of scrutiny applies when the injury is to economic rights. Here the true test is whether the objective is reasonable.

In contrast to the three levels of American law, Canada has developed a unified test. The purpose of the law is fitting if it is directed towards social needs of fundamental importance. It is premature to determine what the Israeli rule will be as to the limitation clause and whether our test should comprise a single level (as in Canada) or multiple levels (as in the United States). It seems to me that for the purposes of the matter before us, it is sufficient to determine that the purpose is fitting if it is intended to fulfill important social goals for the establishment of a social framework that recognizes the constitutional importance of human rights and the need to protect them.

"To an Extent no Greater than is Required"

The final element of the limitation clause is that the injury to the human right must be to an extent no greater than is required. If the previous factor examines the motives of the infringing legislation, this factor examines the means chosen by the legislature. This is a proportionality test. This test examines whether the means chosen by the legislature are appropriate for achieving its objectives (the proper purpose).

Let us assume a law that infringes on a protected human right. Let us further assume that the law accords with the values of the State of Israel and is intended for a proper purpose. How must we decide whether the law infringes human rights "to an extent no greater than is required?" When does a law that infringes a constitutional human right achieve the required proportionality? In the law of other countries, an attempt has been made to concretize the principle of proportionality. It seems to me that we should learn from this attempt, which is common to Canada, Germany, the European Community and the European Court for Human Rights in Strasbourg, for the principle of proportionality does not reflect a unique social history or particular constitutional position. Rather it is a general analytical position according to which we may examine a law infringing constitutional human rights.

Comparative law indicates that the examination of the extent necessary is divided into three sub-tests. The first sub-test determines that a legislative means that infringes a constitutional human right is fitting if it is appropriate to achieving the purpose. This is the fitness test ... or the rational relationship test. There must be a suitable connection between the goal and the means. The means must be tailored to achieve the objective. The means must lead, in a rational manner, to fulfillment of the goal. The second sub-test establishes that the legislative means that infringe the constitutional human right are fitting only if the goal cannot be achieved by other means that would result in a lesser injury to the human right. This is the middle test of minimal harm. It is sometimes described as the principle of need. The third sub-test requires a balancing of the public good against the private harm arising from the means. There must therefore be a suitable relationship between the means and the purpose (proportionality in the strict sense).

The limitation clause imposes upon the Court a difficult task. It requires sensitivity to the necessity of balancing between the rights of the individual and the public interest.... The Court must determine the constitutionality of the law, not its wisdom. The question is not whether the law is good, efficient, or just. The question is whether the law is constitutional.

Comment

The most significant part of this interpretation of the limitation clause is the last portion. The limitation clause provides that any infringement of a basic right be "to an extent no greater than is required." The opinion interprets this to mean that a court should apply the proportionality test, familiar in the constitutional law of some other countries, as described in the opinion. To determine whether an infringement is proportional, the Court applies a test with three sub-parts. The Court determines first whether the infringing law is appropriate to achieving its purpose. In other words, the Court must first determine what purpose the Knesset had in enacting the law and then determine whether the law is designed to achieve this purpose. Determining the legislative purpose may be difficult. Legislative history in Israel is much more abbreviated than that in the United States. Furthermore different parties may have different reasons for voting for proposed legislation, and with multiple parties represented in the Knesset, the law might not have a single purpose. Once the Court identifies what it sees as the purpose of the law, the Court must decide whether the legislation is appropriate to achieving its purpose. In applying this part of the test, the Court must review the legislative decision that the mechanism set out in the law will achieve the purpose of the law.

In applying the second part of the proportionality test, the Court determines whether the infringing legislation causes the minimal amount of harm to the right infringed. A law could pass the first test, in that it could be well designed to achieve its purpose, but it could infringe on the basic right more than is necessary to achieve that purpose. If the Court sees another possible way to get to the purpose with less infringement on the right, then the law will be invalid for failing the second part of the proportionality test.

The third part of the test is a balancing test. The Court balances the harm the law causes to the individual, in the sense of the infringement of rights, against the public good the law will accomplish. This requires the Court not only to define the weight of the private harm, but also to identify the value of the public good. If the relationship between harm and benefit is not suitable, the law is invalid.

We see, then, that the Basic Laws on individual rights, as interpreted in the *Migdal* case, put a tremendous amount of power in the hands of the courts. Rights are defined very broadly and amorphously in the Basic Laws, and the courts determine what specific rights are included in those definitions. The rights are also defined in absolute terms, so that they are easily infringed. Infringement is allowed only if it meets the limitation clause. The courts also apply the proportionality test, which is the third part of the limitation clause. In applying the proportionality test the courts must determine the legislative purpose, decide whether the law will work, decide if a better law was possible, and determine whether the social good sought by the law justifies the individual harm. All these decisions give the courts broad discretion and therefore broad power. This endowment of the courts with such power can be regarded as a second component of the constitutional revolution found in the Basic Laws on individual rights.

The actual holding of the *Migdal* case is much less dramatic than its constitutional law analysis. All nine justices agreed that, whatever the status of Basic Law: Human Dignity and Freedom, the Gal Law met the requirements of the limitation clause and was valid. It would seem then that the long opinions in the case were merely dicta, except that they were afterwards accepted as laying the foundation for the courts examining the constitutionality of statutes. Later decisions applied the reasoning of Chief Justice Barak's opinion to determine the constitutionality of statutes, in some cases finding the statutes invalid.

G. Cases Applying Law on Constitutional Rights

To show how the law of *Migdal* works in practice, two cases applying that law are presented here. In the first case, the Supreme Court examined a claim that a statute enacted by the Knesset infringed on rights protected by the Basic Law: Human Dignity and Freedom. The Court found that there was such an infringement, so it had to determine whether the statute met the requirements of the limitation clause.

Israeli Case

Adalah Legal Centre for Arab Minority Rights in Israel v. Minister of Defense
HCJ 8276/05) (Dec. 12, 2006)[18]

[Under the Civil Torts Law (State Liability), 5712-1952, the State of Israel has the same tort liability as does any incorporated body, absent an express exception under the statute. One exception is for torts resulting from *combatant activities* of the Israel Defense Forces (IDF). The Israeli security forces in the territories (the West Bank and, prior to the summer of 2005, Gaza) engage in policing activities designed to prevent combat or terrorism, such as maintenance of roadblocks and searches. The Supreme Court ruled, in an earlier case, that these are not counted as combatant activities. The Knesset re-acted to that ruling by enacting Amendment 7 to the law, broadening state tort immu-nity to include any activity by the security forces in a conflict zone. Parts of the territories are considered conflict zones; other parts are not. The relevant portion of the amend-ment provided:

> 5C. Claims in a Conflict Zone
>
> (a) Notwithstanding what is stated in any law, the state is not liable in torts for damage that is caused in a conflict zone as a result of an act done by the secu-rity forces [with several listed exceptions].]

Chief Justice Emeritus A. Barak:

[The issue is] whether [section 5C of] Amendment 7 unlawfully violates the Basic Law: Human Dignity and Liberty. This examination, according to our accepted practice, is done in … stages. The *first* stage examines whether the law … violates a human right that is enshrined and protected in a Basic Law. If the answer is no, the constitutional scrutiny ends. If the answer is yes, the constitutional scrutiny passes to the *second* stage. In this stage, we consider the question whether the law containing the violation, in whole or in part, satisfies the requirements of the limitation clause. Indeed, our basic constitu-tional outlook is that not every violation of a constitutional human right is an unlawful violation. We recognize lawful violations of constitutional human rights. These are those violations that satisfy the conditions of the limitation clause. If the violation of the con-stitutional human right is lawful, the constitutional scrutiny ends. If the violation does not satisfy one of the conditions of the limitation clause, the violation is unlawful.

First Stage: The Violation of the Constitutional Right

[The opinion considered whether the Basic Law applied, because the statute purported to govern activities that take place outside of the borders of the State of Israel.] The rights of the residents of the territories which are violated by Amendment 7 are rights that are given to them in Israel. They are rights under Israeli private international law, according to which, when the appropriate circumstances occur, it is possible to sue in Israel, under the Israeli law of torts, even for a tort that was committed outside Israel.

Has a Right Enshrined in the Basic Law: Human Dignity and Liberty Been Violated?

Amendment 7 provides that the state is not liable in torts when the conditions set out therein are satisfied. Does this denial of liability for torts violate rights that are enshrined

---

18. This translation is based on that on the website of the Supreme Court, at http://elyon1.court.gov.il/files_eng/05/760/082/a13/05082760.a13.htm.

in the Basic Law: Human Dignity and Liberty? The answer is yes. There are two main reasons for this. *First*, the right in torts that is given to the injured party (or to his heirs or dependants) and that was denied by Amendment 7 is a part of the injured party's constitutional right to property. Indeed, the word "property" in section 3 of the Basic Law: Human Dignity and Liberty—"A person's property shall not be harmed"—means a person's property rights.... The right of an injured party under the law of torts is a part of his property rights and therefore part of his "property." ... *Second*, liability in torts protects several rights of the injured party, such as the right to life, liberty, dignity, and privacy.

Second Stage: Is the Violation of the Constitutional Rights Lawful?

(1) The Limitation Clause

The second stage of the constitutional scrutiny considers the limitation clause in the Basic Law: Human Dignity and Liberty, which states:

> 8. Violation of rights
>
> The rights under this Basic Law may only be violated by a law that befits the values of the State of Israel, is intended for a proper purpose, and to an extent that is not excessive, or in accordance with a law as aforesaid by virtue of an express authorization therein.

This provision plays a central role in our constitutional system. It has two aspects. It protects the human rights that are set out in the Basic Law and also determines the conditions for violating the basic right. The limitation clause is based on the outlook that in addition to human rights there are also human obligations; that the human being is a part of society; that the interests of society may justify a violation of human rights; that human rights are not absolute, but relative. The limitation clause reflects the approach that human rights may be restricted, but there are limits to such restrictions.

Is the purpose underlying the provisions of section 5C of Amendment 7 a proper purpose? In my opinion, the answer to this question is yes. Indeed the ordinary law of torts was not designed to contend with tortious acts that are caused during the combatant activities of the security forces outside Israel in an armed conflict. Excluding liability in torts in situations of combatant activity is also accepted in other legal systems. An arrangement whose purpose is to adapt the law of torts to the special circumstances that prevail during the combatant activity of the security forces is an arrangement that is intended for a proper purpose.

Is section 5C of Amendment 7 proportionate? The *first* sub-test, which concerns a rational connection between the proper purpose and the provisions of section 5C, is satisfied. The exclusion of liability in torts provided by section 5C of Amendment 7 removes the damage caused by the security forces in a conflict zone from the scope of the ordinary law of torts. This realizes the proper purpose that Amendment 7 sought to achieve.

Does section 5C of Amendment 7 satisfy the *second* sub-test of proportionality? According to this test, the statute should adopt the measure that is least harmful. Does section 5C satisfy this constitutional requirement? My answer is that it does not. In order to realize the purpose underlying section 5C of Amendment 7, it is sufficient to provide legal arrangements that the state is exempt from liability for combat activities. The ordinary law of torts is not suited to addressing liability for tortious acts in the course of combat. Arrangements of this kind were provided in section 5 of the original Torts Law, which determined that the state is not liable in torts for an act done in the course of the combatant activity of the Israel Defense Forces.... Amendment 7 ... excludes liability in torts for all damage that is caused in a conflict zone by the security forces, even as a result of acts that were not done in the course of the combatant activity of the security forces. This amplification of the state's exemption from liability is unconstitutional. It does not adopt the least harmful measure that achieves an exemption from liability for combatant activities. It releases the state from liability for tortious acts that are in no way related to combatant activities, no matter how broadly the term is defined. Nothing in the ordinary activities of law enforcement that are carried out by the security forces in a territory controlled by them justifies an exclusion from the ordinary law of torts. This is certainly the case when the tortious act is totally unrelated to security activity. Only combat activities justify, as the purpose of Amendment 7 indicates, an exclusion of the arrangements in the ordinary law of torts. Excluding tortious acts in which the security forces are involved but which have no combatant aspect does not realize the proper purpose of adapting the law of torts to combat situations. It seeks to realize an improper purpose of exempting the state from all liability for torts in conflict zones.

Exempting the state from liability under section 5C does not adapt the law of torts to the state of war.

Indeed, the proportionate approach is to examine each incident on a case by case basis. This examination should consider whether the case falls within the scope of combatant activity, however this is defined. It is possible to extend this definition, but this case-by-case examination should not be replaced by a sweeping exemption from liability.... [The exceptions provided in section 5C are not sufficient to save the provision from being disproportionate.]

Does section 5C of Amendment 7 satisfy the *third* sub-test of proportionality, the test of proportionality in the narrow sense? Is the benefit to the public interest from excluding the state's liability for the damage caused in a conflict zone commensurate with the loss caused to individuals who are injured as a result of tortious acts of the security forces? ... The question that we should ask ourselves is the following: Is the benefit to the public interest that is afforded by excluding the state's liability for a tort that was not caused by combatant activities commensurate with the damage that is caused to someone who is injured as a result of this tort?

The immunity from liability for combatant activities in its broad sense is sufficient in order to adapt the law of torts to a situation of war and in order to release the state from the burden of liability for claims arising from war damage. It would appear that the main benefit does not lie in realizing these purposes, but in releasing the state from conducting legal proceedings in order to determine the question of whether there were combatant activities. Indeed giving the state a sweeping immunity makes it unnecessary to conduct many proceedings in which the state is required to prove that the damage for which it is being sued was caused by combatant activities. But this benefit to the public interest—a benefit that lies mainly in a savings of administrative resources—is disproportionate in comparison to the damage to the various individuals, which was caused by non-combatant activities. This damage often involves great suffering. Injured parties suffer major injuries; they become seriously disabled; their ability to earn a livelihood is significantly impaired. All of these—and of course the loss of life—are far greater than the limited benefit that arises from releasing the state from liability and from the need to defend its position in court, both when the damage is caused by combatant activities and when it is caused by non-combatant activities.

[All nine justices agreed to the constitutional analysis.]

Comment

The Court easily found that the right to a remedy in tort was a protected basic right. The opinion contains a more detailed discussion of how the limitation clause applies to the case. The opinion did not directly consider the first two parts of the clause, as identified in the *Migdal* case. The first part is whether "the infringement is made by law or in accordance with law and by means of an express authorization." Section 5C of Amendment 7 clearly met this requirement because it was in a statute. The second part is whether the infringing law is "consistent with the values of the State of Israel." The opinion reviewed the events of the first and second intifadas, or Palestinian uprisings, and the loss of life during those periods. It implicitly recognized that it was important to the state to control actions, as well as all terrorist activity, and that it needed its security forces to be free from tort liability for harm caused by combat activity.

Questions

8. In *Adalah Legal Centre*, the Court found that section 5C failed to meet either the least harmful means or the balance of interest (commensurate harm) portions of the proportionality test. The Court ruled that a case-by-case analysis of tort claims would cause less harm to tort claimants' basic rights, so the statute did not adopt the least harmful means of achieving its purpose. If the Knesset now amends the statute to require a case-by-case analysis of tort claims, would the amended statute be constitutional?

9. Notice how easily the Court found that the Basic Law: Human Dignity and Freedom applied to actions of the Israeli security forces outside of Israel. Is the analysis of the extraterritorial application of the Basic Law is complete?

In the following case, the Court found a violation of only the third sub-part of the proportionality test:

Israeli Case

Academic Center of Law and Business, Human Rights Division v. Minister of Finance

HCJ 2605/05 (Nov. 19, 2009)[19]

[The Prisons Ordinance Amendment Law (no. 28), 5764-2004 (Amendment 28) provided that the state would establish a prison to be operated by a private corporation rather than by the state. Petitioners claim the statute is unconstitutional.]

Chief Justice D. Beinisch:

We have reached the conclusion that the actual transfer of powers to manage a prison from the state, which acts on behalf of the public, to a private concessionaire that is a profit-making enterprise, causes a serious and grave violation of the inmates' basic human rights to personal liberty and human dignity—a violation that should, of course, be ex-

---

19. This translation is based on that on the website of the Supreme Court, at http://elyon1.court.gov.il/files_eng/05/050/026/n39/05026050.n39.htm.

amined from the viewpoint of the limitation clause. Let us now turn to clarify our reasons for this conclusion.

The Violation Caused By Amendment 28 to the Constitutional Right to Personal Liberty

Sending someone to prison—whether it is managed privately or by the state—first and foremost violates the constitutional right to personal liberty. This right is set out in section 5 of the Basic Law: Human Dignity and Liberty.

When the power to deny the liberty of the individual is given to a private corporation, the legitimacy of the sanction of imprisonment is undermined, since the sanction is enforced by a party that is motivated first and foremost by economic considerations—considerations that are irrelevant to the realization of the purposes of the sentence, which are public purposes.

When we examine the extent of the violation of the right to personal liberty inherent in placing a person under lock and key, we should take into account not merely that person's actual loss of personal liberty for a certain period but also the manner in which he is deprived of liberty.

An examination of the provisions of Amendment 28 shows that the private concessionaire was given wide-ranging powers with regard to the day-to-day management of the prison, including the enforcement of order and discipline therein.

The conclusion that we have reached is that Amendment 28 causes an additional independent violation of the constitutional right to personal liberty beyond the violation that arises from the imprisonment itself. It can therefore be said that our position is that the scope of the violation of a prison inmate's constitutional right to personal liberty, when the entity responsible for his imprisonment is a private corporation motivated by economic considerations of profit and loss, is inherently greater than the violation of the same right of an inmate when the entity responsible for his imprisonment is a government authority that is not motivated by those considerations, even if the term of imprisonment that these two inmates serve is identical and even if the violation of the human rights that actually takes place behind the walls of each of the two prisons where they serve their sentences is identical.

Amendment 28 Violates the Constitutional Right to Human Dignity

In addition to the violation of the right to personal liberty, Amendment 28 also violates the constitutional right to human dignity that is enshrined in section 2 of the Basic Law: Human Dignity and Freedom.

It is hard to deny that imprisoning someone under lock and key and imposing upon him the rules of conduct in the prison violates his human dignity. This violation is caused whether that person is imprisoned in a public prison or in a privately managed prison. Therefore the question that we need to decide in this case is whether imprisoning a person in a privately managed prison causes a greater violation of his human dignity than imprisoning him in a public prison.

Imprisoning persons in a privately managed prison leads to a situation in which the clearly public purposes of the imprisonment are blurred and diluted by irrelevant considerations that arise from a private economic purpose, namely the desire of the private corporation operating the prison to make a financial profit. There is therefore an inherent and natural concern that imprisoning inmates in a privately managed prison that is run with a private economic purpose *de facto* turns the prisoners into a means whereby the corporation that manages and operates the prison makes a financial profit. It should be noted that the very existence of a prison that operates on a profit-making basis reflects a lack of respect for the status of the inmates as human beings, and this violation of the human dignity of the inmates does not depend on the extent of the violation of human rights that actually occurs behind the prison walls.

Does Amendment 28 Satisfy the Limitation Clause Tests?

The first condition provided in the limitation clause [is] the demand that the violation of the protected constitutional right should be made by a law—no one disputes that Amendment 28 satisfies this condition.

The second condition provided in the limitation clause, according to which the law that violates the constitutional right should befit the values of the State of Israel, does not give rise to any real difficulty in our case.... The Petitioners' claims in the petition before us did not focus on the question of whether this condition is satisfied, and it is indeed hard to see how this condition may be violated by anything other than unusual and exceptional circumstances; it is therefore possible to assume that Amendment 28 satisfies the condition of befitting the values of the State of Israel.

The third condition provided in the limitation clause is that the violation of the constitutional right should be done for a proper purpose.... According to the State, the purpose of Amendment 28 is to bring about an improvement of inmates' prison conditions at a reduced budgetary cost. This purpose of improving the prison conditions of inmates in Israel—even if it is combined with an economic purpose—is a proper purpose. It should be noted that the Petitioners' claim with regard to the requirement of the proper purpose is that the purpose of economic efficiency does not in itself constitute a proper purpose that justifies a violation of constitutional rights. This claim of the Petitioners is too sweeping, since there are situations in which an economic purpose will be considered a proper purpose that justifies a violation of human rights, depending on the type of purpose, its importance to the public interest, and the extent of the violation of the constitutional right.

The fourth condition provided in the limitation clause is that the infringement of the protected constitutional right shall not be excessive. We focus our discussion on this requirement. This condition addresses the proportionality of the violation of the constitutional right. In other words, even if the violation of the constitutional right is effected by a law that befits the values of the State of Israel and that is intended for a proper purpose, the law may still be found to be unconstitutional if its violation of the constitutional right is disproportionate. The requirement of proportionality therefore examines the means chosen by the legislature to realize the (proper) purpose of the legislation.

The case law of this Court has recognized three sub-tests that are used to examine the proportionality of the violation of a protected constitutional right by an act of legislation.

With regard to the first sub-test of proportionality—whether the legislative measure chosen is consistent with the legislative purpose—the dispute between the parties focuses on the question of whether Amendment 28 is expected to realize the economic aspect of its purpose.... At this stage of the privatization planning process, the state cannot prove that better conditions for the inmates will indeed be achieved with the expected budgetary savings, nor are we able to determine that Amendment 28 is not *prima facie* capable of realizing the purposes of an economic saving and improving the prisons conditions of inmates that it was designed to achieve. Therefore we are prepared to assume for the sake of argument that the rational connection regarding the purpose of Amendment 28 does exist.

The second test of proportionality is, as we have said, the least harmful measure test, which requires that of all the possible measures for realizing the purpose of the legislation, the measure that violates the protected constitutional right to the smallest extent should be chosen. With regard to this sub-test, the Petitioners argued that it is possible to achieve the economic purpose underlying Amendment 28 with measures that violate human rights to a lesser degree.

We are unable to determine in what less harmful way it is possible to achieve the combined purpose of improving prison conditions while making a budgetary saving, which according to the state, underlies the purpose of Amendment 28, and since this issue naturally requires proof that we do not have before us, the conclusion that follows is that Amendment 28 also satisfies the second sub-test of proportionality.

The third sub-test of proportionality is the test of proportionality in the narrow sense. This test is essentially an ethical test in which we are required to examine whether the public benefit that arises from the legislation whose constitutionality is under discussion is commensurate with the damage to the constitutional right caused by that act of legislation.

In the case before us, we are required, within the context of the test of proportionality in the narrow sense, to examine the relationship between the public benefit that arises from Amendment 28 and the degree to which Amendment 28 to the infringes on the constitutional rights to personal liberty and human dignity of inmates in the privately managed prison.

We have already discussed ... the special significances of the violation of liberty as a result of privatization of the prison. *Inter alia*, we clarified that the violation of the rights to liberty and dignity deriving from introducing a private prison system is not reflected in the actual power of imprisonment, which is invasive in itself, since the actual violation of the personal liberty also occurs when the imprisonment takes place in a state managed prison. In the case of a privately managed prison, the violation lies in the identity and character of the body to which powers are given to violate liberties in the format provided in Amendment 28 of the Prisons Ordinance.

We mentioned the democratic legitimacy of the use of force by the state in order to restrict the liberty of individuals and to deny various rights that they have, when this violation is carried out by the organs of the state and for the purposes of protecting the public interest. By contrast, as we have already indicated, when the power to deny the liberty of the individual is given to a private corporation, the legitimacy of the sanction of imprisonment is undermined and the extent of the violation of liberty is magnified.... Imprisonment that is based on a private economic purpose turns the inmates, simply by imprisoning them in a private prison, into a means whereby the concessionaire or the operator of the prison can make a profit; thereby, not only is the liberty of the inmate violated, but also his human dignity.

Now that we have addressed the violation of human rights that will be caused by Amendment 28, we need to examine, within the framework of the third sub-test of proportionality, what lies on the other pan of the scales, namely the public benefit that Amendment 28 is intended to advance. The state argued that this benefit is a two-fold benefit—achieving a significant financial saving, which according to the state is expected ... to reach the amount of NIS 290–350 million, while improving prison conditions for the inmates. In other words, it can be said that the state, in enacting Amendment 28, was aware of the need to contend with the serious overcrowding that exists in Israeli prisons.... The state had to choose the means it should adopt in order to contend with this crisis, and in these circumstances, the state chose a measure that in its opinion is the most economically viable. The purpose underlying the enactment of Amendment 28 and the special arrangements provided in it was, therefore, an economic purpose. In our opinion, this is the main public purpose that Amendment

28 sought to achieve and it is the *raison d'être* that underlies it; had the economic savings not been the main consideration taken into account by the legislature, there would have been no need to enact Amendment 28, and it would have been possible to contend with the problem of overcrowding in the prisons by building additional state managed prisons or by improving the existing prisons, in accordance with the normative framework that existed prior to the enactment of Amendment 28. We are prepared for the purposes of our deliberations to assume that the economic benefit underlying Amendment 28 will indeed be realized.

Different countries may have different approaches to the question of the scope of state responsibility in various fields. They may also have different approaches to determining the relationship between activities managed by the public sector and those carried out by the private sector. These different approaches are determined, *inter alia*, by political and economic ideologies, the special history of each country, the structure of the political system and the government, and various social arrangements. These differences between the various countries are expressed in the content of the constitutional arrangements laid down in each country. The role of this Court, which is required to interpret and give content to the various constitutional arrangements is not, of course, to decide between various economic and political ideologies; notwithstanding, the Court is required to reflect the values enshrined in the social consensus and in the ethical principles that are common to the members of society, to identify the basic principles that make society a democratic society and identify what is fundamental and ethical, while rejecting what is transient and fleeting.

As to whether Amendment 28 satisfies the test of proportionality in the narrow sense, we have reached the conclusion that the relationship between the intended social benefit of achieving an improvement in prison conditions while making a maximum financial saving by using a private concessionaire ... and the degree of the violation of human rights caused by the provisions of Amendment 28 is a disproportionate one. The violation of the inmates' human rights that is caused by establishing a privately managed prison in which the private concessionaire's employees are given extensive powers to use force, which is in essence a sovereign power, is not a violation that is limited to a single issue or an isolated incident. Amendment 28 results in the establishment of an organizational structure whose very existence seriously violates the personal liberty of the inmates of the privately managed prison, to an extent that exceeds what is required by imprisonment itself, and the human dignity of those inmates in the basic and fundamental sense of this concept. This violation is an ongoing violation that occurs continuously for as long as an inmate is confined within a prison where he is subject to the authority of the employees of a private concessionaire. As we have said, this violation is exacerbated by the invasive character of the powers given to the private concessionaire.... In other words, in view of the great social importance of the principles underlying the granting of power to imprison offenders and the invasive powers that derive from it solely to the state, in comparison to the result achieved by realizing the goal of improving prison conditions while making as large a financial saving as possible for the state, the *additional* violation of the constitutional rights to personal liberty and human dignity deriving from granting the powers described to a private profit-making corporation is disproportionate to the *additional* public benefit that will allegedly be achieved by Amendment 28.

We are led to the conclusion that the violation of the constitutional rights to personal liberty and human dignity caused by Amendment 28 is a disproportionate one that does not satisfy the conditions of the limitation clause. Amendment 28 is therefore unconstitutional.

Comment

This opinion finds that economic factors cannot outweigh the added infringement on liberty and human dignity caused by privatization of prisons. Notice that the Court is careful to examine only the marginal adverse impact on human rights caused by privatization; it excludes the impact of any incarceration.

Questions

10. The case raises the claim that incarceration in a private prison is unconstitutional, but not the claim that incarceration in a public prison is unconstitutional. Is incarceration in a public prison constitutional?

11. Are the decisions in *Luzon* and in *Academic Center of Law and Business* consistent in the way they treat economic considerations and the balancing of various social goods?

12. Chief Justice Beinisch, in applying the third sub-part of the proportionality test, says it is essentially an ethical test. According to the opinion, who determines the ethical values of the state? Who else might be charged with making this determination? Who is best able to make it?

After the legal analysis presented in the previous excerpt, Justice Beinisch examined the law of other countries on privatization of prisons. Here is what she wrote about the United States:

Israeli Case

Academic Center of Law and Business, Human Rights Division v. Minister of Finance
HCJ 2605/05 (Nov. 19, 2009)[20]

Chief Justice D. Beinisch:

The possibility of entering into a contract with private enterprises in order to manage and operate prisons is regulated in legislation, *inter alia*, in the United States (both at the federal level and at state level) and Britain. The various acts of legislation that regulate the privatization of prisons differ from one another, *inter alia*, in the scope of the powers given to the concessionaire in fields that have a potentially significant effect on the human rights of the inmates. In the United States, it is possible to give the private concessionaire the responsibility for all aspects involved in managing and operating the prison, including the enforcement of discipline in the prison and the use of force against inmates, although some states take a more limited approach. Some states have through legislation set limitations on to power of private prison operators to determine the dates of the inmates' release, set disciplinary rules, define disciplinary offences, and decide which inmates can obtain various benefits. Different states also exercise differing degrees of public supervision over the activities of private prison operators. *See* W.L. Ratliff, *The Due Process Failure of America's Prison Privatization Statutes*, 21 Seton Hall Legis. J. 371 (1997).

---

20. This translation is based on that on the website of the Supreme Court, at http://elyon1.court.gov.il/files_eng/05/050/026/n39/05026050.n39.htm.

It would appear that the courts in the United States have not hitherto held that any of the various legislative arrangements in force in the United States regarding the privatization of prisons are unconstitutional. Indeed it would appear that the premise of the courts in the United States when considering matters concerning the privatized prisons is that the privatization of the prisons does not in itself give rise to any constitutional difficulty. A good example of this is the judgment of the Federal Court of Appeals for the Seventh Circuit in *Pischke v. Litscher*, 178 F.3d 497, 500 (7th Cir. 1999), in which Judge Posner explained that inmates who raised a constitutional argument against their transfer from a state prison to a private prison "would be foolish to do so." See also *Montez v. McKinna*, 208 F.3d 862, 866 (10th Cir. 2000); *White v. Lambert*, 370 F.3d 1002, 1013 (9th Cir. 2004). The Supreme Court of the State of Oklahoma rejected a claim that giving a permit to counties in the state to enter into contracts with private enterprises in order to manage and operate prisons was an unconstitutional delegation of powers by the legislature. *Tulsa County Deputy Sheriff's Fraternal Order of Police v. Board of County Commissioners of Tulsa County*, 959 P.2d 979 (1998). It would therefore seem that the main questions that have been considered by the courts in the United States regarding the privatization of prisons concerned the scope of the tortious liability of the private prisons and their employees in relation to that of the state prisons and their employees (*see Richardson v. McKnight*, 521 U.S. 399 (1997)); *Correctional Services Corporation v. Malesko*, 534 U.S. 61 (2001). It should be noted, however, that several judgments in the United States have held that the public nature of the role fulfilled by the corporations that operate private prisons makes them subject to the provisions of the constitution (*see Skelton v. Pri-Cor, Inc.*, 964 F.2d 100, 101–102 (6th Cir. 1991)); *Rosborough v. Management and Training Corporation*, 350 F.3d 459 (5th Cir. 2003).

Comment

In February 2012, the Supreme Court applied the proportionality test in striking down an important and controversial statute providing draft deferrals to Ultra-Orthodox men. The statute maintained the draft deferrals, which functioned as exemptions because the deferrals lasted until the men were at an age at which they would not be drafted, but also provided a variety of mechanisms to encourage Ultra-Orthodox men to agree to serve either in the army or in national service. In HCJ 6298/07 *Ressler v. Knesset of Israel* (Feb. 21, 2012), the Court found that the purpose of the statute was fourfold: to establish the rules on draft exemptions for Ultra-Orthodox in a statute, rather than in administrative orders as had been done prior to the enactment of the statute; to increase the number of Ultra-Orthodox serving in the army and in national service so as to reduce the inequality caused by the deferrals; to increase Ultra-Orthodox participation in the workforce by giving them an alternative to the exemptions which required them to study full-time and prohibited gainful employment; and to find a solution to the problems associated with the Ultra-Orthodox exemptions without using ineffective force against the Ultra-Orthodox. The Court found that ten years of experience in implementing the law showed that the large majority of Ultra-Orthodox men continued to take advantage of the exemption and did neither military nor national service. This finding showed that in practice the statute reached none of its goals except the first.

To determine whether the statute was constitutional, the Court recognized that the statute infringed on the constitutional principle of equality and therefore held that it was constitutional only if it met the limitation clause. The Court did not question whether the infringement was by law, was consistent with the values of the State of Israel, or was for a proper purpose. It applied the proportionality test and held that the statute failed the first part of that test because it had no rational relation to its goal. The results of ten years of experience with the law showed that implementation of the statute would not attain the last three goals. Therefore the statute was unconstitutional. The court further ruled that the statute would remain in force until August 1, 2012. As of the end of September 2012, the expired statute had not been replaced nor had the military begun widespread draft of Ultra-Orthodox men.

The proportionality test raises a number of interesting issues, but discussion of these issues is put off until the end of the next chapter, which discusses the use of the this test in administrative law.

H. Institutional Aspects of Constitutional Law

Constitutional law is concerned not only with individual rights, but also with institutional arrangements. A constitution *constitutes* a regime; it sets up its structure. We have seen that it was expected that the Constituent Assembly would write a constitution that established the structural institutions for the state, and that it failed to do so. We have also seen that a series of Basic Laws set the structure for the main state institutions.

Israeli case law is close to silent on the constitutional aspects of the relationships among the governmental institutions. Cases include some reference to separation of powers and to checks and balances, but mainly in the context of administrative law and the power of the courts to review administrative actions. Israel case law allows the Knesset to delegate to an administrative agency the power to make basic policy choices.

> It is presumed that that legislature has chosen to retain the general authority to set out primary arrangements and to delegate to the administrative authority to determine the practical aspects of a matter, but this presumption can be overcome. As long as it does so explicitly, the legislature has the power to authorize an administrative body named in a statute to determine the basic requirements on a matter even though, in the normal course of things, it would be more appropriate for the legislature to determine the basic requirements.[21]

The national government is the only inherently sovereign unit of government in the Israeli system; the local governments derive their authority from national laws enacted by the Knesset. As a result, there is no constitutional issue parallel to that which arises in the United States regarding the division of power between the federal government and the states. The only meaningful limits on the national government are in the law relating to individual rights. Recall that Chief Justice Meir Shamgar's opinion in the *Migdal* case based the constituent authority of the Knesset on the unlimited sovereignty of that body.

Perhaps as constitutional law develops, institutional arrangements will receive more attention from the courts. For now, the overwhelming concentration of constitutional law is on the matter of individual rights.

---

21. HCJ 244/00 Organization for a New Conversation v. Minister of National Infrastructure 56(6) PD 25 [2002].

Chapter 9

Administrative Law

A. The Nature of Administrative Law

Administrative law is the law that governs how agencies go about making decisions. Israeli administrative agencies include, for example, the Ministry of Environmental Defense, the Ministry of Education, the National Building and Planning Commission, and the National Insurance Institute (the Israeli equivalent of the United States Social Security Administration). They engage in a variety of activities. The Ministry of Environmental Defense, which is similar to the Environmental Protection Agency in the United States, enacts regulations setting air quality standards for a variety of air pollutants; the Ministry of Education licenses schools; the National Building and Planning Commission, which has no parallel on the national level in the United States, determines the adequacy of national plans, such as the national plan for airports; and the National Insurance Institute, similar to the US Social Security Administration, decides whether an applicant qualifies for an old-age public pension. An agency goes through some sort of procedure in reaching a decision on any of these matters, and administrative law dictates what that procedure is. What information must the agency gather before making a decision? Do those affected by the decision have the right to some sort of hearing before it is made? With whom must the agency consult in reaching the decision? All of these are procedural matters covered by administrative law.

Administrative law also deals with judicial review of agency decisions. Generally a person dissatisfied with an agency decision can petition a court to review it. This is a request for the court to determine that the agency decision is illegal because of some inadequacy in what the agency did. For example, the petition might claim that the agency used improper procedure in making the decision, such as a claim that the agency had to hold a hearing before denying a person a public pension, but failed to do so. Or the petition might claim that the agency lacked legal authority to make the decision, such as claiming that a statute said the agency could license schools for children but not vocational schools for adults. The petition might also claim that the agency based its decision on considerations that were not consistent with those required by law, such as claiming that the commission decided whether to approve a plan for airports based on whether the airports were close to the homes of the members of the commission. In addition, the petition could claim some other sort of defect in the way the agency reached its decision. In all of these cases, if the court finds that the agency decision is defective under the applicable legal standards, it can rule that the decision is invalid.

Administrative law in Israel is enormously important. Due to the history of governmental control of many aspects of the economy, economic activity is highly regulated and people must obtain permits or licenses to engage in a great variety of activities. Government regulation of private activity is extensive, if not always effective. In addition, the government is the source of financial support for many private endeavors. Governmental decisions on all these matters are subject to the rules of administrative law.

B. Agencies and Other Bodies Subject to Administrative Law

The requirements of administrative law apply to the national Government, the ministries, and all subunits of the ministries, as well as to local governments. In addition, many other bodies are subject to some or all of the same legal requirements. These include temporary institutions established by the Knesset, such as commissions of inquiry, and also permanent organizations established by the Knesset that do not operate in corporate form, such as the Red Star of David (the Israeli affiliate of the Red Cross) and the National Insurance Institute. Government corporations, which are corporations established by statute and in which the state controls more than half the shares or more than half of the members of the board of directors, are subject to administrative law when engaged in an activity authorized by statute. Knesset committees are subject to administrative law when they are making quasi-judicial decisions, such as removing the immunity of a specific member of the Knesset, and to a limited extent when they make procedural decisions. Even private corporations are subject to judicial review under the rules of administrative law when they fulfill necessary public functions, such as burial.[1] In some circumstances, private corporations are subject to the rules of administrative law if they are acting under government contract; in such a case, the government cannot avoid the obligation to comply with the requirements of administrative law by contracting out some tasks.[2] It is clear from the foregoing that administrative law applies very broadly.

In the United States, the reach of administrative law is less extensive than in Israel. Federal administrative law applies to federal agencies, and state administrative law applies to state agencies. Whether government corporations are subject to administrative law depends not on the function they serve but on the provisions of the statutes establishing them. Generally they are free from the restraints of administrative law. Private entities do not have to meet administrative law rules.

C. Sources of Administrative Law

There are three sources of administrative law: constitutional law, statutory law and judge-made law (case law). In Israel, much of the law on the procedures agencies must use, and essentially all the law on judicial review of agency decisions, comes from case law. In the United States, in contrast, most administrative law comes from statutes. Some additional requirements are based on constitutional law. Case law is important in interpreting the statutory and constitutional provisions, especially where the statutory or constitutional language is imprecise, but it does not impose independent requirements.

---

1. CA 294/91 *"Jerusalem Community" True Loving-Kindness Burial Society v. Kastenbaum* 46(2) PD 464 [1992].
2. HCJ 6698/95 *Kadan v. Israel Lands Authority* 54(1) PD 258 [2000].

Three types of statutes lay out administrative law requirements. The *first* is a general statute that applies across the board to almost all agencies and covers most areas of administrative law. The Administrative Procedure Act (APA) in the United States is this type of statute. It prescribes the procedures federal agencies must follow in reaching decisions. In addition, the APA provisions on judicial review set out the rules for when a reviewing court can hold an agency decision invalid. State administrative procedure acts have similar types of provisions. There is no equivalent in Israel.

The *second* type is a statute that applies to a large number of agencies but covers only a limited topic, setting procedures and sometimes standards for judicial review for a specific type of action. The National Environmental Policy Act in the United States is a statute of this type. It not only requires agencies to consider the environmental impacts of their actions, but sets out the procedures for such consideration. Israel also has a number of statutes of this type. The following statute is one of them:

Israeli Statute

Freedom of Information Act, 5758-1998

7. Procedure for Submitting Requests and for Responding to Them

(a) A request to obtain information shall be submitted in writing to the responsible official, or to the person authorized to receive requests; the person requesting information is not required to give the reason for the request.

(b) The public authority shall respond to a request without delay, but not later than 30 days from receiving the request, stating its decision as to whether to supply the information requested. The head of the public agency, or his authorized representative, may extend this period, if needed, for an additional 30 days, provided that notice is given in writing to the requesting party including the reasons for needing the extension.

(c) If an extension is needed due to the scope or complexity of the requested information, the head of the public authority may extend the time for an additional period by a reasoned decision sent to the requesting party during the period of the original extension, provided that the extension shall be for no longer than needed for the grounds stated, and in no case shall the extension exceed 60 days.

(d) If the public authority decides to provide the information to the person requesting it, the information shall be provided within a reasonable time, taking into consideration the circumstances, but not later than 15 days, unless the responsible official determined, based on special grounds, that the decision shall be implemented at a later time. In that case, the authority shall notify the requesting party how and when the information will be provided.

(e) The information shall be provided in the form in which it is held within the authority and the authority is not required to process the information in a way that makes it more useful to the requesting party. If the information is computerized, it shall be provided through means normally used by the authority.

(f) If the public authority decides to reject the request in whole or in part, a written notice shall be sent to the person making the request and shall include the reasons for rejecting the request, and shall include notice to the requesting party of the right to appeal the decision under the Administrative Courts Law, 5760-2000.

Comment

This provision applies to a large number of agencies that are included in the definition of "public authority" found elsewhere in the statute. When any of these authorities receives a request for information under the Freedom of Information Act, it must follow the procedures set out for responding to the request. The procedures address when and how the agency must respond. The number of agencies to which the law applies is large, but the procedural requirements are limited to one specific type of decision.

The *third* type of statute setting out administrative law provisions is an enabling act, or a statute authorizing a specific agency to act. An enabling act grants the agency substantive authority to engage in some activity, such as promulgating a rule on a defined topic or issuing an order to undertake a defined action. The enabling act may also specify the procedures the agency should use when it engages in the activity, and those can be different from the procedures set out in another, more general statute. For example, in the United States, the APA specifies that the public must be given the opportunity to comment in writing on a proposed rule. An enabling act addressed to a specific agency may require that the agency also take oral comments. When an enabling act sets requirements different from those in a more general statute, the enabling act is controlling. In Israel, as in the United States, enabling acts sometimes set out procedural requirements.

Where administrative law is covered by statute, courts are involved in determining the proper interpretation of the statute. For matters not covered by statute, agencies are usually free to choose their own procedures. In the United States, the courts generally take a hands-off attitude towards these choices.[3] In Israel, courts likewise interpret the administrative law provisions in statutes, but they also take an active role in deciding whether procedures chosen by agencies are appropriate. Similarly Israeli courts are deeply involved in deciding how to review decisions of administrative agencies and for developing the rules on when to hold those decisions invalid. As a result, most of the administrative law in Israel is judge-made law.

In Israel, one other source affects the administrative procedures used by agencies: the Guidelines of the Attorney General. The attorney general issued these guidelines as management directives to the governmental ministries. Because they are guidelines and not regulations, they may not be enforceable in court.

D. Procedures in Administrative Agencies

Agencies make decisions on a variety of matters. They promulgate regulations, which, like statutes, prescribe legal rules that everyone must follow, but are generally more specific than statutes. Agencies also issue orders requiring an individual person (including a regulated company) to take specified action, issue permits and licenses, and decide whether to grant money or goods or services to specific applicants. They also enter into valuable contracts with private persons for construction of buildings, provision of services, etc. Administrative law may dictate the procedures agencies must follow in each of these activities.

---

3. *See* Vermont Yankee Nuclear Power Corp. v. Natural Resources Defense Council, Inc., 435 U.S. 519 (1978).

Israeli ministries are the most important of the administrative agencies. When they promulgate regulations, they follow procedures set out in the following Guidelines of the Attorney General:

Israeli Provision

Guideline No. 2.3100

Attorney General, Guidelines of the Attorney General (Nov. 9, 2003)[4]

11.2. Coordination among Ministries as a Requirement of the Principles of Sound Administration

Even when the enabling act does not require collaboration between more than one ministry in promulgation of regulations, the principles of sound administration require inter-ministerial coordination in such matters. A basic principle of the constitutional structure of Israel, based on section 4 of the Basic Law: The Government, is that the Government has shared responsibility to the Knesset. Due to this provision, and due to the fact that promulgation of regulations by one ministry is likely to affect matters for which another ministry is responsible, coordination among ministries is required. Promulgation of regulations by one ministry without such coordination is likely to have a negative effect on other ministries and even on the public. The guideline on coordination between ministries is meant to prevent administrative problems and any injury to the public good.

11.3. Coordination Among Ministries that Have a Direct Interest in Regulations

a) A ministry that is engaged in preparation of regulations shall determine which other Government ministries have a direct interest in those regulations. The question of whether another ministry has a direct interest in specific regulations depends on the subject matter and the content of the regulations. In general, if the regulations are liable to affect a matter found within the authority of another ministry, that ministry should be seen as one that has a direct interest in the regulations.

c) The general counsel of a ministry promulgating the regulations shall send a draft of the regulations to the other ministries that have a direct interest in the regulations, together with a letter requesting that comments be submitted by a specified date. After receiving comments from all relevant ministries, the draft shall be sent to the person in the ministry of justice responsible for overseeing promulgation of regulations.

d) If no comments are received from some ministry by the date set out in the letter, it will be treated as though that ministry does not object to the draft regulations as proposed.

e) If a ministry made comments on the draft regulations, and its comments were not accepted in their entirety or in part, the general counsel to the ministry promulgating the regulations shall notify the objecting ministry of this fact at least a week before the regulations are prepared for signing, so as to allow the objecting minister to consider what it will do. The objecting ministry can take any one of the following steps:

1) It can initiate contacts between the senior officials of the two ministries, including at the level of the ministers, in an effort to come to some agreement;

2) It can bring the dispute before the prime minister or can raise the issue at a meeting of the Government.

---

4. *Available at* http://www.justice.gov.il/NR/rdonlyres/5C816E7D-1BAC-4452-A696-34CBFA029A38/0/23100.pdf.

These steps do not obligate the ministry promulgating the regulations to delay its work or promulgation of the regulations.

Comment

Even though courts do not force agencies to follow the procedures set out in these guidelines, agencies follow them for political reasons, and the procedures required by the guidelines have a strong influence on the content of rules.

Some enabling acts require an agency to consult with a specific official or an organization before promulgating a regulation. The agency may be required to consult with another ministry (prior to the coordination required by the guidelines), an expert committee, a non-governmental organization (NGO), or with an industry group. Courts enforce these requirements when they are found in statutes. There are no requirements to take comments from the public. By comparison, the United States Administrative Procedure Act requires that the entire public be allowed to comment on most proposed rules.

When an Israeli agency makes a decision that affects a specific individual, such as by issuing an order or deciding whether to grant a license, it must follow the *rules of natural justice*. Israel has no constitutional or statutory equivalent to the procedural due process requirements of American constitutional law. Under the Due Process clauses of the Fifth and Fourteenth Amendments to the US Constitution, federal and state agencies must provide a person with certain procedural protections before making a decision that will deprive that person of life, liberty, or property. Israel has developed a comparable, although not identical, set of rules under the judicially-imposed requirement that agencies observe the rules of natural justice. These rules, like due process, usually require that the agency provide some sort of hearing before taking an action that directly affects an individual. The rules also require that the hearing meet court-developed standards of fairness. In addition, some enabling acts also require consultation before an agency issues an order, a permit, etc. For example, before a local government issues a business license that may adversely affect the environment, it must consult with the minister of environmental defense.

Israeli administrative law also includes detailed requirements on the procedures for government contracts. These rules require publication of tenders (requests for proposals to enter the contract) and a fair and open process of decision-making on who will get the contract.

E. Challenges to Administrative Actions— Preliminary Issues

1. Jurisdiction

As was described in chapter 5, many direct challenges to administrative actions are heard by an administrative law court, which is a special sitting of the district courts. Judges of each district court sit on administrative law cases, deciding those cases under the special rules that apply to administrative law. The administrative courts hear cases assigned to them under the Administrative Courts Law, 5760-2000. These tend to be cases of a more routine, repetitive nature, such as those involving grant or denial of business licenses, public tenders (public contracting), and decisions of local councils. Since the law was enacted, it has been amended numerous times, expanding the types of cases assigned to the administrative law courts. The Supreme Court has original jurisdiction over all other administrative law cases and appellate jurisdiction over cases heard in the administrative law courts. The Israeli Supreme Court decides a large number of administrative law cases each year. In comparison, many administrative law cases in the United States do not go beyond the courts of appeal.

2. Standing

When an administrative law case comes before a court, the court will consider whether the person petitioning for judicial review of the agency decision has *standing*. Generally only those with a direct interest in the outcome of the case have standing to petition a court for judicial review. In Israel, special rules regarding standing have been developed in administrative law cases. Standing is a crucial problem in administrative law. Many actions of administrative agencies have a small impact on a large number of people. It is not worthwhile for any one of them to sue the agency even when the agency makes a legally invalid decision. Therefore the court would never be able to review the agency action and hold it invalid if the requirement of a direct interest were strictly applied. In response to this problem, the Supreme Court of Israel considered whether to expand the concept of standing.

Israeli Case

Ressler v. Minister of Defense
HCJ 910/86, 42(2) PD 441[1988][5]

[As described in chapter 2, Israel has nearly universal military service. From the time of the establishment of the state, the minister of defense granted deferrals to full-time yeshiva students.[6] At first, the deferrals were justified by the need to revive study of Jewish texts, which was seriously diminished by the destruction of the main yeshivas in Europe during the Holocaust. If young men studying in yeshivas were drafted, they would miss their prime age for study and might never return to that pursuit. At first, the deferral was limited to four hundred students a year. With time, the limit was abandoned and the number of students taking advantage of the deferral grew to 1600 by the time of this case. Jewish study had become widespread in Israel, so there was no longer a need for its revival. With that change, the rationale for the deferral changed. On the one hand, Ultra-Orthodox authorities wanted to maintain such expanded study, and they also feared that exposure of their insulated students to the largely secular world of the army would lead the students away from religious life. At the same time, the army was hesitant to draft Ultra-Orthodox students, fearing that the students would not adjust well to the military environment and that accommodating their religious needs would be too burdensome for the military establishment.[7] Deferrals were in effect the same as exemptions because

---

5. The case is found in English on the website of the Supreme Court at http://elyon1.court.gov.il/files_eng/86/100/009/Z01/86009100.z01.htm.

6. As explained in the previous chapter, a yeshiva is an institution dedicated to learning Jewish texts. Jewish law values the study of these texts, independent of any utilitarian goal for such study.

7. *See* HCJ 3267/97 Rubenstein v. Minister of Defense 52(5) PD 481, 491 (1998). This case is found in English at http://elyon1.court.gov.il/files_eng/97/670/032/A11/97032670.a11.htm.

the yeshiva students kept their deferrals from year to year until they were beyond the age for military service. The issue of the propriety of the deferrals was the subject of considerable debate in the Knesset throughout the years.

The authority for the deferrals in effect at the time of the case was in the Law on Military Service (Consolidated Version), 5746-1986 (referred to in the case as "the statute"), section 36, which provided:

> The minister of defense, if he sees a need to do so for reasons related to the size of the enlisted forces or the military reserves of the Israel Defense Forces, or for reasons related to the needs of education, security settlements, or the national economy, or for family reasons or for other reasons, is authorized to issue an order
>
> (1) to exempt a person of draft age from the military service, or to reduce the period of the person's service;
>
> (2) to exempt a person of draft age from the requirement of serving in the military reserves ...;
>
> (3) to defer ... the date on which a person must appear ... for registration, physical examination, or to begin military service.

It was under this authority that the minister of defense had issued the deferral for yeshiva students.[8]]

Justice A. Barak:

Is the deferral of military service for yeshiva students legal? This question, which was previously put before this Court, is before us again. Should we deal with the substantive issue, or should we decline to consider it due to a lack of standing or lack of justiciability?[9]

This case presents three questions for our determination: *first,* do Petitioners have standing; *second,* is the subject of the petition justiciable; and *third,* is the minister of defense's decision lawful, that is, does the minister have the power to defer the military service of yeshiva students, and if so—did he make lawful use of his power. We will address each question separately, beginning with the question of standing.

Past Petitions

The petition before us is not the first to be brought before this Court on the subject of deferral of military service for yeshiva students. The first petition was considered 18 years ago. The petition was rejected without even hearing the government's attorney. Justice Vitkin based the decision on the petitioner's lack of standing. He held that "the more a petition raises an issue that is public in its nature, of the type that is assigned to the political branches and is discussed by the Government and the Knesset, the stricter we should be in requiring that the petitioner suffers a real individual injury before we grant him standing before the judicial branch." Justice Vitkin explained that, in his opinion, the Petitioner had not succeeded in demonstrating a real personal injury. The Petitioner's grievance was "a general public grievance and the Petitioner is no different from all other persons who see as impermissible the exemption of men who, in their eyes, are nothing but draft evaders." He thought that the Court need not respond to such a grievance.

---

8. The *Ressler* case preceded by 18 years the case of Movement for Quality Government in Israel v. Knesset, HCJ 6427/02, 61(1) PD 619 [2006], set out in the chapter on constitutional law. The connection between the two cases is explained below in the comments on justiciability.

9. Justiciability is considered in the following section of the text.

More than ten years passed after this petition was rejected, and at the beginning of the 1980s a second petition was brought before this Court on the subject of deferral of military service of yeshiva students, this time by Mr. Ressler, who is one of the Petitioners in the present case. Affidavits of two senior officers were attached to that petition, claiming that, were all yeshiva students drafted into the IDF [Israel Defense Forces], this would add another division of soldiers on mandatory duty. This would lead to a substantial reduction in the time of active duty for all reserve soldiers and for the petitioner. The Supreme Court rejected the petition [relying on the earlier case.] The Court rejected the Petitioner's claim that the burden of reserve duty would be reduced as a conclusion without basis in substantiated facts. It is possible that the Petitioner believes this to be true, but this is not sufficient to show a real injury to his interests. [One of the justices] stated that "it is clear that the objective of this petition is to drag this Court into a public political debate on a sensitive and stormy matter, as to which there are sharp differences in opinion among members of the public. The Petitioners cannot succeed in this endeavor both because they have no standing and because the matter is not justiciable."

The Current Petition

The petition before us, like the former petitions, is on the deferral of military service for yeshiva students.... The Petitioners claim that they have standing. They attached an affidavit from Major General (Reserves) Dr. Emanuel Wald, who served for many years as the head of the Human Resources Planning Branch in the Planning Section, Human Resources Division of the General Staff. The affiant declares that

> There is a direct connection between drafting of yeshiva students into active duty and afterwards into the reserves and the period of time that the Petitioners will each individually serve in their reserve positions. Were the draft of yeshiva students not deferred, as requested in the petition, the amount of time that the Petitioners would serve each year would be shortened.

Based on these facts, the Petitioners claim they have established standing.

Standing

a. Background

As we have seen, in the past, petitions on deferral of the draft for yeshiva students have been rejected because of the rules of standing. Should we also reject the petition before us for the same reason? My answer is in the negative. In my opinion, the Petitioners have standing, and if the matter is justiciable, it is proper for us to consider it.

In order to set out the basis for my conclusion, we should consider the rules of standing. We begin with subsections 15(c) and (d) of the Basic Law: the Judiciary. These subsections grant the High Court of Justice jurisdiction to consider a matter when, in the interest of justice, it is necessary to provide a remedy and the matter is not in the jurisdiction of another court (subsection (c)). Similarly this section authorizes the High Court of Justice to issue orders to governmental authorities "to act or to refrain from acting in lawful fulfillment of their positions" (subsection (d)). These two provisions do not create administrative rights or administrative duties, and they clearly do not relate to the standing of a petitioner to claim violation of a right or duty. The parliament created jurisdiction in the Court based on the assumption, like that of the English common law tradition, that grant of jurisdiction to hear a matter includes a sort of delegation of authority to create legal rules relating to jurisdiction in the matter.

Within the framework of this power, the High Court of Justice created a series of legal rules that relate to the manner in which it exercises its discretion. Among these are the rules on standing.

Therefore the rules of standing are legal rules. Nothing in the Basic Law: The Judiciary requires adoption of a specific rule or position on this matter.... Unlike in the United States, where the rules of standing grew out of interpretation of a provision in the Constitution, our standing rules developed without any statutory source. The opposite is true: On its face, the language of the statute is broad, and it authorizes the High Court of Justice to consider every violation of the law by a governmental agency, without regard to the standing of the petitioner. Therefore the standing rules developed by this Court represent self-imposed limits on the High Court of Justice's exercise of its jurisdiction.

b. The Origins of the Problem

The rules of standing are in a state of flux.... The rules of standing are different if the appropriate model for judicial review [of administrative action] is that of defending the rights of a private person from the rules of standing if the appropriate model for judicial review is one of protecting the rule of law and the legality of actions of the government.... A judge whose judicial philosophy is based only on the understanding that his job is to decide disputes between people with different existing rights is unlike a judge whose judicial philosophy is based on a recognition that the job of the judge is to create rights and to ensure the rule of law.

c. The Classical Position

[There has been] liberalization in the rules of standing in the last decades.... In order to obtain standing, a petitioner does not have to demonstrate an impairment of his own legal *right*.... It is sufficient if he demonstrates an injury to some *interest* of his. Furthermore this interest need not be peculiar to the petitioner, and his standing will be recognized if his interest is injured, even if he and many others share the same interest.... Finally in order to lay the evidentiary basis to show an injury to an interest, the petitioner need not show with certainty that his interest has been injured. It is sufficient if he demonstrates a reasonable chance that his interest will be injured.

d. The Conventional Exceptions

The debate focuses on identifying those special situations (exceptions) in which a petitioner's standing will be recognized even if he cannot demonstrate that some interest of his has sustained an injury. Even on this matter, most judges agree on a number of points: First, a petitioner's standing will be recognized when his substantive claim is one of corruption at some governmental agency.... Thus, if a governmental agency acts on the basis of favoritism or a conflict of interests, the standing of petitioner who has no interest in the matter will be recognized.... Second, this Court will recognize the standing of a petitioner who raises a claim of a clear constitutional problem with an agency decision.

e. Liberalization of the Exceptions

Therefore the main dispute is on the scope of the exceptions, which provide for cases in which standing of a *public petitioner* is recognized. In regard to this, three questions arise: First, is the exception relating to corruption limited to just a claim of corruption, or can it be broadened to include all claims based on a serious defect in the operation of an administrative authority? Second, is the exception for a claim of a clear constitutional problem limited just to constitutional claims, or can it be expanded to all claims of a public nature that have a direct connection to the rule of law? Third, is it appropriate to recognize additional exceptions, or are we limited to only these two? On each of these questions we find differing opinions among judges. On each of the questions, I take a liberal position. In my opinion, the first exception is not limited to government corruption alone, and it can be expanded to include every case in which the petitioner claims a serious defect in the administrative action. Similarly my opinion is that the second exception is not limited to constitutional questions, but applies in every case in which "the issue raised is of a public nature and directly relates to promoting the rule of law and assuring its implementation in practice," and to all those "legal issues of an exceptional nature that relate to the rule of law." ... Finally in my opinion the exceptions to the rule of not recognizing public claims are not limited to the two exceptions that I described. We should not create fixed categories of exceptions. We should leave the matter flexible, leaving the door open for recognizing other situations in which to recognize the standing of a petitioner who has no direct interest in a matter. So for example, there are situations in which, due to the nature of the case, there is no person with an interest under the accepted tests. In such situations, we should sometimes recognize the standing of a *public petitioner.*

In a dispute that arises before a court, the court must assure that all governmental branches—the legislative, the executive, and the judicial—function within the law. When it does this, the court is not transgressing the principle of separation of powers, but rather implementing that principle.... In my opinion, the meaning of separation of powers is not that a problem of a public nature is to be treated exclusively in the legislative and executive branches and not in the judicial branch. The meaning of separation of powers is that, in the absence of legal limitations, the legislative branch is allowed to determine the legal framework through which a matter of public interest will be managed, and the executive branch should solve public problems within that legal framework. Once such a framework is established, the court is to determine whether the legal framework that has been established is being observed. This is the task of the courts as one of the branches of government. Nothing in the principle of separation of powers allows any one of the branches to operate in violation of the law. Nothing in the principle of separation of powers obligates the judicial branch to desist from all involvement in matters of public interest, especially when this involvement relates to the lawfulness of the action of another branch.... Therefore evaluation of the legality of an action, whether or not it is a matter of public interest, is the job of the judicial branch, and this functions as a way of realizing the objective of the separation of powers arrangement. In this connection, I cannot accept the position, taken by Justice Alon, that the main and fundamental task of the judicial branch is to decide disputes that revolve around a claim of one person's deprivation of a legal right at the hands of another. The source of this position is in private law, in which a litigant is a person who was deprived of a right.... This position is not at all acceptable in public law. The *classic* law of standing, based on the interest of the person who sustained an injury, does not require the plaintiff to demonstrate that he has been deprived of a right before a court will deal with the case. The exceptions that are universally recognized are not based on a claim of deprivation.

f. The Pragmatic Balance

This view of the judicial function should lead to our recognizing public petitions for all sorts of matters, and not just in exceptional cases. Yet I have explained that I do not find this acceptable. Nothing in jurisprudential theory or in the theory of separation of powers prevents a public court from opening its doors to a public petitioner. Opposition to a general opening of the doors is not based on jurisprudential theory or on separation of powers, but on considerations of judicial policy. There is a concern that the courts will be swamped with public petitions; precious judicial resources will not be sufficient and, as a result, there will be delays in consideration of cases involving parties claiming an interference with their rights. Furthermore sometimes a person who has no personal stake in the outcome of a case will not be able to present the court with the necessary factual basis for making a decision.

These concerns and others are not based on principle but on pragmatic considerations that differ from case to case. Some of them are more substantial and some less. Taken together, they sometimes create a practical problem. The solution is found in the striking the appropriate balance between the principled position and the pragmatic position.... To the extent that the defect in the administrative action is more serious, that the dispute is more of a public nature, and that fewer people can claim a private injury, then the issue is one of a general public nature, and arguments in favor of recognizing a public petitioner prevail.

In my opinion we should not recognize a public petitioner in a case where the petitioner's claim is simply that the law has been violated. That claim is necessary for recognition of a public petitioner, but it is not sufficient. The petitioner must claim something more, as required by the liberal position to the exceptions.

I am aware that this flexible liberal position creates a number of difficulties: First, it creates uncertainty, stemming from the need for a court to apply the *expert sense of the jurist* in deciding the matter of standing.... We can assume that this uncertainty will be reduced with the passage of time as the line between those who have standing and those who do not is more clearly defined. Furthermore I find nothing objectionable in this lack of clarity. As I see it, the rules of standing are pragmatic rules, designed to protect the efficient operation of the court, and not rules designed to create dead areas in which, due to the lack of standing of any petitioner to protest, the government can operate without observance of law. Governmental authorities should assume that every petitioner has standing, and they must operate on this assumption. The court must raise the issue of standing in cases in which it seems to the court appropriate, as a means of self defense in order to protect the efficiency of its operations.

Second, I understand that there is a practical difficulty in distinguishing between those public petitioners who turn to the courts only for the purpose of obtaining publicity (and whose petitions we should refuse to consider) and those petitioners who turn to the courts in order to insure the rule of law (whose petitions we should hear). [The experience in other countries has been that a loosening of the rules on standing does not bring a flood of inappropriate cases.] Of course, we must not ignore this practical problem, which concerns many judges and prevents them from taking a more liberal position to the matter of the public petitioners. But this practical consideration is not of sufficient import to be, by itself, determinative. Petitioners who raise claims of a serious violation of the law that is harmful to the public should not find the doors of the courthouse locked because of the workload of the court.

Third, I understand that it is difficult to set criteria for when a matter raised in a petition is of a public nature and when it is not, when the defect in operation of the administrative authority is serious and when it is not. This difficulty also creates a lack of certainty that will be reduced with the passage of time.... Determining when a matter is of a public nature and when it involves a serious defect is not simple. I accept the position that a complaint that the law was violated and the rule of law implicated is not sufficient to give a petitioner standing. A claim of a violation of the rule of law is a necessary but not sufficient condition for finding that a petitioner has standing as a public petitioner. Similarly a claim by the petitioner that a matter seems to be of a public nature is not sufficient. In addition to a claim of a violation of the rule of law, one must claim something more, such as a serious violation of law in the actions of an administrative authority, or a matter of a public nature, or a matter that relates to the rule of law, as to which there is no petitioner who has a private interest in the matter. As we have seen, this list is not closed, and this creates a degree of uncertainty as to the type of claims that should be included in the list and as to their limits. Still, this position seems to me preferable to a position that locks the courtroom doors in such cases.

g. From the General to the Particular

(1) The Petitioners Have Standing Under the Classic Position

Through their affidavits, the Petitioners have laid a factual basis from which we may conclude that if they succeed in their petition and the induction of the yeshiva students is not delayed, the reserve duties of the Petitioners will be reduced to some degree. Thus they have standing under the classical position.

(2) The Petitioners Have Standing Under the Accepted Exceptions

The question of the legality of freeing an entire segment of the population from the draft falls within the framework of a clear constitutional question, and it thus falls within the framework of one of the usual exceptions [to the rule of not granting standing to a person without a personal stake in the outcome of the case].

(3) The Petitioners Have Standing Under the Liberalization of the Exceptions

The present case raises a constitutional problem, of a public nature, that relates directly to the rule of law, and as to which no one has a better claim of standing than that of the Petitioners. The joining of all these factors justifies recognition of the standing of the Petitioners.

Comment

Both the technique used in the opinion and the substance of standing rule it establishes are interesting. Justice Barak's technique was to set up three positions on the matter of standing. The opinion began by stating that the Israeli cases accepted two of these positions. The first position was the classical position, which held that a person has standing to challenge the decision of an administrative agency only if the person suffered a personal harm resulting from the decision challenged. The second position was one that recognized a limited number of defined exceptions to the classical position. A person who was not personally injured by an agency decision could still challenge the decision if the person alleged that the agency action was the result of corruption or that it presented a clear constitutional problem. The opinion then adds a third, liberal position, which allows a court to recognize standing of petitioners even when they do not have standing under either of the first two positions.

Justice Barak finds that under even the classical position, the petitioners have standing. If that is so, why is the rest of the analysis necessary? Justice Barak could just have said that the petitioners have shown that they serve more time in reserve duty than they would if the minister of defense had not granted a deferral to yeshiva students, so they are harmed by the minister's decision and have standing. The added discussion of the other two views of standing was unnecessary.

There are three answers to this question of why the opinion goes beyond simply finding that the petitioners have standing under the classical rule. First, it is not so clear that they do have standing under the classical rule. Despite the affidavit submitted by the petitioners saying that there is a connection between drafting of yeshiva students and the time the petitioners will have to serve in the reserves, the finding that they have adequately shown an injury is a questionable finding. It is hard to demonstrate that the induction of more soldiers would lead to fewer days of reserve duty for the specific petitioners. Soldiers on regular duty do not always do the same jobs as reservists do, so more enlisted soldiers would not necessarily free the petitioners from their work in the reserves. The presence of more reserve soldiers also might not help them. Soldiers in some units do more reserve duty than others. It depends on the needs of the army at any point in time. If the new reservists were not in the same units, the reserve duty of the petitioners might not be affected. Moreover Ultra-Orthodox men tend to marry young and have many children, and the army generally excuses people in this situation from reserve duty.

Second, the determination in *Ressler* that the reservists had standing under the classical rule is not convincing because it conflicts with an earlier Court determination. In a prior, almost identical case, the Court had determined that reserve soldiers do not have standing to challenge the deferrals. Affidavits such as the one submitted by the petitioners in *Ressler* were rejected by this Court in the earlier case as not providing an adequate showing of a connection. Strictly speaking, this is not a legal problem because under the Basic Law: The Judiciary, section 2, set out in chapter 5, "case law laid down by the Supreme Court obligates all lower courts, but not the Supreme Court." But the prior determination was arguably one of fact and not of law, and it looks odd when the Court directly contradicts its prior factual determination.

The third probable reason the opinion goes beyond the simple determination that the petitioners have standing under the classical position is that the Court wanted to set out a new, more expansive rule of standing. It set this position out in dicta. Recall from chapter 5 that dicta in Supreme Court decisions is generally treated as binding on lower courts. Furthermore while the dicta are not binding on the Supreme Court itself, it is usually followed, especially when it stems from the opinion of a prestigious justice such as Justice Barak.

Why, then, did the opinion bother to argue that the petitioners have classical standing, since that claim is questionable and, in any case, unnecessary? Presumably this portion of the opinion serves the purpose of making the Court look less revolutionary and therefore more judicial. The Israeli Supreme Court was undoubtedly well aware of the fact that it was extending the existing law, and it was necessary not to damage the public respect for the Court. Showing that the petitioners would have had standing anyway helped protect the Court from criticism that it was being too active in making new law.

As to the substantive law of standing, the opinion adopts the liberal position that a person who does not suffer an injury has standing if: (1) that person claims a serious defect in administrative action, or raises an issue of a public nature directly relating to the promotion and implementation of the rule of law, or raises other claims yet to be defined, and (2) there is no petitioner who has a private interest who would have standing under the classical rule. This position leaves open a number of questions:

- What type of defect in an administrative action qualifies as a "serious" defect?
- What types of issues are of a "public nature"?
- Does it depend on how many people are affected?
- What about a highly publicized issue that affects the public's perception of the quality of government, even though very few people are actually affected?
- What is the nature of the issues that affect the rule of law?

- Is it necessary in all cases that there be no private person who would have standing under the traditional rules?

- What if an administrative decision has a direct adverse effect on three people and none of them is interested in suing the government?

- What if the issue affects half a million people, but the effect on each one is so small that no one will file a petition to review the agency decision?

The *Ressler* case does not answer any of these questions, leaving the development of answers to future case law. Indeed there have been a very large number of cases where petitioners have claimed standing as public petitioners under the rationale of *Ressler*. The courts determine whether such petitioners have standing on a case-by-case basis, and the decisions tend to be highly fact sensitive.

In effect, then, the requirement of standing has been abolished in cases reviewing administrative decisions. Because the liberal position leaves so many open questions on when a petitioner's standing as a public petitioner will be recognized, and because the practice is to answer these questions on a case-by-case basis, the Court has full discretion to decide when to hear a case. Even Supreme Court justices not known for judicial activism recognize that this is the situation. Justice Elyakim Rubenstein stated, "Over the years ... the Court has basically abolished the 'standing' requirement."[10] Perhaps it is more precise to say that the Court has abolished a mandatory standing requirement. The Court still refuses to hear many petitions for judicial review on the grounds that the petitioner does not have standing. The important point is not that there is no standing requirement, but rather that the Court is not bound by formal doctrine in deciding who has standing and who does not. Another way to look at the liberal standing rules in Israel is that they have shifted the focus from the person bringing the petition for judicial review to the subject of the petition.

The abolition of a defined standing requirement has had a marked effect. Numerous political action NGOs regularly seek, and often obtain, judicial review of administrative decisions. This includes review of operational decisions of the Israel Defense Forces during time of armed conflict in the territories as well as review of a wide variety of types of purely domestic administrative decisions.

Standing rules in federal courts in the United States are quite different. They have a strong constitutional dimension derived from Article III of the US Constitution, which gives federal courts jurisdiction over cases and controversies. This is understood to mean that if there is not a case or controversy, the federal courts have no jurisdiction. An excerpt from the leading case, involving a challenge to an administrative agency decision, is set out here:

US Case

Lujan v. Defenders of Wildlife
504 U.S. 555 (1992)

While the Constitution of the United States divides all power conferred upon the Federal Government into "legislative powers," art. I, § 1, "[t]he executive power," art. II, § 1, and "[t]he judicial power," art. III, § 1, it does not attempt to define those terms. To be

---

10. Malvina Halbertam, *Judicial Review, A Comparative Perspective: Israel, Canada, and the United States*, 31 Cardozo L. Rev. 2393, 2413 (2010) (quoting Justice Elyakim Rubenstein).

sure, it limits the jurisdiction of federal courts to "cases" and "controversies," but an executive inquiry can bear the name "case" (the Hoffa case) and a legislative dispute can bear the name "controversy" (the Smoot-Hawley controversy). Obviously then, the Constitution's central mechanism of separation of powers depends largely upon common understanding of what activities are appropriate to legislatures, to executives, and to courts. In The Federalist No. 48, Madison expressed the view that "[i]t is not infrequently a question of real nicety in legislative bodies whether the operation of a particular measure will, or will not, extend beyond the legislative sphere," whereas "the executive power [is] restrained within a narrower compass and ... more simple in its nature," and "the judiciary [is] described by landmarks still less uncertain." The Federalist No. 48, p. 256 (Carey and McClellan eds. 1990). One of those landmarks, setting apart the "cases" and "controversies" that are of the justiciable sort referred to in Article III ... is the doctrine of standing. Though some of its elements express merely prudential considerations that are part of judicial self-government, the core component of standing is an essential and unchanging part of the case-or-controversy requirement of Article III.

Over the years, our cases have established that the irreducible constitutional minimum of standing contains three elements. First, the plaintiff must have suffered an "injury in fact" — an invasion of a legally protected interest which is (a) concrete and particularized and (b) "actual or imminent, not 'conjectural' or 'hypothetical.'" Second, there must be a causal connection between the injury and the conduct complained of—the injury has to be "fairly ... trace[able] to the challenged action of the defendant, and not ... th[e] result [of] the independent action of some third party not before the court." Third, it must be "likely," as opposed to merely "speculative," that the injury will be "redressed by a favorable decision."

Comment

The American constitutional rule is similar to the Israeli classical rule. In the United States, a generalized interest in seeing that the law is enforced does not provide a basis for standing. The injury in such a case is not sufficiently concrete and particularized. Congress may further restrict standing and so may the courts under the doctrine of prudential standing, but neither may expand standing doctrine by granting standing to someone who would not meet the constitutional case or controversy requirement.

Under US standing doctrine, an association, including an NGO, has standing if one of its members would have standing under Article III, the lawsuit seeks to promote interests germane to purposes of the association, and the individual member's participation is not required for either the claim asserted or the relief requested.[11] In other words, an NGO can sue in place of one of its members, but only if it has a member that meets the injury in fact and other requirements of *Lujan v. Defenders of Wildlife*.

In contrast, the standing rule for administrative law cases set out in *Ressler* is governed by neither constitutional law nor statutory law, but rather is a rule developed by case law. At the time of the *Ressler* decision, it was not clear whether Israel had constitutional law. Even today, after the determination in *United Mizrachi Bank v. Migdal Communal Village*[12] that Israel has a written constitution, constitutional law on institutional power is

---

11. *See Hunt v. Washington State Apple Advertising Commn.*, 432 U.S. 333 (1977); *Natural Resources Defense Council v. EPA*, 489 F.3d 1364 (D.C. Cir., 2007).

12. CA 6821/93 *United Mizrachi Bank v. Migdal Communal Village* 49(4) PD 221 [1995], set out and discussed in chapter 8.

not well developed, and it is institutional power issues that are central in the doctrine of standing. The *Ressler* opinion addresses the separation of powers doctrine as it is understood in Israel and finds it non-determinative on standing. According to the opinion, separation of powers requires that the agencies of the executive branch of government comply with the law, and when a court exercises judicial review of administrative actions, even at the bequest of a public petition, the court is enforcing the separation of powers principle. As to statutory law, the opinion examined the High Court of Justice's statutory authority to hear petitions against administrative agency decisions and found that the statute imposed no limits on standing. Therefore the Court was free to develop standing rules on its own.

Today some administrative law cases are heard in the administrative courts, but they use the same standing rule as does the High Court of Justice.

Questions

1. In administrative law cases, what are the advantages and disadvantages of the Israeli position on standing as compared to the American rule?

2. How does the difference in legal, political, and social milieu in Israel and in the United States contribute to the differences in standing law?

3. Justiciability

Justiciability is the issue of whether a court will hear a case, even if it has jurisdiction and the petitioner has standing. A court can decline to hear a case and leave the matter to be resolved by other branches of government. The *Ressler* case provided the definitive ruling on this issue as well.

Israeli Case

Ressler v. Minister of Defense
HCJ 910/86, 42(2) PD 441[1988]

Justice A. Barak:

Justiciability

A. The Parties' Claims

The Respondent's second argument is that the subject matter of the petition is not justiciable, so the Court may not consider the petition. The Respondent claims that issue of enlistment deferment for yeshiva students is among those topics which the Court prefers not to determine. This is a question over which the public is divided in its views, and should be settled by other authorities, in the manner accepted in a democratic society. The question whether yeshiva students should be drafted is a political question, and the practice of not drafting them is a long-standing one. According to the Respondent, any change in this practice requires a political decision. Therefore a judicial determination is inappropriate. A court's intervention in this question will fan the flames of public controversy, and accordingly judicial restraint is appropriate. In the opinion of counsel for the Respondent, the relationships among governmental authorities and the need for mutual respect among them should lead the Court to leave the determination of this question in the hands of the other branches of government—the Government and the Knesset.

In their response, Petitioners claim that the subject matter of the petition is justiciable. True, the petition contains public and political aspects, but this does not bar the hearing of a petition in the High Court of Justice. Even a subject of a clear public nature, which radiates a political aura and is likely to give rise to a strong public reaction, is justiciable. Only thus is it possible to ensure that the executive branch observes the law. Such judicial supervision does not harm the separation of powers. On the contrary: it is in the very soul of every democratic regime.

B. Various Meanings of the Concept of Justiciability

We can distinguish between two different meanings of justiciability. One can be called normative justiciability; the other can be called institutional justiciability. Normative justiciability is designed to answer the question of whether there is a legal standard that can be used to decide a dispute that is brought before a court. Institutional justiciability is designed to answer the question of whether the court is the appropriate institution to resolve a dispute, or whether it is better that the dispute be resolved by another institution, such as the legislature or the executive.

C. Normative Justiciability

A dispute is justiciable in the normative sense if there are legal standards under which it can be resolved. A dispute is not justiciable in the normative sense if no legal standard exists under which it can be resolved. Therefore normative justiciability deals with the ability of the law and of the court to resolve a dispute. The question is not whether it is appropriate for the dispute to be resolved by law and in a court, but rather if it is possible to resolve the dispute by law and in a court. Normative justiciability deals not with what is appropriate but rather with what is possible.

The analysis of normative justiciability (or lack thereof) begins with the concept that law is a system of prohibitions and permissions. In the realm of law, every action is either permitted or forbidden. There is no such thing as an action to which the law does not apply.... There is no legal vacuum in which an action is undertaken without the law taking some position on the action.... Even when there is a lacuna in the law, the law itself provides a means of filling the lacuna. Under this view of matters, there is always some legal norm that applies to an action. It does not matter what type of action is involved, whether it is political or not, or whether it is a matter of policy or not. Every action—be it political or a matter of policy—is included within the realm of law, and there is a legal norm that applies to it, determining whether it is permitted or forbidden.... Take for example, the government's decision to establish diplomatic relations with West Germany.[13] This was certainly a clearly political decision. Yet the law also addressed the matter. This was not an action outside of the realm of law. So, for example, the law addresses the question of what unit of government is authorized to decide on behalf of the state on establishing diplomatic connections with West Germany. It would be inconceivable to claim that this is a po-

---

13. The question of whether Israel should establish diplomatic relations with West Germany was highly controversial among the Israeli public. When the government decided to establish ties in 1965, a petition was brought against admission of the designated West German ambassador to Israel because he had served in the German army in World War II. The Court held that the question of whether to establish diplomatic ties with a country and the question whether to accept a country's ambassador were political questions and not legal questions. In a very brief opinion, the Court dismissed the petition. HCJ 186/65 Reiner v. Prime Minister 19(2) PD 485 [1965].

litical and not legal issue. The question of authority is a legal matter that has political implications, just as it is a political matter that has legal implications.

In my opinion, in the vast majority of cases, the political nature of an action does not affect its normative evaluation. Thus we have expressed the opinion that, for example, even the Knesset is subject to the rules of reasonableness and fairness when it decides on the immunity of one of its members. There may be exceptional cases. It may be that we will not review decisions such as that to make peace or to go to war, for example, under the usual rules that apply to an administrative exercise of discretion. In such cases we would dismiss a petition, not because of the lack of a legal norm, but because there is a legal norm that permits the government to decide to go to war and no legal norm prohibits such a decision. The action is not lacking justiciability; it is justiciable and legal.

Let us examine again the question of establishing diplomatic relations with West Germany. It was held that this question could not be reviewed on the basis of a legal standard. It seems that no one would claim that no legal standard applies to the question of which unit of government is authorized under Israeli constitutional law to decide whether to establish diplomatic relations. Similarly I assume that no one would claim that the matter is not justiciable if the question were the legality of taking a bribe in relation to establishing diplomatic relations. What then is the law if the claim is that it is not appropriate to establish diplomatic relations with West Germany? Are there legal standard to apply? To answer this question it is necessary to examine the nature of the legal norm applicable to the issue. The political plea that the decision was improper has to be translated into the legal norm that measures impropriety of government action. As we have seen, the political plane and the legal plane are distinct. Examination of the example I have cited reveals that the closest legal norm is that which states that every governmental decision, including that concerning diplomatic relations with West Germany, must be reasonable. The political claim that "it is improper to establish diplomatic ties with West Germany" is translated into the legal argument plea that "it is unreasonable to establish diplomatic ties with Western Germany."

The question is therefore the following: If a general norm in fact exists which imposes on government the duty of reasonableness, and if in fact this general norm applies also to the decision to establish diplomatic ties, how can it be said that there are no standards and criteria to assess the question of whether governmental conduct is reasonable or unreasonable? In my opinion, the existence of the reasonableness norm implies that standards to assess the reasonableness of an action exist. It cannot be that a norm prohibits unreasonable action, but there are no standards to decide the question of whether or not an action is unreasonable. We are concerned with an interpretative activity requiring that normative content be given to the principle of reasonableness and that standards be established for its realization. The argument that there are no standards to determine the reasonableness or unreasonableness of a particular action is equivalent to the argument that the norm of reasonableness does not apply to a particular action.

On the basis of this conception, it is possible to examine the plea of *non-justiciability* which was raised and admitted in [a case where the petitioner claimed] that the army was not employing the correct method of debriefing its soldiers and deriving lessons from its experience in the conduct of the Yom Kippur War. [The petitioner claimed that the method of debriefing which the army used was ineffective.] ... The first question I would have posed is: What is the relevant legal norm for deciding the petitioner's claim? To the best of my knowledge, there is no norm which states that an ineffective governmental action is illegal. Therefore if the sole plea is lack of effectiveness, as such, the petition must be dismissed for lack of a cause of action, because the petitioner did not indicate any norm according to which an ineffective military action is also illegal. However, it seems that the correct legal framework which encompasses this petitioner's plea is that the army is acting unreasonably. His legal argument is therefore that an army which does not conduct debriefing and does not derive lessons as he alleges, is an army which is acting unreasonably.

The reasonableness test is a familiar one. Under it, the court does not replace the military authorities' exercise of discretion with its own. Under this test, the court asks whether a reasonable army would have taken the actions which the army took, or the actions which the petitioner requests the army to take.

In most cases where the respondent claims that a petition is non-justiciable, the question really relates to whether the government action should be reviewed under the standard of reasonableness. Given this, we should examine the issue of reasonableness more closely. Today everyone agrees that government must act reasonably. This means that governmental authorities must choose that course of action which a reasonable governmental authority would have chosen under the circumstances of the matter. Frequently a number of reasonable courses of action exist, and then it is incumbent on the authority to choose that course of action which it deems best. We refer to its realm of choice as *the scope of reasonableness*. The boundaries of the scope of reasonableness are determined pursuant to the proper balance between the various interests and values, and in particular the individual's interests and values on the one side, and those of the public on the other. The relevant interests and values are determined based on the specific issue at hand and on the basis of the fundamental principles of the system as understood by the enlightened public. The scope of reasonableness is determined by giving each of these interests its proper weight in balancing them against each other. Determining what is reasonable is therefore not just a technical consideration, but rather a substantive one. The proper balance between competing values depends not just on logic and rationality, but also on legal policy.

The determination of what interests and values are relevant to the decision of the government authority is a question of law. It requires interpreting the relevant norm, such as a statute, and ascertaining what interests and values are relevant to the decision at hand. This is a routine type of judicial inquiry. For example, a decision might involve weighing the need for public order against the value of free expression. The main difficulty arises in deciding the proper weight to be given to competing interests and how they should be balanced against each other.

The question is whether, practically speaking, a court is incapable of carrying out the process of the weighing and balancing. I think the answer is in the negative. If the legislature has not spoken to the issue, the court must consider the fundamental values of the nation, its credo, its national way of life, and the sources of the people's national self-awareness. In doing so, the judge will consider the outlooks accepted by the enlightened public. At times, the judge will find that those sources do not provide sufficient guidance. In such situations, the judge must exercise his own discretion. This task is sometimes difficult.

The judge in this situation must consider all values and interests and give them the weight he thinks best reflects their meaning in society.

Some legal norm applies to every governmental action, and within the framework of the applicable norm it is always possible to formulate standards for evaluating the action. It is possible to determine whether the governmental authority was within its jurisdiction when it undertook the action, whether it considered the proper facts, and whether its conduct was reasonable.... The authority's action will be examined on its merits pursuant to these standards, without any recourse at all to the claim of normative justiciability (or non-justiciability).

D. Institutional Justiciability

A dispute is institutionally justiciable if it is appropriate for a court to make a determination in the matter based on the law. A dispute is not institutionally justiciable if it is inappropriate for it to be determined according to legal standards before a court. Institutional justiciability is therefore concerned with the question of whether the law and the courts constitute the appropriate framework for the resolution of a dispute. The question is not whether it is possible to decide the dispute by law in court; the answer to this question is in the affirmative. The question is whether it is desirable to decide the dispute—which is normatively justiciable—in a court applying legal standards.

Nothing in the separation of powers principle justifies rejection of judicial review of governmental acts, whatever their character or content. On the contrary: the separation of powers principle justifies judicial review of government actions even if they are of a political nature, since it ensures that every authority acts lawfully within its own domain, thereby ensuring the separation of powers.

A democratic regime is one which strikes the proper balance between majority rule and individual rights. The first principle, majority rule, ensures that the government acts in accordance with majority opinion, meaning, *inter alia*, that political decisions are made by the political organs chosen, directly or indirectly, by the people. The second principle, individual rights, ensures that the majority, by means of the political organs, does not infringe the fundamental rights of the individual. Judicial review, which ensures that the political bodies act within the scope of the authority granted to them by the democratic regime, is not contrary to this democratic conception. Judicial review safeguards the proper realization of the democratic formula. It ensures, on the one hand, that majority opinion is effectuated within the legal framework developed for this purpose in the regime, whether it be the Constitution, statutes, regulations or administrative orders ... ; on the other hand, it ensures that the majority does not infringe individual rights, unless it has lawful authorization to do so. It follows that no harm is caused to the democratic regime when judicial review holds illegal the actions of governmental bodies which take into account political considerations, if these bodies act unlawfully. To be more precise: the court does not review the internal logic and practical efficacy of the political consideration. The court examines the legality of such considerations. This examination in no way harms the democratic regime. There is nothing in the democratic regime which holds that the majority is entitled to act contrary to statutes that it enacted, or that political decisions can violate the law. Even the most political determination must be based on a lawful decision. In a democratic regime, there are no politics without law. There is therefore nothing in democratic principles that can justify institutional non-justiciability.

We are left only with the contention that institutional non-justiciability as to political issues is justified because it protects the court from the politicization of the judiciary and from impairment of public confidence in judicial objectivity. I regard this argument as problematic.... The role of the administrative court is to protect the rule of law and the public confidence in the rule of law.

Despite this critique of the institutional non-justiciability doctrine, it is difficult to ignore the fact that the public is unlikely to make a distinction between judicial review and political review; it is likely to identify judicial review of a political issue with the issue itself; it is likely to identify judicial determination that a governmental action is lawful with a judicial position that the governmental action is desirable; it is likely to maintain that a judicial determination that a governmental action is not lawful is equivalent to the judiciary's negative position towards the action itself; it is likely to find that the judicial determination that a governmental action is reasonable is equivalent to a judicial determination that that position is desirable; it is likely to equate the legal determination with a political viewpoint.

The key question is, what weight should we give this fear? ... In my opinion, only in special circumstances, in which the fear of harm to public confidence in the judges outweighs the fear of harm to public confidence in the law, should use of [the doctrine of institutional justiciability] be considered. The list of such circumstances is not closed, and is to be determined by the judicial life experience and according to the judge's expert sense.

Comment

Justice Barak's opinion was the opinion of the Court and is now accepted doctrine in Israeli law. It says that there are two aspects to justiciability: *normative justiciability*, or the question of whether a court has the capacity to review an administrative decision, and *institutional justiciability*, or the question of whether a court should undertake to review an administrative decision.

Normative Justiciability: The portion of the decision on normative justiciability includes a discussion of the substantive standards of judicial review. The basic argument on normative justiciability is that a court is always capable of exercising the power of judicial review over administrative decisions because, in every case, (a) the decisions must be made in accord with legal rules and (b) it is the task of a court to be sure those legal rules are observed. The opinion then discusses what some of those legal rules are. It mentions five:

1. The administrative agency must have authority, or jurisdiction, to make the decision.

2. The administrative agency must not act in a corrupt manner. This means that it cannot take a bribe, cannot exhibit favoritism for relatives of the decision-maker, etc.

3. The agency must consider all factors set out as relevant in the law authorizing it to act. For example, a law on allocation of water rights may require the agency to consider the importance of a specific use for which a person is seeking an allocation. The agency must consider the importance of a use in making the allocations.

4. The agency must consider factors that are part of the general values of the state. These are relevant to every administrative decision whether or not a specific statute makes them relevant. For example, an agency cannot make a decision that adversely affects freedom of expression without at least considering the impact of the decision on freedom of expression. It does not matter whether the statute that authorized the agency action required it to consider freedom of expression. Protection of freedom of expression is a general value in Israel, and it must always be considered.

5. Once the agency has identified all relevant considerations, if there are conflicts among them, it must balance them, assigning to each one the proper weight. A decision that properly balances the various competing considerations is reasonable. One that does not is unreasonable.

Justice Barak goes on to posit that in every case of a challenge to an administrative decision, at least one of these issues, the final one, arises. A court can review all administrative decisions to determine whether they are reasonable. Therefore normative justiciability is present in all challenges to administrative action.

Institutional Justiciability: Even if a court could review an administrative decision on the above grounds, or on other administrative law grounds, the question is whether there are occasions in which it should refrain from doing so. Justice Barak thinks that, in an ideal world, a court would never refrain. The argument for a court refraining is that it would otherwise be entering into the realm of another branch of government, deciding political issues that should be left to the legislative or executive branch. Justice Barak would like to reject this argument for two reasons. First, if a court desists from reviewing an administrative action, then the agency is left free to do whatever it wants without the proper judicial oversight that the system of checks and balances requires. Allowing agencies to act illegally without judicial oversight can even lead the public to lose confidence in the law. In this sense, he means a loss of public confidence in the rule of law: the assurance that government will be conducted according to legal standards. Second, when a court reviews the decision of an agency, even if it is a highly politically charged decision, it is not deciding a political issue. It is only deciding the underlying legal issues, applying the legal tests, including the test of reasonableness, to determine whether the decision is legally valid. It is not deciding the political issue of whether the decision is wise.

But Justice Barak admits that the public does not see things this way and is concerned that, in misunderstanding what a court is doing, the public may come to disrespect the courts as a public institution, wrongfully thinking that they have strayed into the political realm. Therefore Justice Barak does not advocate ignoring this public misunderstanding. Rather, he suggests that to determine whether a court should hear a politically charged case it should balance one evil against the other. Specifically it should balance the harm that will be caused to the public confidence in the rule of law if the court desists from hearing the case against the harm to public confidence in the political neutrality of the courts if the court does hear the case. Only when the latter value exceeds the former should a court decline to hear a case because of a lack of institutional justiciability.

In summary, a court always has something to say about the legality of administrative action, but occasionally, it may refrain from saying it.

The claim that normative justiciability exists in all cases depends on the demarcation between legal issues and political issues being clear, at least conceptually, even if it is not always clear to the public. Arguably the demarcation is not so clear. It is easy to see that the issue of jurisdiction is a fairly pure legal issue. So is the issue of what constitutes forbidden, corrupt practices. The question of what factors a statute requires an agency to consider is also a legal issue: it requires interpretation of a statute, and statutory interpretation is a legal task in which courts often engage. As to the next two legal rules discussed in the opinion, the matter is less clear. In determining whether an agency considered the general values of the state, and in determining whether the agency gave these values the proper weight, a court must first determine what the values are and then decide how important, or weighty, they are. A court finds these in "the fundamental values of the nation, its 'credo,' its 'national way of life,' and 'the sources of the people's national self-awareness.'" How is a court, which is a non-majoritarian institution, supposed to identify the "national self-awareness"? What expertise does a court have in understanding the "national way of life"? Undoubtedly Justice Barak would answer that this is not an empirical exercise that tests what the people want. Justice Barak would look for these values in legal documents, such as the Declaration of the Establishment of the State. But this is not enough. So "the judge will consider the outlooks 'accepted by the enlightened public.'" Is identification of which segments of the public are enlightened a legal process or a political process? Furthermore, "At times, the judge will find that those sources do not provide sufficient guidance. In such situations, the judge must exercise his own discretion." Is exercise of this discretion a purely legal act? What will a judge consider in exercising his own discretion? If it is not, then the demarcation between legal analysis and political analysis of the issues raised in a case begins to blur.

The Outcome: Although the Supreme Court in *Ressler* found that the petitioners had standing and that the issue was justiciable, it declined to invalidate the decision of the minister of defense to grant deferments to yeshiva students. The issue was revisited ten years later in a similar petition in *Rubenstein v. Minister of Defense.*[14] Again, the Court decided the case on the merits of the claim, but this time it decided that the deferments were not legal. The minister of defense was acting under a statute that gave him authority to grant deferments for several specified reasons or for "other reasons." The deferment for yeshiva students did not fall under any of the specified reasons, so the minister of defense granted them under the authority to consider "other reasons." The Court ruled that a matter as controversial as the deferments could not be decided by the minister of defense under such general authority. The deferments had to be specifically authorized by statute. Because they were not, the deferments were invalid.

The Court gave two reasons for deviating from the earlier substantive ruling in *Ressler* that the deferments were permissible. First, the development of constitutional law in the intervening years showed the importance of having the Knesset set any legal rules that impinge on individual rights. The deferments affected two conflicting individual rights: freedom of religion and the right to equality. Therefore the Knesset had to make a decision on the matter and could not leave it to the discretion of the minister of defense to decide whether or not to grant the deferments. Second, the number of deferments had increased substantially in the intervening years, to more than 20,000, so the issue had become more critical.

The Court in *Rubenstein* did not invalidate the deferments immediately, but gave the Knesset a defined period of time to enact a new statute. After several extensions of time, the Knesset enacted a statute that continued most deferments for yeshiva students. The statute was highly controversial. *Movement for Quality Government in Israel v. Knesset,*[15] set out in the previous chapter, involved a challenge to that statute. While that challenge did not succeed, a later one did on constitutional law, not administrative law, grounds. The case, HCJ 2698/07 *Ressler v. Knesset of Israel* (Feb. 21, 2012), was discussed in chapter 8.

In the United States, the issue of justiciability arises under the rubric of the political question doctrine. A case that would require a court to decide a matter that the Constitution has committed to one of the political branches of government, either the legislative or the executive branch, raises a political question, and courts will not decide such cases. The leading case is *Baker v. Carr,*[16] a case that found the issue presented not to be a political question, but in which the Court reviewed and categorized the political question types of cases. More recently, a number of political question cases have been decided

---

14. HCJ 3267/97 Rubenstein v. Minister of Defense 52(5) PD 481 [1998].
15. HCJ 6427/02 Movement for Quality Government in Israel v. Knesset 61(1) PD 619 [2006].
16. 369 U.S. 186 (1962).

by the D.C. Circuit. Some do not involve review of administrative action, so they are not readily comparable to the type of issues the Israeli Supreme Court considered in *Ressler*. In the following case, though, the court reviewed the decision of the secretary of state, an administrative official.

US Case

Zivotofsky v. Secretary of State
571 F.3d 1227 (D.C. Cir. 2009)

GRIFFITH, Circuit Judge:

It has been the longstanding policy of the United States to take no side in the contentious debate over whether Jerusalem is part of Israel. In this case, the federal courts are asked to direct the secretary of state to contravene that policy and record in official documents that Israel is the birthplace of a US citizen born in Jerusalem. Because the judiciary has no authority to order the Executive Branch to change the nation's foreign policy in this matter, this case is non-justiciable under the political question doctrine.

I.

That the United States expresses no official view on the thorny issue of whether Jerusalem is part of Israel has been a central and calibrated feature of every president's foreign policy since Harry S. Truman.... Although the State Department typically records a passport holder's birthplace as the nation with sovereignty over his city of birth, *see* 7 US Department of State, Foreign Affairs Manual § 1383.1, passports issued to US citizens born in Jerusalem note only the city, *see id.* § 1360, app. D ("For a person born in Jerusalem, write Jerusalem as the place of birth in the passport. Do not write Israel.").

In 2002, Congress passed the Foreign Relations Authorization Act, Fiscal Year 2003, Pub.L. No. 107-228, 116 Stat. 1350 (2002) (codified at 22 U.S.C. § 2651 note (2006)). Section 214 of the act, entitled "United States Policy with Respect to Jerusalem as the Capital of Israel," challenges the executive's position on the status of Jerusalem. *Id.* § 214, 116 Stat. at 1365. Under subsection 214(c), Congress forbids the Executive from using appropriated funds for "publication of any official governmental document which lists countries and their capital cities unless the publication identifies Jerusalem as the capital of Israel." *Id.* § 214(c), 116 Stat. at 1366. And subsection 214(d), the provision at issue in this case, states:

> Record of Place of Birth as Israel for Passport Purposes. — For purposes of the registration of birth, certification of nationality, or issuance of a passport of a United States citizen born in the city of Jerusalem, the Secretary [of State] shall, upon the request of the citizen or the citizen's legal guardian, record the place of birth as Israel.

Id. § 214(d), 116 Stat. at 1366. In a written statement issued when he signed the bill into law, the president took the view that section 214 is merely advisory because a congressional command to the executive to change the government's position on the status of Jerusalem would "impermissibly interfere with the president's constitutional authority to formulate the position of the United States, speak for the nation in international affairs, and determine the terms on which recognition is given to foreign states." President George W. Bush,

Statement on Signing the Foreign Relations Authorization Act, 38 Weekly Compilation of Press Documents 1659 (Sept. 30, 2002). Even in signing the act, the president made clear that "US policy regarding Jerusalem has not changed." *Id.*

In October 2002, Menachem Zivotofsky was born in Jerusalem to parents who are US citizens, making him a citizen as well. *See* 8 U.S.C. § 1401(c) (2006). In December 2002, Menachem's mother applied for a US passport and a Consular Report of Birth for her son at the US Embassy in Tel Aviv, Israel. She requested that both documents record her son's place of birth as Jerusalem, Israel. US diplomatic officials told Mrs. Zivotofsky that State Department policy forbade them from recording "Israel" as her son's birthplace. Consistent with its policy, the State Department issued a passport and Consular Report of Birth identifying "Jerusalem" as Menachem's place of birth without reference to Israel.

In September 2003, Menachem (by his parents) filed this action for declaratory and injunctive relief ordering the State Department to comply with the directive in section 214(d) and record "Jerusalem, Israel," as his birthplace in both his passport and Consular Report of Birth.

II.

The issue before us is whether the State Department can lawfully refuse to record [Zivotofsky's] place of birth as "Israel" in the face of a statute that directs it to do so.

It is well established that the Constitution's grant of authority to the president to "receive ambassadors and other public ministers," US Const. art. II, § 3, includes the power to recognize foreign governments. *See, e.g.,* Louis Henkin, *Foreign Affairs and the United States Constitution* 38 (2nd ed. 1996) (explaining that the ambassadorial receipt clause in Article III "implies [the] power to recognize (or not to recognize) governments"). That this power belongs solely to the president has been clear from the earliest days of the republic.

The president's exercise of the recognition power granted solely to him by the Constitution cannot be reviewed by the courts. A decision made by the president regarding which government is sovereign over a particular place is an exercise of that power.

Thus the president has exclusive and unreviewable constitutional power to keep the United States out of the debate over the status of Jerusalem. Nevertheless Zivotofsky asks us to review a policy of the State Department implementing the president's decision. But as the Supreme Court has explained, policy decisions made pursuant to the president's recognition power are non-justiciable political questions. *See United States v. Pink,* 315 U.S. 203, 229 (1942).... The State Department's refusal to record "Israel" in passports and Consular Reports of Birth of US citizens born in Jerusalem implements this longstanding policy of the executive. By asking the judiciary to order the State Department to mark official government documents in a manner that would directly contravene the president's policy, Zivotofsky invites the courts to call into question the president's exercise of the recognition power. This we cannot do. We therefore hold that Zivotofsky's claim presents a non-justiciable political question because it trenches upon the president's constitutionally committed recognition power.

Comment

The D.C. Circuit relied heavily on constitutional considerations in finding that the case raised a non-justiciable political question. The Constitution prevented the court from deciding the case, because a decision would require the court to take a position on a question, the recognition of a foreign government, assigned by the Constitution exclusively to the president. Israel lacks a constitution making such an exclusive assignment, so it is not forced to recognize a mandatory doctrine of justiciability.

This reveals a major difference between the way justiciability is treated in *Ressler* and the way it is treated in *Zivotofsky*. In *Ressler*, the Supreme Court held that it is a discretionary doctrine. The courts have discretion to find cases non-justiciable, but they are not required to do so. The doctrine of non-justiciability discussed in *Zivotofsky* is a mandatory one. The D.C. Circuit held that it lacked the power to make a decision regarding the issue of recognition of a foreign government.

The Supreme Court reversed the decision of the Court of Appeals on the issue of non-justiciability.

US Case

Zivotofsky v. Clinton
132 S.Ct. 1421 (2012)

Chief Justice Roberts:

The lower courts ruled that this case involves a political question because deciding Zivotofsky's claim would force the Judicial Branch to interfere with the President's exercise of constitutional power committed to him alone. The District Court understood Zivotofsky to ask the courts to "decide the political status of Jerusalem." 511 F.Supp.2d, at 103. This misunderstands the issue presented. Zivotofsky does not ask the courts to determine whether Jerusalem is the capital of Israel. He instead seeks to determine whether he may vindicate his statutory right, under § 214(d), to choose to have Israel recorded on his passport as his place of birth.

For its part, the D.C. Circuit treated the two questions as one and the same.... Because the Department's passport rule was adopted to implement the President's "exclusive and unreviewable constitutional power to keep the United States out of the debate over the status of Jerusalem," the validity of that rule was itself a "nonjusticiable political question" that "the Constitution leaves to the Executive alone." *Id.*, at 1231–1233. Indeed, the D.C. Circuit's opinion does not even mention § 214(d) until the fifth of its six paragraphs of analysis, and then only to dismiss it as irrelevant: "That Congress took a position on the status of Jerusalem and gave Zivotofsky a statutory cause of action ... is of no moment to whether the judiciary has [the] authority to resolve this dispute...." *Id.*, at 1233.

The existence of a statutory right, however, is certainly relevant to the Judiciary's power to decide Zivotofsky's claim. The federal courts are not being asked to supplant a foreign policy decision of the political branches with the courts' own unmoored determination of what United States policy toward Jerusalem should be. Instead, Zivotofsky requests that the courts enforce a specific statutory right. To resolve his claim, the Judiciary must decide if Zivotofsky's interpretation of the statute is correct, and whether the statute is constitutional. This is a familiar judicial exercise.

Moreover, because the parties do not dispute the interpretation of § 214(d), the only real question for the courts is whether the statute is constitutional. At least since *Marbury v. Madison*, 1 Cranch 137, 2 L.Ed. 60 (1803), we have recognized that when an Act of Congress is alleged to conflict with the Constitution, "[i]t is emphatically the province and duty of the judicial department to say what the law is."

In this case, determining the constitutionality of § 214(d) involves deciding whether the statute impermissibly intrudes upon Presidential powers under the Constitution. If so, the law must be invalidated and Zivotofsky's case should be dismissed for failure to state a claim. If, on the other hand, the statute does not trench on the President's powers, then the Secretary must be ordered to issue Zivotofsky a passport that complies with § 214(d). Either way, the political question doctrine is not implicated.

Questions

3. Is the Israeli Supreme Court's rule on justiciability consistent or inconsistent with its rule on standing?

4. Taipei is the capital city of the Republic of China, which is commonly known as Taiwan. Taiwan is an island located a little more than a hundred miles off the coast of the mainland. The People's Republic of China (the country on the mainland) claims sovereignty over Taiwan. The People's Republic of China denies the existence of the Republic of China as a separate country. Israel recognizes the People's Republic of China and has an embassy there. It does not have an embassy in the Republic of China but does have a representative in Taipei in the Israel Economic and Cultural Office, which provides visa services. Assume that the foreign minister of Israel, not wanting to take a position on the dispute regarding the status of the Republic of China, had issued a directive stating, "All visas issued in Taipei shall indicate that they were issued in Taipei, without indication of the country of issuance." This directive was issued despite a new statute on visas that provides, "All visas shall indicate the city and country of issuance."

Visas issued in Taipei indicate, under place of issuance, "Taipei." No country is indicated. A Taiwanese NGO dedicated to the continued recognition of the Republic of China as an independent country files a petition against the foreign minister in the High Court of Justice to order that all visas issued by the in Taipei indicate that they were issued in Taipei, Republic of China. A citizen of Israel who is a member of the NGO joins as a petitioner in the suit. The respondent, the foreign minister, claims that the petitioners lack standing and that the Court should not consider the case because it is not justiciable.

How would the Court rule on these two claims and why?

F. Challenges to Administrative Actions — Substantive Review

The most outstanding feature of substantive administrative law in Israel is the way courts review agency exercise of discretion. Assume that an agency, about to issue a rule, decides whether to grant a license to an applicant, determines whether to give a grant to one person or another, or makes another decision, correctly interprets the law that applies to it and properly gathers the relevant facts. The agency now has to decide what to do. In some cases, the answer is clear. For example, the age for obtaining a driver's license in Israel is 17. If a person applies to get a license at age 16, the agency responsible must deny the license. If the applicant is 17 and has passed all the required tests, the agency issues the license. There is no discretion involved. In other cases, agencies have very broad discretion. Consider the case where a statute authorizes an agency to promulgate regulations on how factories can be operated so as to reduce water pollution. Such a statute gives the agency broad discretion. Once the agency promulgates a regulation requiring certain types of factories to install designated pollution control equipment, a person can file a petition for judicial review claiming that the regulation is too stringent, too costly, or too lenient. In effect, the petition seeks judicial review of the agency's exercise of discretion.

Courts reviewing an agency's exercise of discretion apply three main tests to determine whether an agency properly exercised its discretion: the relevant factors test, the reasonableness test, and the proportionality test.

1. The Relevant Factors Test:

Under the relevant factors test, an Israeli court reviewing an agency's exercise of discretion determines whether the agency took into consideration all relevant factors. Such review may seem simple, but is in fact far-reaching. In looking for the factors the agency must consider, the court looks first at the agency's enabling act. The court will determine whether the agency considered all the statutorily mandated factors. This is the beginning of the court's examination, but, as the following case explains, it is not the end.

Israeli Case

Poraz v. City Council of Tel Aviv-Jaffa
HCJ 953/87 42(2) PD 309 [1988]

[In most countries, although not in the United States, the Jewish community is served by a chief rabbi, selected by the Jewish community within the country. In Israel, the office is recognized by law. In fact, the country has two chief rabbis, one of whom is Ashkenazi and one of whom is Sephardic. They oversee the provision of religious services to the Jewish community in Israel. Major cities in Israel also have chief rabbis who oversee provision of Jewish services within the city. This case involves the procedures leading up to the selection of a chief rabbi for a city.]

Justice A. Barak:

The chief rabbi of a city is selected by an elective assembly. One-third of the members of the elective assembly are representatives of the city council. Is the city council permitted to intentionally refuse to elect a woman as one of its representatives to the elective assembly? This is the question before us on this petition.

The composition of the elective assembly is: one-third representatives of the city council, one-third representatives of the religious council, and one-third representatives of the synagogues in the area. [The city council held many discussions about the issue of inclusion of women as representatives of the council to the elective assembly. After many failed attempts at voting for lists of representatives that included women, the council finally voted for a list of 20 representatives, all of whom were male.]

Women in the Elective Assembly

The central question before us is whether the decision of the city council is consistent with the law. We begin by recognizing that the absence of women from among the city's representatives to the elective assembly is not just coincidental and is not a result of the fact that there were no women appropriate for the task. The facts set before us show that the reason for the city council's decision—that is the reason for the majority vote—is based on an affirmative decision not to select any women as representatives of the city council to the elective assembly. The reason the city council decided not to select any women was not that its members desired to discriminate against women. Instead, the council based its decision on two practical considerations. One is the fear that if the chief rabbi of the city is selected by an elective assembly that includes women, he will not be able to fulfill his job properly because the office of the national chief rabbi will then not cooperate with the chief rabbi of the city. The second consideration is that some appropriate candidates for the job of chief rabbi of the city will not present their candidacy if the elective assembly includes women. We determined from the discussions in the city council that these were the reasons for the vote.... The question before us now is whether the decision based on these reasons is legal.

The Law

In my opinion, the decision of the city council is invalid, and therefore void. Here is the reason for my position: When the city council elects its representatives to the elective assembly, it is operating under authority granted to the council in regulations promulgated under the authority of the Law on Religious Services for Jews (Consolidated Version), 5731-1971 (hereinafter Religious Services Law). The city council is therefore fulfilling a public mission under the law. The factors that the city council can consider in reaching a decision are those that fall within the area defined by the Religious Services Law and the regulations promulgated pursuant to that law. The identity of these factors is determined by interpretation of the statute and the regulations. In interpreting the law, we take into account the language of the law and its objectives. The objectives include the specific objectives of the law, which are to be determined from its language and from the legislative history. In addition, in the absence of evidence to the contrary, we assume that the objectives include general objectives that implement the values and principles of our legal system.

Practical Objectives

[As to the specific objective of the statute,] the city council must consider factors related to selection of an elective assembly that will be capable of fulfilling its task of appointing a chief rabbi for the city. Any factor that relates to effectuating that goal is a relevant factor.... If the legislature established the institution of the chief rabbi of the city, our presumption is that the specific goal was that the elective assembly will be constituted in a way that will allow it to select a chief rabbi of the city who will be able to properly fulfill his job. Therefore I am ready to presume that based on the specific goals of the Religious Services Law, nothing prohibits the city council from considering the undesirability of selecting women for the elective assembly. If the participation of women in the elective assembly will adversely affect the ability of a chief rabbi chosen by the assembly to do what is required in his job, I am willing to see this as counting against the selection of women and to allow the city council to take this into consideration. This presumption is not founded on the legislative history or the language of the law, which are silent about this problem. The presumption is based on rational analysis.

Does the legislative history tell us anything? [The rules that were in effect beginning during the British Mandate and continuing through 1974 provided that the chief rabbi of a local community was to be chosen by a committee "composed of men 25 years of age and older." In 1974, new regulations were promulgated under the Religious Services Law.] These regulations are not like the old regulations on the selection of the chief city rabbis. Rather, they set up a new system of elections, partly based on the old one. For the purpose of our analysis, we note that ... the new regulations have no requirement that the elective assembly be composed of men aged 25 and older. We do not know what led to this change. To my great sorrow, we do not publish proposed rules, and there are no written documents explaining the rules available to the public. We do not know if the change was accidental or intentional. Still, we can see from this legislative history that while in the past there was a requirement that only men aged 25 and older could serve on the body that chose the rabbis, such a requirement no longer exists. This creates the presumption that the change was not coincidental, and that the party promulgating the regulations did not want to perpetuate this limitation. Therefore the legislative history supports the view that membership in the elective assembly should not be limited to men alone.... Nonetheless this presumption is not a strong one, and based on it alone I would not reach a conclusion one way or another.

Therefore based on the language of the Religious Services Law and on the practical goals of the law, we cannot find a clear solution to our problem. On the one hand, the nature of the city council and its limited task in selecting the elective assembly that chooses the chief rabbi of the city suggest that we should not discount practical considerations that are designed to allow the elective assembly to fulfil its job. In this light, the refusal to select women does not seem an improper consideration. On the other hand, the legislative history, from which we learn that the limitation of membership in the elective assembly to men aged twenty five or older was dropped, suggests that the goal was to eliminate the limitation of the elective assembly to men only. It seems to me that these two opposing goals are both weak ones, and they cannot form the basis for reaching a final decision on the matter before us. With this in mind, it is appropriate for us to turn to the general goals that we can presume that the legislature intended to serve.

General Presumptions

We presume that every law is intended to effectuate the basic values accepted in our legal system and to be consistent with them. Among these values is the principle of equality, including equality between the sexes.

Basic Values of the System

It is presumed that every statute and rule is designed to effectuate the basic values of the system and not to work in opposition to them.... The list of basic values is not a closed one. It varies with changes in the national way of life. Case law identifies equality, justice, and ethics as accepted basic values. Addition basic values are the democratic nature of the state, separation of powers, freedom of association, freedom to strike, freedom of expression, freedom to demonstrate, freedom of religion, protection of property rights, freedom of occupation, dignity of man, and neutrality of the judge. In addition, this Court has repeatedly identified good faith, natural justice, fairness, reasonableness, impartiality, and the absence of conflicts of interest as basic values that every law seeks to effectuate.

Equality is among these basic values which we have recognized.... Equality relates to all areas of life and to actions of the state. Equality should be maintained between those of different religions, nationalities,[17] sectors, races, parties, outlooks, and various groups. Even this is not a full list. We derive the requirement to assure equality in Israel from var-

---

17. Many Jews and Arabs in Israel see themselves as part of different nationalities, even though they are all Israeli. In this way, nationality means something different in the Israeli context than in the American context. See the discussion in chapter 2.

ious sources. The primary source is the Declaration of Independence,[18] which provides that the State of Israel "will ensure complete equality of social and political rights to all its inhabitants irrespective of religion, race, or sex." In addition to this source, we can point to the democratic nature of the state as requiring implementation of the principle of equality, to the nature of man as aspiring to equality, and to our national tradition. All of these have found expression in a number of statutes designed to implement the principle of equality in different areas.

One of the important aspects of equality is equality between the sexes. The Declaration of Independence expressed this.... Israeli law gives expression to this principle in a number of statutes (see, for example, Law on Equal Pay for Male and Female Employees, 5724-1964; Law on Equal Retirement Age for Male and Female Employees, 5747-1987; Law on Equal Work Opportunity, 5748-1988). The most important law of this type is the Law on Equal Rights for Women, 5719-1951.

It seems to me that we must presume that in enacting the Religious Services Law and its regulations, the Knesset and the minister who promulgated the regulation sought to implement the principle of equality. We must presume, therefore, that in authorizing the city council to select representatives to the elective assembly, the minister meant that the selection should follow the principle of equality and should not involve discrimination. We must presume, therefore, that the decision of the city council not to have female representatives to the elective assembly violates the principle of equality and therefore deviates from the goals of the law that authorizes the city council to act.... Of course, the presumption about the goal of law can be rebutted by a clear statement of specific contradictory goals. As we have seen, such clear contradictory goals are not found in the matter before us. The presumption remains that gender equality is among the basic values that should inform the actions of the governmental authorities in choosing representatives to the elective assembly. We note that the city council did not purposely try to violate the principle of equality or treat this as an irrelevant matter. The opposite is true. Many of the city council members indicated that they agree with the principle of equality, but they were not ready to implement it. In this way, they violated it. It is not just the motivation of those making the decision that is relevant, but also the result of the decision. The decision is invalid not only when there is intent to discriminate, but also when there is no such intent, but in fact the principle of equality is violated.

What is the conclusion to be reached from our analysis? I conclude that the Religious Services Law and the regulations are to be interpreted in light of both their specific and their general objectives. Such interpretation requires that representatives of the local council to the elective assembly be selected after taking into consideration the principle of gender equality. Every exercise of discretion that does not weigh this factor contradicts the goal of the law and is therefore invalid.

Comment

In *Poraz*, the Supreme Court treated the city council of Tel-Aviv-Yaffo as an authority subject to the rules of administrative law. The Court reviewed the council's decision not to include women among the council's representatives to the elective assembly for selecting the chief rabbi of the city. The Court examined the decision of the council to see if it considered the proper factors in reaching this decision. It found that it considered some

---

18. The document officially titled "The Declaration of the Establishment of the State," set out in chapter 4, is often referred to as the Declaration of Independence.

relevant factors, but not all of them. The council considered a goal that related to the specific law: to make the selection system work so that the chief rabbi selected would be able to fulfill the jobs assigned to the chief rabbi of a city. Other factors that had to be considered derived from the general goals of the state. These included promotion of equality. Because the council did not properly consider the importance of promoting equality between the sexes, the decision was invalid.

The city council decided not to put any women on the elective assembly because it feared that the chief rabbis of the country would have disdain for a chief city rabbi selected by a group that included women. This was a reasonable fear, given the very conservative nature of the national chief rabbis' office at the time of the decision. The attitude in this office did not reflect the majority attitude in the country toward women, but it did reflect the attitude of many in the religious establishment. The Court held that it was reasonable for the city council to consider this problem, but that such consideration could not be the only one taken into account. Furthermore it had to be weighed against the value of equality between the sexes. Nothing in the laws applying to the selection of the chief rabbi of a city prevented consideration of gender equality. Because the value of promoting gender equality was so important, had it been considered, it would have trumped the concern about the adverse effects of having women in the elective assembly.

In *Poraz*, the Court treated the right to equality as a general right that derived from the Declaration of the Establishment of the State and from a variety of other sources. Fourteen years after *Poraz* was decided, the Court decided that there is a constitutional right to some aspects of equality.[19]

The rule of the *Poraz* case is far-reaching. It requires all administrative agencies to consider promotion of gender equality in all of their decisions, unless specifically told not to do so by statute. Other cases apply analysis used in *Poraz* to require all agencies to consider equality not only between the sexes, but also equality between Jews and Arabs. An agency may even be required to consider the value of affirmative action.[20] Case law has also required government decisions to reflect considerations of distributive justice, or equal treatment of different social sectors.[21]

The general considerations that agencies must take into account are not limited to those associated with equality. Agencies are also required to consider other values related to individual rights, both those that are recognized as constitutional rights and those derived from other sources. While most cases addressing the requirement to consider general values of the state relate to individual rights, some go beyond this realm. In *Medinvest Medical Center Herzliya Ltd. v. Director General of the Ministry of Health*,[22] the petitioner had requested a license to open a new hospital to be financed largely by foreign investors. The plan was for the hospital to hire both Israeli doctors and foreign doctors who wanted to move to Israel. The respondent had refused to grant a license, giving as the reason the fact that there was no need for another hospital. The Supreme Court held the decision invalid, pointing out that the respondent had failed to take into consideration a number

19. HCJ 6427/02 Movement for Quality Government in Israel v. Knesset 61(1) PD 619 [2006]. This case was discussed in chapter 8 on constitutional law.

20. See HCJ 6924/98 Association for Civil Rights in Israel v. Government of Israel 58(5) PD 15 [2001] (recognizing as a general principle the need for affirmative action for Arabs).

21. See HCJ 244/00 Ass'n for New Deliberation for Democratic Deliberation v. Minister of Nat'l Infrastructure 56(6) PD 25 [2002].

22. HCJ 256/88 Medinvest Medical Center Herzliya Ltd. v. Director General of the Ministry of Health 44(1) PD 19 [1989].

of factors related to general values of the country, and not just to the specific statute regarding hospital licensing. These factors were obtaining foreign investment, the importance of providing additional places of work to discourage Israeli doctors from leaving the country in search of employment, encouraging immigration of Jewish doctors, and reducing the large number of people waiting for elective surgery. None of these considerations are based on individual rights.

Under the approach seen in *Poraz*, a court can identify general values, determine that they are incorporated into legislation that does not speak explicitly to these values, and invalidate any agency decision that does not take these values into account. This allows courts to prevent agencies from making parochial decisions that impinge on freedoms and values that most Israelis prize. Yet it leaves agencies in a conundrum. It is hard for an agency to know just what factors it must take into account in reaching a decision. The general values derive not from the language or legislative history of the specific statute, but from a variety of external sources. In the excerpt from *Poraz*, the Court relies on the Declaration of the Establishment of the State, a variety of statutes, the democratic nature of the state, the nature of man, and the national tradition to identify the general value of equality. Omitted portions of the decision cite case law, as well as Israeli and foreign legal literature as additional sources of general values. Even if an agency wanted in good faith to interpret its enabling act as requiring it to consider all general values, it may have a difficult time determining just what those general values are. This makes decision-making at agencies challenging. It also poses a problem for a person trying to get something from an agency, whether the person wants a new rule, an order, a license, or something else. Without having a clear idea of what the agency must consider in making a decision, it is almost impossible to predict how the agency will decide on a matter.

The great advantage of *Poraz* is that it inserted into Israeli jurisprudence the requirement that agencies do not discriminate even though no explicit requirement existed in positive law. The problem is that it did this in a way that leaves the law unpredictable.

Under the comparable doctrine in United States law, the APA requires that agencies consider all relevant matter submitted.[23] In any exercise of discretion, agencies must base their decisions on relevant factors.[24] In applying this test, courts do not engage in a far-reaching examination of factors that were not part of the record before the agency. *Poraz*, in contrast, requires the agency on its own to identify all general factors that are not evident on the face of the statute under which the agency acts. In part, this reflects the fact that the law does not require Israeli agencies to engage in extensive procedures providing outside input to the agency. In part, though, it reflects the Israeli view that every agency should know the general values of the state and should always take them into account.

Part of the *Poraz* decision goes beyond looking at the deliberative process of the agency and examines instead the outcome of those deliberations. This is found in the following language:

> Many of the city council members indicated that they agree with the principle of equality, but they were not ready to implement it. In this way, they violated it. It is not just the motivation of those making the decision that is relevant, but also the result of the decision. The decision is invalid not only when there is in-

---

23. 5 U.S.C. §553(c) (for informal rulemaking) and §706(2)(E) (for formal rulemaking and formal adjudication).

24. Motor Vehicle Mfrs. Ass'n. v. State Farm Mutual Auto. Ins. Co., 463 U.S. 29 (1983).

tent to discriminate, but also when there is no such intent, but in fact the principle of equality is violated.

The Court does not emphasize this aspect of the decision. Still, it shows a tendency of the Israeli Court to judge the actual decision, free of examination of the decision-making process. In this regard, the American approach to administrative law shows a stronger concentration on the decision-making process. American courts generally desist from judging the correctness of agency decisions. They do not examine the legality of the decision itself except to see if it contradicts the statute authorizing the agency to act, another statute, or the Constitution. American administrative law depends more on concepts of procedural justice, assuming that if the decision-making procedure is correct, the decision is likely to be correct. Furthermore American courts, when examining the substance of a decision, look at the agency explanation for that substance to see if the analytic process makes sense.[25] Because Israeli agencies are not required to explain their decisions, courts look more at the actual decision.

Question

5. You are the general counsel for the Ministry of Environmental Protection. The statute on hazardous waste requires that hazardous waste be removed from the premises where it is generated as soon as possible and in no case later than six months after generation, and the waste be sent to a special facility for handling hazardous waste. The specific requirement for each facility generating hazardous waste is included in the business license for that facility. A small metal cleaning factory generates small quantities of a type of hazardous waste that deteriorates in a period of 45 days into an explosive form. The ministry determined that removal of the waste every month is both necessary and possible. As a result, the factory's business license requires it to remove the hazardous waste from the factory premises every month. The factory has not been doing so. The minister is considering issuing an order to the factory requiring immediate compliance with the business license. The factory owner claims that monthly removal of small amounts of waste is far too expensive, that the factory accumulates sufficient amounts of waste to justify removal costs only every six months, and that the factory will have to shut down if forced to remove wastes every month. At present, the factory employs 15 workers. The head of the hazardous waste division of the ministry takes the position that none of these claims are relevant and that the factory must comply with the law. If the order is issued and the factory violates it, it will be subject to substantial daily penalties. The minister, who is sympathetic to the claims of the factory owner, wants to know if she can consider these claims in deciding whether to issue the order. You should also give her advice on what other factors she should consider. Focus on principles of administrative law in formulating your advice.

2. The Reasonableness Test

An Israeli court reviewing an agency decision determines whether the agency exercised its discretion in a reasonable manner. The test for reasonableness is interpreted to relate to the proper weighing of various factors in reaching a decision and is set out in the following case.

---

25. *Citizens to Preserve Overton Park v. Volpe*, 401 U.S. 402 (1971); *Motor Vehicle Mfrs. Ass'n. v. State Farm Mutual Automobile Ins. Co.*, 463 U.S. 29 (1983).

Israeli Case

Ganor v. Attorney General
HCJ 935/89 44(2) PD 485 [1990]

[Another part of this case was presented in chapter 6 on procedure. Several banks and bankers had been involved in a scheme that artificially ran up the value of bank shares. When the value of these shares began to plummet, the government had to purchase the shares to prevent a major financial crisis. A committee was appointed to investigate the matter and found that banks and their bankers had acted inappropriately. The attorney general decided not to indict the banks and the bankers because it would not be in the public interest to do so. In the case before us, the Court has been asked to review this decision. We saw in chapter 6 that the Court decided that the decision of the attorney general was subject to judicial review. The portion presented below discusses how the Court exercised that review.]

Justice A. Barak:

Reasonableness of Exercise of Discretion

Every governmental exercise of discretion must be reasonable. This includes the prosecutor's decision whether to indict a person. Reasonableness is not a physical or a metaphysical concept; it is a normative concept. It means that all relevant factors were considered and given the appropriate weight.

The appropriate weight is not set through deductive logic. [As I have said elsewhere:]

> The administrative authority must balance the various interests within the general normative framework set out by the legislature. The balance performed by that administrative authority is reasonable if the authority gives each factor the proper weight; that is, the weight required by interpreting the legislative norm which the authority is implementing.

Sometimes it is possible to achieve the goal of the statute in various ways. In such cases, it may be that there are several different appropriate ways of balancing the various factors. In such cases, a number of different administrative decisions may all be reasonable, without any one of them being best. In such a case, there is a *range of reasonableness*, that is, a range of possible decisions, each of which is reasonable.

Application to the Present Case

We must evaluate the decision of the attorney general on the basis of these principles.

In our opinion, the decision of the attorney general is defective because his conclusion that there is no "public interest" in prosecuting the banks and the bankers is substantially lacking in reasonableness. True, the attorney general did not consider any irrelevant facts, but only factors that are properly related to the issue. Nonetheless the weight he gave to the various factors is outside of the range of reasonableness. As a result, he decided that there was no public interest in the prosecution, and this distorted the weighing of the various factors. The crimes of which the banks and the bankers are accused, relating to securities, are, under the circumstances, serious crimes. The criminal behavior of which they are accused continued over a long period of time. It was done secretly. Their actions caused serious damage to thousands of people who lost their money and to the state treasury that had to put out huge sums of money in the bailout. The adverse effects on the state economy were extremely serious. All of these factors argue for giving great weight in favor of indicting the defendants. There is a very substantial public interest in punishing the responsible parties and in deterring banks, bankers, and others in the financial markets. If this earth-shaking case does not lead to an indictment, are there any circumstances under which it would be justified to indict banks and bankers said to violate the security laws? The factors which the attorney general considered are not of sufficient weight to counterbalance the factors which argue for filing an indictment. Let us examine those factors.

In deciding that an indictment would not be in the public interest, the attorney general gave substantial weight to the fact that the suspects have been subject to judgment in both administrative and public forums. This occurred in the decision of the Biyeski Commission [a public commission set up to investigate the affair] "that brought the imposition of serious sanctions on those involved with the affair, including dismissal from their positions and separation from the profession of banking." The attorney general also stated that the Biyeski Commission had already denunciated them for following unacceptable standards in their work, and thus not only punished the banks but also deterred others. These considerations are not relevant as to the banks themselves. The banks suffered no sanctions, not of dismissal and not of separation from their work. These considerations are partially relevant as to the bankers, but under the circumstances of the case, they are not of substantial weight. The imposition of administrative sanctions can reduce the public interest in the filing of an indictment where the matter at hand is not serious, and when the administrative sanctions have a sufficient deterrent effect on both the suspect and also on potential violators. Nonetheless the administrative sanction cannot meaningfully reduce the public interest in the filing of an indictment if the crime of which a suspect is accused is serious and if the degree of general deterrence is not substantial.

The bankers owe a debt to society and to the rule of law for the criminal acts of which they are accused. This debt has not yet been paid. The public has a strong interest in having them stand trial, so that what they did will be seen and known, so that this will not happen again. The judicial process that determines facts and imposes criminal liability determines the standards for appropriate behavior and expresses the public interest in establishing legal responsibility and in deterring potential criminals. Failing to put the bankers on trial in a case like this and leaving the matter to the administrative sanctions does not provide the same degree of establishment of legal rules that is needed for those suspected of causing such extensive damage to society. Furthermore the administrative sanction does not have the same deterrent effect that is so necessary to the continued functioning of society. In fact, the opposite is true; leaving the matter to an administrative sanction is an invitation to potential criminals to take a chance on committing a crime.

The attorney general gave great weight to the fact that the guilt for the affair lies not only at the door of the banks and the bankers, but also falls on the governmental authorities that are responsible for the stock exchange and for the economy. They knew what was happening and did nothing meaningful to prevent it. Of course, this is a proper factor to be considered, but under the circumstances, the weight of this consideration is not substantial. This is so for two reasons: First, to the degree that those working in such agencies are responsible for committing criminal acts, it is appropriate to consider indicting them as well. From the material before us, it appears that the public authorities did not cause the problem, but only failed to prevent it. This does not make their liability equal to that of those who caused the problem.... Second, the public officials knew generally what was happening, but did not know the specifics about the criminal offenses that were committed.

The attorney general, in his opinion, gave substantial weight to the long period of time that has passed since the commission of the crimes of which the banks and bankers are accused, writing that, "I do not see that it serves the public interest to go back over the matters and to impose on the public the costs and the distastefulness and effort of revisiting the affair after so much time, with the only goal being to gain an additional measure of punishment." These are appropriate considerations but, under the circumstances, they should not be afforded great weight. As for the time that has passed, this is partially because the attorney general put off making a decision on the matter in order to gain the perspective of distance from the affair. Without deciding whether waiting to gain perspective was appropriate, we can say that the resulting delay cannot be considered as a factor in deciding not to indict the banks and the bankers. Moreover the affair and the crisis that occurred in its wake caused so much turmoil that the passage of time has not weakened the aftermath of the affair and has not reduced its seriousness. Therefore the passage of time does not justify the failure of holding the responsible people liable at law.... In addition, even if considerations of efficiency require concentrating legal efforts on the main offenders, and leaving out those who were not as centrally involved, administrative efficiency can in no way justify completely abandoning the legal process in so sensitive a matter.

A decision about whether an indictment serves the public interest is reasonable if the benefit, from the point of view of the values and principles served by the criminal law, exceed the degree to which these values and principles are damaged. Under this standard, the attorney general's decision that there is no public interest in indicting the banks and the bankers is not reasonable. The damage to the values of the criminal law is substantial. Suspects who committed serious crimes would not be brought to justice. Those who caused "a business failure of rare magnitude, to which nothing in the Israeli experience is comparable," and who apparently committed a series of criminal acts under suspicious circumstances would not be subject to criminal liability. No deterrent lesson would be learned. The sense that all are equal before the law would be lost. The ability of the criminal law to direct social behavior would be damaged. Public trust in governmental authorities would be undermined. Behavior that had a destructive effect on the economy and on social life would go without proper punishment. This damage was considered insufficient to outweigh the social and private interest in not indicting the banks and bankers. It is proper to consider the suffering of the bankers since the crisis. It is proper to consider the price they paid under the recommendations of the Biyeski Commission and the values associated with not indicting them.... It is proper to consider the value of not imposing on the public the difficult task of presenting an indictment and conducting a criminal proceeding. But this value is nothing compared to the damage that will be caused to the public by failure to try the banks and the bankers. The scales are not of equal weight.

Scope of Review

We have come to the conclusion that the decision of the attorney general is not reasonable. The unreasonableness is not based on a slight deviation from the proper weighting of the various factors. The unreasonableness is found on a substantial deviation that reaches the very roots of the matter, so that the entire decision must be rejected as completely unreasonable. We have before us a serious departure from the proper balancing of consideration. Such a lack of reasonableness leads us to invalidate the decision of the attorney general, and also justifies our decision to interfere in this matter.

Comment

In *Ganor*, the Court looked at how the attorney general explained his decision in order to determine what weight he had given to various factors. In many cases, though, the agency under review has not prepared a full written justification for its decision. The reviewing court must then look at the explanations the agency offers in court, any other evidence of the weight the agency gave to various factors, or the substance of the agency's decision. American courts look only at the agency's contemporaneous explanation for its decision.

Question

6. Consider the same fact situation as is set out in question 5. Assume the minister decided to consider the factory owner's claims in deciding whether to issue the order. How much weight should she give to those claims? Assume she gives them great weight and does not issue an order, and an environmental group sues to reverse her decision because it is unreasonable. What is a court likely to decide? What if she gives the factory owner's claims little weight and issues the order, and the factory owner sues to have the order declared invalid because it is unreasonable? What is a court likely to decide?

It is hard to predict what a court would do in either scenario presented in the last question. This is another indicator that the law gives the agency little guidance. The agency cannot adjust its decision so as to avoid reversal on judicial review. In the United States, agency lawyers use case law to help guide the agency into making decisions that will withstand judicial review. That is a more difficult task under Israeli law.

Most of the time the Supreme Court does not interfere with an agency's choice of what factors to consider or how to weigh those factors against each other in economic or environmental decisions. An example of a case involving economic and environmental issues where the Supreme Court declined to substitute its judgment for that of the agency because the matter within the expertise and professional knowledge of the agency is *Zera Company (1939) v. National Building and Planning Commission.*[26] The case involved a petition against a plan for a new park. The petitions claimed that the plan was economically infeasible, that as a result the park would not actually be built, and that the area designated for the park would remain undeveloped to the disadvantage of residents of the area. The Court refused to second guess the way the agency weighed economic factors in approving the plan.

3. Proportionality Test

Although the opinion in the *Ganor* case says it is looking only at how the agency weighted various factors, it includes language that suggests that it is going beyond this type of examination. The Court stated, "A decision about whether an indictment serves the public interest is reasonable if the benefit, from the point of view of the values and principles served by the criminal law, exceed the degree to which these values and principles are damaged." In other words, a court should do a cost-benefit analysis and determine whether the good to come from the decision exceeds the bad that comes from it. The Court in *Ganor* did not follow through on this suggestion, but later cases did. The cost-benefit analysis of administrative decisions became part of the proportionality test.

We already saw in chapter 8 that the courts use the proportionality test to determine whether a law infringing on a basic right is constitutional. The infringement must be pro-

---

26. HCJ 3017/05 (March 23, 2011).

portional. The following case demonstrates how the proportionality test is used to determine the validity of an administrative decision based on an exercise of discretion. This test applies to administrative actions even when they do not infringe on basic rights. In the case that follows, the Court reviewed a decision to build a separation fence between Palestinians living outside of Israel and Israeli communities. The Court did not consider whether the fence infringed on basic rights. The petitioners claiming injury from the fence were neither citizens nor residents of Israel, and it would have required an extension of existing law to hold that they have basic rights under Israeli law. The Court instead applied rules of Israeli administrative law, and specifically the proportionality test, to review the decision of the military commander of the Israel Defense Forces.

Israeli Case

Beit Sourik Village Council v. Government of Israel
HCJ 2056/04, 58(5) PD 807 [2004][27]

Chief Justice A. Barak

The Commander of the IDF Forces in Judea and Samaria issued orders to take possession of plots of land in the area of Judea and Samaria. The purpose of the seizure was to erect a separation fence on the land. The question before us is whether the orders and the fence are legal.

Background

Since 1967, Israel has been holding the areas of Judea and Samaria (hereinafter the area) in belligerent occupation. In 1993 Israel began a political process with the Palestinian Liberation Organization (PLO),[28] and signed a number of agreements transferring control over parts of the area to the Palestinian Authority. Israel and the PLO continued political negotiations in an attempt to solve the remaining problems. The negotiations, whose final stages took place at Camp David in Maryland, USA, failed in July 2000.

From Respondents' affidavit in answer to *order nisi* we learned that, a short time after the failure of the Camp David talks, the Israeli-Palestinian conflict reached new heights of violence. In September 2000, the Palestinian side began a campaign of terror against Israel and Israelis. Terror attacks take place both in the area and in Israel. They are directed against citizens and soldiers, men and women, elderly and infants, regular citizens and public figures. Even now, terror attacks are carried out everywhere: in public transportation, in shopping centers and markets, in coffee houses, and in restaurants. Terror organizations use gunfire attacks, suicide attacks, mortar fire, Katyusha rocket fire, and car bombs. From September 2000 until the beginning of April 2004, more than 780 attacks were carried out within Israel. During the same period, more than 8200 attacks were carried out in the area.

The armed conflict claimed (as of April 2004) the lives of 900 Israeli citizens and residents. More than 6000 were injured, some with serious wounds that have left them se-

---

27. The translation is based on that on the website of the Supreme Court, http://elyon1.court.gov.il/files_eng/04/560/020/A28/04020560.a28.htm (last visited March 24, 2011).

28. The PLO is an organization founded in 1964 to represent the interests of the Palestinians. The Palestinian Authority is an authority established in 1994 as a result of negotiations between Israel and the PLO to administer areas transferred to its control by Israel.

verely handicapped. The armed conflict has left many dead and wounded on the Palestinian side as well. Bereavement and pain wash over us.

These terror acts caused Israel to take security precautions on several levels.... The attacks did not cease. Innocent people paid with both life and limb. This is the background behind the decision to construct the separation fence.

The Decision to Construct the Separation Fence

The Ministers' Committee for National Security reached a decision (on April 14, 2002) regarding deployment in the *seamline area* between Israel and the area....[29] As a temporary solution, it was decided to erect an obstacle in the three regions found to be most vulnerable to the passage of terrorists into the Israel: the Umm El-Fahm region [in the Galilee]; the Qalqilya-Tulkarm region [close to the Israeli cities of Kfar Saba and Netanya]; and the Greater Jerusalem region. It was further decided to create a team of ministers, headed by the prime minister, which would examine long-term solutions to prevent the infiltration of Palestinians, including terrorists, into Israel.

The Ministers' Committee on National Security decided (on September 5, 2003) to construct stage three of the obstacle in the Greater Jerusalem area (except in the Ma'ale Adumim area). The length of this obstacle is 64 km.

The location of this fence, which passes through areas west of Jerusalem, stands at the heart of the dispute between the parties.

The Separation Fence

The seamline obstacle is composed of several components. In its center stands a *smart fence*. The purpose of the fence is to alert the forces deployed along its length of any attempt at infiltration. On the fence's external side lies an anti-vehicle obstacle, composed of a trench or other structure intended to prevent vehicles from breaking through the fence by slamming against it. There is an additional delaying fence. Near the fence a service road is paved. On the internal side of the electronic fence, there are a number of roads: a dirt road (for the purpose of discovering the tracks of those who pass the fence), a patrol road, and a road for armored vehicles, as well as an additional fence. The average width of the obstacle, in its optimal form, is 50–70 meters. Due to constraints, a narrower obstacle, which includes only the components supporting the electronic fence, will be constructed in specific areas. In certain cases the obstacle can reach a width of 100 meters, due to topographical conditions. In the area relevant to this petition, the width of the obstacle will not exceed 35 meters, except in places where a wider obstacle is necessary for topographical reasons.[30] In the area relevant to this petition, the fence is not being replaced by a concrete wall. Efforts are being made to minimize the width of the area of which possession will be taken *de facto*. Various means to help prevent infiltration will be erected along the length of the obstacle. The IDF and the border police will patrol the separation fence, and will be called to locations of infiltration, in order to frustrate the infiltration and to pursue those who succeed in crossing the security fence. Hereinafter we will refer to the entire obstacle on the seamline as the *separation fence*.

---

29. The term *seamline* refers to what is commonly called the *green line* in the US press. It is the armistice line between Israel and the Arab states at the end of the War of Independence in 1949. See chapter 2. Israelis live in separate communities in many areas beyond the green line. These are usually referred to as *settlements* in the American press. They vary from cities with high rises and shopping centers to groupings of mobile homes.

30. This explains how the fence is constructed in most areas. In short segments, where Israeli and Palestinian areas are very close and there is not space between them for all these structures, the fence is replaced by a concrete wall.

The Petition

The petition, as originally worded, attacked the orders of seizure regarding lands in the [Palestinian] villages of Beit Sourik, Bidu, El Kabiba, Katane, Beit A'anan, Beit Likia, Beit Ajaza, and Beit Daku.[31] These lands are adjacent to the towns [with Israeli residents] of Mevo Choron, Har Adar, Mevasseret Zion,[32] and the Jerusalem neighborhoods of Ramot and Giv'at Zeev, which are located west and northwest of Jerusalem. Petitioners are the landowners and the village councils affected by the orders of seizure. They argue that the orders of seizure are illegal. As such, they should be voided or the location of the separation fence should be changed. The injury to Petitioners, they argue, will be severe and unbearable. Over 42,000 dunams[33] of their lands will be affected. The obstacle will pass over 4,850 dunams, and will separate between Petitioners and more than 37,000 dunams, 26,500 of which are agricultural lands that have been cultivated for many generations. Access to these agricultural lands will become difficult and even impossible. Petitioners' ability to go from place to place will depend on a bureaucratic permit regime which is labyrinthine, complex, and burdensome. Use of local water wells will not be possible. As such, access to water for crops will be hindered. Shepherding, which depends on access to these wells, will be made difficult. Tens of thousands of olive and fruit trees will be uprooted. The fence will separate villages from tens of thousands of additional trees. The livelihood of many hundreds of Palestinian families, based on agriculture, will be critically injured. Moreover the separation fence will injure not only landowners to whom the orders of seizure apply, but also the lives of 35,000 village residents will be disrupted. The separation fence will harm the villages' ability to develop and expand. The access roads to the urban centers of Ramallah and Bir Naballa will be blocked off. Access to medical and other services in East Jerusalem and in other places will become impossible. Ambulances will encounter difficulty in providing emergency services to residents. Children's access to schools in the urban centers and students' access to universities will be impaired. Petitioners argue that these injuries cannot be justified.

Petitioners' argument is that the orders are illegal in light of Israeli administrative law, and in light of the principles of public international law which apply to the dispute before us.

The Response to the Petition

Respondents, in their first response, argue that the orders of seizure and the route through which the separation fence passes are legal. The separation fence is a project of utmost national importance. Israel is in the midst of active combat against a wave of terror that is supported by the Palestinian population and leadership. At issue are the lives of the citizens and residents of Israel, who are threatened by terrorists who infiltrate into the territory of Israel. At issue are the lives of Israeli citizens residing in the area. The construction of the separation fence system must be completed with all possible speed. The separation fence has already proved its efficacy in areas where it has been erected. It is urgent that it also be erected in the region of Petitioners' villages. Respondents claim that a number of terror attacks against Jerusalem and against route 443, which connects Jerusalem and the [Israeli] city of Modi'in,[34] have originated in this area. The central consideration in choosing the route of the separation fence was the operational-security con-

---

31. All of the Palestinian towns are in the areas; i.e., outside the green line.

32. Mevo Choron and Har Adar are towns with Israeli residents located in the areas; i.e., over the green line. Mevasseret Zion is an Israeli town located on the Israeli side of the green line.

33. A dunam is 1000 square meters. It is a measure of land area used in the Ottoman Empire. There are approximately four acres per dunam.

34. Route 443, one of two main arteries connecting the capital city of Jerusalem to the coastal plain, is a heavily travelled road.

sideration. The purpose of the fence is to prevent the uncontrolled passage of residents of the area into Israel and into Israeli towns located in the areas. The separation fence is also intended to prevent the smuggling of arms and the infiltration of Palestinians, both of which are likely to lead to the establishment of terror cells in Israel and to recruiting new members for existing cells. Additionally armed forces stationed along the obstacle, and Israeli towns on both sides of it, must be protected. Security considerations dictate that the area of the separation fence must have topographic command of its surroundings. This allows surveillance and prevents attacks upon the forces guarding it. To the extent possible, a winding route must be avoided. In addition, a security zone is required to provide warning of possible terrorist infiltration into Israel.

Respondents explain that, in planning the route of the separation fence, great weight was given to the interests of the residents of the area in order to minimize, to the extent possible, the injury to them.... An effort is being made to refrain from cutting lands off from their owners. In the event of such a cutoff, agricultural gateways will allow farmers access to their lands. New roads will be paved which will provide for the needs of the residents. In cases where damage cannot be avoided, landowners will be compensated for the use of their seized lands. Efforts will be made to transfer agricultural crops instead of cutting them down. Prior to seizure of the land, the inhabitants will be granted the opportunity to appeal. Respondents assert that they are willing to change the route in order to minimize the damage. Respondents declare, in addition, that they intend to erect permanent checkpoints east of certain villages, which will be open 24 hours a day, every day of the year, and which will allow the preservation of the fabric of life in the area. It has also been decided to improve the road system between the villages involved in this petition, in order to tighten the bonds between them, and between them and Ramallah.

Respondents do not deny the need to be considerate of the injury to the local population and to keep that injury proportionate; their claim is that they fulfill these obligations. Respondents deny the severity of the injury claimed by Petitioners. The extent of the areas to be seized for the building of the fence, the injury to agricultural areas, and the injury to trees and groves, are lesser—by far—than claimed. All the villages are connected to water systems and, as such, damage to wells will not interrupt the supply of water for agricultural and other purposes. The marketing of agricultural produce will be possible even after the construction of the fence. In each village there is a medical clinic, and there is a central clinic in Bidu. A few archeological sites will find themselves beyond the fence, but these sites are neglected and not regularly visited. The educational needs of the local population will also be taken into account. Respondents also note that, in places where the separation fence causes injury to the local population, efforts are being made to minimize that injury. In light of all this, Respondents argue that the petitions should be denied.

The Hearing of the Petition

Petitioners submitted a motion to file additional documents, the most important of which was an affidavit prepared by members of the Council for Peace and Security, which is a registered society of Israelis with a background in security, including high ranking reserve officers.... The society, which sees itself as nonpartisan, was, it argued, among the first to suggest a separation fence as a solution to Israel's security needs. The affidavit included detailed and comprehensive comments regarding various segments of this route and raised reservations about them from a security perspective. The claims in the affidavit were serious and grave.

Petitioners, pointing to the affidavits of the Council for Peace and Security, argue that the route of the separation fence is disproportionate. It does not serve the security objectives of Israel, since establishing the route adjacent to the houses of the Palestinians will endanger the state and its soldiers who are patrolling along the fence, as well as increasing the general danger to Israel's security. In addition, such a route is not the least injurious means, since it is possible to move the route farther away from Petitioners' villages and closer to Israel. It will be possible to overcome the concern about infiltration by reinforcing the fence and its accompanying obstacles.

A number of residents of Mevasseret Zion, a town adjacent to the Beit Sourik village, joined as petitioners in this petition. They claim that the fence route should be immediately adjacent to the green line, in order to allow residents of the Beit Sourik village to work their land. In addition, they claim that the gates which will allow the passage of farmers are inefficient, that they will obstruct access to the fields, and that they will violate the farmer's dignity. Furthermore they point out the decline of relations with the Palestinian population in the area which, as a consequence of the plan to construct the separation fence on Palestinian land, has turned from a tranquil population into a hostile one. On the opposing side, Mr. Efraim Halevy joined as a respondent in the petition. He argues that moving the route of the fence adjacent to the Green Line will endanger the residents of Mevasseret Zion. It will bring the route closer to the houses and schools in the community. He also calls our attention to the terrorist activity that has taken place in the Beit Sourik area. Thus, the alternate route proposed by Petitioners should be rejected. He claims that his position reflects the opinions of many residents of Mevasseret Zion. After reading the motions, we decided to accept them, and we considered the arguments they presented.

The Normative Framework

Authority to Erect the Separation Fence

[The Court held that under international law, the State of Israel had authority to erect the separation fence, which was militarily rational.[35]]

The Route of the Separation Fence

The focus of this petition is the legality of the route chosen for construction of the separation fence.

Proportionality

[International law requires that the security needs of the state be balanced against the harm to the local population under the principle of proportionality.]

Proportionality is not only a general principle of international law. Proportionality is also a general principle of Israeli administrative law. At first a principle of our case law, then a constitutional principle, enshrined in article 8 of the Basic Law: Human Dignity and Freedom, it is today one of the basic values of Israeli administrative law. The principle of proportionality applies to every act of the Israeli administrative authorities. It also applies to the use of the military commander's authority pursuant to the [international] law of belligerent occupation.

The Meaning of Proportionality and its Elements

Under the principle of proportionality, the decision of an administrative body is legal only if the means used are in proper proportion to the objective that the government

---

35. This was contrary to an advisory opinion of the International Court of Justice, which found that construction of the fence was illegal. Legal Consequences of the Construction of a Wall in the Occupied Palestinian Territory, Advisory Opinion, 2004 I.C.J. 136 (July 9) *available at* http:www.icj-cij.org under Cases, Advisory Opinions, Advisory Opinion of 9 July 2004 (main opinion plus seven separate opinions).

seeks to realize. The principle of proportionality focuses, therefore, on the relationship between the objective of the administrative decision and the means used to achieve it.... Three sub-tests grant specific content to the principle of proportionality.

The first sub-test is that the objective must be related to the means. The means that the administrative body uses must be constructed to achieve the precise objective which the administrative body is trying to achieve. The means used by the administrative body must rationally lead to the realization of the objective. This is the *appropriate means* or *rational means* test. According to the second sub-test, the means used by the administrative body must injure the individual to the least extent possible. In the spectrum of means which can be used to achieve the objective, the least injurious means must be used. This is the *least injurious means* test. The third sub-test requires that the damage caused to the individual by the administrative decision must be of proper proportion to the gain brought about by that decision. That is the *proportionate means* test (or *proportionality in the narrow sense*) The test of proportionality in the narrow sense is commonly applied with absolute values, by directly comparing the advantage of the administrative act with the damage that results from it. However, it is also possible to apply the test of proportionality in the narrow sense in a relative manner. Under this approach, the administrative act is tested vis-à-vis an alternate act, whose benefit will be somewhat smaller than that of the former one. The original administrative act is disproportionate in the narrow sense if a certain reduction in the advantage gained by the original act—by employing alternate means, for example—ensures a substantial reduction in the injury caused by the administrative act.

It is possible to say that the means used by an administrative authority are proportionate only if all three sub-tests are satisfied. Satisfaction of one or two of these sub-tests is insufficient. All three of them must be satisfied simultaneously. Not infrequently, there are a number of ways that the requirement of proportionality can be satisfied. In these situations, a *zone of proportionality* must be recognized (similar to a zone of reasonableness). Any means chosen by the administrative body that is within the zone of proportionality is proportionate.

The Military Nature of the Route of the Separation Fence

In our examination of the contrasting military considerations in this case, we give special weight to the fact that the commander of the area is responsible for security. Even though we adopt this position, we are of the opinion—the details of which we shall explain below—that Petitioners have not carried their burden and have not convinced us that we should prefer the professional expert opinion of members of the Council for Peace and Security over the security stance of the commander of the area. We are dealing with two military opinions. Each of them has military advantages and disadvantages. In this state of affairs, we must place the expert opinion of the military commander at the foundation of our decision.

From the General to the Particular

This oversight applies to the case before us. The military commander is the expert regarding the military quality of the separation fence route. We are experts regarding its humanitarian aspects. The military commander determines where, on hill and plain, the separation fence will be erected. That is his expertise. We examine whether this route's harm to the local residents is proportional. That is our expertise.

Order TH/104/03; Order TH/103/03; Order TH/84/03 (The Western Part of the Order)

These orders apply to more than 10 kilometers of the fence route. This segment of the route surrounds the high mountain range of Jebel Muktam. This ridge topographically controls its immediate and general surroundings. It towers over route 443 which passes north of it, connecting Jerusalem to [the Israeli city of] Modi'in. The route of the obstacle passes from southwest of the village of Beit Likia, southwest of the village of Beit Anan, and west of the village of Chirbet Abu A-Lahm. Respondent explains that the objective of this route is to keep the mountain area under Israeli control. This will ensure an advantage for the armed forces, who will topographically control the area of the fence, and it will decrease the capability of others to attack those traveling on route 443.

Is the injury to the local inhabitants by the separation fence in this segment, according to the route determined by Respondent, proportionate? Our answer to this question necessitates examination of the route's proportionality, using the three sub-tests. The first sub-test examines whether there is a rational connection between the objective of the separation fence and its established route. Our answer is that such a rational connection exists.... By our very ruling that the route of the fence passes the test of military rationality, we have also held that it realizes the military objective of the separation fence.

The second sub-test examines whether it is possible to attain the security objectives of the separation fence in a way that causes less injury to the local inhabitants. There is no doubt— and the issue is not even disputed—that the route suggested by the members of the Council for Peace and Security causes less injury to the local inhabitants than the injury caused by the route determined by the military commander. The question is whether the former route satisfies the security objective of the security fence to the same extent as the route set out by the military commander. We cannot answer this question in the affirmative. The position of the military commander is that the route of the separation fence, as proposed by members of the Council for Peace and Security, grants less security than his proposed route. By our very determination that we shall not intervene in that position, we have also determined that there is no alternate route that fulfills, to a similar extent, the security needs while causing lesser injury to the local inhabitants. In this state of affairs, our conclusion is that the second sub-test of proportionality, regarding the issue before us, is satisfied.

The third sub-test examines whether the injury caused to the local inhabitants by the construction of the separation fence stands in proper proportion to the security benefit from the security fence in its chosen route. This is the proportionate means test (or proportionality in the narrow sense).

This sub-test weighs the costs against the benefits. According to this sub-test, a decision of an administrative authority must reach a reasonable balance between communal needs and the damage done to the individual.... The question before us is: Does the severity of the injury to local inhabitants, by the construction of the separation fence along the route determined by the military commander, stand in reasonable (proper) proportion to the security benefit from the construction of the fence along that route?

Our answer is that the relationship between the injury to the local inhabitants and the security benefit from the construction of the separation fence along the route, as determined by the military commander, is not proportionate. The route undermines the delicate balance between the obligation of the military commander to preserve security and his obligation to provide for the needs of the local inhabitants. This conclusion is based on the fact that the route which the military commander established for the security fence—which separates the local inhabitants from their agricultural lands—injures the local inhabitants in a severe and acute way, while violating their rights under humanitarian international law. Here are the facts: More than 13,000 farmers (*falahin*) are cut off from thousands of dunams of their land and from tens of thousands of trees which are their livelihood, and which are located on the other side of the separation fence. No attempt was made to seek out and provide them with substitute land, despite our oft-repeated proposals on that matter. The separation is not hermetic. The military commander announced that two gates will be constructed, from each of the two villages, to its lands, with a system of licensing. This state of affairs injures the farmers severely, as access to their lands (early in the morning, in the afternoon, and in the evening), will be subject to restrictions inherent to a system of licensing. Such a system will result in long lines for the passage of the farmers themselves; it will make the passage of vehicles (which themselves require licensing and examination) difficult, and will distance the farmer from his lands (since only two daytime gates are planned for the entire length of this segment of the route). As a result, the life of the farmer will change completely in comparison to his previous life. The route of the separation fence severely violates their right of property and their freedom of movement. Their livelihood is severely impaired. The difficulties they suffer, due, for example, to high unemployment in that area, will only become more severe.

These injuries are not proportionate. They can be substantially decreased by an alternate route, either the route presented by the experts of the Council for Peace and Security, or another route set out by the military commander. Such an alternate route exists. It is not a figment of the imagination. It was presented before us. It is based on military control of Jebel Muktam, without bringing the separation fence towards that mountain. Indeed, one must not forget that, even after the construction of the separation fence, the military commander will continue to control the area east of it. In the opinion of the military commander — which we assume to be correct, as the basis of our review — this route will provide less security in that area. However, the security advantage reaped from the route as determined by the military commander, in comparison to the proposed route, does not stand in any reasonable proportion to the injury to the local inhabitants caused by this route. Indeed the real question in the relative examination of the third proportionality sub-test is not the choice between constructing a separation fence which brings security but injures the local inhabitants, or not constructing a separation fence and not injuring the local inhabitants. The real question is whether the security benefit reaped by the acceptance of the military commander's position (that the separation fence should surround Jebel Muktam) is proportionate to the additional injury resulting from his position (with the fence separating local inhabitants from their lands). Our answer to this question is that the military commander's choice of the route of the separation fence is disproportionate. The gap between the security provided by the military commander's proposal and the security provided by the alternate route is very small, as compared to the large difference between a fence that separates the local inhabitants from their lands, and a fence which does not separate the two (or which creates a separation which is smaller and possible to live with). Indeed, we accept that security needs are likely to necessitate an injury to the lands of the local inhabitants and to their ability to use them. Nonetheless both international humanitarian law and the basic principles of Israeli administrative law require making every possible effort to ensure that injury will be proportionate. Where construction of the separation fence demands that inhabitants be separated from their lands, access to these lands must be ensured in order to minimize the damage to the extent possible.

We have reached the conclusion that the route of the separation fence, which separates the villages of Beit Likia and Beit Anan from the lands which provide the villagers with their livelihood, is not proportionate.

[The Court examined the route of six other segments of the separation fence. As to one segment, the route was uncontested and the Court let that route stand. It held invalid the route chosen for each of the other five segments on the same grounds as were discussed above.]

Epilogue

Our task is difficult. We are members of Israeli society. Although we are sometimes in an ivory tower, that tower is in the heart of Jerusalem, which is not infrequently hit by ruthless terror. We are aware of the killing and destruction wrought by the terror against the state and its citizens. Like all Israelis, we recognize the need to defend the country and its citizens against the wounds inflicted by terror. We are aware that in the short term, this judgment will not make the state's struggle against those rising up against it easier. But we are judges. When we sit in judgment, we are subject to judgment. We act according to our best conscience and understanding. Regarding the state's struggle against the terror that rises up against it, we are convinced that at the end of the day, a struggle according to the law will strengthen the state's power and her spirit. There is no security without law. Satisfying the provisions of the law is an aspect of national security.... Only a separation fence built on a base of law will grant security to the state and its citizens. Only a separation route based on the path of law, will lead the state to the security so yearned for.

Comment

The decision on proportionality of the fence route in *Beit Sourik* has received warm praise and sharp criticism. Professor Owen Fiss wrote of the decision,

> [Chief Justice Barak's] method was to demand, systematically and relentlessly, that any sacrifices of rights required by a proper regard for human dignity be fully and rationally justified. In so doing, Barak revealed a deep and profound commitment to reason — the common element that unites his life as a professor and as a judge and that defines his unique place in Israeli society and the world legal community.[36]

Another writer has praised the use of the proportionality test in a case like this as allowing the state to maintain its basic values as a liberal democracy.[37] In contrast, it has been argued that the Supreme Court should have given greater deference to the military than it did in the decision.[38] The case is also criticized because, "The vague nature of the substantive sense of the proportionality tests may cause judicial decisions to assume a subjective character, thus violating the democratic principle according to which fundamental decisions should be determined by the people's elected representatives."[39]

The proportionality test, as used in *Beit Sourik*, requires not only cost-benefit analysis, but marginal cost benefit analysis. The fence route may provide benefits that outweigh its negative effects, but still is not justified if another fence route would provide a better cost-benefit ratio. In other words, if the present route has costs of 40 and benefits of 80, but an alternative route would have costs of 20 and benefits of 70, the military authorities must choose the alternative route.

---

36. Owen Fiss, *Tribute, Law is Everywhere*, 117 YALE L.J. 256, 278 (2007).

37. Emanuel Gross, *The Struggle of a Democracy against the Terror of Suicide Bombers: Ideological and Legal Aspects*, 22 WIS. INT'L L.J. 597 (2004).

38. *See* Note, Jason Litwack, *A Disproportionate Ruling for All the Right Reasons: Beit Sourik Village Council v. Government of Israel*, 31 BROOK. J. INT'L L. 857 (2006).

39. Moshe Cohen-Eliya, *The Formal and Substantive Meanings of Proportionality in the Supreme Court's Decision Regarding the Security Fence*, 38 ISR. L. REV. 262, 263 (2005).

Of course, the calculations are not this simple, because values cannot easily be translated into numerical values. The opinion weighs costs of disruption of life of the Palestinians and infringement on their rights under humanitarian international law against the benefits of security to Israeli civilians and the army. But the numbers help illustrate the effect of the opinion: the alternative route is preferable even if it provides a reduced degree of security as long as it produces a better ratio between disruption costs and security benefits.

Following the *Beit Sourik* decision, the Israel Supreme Court reviewed the route of many other segments of the separation fence. It has approved the routes of some segments and rejected others.

Questions

7. Assume the facts given in question 5. The minister issued the order requiring compliance with the business license providing for removal of hazardous wastes within one month of generation. Does the order comply with the requirement of proportionality in administrative law?

8. In the opinion in *Ressler v. Minister of Defense*, Justice Barak wrote, "The meaning of separation of powers is that, in the absence of legal limitations, the legislative branch is allowed to determine the legal framework through which a matter of public interest will be managed, and that the executive branch should solve public problems within that legal framework. But, once such a framework is established, a court is to determine whether the legal framework that has been established is being observed." Is the later opinion in *Beit Sourik* consistent with this statement, or did it indicate that Justice Barak, and the Supreme Court, changed their minds?

———

In the United States, courts use a different test, set out in the APA, to evaluate an administrative agency's exercise of discretion.[40] Here is the language of the definitive case explaining the meaning of that test.

US Case

Motor Vehicle Manufacturers Assoc. v. State Farm Mutual Automobile Ins. Co.

463 U.S. 29 (1983)

Justice White:

The scope of review under the "arbitrary and capricious" standard is narrow and a court is not to substitute its judgment for that of the agency. Nevertheless the agency must examine the relevant data and articulate a satisfactory explanation for its actions including a "rational connection between the facts found and the choice made." In reviewing that explanation, we must "consider whether the decision was based on a consideration of the relevant factors and whether there has been a clear error of judgment." Normally an agency rule would be arbitrary and capricious if the agency has relied on factors which Congress has not intended it to consider, entirely failed to consider an im-

———

40. See 5 U.S.C. § 706(2)(A).

portant aspect of the problems, offered an explanation for the decision that runs counter to the evidence before the agency, or is so implausible that it could not be ascribed to a difference in view or the product of agency expertise. The reviewing court should not attempt to make up for such deficiencies: "We may not supply a reasoned basis for the agency's action that the agency itself has not given."

Comment

In other words, in the United States, courts review the record of the agency's decision to see whether the agency considered the proper factors and whether it has fully and plausibly explained the decision. The record is that before or created by the agency at the time of making the decision. Sometimes a similar standard called the *substantial evidence test* is used to review agency exercise of discretion, but that too is limited to review of the agency record. Furthermore a court does not engage in a far-reaching evaluation of whether the administrative decision is justified by some cost benefit analysis, but rather looks at how the agency justified its decision and determines if that justification is plausible. This is a more hands-off approach by the court, and it concentrates more on the adequacy of the agency decision-making and less on the adequacy of the agency's decision.

G. Judicial Activism in Constitutional and Administrative Law

The Israeli Supreme Court is widely perceived as a very activist court in public law areas. The materials presented here show why the Court is so regarded. Having rejected all formal barriers to standing and justiciability, the Court leaves the judiciary free to review the validity of statutes and of administrative decisions whenever it finds it appropriate to do so. The Court declared that the Basic Laws on human rights form a constitution, even though the Knesset did not seem to be conscious of enacting a constitution when it passed those laws. The Court uses the proportionality test to determine the validity of statutes that infringe on human rights, and defines those human rights so broadly that many, if not most statutes constitute an infringement. It uses the same proportionality test to judge the validity of administrative decisions. In both cases, the proportionality test, particularly the third cost-benefit subsection, gives a court fairly unstructured authority to determine whether actions of the other branches of government are legally valid.

There are several possible reasons why the Israeli Supreme Court has taken on such an activist role. They all relate to the history, social milieu, and governmental arrangements in Israel and to the domestic and international political issues that affect the country.

First, the Court sees itself as the defender of individual rights against the majoritarian branches of government. While it is the main job of the Knesset and of the ministries and other government agencies to react to what the electorate wants, it is the job of the courts to defend the individual against unfair treatment by the majority. It is not surprising that the Supreme Court in Israel is highly sensitive to the need to protect the individual. Most Jews who have arrived in Israel over the years came from countries where Jews were discriminated against, oppressed, or killed. Former Chief Justice Barak, a survivor of the Holocaust, has called the protection of human rights "substantive democracy," as opposed to requirement that government act through representatives chosen by the people, which he calls "formal democracy."[41] He also wrote,

> A key historical lesson of the Holocaust is that the people, through their representatives, can destroy democracy and human rights. Since the Holocaust, all of us have learned that human rights are the core of substantive democracy. The last few decades have been revolutionary, as we have learned the hard way that without protection for human rights, there can be no democracy and no justification for democracy.[42]

Schnitzer v. Chief Military Censor, discussed in the previous chapter on constitutional law, is a case of this sort.

Protection of individual rights is perceived of as important in other ways as well. Israel has a large Arab minority that suffers from discrimination on some matters, and the Court sees the need to correct this. The Court also wanted to allow Palestinian residents of the territories to seek judicial review of decisions that adversely affected their lives and their rights under international humanitarian law.[43] The question of whether these Palestinians, who are neither Israeli citizens nor residents of Israel, have standing presents some sticky legal issues, and their claims often involve political issues. By making the requirements of standing and justiciability discretionary with the Court, it became possible to avoid these issues and to allow the Court to hear substantive challenges to actions of the military authorities.

The Court is undoubtedly aware that without expanded rules on standing and justiciability, many cases involving individual rights would not be heard. Government action that infringes on individual rights often causes such small infringements to each individual that no one will bring a petition for review, even though the overall adverse effect is large. It is only by recognizing the role of public petitioners that the Court can increase the chance that a petition for review will be filed. The Court is aware that Israel has a significant number of NGOs who engage in legal work, and they will file the cases if they are granted standing and if justiciability barriers are removed to allow their cases, which often raise political issues, to be heard.

Another reason the Court has taken on an activist role may be that it sees the need to protect the majority from the anti-majoritarian decisions of the legislative and executive branches.[44] As explained in chapter 3, because of the way the coalition Governments of Israel are structured, small parties have an influence that exceeds the size of the electorate they represent. The larger parties need several of the small ones to form a coalition, so the large parties often agree to enact laws advancing the partisan agendas of the small parties, even if they do not serve the interests of the majority of the population. This is particularly true of the laws demanded by some of the Jewish religious parties. Similarly ministers from the small parties sometimes take administrative decisions that serve the group they represent but not the society as a whole. In such cases, the Court steps in to

---

41. Aharon Barak, *Forward: A Judge on Judging: The Role of a Supreme Court in a Democracy*, 116 Harv. L. Rev. 16, 20 (2002).

42. *Id.* at 20–21.

43. *See* Halbertam, *supra* note 10.

44. *See* Daphne Barak-Erez, *From an Unwritten to a Written Constitution: The Israeli Challenge in American Perspective*, 20 Colum. Hum. Rts. L. Rev. 309, 321–22 (1995). *See also* Eli M. Salzberger, *Judicial Activism in Israel*, http://papers.ssrn.com/sol3/papers.cfm?abstract_id=984918 (last visited March 28, 2011) (especially the discussion on page 13 at footnote 18).

limit the impact of these small groups. Both *Ressler v. Minister of Defense* and *Poraz v. City Council of Tel Aviv-Jaffa* involve such concerns.

A third concern motivating the Court seems to be its perception of the need to prevent corruption in government. Israel has had serious problems with corruption in high government office, resulting in criminal investigations and sometimes prosecutions. The Court seems determined to limit back-room dealing and help develop clean, transparent government.[45] The case of *Ganor v. Attorney General* appears to be of this sort. The Court seemed to be saying that it just could not believe that a fair assessment of the facts would lead to a conclusion that there was no public interest in filing an indictment.

Fourth, it is likely that the Court is influenced by the security situation in Israel and the difficulty it sees in properly balancing between the urgent need to protect the country from terrorism and the need to protect individual freedoms.[46] Many democracies face this problem, but Israel has been dealing with it longer than most western countries. The issue is particularly severe in Israel's dealing with the areas it holds that are not part of the state, but which are the source of most terrorist attacks. The Court has taken upon itself the role of protecting the non-Israelis living in these areas from security measures that would negatively affect their lives. Both *Adalah Legal Centre for Arab Minority Rights in Israel v. Minister of Defense*, discussed in the previous chapter on constitutional law, and *Beit Sourik Village Council v. Government of Israel*, discussed in this chapter, are cases of this sort.

Fifth, the Court may not have taken the activist role on itself, but may have been prodded (and not unwillingly) into this role by the enactment of the Basic Laws on human rights, which had as their purpose the empowerment of the Court to intervene in more areas of Israeli life. The enactment of these laws, it has been argued, was promoted by the Ashkenazi secular elite that had long held the balance of political power in Israel but that had lost that power by the beginning of the 1990s. By this time, the religious groups, the Mizrahi Jews, and, a bit later, the immigrants from the areas of the former Soviet Union all acquired greater political power. The secular elite establishment, seeing that it has lost control of the political branches of government, wanted to see the Basic Laws on human rights enacted as a way of moving power into the hands of the Supreme Court, which were still controlled by that establishment.[47]

Finally it has also been argued that the Court has become activist because it is the only counterweight to the other parts of government, which are closely connected, with no real separation against them.[48] Under Israel's parliamentary system, the legislature and the executive are not really separate branches of the regime. Because the local governments are created by and get their powers from the Knesset, the Israeli system also lacks vertical separation between the national government and regional or local government.

---

45. *See* Richard A. Posner, *Enlightened Despot*, The New Republic, April 23, 2007, at 53, *available at* http://www.tnr.com/article/enlightened-despot (suggesting one of the unstated reasons for the Court taking on such an active role may be its perception of the need to stem corruption in government).

46. *See* Barak, *supra* note 41, at 21.

47. See Ran Hirschl, *The Struggle for Hegemony: Understanding Judicial Empowerment Through Constitutionalization in Culturally Divided Polities*, 36 Stan. J. Int'l L. 74, 89–96 (2000).

48. Eli M. Salzberger, *Judicial Activism in Israel*, http://papers.ssrn.com/sol3/papers.cfm?abstract_id=984918 (last visited March 28, 2011) (especially see discussion at page 12 and footnote 17).

This analysis explains why the Israeli Supreme Court has taken such an activist stand on public law, but it does not ask the question of whether it is wise for the Court to have taken on such an activist role. The answer to that question requires not only identification of the advantages of judicial activism, but also consideration of the disadvantages. A highly activist court presents a danger to a democratic society. The protection of freedom requires that all governmental institutions be limited.

Article

Marcia Gelpe, Constraints on Supreme Court Authority in Israel and the United States: Phenomenal Cosmic Powers; Itty Bitty Living Space

13 Emory Int'l L. Rev. 493, 493, 496–499 (1999)

Near the beginning of the movie *Aladdin*,[49] the good, powerful Genie complains about having to live in a tiny lamp. "Phenomenal cosmic powers; itty bitty living space," he laments. This line is crucial later in the film, when the evil vizier Jafar turns into a Genie. Jafar's ability to use his new powers to his own nefarious ends is thwarted when the commoner, Aladdin, holds up the lamp, thus forcing Jafar into its cramped quarters. Aladdin says slyly, "phenomenal cosmic powers; itty bitty living space." The structural constraints on the powers prevent their use for evil purposes and save the world.

This movie carries a marvelous lesson about governmental structure in a democratic regime. In order to prevent abuse of the extensive powers of the state, all governmental powers should be subject to structural constraints. This need for constraints exists even when the powers are in the hands of good people. The identity of those holding the power can change. If it does, it is the structural constraints that stand between the people and tyranny.

Reasons for Constraining Judicial Power

Judicial power should be constrained in order to prevent excessive concentration of power, to prevent arbitrary exercise of power, and to protect the judiciary's ability to function. The first two of these reasons apply to all institutions in a democratic regime. The third applies specifically to the courts.

A. Preventing Excessive Concentration of Power

One of the basic themes of democratic government is that the power of the government over the individual should be limited in order to maximize individual freedom. A government that is too powerful tends toward tyranny and endangers the freedom of its citizens. The doctrine of separation of powers, adopted in both the United States and Israel, is designed to protect against tyranny by preventing concentration of all governmental powers in the hands of any individual or institution. The judicial, legislative, and executive powers are given to separate institutions. An institution assigned one power may exercise one of the others to a small degree because absolute separation is not feasible, but both legal rules and traditions limit the amount of overlap.

---

49. *Aladdin* (Walt Disney Pictures 1993).

B. Preventing Arbitrary Exercise of Power

A power is exercised arbitrarily if it is exercised in any manner other than to advance the good or will of the public. Exercise of power is arbitrary if it furthers private interests, such as the personal good of those exercising the power, yet fails to also serve the public good. An institution with a great concentration of power is likely to exercise that power in an arbitrary manner if no other institution, or combination of institutions, is strong enough to stop the arbitrary exercise. This suggests two ways of preventing arbitrary exercise of power. One is to prevent any institution from accumulating a great deal of power. This will help by preventing the institution from causing a great deal of harm. But this is not enough: even an official with limited powers might exercise them in an arbitrary manner. Therefore it is necessary also to provide other institutions with power to prevent or reverse arbitrary exercises of power. Both the United States and Israel use a system of checks and balances to accomplish this task. Under the system of checks and balances, each of the three main governmental institutions oversees and limits the ways the other institutions perform their functions. This allows each institution to operate as a check on the arbitrary exercise of power by either of the other institutions.

C. Protecting the Judiciary's Ability to Function

The judiciary is an important institution but has an inherent weakness. The courts decide disputes, apply the law to individual cases, interpret the law, attempt to assure that the other institutions respect the rule of law, and protect the individual from excessive exercise of power. But the courts lack any real coercive power to enforce their decrees. If litigants do not do as ordered by the courts, the courts by themselves are essentially powerless to make them comply. Courts depend on voluntary compliance and on the coercive powers of other branches of government. If people generally do comply with court orders, it is largely because courts are well-respected institutions.

If the judiciary does not operate in a restrained manner, it risks losing the respect of the people. Losing litigants, lower courts, the executive, and the legislature may then simply ignore the pronouncements of the courts. The courts, lacking enforcement powers, will be left without any way to exercise authority. This is troublesome for courts in general. We need effective courts to settle disputes that cannot be settled as readily, as determinatively, or as authoritatively by other means. It is especially important to protect a Supreme Court's ability to exercise authority.... In Israel, the Supreme Court has considered socially and politically important issues such as the enforceability of coalition agreements, the relations between religious and nonreligious Jews, and the validity of draft exemptions. Each society needs its Supreme Court to be able to speak authoritatively to important questions of this sort. The loss of respect can mean the loss of power to settle such issues.

Comment

Two other objections to Supreme Court activism are not covered in the above excerpt. One is that judges who are not elected by the people take on themselves the authority to overrule the policy-based decisions of the majoritarian branches of government. Of course, this is exactly what we want a court to do when it is protecting individual rights, but the activism of Israel's Supreme Court has extended beyond individual rights issues.

The other additional problem is that judges who engage in activist review of administrative decisions must necessarily examine issues on which they have no expertise. It is questionable whether they can fully understand all the implications of their decisions. Because there is not always a full record for Israeli administrative decisions, the information before the court may be limited to that presented in the arguments of the sides to the litigation. Judges may lack the ability to understand all of those arguments, or to perceive what information has not been presented that may be relevant to the decision.

The issue is how to balance the advantages and disadvantages of judicial activism. In Israel today, the advantages have been given greater weight. Whether this will hold in the long run has yet to be seen.

Question

9. It has been suggested that this chapter could be titled "Administrative Law and the Quest for Substantive Democracy." Another suggested title is "Administrative Law and the Removal of all Limits on Judicial Power." Which title is more appropriate?

Chapter 10

Public International Law

Public international law is based mainly on treaties and customary law. Treaties are agreements between nations. Customary international law is general practice that enters international law by virtue of being accepted as law by most nations. The degree to which international law is binding within a country depends on the internal law of the country. A refusal by a country's courts to apply some rule or principle of international law may be valid as a matter of the internal law of that country, although it may constitute a breach of the country's international obligations.

The terminology in international law can be confusing for those not accustomed to it. Because international treaties are also called *conventions*, treaty-based international law is sometimes called *conventional law*. The internal law of a country is also called *national law*, *domestic law*, *municipal law*, or *state law*. State law, in this sense, is different from the law of a state of the United States.

This chapter examines first the Israeli law on how Israel can make treaties with other countries. It then presents the Israeli law defining the effect of treaty and customary international law on Israeli national law.

A. The Power to Make Treaties

Treaty-making involves two legal steps. First, countries involved in discussions on the formulation of the treaty *sign* the treaty. Later, these countries, and others, may *ratify* the treaty. The meaning of signing and of ratification, and how a treaty may be ratified, are essential matters. They determine when a country is obligated to observe the treaty as a matter of international law and may also affect the treaty's applicability under a country's national laws. The following materials explore the meaning of signing and ratification and the question of how treaties are ratified under Israeli law.

Israeli Statute

Basic Law: The President of the State

11. Functions and Powers

(a) The president of the state—

(1) shall sign every law, other than laws relating to the powers of the president;

(2) shall fulfill the functions assigned to the president under the Basic Law: The Government [relating to formation of the Government];

(3) shall receive from the Government a report on its meetings;

(4) shall accredit the diplomatic representatives of the state, shall receive the credentials of diplomatic representatives sent to Israel by foreign states, shall empower the consular representatives of the state, and shall confirm the appointments of consular representatives sent to Israel by foreign states;

(5) shall sign treaties with foreign states that have been ratified by the Knesset;

(6) shall fulfill every function assigned to him by law in connection with the appointment and removal from office of judges and other office-holders.

(b) The president of the state shall have power to pardon offenders and to lighten punishments by the reduction or commutation.

(c) The president of the state shall carry out every other function and have every other power assigned to him by law.

Israeli Case

Kamiar v. State of Israel
CrimA 131/67, 22(2) PD 85 [1968]

[Israeli law allows extradition of a person to another country if several conditions are met. For example, a person who would not be subject to capital punishment in Israel cannot be extradited to a country that might impose capital punishment unless the other country agrees it will not do so. Before extradition, a court must declare that a person is extraditable; i.e., that all of the conditions for extradition are met. After a court declares a person extraditable, the minister of justice is authorized to extradite the person.]

Justice Cohen:

The Appellant was declared extraditable in the District Court of Jerusalem, in accordance with section 9 of the Extradition Law, 5714-1954 (hereinafter *the statute*).[1] He claims that this declaration is not valid because ... there is no extradition agreement in force between Israel and Switzerland, the country seeking his extradition.

An extradition agreement (hereinafter *the treaty*) between Israel and Switzerland was published in Reshumot [the official publication of the government of Israel]. In addition, a notice was published there ... that the treaty entered into force on December 15, 1959.

The Appellant claims that there are two reasons why the treaty is invalid and of no force:

(1) It was signed on behalf of the State of Israel by Joseph Y. Linton, who was not authorized to sign on its behalf;

(2) It was ratified on behalf of the State of Israel by the Government, and the Government is not authorized to ratify international treaties.

[As to the first question, I would find that Linton, who was the Israeli Ambassador to Switzerland when he signed the treaty, had authority to sign on behalf of the State of Israel.][2]

---

1. Section 9 of the Extradition Law provides that a court shall declare that a person is extraditable if it finds that all the conditions for extradition set out in the statute have been met. One of the conditions is found in section 2, which is discussed later in the case.

2. All the justices agreed on this point.

[I turn to the second claim.] Under section 2 of the Extradition Law, a person can be extradited from Israel to another country if "there is an agreement between Israel and the country seeking extradition that establishes mutual obligations as to extradition of criminals."

The question is whether the government is correct in its position that the treaty is in force and subject to execution.

The attorneys claim that the answer depends on a constitutional question, which is whether a treaty may be ratified by the Government or whether this must be done by the Knesset or the president.

First: We have already determined that the treaty was properly signed on behalf of the government of Israel, which means that there is a legal agreement between the government of Israel and the government of Switzerland. No one claims that the Government is not authorized to sign an international treaty, or that the government of Switzerland did not legally sign the treaty. Therefore, in accordance with the language of section 2 of the statute, there is an agreement between Israel and Switzerland. Under the Israeli law of contracts, an agreement is formed when it is signed by the parties to it. Under the position taken by most scholars of international law, an agreement is formed when signed, even if it still requires ratification. Even the attorney for the Appellant admitted before us, although for a different purpose, that upon signing a treaty, a contract is formed between the two countries; that is why he insisted that the treaty was not properly signed. If "there is an agreement" as stated in section 2 of the statute, it does not matter for the purpose of implementing the statute whether the agreement was ratified or what form the ratification took. This is different from the question of what is required to implement a treaty. At this stage, we are only dealing with activities preliminary to implementing the treaty, which occur after it becomes effective. As long as we do not extradite a person before the agreement becomes effective, we can take whatever steps are needed prior to the actual extradition.

Second, and importantly: Were we to say that there is no agreement as long as the treaty has not entered into force, we would then need to determine the nature of the required ratification.

The government of Israel takes the position that ratification of international treaties is a matter for the Government alone. Because the Government ratified the treaty at stake in this case, and there is no doubt as to whether it did so, the requirements of the treaty apply. If we look to the requirement of the treaty, all that was necessary under its terms for its ratification was done.

But it may be claimed that the issue is not one of interpreting the requirements of the treaty, but rather a general constitutional question, and that the actions required for ratification cannot be determined by the parties to the treaty, but rather must be determined under the law of Israel. Even if we accept this position, I would conclude that the Government is authorized to ratify the treaty. It is true that this is not a unique authorization. We see from section 11(a) (5) of the Basic Law: President of the State ... that some treaties are to be ratified by the Knesset, and these are the only ones which require the signature of the president of the state. This provision does not grant authority or impose a task on any institution except on the president. It only provides that if, under the law that applies, a treaty must be ratified by the Knesset, or if it was in fact ratified by the Knesset, then the president is authorized to sign the treaty, and it is the president's job to do so. This does not tell us which treaties require ratification by the Knesset, and certainly does not provide that all treaties require ratification by the Knesset.

The Knesset is the legislature, while the Government is the executive branch of the state. The executive branch cannot function without the confidence of the legislature, but as long as it has the confidence of the Knesset, the executive branch administers the functions of the state, aside from legislation and formulation of the budget.

Establishment and maintenance of international relations in general, and formulation of international agreements in particular, are clearly assigned to the executive branch and are not within the purview of the legislative branch. In this matter, our situation is different from that in those countries where international treaties have the status of statutes, or of statutes of a higher status. In such countries, formation of an international treaty is a type of act of legislation. This is not the law in Israel, where no international treaty has the status of a statute until it is given such status by an express statutory enactment of the Knesset. In this way, the separation of powers is assured. If an international treaty requires legislation either because it would affect an existing statute or because it would impose an affirmative obligation to act that could not be enforced without legislation, the Knesset must enact a statute or authorize an administrative agency to promulgate a regulation. If it does not, the treaty cannot be implemented. But a treaty that can be implemented by the Government in conducting the affairs of state, or a treaty that reflects existing law, or treaties—such as extradition treaties—that are entered within the existing framework of a statute enacted for such a purpose, are not matters that require the involvement of the Knesset, but concern only the Government.

These determinations are based on the way the state and its various branches were first established and on the constitutional arrangements set out in the Law and Administration Ordinance and in the Transition Law.[3] I am not merely giving my opinion on the appropriate allocation of authority among the various state institutions, nor I am examining analogous arrangements among countries that were governed by the British or that were part of the Mandate system prior to becoming countries in their own right. This might lead us to the wrong conclusions.

As to international law on the matter, the two lawyers who appeared in this case have shown that there is no uniformity in the laws of various states as to what governmental body is authorized to enter an international treaty on behalf of a country. This shows that international law leaves this matter to the internal law of the various countries. Were there one uniform rule accepted by all countries, we might hold that the same rule applies in Israel, as long as it would not violate Israeli statutory law. Thus, were there an international rule that the *head of the state* is authorized to enter international treaties (as one of the attorneys before us has claimed), this would not be sufficient to authorize the president of Israel to do so, because under Israeli law, the president has no independent powers, and the person designated as the head of state as that term is used in international law is a person with executive power within the state.

[According to a noted authority on international law,] when the constitutional arrangements within a given country are that the head of state is not authorized to enter into international treaties, then the Government is the body authorized to act on behalf of the state and to ratify treaties. This is precisely the situation in Israel.

The facts presented to us by the attorney general prove that this is the constitutional practice of the state. Until now, in the name of the State of Israel, the Government has entered into 780 international agreements, of which 356 are treaties that required ratification, and all were ratified by the Government.

---

3. Both of these statutes are discussed in chapter 4.

The conclusion is that not only was the treaty legally signed, but also that it was legally ratified.

Justice Levy:

The main question in this appeal is whether "there is an agreement" as provided in section 2 of the Extradition Law, 5714-1954; that is, "whether there is an agreement between Israel and the country seeking extradition [Switzerland] that establishes mutual obligation as to extradition of criminals." Section 1 of the treaty between Israel and Switzerland establishes a mutual obligation as to extradition of criminals.

The first question is one of choice of law. Which law controls the question of the validity of the treaty? The treaty is an agreement between two sovereign countries, an international agreement, and therefore we must consider its validity. As a principle of international law, every international agreement is a creation of international law, and its validity, or power to create obligations, or its existence, flows from international law. The questions of whether an agreement exists under section 2 is therefore, first of all, a question of international law, and the internal or municipal law of a country is relevant only to the extent that international law makes it relevant. In my opinion, it does not matter that the Extradition Law is a municipal law, or that this court is a municipal court, or that the subject before us is the right and freedom of an individual under Israeli law. The Extradition Law itself establishes the rights of the Appellant (section 1: "A person who is in Israel shall not be extradited to another country except according to the provisions of this statute"), and it refers us to international law when it provides in section 2 that "it is permissible to extradite such a person, if there is an agreement between Israel and the country seeking extradition that establishes mutual obligations as to extradition of criminals." If "there is an agreement" between the two countries as provided, it is permissible to extradite the Appellant, as long as all the other conditions set out in the statute are met. If there is no such agreement, it is not permissible to extradite him.

The law applicable to the Appellant under the Extradition Law, as I interpret sections 1 and 2 of the statute, depends on the existence of an international agreement.

The Appellant's ... main argument against the validity of the treaty is that the Government was not authorized to ratify it because the exclusive authority to ratify an international treaty is given to the Knesset. In my opinion, there is no need to consider this constitutional claim. Even if that were what should be done (and I do not think it is), it would be insufficient to invalidate the extradition treaty between Israel and Switzerland that has been signed by the Government. Here are my reasons for this conclusion.

As the learned General Counsel described, since its founding, the State of Israel has entered 356 international treaties that required ratification, and none were ratified by the Knesset. All were ratified by the Government. Were Appellant's claim accepted, all of these treaties, which form the system of Israel's international rights and obligations, would be of no force and effect!

Furthermore, in response to the request of the Secretary General of the United Nations, 86 countries, including Israel, presented official documents on their laws and practices as to formation of treaties. These documents, including a memorandum of the Government of Israel dated March 11, 1951, were published by the United Nations in 1953 in the volume Law and Practices Concerning the Conclusion of Treaties (United Nations Legislative Series, St/Leg/Ser.B/3). The Israeli memorandum provides:

> 1. The situation in Israel is at present characterized by the absence of clear and specific provisions of a legislative character.

7. The authority which in this way is vested exclusively in the Government of Israel extends not only to negotiating and signing international treaties, whether or not they are subject to ratification. It also includes ratifying international treaties requiring ratification.

9. The president's functions in connection with the exercise of the treaty-making power are governed by section 6 of the Transition Law, 5709-1949, under which "the president of the state shall sign treaties with foreign states that have been ratified by the Knesset."[4] This means that when in fact the Knesset has expressed its approval of the ratification of the treaty, the act of ratification will be signed by the president. In other cases, the act of ratification may be signed by the president or by the foreign minister.... It is to be observed that this provision is one relating to the powers of the president. It does not import any modification of the general law about treaty-making or about the authority of the Knesset to ratify treaties. This aspect is not regulated by any law passed by the Israeli legislature and therefore remains as described above.

11. The position can therefore be summarized in the following way:

(A) The legal power to negotiate, sign and ratify international treaties on behalf of Israel is vested exclusively in the Government of Israel and is in the charge of the minister of foreign affairs;

(B) Where the Knesset has given its approval to the ratification of a treaty, the act of ratification is signed by the president of the state.

In light of this representation, upon which the nations of the world, including Switzerland, have relied in entering treaties with Israel, Israel should not now take the position that a treaty that has been ratified by the Government and not by the Knesset lacks legal force.

Two factors, taken together, lead to the conclusion that the extradition treaty between Israel and Switzerland is of full validity, and these two factors are: (1) Israel's express representation that under Israeli constitutional law the Government has authority to ratify treaties, and (2) the continuous practice of Israel, ever since the establishment of the state, of ratification of treaties by the Government.

[Justice Levy then shows that under international law, one country may rely on another country's ostensible authority to enter into a treaty in the manner in which it has done so.]

Justice Landau:

As to the Appellant's claim that the treaty between Israel and Switzerland is not valid, I agree with the opinion of my honorable colleague Justice Levy that the first question is one of classification: When the Knesset enacted section 2 of the Extradition Law, 5714-1954, providing that one of the conditions for extradition is that "there is an agreement" that provides mutual obligations for extradition of criminals, did it mean that the agreement should be in force under international law or under internal Israeli (municipal) law?

My colleague is of the opinion that the legislature meant here to refer to international law. I doubt that this was the intent. It is presumed that national legislature speaks in terms of the internal law of the state, without sending the person who must interpret the law to sources outside that framework. Section 2 contains no clear indication of intent to deviate from this presumption. For example, were an international treaty ratified by the

---

4. The same provision now appears as section 11 (a) (5) of the Basic Law: The President of the State.

Knesset, and if the president of the state did not sign that treaty as required by section 11 (a) (5) of the Basic Law: The President of the State, would not an Israeli court have to declare that there is no such treaty for the purposes of section 2 of the Extradition Law, even if under the rules of international law, someone could claim that the treaty obligated the state?

I do not mean to say that there is no meaning to international law. Our common law rule is that an Israeli court will interpret an Israeli statute in a way that eliminates any contradiction between internal Israeli law and the recognized principles of international law, so that Israeli law will be consistent with the state's obligations under international law. But when there is a conflict between internal law and international law, the court must give preference to the internal law.

My colleague Justice Levy has shown that under international law the extradition agreement that is the subject of this case is valid. If internal Israeli law had clearly established who can enter an international treaty on behalf of the state, there might be a situation in which the internal law on this matter conflicted with the international law. But if the two sides to this case agree on anything, it is that the Israeli law on the matter is not clear. In such a case, it cannot be said that Israeli law conflicts with international law, which recognizes the validity of the agreement that was ratified by the Government of Israel. In my opinion, that is sufficient reason to reject the Appellant's claims.

I reach the same result without relying on the presumption that the internal Israeli law is consistent with the rules of the international law.... [As to the question of] which Israeli authority can enter into an international treaty ... the Israel statutory law gives us only a partial answer in ... section 11 (a) (5) of the Basic Law: President of the State. Under this section, the president is to sign treaties that were ratified by the Knesset. This section addresses the authority of the president and not the authority of the Knesset. We can only infer indirectly from this provisions that the Knesset can ratify international treaties. The Knesset's power of ratification is not an exclusive power; if it were, the legislation would provide that the president of the state shall sign treaties "after they are ratified by the Knesset," or would use similar wording. From the way the section is presently worded, we do not know whether the Knesset is authorized to ratify international treaties of a certain type, or if Knesset authorization depends on whether the Government chooses to refer the treaty to the Knesset for ratification or to ratify the treaty itself. The minister of justice has adopted the latter position in all Knesset debates on the matter. His position has been that formation of international treaties is by its nature among the tasks assigned to the executive branch. Some in the Knesset and outside of the Knesset have disputed this position, but [the Knesset enacted] section 11 (a) (5) of the Basic Law: President of the State [adopting language identical to that found in an earlier statute]. The Knesset was aware of the established practice in this matter, under which the Government has ratified all the many international treaties that have required ratification, and not one of them has been ratified by the Knesset.... We must understand this action by the Knesset, and its decision not to adopt several private proposed laws that would have changed the arrangements as to ratification of treaties, to be a clear expression of the legality of the existing situation under which treaties have been ratified by the Government and a decision to continue such an arrangement.

Chief Justice Agranat:

[Under international law, the executive branch of a state has the power to ratify treaties. Different states place the executive authority in the hands of different state institutions. National law may impose additional requirements.]

When a claim is raised before a national court that ratification of a treaty under discussion required legislative approval, the court has no choice but to examine the internal constitutional law of its own country in order to determine whether or not such a claim is correct. Clearly if the court is convinced that there is such a requirement, and it has not been fulfilled, it must rule that ratification of a treaty by the Government is devoid of constitutional authority and ultra-vires. In this case, the treaty would have no legal effect. For the concrete case that is before us, we can phrase the legal issue as follows: In order to determine whether "there is an agreement" between Israel and Switzerland as to extradition of criminals, first we need to decide whether the Government had the power to ratify the treaty, or whether the ratification required the agreement of the Knesset. The answer depends solely on interpretation of the relevant Israeli law.

The dispute before this Court is not a dispute between Israel and Switzerland.... This dispute involves only local law, depends on the validity of the treaty only in relation to the provisions of Israeli law. It is not about the relations between Israel and Switzerland, but rather about the right of Israel to extradite a citizen to Switzerland.

We find that when the legislature provided in section 2 of the Extradition Law that a person can be extradited to another country if there is an extradition agreement between that country and Israel, the legislature clearly referred to an extradition agreement that was entered into in accord with the law of Israel. This includes the Israeli law that determines what authority of the state has the power to decide whether to enter into such an agreement.

The reasoning set out by Justice Cohen is correct ... that under the parliamentary system of Israel, the Government is given the treaty-making power. The Knesset has the supervisory authority over the Government that it can exercise in two ways. First, it can exercise its power to express its lack of confidence in the activities of the Government. Second, under Israeli law, an international treaty to which Israel is a party cannot be implemented internally by a court until it has undergone the process of *transformation* into a law of the state. This process is unnecessary as to an extradition agreement.

In conclusion, the system followed in Israel is similar to that in England, as described in Canada v. Ontario, (1937), A.C. 326, 347–348:

> Unlike some other countries, the stipulations of a treaty duly ratified do not within the empire, by virtue of the treaty alone, have the force of law. If the national executive, the Government of the day, decide to incur the obligations of a treaty which involve alteration of law they have to run the risk of obtaining the assent of parliament to the necessary statute or statutes. To make themselves as secure as possible they will often in such cases before final ratification seek to obtain from parliament an expression of approval.... Parliament ... has a constitutional control over the executive but it cannot be disputed that the creation of the obligations undertaken in treaties and the assent to their form and quality are the function of the executive alone. Once they are created, while they bind the state as against the other contracting parties, parliament may refuse to perform them and so leave the state in default. In a unitary state whose legislature possesses unlimited powers the problem is simple. Parliament will either fulfill or not treaty obligations imposed on the state by its executive. The nature of the obligations does not affect the complete authority of the legislature to make them law if it so chooses.

The conclusion is therefore that the Government had the power to decide whether to ratify the treaty under discussion in this case. The ratification by the foreign minister was completely in accordance with the law and was sufficient to bind Israel to the treaty.

Justice Berenson:

I join the opinions of my esteemed colleagues, Justice Landau and the Chief Justice.

Comment

Justice Cohen presents several different arguments for finding the agreement between Israel and Switzerland sufficient to support the lower court's decision that Kamiar is extraditable. (1) The statute requires only an "agreement" between Israel and Switzerland. Under the rules of Israeli contract law, a signed treaty between the two countries qualifies as an agreement. (2) Determining that Kamiar is extraditable is not the same as extraditing him. A court can determine that all the conditions for extradition set out in the law exist (and there are a number of such conditions), so that he can be extradited as soon as a treaty goes into effect. (3) The treaty is in effect because it was ratified according to its own requirements on ratification. (4) The treaty is in effect because it was ratified in accordance with the Israeli law on ratification. Israeli law assigns the task of ratification of treaties, at least those that do not need legislative implementation, to the Government. The last argument is the essential one and became accepted Israeli law.

The problem with the last argument is that the treaty was ratified by the Government, but section 11 (a) (5) of the Basic Law: President of the State refers to ratification by the Knesset and signature of the president. The opinion did away with this problem by holding that section 11 (a) (5) referred only to treaties that require ratification by the Knesset; it does not provide that all treaties need such ratification. It then distinguished between those treaties that would need ratification by the Knesset and those that would not, concluding that this treaty fell into the second category.

Justice Levy's approach is different. He reaches the same conclusion—that the Government may ratify treaties—but bases his analysis on international, and not national, law. He uses an estoppel type of analysis. Given (a) the past practice of the Government in ratifying treaties, (b) the representations of Israel to other countries that the Government has the right to ratify treaties, (c) the reliance of other countries on this practice and this representation, and implicitly, (d) the detriment that would occur if such reliance were not affirmed, the Court will not now hold that ratification by the Government makes a treaty invalid. In short, presumably Switzerland relied on Israel's assertion that its Government could ratify the extradition treaty.

Justice Landau reasons that international law is not decisive in determining who can ratify treaties. International law is relevant in applying the Israeli common law rule that national law should be interpreted in a manner consistent with international law where possible. Since Israeli law on who can ratify a treaty is unclear, it will be interpreted to be consistent with the international law, which recognizes ratification by the Government. Justice Landau offers, in addition, an alternative analysis that does not rest on international law at all. Under this second analysis, he maintains that the legislature can assign the task of treaty ratification to any branch of government. Although the Knesset has not expressly made such an assignment, Justice Landau finds that it has implicitly given the task to the Government. This finding is based on the fact that the Government has in fact been ratifying treaties, and the Knesset has not objected, despite having had the clear opportunity to do so.

Chief Justice Agranat agrees with Justice Landau that international law does not determine the validity of the treaty as a matter of Israeli law. Israeli law determines whether a treaty is valid and applicable in internal litigation and also controls on the question of what body must ratify a treaty. Under Israeli law, the Government ratifies treaties because the treaty-making power is part of the executive power assigned to the Government. His view of Israeli law is slightly different from that of Justice Landau in that it is based on what he sees as an affirmative assignment of the task to the Government, rather than an implication to be inferred from the Knesset's failure to react to the Government practice of ratifying treaties.

Thus, while all justices agree that the treaty was valid, they do not agree on the reasons. The essential disagreements are on whether national or international law controls the means of ratification and on the source of the national law giving the Government the power to ratify treaties. Nonetheless the *Kamiar* case is accepted as establishing the rule that Israeli law provides that the Government can ratify treaties.

The Government's memorandum to the United Nations, quoted in Justice Levy's opinion, represents that the foreign minister can in some cases ratify treaties on behalf of the Government. Israeli law allows the Government to delegate its power to the foreign minister.

Shortly after the decision in the above case, the Knesset enacted the Basic Law: the Government, which contained a provision on the residual power of the Government. The same language is now found in section 32 of a later version of that Basic Law. This provision reinforces Justice Agranat's approach to the question of whether the Government has the power to ratify treaties.

Israeli Statute

Basic Law: The Government

32. Residual Powers of the Government

The Government may, in the name of the state, undertake all acts, subject to law, that are not assigned to another branch of government.

Comment

In the United States, the matter is much clearer.

US Law

US Constitution, Article II

Section 2. (1) The president shall be Commander in Chief of the Army and Navy of the United States.

(2) He shall have power, by and with the advice and consent of the Senate, to make treaties, provided two thirds of the Senators present concur.

Comment

The major difference between the Israeli and American systems for treaty ratification is that Israel does not provide for mandatory legislative participation, but the United States does. Arguably the difference may not be as great as it seems. As both Justice Cohen and Justice Agranat noted in the *Kamiar* case, in Israel's parliamentary system, the legislature has control over the executive through the power of a no-confidence vote, so that the legislature is indirectly involved in treaty ratification. The US presidential system does not provide for votes of no-confidence; the president serves for a fixed term. On the other hand, the parliamentary involvement through the no-confidence vote is minimal. In order to express displeasure over ratification of a treaty, the Knesset would have to bring down the Government. This is too blunt a tool to be effective in all but the most extreme cases.

Another factor that may moderate the difference is the fact that in Israel's parliamentary system there is much less separation between the executive and the legislative branches than in the presidential system in the United States. Thus the legislative branch is involved in treaty ratification because a significant number of Knesset members are in the Government. On the other hand, the task of treaty ratification is generally delegated by the Government to the foreign minister. It is not clear how extensively other members of the Government are involved in decisions whether to ratify treaties.

Questions

1. The majority of justices in *Kamiar* ruled that national Israeli law, and not international law, determines what steps Israel had to take to ratify a treaty. Does the United States take the same position?

2. What are the advantages of the Israeli system of ratification and what are the advantages of the American system?

B. The Incorporation of Treaties into Israeli Law

The prior section dealt with the question of what acts bind Israel to a treaty. This section considers further the effect of a treaty on Israeli domestic law. Assuming that Israel has taken the proper steps to become bound to a treaty as a matter of international law, to what extent are those treaty provisions enforceable in litigation in an Israeli court?

Israeli Case

Custodian of Absentee Property v. Samara
CA 25/55, 10 PD 1825 [1956]

[The 1949 Armistice Agreement between Jordan and Israel after the Israeli War of Independence (the Rhodes Agreement) provided for an exchange of territories between

Israel and Jordan. The Appellants were three individuals, who lived in villages that were located in Jordan before the exchange, and claimed rights to lands that were within the area of Israel even before the exchange. After the exchange, their villages also became part of the territory of Israel. They all claimed that the Rhodes Agreement provided them with certain protected rights as to their lands. The Court at first considered whether the Rhodes Agreement covered these lands and decided it did not. The Court then turned to an alternative approach to the dispute, finding that it did not matter whether the treaty covered these lands because it was not a law that could be enforced in an Israeli court.]

Justice Berenson:

The Rhodes Agreement is a treaty between the State of Israel and another country. Whatever the validity of such an agreement under international law, it is not a law that our courts will refer to or will give force to in their decisions. The rights and obligations it creates are rights and obligations of the countries that are sides to the agreement, and their implementation can be obtained by the countries themselves only through the special mechanisms of international law. Such an agreement is not to be enforced by national courts unless the rights and obligations under the agreement were transformed through national legislation into statutory obligations. In a case like this, we need to consider not the international agreement, but rather the statute that gives life to its contents as a matter of our municipal law. If there is a both a statute and an international agreement, and they are not completely consistent with each other, even if it is clear that the statute was meant to implement and apply the international agreement, our courts will give preference to the terms of the statute, which our courts must follow. The courts will base their judgments on the statute alone. Furthermore, even if an agreement between two states, or an international agreement, grants rights to certain individuals, the undertakings set out in the agreement remain solely undertakings of the state in the international arena. Individuals do not by virtue of the agreement acquire rights that they can effectuate in the courts.

These principles are the same as those found in a long line of cases in England. *Hoani Te Heuheu Tukino v. Aotea District Maori Land Board*, (1941) A.C. 308, 324–25 P.C. expresses this:

> When a territory is acquired by a sovereign state for the first time, that is an act of state. It matters not how the acquisition has been brought about. It may be by conquest, it may be by cession following on treaty, it may be by occupation of territory hitherto unoccupied by a recognized ruler. In all cases the result is the same. Any inhabitant of the territory can make good in the municipal courts established by the new sovereign only such rights as that sovereign has, through his officers, recognized. Such rights as he had under the rule of predecessors avail him nothing. Nay more, even if in a treaty of cession it is stipulated that certain inhabitants should enjoy certain rights, that does not give a title to those inhabitants to enforce these stipulations in the municipal courts. The right to enforce remains only with the high contracting parties.

Similar rulings are found in other countries. In fact, the rules and principles expressed here are almost universal. See, for example, the statements of Justice Lamont of the Supreme Court of Canada in *Arrow River & Tributaries Slide & Boom Co. v. Pigeon Timber Co.*: (1932) S.C.R. 495, 510:

The treaty in itself is not equivalent to an Imperial Act and, without the sanction of Parliament, the Crown cannot alter the existing law by entering into a contract with a foreign power. For a breach of a treaty a nation is responsible only to the other contracting nation and its own sense of right and justice. Where, as here, a treaty provides that certain rights or privileges are to be enjoyed by the subjects of both contracting parties, these rights and privileges are, under our law, enforceable by the courts only where the treaty has been implemented or sanctioned by legislation rendering it binding upon the subject. Upon this point I agree with the view expressed by both courts below: that, in British countries, treaties to which Great Britain is a party are not as such binding upon the individual subjects, but are only contracts binding in honour upon the contracting states.

In the absence of affirming legislation this provision of the treaty cannot be enforced by any of our courts whose authority is derived from municipal law.

Similar rules are found in [courts of Italy, Greece, and Australia].

It may appear that things are different in the United States (and in other countries that are similar in the nature of their constitutions), but that is not really so. The US Constitution explicitly raises every treaty made in the name of the United States to the level of the supreme law of the land. Under this provision, US federal and state courts enforce treaties and even give them priority over conflicting state statutes. This is a direct result of the constitutional provision. In this way, the US courts are following the universal principle we set out above. They also implement treaties on behalf of private individuals only to the extent that their own law requires that they do so, although due to the general provision in the US Constitution, there is no need for their law to express such a requirement for each individual treaty. *Edye v. Robertson*, 112 U.S. 580 (1884).

As for the Rhodes Agreement, there is no statute that gives it effect or that makes it, or any portion of it, part of the law of the state. Therefore it cannot be relied on in court as a source of private rights or of obligations of the state or of any of its agencies.

[Israeli statutes that exist independent of the Rhodes Agreement do not recognize the Appellants' claims to the land in question.]

Comment

This case involved the question of whether an individual could effectuate rights granted in a treaty and whether the state was bound to fulfill obligations as to individuals undertaken in a treaty. The Court held that the individual could not effectuate rights and the state was not bound to fulfill such obligations without implementing national legislation. This rule does not affect the question of whether the state itself is bound to other countries due to the treaty; even without implementing legislation, the state is bound. Furthermore, if Israel already has domestic legislation that meets the requirements set out in the treaty, it does not need to enact new legislation after treaty ratification. In this case, also, it is the domestic legislation that is enforceable in Israeli courts, not the international treaty.

In this regard, consider again the following statement in Justice Cohen's opinion in the *Kamiar* case, set out earlier in the chapter.

If an international treaty requires legislation either because it would affect an existing statute or because it would impose an affirmative obligation to act that could not be enforced without legislation, the Knesset must enact a statute or authorize an administrative agency to promulgate a regulation. If it does not, the treaty cannot be implemented. But a treaty that can be implemented by the Government in conducting the affairs of state, or a treaty that reflects existing law, or treaties — such as extradition treaties — that are entered within the existing framework of a statute enacted for such a purpose, are not matters that require the involvement of the Knesset, but concern only the Government.

The last statement might appear to contradict the rule that treaties must be implemented by the Knesset. On closer examination, though, the statement can be understood as consistent with the rule. The *Kamiar* case involved an extradition treaty. Israel already had a domestic statute that provided that a person could be extradited to a country with whom Israel had an extradition treaty. In other words, there was prior Knesset legislation that stated the effect of any extradition treaty that the Government might later ratify. No further Knesset action was needed not because the Government could bind the Israeli courts without the Knesset, but rather because the Knesset had already enacted the necessary legislation.

At first consideration, the rule in *Samara* may seem unfair because it lets the Government say one thing in the international arena without being bound to its own word. It allows the Government not to be bound by its own international undertakings as long as they are not implemented by statute. On the other hand, it is justified by the need to prevent the Government, which is a political body not directly elected by the people, from binding future Governments to actions that the majority does not want.

Israel is, of course, under political pressure to implement its international treaty obligations with domestic legislation. Such pressure can come from both inside and outside of the country.

The rule that Israeli courts will not apply international treaty law without implementing Israeli legislation is subject to two significant exceptions.

1. As discussed in the next section, customary international law is applied by Israeli courts without implementing legislation. Many treaties, or provisions of treaties, simply incorporate customary law. In such cases, the treaty provisions are enforceable as customary law even in the absence of implementing legislation.

2. In cases involving the human rights, particularly in cases involving human rights of the residents of the territories, the Israeli Supreme Court tends to apply "norms" of international law without close examination of whether those norms derive from treaty law or from customary law. In that way, the Court expands the influence of international law in the Israeli judicial decisions.[5]

In the United States, treaty law is applied by the courts without implementing statutes. The *Samara* case claims that the US Constitution functions as the implementing law, without requiring any action by Congress.

---

5. *See* Daphne Barak-Erez, *The International Law of Human Rights and Constitutional Law: A Case Study of an Expanding Dialogue*, 2 INT'L J. CONST. L. 611 (2004).

US Law

US Constitution, Article III

Section 1. The judicial power of the United States shall be vested in one Supreme Court and such inferior courts as the Congress may from time to time ordain and establish.

Section 2. (1) The judicial power shall extend to all cases, in law and equity, arising under this Constitution, the laws of the United States, and treaties made, or which shall be made, under their authority ...

Article VI

(2) This Constitution, and the laws of the United States which shall be made in pursuance thereof; and all treaties made, or which shall be made, under the authority of the United States, shall be the supreme law of the land; and the judges of every state shall be bound thereby, any thing in the Constitution or laws of any state to the contrary notwithstanding.

Comment

Article III, section 1 provides that federal courts have the "judicial power of the United States," and section 2 that this includes all cases arising under treaties. In case there is any doubt as to what this means, Article VI, section 2 provides that treaty law is the supreme law of the land. It is therefore enforced by federal courts under Article III and by state courts under Article VI, section 2.

This automatic absorption of treaty law into federal law is not absolute. The effect of a treaty that violates the US Constitution may be limited by a constitutional requirement.[6] In addition, a treaty provision that is not self-executing does not become law until implemented by legislation.[7] For example, a treaty imposing a penalty on individuals generally must be implemented through domestic legislation and, when it is, it is the legislation and not the treaty that is enforced.[8] The extent of the self-executing exception is highly controversial.[9]

Questions

3. What justifies the Israeli position, which is characterized as almost universal, that rights and obligations under a treaty cannot be enforced without implementing domestic legislation? In this regard, consider the discussion in *Kamiar*.

4. The Israeli Government Code of Procedure is a document adopted by the Government that relates to how it will conduct business. Section 6 of the code requires that the Government shall give two weeks' notice to the Knesset before deciding whether to ratify a treaty.[10] In light of this provision, which provides the Knesset with the opportunity

---

6. *See* Reid v. Covert, 354 U.S. 1, 16 (1957).

7. Medellin v. Texas, 552 U.S. 491, 491–92 (2008); Foster v. Neilson, 27 U.S. (2 Pet.) 253, 314 (1829), *overruled in part on other grounds.*

8. *See* Hopson v. Kreps, 622 F.2d 1375, 1380 (9th Cir. 1980).

9. See Carlos Manuel Vázquez, *Treaties as the Law of the Land: The Supremacy Clause and the Judicial Enforcement of Treaties*, 122 Harv. L. Rev. 599 (2008).

10. Government Code of Procedure, The 32nd Government (Apr. 4, 2009) (in Hebrew), *available at* http://www.pmo.gov.il/NR/rdonlyres/6131A66F-297B-4C38-8ACC-368658178CEB/0/tak050409.doc.

to prevent treaty ratification, should the law be changed so that treaties become national Israeli law without implementing legislation?

C. The Incorporation of International Customary Law into Israeli Law

Israeli Case

Afu v. Commander of IDF Forces in the West Bank
HCJ 785/87, 845/87, 27/88, 42(s) PD 1 [1988]

[Petitioners were three residents of the territories (the West Bank and Gaza Strip). At the time of the case, these areas were under Israeli military rule. The petitioners had been tried in military courts and found guilty of acts of violence, incitement of others to acts of violence, and engaging in activities for a terrorist organization. All of these actions violated military regulations in force in the territories. When the petitioners continued their actions after release from prison, the Commanders of the Israel Defense Forces in the territories issued orders for their deportation, as permitted under the regulations. The petitioners sought review of the deportation orders in the Supreme Court, arguing that the deportations violated international law.]

Chief Justice Shamgar:

On the matter of the relationship between international and domestic law, Israeli law distinguishes between customary law and conventional law.

According to the consistent case law of this Court, customary international law is part of the law of the state so long as there is not conflicting Israeli law.

In the matter of the status of conventional international law in our state law, Justice Berenson discussed the matter. [The opinion thus sets out the same language of Justice Berenson in the *Samara* case as is set out above.]

One might think that there are rules of *conventional* international law, derived from legal treaties, that *automatically* become rules of municipal law in Israel, even without requiring legislation. Such a conclusion would be founded in error. We accept the classification of treaties as declarative or constitutive, and it is important to be precise in distinguishing between them.... As Professor N. Feinberg has made clear in his article [in Hebrew],

> In international law there is a fundamental distinction between a declarative treaty, that transfers existing norms from the realm of customary law to the realm of conventional law, and constitutive treaties, that created entirely new norms. Constitutive treaties may also create new norms that are founded in the conduct of states but are customs that have not yet reached the degree of definition that make them part of the customary law.

In summary, under Israeli law, an international treaty does not become part of the law of the land unless—

(1) its provisions were enacted in legislation, and then only to the extent that they are so enacted, or

(2) the provisions are only a restatement or declaration of the existing customary law; that is, a codification of an existing custom.

[The Court then found that the international law which the petitioners wanted the Court to consider was conventional law that was not implemented by Israeli legislation. The Court reviewed the factual basis for the deportation orders and found that the deportations were not a misuse of authority, were neither arbitrary nor discriminatory, and were not subject to any other legal defect that would invalidate the orders.]

Comment

Most countries follow the same rule that applies in Israel: customary international law becomes domestic law without implementing legislation. There are two exceptions to this rule: customary law does not bind a country that has indicated from the beginning that it does not intend to be bound by it. In addition, at least in Israel, if domestic law based on statute conflicts with international customary law, the Israeli courts follow the Israeli law.

Despite the near-universality of the rule, the rationale for automatic adoption of customary law is not clear.[11] It is easier to give a negative justification for the rule than to provide a positive one. If treaty law were automatically absorbed into domestic law, that would allow the Government to make law without involvement of the legislative branch, the Knesset. The absorption of customary law presents no such problem: the Government is not involved in making the customary law; the law is made by implicit or explicit assent of most nations. Still, this negative rationale does not explain why "assent of most nations" provides sufficient justification for bypassing the legislative process. Furthermore, the Government is involved to some extent in imposing customary law on courts of the state, because an objection by the Government at the beginning of the formation of the custom would make it inapplicable to Israel. Nonetheless the rule is clear: customary law applies in Israeli courts.

A more difficult question in practice is distinguishing customary law from treaty law, especially since, as the *Afu* case indicates, a treaty may simply restate or *declare* customary law. In that case, the provisions of the treaty are applicable in Israeli courts as customary law.

The issue of when an Israeli statute conflicts with customary international law has arisen in some cases. The Israeli courts try to construe Israeli legislation in such a way that there is no conflict. For example, in *Shalom v. Attorney General*,[12] an Israeli belly dancer filed a tort claim against the Egyptian Ambassador to Israel, seeking damages for assault and false imprisonment. The Egyptian Ambassador's counsel argued that the Ambassador had diplomatic immunity from the claim. Neither Israel's tort statute nor any other law provided for such immunity. The tort statute included a list of defenses, and diplomatic immunity was not among them. The Court had to consider whether the list of defenses was exclusive. Although normal rules of statutory construction might lead to the conclusion that the list was exclusive, the Court here held that it was not and that the Court should apply the customary international law rule of diplomatic immunity to bar the claim.

The analysis of when customary law enters Israeli law explains the following statement by Justice Cohen in the *Kamiar* case, discussing whether Israeli law authorizes the Government to ratify treaties:

---

11. *See* Yaffa Zilbershats, *The Adoption of International Law into Israeli Law: The Real is Ideal*, 25 ISRAEL YEARBOOK ON HUMAN RIGHTS 243, 245–46 (1996).

12. CA (T.A.) 4289/98 Shalom v. Attorney General, PM 58(3) PD 1 (1999).

As to international law on the matter, the two lawyers who appeared in this case have shown that there is no uniformity in the laws of various states as to what governmental body is authorized to enter an international treaty on behalf of a country. This shows that international law leaves this matter to the internal law of the various countries. Were there one uniform rule accepted by all countries, we might hold that the same rule applies in Israel, as long as it would not violate Israeli statutory law. Thus, were there an international rule that the *head of the state* is authorized to enter international treaties (as one of the attorneys before us has claimed), this would not be sufficient to authorize the president of Israel to do so, because under Israeli law, the president has no independent powers, and the person designated as the head of state as that term is used in international law is a person with executive power within the state.

In other words, there is no customary international law on what authority of a state can ratify treaties, but even if there were, it would not apply in Israel. While customary international law ordinarily becomes part of the domestic law of Israel without any action by the Knesset, this is not the case where the customary international law contradicts Israeli law. Were customary international law to provide that the head of state can ratify treaties, this would not authorize the president of Israel to ratify treaties for one of two reasons. The first reason is that the term head of state as used in international law does not apply to the president of Israel. The term, as used in international law, means a person with executive authority, and the president of Israel does not have executive authority. Alternatively the Israeli law that denies the president independent authority contradicts customary international law that would give treaty power to the president as head of state.

In the United States, customary law is automatically incorporated into domestic law and treated as federal law.[13]

---

13. Restatement (Third) of Foreign Relations Law of the United States § 111, cmt e & Reporters' Note 3 (1987).

Chapter 11

Criminal Law

Criminal law is based on statute. The main criminal law statute is The Penal Law, 5737-1977. It is heavily based on the British criminal statute from the period of the Mandate. This is a long and detailed statute that sets out general principles of criminal law (e.g., Section 1: "There is crime and no punishment except as specified in a law."), defines specific criminal violations, and establishes punishments. Many other statutes, such as the environmental statutes, also include provisions defining criminal violations.

Some of the most interesting features of Israeli criminal law are illustrated by the most notorious criminal proceeding in Israel's history, the trial of Adolf Eichmann. Use of this trial to examine principles of criminal law also teaches about the Holocaust, which deeply influences the Israeli psyche. Some brief background material on the Eichmann trial is presented in the first section of this chapter. The remaining sections of this chapter examine legal issues that arose during the trial or that are illustrated by the case.

A. The Eichmann Trial — Overview

Adolf Eichmann was in charge of the Jewish Department of the Nazi security police during World War II. In this capacity, he was in charge of the *Final Solution* for the Jews of Europe. After the war, he assumed a false identity and escaped Germany. By 1950 he was living in Argentina. In May 1960 he was abducted from Argentina by Israeli agents and flown to Israel. The prime minister of Israel announced in the Knesset that Eichmann had been located and would be put on trial for his part in the Final Solution. Argentina objected to the violation of its territorial sovereignty and brought the matter before the Security Council of United Nations, but the matter was resolved when the Government of Israel issued a communication of regret and the two countries issued a joint communiqué stating that the dispute between them was closed.

Eichmann was tried before the District Court of Jerusalem in the spring and summer of 1961 for violation of an Israeli statute, the Nazi and Nazi Collaborators (Punishment) Law, 5710-1950. He was convicted and sentenced to death. Eichmann appealed to the Supreme Court of Israel, which upheld both the conviction and the sentence. He was executed by hanging and his ashes scattered at sea.

Throughout the trial and the appeal, Eichmann did not deny the facts presented about what he was done, but raised numerous legal objections to his conviction. The Supreme Court's treatment of the legal objections illuminates many important principles of Israeli criminal law.

Israeli Statute

Nazis and Nazi Collaborators
(Punishment) Law, 5710-1950

1. Crimes against the Jewish people, Crimes against Humanity, and War Crimes

(a) A person who committed one of the following offenses is subject to the death penalty—

(1) committed an act constituting a crime against the Jewish people in an enemy country during the period of the Nazi regime;

(2) committed an act constituting a crime against humanity in an enemy country during the period of the Nazi regime;

(3) committed an act constituting a war crime in an enemy country during the period of the Nazi regime.

(b) In this section—

"Crime against the Jewish people" means any one of the following acts that was done with the intention to destroy the Jewish people in its entirety or in part:

(1) killing of Jews;

(2) causing serious bodily or mental harm to Jews;

(3) inflicting on Jews conditions of life calculated to bring about their physical destruction;

(4) imposing measures intended to prevent Jewish births;

(5) destroying or desecrating Jewish religious or cultural property or values;

(7) inciting hatred of Jews.

"Crime against humanity" means any of the following acts:

Murder, destruction, enslavement, starvation and deportation of a civilian population, and any other inhuman act done to a civilian population, and also persecution for reasons of nationality, race, religion, or politics.

"War crime" means any one of the following acts:

Murder or persecution and deportation as forced labor, or for any other reason, of the members of a civilian population of an occupied territory or within an occupied territory; murder and deportation of prisoners of war or of persons on the high seas; killing of hostages; theft of personal or private property; wanton destruction of cities, towns or villages, and demolition not justified by military necessity.

8. Provisions that Do Not Apply

Section ... 19 of the Criminal Law shall not apply to a criminal offense under this law.

Israeli Statue

Penal Law, 5737-1977

[Section 19 of the Criminal Law was moved to the following provision when the criminal code was recodified in 1977.]

34m. Justification

A person is not criminally liable for an act done under one of the following conditions:

(2) The act was done pursuant to an order of a competent authority which the accused was obligated by law to obey, unless the order was manifestly unlawful.

Comment

The language used to define a crime against the Jewish people is derived from international law. In 1949, Israel signed the Convention on the Prevention and Punishment of the Crime of Genocide. The following year, Israel ratified it, enacting the Law on Prevention and Punishment of Genocide, 5710-1950 (hereinafter the Genocide Law) in fulfillment of its obligations under the Convention. That statute is set out and discussed in section F of this chapter. The definition of *genocide* in the Genocide Law is almost identical to that in the Convention.

A few months later, the Knesset enacted the Nazis and Nazi Collaborators (Punishment) Law (hereinafter the Nazi Punishment Law). The Nazi Punishment Law copied the language on prohibited acts from the Genocide Law, but made those acts relate specifically to crimes against the Jewish people. Israel now has two laws dealing with genocide, the Genocide Law, which treats genocide against any group, and the Nazi Punishment Law, which treats genocide against Jews specifically, but also has a broader application to crimes against humanity and to war crimes. Thus, the two laws overlap.[1]

Israeli Case

Attorney General v. Eichmann
CrimC (Jer) 40/61, 27 PM 169 (1961)[2]

[This is the final portion of a long opinion by the district court.]

(1) We therefore find the Accused guilty under of the first count of the indictment of a crime against the Jewish people, a criminal offense under section 1(a)(1) of the Nazis and Nazi Collaborators (Punishment) Law 5710-1950, in that during the period from August 1941 to May 1945, he, along with others, caused the killing of millions of Jews in Germany, in the Axis nations, in the areas occupied by Germany and by the Axis nations, and in areas under the authority of Germany and of the Axis nations.

We acquit the Accused of guilt for the criminal acts against the Jewish people of which he is accused in this count during the period prior to August 1941. His criminal actions during that same time shall be included in his conviction for crimes against humanity under paragraph (5) below.

(2) We find the Accused guilty under of the second count of the indictment of a crime against the Jewish people, a criminal offense under section 1 (a)(1) of the same statute, in that during the period from August 1941 to May 1945, he, along with others, inflicted conditions of life likely to bring about their physical destruction upon millions of Jews in the same areas listed in paragraph (1) above, all in order to carry out the program called "The Final Solution of the Jewish Problem" and with the intention of destroying the Jewish people.

We acquit the Accused of guilt for the criminal acts against the Jewish people of which he is accused in this count during the period prior to August 1941.

(3) We find the Accused guilty under of the third count of the indictment of a crime against the Jewish people, a criminal offense under section 1 (a)(1) of the same statute,

---

1. The history of the Nazi and Nazi Collaborators (Punishment) Law is discussed in CrimA 347/88 Demjanjuk v. State of Israel, 47 (4) PD 221, 286 (1993).

2. A different translation of the full case is available at http://www.nizkor.org/hweb/people/e/eichmann-adolf/transcripts/. An English language summary of the trial court proceedings is found at 36 INT'L L. REP. 5 (1968) (summary prepared by A. Munkman).

in that during the period from August 1941 to May 1945, he, along with others, caused serious physical and mental injury to millions of Jews, with the intention of destroying the Jewish people, in the same areas listed in paragraph (1) above.

We acquit the Accused of guilt for the criminal acts against the Jewish people of which he is accused in this count during the period prior to August 1941.

(4) We find the Accused guilty under of the fourth count of the indictment of a crime against the Jewish people, a criminal offense under section 1 (a)(1) of the same statute, in that during the years 1943 and 1944, he imposed measures intended to prevent Jewish births in his orders forbidding birth and requiring termination of pregnancies of the Jewish women in the Terezin ghetto, with the intention of destroying the Jewish people.

We acquit the Accused of guilt for the other actions set out in the fourth count of the indictment.

(5) We find the Accused guilty under the fifth count of the indictment of a crime against humanity, a criminal offense under section 1(a)(2) of the same statute, in that during the period from August 1941 to May 1945 he, along with others, caused the murder, destruction, enslavement, starvation and deportation of the civilian Jewish population in the same lands and areas listed in paragraph (1) above.

We also find the Accused guilty of a crime against humanity, a criminal offense under section 1(a)(2) of the same statute, in that during the period from March 1938 to October 1941 he, along with others, caused the deportation of Jews from their homes in the area of the old Reich, in Austria, and in the Protectorate of Bohemia-Moravia, by forced emigration through the centers for emigration in Vienna, Prague, and Berlin.

We also find the Accused guilty of a crime against humanity, a criminal offense under section 1(a)(2) of the same statute, in that during the period from December 1939 to March 1941 he caused, along with others, the deportation of the Jews of Lenisko and the deportation of the Jews from the areas that had been added to the Reich in east and in the Reich itself to the occupied areas of Germany in the east.

(6) We find the Accused guilty under the sixth count of the indictment of a crime against humanity, a criminal offense under section 1(a)(2) of the same statute, in that in his execution of the actions listed in paragraphs 1 to 5 above, he persecuted Jews for reasons of nationality, race, religion and politics.

(7) We find the Accused guilty under the seventh count of the indictment of a crime against humanity, a criminal offense under section 1(a)(2) of the same statute, in that during the period from March 1938 to May 1945 he, along with others, was responsible for the theft of the property of millions of Jews through the use of mass terror, along with the murder, destruction, starvation and deportation of these Jews, in the same lands and areas listed in paragraph (1) above.

(8) We find the Accused guilty under the eighth count of the indictment of a war crime, a criminal violation under section 1(a)(3) of the same law, in that he executed malicious acts, the deportation and murder set out in the previous paragraphs, to the extent that they were done during World War II against Jews among the population of the countries that were occupied by Germany and the rest of the Axis countries.

(9) We find the Accused guilty under the ninth count of the indictment of a crime against humanity, a criminal violation under section 1(a)(2) of the same statute, in that during the years 1940 to 1942 he, along with others, caused the deportation of a civilian population, specifically hundreds of thousands of Poles, from their homes.

(10) We find the Accused guilty under the tenth count of the indictment of a crime against humanity, a criminal violation under section 1(a)(2) of the same statute, in that during 1941 he, along with others, caused the deportation of a civilian population, specifically more than 14,000 Slovenians, from their homes.

(11) We find the Accused guilty under the eleventh count of the indictment of a crime against humanity, a criminal violation under section 1(a)(2) of the same statute, in that during World War II he, along with others, caused the deportation of a civilian population, specifically tens of thousands of Gypsies, from Germany and from areas occupied by Germany and transported them to the areas occupied by Germany in the east. It has not been proven before us that the Accused knew that the Gypsies were being exterminated.

(12) We find the Accused guilty under the twelfth count of the indictment of a crime against humanity, a criminal violation under section 1(a)(2) of the same statute, in that during 1942 he, along with others, caused the deportation of 93 children from the Czech village of Lidice. It has not been proven before us that the Accused is guilty of the murder of these children.

Comment

On appeal, Eichmann raised a number of legal objections to the proceedings. These are examined in the following four sections.

B. Retroactive Application of the Criminal Law

The statute under which Eichmann was convicted, the Nazis and Nazi Collaborators (Punishment) Law, 5710-1950, was enacted in Israel in 1950, but Eichmann's actions which were held to constitute criminal acts occurred earlier, during World War II. Israel was not in existence as a state during that time, so it had no statute at the time of Eichmann's acts.

Israeli Case

Eichmann v. Attorney General

CrimA 336/61, 16 PD 2032 [1962][3]

Chief Justice Y. Olshan, Deputy Chief Justice S. Agranat, Justice M. Silberg, Justice Y. Sussman, Justice A. Witkin:

JUDGMENT

Most of the legal contentions of the counsel for the Appellant revolve around the general claim that the district court acted in violation of the rules of international law in taking upon itself the jurisdiction to try the Appellant for crimes.

---

3. A different translation of the full case is available at http://www.nizkor.org/hweb/people/e/eichmann-adolf/transcripts/. Another translation is found at 36 INT'L L. REP. 277 (Isr. S. Ct. 1962).

[The first contention is that because the] Nazis and Nazi Collaborators (Punishment) Law, 5710-1950, which is the sole source of the court's jurisdiction in this case, constitutes a criminal statute that applies retroactively (*ex post facto*) and makes a crime of acts performed before the state of Israel existed, can be applied by Israel only to its own citizens [because it violates an international law rule against *ex post fact* criminal laws].

The short answer ... is found in the district court's decision: "It is the task of the court to give effect to a law enacted by the Knesset, and we cannot consider a claim that the law violates the principles of international law."

The counsel for the Appellant argues that this response is in error because when there is a conflict between domestic law and international law, it is necessary to give preference to the rules of international law. We disagree. Under Israeli law, which is identical to this matter to English law, the relationship between domestic law and international law is determined under the following rules:

(1) The rule that is asserted is received into and becomes part of domestic law only when it has been generally accepted internationally.

(2) In what case does this apply? When there is no conflict between the domestic law and the international law. If there is a conflict, a court is required to give effect to the instructions of the local legislature. True, it is assumed that the local legislature endeavors to make its laws consistent with the generally accepted principles of international law. But when there is a clear conflict, the principle that domestic and international law are consistent loses its effect and a court must not consider it.

(3) Nonetheless, in consideration of the assumption of consistency, where there is more than one possible interpretation of a domestic statute, it should be interpreted consistently with the rules of international law. This rule is of no effect in the matter before us, because there is no doubt that the statute under consideration, which imposes criminal liability on those who are not Israeli citizens, applies retroactively.

Under the second proposition stated above, we conclude that even if the counsel for the Appellant were correct in claiming that the Israeli statute conflicts with international law, it does not help his position.

We come to the same conclusion under the first proposition. For the sake of clarity, we shall explain this conclusion.... [T]o the extent that principle of *nullum crimen sine lege, nulla poena sine lege*[4] rejects retroactive criminal legislation, that principle has not yet become a rule of customary international law.

It is true that, due to its great moral value, many states follow this principle in their constitutions or codes. In such states, a court may not deviate from the principle in any way. But this is not a universal rule. For example, in England, a country whose system of law and justice is generally acknowledged to be of a very high level, there is no constitutional limitation on the authority of the legislature to give retroactive force to its criminal laws. If it does so, no court can refuse to give effect to the laws. Even though the moral value of the principle of non-retroactivity is recognized, but this recognition is effectuated only in interpretation of laws. In other words, where the intention of the legislature is not clear, a court is required to interpret a statute such that it does not apply to an act committed before enactment of the statute.

As to the ethical aspect of the principle, we can agree that the general feeling as to what is just calls on us to desist from punishing a person for an act done at a time when

---

4. No crime without a law [prohibiting the act], no punishment without a law.

he could not know would result in criminal liability because the act was not yet prohibited by a statute. But this court cannot extend that principle to the types of crimes of which the Appellant was accused, especially when they were of the scope and measure described in the decision of the lower court. In such a case, ethical considerations lead us elsewhere: the sense of justice would certainly be more greatly violated by the failure to punish a person who was involved in such terrible acts, and he cannot claim, as the Appellant cannot claim as to his part in the Final Solution, that he did not know, when he committed the act, that he was violating basic and eternal moral values. [As has been stated:] "If, then, the rules applied at Nuremberg were not previously rules of positive international law, they were at least rules of positive ethics accepted by civilized men everywhere, to which the accused could properly be held in the forum of ethics."

Therefore in the absence of positive international law prohibiting retroactive criminal legislation, and in the absence of a moral justification for prohibiting application of this statute on the crimes that are the subject of this case, the second part of the claim of the counsel for the Appellant—that the state of Israel did not exist at the time at which the crimes were committed and that Israel's authority to impose punishment for such acts is limited to her own citizens—fails as well. As we shall see, the actions of which the Appellant is convicted can be seen as actions that have always been and always will be prohibited by the law of nations. Based on this view, the enactment of the statute in 1950 did not deviate at all from the principle of *nulla poena*. To this point we have succeeded in rejecting the international law claim of the counsel for the Appellant on the first grounds previously mentioned that sets out the relationship between domestic and international law. This rule requires, as we have stated, that the principle that domestic law cannot violate international law has not become part of Israeli domestic law, and this alone justifies rejection of the claim of the Appellant's counsel.

[Under the Nuremberg principles, the crimes against humanity and war crimes of the accused have violated customary international law "since time immemorial."]

Comment

The decision refers to the "rules applied at Nuremberg." This is a reference to the Principles of International Law Recognized by the Charter of the Nuremberg Tribunal and in the Judgment of the Tribunal.[5] These are the principles applied in the trial of Nazis by an international tribunal after World War II.

In the *Eichmann* decision, the Supreme Court of Israel offered six grounds for rejecting Eichmann's claim that the Israeli statute under which he was prosecuted was invalid because it violated the principle against retroactivity of criminal law. These are: (1) International law does not have a rule against retroactivity of criminal law. (2) Were there such a rule in customary international law, the only possible source of such a principle as applied to Israel, the Israeli court would have to give preference to a conflicting Israeli law. (3) Israeli law, like the law of the United Kingdom, has no absolute prohibition on retroactivity of criminal law. (4) Any ethical defect in applying a criminal prohibition retroactively is dwarfed by the ethical affront that would be involved in leaving a person who did what Eichmann did free from punishment. (5) Israel's statute did not make illegal actions that were legal prior to enactment of the statute. (6) The Israeli statute advanced a recognized principle of international law.

---

5. 2 Y.B. Int'l L. Comm'n, 377, U.N. Doc. A/CN. 4/SER.A/1950/Add.1, *available at* http://untreaty.un.org/ilc/texts/instruments/english/draft%20articles/7_1_1950.pdf. The principles were adopted by the International Law Commission in 1950.

The Court's treatment of the rule of retroactivity should not be understood to mean that retroactivity is generally allowed in Israeli criminal law. The opposite is true. The usual rule in Israeli law is that criminal laws cannot be retroactively applied. The *Eichmann* case, though, involved a special problem. It was not that the Israeli law existing at the time of Eichmann's criminal acts allowed those acts but later law disallowed them. Rather, there was no Israeli law at the time because the state did not exist. The way out of this bind in the *Eichmann* case was easy; Eichmann's actions were not permitted at the time he engaged in them. Under the Nuremberg principles, it had been decided that crimes against humanity such as those in which the Nazis engaged violated international law. Furthermore, the heart of the principle of retroactivity is that people should be warned of what they cannot do, and Eichmann could hardly claim that he thought what he was doing was innocent.

The case, then, does not resolve the underlying problem of retroactivity. Can a person who engages in acts less obviously reprehensible be held criminally liable if those acts were not defined as criminal at the time the person engaged in them? The general answer is that he may not.

The problem that arises in Israel, as in England, is the extent to which judicial interpretation of statutes affects this principle. In common law systems, courts have a degree of leeway in defining statutory provisions. If a court interprets a criminal statute in a way that was not completely obvious at the time a person acted, and according to that interpretation the action is a crime, is the law as newly interpreted being applied retroactively? The problem arises when there was another possible interpretation of the statute, under which the person's action would not be a criminal offense. Israeli law deals with this problem through the following provision and case:

Israeli Statue

Penal Law, 5737-1977

1. No Crime Except as Prescribed by Law

There is no crime and no punishment for a crime except as specified in a statute or pursuant to a statute.

2. Punishment Under an Administrative Regulation

(a) The authority granted [to an agency] to promulgate regulation to implement a statute includes the authority to stipulate that violation of the regulations is a criminal offense and to set the punishment for violating the regulations, provided that the period of incarceration set in the regulation shall not be for more than six months, and if there is a monetary penalty, its shall not be for more than [a statutorily determined amount that is relatively small].

(b) Rules that provide criminal offenses and criminal sanctions require the approval of a Knesset committee.

3. No Retroactive Punishment

(a) A law [statute or regulation] that creates a crime shall not apply to an act done before the day the law was properly published or the effective date of the law, whichever is later.

(b) A law [statute or regulation] that sets out a punishment for a crime that is more serious than that which was set out in the law at the time of the criminal act will not apply to an act done before the date of proper publication of the law or before its effective day, whichever is later.

Israeli Case

Cohen v. State of Israel
CrimA 766/07 (Nov. 19, 2007)

Justice A. Grunis:

Two appeals on judgments of the District Court of Jerusalem have been joined for our consideration. The underlying question is the same in both appeals: At the relevant time, was the Appellant a "public servant" as that term is defined in Section 290 of the Penal Law, 5737-1977 (hereinafter the Penal Law)?

The Appellants claim that the lower court erred in its legal determination. First of all, the Appellants claim that the court below adopted a position based on a problematic principle, using in the area of the criminal law rules of interpretation that belong to other areas of law. In their view, the approach taken by the court below deviates from the principle of legality, which requires a narrow interpretation of a criminal statute. The Appellants object to the interpretation that allowed that court to treat Cohen as a public servant. The Respondent is of the opinion that the method of interpretation of the court, which aimed to realize the objective of the criminalization of bribery, is appropriate and is consistent with the principle of legality. On the substance of the matter before the court, the Respondent claims that the interpretation of the relevant statutory provisions by the court below was correct and was in fact the only interpretation that would effect the purpose of the statute.

The Principle of Legality and Interpretation of a Criminal Statute

The court has the responsibility to interpret statutes. Sometimes this is a simple task and the meaning of the statute is apparent from its working. But in some cases that are not so rare, the correct interpretation is not so obvious. In these cases, we must determine how the statute should be interpreted and what sort of facts the court should consider in determining the correct interpretation. In our system, it is accepted that in interpreting a statute, we should consider not only the language, but also the purpose, goals, and interests that the statute is intended to effectuate. Sometimes a judge must also exercise judicial discretion. Under this approach to interpretation, the court is not limited to the technical meaning of the words of the statute. The court has some measure of freedom within defined boundaries to interpret the statute in a way that implements its objective. Much has been written on the justifications for this approach to interpretation and on its advantages and disadvantages. One of the central justifications, in my opinion, is a practical one. The legislature is trying to effectuate some interest or defend some value, and it is not practical to stipulate every single set of circumstances in which the matter might arise. Therefore the legislature must be satisfied to set a standard through the wording of a general provision and leave to the court the job of interpreting the provision and deciding how it applies to a given situation. This understanding of how the legislature works justifies our pursuing the goal of the statute, sometimes even by being somewhat flexible in the way we relate to the simple meaning of the language. This approach to interpretation also has its disadvantages. One of them is that to the extent it leads us to deviate from the simple meaning of the language and grants interpretative discretion to the court, it impinges to some degree on the value of judicial certainty.

Overall, though, we cannot avoid considering the goal of the statute and the purpose of the legislator, even if this has some cost in terms of judicial certainty.

When the subject is the interpretation of a criminal law, even though the aspiration remains that of implementing the goal of the law, there is room for giving a different weight to the language of the statute, based on a different balance [between being true to the language and being true to the goal of the statute]. The principle of legality is a foundation stone of criminal law doctrine. This principle is now expressed in section one of the Penal Law, that provides, "There is no crime and no punishment for a crime except as specified in a statute or pursuant to a statute." Similarly section 3 of the statute prohibits retroactive punishment. It has been posited that this principle is constitutional in nature. The principle of legality formally requires that a statute or rule defining a crime set out the basic components of the criminal violation and the punishment one who violates the law can expect. A clear expression of this principle in the case law, from the period before it was expressed in a statute, is found in a decision of the Supreme Court:

> It is a major rule in the penal law: "There is no punishment without a law." Punishment is not established by rules of interpretation, such as *a fortiori* inference,[6] and not from verbal analogy,[7] and not from any other rule of comparison or analogy, but only from the statute as written and enacted. It is the statute that can transform a given act, under defined conditions, to a criminal violation. No interpretation, analogy, and logic can do what the law does not do in clear and explicit language. These are first principles, and we do not need to belabor them.

The principle of legality is not limited to the formal requirement that the criminal prohibition be set out in a statute. The principle of legality also has a substantive aspect that imposes several different requirements on criminal law. One of the derivatives of the principle of legality is the interpretive rule of leniency with the accused. This principle is found today in section 34u of the Penal Law: "If in accordance with its purpose, a law can be interpreted in several different ways, it shall be interpreted in the manner most lenient to the person who is to be held liable under the law." Another sub-principle derived from the principle of legality is that a criminal statute should use clear language and should not use vague and ambiguous terms. This implies that the judge, as interpreter, should act with special care.

Comment

In the *Cohen* case, even under these principles the justices did not agree on how to interpret the term *public servant* as applied to the Appellant.

---

6. The term used in Hebrew is *kal v'chomer*, which literally translated means lenient and strict. This is a rule for deriving one rule from another that is used in the Talmud, one of the foundational books of Jewish law. An *a fortiori* inference is "a rule of logical argumentation by means of which a comparison is drawn between two cases, one lenient and the other stringent. [The rule] asserts that if the law is stringent in a case where we are usually lenient, then it will certainly be stringent in a more serious case; likewise, if the law is lenient in a case where we are usually not lenient, then it will certainly be lenient in a less serious case." ADIN STEINSALTZ, THE TALMUD: THE STEINSALTZ EDITION: A REFERENCE GUIDE 153 (1989).

7. The term used in Hebrew is "*gezerah shavah*," literally meaning "an equal edict." It is also a principle used in the Talmud for deriving one rule from another. "If the same word or phrase appears in two places in the Torah [the Bible], and a certain law is explicitly stated in one of these places, we may infer on the basis of 'verbal analogy' that the same law must apply in the other case as well." *Id.* at 150.

Question

1. Should criminal law observe an absolute rule against retroactivity?

C. The Defense of Following Orders

Israeli Case

Eichmann v. Attorney General
CrimA 336/61, 16 PD 2032 [1962][8]

The counsel for the Appellant [claimed] the defense of superior orders. His claim is that the Appellant was led to act as he did by the oath he swore upon entering the SS [the Schutzstaffel, a powerful paramilitary organization under Hitler that carried out many of his programs during World War II] and by the need to comply with Hitler's order to effect the complete destruction of the Jews, an order passed through the chain of command of that organization and communicated to him by those under whom he served. At this stage, we consider the legal validity of such a claim. Our main objectives are to distinguish between this defense and that of an act of state, and to clarify the meaning and value of the claim of obedience to superior orders under international law.

(a) The defense of obedience to superior orders is distinguished from that of an act of state in three ways: (1) The latter is a claim that the criminal act should not be attributed to the individual who performed it at all, but rather to the state alone. The former is a claim that the act of the individual should be seen as justified under the law because it was performed under the compulsion of an order of the proper authority to which the actor was subject.

(2) The doctrine of an act of state provides the agent with a defense only because the highest authority of the state (the head of state, for example) commanded or authorized the act in question. This requirement does not necessarily apply for the defense of superior orders, under which the criminal act is justified only when the direct commander of the person who committed the act gave the order and the person who acted was required to carry out that order.

(3) The doctrine of act of state is not understood to require that the agent acted under ministerial instructions which left him no discretion. The fact that the act was done within the framework of the authorization by the regime is sufficient to give it the character of an act of state. In contrast, the claim that an action was done under superior orders assumes that the actor had no choice but to fulfill the order he received from his commander, either under the law or under the requirements of the well-disciplined body (the army, etc.) of which he was a member.

So far we have not addressed the legality of the claimed defense, but only the differences between it and another type of defense. The third distinction shows that the claim of superior orders cannot serve as a defense to the Appellant, given that when we analyze the facts, we see that in administering the Final Solution, the Appellant operated in an in-

---

8. A different translation of the full case is available at http://www.nizkor.org/hweb/people/e/eichmann-adolf/transcripts/. Another translation is found at 36 Int'l L. Rep. (Isr. S. Ct. 1962).

dependent manner and even went beyond the tasks with which he was charged through the official chain of command.

(b) The question of whether the public good requires recognition of the defense of superior orders raises the following two difficulties: On the one hand, maintenance of order in the disciplined organization to which the Accused belonged requires that he should not rebel against the person in command and should not have to ponder the legality of every order he receives from his commander, lest the objective be lost. On the other hand, the harm that will be caused to the public from wrapping the crime that was committed in the protection of an order requires that a person not be allowed to follow an order automatically and that he should do so only if he is convinced rationally that it is a lawful order.

There is also the personal problem of the soldier himself, who is put in a dilemma. If he rebels against his commander and it turns out that the order given him was legal, he will be made to answer to a military court. If he follows the order and it turns out that it was not legal, he can expect to be punished under the general criminal law. This difficulty is likely to be a serious one given the fact that the simple soldier is not always capable of determining on the spot whether an order he receives is illegal or not.

All three of these difficulties teach us that the main problem in recognizing the defense of superior orders is in determining whether and to what extent we should consider the mental state of the accused at the time of commission of the act; in other words, the problem is how we should relate to the question of whether he knew that the order under which he acted was illegal. The solution under Israeli criminal law in general, like that in English law, is that the defense of superior orders is recognized if the order was not manifestly illegal. But in section 8 of the Nazi and Nazi Collaborators (Punishment) Law, 5710-1950, the legislature provided that for offenses under this statute, the defense of superior orders shall not apply, just as the defense of constraint and necessity shall not apply. Section 11, on the other hand, provides that it is permissible, under certain conditions, to consider these factors in mitigation of the sentence.

We agree with the determination of the district court that even were this case decided under the rules of the general criminal law, it would be necessary to reject the defense of superior orders, not only because the order for the physical destruction was manifestly illegal, as were all the other orders for persecution of the Jews that conflicted with the basic concepts of law and justice, but also because the Appellant was fully aware when he did these things that he was participating in the most serious and terrible criminal acts. Indeed, the district court decision cited the Accused's testimony in which he himself admitted this: "Already I saw in this solution an illegal use of force, a terrible thing, but regretfully I had to deal with the matter of transport due to my oath of loyalty which I was not free to violate." [The Court further found that Israeli law on the defense of superior orders is in accord with international law.]

Comment

The *Eichmann* case was an easy case on the defense of orders issue. No one may commit such heinous acts and then claim he is immune from punishment because he was operating under orders. Israeli law, like international law, disallows the defense for manifestly illegal orders, and Eichmann's orders, if indeed he was subject to superior orders, were manifestly illegal.

How does this apply, though, to a more marginal case? The validity of the defense of following orders is important in Israel. In a perpetual state of conflict, and in some cases war, with some of its neighbors, Israel depends for its daily existence on its strong army. Armed forces depend on discipline among soldiers, and soldiers must follow orders. If every soldier were free to decide for him or herself whether an order were legal, ethical, or acceptable, there would be no effective discipline. Soldiers need to know they can depend on each other to act in concert; otherwise, the lives of the soldiers themselves, as well as of the people they are sworn to defend, are at risk.

On the other hand, against the background of the Holocaust, Israelis are painfully aware that military orders can be morally wrong. In addition, the moral quality of military actions in the conflict with the Palestinians is the subject of daily debate in the Israeli press. For this reason, and because of almost universal military service, virtually the entire population of Israel is concerned about the values of the military.

Questions

2. Under Israeli law, for crimes other than those defined under the Nazis and Nazi Collaborators (Punishment) Law, the accused can claim as a defense that they were following orders, unless the orders were manifestly illegal. Is this law appropriate?

3. Given the fact that Israeli law generally allows a defense of following orders unless the order is manifestly illegal, why do you think that defense is not allowed under the Nazis and Nazi Collaborators (Punishment) Law? Is the law wrong in disallowing the defense to liability, confining it only to determination of the severity of the punishment?

D. Inability of Victims to Judge the Perpetrator

One of the claims raised in Eichmann's defense on appeal was that, "the judges of the district court, being Jews and feeling a sense of affinity with the victims of the plan of extermination and Nazi persecution, were psychologically incapable of giving the Appellant an objective trial." The following excerpt shows how the Israeli Supreme Court handled this claim.

Israeli Case

Eichmann v. Attorney General
CrimA 336/61, 16 PD 2032 [1962][9]

We have yet to respond briefly to the claim of the counsel for the Appellant that the district court judges, and similarly the justices of this Court, are not psychologically capable of exercising judgment in an objective manner in this case.

Like the district court, we reject this claim. The response of the district court is also our response:

---

9. A different translation of the full case is available at http://www.nizkor.org/hweb/people/e/eichmann-adolf/transcripts/. Another translation is found at 36 INT'L L. REP. 277 (Isr. S. Ct. 1962).

As to the Accused's fear of our reaction to the matters that will arise in this case, we reiterate a position that applies to the ability of every judicial system that can fairly claim to function as such. While it is true that the judge sitting on the bench does not stop being a human being, with feelings and urges, but the judge is required by law to overcome these feelings and urges. If a person cannot do this, no judge will ever be qualified to sit on a criminal case that raises feelings and revulsion, such as cases involving treason, murder, or any other serious crime. It is true that the memory of the Holocaust shocks every Jew deeply, but when this case was brought before us, we were obligated to overcome even these feelings while sitting in judgment. We shall meet this obligation.

Indeed, the learned judges did fully and completely meet this obligation.

Comment

Gabriel Bach was one of the attorneys who worked on prosecution of the *Eichmann* case. He addressed the claim that Israel as the Jewish state should not have exercised jurisdiction over the *Eichmann* case in an article he wrote twelve years after the decision. In 1982, Bach became a justice of the Israel Supreme Court.

Law Review Article

Gabriel Bach, Development of Criminal Law in Israel during the 25 Years of Its Existence
9 Isr. L. Rev. 568 (1974)

Characteristic for the attitude of those who criticized the assumption of jurisdiction by Israeli courts over Nazi criminals on the ground that the victim of the crime was unfit to judge the criminal, was the reaction of those same critics when they saw the indictment we had filed against Adolf Eichmann. They pointed with astonishment at those counts under which we had charged the accused with persecution and annihilation of Polish and Czech citizens and of gypsies and asked us: "What has that got to do with you? Why not leave that to the Polish or Czech courts?" In other words, they saw nothing strange in the court of the victims judging the accused, as long as they were Czech or Polish courts. Only the trial of Nazis before a Jewish court seemed repugnant to them. But actually the number of those critics gradually declined to an insignificant few.

E. Other Objections

Eichmann's defense raised three legal objections based on international law. The first was that under international law, Israel could not try Eichmann for acts committed outside of Israel, and that he had to be tried in Germany. The Court rejected this on numerous grounds: No rule of international law prohibits a state from trying a person for acts committed outside of its territory. If there were such a rule, a state could raise it but an individual could not. The West German government, asked by the defendant to demand extradition of Eichmann, had refused to do so. If Germany could demand extradition, so could other countries where Eichmann's crimes had occurred, and Israel should not be put in the position of having to decide to which country to extradite Eichmann. In fact, no country had asked for Eichmann's extradition. Due to its link with the Jewish people, Israel had a right to try Eichmann for his crimes specifically against Jews. Eichmann must be tried somewhere for his crimes which violated international law.

The second objection based on international law was that Israel should not try him because it had abducted him from Argentina. The Court held that the abduction might involve a problem between the states of Israel and Argentina, but such problem did not prevent Israel from trying Eichmann. In any case, the dispute between Israel and Argentina about the abduction had been resolved.

The third international law claim was that Eichmann was protected by the international law doctrine of *act of state*. Under this doctrine, it was claimed, certain actions are acts of the state and not of the individual who carries them out on behalf of the state. In these cases, the individual cannot be held guilty for a criminal act. The Court replied that act of state is not an absolute defense and does not apply to acts, such as those performed by Eichmann, which are prohibited under international law.

F. Death Penalty

Israeli law provides the death penalty under five statutes, all of them dealing with unusual cases. The first is the Nazi and Nazi Collaborator's (Punishment) Law. The death penalty was imposed on Adolph Eichmann under this statute. Here is the language of the district court's decision on sentencing in the Eichmann trial:

Israeli Case

Attorney-General v. Eichmann
CrimC (Jer) 40/61, 27 PM 169 (1961)[10]

Judge Landau:

Having come to the end of the lengthy discussion of this case, we must determine the punishment to be imposed on the Accused.

The Attorney General asks that we impose the death sentence on the Accused. His first claim is that this is the punishment the court must impose under law on one who is found guilty of criminal offenses under section 1 of the Nazis and Nazi Collaborators (Punishment) Law, 5710-1950, and therefore the court has no discretion in determining the punishment.

We are of the opinion that although this was the law when the statute was first enacted ... there was a change after enactment of the amendment to Punishments Law 9 (Methods of Punishment), 5714-1954. Under section 1 of that statute, the punishment set out in a statute is the maximum punishment.

We have considered the question of the appropriate punishment for the Accused and are aware of the heavy burden of our responsibility. We have come to the conclusion that

---

10. A different translation of the full case is available at http://www.nizkor.org/hweb/people/e/eichmann-adolf/transcripts/.

for punishing the Accused and for deterring others it is appropriate to impose the maximum punishment set out in the statute. We have described in the judgment the crimes in which the Accused participated. They are terrible beyond comparison in both their nature and their scope. The objective of the crimes against the Jewish people of which the Accused has been found guilty was the eradication of an entire people from the face of the earth, and in this the crimes are different from those committed against individuals. It can be said that comprehensive crimes such as these and crimes against humanity that are directed against a group of people because of their identity as a group are more serious than all the individual criminal acts of which they are composed.

But at the stage of setting the punishment, we should also, or perhaps mainly, consider the injury these crimes caused to the victims as individuals and the immeasurable suffering of the victims and their families both then and now as a result of these crimes. These involved the Accused's dispatch of every train containing a thousand souls to Auschwitz or to any other place of destruction and the direct participation of the Accused in acts of premeditated murder. The measure of the Accused's legal and ethical responsibility for these acts of murder is in no way less than the measure of responsibility of the person who pushed these same people into the gas ovens.

Even if we were to find that the Accused acted under orders, as he claimed, we would still find that a person who participated in crimes of these dimensions over a period of years would be deserving of the maximum penalty under law. No order can justify a reduction of the penalty. Furthermore we found that the Accused personally identified with the orders he received and had a great desire to achieve the criminal objective. In our opinion, in determining the punishment for shocking crimes such as these, it does not matter how the identification and desire arose or whether they were the result of the conceptual education given to the Accused by the regime that promoted him as his defense attorney claims.

This court sentences Adolf Eichmann to death for the crimes against the Jewish people, the crimes against humanity, and the war crimes of which he was convicted.

Comment

The death penalty was imposed by a trial court in another case brought under the Nazis and Nazi Collaborators (Punishment) Law, but in that case, the penalty was never implemented. John Demjanjuk, who lived in the United States, was accused of being the Ivan the Terrible, a guard at the Nazis' Treblinka death. He was extradited from the United States. After his conviction and sentencing to death for the deeds ascribed to Ivan the Terrible, Demjanjuk appealed to the Supreme Court. During the period of the appeal, new information came to light. Prior to Israel's trial of Demjanjuk, Israeli prosecutors had sought information on his activities during World War II from the former Soviet Union. The Soviet government did not supply the information requested.[11] During the appeal, new allegations relevant to Demjanjuk's defense were brought before the Supreme Court. Israeli prosecutors again turned to the Soviet Union to obtain information. With the warming relations between the two countries (this was during the period of the disintegration of the Soviet Union), the

---

11. CrimA 347/88 Demjanjuk v. State of Israel, 47 (4) PD 221, 265 (1993).

Israeli prosecutors were allowed to enter the Soviet Union and gather documents. The new documents cast a reasonable doubt on whether Demjanjuk was Ivan the Terrible, and the Supreme Court acquitted him. Israel did not bring new charges against Demjanjuk for deeds other than those committed by Ivan the Terrible.[12]

Another statute similar to the Nazi and Nazi Collaborators (Punishment) Law also provides for the death penalty.

Israeli Statute

Law on Prevention and Punishment of Genocide, 5710-1950

1. Definition of Genocide

(a) In this statute, "genocide" means any of the acts listed below if done with the intention to destroy, completely or partially, a national, ethnic, racial or religious group (hereinafter *group*) because it is such a group.

These are the acts:

(1) Killing members of the group;

(2) Causing serious bodily or mental harm to members of the group;

(3) Inflicting on a group conditions of life calculated to bring about its physical destruction, in whole or in part;

(4) Imposing measures intended to prevent births within a group;

(5) Forcibly transferring children of a group to another group.

(b) In subsection (a), "child" means a person under the age of eighteen.

2. Penalty for Genocide

A person guilty of genocide is subject to the penalty of death, but if the act was done under conditions which, but for section 6 [making inapplicable the defenses of necessity, compulsion, and justification], would excuse the person from criminal responsibility or would serve as an excuse for the crime, and the person did all they could to alleviate the seriousness of the results caused by their action, the penalty shall be imprisonment for not less than ten years.

3. Conspiracy, Incitement, Attempt, and Complicity in Genocide

(a) A person guilty of one of the following acts is punished as a person guilty of genocide. These are the acts:

(1) Conspiracy to commit genocide;

(2) Incitement to commit genocide;

(3) Attempt to commit genocide;

(4) Complicity in genocide.

---

12. Demjanjuk was returned to the United States. Based on new information, Germany sought his extradition to try him on crimes committed at a different death camp, Sobibor. That trial began in 2009. In 2011, Demjanjuk was found guilty and sentenced to five years in prison, with the sentence is to be reduced by the two years he spent in jail prior to the sentencing. Demjanjuk died in March 2012 while free pending a decision on his appeal.

4. Responsibility for Genocide

A person guilty of a crime under this statute shall be punished whether the person is a responsible ruler under law, a member of the legislature, a public official, or a private person.

10. Effective Date

This law, which is enacted pursuant to the Convention on the Prevention and Punishment of the Crime of Genocide that was adopted by resolution of General Assembly of the United Nations on the seventh of Kislev[13] 5709 (December 9, 1948), that was signed by the State of Israel and ratified by the State of Israel according to the decision of the Knesset, shall enter into effect on the day of its publication in [the official gazette of the government] and shall remain in force whether or not the Convention shall enter into effect or remain in effect.

Comment

Two statutes that are similar to each other provide the death penalty for treason in times of war. One of these is set out here:

Israeli Statute

Penal Law, 5737-1977

Part 2: Treason

97. Injury to the Sovereignty or Physical Integrity of the State

(a) A person who committed an act that may injure the sovereignty of the state, with intention to so injure its sovereignty, is subject to death or life imprisonment.

(b) A person who committed an act that may cause the state to lose sovereignty over any of its territory or that may cause another state to gain sovereignty over any of its territory, with intention to bring about this result, is subject to death or life imprisonment.

98. Causation of War

A person who committed an act that may bring about a military action against Israel, with intention to bring about this result, is subject to imprisonment for fifteen years; a person who in doing so intended to aid an enemy is subject to death or life imprisonment.

99. Giving Aid to an Enemy in Time of War

(a) A person who committed an act that aids an enemy making war against Israel, with intention to do so, is subject to death or life imprisonment.

Comment

The other statutory provision allowing the death penalty for treason is section 43 of the Military Adjudication Act, 5716-1955. That section applies to soldiers who assist the enemy in time of war.

The final statute providing the death penalty is an obscure emergency provision, Defense Regulation (Emergency) number 58, left over from the days of the British Mandate.

---

13. Kislev is the name of a Hebrew month that occurs in winter.

In fact, the death penalty has been carried out only twice, and the first time by an illegally constituted ad-hoc court during the War of Independence.[14] The only other imposition of the death penalty, this time by a properly constituted court, was that of Adolf Eichmann. Israel does not use the death penalty for terrorists, even those who kill large numbers of people. When the prime minister was assassinated in 1995, the death penalty was not even possible for his assassin, since Israeli law does not allow use of the death penalty for single murders.

Some members of Israeli society periodically call for expanding the death penalty to cover terrorists, but the Knesset has not changed the law. In fact, it is widely posited that the death penalty for any additional offense would be unconstitutional. Under constitutional law doctrine, a law prescribing the death penalty, which undoubtedly infringes on rights protected in the Basic Law: Human Dignity and Freedom, would have to meet the requirements of the limitation clause. One requirement of this clause is that the law be consistent with the values of Israel as a Jewish and democratic state. It is doubtful whether the death penalty could be reconciled with Jewish values.[15] Another requirement is that the law must accomplish its objective in a way that causes minimal harm. A court would probably find that the same objective could be accomplished by life imprisonment. Finally the public value of the law must outweigh the harm to the individual. Again, a court may well find that the marginal benefit to the public of imposing the death sentence does not outweigh the marginal detriment to the individual, which is death rather than life in prison.[16]

Question

4. Should Israel expand the death penalty to cover other cases? Should it abolish the death penalty completely?

G. The Use of the Criminal Law

Israel saw the importance of the prosecution of Adolf Eichmann not only in penalization of Eichmann for the crimes he committed, but also in educating Israeli youth and people in the rest of the world about what had happened.[17] In fact, it had just such an effect.[18] Not all Israelis had known about the Holocaust. Many people in the generation of survivors did not talk about their experiences in the war. In addition, many Israelis came from areas outside of Europe that were not subject to the Holocaust. Other Israelis knew

---

14. Meir Tobianski, an officer in the Israeli Defense Forces, was accused of espionage and "tried" in a hurriedly assembled and illegal court martial proceeding. He was sentenced to death and killed by firing squad. It was soon revealed that Tobianski was innocent, and the officer who gave the orders for his execution was convicted of manslaughter, although he did not serve any time for the offense. *See* SHABTAI TEVETH, BEN GURION'S SPY 17–31 (1996).

15. *See* Michelle M. Sharoni, *A Journey of Two Countries: A Comparative Study of the Death Penalty in Israel and South Africa*, 24 HASTINGS INT'L & COMP. L. REV. 257, 258–65 (2000–2001). This article purports to describe Jewish law, although it discusses the law of Israel.

16. *See* Guy E. Carmi, *On the Constitutionality of the Death Penalty in Israel*, http://www.irmgard-coninx-stiftung.de/fileadmin/user_upload/pdf/archive/Guy_Carmi_III.pdf.

17. *See* Jon Immanuel, *Catharsis or Neurosis?*, JERUSALEM POST, April 8, 2011, (Magazine) at 14.

18. *See id.*; Gabriel Bach, Deputy Prosecutor for the State of Israel in the Eichmann case and former justice, Israel Supreme Court, The Eichmann Trial, Fuchsberg Center for Conservative Judaism, Jerusalem, Israel (Mar. 7, 2011).

about the Holocaust but did not understand why the Jews had not offered more resistance. Young Israelis raised on an ethic of self-reliance were not aware of the conditions which made confrontation of the perpetrators of the Holocaust so difficult. The trial painted for them a picture of how difficult resistance was.[19] In addition, the trial showed Israeli youth the importance of having an independent Jewish state.

The trial was also an important educational tool outside of Israel. The controversy that followed the trial over how to interpret the Holocaust led to an enormous growth in Holocaust education and taught both Jews and non-Jews outside of Israel about what had happened during World War II. This was especially important in areas such as Russia, where such information had not been previously available to the population at large.[20]

Question

5. Was it appropriate for Israel to use the criminal trial of Eichmann as a tool for educating young Israelis and the world about what happened during the Holocaust? How was this similar to or different from the general deterrent function of criminal law?

---

19. *See* Deborah E. Lipstadt, The Eichmann Trial 194–98 (2011).
20. *See* Immanuel, *supra* note 17.

Part Four

Religious Law and Israel as a Jewish State

Chapter 12

Religious Law as State Law

A. The Nature of Religious Law

This chapter discusses the role of religious law in Israeli law. Before examining the role of religious law, it is necessary to understand what it is. This chapter discusses the nature of religious law as distinct from other types of law. It also briefly describes the religious law of the main religious communities in Israel.

Definition of the term religious law is not simple because no single definition seems to describe religious law fully or to distinguish it absolutely from law that is not religious. When we use the term religious law, we usually mean a set of rules that are followed by a group we define as a religion. This simple definition creates two problems. First, it requires a definition of religion, a term which itself is difficult to define. Second, it assumes that all members of the religion follow the rules, which is generally not true.

There is a tendency to think of a religion as a set of beliefs about the divine, but that is not an accurate definition for all religions. Judaism, for example, counts among its members a person born to a Jewish mother, without regard to that person's beliefs.[1] For the same reason, we cannot define a religious group by the way people identify themselves. Again, Judaism is an example of why this is not possible. A person who is born Jewish is considered a Jew even though that person does not identify as a Jew and, on the other hand, a person who identifies as a Jew is generally not considered to be one unless the person is either born as a Jew or went through a valid conversion.

Similarly we cannot define religion as a shared set of observances. Here too Judaism is an example of why this definition is not universally valid. A person born a Jew remains a Jew even though the person does not engage in any of the observances associated with Judaism.[2] In addition, many religious communities have within them different sub-

---

1. American Reform Judaism and Reconstructionist Judaism also count a person born to a Jewish father as a Jew under some, but not all, circumstances. Central Conference of American Rabbis, *Report of the Committee on Patrilineal Descent on the Status of Children of Mixed Marriages*, in YEARBOOK OF THE CENTRAL CONFERENCE OF AMERICAN RABBIS 90 (1983); *see* Richard A. Hirsch, *Jewish Identity and Patrilineal Descent; Some Second Thoughts*, 49 RECONSTRUCTIONIST 25 (1984), *available at* http://jrf.org/resources/files/Jewish%20idenity%20and%20patrlineal%20descent%20-%20some%20second%20thoughts.pdf. Both American Reform Judaism and Reconstructionist Judaism may not count as Jewish a person born to a Jewish mother and a non-Jewish father in some circumstances, although those circumstances do not depend on a test of belief.

2. American Reform Judaism may not agree to this statement for a person born of a Jewish mother and a non-Jewish father. Central Conference of American Rabbis, *supra* note 1.

groups with different definitions of what observances are required. A definition of religion based on a shared set of observances would create a very large number of different religions within each group that we usually identify as one religion.

In order to avoid the need to define the term religion, we could define religious law by the characteristics of the legal system, rather than by the characteristics of its adherents. In this way, a religious legal system may be defined as one that claims that its rules are based on dictates of the divine. Again, this definition encounters difficulties. Some religious legal systems include rules based on interpretations, amendments, and additions that are made by people. For example, this is true in both Jewish law and in Islamic law. While the religious legal system may claim that these legal rulings are interpretations of divine will, the role of people in determining the will of the divine brings into question the utility of the definition. Furthermore, if the discussion is about a legal system, and not just about divine texts, the issue of compliance is central. In a religious legal system, while the rules may come from the divine, the obligation to follow them does not necessary flow from this source. Again, Jewish law is an example. The obligation of the Jewish people to comply with the law is seen by some as based at least partly on their binding agreement to do so.[3] In other words, the obligation is based not on divine dictate alone, but also on the agreement of those who are bound.

Religious law could be defined by the subjects it treats. It might be said that religious law is law on how people should relate to the divine. This definition is not without ambiguity. It raises the question of what is meant by relationship to the divine. Normally this is thought to relate to modes of worship or religious ritual, but religious legal systems may treat subjects far beyond the usual boundaries of these terms. Both Jewish law and Islamic law, the predominant religious law systems in Israel, cover commercial affairs and other matters, considering them all related to what the divine wants of people. These are all-encompassing legal systems and cannot be distinguished from other legal systems by the subjects to which they relate.

Due to these difficulties in definition, this book will discuss religious law without a precise definition of the term, using a general sense that Jewish law is the law of the Jews, Islamic law is the law of Muslims, etc.

B. Jewish Law

1. Distinction between Jewish Law and Israeli Law

Israeli law is the law of the State of Israel. It is analogous to US law, French law, or German law. Jewish law is the legal system of the Jewish people. It applies to Jews everywhere, including, but not limited to, the Jews in Israel. It is analogous to (although much broader than) canon law. Israeli law is distinct from Jewish law. This chapter and the next describe the features of Israeli law that are based on Jewish law. Most Israeli law is not based on Jewish law.

---

3. *See* Hanina Ben-Menahem, *Is Talmudic Law a Religious Legal System? A Provisional Analysis,* 24 J.L. & RELIGION 379, 383–85 (2008–2009).

2. Structure of Jewish Law

The formal term for the whole of the Jewish legal system is *Halacha*. Halacha, meaning *the way to go*, is commonly divided into law relating to ritual matters and the law relating to other matters, the latter called by the somewhat misleading term *monetary matters*. This term is misleading because the law is not limited to financial issues. Broadly speaking, the law on ritual matters relates in a narrow sense to the relationship between a person and the divine, while the law on monetary matters relates to all aspects of the relationships among people, including what we would characterize in modern law as commercial law, contracts, property law, torts, criminal law, family law, and individual rights law. The separation between the ritual law and the law on monetary matters is not complete, and rulings in one area are sometimes based on the rules in the other. This is because the system of Jewish law is seen as a singular system. On the other hand, there is some difference in the rules of interpretation for laws on ritual matters and laws on other matters. Formally the term Jewish law (Hebrew *mishpat ivri*) is used only for the law regulating relationships among people. For simplicity, this book uses the term Jewish law for the law on all matters.

Jewish law is a very old legal system and has accumulated numerous sources over the years, all of which may be relevant to modern discussion of its content. To understand the types of sources, it is important to understand that Jewish law is based on the assumption that two types of law were received at Sinai: the *written law*, which is found in the Bible, and the *oral law*, which contains interpretations and applications of the written law, as well as additional legal rules. For many years, the oral law was transmitted from teacher to student without being written down. The oral law was first systematically recorded in writing in the *Mishna*, which is described below. In later years, more of the oral law was written, so now people look to the written, or *literary*, sources of the oral law. In other words, although the oral law is now written, it is still referred to as the oral law because it was first transmitted orally. It is important to understand that both the written law and the oral law are traditionally viewed as authoritative, so that to make a ruling on Jewish law, it is inappropriate to consult only the Bible without consulting sources of the oral law as well.

The primary literary sources of Jewish law, or the places were source material is found in writing, are:

- The Bible: This refers to what Christians call the Old Testament, a term Jews, who have no New Testament, do not use.

- The Mishna: The Mishna was written in about 200 CE by the leader of the Jewish community in the Roman province of Palestine. It summarizes the oral law in a highly abbreviated form.

- The Talmud: There are two versions of the Talmud, both written after the Mishna: the Jerusalem Talmud, redacted in Palestine in about 400 CE, and the Babylonian Talmud, redacted in Babylonia in about 500 CE. Each expands on the discussion in the Mishna. The Palestinian and Babylonian Jewish communities were in contact with each other and the two versions are similar, although they have some important differences in language and subjects covered.

- Commentaries: Commentaries on the Bible, the Mishna, and the Talmud have been written by various scholars in various places. The process continues, with new commentaries being written at the present time.

- Codes: From time to time, prominent scholars have gathered the material found in the various sources and prepared organized legal codes setting out the rules derived from the other, more narrative sources.

- Responsa: Beginning in the seventh or eighth century, it became the practice to send questions on legal issues to recognized legal scholars, who would provide answers, or *responsa*. Many of these questions and answers have been preserved in writing and form part of a broad literature, containing more than 300,000 responsa. The practice of writing responsa is ongoing.

This list of sources is quite different from the types of sources that are used in American law. The primary sources, the Bible, the Mishna, and the Talmud, do not look anything like any sources of American law. The Bible contains a great deal of narrative material and the legal rules are not set out in any systematized way. The Mishna and the Talmud are even more unlike American legal materials. Both record discussions of legal scholars on various issues of law. Especially in the Talmud, the discussions are only loosely arranged by topic. The discussions in the Talmud pit opinions of scholars of one generation and location against those of another generation and location. The analysis is very exacting. Furthermore, the discussions contain not only analysis of legal rules, but also significant narrative material, including stories about specific scholars, descriptions of events, etc. These narrative portions are sometimes treated as allegorical and are also sometimes referenced in discussions of the law.

Jewish law places a much heavier emphasis on the commentaries of scholars than does American law. The commentary literature is extensive and no discussion of the law can ignore the work of the major commentators. Contradictions in the positions of different scholars must be resolved or reasons given for preferring one position over competing positions.

Another difference between American law sources and the sources of Jewish law is that in American law, codes are primary source material, whereas in Jewish law, the codes are derivative. Various scholars analyzed the primary materials on the written and oral law and derived the codes from them. The codes were not enacted as such.

The list of major sources of Jewish law does not include case decisions. Responsa are not the same as case decisions. Not all responsa are based on actual disputes; sometimes they are answers to questions on what action should be undertaken in the future or to theoretical questions. They are not the result of an adversary process. Even when they address a dispute, they consist of advice given to the person who must decide an actual dispute and not the practical decision itself.

The Jewish law system has Jewish courts that hear cases, but case decisions are not major sources of Jewish law. First, there is a heavy emphasis in Jewish law cases on using mediation and accommodation, rather than actual legal rulings, to settle disputes. Second, there is no system for recording all case decisions. Third, the decision in one case is not considered binding precedent for another.

With its major emphasis on opinions of scholars, and without any contemporary lawmaking hierarchy, the authority to make, to interpret, and to apply Jewish law is diffuse. Rabbis operating in their own communities make rulings for that community. When there is disagreement among rabbis, there is no defined body with authority to settle the dispute. Furthermore, Jewish law allows some degree of change of how the law is applied as circumstances change over time.[4]

---

4. *See* Eliezer Berkovits, Not in Heaven: The Nature and Function of Halakha (1983).

Jewish law is traditionally understood as applying to all Jews but, with the exception of seven legal precepts, it does not make a claim of application to non-Jews. The seven precepts which Jewish law claims have universal application are not to worship idols, not to engage in blasphemy, not to murder, not to engage in immoral sexual practices, not to steal from another person, not to eat meat torn from a living animal, and to establish a court system. The six prohibitions in this list apply to the individual; the seventh is an affirmative requirement of society. Even these precepts are not enforced against non-Jews; instead, Jewish law allows Jews to engage in certain relationships with non-Jews only if they observe the seven precepts. In legal terms, it can be said that non-Jews are not under the jurisdiction of Jewish law. It is assumed that they govern their own affairs.

Not all Jews believe that they are obligated to meet all the requirements of Jewish law. In fact, most Jews in Israel are largely non-observant and probably do not believe that they are violating mandates that apply to them. Furthermore, many Jews who believe themselves obligated do not in fact meet all the requirements set out in the law. As stated earlier, non-belief and non-observance do not exclude a person from being considered a Jew.

The obligations imposed by Jewish law apply to Jews wherever they are, with one exception. Jewish law allows for community-based rules that apply only to Jews within a specific community. In some cases, the community is defined by current location; in others, it is defined by community of origin.[5]

Judaism provides for the existence of courts to apply Jewish law. In fact, Jewish law includes extensive provisions on criminal and civil procedure. In most countries where Jewish courts exist today, they are outside of the state court system. Therefore they exercise no criminal jurisdiction. They exercise civil jurisdiction over matters that litigants bring before them. Even if their decisions may not be formally enforceable in state courts, they may be considered and treated as binding by parties who accept the Jewish law system. The position of Jewish courts in Israel is different because, as described in part G of this chapter, Israeli state law assigns them jurisdiction over certain matters relating to marriage and divorce for Jews.

C. Islamic Law

Islamic law is the law of Islam. Like Jewish law, it is all-encompassing, addressing all aspects of life. Islam does not distinguish between rituals and the every-day aspects of conduct; all are to be done according to the will of *Allah*, as set out in Islamic law. Allah is the Islamic conception of the divine.

The *Qur'an* is the highest authority of Islamic law; it consists of verses considered to be the word of Allah as revealed to the Prophet Muhammad between 610 and 632 CE. The *Sunnah* is the other primary source of law; it includes reports of what the Prophet Muhammad (570–632 CE) said and did, as chronicled by his followers over several centuries in the *hadith* literature.[6] The Qur'an and the Sunnah are referred to as the *Shari'a*, a term which literally means *way*, as in the path to follow. The Shari'a is regarded as Allah's law.

Islamic law is based on the Shari'a, but also on human interpretations of the Shari'a, referred to as the *fiqh*, or Islamic jurisprudence. The Shari'a authorizes use of reasoning

---

5. A more extensive examination of the structure of Jewish law is found in Menachem Elon, Jewish Law: History, Sources, Principles (1994).

6. Sometimes the term *hadith* is used to refer only to reports of Muhammad's statements.

to interpret and apply Shari'a principles where these matters are not explicitly covered by the Shari'a. A process of mental reasoning, called *ijtihad*, can be used in applying principles of Islamic law to new situations. Both the process of using ijtihad to find new legal rules, and the jurisprudence it produces, are called *fiqh*. Law of the Shari'a is regarded as permanent and infallible; the fiqh may change depending on circumstances and perhaps on re-evaluation of issues.

There are several schools of Islamic jurisprudence. Most prominent are the *shi'a* (Shiite) school (called the Jafari school) and four major *sunni* schools (Hanafi, Maliki, Shafi'i, and Hanbali). On some questions of Islamic law, the scholars of all groups agree. On other questions, they take different positions. The schools differ in their views of ijtihad as an ongoing process. The shi'a continue to use ijtihad, while the sunni do not.

One interesting feature of Islamic law is that it not only delineates what actions are required and which are forbidden, but also those which are recommended, permitted, and discouraged. Here are the options:

- A required act is rewarded and failure to do it is punished.
- A recommended act is rewarded, but failure is not punished.
- A permitted act is neither rewarded nor punished.
- A discouraged act is not punished, but avoidance is rewarded.
- A forbidden act is punished and avoidance is rewarded.[7]

In modern times, Islamic law is important as an element of state law in many countries. In some, state law is Islamic law in a rather pure form; in others, state law is Islamic law that has taken on some feature of other law systems.

The Islamic law system includes special courts. In Israel, these are called Muslim Religious courts or Shari'a courts. Like Jewish courts, they have jurisdiction over certain subjects assigned to them by state law, but they exert their jurisdiction only over Muslims.

D. Druze Law

The Druze religion, like Judaism and Islam, is monotheistic. The Druze separated from Islam in the tenth century and adopted a faith and practices that have some similarities to Islam but that are also different in a number of significant ways. The Druze have their own religious texts, called Kutab al-Hikma (the Book of Wisdom) or Rasa'il al Hikma (the Epistles of Wisdom). These books are not open to either those outside the Druze community or to most Druze. The Druze distinguish between the religious sages (*Uqqal*) and secular people (*Juhhal*). Only the former are allowed to study the religious text and to take part in other activities.

Druze courts are found in several countries with Druze communities. In Israel, Druze courts are established by state law.

---

7. A fuller, but still brief, description of Islamic law is found in Irshad Abdal-Haqq, *Islamic Law: An Overview of its Origin and Elements*, 7 J. ISLAMIC L. & CULTURE 27 (2002).

E. Law of Christian Religious Communities

Israeli law recognizes ten Christian communities, each with their own set of legal doctrine, although the reach of those doctrines may not be as all-encompassing as the reach of Jewish law and Islamic law. The legal doctrines of each of these groups are not set out here, but the religious communities are briefly described.

- The Greek Orthodox Church (Eastern Orthodox Church), which is an Eastern Orthodox church, is the most prominent Christian church in Israel. It is a *Chalcedonian* church, which means it accepted the decrees of the Council of Chalcedon of 451 CE relating to the nature of Christ. Most of its members are Arabic speaking. It includes the Russian Orthodox Church within its jurisdiction.

- The Armenian Orthodox Church (Armenian Gregorian Church) is also an Eastern Orthodox church, but is non-Chalcedonian. The community has been present in Jerusalem since the fifth century.

- The Syriac Orthodox Church (Syrian Orthodox Church) is also among the non-Chalcedonian, Eastern Orthodox churches. Successor to the Church of Antioch, it is one of the oldest churches in the Middle East and uses a very old language, related to Aramaic, in its rituals.

- The Latin Church was not established in Jerusalem until the Crusades. It was renewed in the mid-nineteenth century. It is affiliated with Rome and is what Americans know as the Catholic Church.

- The Maronite Church is an Eastern church affiliated with Rome. It retains its own language, liturgy, and canon law. Most members live in the northern part of the country.

- The (Melkite) Greek Catholic Church is another Eastern church with an affiliation with Rome. It broke away from the Greek Orthodox Church in 1724.

- The Syriac Catholic Church (Syrian Catholic Church) formed as a result of a break with the Syriac Orthodox Church. It, too, is an Eastern church affiliated with Rome.

- The Armenian Catholic Church broke with the Armenian Orthodox church and is affiliated with Rome.

- The Chaldean Catholic (Uniate) Church is a break away from the Assyrian Apostolic Church of the East and, like the other Catholic churches, is affiliated with Rome.

- The Anglican Episcopalian Church is the largest Protestant denomination in Israel. Its presence dates from 1841 as a joint church with the Prussian Lutheran Church. The union later dissolved.

The recognized Christian religious communities in Israel are free to set up their own administrative and legal systems. State law does not set out the structure for their courts.

F. Law of the Baha'i Faith

Israeli law also recognizes Baha'i as a religious community. The Baha'i faith developed out of Islam in Iran in the nineteenth century. After persecutions in Iran, an early leader fled to cities of the Ottoman Empire and was banished by the Ottomans to Acre in 1868. Acre is a city on the northern Mediterranean coast of Israel. Since then, the Baha'i have established their administrative World Center and a major shrine in Haifa, a large Israeli city near Acre.

Baha'i law is different from Islamic law in several fundamental features. It does not accept human interpretations as binding on all adherents, but relies on each individual's understanding of the written texts of the religion. In many areas, the legal system sets out principles but leaves it to the individual to decide how to implement them. The legal system also has a significant degree of flexibility in adapting to local conditions.[8]

G. Areas in Which Religious Law Is State Law

Religious law is the law of the State of Israel only in areas in which Israeli law provides that religious law will be followed. Israeli law adopts religious law on issues of personal status, mainly marriage and divorce. The statutes authorizing use of religious law in these areas are presented here. The next chapter touches on a few other areas in which Jewish religious law controls.

Israeli state law provides that on matters of personal status, religious courts have exclusive or concurrent jurisdiction. When religious courts consider marriage and divorce, they apply religious law. Under this system, Israel does not apply the law of one particular religion to marriage and divorce; rather the law of each of the recognized religious communities applies to people within those communities.

This arrangement originated during the rule of the Ottoman Empire, prior to its defeat in 1917. The British adopted essentially the same system, which was codified in the Palestinian Order of Council, 1922, set out below. When Israel became a state, it left this law, like most other British laws of the Mandate, in place. Over time, most British laws were revised or replaced. This also occurred in the area of religious law and personal status law, but the revised laws retained the basic principle of leaving each religious community to manage its own affairs as to marriage and divorce, and sometimes as to other personal status matters as well. In this way, Israel, as a Jewish state, refrained from interfering with the most intimate arrangements of members of its non-Jewish communities. Furthermore, it retained the strictures of Jewish marriage law for the Jewish population, a matter which is very important to some parts of the Jewish community, although it is opposed by others.

The relevant statutes are set out below.

---

8. The material presented here on the Baha'i faith is based on Peter Smith, An Introduction to the Baha'i Faith (2008).

Israeli Statute

Palestinian Order in Council, 1922
3 Laws of Palestine 2569, 2581–82
Part 8 — Legal Institutions

2. Definitions

"Religious community" means every community listed in the second appendix to this order and every community declared to be a religious community by the Government.

51. Religious Courts, Jurisdiction, Definition of Personal Status

(1) Jurisdiction in matters of personal status shall be exercised by the courts of the religious communities, in accordance with the provisions of this part. For purposes of these provisions, personal status means legal actions regarding marriage or divorce, alimony, maintenance, guardianship, determinations of legitimacy of minors, prohibitions on use of the property of legally incompetent persons, and administration of property of absentee persons.

52. Muslim Religious Courts

Muslim religious courts shall have exclusive jurisdiction in matters of the personal status of Muslims who are Israeli citizens, or who are aliens subject under the law of their place of citizenship to the jurisdiction of Muslim courts.... In addition, ... they shall have exclusive jurisdiction in matters of creation of a waqf or the internal administration of a waqf created for the benefit of Muslims subject to the jurisdiction of a Muslim religious court.[9]

A decision issued by a qadi's[10] court [a court of first instance in the Muslim religious courts system] may be appealed to the Muslim Religious Court of Appeals, the decisions of which shall be final.

53. Jewish Religious Courts

The Rabbinical courts of the Jewish community shall have ... exclusive jurisdiction over creation or internal administration of religious endowment properties that were created before the religious court under Jewish law.

54. Christian Religious Courts

The courts of the various Christian communities shall have:

(1) Exclusive jurisdiction in the matters of marriage, divorce, and alimony of members of their community who are not aliens as defined in section 59.

(2) Jurisdiction in all other matters as to the personal status of such persons, in cases in which all parties to a case agree to their jurisdiction.

(3) Exclusive jurisdiction over creation or internal administration of religious endowment properties that were created before the religious court under the religious law of the community if there is such law.

59. Definition of "Alien"

For the purpose of this Part of the Order, the term "alien" means any person who is not an Israeli citizen.

---

9. The *waqf* is a Muslim land trust for certain types of land.
10. A *qadi* is a judge in a Muslim court. The same term is used for a judge in a Druze court.

Second Appendix

Eastern Orthodox Community

Latin Catholic Community

Gregorian Armenian Community

Armenian Catholic Community

Syrian Catholic Community

Chaldean Uniate Church

The United Church[11]

The Greek Catholic Melkite Church

The Maronite Church

The Syrian Orthodox Church

Comment

The above provision was enacted by the British to apply during the British Mandate. It was retained in Israeli law, but changed by amendments. The version given above is that as presently in effect. In the original version, the law had more detail on the jurisdiction of rabbinical courts, which are the Jewish religious courts. Most matters related to the authority of rabbinical courts are now covered in a separate statute. The Palestinian Order in Council, 1922, did not recognize Druze religious courts as having any authority. Modern Israeli law changes this and recognizes the Druze courts. The statutes on the authority of the rabbinical and Druze courts are set out here:

Israeli Statute

Rabbinical Courts Jurisdiction
(Marriage and Divorce) Law, 5713-1953

1. Jurisdiction in the Matters of Marriage and Divorce

Matters of marriage and divorce of Jews in Israel who are citizens or residents of the state shall be within the exclusive jurisdiction of the rabbinical courts.

2. Conduct of Marriage and Divorce

Marriage and divorce of Jews in Israel shall be in accordance with Torah (Jewish) law.

3. Consensual Jurisdiction

In matters of personal status, as defined in section 51 of the Palestinian Order in Council, 1922 or in the Inheritance Ordinance, for which the rabbinical court does not have exclusive jurisdiction under this law, the rabbinical court shall have jurisdiction after all sides to a matter have expressed their agreement to such jurisdiction.

---

11. At one time, the Prussian, then German Lutheran Church had a united presence with the Anglican Church. The United Church is no longer functioning.

Israeli Statute

Druze Religious Courts Law, 5723-1962

1. Definitions

"Court" means a Druze religious court.

"Court of appeals" means the Druze Religious Court of Appeals.

2. Establishment of the Courts

A court and a court of appeals are hereby established.

4. Exclusive Jurisdiction

Matters of marriage and divorce of Druze in Israel, who are citizens of the state or residents, shall be in the exclusive jurisdiction of the court, as well as matters relating to the creation or internal administration of religious endowment properties that were established before a court under Druze law or of Druze endowment properties that were established before the effective date of this law under the Druze custom even though not before a religious or state court.

5. Consensual Jurisdiction

In matters of personal status of Druze, as defined in section 51 of the Palestinian Order in Council, 1922 or in the Inheritance Ordinance, for which the court does not have exclusive jurisdiction under section 4, the court shall have jurisdiction after all sides to a matter have expressed their agreement to such jurisdiction.

6. Jurisdiction of the Court of Appeals

The court of appeals shall determine appeals from the decisions of the court.

Comment

The Israeli Government has issued two orders under its authority in section 2 of the Palestinian Order in Council, one in 1970 declaring the Anglican Episcopalian Church to be a recognized religious community and one in 1971 making a similar declaration as to the Baha'i faith. The recognition of the Anglican Episcopalian Church grants it authority under section 54 of the Palestinian Order in Council to have courts with jurisdiction over personal status issues of members of the church. Section 54 establishes the jurisdiction of the courts of all Christian communities. Because the Baha'i community is not Christian, it may need separate legislation for its courts to have official jurisdiction. The Druze also needed separate legislation and that has been enacted. No such legislation has yet been enacted for the Baha'i faith.

The statutes given above address the issue of subject matter jurisdiction. Although all religious courts have subject matter jurisdiction over issues of personal status, the scope of *exclusive* jurisdiction is different for the different religious courts. Jewish and Druze religious courts have exclusive jurisdiction only over marriage and divorce. Christian religious courts have exclusive jurisdiction over marriage, divorce, and alimony. Muslim courts have exclusive jurisdiction over marriage, divorce, alimony, maintenance, guardianship, legitimacy of minors, and some property issues. The most important of the areas in which religious law applies are marriage and divorce. The substantive law on these topics is discussed in chapter 14.

In those personal status matters where a religious court does not have exclusive jurisdiction, civil courts have concurrent jurisdiction. The parties, together, may agree to have a case tried before a religious court with concurrent jurisdiction; without such agreement, the case will be heard in a regular civil court. For example, two Jews can agree to have a guardianship issue tried before a rabbinical court. Absent such mutual agreement, the case must be tried before a civil court.

On the issue of personal jurisdiction, the statutes provide that each religious court has jurisdiction over issues involving members of its own community. For the major religion of Israel, Judaism, this is a matter of the applicability of the religious law. Jewish law does not apply to non-Jews. A Jewish court, which applies Jewish law, could not apply it to non-Jews because they are not subject to the law. Therefore the Jewish court, as a matter of Jewish law, does not have personal jurisdiction over non-Jews. The state law merely recognizes, but does not create, this limitation on personal jurisdiction. The personal jurisdiction provisions create a hole in the law: two people who are not members of the same religious community are seemingly left with no way to marry or divorce, because both of these are in the exclusive jurisdiction of the religious courts and, for the most part, the religious courts will not marry people of different religions. Israeli law provides a rather inelegant solution to this problem; it is investigated in chapter 14.

Because religious courts apply religious law, the question arises of what happens if religious law and state law conflict. The following case deals with such an alleged conflict.

Israeli Case

Mulhem Naif Mulhem v. Qadi[12] of Akko
HCJ 49/54, 8 PD 910 (1954)

Justice Silberg:

The question in this case is whether polygamy is allowed for Muslims, as it was for all communities until July 26, 1951, or was it forbidden as of that time. On that date, section 8(a) of the Law on Equal Rights for Women, 5711-1951, entered into effect. That section provides, "The limitation on section 181 found in paragraph (3) [of the Criminal Law Ordinance first enacted during the British Mandate] is revoked."

[Section 181 of the Criminal Law Ordinance defined the crime of bigamy.] Paragraph (3) of section 181 provided that a man would have a valid defense to an accusation of bigamy if it were proven "that the marriage law that applied to a husband at the time of a prior marriage and at the time of a subsequent marriage was a law other than Israeli law, and if that other law permitted him to marry more than one woman."

The issue is whether section 8a set out above, the objective of which was to eliminate the discrimination that existed under the Mandatory ordinance and impose a prohibition of bigamy on all the communities living in Israel, prohibits all bigamous marriages or whether this section is limited by section 5 of the Law on Equal Rights for Women that provides, "This law is not meant to impair the laws on what is prohibited and what is permitted as to marriage and divorce."

---

12. The term *qadi* is used for a judge in the Muslim courts and in the Druze courts.

Prohibiting bigamy for Muslims, the attorney for the Petitioner claims, will certainly impair "the laws and what is prohibited and what is permitted as to marriage." In other words, he claims that section 8a ... cannot revoke the general permission that existed beforehand for members of the Muslim community.

The events that brought this issue before us are as follows:

The Petitioner, a Sunni Muslim who is married and a father, wants to marry another woman in addition to his present wife. In March of this year, he applied to the Respondent, a qadi in Akko, to conduct a religious marriage ceremony with his intended second wife. He presented a certificate from the noteworthy members of his village testifying that the Petitioner is an adult of sound mind and that there is no legal obstacle to his marriage, that the young woman he wants to marry is an adult, 22 years old, of sound mind and fit for marriage, and there is no legal obstacle to her marriage to the Petitioner.

The Respondent refused to do as requested by the Petitioner and did not agree to conduct the marriage ceremony. In a letter to the Petitioner's attorney he explained his refusal, stating that "although under the Shari'a law there is no obstacle to this additional marriage, section 8a of the Law on Equal Rights for Women prohibits the marriage, and the police report to the court anyone who authorizes such a marriage and the husband. Therefore we do not conduct weddings of this sort."

Given this refusal, the Petitioner turned to this Court.

Before we deal with the issue described above, we shall deal with a preliminary question which the counsel for the Petitioner addressed. He claimed that prohibiting multiple wives to Muslims would be an infringement of freedom of religion, so the Knesset could not enact such a law.

We do not accept this claim. Without ruling on whether and to what extent the legislature can enact a law that infringes on the freedom of religion of the individual, we observe that in this case, this is no such infringement. The freedom of religion does not mean the freedom to do anything that the religion allows, but rather the freedom to do what the religion commands. Taking multiple wives clearly is not required, but only permitted, by the Muslim religion, although doing as permitted may indeed in certain circumstances allow fulfilling another religious commandment. But that is so as to many permitted acts that the legislature, for some reason, deems necessary to prohibit, and no one can validly raise a legal objection.

We have not ignored the fact that taking of multiple wives is a deeply rooted custom in the lives of most Muslim peoples, and that it is firmly connected to their ideology, mentality, and world outlook, that everywhere where this custom is prevalent or tolerated, it is woven into and integrated into the way of life of that people or that society, and has become an important part of their culture. But there is a great distance between this and a mandatory commandment that an individual must fulfill. Nor should we forget that not every state with a Muslim population permits multiple wives (see, for example, Turkey). There is even an opinion, expressed in the book of Amir Ali, Muhammad's Laws, which the attorney general brought to our attention, that:

> The conditions under which polygamy is permitted (to Muslims) are so difficult to meet that we can, in fact, regard polygamy as forbidden, and that the circumstances that lead to it being permitted in earlier times have either have been revoked or have ceased to exist in modern times, so that polygamy constitutes a violation of the [religious] law.

If a modern state, like the State of Israel, sees the need to eliminate existing discrimination and to forbid multiple wives for all residents of the country, it should not be critiqued for ignoring the religious obligations of its Muslim citizens.

It is to be noted, and not for the purpose of finding authority, but rather as an interesting historical fact, that a very similar question was brought before the Supreme Court of the United States in 1879 in an appeal from the decision of the Supreme Court of the Territory of Utah, as it was called then, before it became a state in 1896. The matter there related to a Mormon, Reynolds, who was accused and found guilty by the Utah court of bigamy, a violation of a congressional law of 1862 known as "The Law to Punish and Prevent the Custom of Multiple Wives in the Territories of the United States and Other Places, Revoking Known Laws of the Legislature of the Territory of Utah." ... Reynolds claimed that the statute contradicted the First Amendment to the United States Constitution, which provides, "Congress shall make no law ... prohibiting the free exercise [of religion]." He claimed that the law prohibiting bigamy was therefore invalid, at least as to the Mormon sect.

His factual claim in both the lower court and the Supreme Court was that male members of the Mormon Church were obligated to take multiple wives because,

> it was the duty of male members of said church, circumstances permitting, to practice polygamy; ... that this duty was enjoined by different books which the members of said church believed to be of divine origin, and among others the Holy Bible, and also that the members of the church believed that the practice of polygamy was directly enjoined upon the male members thereof by the Almighty God, in a revelation to Joseph Smith, the founder and prophet of said church; that the failing or refusing to practice polygamy by such male members of said church, when circumstances would admit, would be punished, and that the penalty for such failure and refusal would be damnation in the life to come.[13]

Therefore the position of the Mormons was much stronger than the position of the Petitioner in the case before us. In that case, a person whose religious belief required him to observe the commandment of polygamy was tried for doing just that. He based his defense on a constitutional provision that explicitly forbid any congressional law that infringed on a citizen's freedom of religion. Nonetheless the American Supreme Court did not accept this claim and allowed the conviction by the lower court to stand. The Supreme Court held that the law against bigamy was within the legislative authority of the Congress, and that those who practice polygamy as part of their religion would not be exempt from punishment. We found two other cases of the Supreme Court, handed down about ten years later, that followed this holding: *Davis v. Beason*,[14] and *Late Corporation of the Church of Jesus Christ v. United States*.[15] As a result of these cases polygamy was finally abolished by law in the state of the Mormons, and Utah was accepted as a state of the United States of America.

The same rule of law applies to the case before us, although ours is a simpler case. Here, as we have seen, there is no infringement of the citizen's freedom of religion, nor is there an infringement of the religion's essential beliefs or of its positive commandments. Muslim polygamy is not like Mormon polygamy. For the Muslims, polygamy does

---

13. Reynolds v. United States, 98 U.S. 145, 161 (1878).

14. 133 U.S. 333 (1890). The case upheld a state statute denying the right to vote to anyone who practiced or advocated polygamy. A later case held *Davis v. Beason* invalid to the extent that it applied to mere advocates of polygamy. Romer v. Evans, 517 U.S. 620, 634 (1996).

15. 136 U.S. 1, 32 (1890).

not constitute part of the Muslim belief nor is it a religious obligation. Previously in the case of Crim.A 112/50 *Yosifof v. Attorney General*,[16] the bigamy provision in the Mandatory law which prohibited polygamy was attacked as it applied to a Jew as an infringement on freedom of religion or freedom of conscience. There also, the claim was rejected, mainly for the reason that the prohibition of polygamy did not interfere with any religious obligation of the accused or of members of the accused's community.

We now turn to the other claim of the Petitioner, which is his main claim, that there is a contradiction between section 5 and section 8a of the Law on Equal Rights of the Woman, 5711-1951.... It cannot be the case that there is no way to read two sections within one law so that they do not contradict each other. Clearly the contradiction is only alleged; we must closely examine the law to find common ground between the two sections.

It is not difficult to resolve this apparent contradiction. [Under Muslim law, a man may marry a second wife, but a woman cannot marry a second husband. Under Jewish law,] in certain circumstances a Jewish man can obtain a permit from a hundred rabbis to marry a second wife while still married, but a woman cannot do so. The Law on Equal Rights of Women, as a statute of the Knesset, obligates all residents of the state.... Without section 5 it would prohibit the kind of discrimination described in these examples. [Therefore if either a Muslim or a Jewish man had married a second wife, the law would retroactively invalidate that second marriage.]

The Israeli parliament did not want to go this far.... Therefore it enacted section 5 of the statute that provides that, despite the provision of equal rights for women that stands as the foundational principal of the law, "this law is not meant to impair the laws on what is prohibited and what is allowed as to marriage and divorce." ... There is no conflict between the true meanings of the two sections of the law, and section 5 does not deprive section 8 of its force and power. Section 5 is intended to protect the specific legal discrimination described above that exists, whether in the personal status provisions of Jewish law or in the personal statues provision of another recognized religious community. The result is that if the Petitioner before us had succeeded in marrying a second wife, the marriage would be valid. But the meaning of section 5 is not to abolish the revocation of discrimination as declared in section 8a of the law. The latter section contains a clear and explicit requirement, and it cannot be that the legislature meant to abolish it with another provision.

For these reasons, we reject the petition.

Comment

The *Mulhem* case refers to an earlier case, *Yosifof v. Attorney General*, involving the prohibition on polygamy in a different law. That law prohibited polygamy, but contained some exceptions to allow it where it was permitted under religious law. Yosifof was a married Jew who married a second wife. He did this by lying to the rabbinical authorities and telling them he was single. The marriage was clearly impermissible under Jewish law, which permits a man to take a second wife only under very restrictive conditions that did not apply in this case.[17] Yosifof was convicted of the crime of bigamy and sentenced to a year of imprisonment. He claimed that the law under which he was convicted was in-

---

16. Crim. A 112/10, 5 PD 481 (1951).

17. A man is on rare occasions allowed to take a second wife, such as when he cannot divorce his first wife because she is insane or when a court has ruled that he is entitled to a divorce and she refuses to accept one.

valid because it discriminated against him and because it interfered with his freedom of conscience and religion. The discrimination claim was based on the fact that, due to an exception in the law, a Muslim who took a second wife, as permitted by his religion, would not be subject to punishment as a bigamist, but Yosifof, as a Jewish man, was being punished. The Court rejected this claim on the grounds that the difference was justified by the application of religious law to the matter of marriage.

As to Yosifof's claim that the law interfered with his freedom of conscience and religion, the Court rejected the claim on the same grounds that the *Mulhem* Court later used to reject a similar claim from a Muslim. The case arose as to a Muslim only after the enactment of the new law discussed in *Mulhem*; before that law was enacted, Muslim men in Israel could marry more than one woman. In each case, the Court pointed out that there was no interference with religion because neither Judaism nor Islam requires that a man marry more than one wife.

Although we know that polygamy was practiced during the early Biblical period, Jewish law developed prohibitions on polygamy for most Jewish communities. This prohibition was never applied to the rather isolated Jewish community in Yemen. When Yemenite Jews were brought to Israel after the founding of the country, some arrived in families that included a husband with more than one wife. The law did not break up existing families of this sort, but the question was whether Yemenite Jewish men could marry more than one woman in the future. We see in *Mulhem* that the Court touches on this problem indirectly; it says that existing polygamous marriages are valid, even though in the future, polygamy is banned.

Still, the issue in the *Mulhem* case is arguably more complex than Justice Silberg admits. He compares the rule in Israel to the Supreme Court's ruling on the Mormons in the United States. Israel is not the United States. In Israel, the state law allows each religious community to control marriages within its community. No such law exists in the United States, where states simply recognize marriages performed by religious officials but do not provide religious communities with exclusive authority over marriage. The real question in Israel is whether the anti-polygamy provision interferes with the autonomy of the religious communities, not whether it interferes with an individual's freedom of religion. Some Muslim authorities think Israeli law does interfere with the autonomy of Islamic law in the field of marriage and divorce.[18]

It is widely reported that polygamy is still practiced among the Bedouin living in the southern Negev, a group of Israeli Muslims with a distinctive culture, and that the state does not enforce the law banning polygamy against men who are members of this group.[19]

Question

1. Should Israeli law displace Islamic law, which allows polygamy but puts some limits on its practice?

The Jewish law courts system, the Muslim law courts system, and the Druze law courts system all have courts of original jurisdiction and a court of appeals. Section 52 of the

---

18. *See* Mousa Abou Ramadan, *The Shari'a in Israel: Islamization, Israelization and the Invented Islamic Law,* 5 UCLA J. Islamic & Near E.L. 81, 106–07 (2005–06).

19. *See, e.g.,* Ruth Sinai and Haaretz Correspondent, *State Program to Tackle Problem of Polygamy in Bedouin Community,* Haaretz, March 27, 2008, http://www.haaretz.com/print-edition/news/state-program-to-tackle-problem-of-polygamy-in-bedouin-community-1.242837.

Palestinian Order in Council provides that decisions of the Muslim Religious Court of Appeals are final. In fact, no statute provides that decisions of any of the religious courts can be appealed to a non-religious court. On the other hand, decisions of the highest religious court for each system, including Muslim courts, are subject to judicial review by the Supreme Court sitting as the High Court of Justice. Judicial review is different from review by way of appeal. It is similar to Supreme Court review of decisions of administrative agencies, although it is probably less intrusive. The Supreme Court does not review determinations under religious law, but does review whether the religious courts acted within their jurisdiction.[20] In cases in which religious courts applied non-religious law, the Supreme Court determines whether they did so properly (such as in the *Mulhem* case).[21] The Supreme Court also decides whether the religious courts complied with applicable rules of constitutional and administrative law. Thus, a religious court decision can be tested to determine if it complies with the rules of proportionality,[22] the rules of natural justice,[23] the requirement of reasonableness,[24] and other rules of administrative law.

---

20. *See* Basic Law: The Judiciary, § 15(d).
21. *See* also HCJ 323/81 Vilozhni v. High Rabbinical Court, 36(2) PD 733 (1982).
22. *See* HCJ 5227/97 David v. High Rabbinical Court, 55(1) PD 453, 458 (1998).
23. *See id.* at 457.
24. *See* decision of Justice S. Joubran in HCJ 6124/07 Anonymous v. High Rabbinical Court (Nov. 22, 2007).

Chapter 13

Israel as a Jewish State

A. Israel as a Jewish State

From the time of its establishment, Israel has identified itself as a Jewish state. Israel is the only country with a Jewish majority, but its claim to be a Jewish state is based on more than the identity of the majority of its citizens. It is based on seeing Jews as a people entitled, as any other people, to a state of their own. The country is located where the Jews had their own land in ancient times, in a place to which they have had a connection for more than 3,500 years.

This section sets out the legal documents providing that Israel is a Jewish state and explores the meaning and implications of being a Jewish state.

Israeli Document

Declaration of the Establishment of the State of Israel, 5708-1948
1 LSI 3 (1948)[1]

We ... hereby declare the establishment of a Jewish state in Eretz-Israel [the land of Israel], to be known as the State of Israel.

Israeli Statute

Basic Law: Human Dignity and Freedom, 1992

1a. Purpose

The purpose of this Basic Law is to protect human dignity and freedom in order to secure in a Basic Law the values of the State of Israel as a Jewish and democratic state.

Israeli Statute

Basic Law: Freedom of Occupation

2. Purpose

The purpose of this Basic Law is to protect the freedom of occupation in order to secure in a Basic Law the values of the State of Israel as a Jewish and democratic state.

---

1. The English translation presented in Laws of the State of Israel (LSI) is the official translation.

Comment

The declaration of Israel as a Jewish state was based on the historical connection of the Jewish people with the land of Israel. This is made explicit in the full text of the Declaration of the Establishment of the State of Israel, set out in chapter 4. The declaration of Israel as a Jewish state was consistent with the United Nations General Assembly Resolution 181 (II): Future Government of Palestine, also set out in chapter 4, which provided for the termination of the British Mandate and the establishment, in the area it had covered, of two states, one Arab and one Jewish.

It has been clear from the beginning that Israel's identity as a Jewish state did not mean that it was to be governed by Jewish law. Israel views itself as the national homeland of the Jewish people, a people with a shared religion, but not as a religious state. Nonetheless some of the laws reflect Jewish religious doctrine. Others reflect the cultural values of the Jewish people. Most of these laws would not exist in a state that is not a Jewish state.

One study lists sixty-three countries, including Israel, as having state religions. Among these countries are most other countries of the Middle East; most countries of Eastern Europe; many countries in Northern, Western and Central Europe, including Denmark, Norway, Spain, Italy, the United Kingdom (England and Scotland only); and a number of countries of South America.[2] In fact, Israel does not have an officially adopted state religion. On the other hand, a number of laws and features of public life are based on Jewish law, tradition, or culture. In this way, the state and the Jewish religion are intertwined. Yet the Jewish character of the state is not based solely, and even not primarily, on considerations that are typically seen as religious.

It has also been clear from the time of the establishment of the state that Israel would be democratic. Early case law refers to the democratic nature of the state, as do the later-enacted Basic Law: Human Dignity and Freedom and the Basic Law: Freedom of Occupation. The following case considers what it means for Israel to be a Jewish state and how its nature as a Jewish state is harmonized with its nature as a democratic state.

Israeli Case

Central Election Comm. of the Sixteenth Knesset v. Tibi
Election Authorization 11280/02, 57(4) PD 1 [2003]

[Under Israeli law, a person who claims that a candidate for election to the Knesset does not meet the legal requirements for candidacy can bring the claim before the Central Election Committee. The committee can rule that the candidate should be prevented from running or allow the candidate to run. Similarly, the committee can consider claims that a party fails to meet the legal requirements for participation in an election. If the committee decides that a candidate or party should not run, the matter is transferred to the Supreme Court, which decides whether the candidate or party will be allowed to run in the election.

Objections were raised before the Central Election Committee to two candidates and one party, in part because they advocated the position that Israel should be a "state of all

---

2. Robert J. Barro & Rachel M. McCleary, *Which Countries Have State Religions?*, 120 THE QUARTERLY JOURNAL OF ECONOMICS 1331, (2005), *available at* http://www.economics.harvard.edu/faculty/barro/files/state%20religion%2001-05.pdf.

its citizens." That term is often understood in Israeli politics as advocating that the state should not be a Jewish state and should not give any special status or consideration to Jews and Judaism. This case deals with the Supreme Court's reaction to the Central Election Committee's determination that these two candidates and one party should not run in the election.]

Chief Justice A. Barak:

Decisions of the Central Election Committee to prevent a candidate or a list[3] from participating in the elections must come before us for authorization. [In other words, the decision of the Committee is not effective without Supreme Court authorization.] A decision of the Central Election Committee to allow a candidate to run is effective on its own, but can be brought before this Court as an appeal of the Committee decision.... We begin by setting out the normative framework of the law that applies. After that, we shall consider each decision separately.

The General Normative Framework

Section 7a of the Basic Law: The Knesset, under which the Central Election Committee made the decisions we must consider, provides:

7a. Prevention of Participation in Elections

(a) A list of candidates shall not participate in elections to the Knesset, and no person shall be a candidate for the Knesset, if the goals and actions of the list or the actions of the person, constitute either explicitly or implicitly one of the following:

(1) rejection of the existence of the State of Israel as a Jewish and democratic state;

(2) incitement to racism;

(3) support of an armed struggle against the State of Israel by an enemy state or a terrorist organization.

(b) The decision of the Central Election Committee that a candidate is prohibited from participating in the elections requires the authorization of the Supreme Court.

The interpretation and application of this provision lies at the heart of this case.

Section 7a of the Basic Law, like similar provisions in the constitutions of democratic countries, is designed to solve a difficult dilemma, a sort of paradox, that faces democratic states. The dilemma relates to the tension between two opposing principles. On the one hand we have the principle that democracy should be based on the free market of ideas. A party list of candidates, even if it seeks to reject or impair democracy, is entitled to present its ideas and to compete on an equal basis in elections that determine the structure of the society. Based on this principle, preventing an anti-democratic list from participating in the elections is inconsistent with the democratic ideal. It is in apparent conflict with the basic idea of a free marketplace of ideas. Furthermore, when the existing majority prevents the participation of an anti-democratic list, it raises a fear of misuse of the power of the majority to suppress the political power of the minority. It also may appear to be a magic solution that does not deal with the root of the problem but rather shuts off its expression; this can encourage anti-democratic lists to engage in even more extreme ac-

---

3. The election system in Israel and the role of the party lists of candidates are described in chapter 3.

tivities. On the other hand we have the principle that a democracy should be allowed to defend itself against those who rise up against it. A democracy has a right to prevent the participation in a democratic process by a list that denies the value of democracy itself. A democracy does not have to sacrifice itself in order to prove its vitality. Moreover one cannot demand the right to participate in the democratic process based on the very principles that the person or list does not accept. This tension ... lies at the basis of the democratic paradox. How is it possible to deal with this paradox?

Different democratic countries adopt different solutions. Some have abstained from setting forth any constitutional solution. This is the case in the United States, Canada, and England. Some have constitutional provisions that allow steps to be taken against undemocratic parties. The provisions of the German constitution on this matter are well known. Enacted after World War II, they reflect the terrible experience of the war and the Holocaust. Section 21(2) provides:

> Parties which, by reason of their aims or the behavior of their adherents, seek to impair or abolish the free democratic basic order or to endanger the existence of the Federal Republic of Germany shall be unconstitutional. The Federal Constitutional Court shall decide on the question of constitutionality.

Interpreting this provision, the German Constitutional Court said:

> The Basic Law represents a conscious effort to achieve a synthesis between the principle of tolerance with respect to all political ideas and certain inalienable values of the political system. Article 21(2) does not contradict any basic principle of the Constitution; it expresses the conviction of the [founding fathers], based on their concrete historical experience, that the state could no longer afford to maintain an attitude of neutrality toward political parties. [The Basic Law] has in this sense created a "militant democracy," a constitutional [value] decision that is binding on the Federal Constitutional Court. Bundesverfassungsgericht [Federal Constitutional Court], *The Communist Party Case*, 5 Entscheidungen des Bundesverfassungsgericht [BVerfGE] 85, 392 (1956) (Ger.).

Other countries prohibit the activities of parties with special characteristics, such as fascist parties (Italy), Nazi and fascist parties (Poland), parties that do not respect the national sovereignty and democracy (France), and parties whose goals or activities are unconstitutional or that support terror (Spain). Some countries require parties to respect political democracy (Portugal) or basic democratic values (Czech Republic) and even to respect the constitution and the requirements of constitutional law (Hungary).

Rejection of the Existence of the State of Israel as a Jewish and Democratic State

The first cause for preventing a list of candidates or an individual candidate from participating in elections for the Knesset is that the goals and actions of the list, or the actions of the candidate, constitute "a rejection of the existence of the State of Israel as a Jewish and democratic state." ... The term "the State of Israel as a Jewish and democratic state" appears in the Basic Law: Human Dignity and Freedom and in the Basic Law: Freedom of Occupation. Nonetheless the meaning of the term in section 7a of the Basic Law: the Knesset is different from that in the two Basic Laws on human rights. The reason is that the term is used for different purposes in the different laws. As we shall see, the term as used in the Basic Law: the Knesset should be given a narrow meaning because it restricts the basic right to vote and to be elected. In contrast, the term as used in the Basic Law: Human Dignity and Freedom should be given a broad meaning because it is designed to protect human dignity and freedom. Nonetheless we can use our understanding of the term in one context to aid in our understanding of the same term in the other context.

One common element is that the term "the State of Israel as a Jewish and democratic state" is interpreted as one phrase with two components (Jewish and democratic). There should be a synthesis and harmony between these two components. It is the task of judges, as interpreters of the constitutional text, to maintain such a synthesis. A clear expression of this idea is found in the words of Chief Justice Shamgar:

> The claim that there is an apparent contradiction between the various provisions of section 7a of the Basic Law: The Knesset is not correct. The existence of the State of Israel as the state of the Jewish people is not inconsistent with its democratic nature, just as the *Frenchness* of France is not inconsistent with its democratic nature.... (Election Appeal 1/88 *Neiman v. Chairman of the Election Committee of the Twelfth Knesset* 43(4) PD 177 [1988]).

It is natural that if each of the components is given its broadest possible meaning, then there may be some points of conflict between them, so we must search out the core concepts of each of the two components.

Rejection of the Existence of the State of Israel as a Jewish State

There are many democratic countries. Only one of them is a Jewish state. Indeed, the reason for Israel's existence is its identity as a Jewish state. This characteristic is central to her existence and is, as Justice M. Cheshin stated before the Central Election Committee, "axiomatic" for the state. We see it as a "basic principle of our law and our system." Rejection of Israel as a Jewish state prevents a list or a candidate from running in elections for the Knesset. The characteristics of Israel as a Jewish state are many and varied. Only the core or minimal characteristics are relevant to the issue of running in the elections. As we have stated before, "the very foundations of the Jewish or democratic nature of the state must be threatened.... The threat must be to the core characteristic of the state as Jewish and democratic. It must threaten matters that are of the first order as to this characteristic."

What are the core characteristics that mold the minimal definition of what it means for the State of Israel to be a Jewish state? These characteristics have both a Zionist and a traditional aspect. The right of every Jew to make aliyah (to immigrate) to the land of Israel is central, as is the concept that Jews shall constitute a majority. Hebrew is the main official language of the state. Its main holidays and symbols reflect the national resurrection of the Jewish people. The heritage of Israel is a central component, expressed in Israel's religious and cultural traditions. A candidate list or an individual candidate cannot participate in elections if abolition or rejection of these characteristics is central and dominant in its aspirations or its activities, if the list or party works diligently to implement these aspirations, and if it is possible to prove all this with clear, unambiguous, and convincing evidence.

Is a list or a candidate disqualified from participation in elections due to rejection of the nature of Israel as a Jewish state if one of its dominant goals is to advance the view of the State of Israel as a state of all its citizens? We cannot answer this question without understanding the term "a state of all its citizens." If this refers only to equality among all citizens, this goal does not infringe on the nature of Israel as a Jewish state.

The assertion that the State of Israel is the "state of all its citizens" does not negate the existence of the State of Israel as a Jewish state. Would the claim that Israel is not the state of all its citizens be accepted? Can it be claimed that the State of Israel is the state of a portion of its citizens? Equality among citizens is a basic principle of democracy.

In the same spirit, we said in another case that

we do not accept the view that the values of the State of Israel as a Jewish state justify ... state discrimination among citizens of the state.... The values of the State of Israel as a Jewish and democratic state do not require that the state discriminate among its citizens. Jews and non-Jews are citizens with equal rights and duties in the State of Israel.

In the same case we stated, "It is not only that the values of the State of Israel as a Jewish state do not require discrimination based on religion or nationality, but that these values themselves prohibit discrimination and require equality among religions and nationalities." I added that

the State of Israel is a Jewish state in which there are minorities living, among them the Arab minority. All members of the minorities living in Israel enjoy complete equality of rights. It is true that the Jewish people have a special right to enter the country (see the Law of Return), but once a person is legally here and a citizen, he enjoys equal rights with all others.

Based on this, we see that if the goal of having a "state of all its citizens" means just that equal rights of all citizens within the state shall be assured by recognition of the rights of the minority living there, this involves no negation of the existence of the State of Israel as a Jewish state. On the other hand, if the goal of having a "state of all its citizens" means more than this, it does infringe on the basic rationale for establishing the state and, in this way, negates the nature of the State of Israel as the state of the Jewish people. In this case, there is an infringement on the minimal core characteristics of the State of Israel as a Jewish state.

Comment (More Information on the Case)

In the decision set out above, the Committee had decided in three cases to prevent a candidate or party from running in the elections, and these decisions came before the Supreme Court for authorization. In an authorization proceeding, the Court makes the decision on whether to allow the candidate to run without deferring to the committee decision. In the first case, the Central Election Committee had decided that Knesset Member Azmi Bishara of the Balad party,[4] one of the Arab political parties, should not run again because he denied the existence of the State of Israel as a Jewish state and because he supported the armed struggle of terrorist organizations against Israel. The Supreme Court rejected this determination, finding that the statements and writings of Knesset Member Bishara did not support the determination. The Court allowed Knesset Member Bishara to run.

In the second case, the Central Election Committee had decided that the Balad party could not participate in the elections for reasons similar to those that applied to Knesset Member Bishara. The Supreme Court rejected this decision on the same grounds on which it rejected the decision against Knesset Member Bishara.

In the third case, the committee would have prevented Knesset Member Ahmed Tibi, who was associated with a different Arab party, from running in the elections due to support of terror organizations. The Court also rejected this decision, finding the evidence of such support insufficient, and allowed Knesset Member Tibi to run.

---

4. Balad stands for the National Democratic Covenant. Its website, which is only in Arabic, is found at http://www.tajamoa.org/?mod=arch&ID=21.

When the Election Committee decides to allow someone to run for office and the decision is appealed to the Supreme Court, the Court sits as an appellate body and gives substantial deference to the committee decision to allow a person to run. A portion of the *Central Election Comm. of the Sixteenth Knesset v. Tibi* case that is not included here dealt with one such appeal. The Central Election Committee had been asked to prevent Baruch Marzel from running in the elections due to allegations of anti-Arab racism that constitute both the rejection of Israel as a Jewish and democratic state and incitement to racism. The committee decided not to prevent Marzel from running, finding that although he had been associated with a racist organization in the past, he was no longer associated with that organization or its views. On appeal of this decision by those who opposed Marzel's participation in the elections, the Court said its review of a decision to allow someone to run had to be very narrow, because the presumption is in favor of allowing candidates to run. In this case, it did not find sufficient basis to overturn the decision of the committee.

All three candidates ran in the election. Both Azmi Bishara and Ahmed Tibi were elected; Baruch Marzel was not. In 2007, while under police investigation for passing information to Hezbollah while it was fighting against Israel during the Second Lebanese War of 2006, Bishara fled the country and resigned his Knesset seat by letter. As of the summer of 2011, three other members of Balad were serving in the Knesset and Ahmed Tibi continued to serve in the Knesset and was a Deputy Speaker. Baruch Marzel ran again in the elections for the seventeenth Knesset and was not elected.

Comment (Definition of a Jewish State)

The opinion recognizes five core characteristics of Israel that derive from its nature as a Jewish state. These are:

1. Jews everywhere have the right to live in Israel. This concept derives from the view of Israel as the traditional homeland of the Jewish people and the idea that the movement of a Jew to Israel is a return to the resurrected Jewish national state.

2. Jews shall constitute a majority. This requirement derives from two ideas. First, it reflects the idea that Israel cannot claim to be a Jewish state that will retain the other characteristics without a Jewish majority. Second, it derives from the Jewish experience in other lands where Jews were not a majority. Jews were massacred, expelled, and subjected to severe discrimination in many countries on different continents. Israeli Jews see their majority status as guaranteeing them the ability to defend themselves from such scourges. Indeed, most Jewish Israelis see maintenance of a Jewish majority in Israel as essential.

3. Hebrew is the main official language. Hebrew was the common language of the Jewish people in ancient times and the Bible is written mainly in Hebrew.[5] The language was preserved in religious texts and in Jewish prayer but had largely ceased to be a spoken language. Its revival began in the nineteenth century. Today it is the main language of Israel. Hebrew is important because of its connections to both the history and the religion of the Jewish people. Immigrants to Israel are expected to learn and function in Hebrew, which serves as a cement for a very diverse population. It is the language of all governmental proceedings. Arabic is also an official language, but its use is not as extensive. While instruction in the primary and secondary schools in the Arab sector is in Arabic,

---

5. A few verses, mainly in the books of Daniel and Ezra, are written in Aramaic, another language of the ancient Near East.

Hebrew is taught as a required second language beginning in the third grade. Most higher education is in Hebrew.

4. The main public holidays are Jewish. The official Israeli holidays are all Jewish religious or Jewish national holidays. Just as the Christian holiday of Christmas is a day off in the United States, Jewish holidays are days off in Israel. Public institutions, schools, and most private businesses are closed. In the same way that Sunday is the day off in the United States, Saturday, the Jewish Sabbath, is the day off in Israel. While observant Jews spend Saturdays and most holidays in religious observance, the less-observant Jewish majority may have a family meal and then spend time at the beach, at parks, in bars and restaurants, and in family activities. The main Muslim holidays are not official days off, but Muslims are allowed to be absent from work and school as required for religious observance. The same is true of Christians for Christian holidays.

5. The state's symbols reflect the national resurrection of the Jewish people. The state flag has a six-pointed Jewish star, called in Hebrew a *Shield of David*. The term Shield of David refers to King David, the second king of the Jewish people who reigned about three thousand years ago, although it is not know that he used a shield with such a star. The star has been a Jewish symbol for several centuries, although it has no deeper historical and no religious connection. On the flag, the star is blue and is on a field of white with two horizontal blue stripes. This field is based on the *tallit*, the Jewish prayer shawl. The official state symbol is a seven-branched candelabrum called a menorah. Although Americans commonly refer to the eight-branched candelabrum that Jews use as part of their observance of Hanuka as a menorah, this reference is technically not correct. The true menorah was a ritual object associated with the ancient Jewish temple worship. The candelabrum for Hanuka is properly called a *hanukia*.

In identifying the characteristics listed above as important ones, the opinion contains references to the history of the Jewish people, to Zionist political philosophy, and to tradition. Notably it does not refer to Jewish law. Some of the Jewish religious parties argue that the requirements of religious law should play a greater role in defining the contours of a Jewish state, but this view has not been accepted. In fact, one of the other Justices sitting on the *Tibi* case, Justice Yitzhak Englard, who is religiously observant, agreed with Chief Justice Barak's analysis.

The Court says that these are only the "core" characteristics, and that there are other characteristics of Israel as a Jewish state. It states that, "the heritage of Israel is a central component [of what it means to be a Jewish state], expressed in Israel's religious and cultural traditions." The term "religious and cultural traditions" is vague, but other cases go further on defining this term and in recognizing additional Israeli customs and laws as characteristics of Israel as a Jewish state. Some of these laws and cases will be encountered in the remainder of this chapter.

Questions

1. The United States Constitution has no provision limiting candidates based on the ideas they advocate. The German constitution has such a provision. What explains the difference? Does the difference provide a justification for the provision in Israel's Basic Law: The Knesset preventing the participation of a candidate who denies the existence of Israel as a Jewish state?

2. The Court says it is giving the term *Jewish state* a restricted meaning as it is used in the Basic Law: The Knesset, but would give it a broader meaning in the context of the Basic Law: Human Dignity and Freedom and Basic Law: Freedom of Occupation. What justifies this unusual approach to statutory construction?

Israeli Case

Solodkin v. Mayor of Tiberias

HCJ 953/01, 58(5) PD 595 [2004][6]

Chief Justice A. Barak:

A local law of the Tiberias Municipality prohibits the sale of pork in all areas within the municipal boundaries. Local laws of the Beit Shemesh Municipality and the Carmiel Municipality prohibit the sale of pork in some areas within the municipal boundaries, while permitting the sale of pork in other areas. The question before us is whether these local laws are legally valid.

Background

Since the nineteen-fifties, the question of the sale of pork within the boundaries of local authorities has been on the political, legal and judicial agenda in Israel. Several local authorities made a licence to run a business conditional upon not selling pork within their boundaries. When the legality of this condition was brought before the High Court of Justice, it was held that a local government does not have the power to make a business licence conditional upon not selling pork. Chief Justice Olshan said that the sale of pork within the boundaries of the local government "is in our opinion a general and national problem, which is not unique to any particular place, and its solution rests with the sole jurisdiction of the national legislature, unless the national legislature has seen fit to delegate this authority to the local authorities." HCJ 122/54 *Axel v. Mayor, Council Members and Residents of the Netanya Area* 8 PD 1524, 1531 [1954]. The Court rejected the claim that the power of the local government to prohibit the sale of pork derived from its duty to maintain order and security within its boundaries.

In addition to refusing a licence to open a business that sold pork pursuant to general powers, several local governmental units adopted a direct measure: they enacted local laws that expressly prohibited the sale of pork within the boundaries of the local government. The legality of these local laws came before the Supreme Court in the middle of the nineteen-fifties. It was held that a local government does not have the power to prohibit the sale of pork by means of local laws.

The Enabling Law

The regulation of the sale of pork passed therefore to the Knesset, which enacted the Local Authorities (Special Authorization) Law, 5717-1956. The law contains six sections. It deals with the prohibition on raising pigs and the prohibition of selling pork. The first issue was regulated several years later in the Prohibition against Raising Pigs Law, 5722-1962, and the provisions on this matter were removed from the Local Authorities (Special Authorization) Law, which was limited to the sale of pork only. The main provisions on this matter are as follows:

---

6. The translation is based on that on the Supreme Court website, http://elyon1.court.gov.il/files_eng/01/530/009/A19/01009530.a19.pdf.

1. Prohibition on the Sale of Pork and Pork Products

Notwithstanding what is stated in any other law, a local government shall be competent to enact a local law that will restrict or prohibit the sale of pork that is intended for consumption.

2. Commencement of the Prohibition

A local government may impose a restriction or prohibition as stated in section 1 on the whole area of its jurisdiction or on a specific part thereof, provided that restriction or prohibition shall apply to the whole of the population in that area or in that part.

Additional provisions in the enabling law grant a local government ancillary powers and state that whoever breaches a provision of the local law is criminally liable.

On the basis of the enabling statute, a large number of local authorities enacted local laws restricting the sale of pork. Many local laws imposed a complete prohibition of the sale of pork within the boundaries of the local government. Others limited sales to a certain area within the local jurisdiction. Attempts were made in the Knesset to replace the Local Authorities (Special Authorization) Law with a general prohibition (see, for example, the draft Prohibition against Raising Pigs Law (Amendment), 5785-1985). These proposals did not become law.

During the nineteen-nineties, the sale of pork became significantly more widespread, notwithstanding the prohibitions contained in the municipal local laws. It is possible that one of the reasons for this is the large wave of immigration from the former Soviet Union. Some of these immigrants, who were accustomed to consuming pork in their countries of origin, brought with them a demand for pork in the places where they settled. In response, there was an increase in the number of shops selling pork in cities where large numbers of immigrants from the former Soviet Union were concentrated. Several local authorities filed criminal actions on account of offences against the local laws prohibiting the sale of pork.

The Petitions

We have before us four petitions against local laws limiting the sale of pork by three local governmental units.

The Normative Framework

The enabling statute constitutes a compromise between conflicting objectives of different groups. Some wanted to totally prohibit the consumption of pork throughout Israel, similar to the prohibition that was enacted shortly afterwards on the raising of pigs throughout the State of Israel, except in specified communities (Prohibition against Raising Pigs Law, 5722-1962). Others wanted to refrain from any national legislation on the matter. In light of the case law from the nineteen-fifties, this would mean that no local government could limit the sale of pork. The compromise arrangement that was reflected in the enabling law refrained from imposing a national prohibition on the consumption of pork and instead authorized local governments to determine what would happen in each locality. The enabling statute thus rejected the approach that would leave the decision whether to sell pork to the personal choice of each individual.

The enabling law solved the problem of authorization that had arisen in the past. The local governments were specifically authorized to regulate the sale of pork. The legal question moved therefore from a question of authorization to regulate the sale of pork to the question of the scope of discretion that the local government has when it wishes to regulate this matter ... [Petitions were filed claiming that local governments had imposed bans that were too extensive as to the areas to which they applied.]

The scope of a local government's discretion when it decides upon the enactment of a local law in the matter of the sale of pork is determined by the enabling law, which we are charged with interpreting. We interpret the language of the enabling law in a way that realizes the purposes of the law—the specific and general purpose, both subjective (the intention of the legislator) and objective (the intention of the law). What are these purposes? Consideration of the facts gives rise to several purposes that should be taken into account.

The *first* purpose of the enabling law is to protect the feelings of Jews who regard the pig as the symbol of impurity. This outlook is, of course, religious in origin. The pig has always been considered a symbol of abhorrence, abomination and disgust by the Jewish person. A similar approach is also accepted by the Islamic religion. Notwithstanding, the Jewish approach is not based only on Jewish dietary laws, which contain other restrictions besides the one that prohibits eating pork. The prohibition on eating pork also includes a national factor, which goes beyond the religious perspective relating to the laws of kosher food, and which is shared by many who are not religious. Justice Olshen stated that the prohibition on the sale of pork is based on a perception of "the prohibition on consuming pork as a holy matter or as a matter that is in the national soul...." The story is well-known of the civil war between Hyrcanus II and Aristobulus, the sons of Yannai (Alexander Jannaeus) and Shlomtzion (Alexandra Salome), which preceded the Roman conquest. According to the story, a pig was sent up to the besieged Jews instead of a sheep.... The pig as a symbol is therefore closely connected with the Roman conquest and the loss of Jewish national independence. Jewish history is full of heroic stories of Jews who preferred death to eating pork. The story of Hannah and her seven sons who sacrificed their lives rather than eat pork is well-known (Maccabees 2, 7:1). Professor Barak-Erez rightly pointed out that "engraved in the collective memory of the Jewish people is the consciousness that the enemies of the Jewish people throughout the generations made use of the pig as a part of the persecutions and humiliations of Jews." Daphne Barak-Erez, *The Transformation of the Pig Laws: From a National Symbol to a Religious Interest?*, 33 Hebrew Univ. L. Rev. (Mishpatim) 403, 413 (2003).

Indeed, the pig has become a symbol of the hatred of Jews, the loss of national independence and the degradation of Jews. The purpose of the enabling law is to protect the feelings of Jews, believers and non-believers, who are seriously injured by the sale of pork.

The *second* purpose of the enabling law is to protect the liberty of the individual. This was the subjective purpose of the enabling law. This is also an objective purpose of this law, just as it is an objective purpose of every other law in Israel. This liberty has been recognized in the abundant case law of this Court since the founding of the State. It is today enshrined in the Basic Law: Human Dignity and Liberty. This liberty includes the liberty of every individual to determine his own lifestyle and consequently the freedom to decide what food he will buy and eat, and what food he will not buy or eat. The prohibition of the sale of pork harms this liberty. Because the prohibition is motivated by religious considerations, it also harms freedom of conscience and freedom from religion. Underlying this purpose is the outlook that there is no justification for the intervention of the State in the liberty of the individual. Moreover the seller's freedom of occupation should be guaranteed. The prohibition of the sale of pork harms this freedom of the seller. Indeed, underlying the enabling law is the presumption that every person in Israel has freedom of conscience and freedom from religious or any other coercion. "It is a supreme principle in Israel, originating in the rule of law (in the substantive sense) and the case law made by the Court, that citizens and residents have both freedom of religion and freedom from religion.... We do not coerce religious obligations on someone who is not religiously observant or who does not want to observe religious obligations ..." A person also has "a natural right to engage in the work or profession that he chooses for himself...." This is the freedom of occupation that is enshrined today in the Basic Law: Freedom of Occupation. It is derived from the autonomy of the individual will and is an expression of a person's self-determination.

The *third* purpose, on which the compromise underlying the enabling law is based, is to empower local governments to determine provisions with regard to the sale of pork. Unlike the prohibition on raising pigs, with regard to which a national rule was adopted, a local approach was chosen for the prohibition on selling pork. The purpose was therefore that the balance between the conflicting purposes—the considerations concerning the protection of religious and national sensibilities, on the one hand, and the consideration of individual liberty, on the other—would not be made on a national level. Instead, the purpose was to provide that the conflicting interests would be balanced at the local level. In this local balancing, the character and changing conditions of the local area would be taken into account. The result therefore is that the task of resolving the tension between the first two purposes of the law was transferred to the local level. The discretion was given to the local government. What is the scope of this discretion, and how should it be exercised? We now turn to consider these questions.

The Discretion of the Local Government

The discretion of the local government is not absolute. It may not simply make whatever decision it wants. The discretion of the local government, like any administrative discretion, is always limited. A local government must exercise its discretion in a manner that effectuates the purpose underlying the law that gave it the discretion. In the case before us, it must exercise the discretion in a manner that reflects the proper balance between the conflicting purposes against the background of the local situation.... This compromise is required by the values of the State of Israel as a Jewish and democratic state. It is reflected in the need to balance, on a local level, the Jewish and national values, on the one hand, against the liberty of the individual in a democracy on the other. It varies from matter to matter and from time to time. It reflects the changes that occur in Israeli society as it moves through history.

The Balance Between Conflicting Purposes

According to the compromise underlying the enabling law, the local government should balance the conflicting purposes against the background of the local conditions. In this balance, in one pan of the scales lies the consideration of religious and national sensibilities. These jointly reflect considerations of public interest. These considerations have great social importance, and they may, in certain conditions, reduce the protection given to human rights. In the other pan lie considerations associated with the liberty of the individual who wishes to sell or buy pork. These are considerations related to human rights. The balance between them must be made in the way dictated by the tests of proportionality and reasonableness. These tests combine two types of criteria that have been developed over the years by the Court.

When analyzing how to apply these tests, we consider a hypothetical case of a local government that contains three villages or three neighborhoods within its boundaries. The distance between the villages or the neighborhoods is not great. There is a regular transport link between the villages or the neighborhoods, and it is possible to go from village to village or from neighborhood to neighborhood within a short time. One village or one neighborhood (village A) is composed of residents whose religious and national sensibilities will be offended if sale of pork in their village is permitted. This village has several residents that will not be offended by this but they are few in number. The second village or neighborhood (village B) is composed of residents who all, with the exception of a small number of opposing residents, wish to buy pork or are not opposed to sale of pork. Village C or neighborhood C is composed of residents of both types without it being possible to separate them on a territorial basis. What does the enabling law say with regard to the discretion of the local government vis-à-vis each of these villages or neighborhoods? This hypothetical case reflects the problematic nature of the case before us. Indeed, the enabling law did not seek to determine an overall balance for the whole of the country. It regards each local government as an independent unit, and it allows an internal division of the territory within the local government's boundaries.

Village A: All the Residents Oppose the Sale of Pork.

Village A is composed of residents, all of whom, apart from a small minority, have feelings that will be injured if the sale of pork is possible in their village. Their feelings are based on religious or national values. Is the local authority entitled to determine in a bylaw that the sale of pork within the geographical boundaries of village A is prohibited? This bylaw would violate the human rights (freedom of occupation) of those people who live outside the village and wish to sell pork in village A. It also violates the freedom of conscience of the residents in the two neighbouring villages and the negligible minority in village A itself, who wish to buy pork in village A, and who are prevented from doing so. Are these violations of human rights lawful? The answer to this question can be determined by applying the principle of proportionality, which seeks to ensure a proper purpose and a proper means of realizing it. Under this test, the restriction of human rights is lawful if it befits the values of the State of Israel as a Jewish and democratic state, is intended for a proper purpose and violates human rights to an extent that is not excessive. It is obvious that the protection of the feelings of those persons who wish pork not to be sold in their village befits the values of the State of Israel as a Jewish state, both because of the injury to religious sensibilities and because of the injury to national sensibilities associated with the sale of pork. The strength of this injury is likely to change from village to village. It is obviously stronger when the religious factor and the national factor unite. It also befits the values of the State of Israel as a democratic state.... I will also assume that the injury to the human rights of those who oppose the prohibition is minimal, since the freedom of occupation of the sellers suffers only a minimal injury. Indeed, the vast majority of the residents of village A in any event would not buy pork in village A, and those persons who live outside village A can, as we will see, buy pork without any difficulty in their own village (village B). Those few residents of village A who wish to buy pork can do so without any difficulty in village B. Their liberty is only harmed a little. It seems to me therefore that in so far as village A is concerned, prohibiting the sale of pork befits the values of the State of Israel as a Jewish and democratic state, notwithstanding the violation of the human rights. It is also intended for a proper purpose, which concerns a protection of these feelings. Is the violation excessive? It is well known that the test of proportionality is composed of three sub-tests. The first of these is the rational connection. The executive measure (prohibition of the sale of pork) must lead, rationally, to the achievement of the purpose (preventing an injury to religious and national sensibilities). The case before us complies with this sub-test. The second sub-test is that the executive measure must violate the right of the individual in the smallest possible degree. The case before us also complies with this sub-test, in view of the possibility of selling pork in the nearby village B. The third sub-test states that the executive measure is improper if its violation of the right of the individual is disproportionate to the benefit that it achieves in realizing the purpose. The case before us also complies with this sub-test.

The conclusion is that in village A, which is composed entirely (apart from a negligible minority) of residents who oppose the sale of pork for religious and national reasons, it is permissible to prohibit the sale of pork. The same conclusion will apply if we are concerned with a city that is divided into different neighborhoods, and in one of the neighborhoods all the residents (apart from a negligible minority) wish to prohibit the sale of pork because of the injury to their religious and national sensibilities. Indeed, the viewpoint of the enabling law is territorial or local, and it is based on the possibility of dividing the city into neighborhoods, by considering each neighborhood as a separate territorial unit for the purpose of exercising discretion under the enabling law.

Village B: All the Residents Wish to Consume Pork and its Products or Do Not Object to the Consumption Thereof.

In village B, which is entirely composed (with the exception of a small minority) of residents who wish to consume pork or who do not oppose this, it is not possible lawfully to prohibit the sale of pork.... The same is true in a city where all the residents of one of its neighborhoods wish to consume pork or are not opposed thereto.

Village C: Some of the Residents Oppose the Sale of Pork, and Some Do Not Oppose the Sale of Pork.

Naturally if it is possible to make a territorial separation in village C between the two camps, the law applying to village A or village B will apply. But what is the law if such a separation is impossible? It would appear that the main purpose of the enabling law is to regulate precisely this situation. Indeed, the enabling law does not seek principally to regulate the sale of pork in village A, where all the residents oppose the sale of pork. The reason for this is practical: there are few cases in which people will wish to sell and buy pork in village A. Indeed, we do not need the enabling law in order to regulate the problem of the sale of pork in the [Ultra-Orthodox] religious neighborhood of Mea Shearim [in Jerusalem]. Likewise, the enabling law does not fulfil an important role in village B, where all the residents oppose a prohibition on the sale of pork. It is inconceivable that the members of the local council will seek to impose a prohibition of the sale of pork in a Christian town. Indeed, the main function and purpose of the enabling law is to authorize a local government to enact a local law that will restrict the sale of pork or to prohibit it in local authorities where residents of both camps live alongside one another, without there being any possibility of a territorial separation. What is the scope of the discretion of the local government under the power given to it in the enabling law?

We analyze this case under the principle that a decision of an executive authority may lawfully violate human rights if the violation is proportionate, namely it befits the values of the State of Israel, is intended for a proper purpose and is not excessive. Are these conditions fulfilled in village C? A prohibition of the sale of pork in village C naturally violates the freedom of occupation and freedom of conscience (freedom from religion) of some of the residents of the village. This violation befits the values of the State of Israel as a Jewish state. Does it befit its values as a democratic state? Is the injury to the feelings of the residents who oppose the sale of pork greater than the level of tolerance that every person in a democracy must accept as part of the social consensus on which society is founded? Naturally the level of tolerance required is not uniform in all circumstances. It varies from right to right, from violation to violation. This was discussed by Justice Zamir, who said:

> The level of tolerance of feelings, such that only an injury above this level will justify protection of feelings, is neither fixed nor uniform for every situation. The level depends, *inter alia*, on the question of what conflicts with the injury to feelings: for example, a fundamental right such as freedom of expression or a mate-

rial interest such as pecuniary gain. Accordingly the level of tolerance required will vary. It can be very high if the protection of feelings necessitates a violation of freedom of expression; it may be lower if the protection of feelings necessitates an injury to pecuniary gain. The level is determined according to the balance between the conflicting interests in light of the circumstances of each case, and it reflects the relative weight—the social importance—of these interests.

In determining the requisite level of tolerance, we must take into account the nature of the specific right that is violated, the extent of the violation, the extent of the injury to feelings, and the likelihood of this injury. With regard to the nature of the right, it has been held that not all rights are of equal status. In this respect, we must take into account various additional parameters, including "the subject-matter of the legislation that inflicts the injury (economic, social, security, etc.), the reasons underlying the protected right and its relative social importance, the nature of the injury to the right and its strength in the specific case, the circumstances and context of the injury and the nature of the conflicting rights or interests" [quoting an earlier case]. With regard to the injury to feelings, we must naturally take into account the strength, scope and depth of the injury. With regard to the likelihood of the injury, this changes from right to right.

Does the prohibition of the sale of pork in village C befit the values of the State of Israel as a democratic state? Because of the many variables, the local characteristics must be examined closely. Different towns may reach different answers even if the ratio of residents opposing the sale of pork is similar. By way of a generalization, villages of type C can reach the conclusion that the sale of pork inside their village or in the neighborhood of residents who oppose this for religious and national reasons exceeds the "level of tolerance" that every resident ought to tolerate as a part of his living in that place. We are dealing, as we have seen, with an injury to religious sensibilities and an injury to strong national sensibilities that characterize the opponents of the sale of pork. This was well expressed by Natan Alterman in his poem "Free Belief and Hooves:"[7]

> In every nation's heart, this nation most,
> Here where it was born—
> Memories of disgust, carved by sword and whip,
> Engraved by reluctant choice.
> So they that care not if hoof uncloven or cloven be,
> They too feel
> A Jewish nation in Israel, a pig sacred? inviolable?
> The generations tremble.
> For reasons of pious and secular alike
> agree, this time, it seems ...
> Strange maybe, but not to be ignored,
> Here religion,
> There ancient geography and some history of many years ...
> The pig, uneasy, in the middle.
>
> 2 Natan Alterman, *The Seventh Column* 237 (1975)

---

7. Natan Alterman, 1910–1970, was a major Israeli poet. His work included political poetry, much of which was published in daily newspapers in Israel. The reference to uncloven hooves relates to the Jewish dietary laws. This is explained in the comment after this case. Animals with uncloven hooves are not permitted under the Jewish dietary laws. The pig has cloven hooves, but is still forbidden for other reasons.

Notwithstanding, in a mixed village, even if there is only a minority whose liberty is infringed if the sale of pork is prohibited, we must ensure that the infringement of the liberty of that minority is proportionate. This condition will be fulfilled by ensuring that there is a place in the village (even if it is on the outskirts), or in another village (such as village B) of the same local government, where it will be possible to buy and sell pork. The location of the sales point will vary from place to place. It will reflect the local characteristics with a proper balance between the right and the violation thereof, under the specific circumstances of the case, and the public interest and the injury thereto in the same circumstances. In all these cases, it must be ascertained that the sales point is accessible, and that it is actually possible to maintain a place for the sale and purchase of pork.

This analysis indicates the relationship between the intensity of the injury to religious and national sensibilities of those who wish to prevent the sale of pork and the intensity of the violation of the liberty, freedom of occupation and conscience and freedom from religion of those who oppose the imposition of the prohibition. This relationship naturally varies from place to place, from village to village. On the basis of the assumptions that I have made, including the existence of a regular transport link between village C and village B and a practical possibility of opening in village B or in the outskirts of village C a shop for the sale of pork, it seems that it is possible to justify in a democracy the violation of the human rights of those who oppose the prohibition on the sale of pork on account of the religious and national sensibilities of those who wish there to be such a prohibition.

Does a local law that prohibits the sale of pork in village C violate the rights of the residents of village C who oppose the prohibition to an extent that is excessive? Is the requirement of proportionality fulfilled? We have discussed the sub-tests of this test. The first sub-test (the rational connection test) is met. Just as in village A, a prohibition against the sale of pork in village C will prevent an injury to religious and national sensibilities. The second sub-test (the smallest violation test) will be met only if it is assured that the residents who wish to sell and consume pork can do so in village B or in the outskirts of village C. The third sub-test (the proportionality test, in the narrow sense) is met, since there is a reasonable relationship between the extent of the violation of the human right, considering the various possibilities, and the degree of injury to feelings.

My conclusion is that if the conditions that I have discussed are fulfilled, of which the main one is proper access to pork in village B or in the outskirts of village C, the local government that incorporates the three villages may prohibit the sale of pork in village A and village C. Underlying my approach is the serious injury caused to the public interest by the sale of pork. This is an injury to religious and national sensibilities together, where the latter strengthen the former. Nonetheless these in themselves are insufficient to justify the violation of human rights. Such a violation will be lawful only if it is guaranteed that it is possible to reduce the extent of the violation by complying with the conditions that I have discussed. This I regard to be a proper balance between the conflicting purposes. We are not concerned with the coercion of religion on those who oppose it, since the purchase of pork is relatively easy.

The Practical Application

The result is that we return the issues that are the subject of the petitions to the respondent municipalities, in order that they may consider them and make new decisions in the light of the criteria that we have discussed, without us adopting any position on the merits of their decision. Until a further decision, the local laws are suspended, as stated in our judgment. Subject to the aforesaid, we decide to deny the petitions.

Comment (Understanding the Issues in the Case)

At one time, it appeared that local governments had two possible means of limiting the sale of pork. Because all food establishments must obtain business licenses issued by the local government, conditions imposing a ban on pork sales could be inserted into those licenses. Alternatively, a local government could pass a local law prohibiting the sale of pork within the area of its jurisdiction. At the beginning of the *Solodkin* opinion, Chief Justice Barak describes two cases that taken together held that local authorities could not regulate the sale of pork by either of these means. These cases arose before the Knesset enacted the Local Authorities (Special Authorization) Law, 5717-1956.

Local governments in Israel have no inherent authority. They are agencies of the national government and have only those authorities granted to them by the state. Prior to 1956, no national legislation explicitly authorized local governments to ban the sale of pork. The national law allowing local governments to put conditions in business licenses addressed other types of issues, such as the need to assure that food businesses did not present a health hazard and that manufacturing businesses complied with environmental standards. It did not explicitly address the issue of whether bans on the sale of pork was permissible. Similarly the national laws allowing local governments to enact local laws on various topics did not authorize local laws about the sale of pork. One law did provide that local governments could enact local laws needed to maintain law and security, but the Supreme Court had found that this did not encompass restrictions on pork sales. In other words, the restrictions imposed by the local governments were ultra vires.

As a consequence of these rulings, it became clear that if the sale of pork were to be regulated, either the national government would have to regulate its sale or the national government would have to enact a law explicitly authorizing local governments to undertake such regulation. The Knesset chose the latter course and enacted the Local Authorities (Special Authorization) Law. This law explicitly granted local governments authority to restrict or prohibit pork sales in local laws. The question in *Solodkin* is whether the respondent local governments exercised that authority in an appropriate manner.

In discussing the Local Authorities (Special Authorization) Law, Chief Justice Barak's opinion identifies the purposes of the statute. Chief Justice Barak refers to the second purpose, to realize individual liberty, as both a *subjective* and an *objective* purpose of the law. A subjective purpose is one which the Knesset actually considered in enacting a law. An objective purpose is one of the general purposes of Israeli law that the Court assumes the Knesset intends to promote in every act of legislation. This concept is set out in *Poraz v. City Council of Tel Aviv-Jaffa*, 42(2) PD 309, 330 [1988], discussed in chapter 9 on administrative law, where the Court said, "We presume that every law is intended to effectuate the basic values accepted in our legal system and to be consistent with them." In *Solodkin*, the basic value is to preserve the freedom of the individual. This is an objective purpose, because it is assumed that achievement of this purpose is part of the general values that the Knesset tries to serve in all legislative acts, whether or not the Knesset members actually thought about that purpose in enacting the legislation.

Comment (Israel as a Jewish State)

Solodkin discusses the meaning of Israel being a Jewish state in two contexts. First, it determines that Israel's nature as a Jewish state gives it an interest in prohibiting the sale of pork. It identifies one of the purposes of the Local Authorities (Special Authorization) Law as protecting the negative feelings many Jews have about pigs. These negative feelings are Jewish feelings related to a Jewish religious prohibition, to Jewish history, and to the collective memory of the Jewish people. In other words, the Court rules that it can look at Jewish history and Jewish perceptions, and even to Jewish poetry to determine the Jewish character of the state. That character includes a Jewish negative attitude about pigs.

Second, it discusses whether the prohibition on the sale of pork befits the values of the State of Israel. The Court decides that the prohibition infringes on basic rights of people to purchase and sell pork, and that this infringement is permissible only if the prohibition meets the requirements of the limitation clauses in the Basic Laws. The limitation clauses define the types of laws that are allowed to infringe on basic rights. The first requirement of the limitation clauses is that the infringing law befit the values of the State of Israel. In *United Mizrahi Bank v. Migdal Communal Village*, CA 6821/93, 49(4) PD 221 [1995], set out in chapter 8, the Court had already said that the values of the State of Israel are its values as a Jewish and democratic state. In *Solodkin*, the Court easily finds that a prohibition on the sale of pork fits within this rubric; for reasons already discussed, it is clear that the prohibition befits Israel's values as a Jewish state.

The Court does not rule that the fact that the prohibition is consistent with Israel's identity as a Jewish state is sufficient to justify the prohibition in all cases. The prohibition infringes on other interests, and the degree of infringement must meet the requirement of proportionality. The Court discusses at length the conditions under which the proportionality requirement is met.

It is clear that the Court's final allowance of a partial prohibition on the sale of pork is a product of Israel's identity as a Jewish state. Although a Muslim state might ban the sale of pork, the reasons for the ban in Israel are not the same as they would be in a Muslim state. The Court's references to Jewish history and sensitivities make this clear.

One interesting feature of this case is that it adjudicates a dispute between different groups of Jews. Generally Muslims do not object to a ban on sales of pork. Christian Arabs would object, but they can both raise pigs and sell pork in their communities. The main tension is within the Jewish community. On the one side stand religious, traditional and other Jews who support the prohibition on the sale of pork for all the reasons set out in the decision. On the other side stand non-observant Jews and immigrants from the former Soviet Union who are not Jewish under Jewish law, but who largely identify themselves with the Jewish community. The Court insists on balancing the interests of these groups. Some Jewish groups find the sale of pork anywhere within Israel inconsistent with the identity of Israel as a Jewish state. The Court rejects this view.

The Prohibition against Raising Pigs Law, 5722-1962, referred to in the case, prohibits raising pigs in Israel except in research facilities and in specified regions that are populated mainly by Christian Arabs. Apparently the permitted facilities raise enough pork to satisfy the demand for the meat. Pork and pork products are found on the menus of numerous non-kosher restaurants, including many in the main Jewish population centers.

The decision refers to several characters and events in Jewish history. Hyrcanus II and Aristobulus were the last of the Jewish rulers of the independent Jewish monarchy established in about 142 BCE. The throne was held by the Hasmonean dynasty, and their assent to power is celebrated by the holiday of Hanukah. The two monarchs ruled during the period from about 67 to 63 BCE and engaged in a civil war against each other. The Romans used the resulting weakness of the kingdom as an opportunity to establish their rule over Judea. One aspect of the struggle during the period of the civil war is described in the Talmud as follows:

> When the Kings of the Hasmonean house fought one another, Hyrcanus was outside and Aristobulus within [the city wall of Jerusalem]. Each day [those that were within] used to let down [to the other party] dinars in a basket, and haul up [in return] animals for the daily offerings. An old man there [on the inside], who was learned in Greek wisdom, spoke with them ... saying, "As long as they carry on the Temple service they will never be delivered into your hands."
>
> On the morrow they let down dinars in a basket and hauled up a pig. When it reached halfway up the wall, it stuck its claws into the wall, and the land of Israel was shaken over a distance of four hundred parasangs by four hundred parasangs.[8] At that time they declared, "Cursed be the man who rears pigs and cursed be the man who teaches his son Greek wisdom!"[9]

The story means that although the forces of the two Jewish kings were fighting each other, they cooperated to allow the sacrificial rites in the Temple continue. Aristobulus forces, ensconced within the walled city of Jerusalem, where the Temple was located, would let down a basket with money in it to pay for animals for the daily sacrifices. Hyrcanus' forces would take the money and purchase the necessary animals and send them back up in some sort of contraption. One day, an old man pointed out that the forces within the wall were being strengthened by the ongoing normal operations in the Temple. Thereafter, Hyrcanus' forces sent up a pig instead of the sheep normally used for the sacrifice. Sacrifice of pigs is not permitted. The entire land shook, expressing its revulsion at this action.

The decision also refers to chapter 7 of Maccabees 2. The book is one of several telling the story of the Jewish Hasmonean war against the repressive Greek regime in Judea and the assimilated Jews who associated themselves with that regime. The Greek king Antiochus tried to force Hannah's seven sons to eat the flesh of pigs. When each in turn refused, they were subjected to horrible tortures before the eyes of their mother.

Chief Justice Barak, the author of the *Solodkin* decision, is secular. His opinion shows that familiarity with these Jewish sources is widespread, at least among educated Jews of his generation. It also shows how deeply contemporary Jews look into history to find their basic values.

Question

3. Bans on sale of different kinds of animal meat are found in the United States as well. Texas bans the sale of horse meat for human consumption.[10] In New Jersey, it is illegal to sell the flesh of a domestic cat or dog for consumption.[11] Are these laws conceptually different from the laws considered in *Solodkin*?

---

8. A parasangs is a Persian mile. According to different sources, it is equal to 2.4 or to 2.9 miles. Adin Steinsaltz, The Talmud: The Steinsaltz Edition: A Reference Guide, 283 (1989). In other words, the resulting quake was felt over an area that included much, if not all, of the Jewish kingdom of that time.

9. Babylonian Talmud, Menachot 64b, available in English at http://www.the-daf.com/gemara-aggadata/menachot-64-josephus-hyrcanus-and-the-pig-on-the-wall/. The translation in the text is from this source.

10. Tex. Agric. Code Ann. § 149.004 (2004).

11. N.J. Stat. Ann. § 4.22-25.4 (West Supp. 2011).

Israeli Case

Design 22 — Shark Deluxe Furniture, Ltd. v. Rozenzweig
HCJ 5026/04, 60(1) PD 38 [2005][12]

[Jewish law prohibits many kinds of work on the Sabbath[13] and on certain Jewish holidays. In other words, a person who observes Jewish law may not only wish to have time off from work to enjoy the Jewish Sabbath or for a Jewish holiday, but will need the time off as a requirement of religious observance.[14]]

Chief Justice A. Barak:

Does the prohibition on employment of Jews on the Sabbath under the Work and Rest Hours Law, 5719-1951, violate the requirements of the Basic Law: Freedom of Occupation? This is the main question in this petition.

Facts

The first Petitioner, a corporation that sells furniture and has branches throughout the country, employs Jewish workers in its branches. Some of its employees are also Petitioners. These branches operate on all the days of the week, including the Sabbath. On March 12, 2003, an administrative fine of NIS 15,000 was imposed on the Petitioners.... due to employment of Jewish workers during the weekly period of rest, in violation of sections 9, 9a, 26(a) and 17 of the Hours of Work and Rest Law (hereinafter *the law*). Upon receiving notice of the fine, the Petitioner turned to the first respondent, the head of the Branch for Sabbath Work Permits in the Ministry of Labor and Social Affairs, and requested a permit to employ Jewish workers on the Sabbath and on holidays. The request was rejected because the Petitioner does not meet the criteria for receiving such a permit. The Petitioner had a choice of paying the fine or of having the matter heard in court and chose to have the matter heard in court. An indictment was brought against the Petitioner.... The Petitioner filed this petition [claiming that the law should be held invalid].

The Normative Framework

Section 7 of the Hours of Work and Rest Law provides:

7. Weekly Rest Hours

(a) A worker shall have at least thirty-six continuous hours of rest each week.

(b) The rest period shall include

(1) For a Jew, the Sabbath;

(2) For someone who is not a Jew, either the Sabbath or Sunday or Friday, depending on which is the person's habitual day of rest.

In addition, the law provides that no one shall employ another person to work or work themselves during the weekly rest period unless a permit has been granted. Similarly, an owner of a workplace may not work there during the weekly rest period.

---

12. The translation is based on that on the website of the Supreme Court at http://elyon1.court.gov.il/files_eng/04/260/050/a02/04050260.a02.htm.

13. The term *the Sabbath* is the term used for the Jewish Sabbath, which begins in most places eighteen minutes before sundown on Friday and ends about forty minutes after sundown on Saturday.

14. This requirement does not apply to medical professionals, police, soldiers, or others engaged in life-saving activities in their work.

9. Prohibition of Employment of Someone to Work During the Weekly Rest Period

Employing a person to work during the weekly rest period is prohibited unless under permit as provided in section 12.

9a. Prohibition on Working During the Weekly Rest Period

(a) During the days of rest ... the owner of a workplace shall not work in his workplace, nor the owner of an industrial plant in his plant, and the owner of a store shall not conduct commercial activity in his store.

12. Permit to Employ a Worker During the Weekly Rest Period

(a) The minister of labor is authorized to permit employment of a worker during the weekly rest period, or during a portion of that period, if he is convinced that complete cessation of work for the full period or for part of it is likely to impair defense of the country or personal safety or the safety of property, or to create great harm to the economy, in the progress of work or in supply of goods or services that are, in the opinion of the minister of labor, essential to the public or to a portion of the public.

(b) A general permit under subsection (a) shall not be given except by decision of a committee of ministers made up of the prime minister, the minister of religions, and the minister of labor.

(c) A special permit under section (a) shall denote the professions or the jobs of the workers who are permitted to work or the divisions that may operate under the permit.

We examine the Petitioners' claims in light of these provisions.

Constitutional Scrutiny

Freedom of occupation has been a basic right in Israeli law since the founding of the state. Before the enactment of the Basic Law: Freedom of Occupation, it was a part of the Israeli common law.

When the Basic Law: Freedom of Occupation was passed, ... freedom of occupation ... became a constitutional super-legislative right. The Knesset (as a constitutive body) restricted the power of the Knesset (as a legislative body) to infringe on the freedom of occupation. It is not sufficient for a law to impose a restriction on the freedom of occupation expressly, clearly and unambiguously. The constitutionality of this restriction must satisfy the requirements of the limitation clause (section 4 of the Basic Law: Freedom of Occupation).

It is accepted that, for the sake of clear and precise analysis, the constitutional scrutiny is carried out in three stages. The first stage examines whether a law violates the freedom of occupation, as it is defined in the Basic Law: Freedom of Occupation.... If there is no violation, the constitutional scrutiny ends. If there is a violation, the constitutional scrutiny proceeds to the second stage. The second stage examines whether the violation of the freedom of occupation satisfies the requirements of the limitation clause. If these requirements are satisfied, the constitutional scrutiny ends. If the requirements of the limitation clause are not satisfied, we must proceed to the next stage. The third stage examines the constitutional remedy. Let us now turn to the constitutional scrutiny that is required in the case before us.

First Stage: Does the Hours of Work and Rest Law Violate the Freedom of Occupation?

Section 3 of the Basic Law: Freedom of Occupation provides:

Every citizen or resident of the state is entitled to engage in any occupation, profession or trade.

In discussing the purpose underlying this provision in another case, I said:

The freedom of occupation as a constitutional right is derived from the autonomy of the individual will. It is an expression of how a person defines himself. By means of freedom of occupation, a person shapes his identity and his status and contributes to the social fabric. This is consistent with the values of the State of Israel as a democratic state. It is also consistent with the values of the state as a Jewish state. Work makes man unique and is an expression of the image of God in him.

Indeed, the freedom of occupation is the freedom of the individual to engage (or not to engage) in any occupation, trade or profession as he sees fit. This is mainly a *protective* right that is usually asserted against a violation thereof by a governmental authority. It follows that any legislative arrangement that restricts the liberty of the citizen or the resident to enter into an occupation, profession or trade, or to manage them as he chooses, violates his freedom of occupation.

Against this background, it follows that the provisions of the Hours of Work and Rest Law that prohibit work during the weekly rest infringe on the freedom of occupation.... The restriction on occupation concerns time. It does not address the content or character of the occupation, but the hours when it takes place. The Hours of Work and Rest Law infringes on the realization of a person's will to develop his business during the hours of the weekly rest. It does not matter whether the business is a sole ownership or a corporation; both have a right to freedom of occupation. Moreover the prohibition of working on the Sabbath also infringes on the freedom of occupation of the worker, who wishes to work in the business on the Sabbath. The prohibition also sometimes infringes on the freedom of competition of the owner of the business. In view of this conclusion, with regard to the existence of a fundamental violation of the freedom of occupation, we do not need to examine whether the Hours of Work and Rest Law violates additional human rights, such as the right to freedom of religion and freedom from religion. Indeed, in the petition before us the constitutional claim focused only on the violation of freedom of occupation by the Hours of Work and Rest Law. The Respondents agreed that "the Hours of Work and Rest Law involves an infringement of the employer's freedom of occupation." Their argument was that this infringement satisfies the requirements of the limitation clause. Let us now turn to this question, which constitutes the *second* stage of the constitutional scrutiny.

Second Stage: Does the Hours of Work and Rest Law Meet the Requirements of the Limitation Clause?

A law that infringes on the freedom of occupation is not unconstitutional for that reason alone. There are many laws that violate constitutional human rights without thereby becoming unconstitutional. For example, the penal laws and the laws concerning arrests and extradition violate the prohibition against denying or restricting "a person's liberty ... by imprisonment, arrest, extradition or in any other way" (section 5 of the Basic Law: Human Dignity and Liberty). No one claims that all these laws are unconstitutional.

The limitation clause in the Basic Law: Freedom of Occupation provides (in section 4):

4. Infringement of Freedom of Occupation

There shall be no infringement of freedom of occupation except by a law befitting the values of the State of Israel, enacted for a proper purpose, and to an extent no greater than is required, or by regulation enacted by virtue of express authorization in such law.

This clause provides that it is possible to infringe on the freedom of occupation, and the infringement will be constitutional, if it satisfies the following conditions: (a) the infringement is in a law or under a law by virtue of an express authorization in the law; (b) the law infringing on the freedom of occupation befits the values of the State of Israel; (c) the law infringing on the freedom of occupation is for a proper purpose; (d) the infringement of the freedom of occupation is not excessive. For a law that infringes on the freedom of occupation to pass the constitutional scrutiny in the limitation clause, it must satisfy the four requirements. Are these requirements satisfied by the Hours of Work and Rest Law?

The *first* requirement of the limitation clause is that the infringement on the freedom of occupation is made "by a law." ... There is no dispute that the Hours of Work and Rest Law is a law. The first requirement provided in the limitation clause is satisfied.

The *second* requirement provided in the limitation clause is that the law that infringes on the freedom of occupation "befits the values of the State of Israel." The limitation clause does not define these values. These can be derived from the purpose clause in the Basic Law: Freedom of Occupation, which provides:

2. Purpose

The purpose of this Basic Law is to protect freedom of occupation, in order to establish in a Basic Law the values of the State of Israel as a Jewish and democratic state.

Thus we see that the "values of the State of Israel" (the limitation clause) are "the values of the State of Israel as a Jewish and democratic state" (the purpose clause). What are these values and does the Hours of Work and Rest Law befit them?

We have no need, within the framework of the petition before us, to examine in detail the combination of constitutional terms "the values of the State of Israel as a Jewish ... state" and "the values of the State of Israel as a ... democratic state." For the purposes of the petition before us the following three points are sufficient. *First*, the State of Israel is a Jewish state.

Second, the State of Israel is a democratic state.

Third, the constitutional interpreter should make an effort to achieve an accord and harmony between the values of the State of Israel as a Jewish state and its values as a democratic state.

Does the prohibition against employing someone and working during the weekly rest, as provided in sections 9 and 9A of the Hours of Work and Rest Law, befit the values of the State of Israel as a Jewish and democratic state? These prohibitions are based on the social need to provide hours of weekly rest to the worker by determining one uniform day of rest that will allow a whole family to be together on the day of rest. This involves a determination based on a religious-national consideration that the weekly rest will include "for a Jew, the Sabbath; for someone who is not a Jew, either the Sabbath or Sunday or Friday, depending on which is the person's habitual day of rest" (section 7). This determination befits the values of the State of Israel, both as a Jewish state and as a democratic state.

The values of the State of Israel as a Jewish state are consistent with the prohibition of employing persons and working during the weekly rest, which is the Sabbath for Jews, and Sunday or Friday for non-Jews. This is the case both for social reasons and for national-religious reasons. An expression of this can be found in the fourth of the Ten Commandments:

> Observe the day of the Sabbath to sanctify it as the Lord your God commanded you. Six days shall you labor and do all your work. And the seventh day is a Sabbath to the Lord your God; you shall not do any work, either yourself or your son or your daughter or your man-servant or your maid-servant or your ox or your ass or any animal of yours or the stranger that is within your gates, so that your man-servant and your maid-servant shall rest as you do. And you shall remember that you were a slave in the land of Egypt and the Lord your God took you out from there with a strong hand and an outstretched arm; therefore the Lord your God has commanded you to keep the Sabbath day. Deuteronomy 5: 11–15. (For a slightly different text, see Exodus 20: 8–11.)

Indeed, the social aspect and the national-religious aspect of a weekly rest is a golden thread that runs through the world of Jewish religious law. The combination of these two led to the observance of the Sabbath becoming a central element of Judaism.... Justice Dorner said:

> Judaism, which bequeathed to mankind the concept of the weekly day of rest, sanctified the Sabbath as the day of rest of the Jewish people. The Sabbath is a national value no less than a religious value. "The Sabbath is the most ingenious creation of the Jewish spirit" wrote Haim Nachman Bialik[15] ... and Ahad HaAm[16] wrote: "Whoever feels in his heart a real connection with the life of the people throughout the generations cannot in any way imagine a reality of the Jewish people without its Sabbath queen."[17]

The restriction on work times set out in the Hours of Work and Rest Law also befits the values of the State of Israel as a democratic state. The social need to ensure hours of a weekly rest for the worker, as well as dictating a uniform day for all the workers in the economy in order to allow joint family activity, befits the values of the State of Israel in a democratic state. So does the choice of the hours of rest against a background of national-religious considerations, with the Sabbath chosen for Jews and Friday or Sunday for non-Jews.

The *third* requirement of the limitation clause is that the infringement on the freedom of occupation should be made in a law "that is intended for a proper purpose." ... What is the purpose of the Hours of Work and Rest Law with regard to the weekly rest, and is its purpose a proper one?

There are two purposes that underlie the arrangements concerning the hours of weekly rest in the Hours of Work and Rest Law, and these complement one another. One purpose is a social purpose, which is concerned with the welfare of the worker and gives him

---

15. Chaim Nachman Bialik, 1873–1934, was born in Russia and moved to Germany and then to Tel Aviv. He wrote poetry and prose in Hebrew, one of the first modern writers to work in that language. He was a prominent literary figure in the pre-state era and had a strong influence on modern Israeli literature. Many Israeli cities and towns have streets named after him.

16. Ahad HaAm (meaning *one of the people*) was the pen name for Asher Tzvi Hersh Ginzburg, 1856–1927. He was born in Russia and lived most of his life there, moving to London and then, late in his life, to Tel Aviv. He was a major thinker of the early cultural Zionist movement and a promoter of the use of the Hebrew language. Many Israeli cities and towns also have streets named Ahad HaAm.

17. Jewish liturgy typically refers to the Sabbath as a queen.

social protection. The law seeks to realize the social purpose involved in ensuring the health and welfare of workers, by preventing them from working to an extent that leads to exhaustion or by requiring rest periods. This day of rest was determined on a uniform basis for the whole economy, thereby promoting the social value whereby the members of the family have the day of rest at the same time. The *second* purpose is a national-religious purpose, which regards the observance of the Sabbath by Jews as a realization of one of the most important values in Judaism that has a national character. In a similar spirit, designating other days of rest for persons who are not Jewish respects their religious outlook. These two purposes have been discussed by the Court on several occasions. Thus, for example, it was held by Chief Justice S. Agranat that the reason underlying the weekly rest arrangement in the Hours of Work and Rest Law is

> the social value involved in ensuring the health and welfare of employees.... It is also clear that it is not a coincidence ... that the "weekly rest" includes, for a Jew, specifically the Sabbath, something that shows that the issue of Sabbath observance was regarded ... as a national treasure of the Jewish people that should be protected in the State of Israel, and also in view, in the words of Justice Berinson, "of the religious feelings, which are held by large sectors of the public" for whom the social value inherent in the legislator's prohibition against employing Jews on the Sabbath is also sacred as a religious value.

In a similar vein Justice M. Elon said that the arrangement concerning the prohibition of employing persons and working on the Sabbath "is based on a whole range of national-religious, social and welfare considerations." The same approach was confirmed by Chief Justice M. Shamgar:

> In determining the principle of having a weekly day of rest and fixing it on the Sabbath the legislator sought to realize two interrelated purposes: first, a social purpose, under which a weekly day of rest should be given to every person so that he can rest from his work, be with his family or with friends and devote time to leisure and recreation according to his choice and preference. The determination of the day of rest is also intended to protect the health of the employee and guarantee him decent work conditions. Second, fixing the day of rest on the Sabbath was done against the background of dictates of Jewish law and Jewish tradition.

Do the two interrelated purposes—the social purpose and the religious purpose—combine to form a "proper purpose"? My answer to this is yes. Guaranteeing a day of rest for the employee and employer, determining a uniform day of rest for the whole economy, in a manner that guarantees the welfare of the family, and fixing this day of rest on a national-religious basis (for a Jew, the Sabbath; for someone who is not Jewish, Friday, Saturday or Sunday, depending on which is the person's habitual day of rest), constitutes a "proper purpose" within the meaning of this expression in the limitation clause. The social purpose serves important public purposes. It is intended to protect the individual (the employee and the employer) and it is intended to guarantee the welfare of the whole family, while also ensuring equality between the religiously observant person and someone who is not religiously observant. I discussed this in one case, where I said:

> The national-religious purpose is also a proper one. It is mindful of the feelings of the religious public in Israel. It gives expression to the national ties that bind us together as one people. It reflects the tradition and customs in Mandatory Palestine and in Israel. Indeed, in many democratic countries there are laws that establish a weekly day of rest in the economy, and as a rule they provide a uniform day that is consistent with the most common religious outlook in that

country (Sunday). See *R. v. Edwards Books and Art* [1986] 2 S.C.R. 713 (Can.); *McGowan v. Maryland* 366 U.S. 420 (1961).

The Petitioners argue that they accept that an employee must be assured of a weekly rest. Notwithstanding, they ask that the hours of rest should be flexible. The meaning of this is that every employer or employee may choose the hours of weekly rest that are convenient for them. According to the Petitioners, the choice that requires uniform hours of rest for all Jews involves an improper purpose. I cannot accept this approach. Determining uniform hours of rest for the whole economy is a social-national interest. It makes it possible to take advantage of the rest and to incorporate it in the welfare of the employee and his family. This was discussed by Chief Justice Dickson of the Supreme Court of Canada in a judgment that considered the constitutionality of laws that required businesses to close on Sunday. Chief Justice Dickson wrote: "I regard as self-evident the desirability of enabling parents to have regular days off from work in common with their child's day off from school, and with a day off enjoyed by most other family and community members." *R. v. Edwards Books and Art*, at p. 770.

Admittedly in determining uniform hours of rest on the Sabbath for Jews, there is an infringement of the freedom of occupation of the employer and the employee. This infringement serves an important social purpose, and therefore it is a "proper purpose" within the context of the limitation clause.

It may be argued that even if it is proper to determine uniform hours of rest, it is not proper to dictate for Jews that this must be on the Sabbath. This involves religious coercion for those who wish to employ persons or work on the Sabbath. This religious coercion is undesirable, and its realization leads to the result that the purpose underlying the Hours of Work and Rest Law is improper. I cannot accept this argument. It has been rejected both in the United States and in Canada. Once we have determined that social considerations rule out a flexible determination of the hours of the weekly rest and justify fixing a day of the week on which the weekly rest can be realized, the fixing of the Sabbath for Jews as the day of weekly rest does not involve religious coercion. The coercion is in the very obligation to have the hours of the weekly rest on the day that the law determines, and not according to the wishes of the individual employer or the employee. The fact that the day chosen to realize this obligation coincides with the Jewish outlook on the Sabbath does not make the coercion religious. This was discussed by Chief Justice Dickson in *R. v. Edwards Books and Art*, where he said:

> Religious freedom is inevitably abridged by legislation which has the effect of impeding conduct integral to the practice of a person's religion. But it is not necessarily impaired by legislation which requires conduct consistent with the religious beliefs of another person. One is not being compelled to engage in religious practices merely because a statutory obligation coincides with the dictates of a particular religion.... Legislation with a secular inspiration does not abridge the freedom from conformity to religious dogma merely because statutory provisions coincide with the tenets of a religion. *R. v. Edwards Books and Art*, at 760–61.

Indeed, fixing the hours of the weekly rest on the Sabbath does not involve religious coercion; it is an expression of the values of the State of Israel as a Jewish state. Moreover the case before us concerns the prohibition of working on the Sabbath. The law prohibits work not only on the Sabbath but also on additional days of rest which are mainly religious holidays. Even in the context of a prohibition of working on religious holidays we should reject an argument that we are speaking of a prohibition that involves religious coercion.

The *fourth* condition for the constitutionality of a law that infringes on the freedom of occupation is that the infringement must be "to an extent that is not excessive." This is a requirement of proportionality. If "the proper purpose" focuses on the purpose of the law that infringes on the freedom of occupation, proportionality focuses on the measures that the law prescribed to achieve the desired purpose. These measures must be proportionate.... According to the accepted approach, the requirement of proportionality is satisfied when the law passes three subtests. We shall discuss these briefly.

The first subtest of proportionality is the suitability test. This test requires that the provisions in the law (the means) are suited to the realization of the proper purpose (the end).... The second subtest of proportionality is the least harmful measure test or the necessity test. The measure chosen by the law should harm the human right to the smallest possible degree.... The third subtest provides that the measure that was adopted by the law and that violates the human right must be proportionate to the purpose.... Within the framework of this subtest "the benefit accruing to the public from the legislation under discussion is weighed against the violation to the constitutional right of the individual as a result of adopting the measure chosen."

Do the provisions of the Hours of Work and Rest Law in so far as they concern the weekly rest period satisfy the proportionality tests? My answer is yes. The first proportionality test (the rational connection test) is satisfied. There is a rational connection between the realization of the purposes underlying the Hours of Work and Rest Law and prescribing a prohibition of employing a worker on the day of weekly rest. The second subtest (the least harmful measure test) is also satisfied in the case before us. A choice of flexible hours of rest would not have realized the purpose of the law. Fixed hours of rest are required. The legislature's choice of the Sabbath for Jews and Sunday and Friday for non-Jews is consistent with the requirements of proportionality. In this respect it should be recalled that an integral part of the Hours of Work and Rest Law are the provisions on those workers who are exempt from the law, such as policemen, civil servants whose jobs require them to be at the state's disposal even outside ordinary working hours, sailors and aircraft personnel. We should also take into account the matters in which the law gives the minister of labor discretion to give permits that allow work during the hours of rest. By virtue of this power, permits have been given to sectors such as hotels, security services, the various emergency services, etc. We should also take into account provisions in various laws, such as the Municipalities Ordinance (New Version), which authorize a municipality to regulate the opening and closing of various businesses, including cinemas, restaurants, theatres and cultural institutions within its municipal boundaries or a part thereof. The third subtest is also satisfied in this case. The law advanced an important social interest, and the infringement on the freedom of occupation is limited.... Since the three subtests are satisfied, the requirement that the infringement on the freedom of occupation is not excessive is satisfied.

In summary, we accept that the Hours of Work and Rest Law, in so far as it concerns the hours of the weekly rest, violates the freedom of occupation of the employer and the workers. This violation does not lead to the unconstitutionality of the law. This is because it satisfies the conditions of the limitation clause. It befits the values of the State of Israel as a Jewish and democratic state. It was enacted for a proper purpose—a social purpose that is achieved by means of realizing a national-religious consideration. The violation of the freedom of occupation is not excessive. It therefore follows that the constitutional argument of the Petitioners should be rejected.

The result is that the petition is denied.

Comment

It is clear that the laws discussed in both *Solodkin* and in *Design 22* reflect the fact that Israel is a Jewish state. But for Israel's being a Jewish state, there would not be laws banning the sale of pork or making the Jewish Sabbath the day of rest. Both cases involved questions of the validity of laws that reflect Jewish practice. In both cases, the Court defined the practices as cultural or traditional or national, and not only as religious. The cases see the Jewish people as sharing a culture and traditions that are derived from the religion of the Jewish people, but are not limited to the religiously observant. Both cases allow coercive laws that are based on Jewish practice where that practice has a strong cultural or traditional element. Although the cases do not say so, it seems much less likely that the Supreme Court would allow coercive practices where the practice had not become absorbed into Jewish culture or non-religious tradition.

In both cases, the main question is how far Israel can go in legislating practices that are religious but also cultural or traditional. The problem in both cases is that people who do not want to observe the practices are forced to do so, or at least inconvenienced by the civil legislation. In *Solodkin*, people who wanted to buy pork in areas where the sale is prohibited had to go to other places to buy pork. People who wanted to sell pork in certain locations were prohibited from doing so. In *Design 22*, an employer who wanted keep his stores open on the Jewish Sabbath could not do so. Jewish employees who want to work on the Jewish Sabbath cannot do so. This statutory coercion, the Court says, is a violation of a basic right, the freedom of occupation or freedom from religion, but that violation is permissible because the coercive laws meet the requirements of the limitation clause.

In *Design 22*, as in *Solodkin*, the main objection was raised by non-observant Jews. The weekly day of rest statute accommodates non-Jews who wish to have another day off: Fridays for Muslims and Sunday for Christians. Certainly in some cases a Christian family living in a Jewish neighborhood with mostly observant Jews, where the sale of pork can be banned under the *Solodkin* rule, will be adversely affected by the ban. Similarly a Muslim who works for a Jewish employer and who takes Friday off may be disadvantaged if the employer closes the business on Saturday, the Muslim is paid hourly, and the employee must work longer days during the week to make up for the lost work time. But for the most part, these problems are more theoretical than actual. For example, some Muslims work on Friday, taking time off only for mandatory prayers. The religious prohibition on Muslims working on Friday is generally understood to apply to work that interferes with prayers and not to be as broad as the Jewish religious prohibition on all work on the Sabbath. Furthermore, many work places are closed on Friday anyway. In any case, most of the legal petitions opposing Jewish religious practice laws are brought by Jews.

In the *Design 22* case, the Court refers obliquely to the fact that the law also solves a problem of equality for religiously observant Jews. Arguably one aspect of a Jewish state, although one to which the Court does not expressly relate, is that it is a state that allows observant Jews to have the same opportunities as others. For observant Jews living in other countries, the need to coordinate religious observance with the demands of work and school creates recurring problems. In a Jewish state, these problems are largely eliminated. It is easy for Jews who observe the Jewish laws that prohibit work on the Sabbath to find employment in a country where most workplaces are closed on the Sabbath. The concern is that if workplaces were to remain open on the Sabbath, employers would favor employers who would work on that day, and observant Jews would have a harder time finding employment.

Besides looking at what Jewish-based kinds of laws are allowed in Israel because it is a Jewish state, there are a few cases indicating what kind of Jewish-based laws are not allowed. *Solodkin* rules that a complete ban on the sale of pork is not allowed. In another case, the Court ruled that a governmental agency could not block the flow of traffic on a main artery for the entire day on the Sabbath, even though the traffic was disturbing to the predominantly Ultra-Orthodox population of the neighborhood. HCJ 5016/96 *Horev v. Minister of Transportation* 51(4) PD 1 [1997].[18] The Ultra-Orthodox Jews, who follow the prohibition on driving or riding in vehicles on the Sabbath, objected to vehicular traffic in their neighborhood on that day. In light of the interference with Jewish religious sensibilities, it would be permissible to block traffic during the times of prayers, but more than that was too great an interference with the rights of others. In another case, the Court rejected the argument that Israel's nature as a Jewish state would allow establishment of exclusively Jewish communities. HCJ 6698/95 *Ka'adan v. Israel Land Administration* 54(1) PD 258 [2000].[19] The Court ruled that equality, not Jewish exclusivity, was a Jewish value.

In the United States, abortion and same-sex marriage are important legal issues seen as related to religion. The abortion issue is not prominent on the Israeli political agenda. Jewish law does not absolutely prohibit abortion. Israeli law allows abortions after approval by a committee, and approvals are fairly freely given. Israel does not allow same-sex marriage. As described in the previous chapter, all marriage is in the hands of the various recognized religious communities, and none of them allow same-sex marriage. On the other hand, two same-sex Israelis who marry abroad in a country where such a ceremony is legal are registered as married in Israel's population registry. HCJ 3045/05 *Ben-Ari v. Director of Population Administration* 61(3) PD 537 [2006].[20] The requirement to recognize the marriage, discussed further in the next chapter, is based not on religious law, but rather on Israeli civil law relating to the functioning of the population registry.

Question

4. Israel is considering a law that would establish Sunday, as well as Saturday, as an official day of rest. The official work week, which is now 45 hours (Israel counts lunch time as part of the work day), would be left in place. Friday, when many but not all businesses are closed, would become a short work day, and hours would be added to the work day on Monday through Thursday. The justifications for the proposed change are that it would make the Israeli calendar more like that of other countries of the western world and that it would provide all Israelis, including observant Jews and Muslims, a common day for family recreational activities. If a Jew challenged the law on the grounds that the change made preparation for Sabbath observance more difficult because of the requirement to work part of the day, would the challenge succeed? Those objecting to the law point out that observant Jews typically spend at least part of Friday shopping and cooking for traditional large Sabbath meals. This would become much more difficult if Friday were a work day, especially in winter when the Sabbath begins as early as 4 pm. Furthermore, it is the custom of a large part of the

---

18. *Available in English at* http://elyon1.court.gov.il/files_eng/96/160/050/A01/96050160.a01.htm.
19. *Available in English at* http://elyon1.court.gov.il/files_eng/95/980/066/a14/95066980.a14.htm.
20. *Available in English at* http://elyon1.court.gov.il/files_eng/05/450/030/a09/05030450.a09.htm.

Jewish population to gather for family meals on the Friday night, and common for family members from different parts of the country to have the meal together. If a Muslim challenged the law on the grounds that it made the requirement to participate in communal prayer at mid-day on Friday more difficult, would the challenge succeed?

B. Laws Giving Special Status to Jews

Israeli Statute

Law of Return, 5710-1950

1. Right of Aliyah[21]

Every Jew has the right to come to this country as an oleh.[22]

2. Oleh's Visa

(a) Aliyah shall be by an oleh's visa.

(b) An oleh's visa shall be granted to every Jew who desires to settle in Israel, unless the minister of immigration is satisfied that the applicant

(1) is engaged in an activity against the Jewish people; or

(2) is likely to endanger the public health or security of the state; or

(3) is a person with a criminal past, likely to endanger public welfare.

3. Oleh Certificate

(a) A Jew who has come to Israel and subsequent to his arrival has expressed his desire to settle in Israel may, while still in Israel, receive an oleh certificate.

(b) The restrictions specified in section 2(b) shall apply also to the grant of an oleh's certificate, but a person shall not be regarded as endangering public health on account of an illness contracted after his arrival in Israel.

4. Residents and Persons Born in this Country

Every Jew who has immigrated into this country before the coming into force of this law, and every Jew who was born in this country, whether before or after the coming into force of this law, shall be deemed to be a person who has come to this country as an oleh under this law.

4A. Rights of Family Members

(a) The rights of a Jew under this law and the rights of an oleh under the Citizenship Law, 5712-1952, as well as the rights of an oleh under any other enactment, are also vested in a child and a grandchild of a Jew, the spouse of a Jew, the spouse of a child of a Jew and the spouse of a grandchild of a Jew, except for a person who has been a Jew and has voluntarily changed his religion.

(b) It shall be immaterial whether or not a Jew through whom a right under subsection (a) is claimed is still alive and whether or not he has immigrated to Israel.

---

21. Aliyah means the return of Jews to live in the historic Jewish homeland. In modern times, it means immigration of Jews to Israel.

22. An oleh is a person who returns by making aliyah. In modern terms, it is a Jew who immigrates to Israel.

(c) The restrictions and conditions prescribed in respect of a Jew or an oleh by or under this law or by the enactments referred to in subsection (a) shall also apply to a person who claims a right under subsection (a).

4B. Definition

For the purposes of this law, "Jew" means a person who was born of a Jewish mother or has become converted to Judaism and who is not a member of another religion.

5. Implementation and Regulations

The minister of immigration is charged with the implementation of this law and may promulgate regulations as to any matter relating to such implementation and also as to the grant of oleh's visas and oleh certificates to minors up to the age of 18 years. Regulations for the purposes of sections 4A and 4B require the approval of the Constitution, Legislation and Juridical Committee of the Knesset.

Israeli Statute

Citizenship Law, 5712-1952

2. Citizenship through Return

(a) Every oleh under the Law of Return, 5710-1950, shall be an Israeli citizen through return, except if he acquired Israeli citizenship through birth … or through adoption.

(b) Citizenship through return shall be acquired

(1) by a person who made aliyah to the country or was born in the country before establishment of the state, beginning upon the day of establishment of the state;

(2) by a person who made aliyah to Israel after establishment of the state, beginning on the day on which the person made aliyah;

(3) by a person born in Israel after establishment of the state, beginning on the day of the person's birth;

(4) by a person who received an oleh certificate under section 3 of the Law of Return, 5710-1950, beginning on the day of grant of the certificate.

5. Naturalization

(a) An adult who is not an Israeli citizen may receive Israeli citizenship by naturalization if the following conditions are met:

(1) The person is present in Israel;

(2) The person was in Israel three out of the five years prior to submitting the request to become a citizen;

(3) The person is entitled to remain permanently in Israel;

(4) The person has settled in Israel or intends to do so;

(5) The person has some knowledge of Hebrew;

(6) The person has given up his previous citizenship or has proven that such citizenship shall cease upon his becoming an Israeli citizen.

(b) If a person has applied for naturalization and all the conditions of subsection (a) are met, the minister of interior shall, if he deems it appropriate to do so, grant the person Israeli citizenship by providing a certificate of citizenship.

(c) Before the granting of citizenship, the candidate shall declare: "I declare that I shall be a loyal citizen of the State of Israel."

7. Naturalization of a Husband and Wife

If either a husband or wife is an Israeli citizen or has applied for naturalization and meets the conditions of section 5(a)..., the other can obtain Israeli citizenship through naturalization even if that person does not meet the conditions of section 5(a).

Comment

These two laws specify that it is much easier for a Jew from outside of Israel to acquire Israeli citizenship than for anyone else from outside of the country. A Jew becomes a citizen by virtue of *return*. All this requires is that the person show up in Israel and meet four conditions: the person must not have engaged in an activity against the Jewish people, must not be a danger to public health, must not be a danger to state security, and must not have the type of criminal past that is likely to endanger public welfare. Such a person gets an oleh visa or oleh certificate under section 2 or 3 of the Law of Return and citizenship under section 2 of the Naturalization Law.

Everyone else not from Israel acquires citizenship only through *naturalization*. The person has to enter the country under some sort of valid visa and meet the more difficult requirements of section 5 of the Naturalization Law. In fact, obtaining a visa that will allow the process to begin is very difficult. Furthermore, citizenship is not automatic, but is granted at the discretion of the minister of interior. Spouses of Israelis can become citizens more easily through naturalization, but another law, Naturalization and Entry into Israel Law (Temporary Provision), 5763-2003, limits even that option if the spouse is from the territories or from Iran, Iraq, Lebanon and Syria. This law was held to be constitutional by a six to five decision of eleven justices of the Supreme Court. HCJ 466/07 *Gal-on v. Attorney General* (Jan. 11, 2012). The majority found that while there was a constitutional right to family life, in cases in which only one spouse was Israeli, the right does not have to be realized within the borders of the state. The majority also recognized that Israeli Arabs are more likely to be affected by the law because they are more likely to marry spouses from the covered areas. Nonetheless the majority found that, to the extent that the law impinges on constitutional rights or the right to equal treatment of all Israelis, that impingement is justified by the security considerations that lay behind the law. The prohibition is on entry of spouses from areas with whom Israel is in a formal state of war or from which terrorist attacks have been launched on Israel. Notably, entry of spouses from Egypt and Jordan, with whom Israel has signed peace treaties, are not specifically limited.

Israel is not the only country that makes citizenship easier for those identified with the majority people of the country. Germany has a law of return for certain people of "German ethnic origin" but more strictly limits naturalization for others.[23] Greece gives

---

23. GRUNDGESETZ FUR DIE BUNDESREPUBLIK DEUTSCHLAND [Grundgesetz][GG] [Basic Law] art. 116 (Ger.).

preference to persons of Greek origin.[24] Poland, Ireland, Bulgaria, Russia, and Latvia are among the countries that give similar preferences in obtaining citizenship.[25]

Section 4A(a) of the Israeli Law of Return, in conjunction with section 2 of the Citizenship Law, gives the non-Jewish spouse, child and grandchild of a Jew (and their spouses) the same rights as a Jew to obtain citizenship by return.[26] It is under this provision that many non-Jews from the former Soviet Union entered Israel. The Jewish population of the areas included within the former Soviet Union was large, and during the communist era intermarriage of Jews was common. When emigration became possible, many descendants of Jews left for Israel.

The provision in the same section disallowing return by a Jew who has voluntarily changed their religion has an interesting history. The provision was not added to the law until 1970. Oswald Rufeisen had been born a Jew in 1922 in Poland and had been persecuted by the Nazis. During World War II he converted to Christianity and became known as Brother Daniel. He moved to Israel and applied for citizenship, claiming rights under the Law of Return. The minister of interior refused to grant him citizenship on this basis, and in HCJ 72/62 *Rufeisen v. Minister of Interior* 16(1) PD 2428 [1962] the Supreme Court upheld the decision. Under Jewish law, a person born a Jew remains a Jew no matter what the person does. Therefore according to Jewish law, Brother Daniel was still a Jew. The Court held that Israeli law, not Jewish law, applies. Applying the usual rules of statutory interpretation, the Court based its decision on the finding that a person who had converted to Christianity is not under the common understanding a Jew. The 1970 amendment wrote this holding explicitly into the statute.

The definition of the term *Jew* in section 4B of the Law of Return has been extremely controversial. Traditional Jewish law defines as Jewish a person born of a Jewish mother or a person who has undergone a valid conversion.[27] As originally enacted, the Law of Return did not define the term Jew, the Knesset having rejected a bid by some religious parties to define the term as it is defined under traditional Jewish law. A case came before the Supreme Court under a different law, regarding registration of the nationality of children on Israeli identity cards. For the purposes of these cards, the term *Jewish* was considered a term of nationality, not religion. The children were born to a Jewish Israeli father and a non-Jewish mother. The governmental ministry in charge of national identity cards refused to register the children as Jewish. The Supreme Court held that the ministry was not to use the Jewish law definition but rather a social and cultural definition. Therefore the children, who were raised as Jewish Israelis, were to be registered as Jewish. HCJ 58/68 *Shalit v. Minister of Interior* 23(2) PD 477 [1969]. The Knesset showed its dissatisfaction with this result by amending the Law of Return, adding the definition in section 4B that adopts the rule of matrilineal descent.

---

24. Kodikas Ellenikes Ithageneias [K.E.I.] [Code of Greek Citizenship] 15 (Greece), *available at* http://www.greekembassy.org/embassy/content/en/Article.aspx?office=11&folder=919&article=20574.

25. *See* Steven Menashi, *Ethnonationalism and Liberal Democracy*, 32 U. Pa. J. Int'l L. 57, 74–78 (2010).

26. In June, 2011, it was reported that the minister of interior refused to accept as an oleh the same-sex spouse of a Jewish immigrant. Ilan Lior, *Israel Refuses Citizenship for Gay Man Married to Jewish Immigrant*, Haaretz, June 28, 2011, *available at* http://www.haaretz.com/print-edition/news/israel-refuses-citizenship-for-gay-man-married-to-jewish-immigrant-1.369936. It is likely that if the minister's decision is challenged in court, the refusal will be found to be illegal.

27. The Reform Movement has adopted a different definition.

The question of what type of conversion qualifies is valid under the same provision has also been controversial. The issue arises when a convert without a Jewish spouse, parent, or grandparent wishes to enter Israel through the Law of Return. Different streams of Judaism have different rules on what is required for conversion. Generally, conversion requires more than just a declaration that a person wants to be a Jew or a declaration of faith. The Supreme Court has interpreted the "has become converted to Judaism" language in section 4B to mean that the person has been converted by a recognized Jewish community outside of Israel. HC 2597/99 *Thais-Rodriguez Tushbaim v. Minister of Interior* (March 31, 2005).[28]

The statutory requirement in section 4B of the Law of Return that, for purposes of that statute, a person is Jewish by birth only if born of a Jewish mother imports Jewish law into Israeli law. Not only that, but it imports the traditional Jewish law, under which a person is Jewish by birth only if born of a Jewish mother. This is the view accepted by both Orthodox and Conservative Jewish communities in the United States. The statute does not accept the view adopted by the Reform Movement, that a person can be Jewish by birth if the father is Jewish. (The Reform Movement did not officially adopt this view until after section 4B was inserted into the Israeli statute.) In other words, section 4B reveals two distinguishable controversies. The first is whether Jewish law should control Israeli law. The second is, where Jewish law does control, which version of Jewish law should be adopted. In section 4B, Jewish law controls, and it is the traditional view of Jewish law which is adopted.

Usually the second of these two controversies is more problematic for those in the American Jewish community, where the Conservative and Reform movements are strong. In Israel, where they are not strong, the first question is often seen as more essential. Many Israeli Jews are not affiliated with any type of synagogue, but have a sense of what it is to be Jewish, and want this sense to be incorporated into the law and not any religious law sense. Furthermore, the second controversy tends to be framed differently for Americans and for Israelis. Americans see it as a dispute between the Orthodox, Conservative, and Reform movements. Israelis are more likely to see it as a dispute between Ultra-Orthodox and national religious views of Jewish law. The Conservative and Reform movements, which are large in the United States, are small in Israel. As a result, they have minimal influence on the Israeli view of what Jewish law requires.

The dispute over what constitutes a valid conversion under the Law of Return reveals similar controversies, although with a different outcome. The Supreme Court interpretation of what type of conversion is valid accepts that Jewish law applies. In requiring that a person must have been converted by a recognized Jewish community, it rejects the idea that people can simply declare themselves to be Jews. It recognizes that some sort of legal process is required. On the other hand, as to the second controversy, it gives force to any version of Jewish law. Conversion by any recognized Jewish community is sufficient to give a person rights under the Law of Return.

In summary, the main importance of the Law of Return, as it works together with the Citizenship Law, is that it gives a clear preference to Jews and their relatives in obtaining Israeli citizenship. This is an expression of Israel's nature as a Jewish state, again relating to Jews as a people or a nation and not just as members of a religion. The concept of return rests on viewing Jews as a people entitled to return to their historic homeland. On the question of who is Jewish, the law takes different approaches. The requirement that

---

28. *Available in English at* http://elyon1.court.gov.il/files_eng/99/970/025/a29/99025970.a29.htm.

a Jew not be a member of another religion is based on common understanding and not on Jewish law. In this way, the requirement is consistent with the approach of the Court in the various cases, examined in Part A of this chapter, that define the meaning of a Jewish state. The requirement that a person who is a Jew by birth be born of a Jewish mother is based on Jewish law, and specifically on the traditional view of Jewish law. The requirement that a person who is a Jew by conversion is one who has been converted by any recognized Jewish community is also based on Jewish law, but accepts any of the multiple views of what Jewish law requires.

C. Laws Facilitating Observance of Religious Law

Israel has a series of laws designed to facilitate observance of Jewish religious law. These laws do not adopt Jewish law as state law, but assist those who want to observe Jewish law to do so. For example, the state provides government religious schools that teach Jewish religious studies along with the usual general curriculum[29] and religious councils that provide religious services such as supervision of food establishments that comply with Jewish dietary laws.[30] While no one is forced to use the government religious schools (non-religious government schools are also state-funded) or the religious services provided by the state, the availability makes religious observance easier. Similarly the law provides that all Jewish soldiers serving in the army will be provided with food that meets Jewish dietary laws.[31] All of these laws have budgetary implications. Israel, as a Jewish state, spends funds on making Jewish religious services available.

Israel does not have the kind of separation of religion and state found in the United States. Of course, it could be argued that the separation is not complete in the United States. Even the use of the term *separation of church and state* indicates a degree of recognition of those religions that have churches. The term *church and state* would not be used, for example, in Israel, where neither of the major religions is associated with churches. More substantially, the nearly complete closure of public services in the United States on Christmas is not devoid of religious overtones.

Nonetheless it is incontrovertible that Israel has less separation between religion and state than does the United States. In some cases, Israel provides religious services or facilitates religious observance by members of all religions. To a large measure, though, state law is designed to facilitate Jewish religious observance. Laws of this sort raise the question of how the state will define the Jewish religious observance that it will facilitate. When the state enacts laws that aid in Jewish religious observance, it must determine whose version of religious observance it will support. The next case deals with this issue. The case after it deals with the problem of unequal funding for Jewish and for non-Jewish religious activities. The third case is on the degree to which non-Jews can be subject to harm from laws facilitating Jewish religious observance.

As indicated previously, one way in which Israel facilitates observance of Jewish law is by providing a system of supervision of compliance with Jewish dietary laws at food es-

---

29. State Education Law, 5713-1953.
30. The Religious Services for Jews Law, 5731-1971.
31. Kosher Food for Soldiers Ordinance, 5708-1948. This statute was enacted by the Provisional Council of State in 1948. It is one of the first laws enacted after establishment of the state.

tablishments. Many Jews in Israel observe the Jewish dietary laws. This includes some who classify themselves as secular; i.e., non-religious. Jewish dietary laws govern what food may be eaten, what foods may be eaten together, and how food must be prepared. Food that complies with the Jewish dietary laws is called *kosher* food. The Jewish dietary laws are referred to as the laws of *kashruth*. The state has set up a system of kashruth certificates. A market, restaurant, or other establishment selling or providing food may apply for a certificate. The facility is inspected and, if found to observe the dietary laws, gets a kashruth certificate and is placed under continuing supervision. No law requires private facilities to have such certificates.

Israeli Statute

Law Prohibiting Fraud as to Kosher Food, 5743-1983

2. Authorization to Grant a Certificate of Kashruth

(a) The following are authorized to grant a certificate of kashruth for the purposes of this law:

(1) The Chief Rabbinical Council of Israel or a rabbi authorized for that purpose by the Chief Rabbinical Council;

(2) A local rabbi who serves in the place in which the food establishment is located.

(b) For the purposes of this section

"Local rabbi" means someone with a written certification from the Chief Rabbinical Council of Israel and who serves as a city rabbi, a local council rabbi, the rabbi of a moshav, or the rabbi of a kibbutz.

3. Prohibition on Fraud at a Food Establishment

(a) The owner of a food establishment shall not represent in writing that the establishment is kosher unless it has a certificate of kashruth.

(b) The owner of a food establishment who has a certificate of kashruth ... shall not serve or sell food that is not kosher under Jewish law.

5. Prohibition on Fraud in Sales

A person who sells foodstuffs to the public shall neither sell nor offer for sale any foodstuff that is not kosher under Jewish law while representing in writing that it is kosher.

11. Limitations on Matters to be Considered

In granting a certificate of kashruth, a rabbi shall consider only the laws on kosher food.

Comment

Under section 1 of this statute, the system of supervision is administered either by a rabbi serving as the official rabbi in the area of a local government, moshav, or kibbutz, or by another rabbi authorized by the Chief Rabbinical Council. The Chief Rabbinical Council is a body comprising sixteen rabbis selected as set out in the Law on the Office of Chief Rabbi of Israel, 5740-1980. The selection process involves religious, governmental, and public representatives.

An establishment, such as a restaurant, bakery, catering hall, or institutional dining hall, with a kashruth certificate may sell only kosher food. The certificate is usually displayed near the entrance. A Jew observing the dietary laws will usually patronize only those establishments displaying a kashruth certificate. The certificate provides assurance that it is possible to eat anything sold in the establishment.[32]

Although the statute is labeled an anti-fraud law, and anti-fraud laws are common in many countries, the specific nature of this anti-fraud law makes it a particular creation of a Jewish state. In the United States, the state of New York also had a series of laws addressing fraud in the kosher food industry, but the Second Circuit struck them down as unconstitutional. The court held that the laws violated the Establishment Clause of the First Amendment because they advanced and inhibited religion and because they lead to an excessive entanglement of the state with religion. The laws required compliance with Orthodox Jewish dietary rules. Because other Jewish groups followed somewhat different rules, the court held that the laws advanced Orthodox Judaism and inhibited non-Orthodox Judaism. The entanglement was found in the fact that the laws

> (1) take sides in a religious matter, effectively discriminating in favor of the Orthodox Hebrew view of dietary requirements; (2) require the State to take an official position on religious doctrine; and (3) create an impermissible fusion of governmental and religious functions by delegating civic authority to individuals apparently chosen according to religious criteria. (*Commack Self-Service Kosher Meats, Inc. v. Weiss*, 294 F.3d 415 (2d Cir. 2002)).

Israeli law does not address the issues in the same manner. Israel has no law requiring separation of religion and state, and it is clear from the cases set out earlier in this chapter that its laws may be designed to protect religious sensibilities. On the other hand, legal doctrine does limit the degree to which the law can protect one version of religious practice. Furthermore, the Israeli Supreme Court clearly sees the state as a civil and not religious actor and tries to minimize state advancement of religion and state entanglement in religious disputes. The following case shows how the Supreme Court does this. The case relates to a law facilitating observance of the sabbatical year laws, which are part of Jewish law and arose in reaction to a debate within the Jewish rabbinical establishment over what these laws require. The Petitioner is asking the Court to resolve the debate.

Israeli Case

Asif Ynov Gidolim, Ltd. v.
The Chief Rabbinical Council of Israel

Sabbatical Year Case
HCJ 7120/07 (Oct. 23, 2007)

[Under Jewish law, every seventh year is a *sabbatical year*. The year is calculated according to the Jewish calendar and begins on the Jewish New Year, which usually falls in September. The rules relating to the sabbatical year prohibit cultivating Jewish-owned land in Israel and forbid Jews from eating produce grown by cultivating such land. Some Jewish law authorities permit Jews to sell land they own to non-Jews through a temporary sale. When land is sold in this way, Jews can still cultivate the land and eat the produce. The

---

32. This is different from the situation in the United States where certification of kosher food is done by private organizations.

permission for this temporary sale arrangement is called a *sale permit* (Hebrew: *heter mechira*). Without the sale permit, Jews can eat only produce grown on land in Israel that is permanently owned by non-Jews, produce grown outside of Israel, or certain other produce, available in small amounts, that is grown through another special process but that must also be handled in a particular, and somewhat burdensome, manner. During the sabbatical year, an establishment cannot obtain a kashruth certificate unless it complies with the sabbatical year rules.

For many establishments, maintaining a valid kashruth certificate is essential to their business. Jews who care about the dietary laws make up a large enough percentage of the customers that the profitability would be negatively affected if those Jews would not purchase food there. Similarly many farmers who do not themselves observe Jewish law want to sell their land through a sale permit so that establishments with kashruth certificates will purchase their produce during the sabbatical year.

As the sabbatical year of 2007 approached, many farmers planned to grow produce during the sabbatical year using the sale permit. They planned to sell their fields to a non-Jew under a temporary sale allowed by the sale permit and continue to cultivate the land and sell the produce. Just seven weeks before the beginning of the sabbatical year, some city rabbis ruled that, based on their understanding of Jewish law, the sale permit was no longer acceptable. These rabbis gave notice that they would not give kashruth certificates to establishments selling produce grown on farms that had been sold under a sale permit. (Of course, they also would not give kashruth certificates to establishments selling produce grown on Jewish farms that had not been sold and had been cultivated.) The Chief Rabbinical Council, which had always accepted the sale permit, would not order a local rabbi to give kashruth certificates to stores selling produce raised on land sold through a sale permit because it could not order a local rabbi to act against his interpretation of Jewish law. For the most part, Judaism lacks a central authority for issuing interpretations that everyone must follow. The Chief Rabbinical Council had always gotten around this problem by using its authority under section 2(a)(1) of the Law Prohibiting Fraud as to Kosher Food to appoint an alternative rabbi to function in the area where a city rabbi refused to accept the sale permit. The alternative rabbi carried authority from the Chief Rabbinical Council to issue a kashruth certificate to stores selling produce raised on land covered by a sale permit. The local city rabbi did not have to act against his own conscience, but the use of the alternative rabbi allowed sale of the produce.

In the late summer of 2007, the Chief Rabbinical Council decided to allow only the local city rabbi to decide on whether to issue kashruth certificates within his city. This decision would have a very substantial effect on the existing arrangements. As a result of this decision, establishments in those cities where the local rabbi would not accept produce grown under the sale permit could not purchase produce as they had in the past. They would have to turn mainly to produce grown locally by non-Jews or to produce imported from abroad. Furthermore, Jewish farmers would lose an important share of their markets and their financial stability would be jeopardized.

There is, as might be suspected, a back story to all of this. The more conservative rabbis, largely associated with the Ultra-Orthodox camp, were the ones refusing to accept the *sale permit*. At the same time, the Chief Rabbinical Council had come to be staffed by more rabbis who identified more closely with the Ultra-Orthodox camp. This became very problematical, not only for the stores, restaurants, and farmers, but also for consumers, including the national religious Jews who did not agree with this conservative approach. Interestingly the justice who wrote the main opinion in the *Sabbatical Year Case*, Justice Elyakim Rubinstein, is a national religious Jew.]

Justice E. Rubinstein:

The two petitions before us are on the same matter. It would be better if we did not need to make a decision on this matter, but we shall fulfill our obligation to do so. The sabbatical year has begun. The issue before us is the validity of the decisions of the Chief Rabbinical Council on August 22, 2007 and August 30, 2007 that a local rabbi can determine, based on his own view of the matter, how matters relating to the sabbatical year shall be conducted within his locality. Specifically the matter relates to the possibility of denying a certificate of compliance with the laws of kashruth to agricultural produce grown under a sale permit, as has been done for many years and as is further explained below. The petitions are against both (1) the Chief Rabbinate of Israel,[33] that permitted local rabbis to make such a decision and that has refused to use its parallel or supervisory legal authority to authorize other rabbis willing to accept the sale permit to grant kashruth certificates in localities were the local rabbis refuse to do so, and also against (2) the local rabbis who are refusing to accept the sale permit.

Background

On July 25, 2007, the city rabbi of Herzliya issued a directive to business owners in his city providing that those who wanted a kashruth certificate for the sabbatical year of 5768 [beginning at sundown on September 12, 2007] must obtain their agricultural products from one of four suppliers [who carried products that complied with the rules of the sabbatical year but that were not grown on land sold through a sale permit].

[In reaction to objections to this directive], we are told that on August 22, 2007, the council decided that rabbis would be appointed to sign kashruth certificates in localities where the local rabbi would not do so, but only with the agreement of the local rabbis. We emphasize that we do not have before us the full version of this decision or the minutes of the discussion, if they even exist, which is to us astounding.

Next, suddenly, on August 30, 2007, the Chief Rabbinical Council conducted a telephone survey, in which twelve of its members participated, and decided "that each city rabbi, and only the city rabbi, can decide for his city on the matter of the sabbatical year, according to his own opinion on the matter."

[The city rabbi of Jerusalem made a decision similar to that of the city rabbi of Herzliya.]

On the Sabbatical Year

It goes without saying that the question before us is the validity of the decisions under the rules of administrative law. We do not decide the rules of Jewish law. For this reason, and because we are already in the sabbatical year and the matter is therefore urgent, the rules of Jewish law that are at the basis of this dispute will be reviewed only briefly.

And the Lord spoke to Moses at Mount Sinai saying: Speak to the children of Israel and say to them: When you come into the land which I am giving you, the land shall observe a Sabbath to the Lord. You shall sow your field for six years and for six years you shall prune your vineyard and gather its produce. The seventh year shall be a Sabbath of rest for the land, a Sabbath to the Lord; you shall not sow your field and not prune your vineyard. That which grows on its own

---

33. Justice Rubinstein uses the terms Chief Rabbinical Council and Chief Rabbinate interchangeably. Both refer to the Chief Rabbinical Council.

you shall not harvest and you shall not gather the grapes of untrimmed vines; it shall be a year of rest of the land for the Lord. And produce of the land on the sabbatical year shall be food for you,[34] for your male servant and for your female servant and for your hired worker and for the stranger living among you, for your cattle and for the animals living freely in your land; all the increase of the fields shall be for food. (Leviticus 25:1–7).

From these verses, and from others in the book of Exodus, the sages derived the laws for the period of rest for the land, or the sabbatical year, which is a commandment for the cycle of years that is parallel to the Sabbath day for the weekly cycle.

The Sale Permit

From the time that the Jewish people were exiled from their land, when there was an almost complete absence of Jewish agricultural activity on the land, the matter of the sabbatical year had no operative meaning.... When Jewish communities that lived off of their agricultural endeavors were established in the 1880s ... the question of the sabbatical year first arose in 1882 [the first sabbatical year after establishment of such communities] and again in 1889. The communities, in which a significant portion of the residents were people who observed Jewish law, faced the question of how they could support themselves if they observed the rules of the sabbatical year. Rabbi Yitzhak Elchanan Spector, the rabbi of Kovno, Latvia, the main Jewish law decisor [person who issues rulings on Jewish law] of his generation, saw the matter as one of saving lives and ruled in 1889 that it is possible to use the sale permit "to allow the sale of the fields and the vineyards and the fruits thereof to non-Jews for a period of only two years,[35] and after this time, they would return to the ownership of their prior owners."

[In later years, many other rabbis agreed that Jews in Israel could continue to use the sale permit during sabbatical years, although some rabbis thought this is not allowable.]

Throughout a number of generations, the Chief Rabbinical Council authorized use of the sale permit.... The sale permit was authorized by the Chief Rabbinate on the national level, and not left to the choice of local rabbis. [This is how the matter was handled in 2007, until the city rabbi of Herzliya issued his directive.] After this, on August 30, 2007, suddenly, as the result of a telephone survey, the decision was made, with the agreement of twelve members of the Chief Rabbinical Council, that "each city rabbi, and only the city rabbi, can decide for his city on the matter of the sabbatical year, according to his own opinion on the matter."

Does the New Policy of the Chief Rabbinate Meet the Requirements of Administrative Law?

The first question before us is whether the Chief Rabbinate made the decision not to use its parallel authority [to authorize rabbis other than the city rabbi to grant a kashruth certificate] in a legally permissible manner. It did not. This answer is not given lightly; this Court honors the position of the Chief Rabbinate and does not make decisions in the area of Jewish law. But it cannot be denied that the Chief Rabbinate is an administrative body subject to the rules of administrative law. The decisions of an administrative body must be made through proper procedures and must meet the requirements of reasonableness and proportionality. Certainly the Chief Rabbinate may change its policy, but ... such a substantial change ... must be made after serious consideration and through the

---

34. This refers to produce that grows naturally, without planting or cultivation.
35. The period of two years rather than one has to do with some technical requirements of the sabbatical year that are not discussed here.

proper procedures, and it must be proportional and it must be reasoned. I fear this has not happened here.

The Decision-Making Procedure

The first decision relevant to the change in policy was that made on August 22, 2007, in which it was decided that the Chief Rabbinate would use its parallel authority only with the agreement of the city rabbi. We have no record of the text of this decision and are not sure whether it was recorded in any written form. We also have no knowledge of whether there was any kind of discussion prior to making the decision and, if there was, of who participated and what was said.... The Chief Rabbinate's response to this petition includes an affidavit by Rabbi Rauchberger that asserts that there was a "special session," but we have no documentation of that.

A policy decision, and especially one that changes policy, must be made through proper procedures. It requires a proper factual basis and the use of appropriate procedures for gathering, verifying, and analyzing the facts. In the case before us, we do not know what kind of discussion preceded the decision or whether the facts relating to the expected damage to the agricultural sector and to consumers from the change in policy were brought before the members of the Chief Rabbinical Council. In a decision such as this one, the administrative body must take into account the important considerations that had led to the Chief Rabbinate's position in all prior years and the possible implications of changing the existing policy. It may also be that it is necessary to hear from representatives of those who would be injured by the decision. In this case, it would have been proper to hear from representatives of the agricultural establishment, either from the Ministry of Agriculture and Rural Development or from other relevant organizations, and this was not done.

Another problem is the timing of the decision. An administrative agency can change its policy ... but, as the sabbatical year approached, and the public, including farmers, business owners, consumers, and governmental ministry, operated according to the existing decisions and policy, the authority to make changes diminished.

If an administrative authority's change in policy contradicts prior procedures on which people have relied and decreases the value of investments made before the change in policy, then the reliance interests must be protected and the decision held invalid, even if there is no other problem with the way the decision is made. In the case before us, the Chief Rabbinical Council did not change its mind about the underlying principle of the validity under Jewish law of relying on the sale permit. Even though the change in policy affected only the use of the parallel authority and not the validity of the sale permit itself, it was an invalid decision given that it would have such damaging effects and was made only a few weeks before the start of the sabbatical year.

The second decision relevant to the change in policy was that of August 30, 2007 (about two weeks before the beginning of the sabbatical year). As distinguished from the August 22 decision, the bottom line of this one was documented. The document provided that a city rabbi had exclusive authority within his city on issues related to the sabbatical year and included the names of twelve members of the Chief Rabbinical Council who had approved this decision. In the presentations before this Court, the Respondents desisted from clearly admitting the fact that this was the result of a telephone survey, perhaps because they were not completely comfortable about the matter, but the State's attorney represented that this was the case and no one has denied it. Telephone surveys, although they are not the preferred manner of decision-making, are also used by other bodies, including the Government. But this is generally done for technical or semi-technical issues. The case before us involves a decision on a clearly substantive issue.

For all the years of operation of the Chief Rabbinate, more than eighty years, and even before that, during the operation of other rabbinical institutions, beginning in the 1880s, altogether for more than one hundred and twenty years, the decision has been to accept the sale permit. This has been the consistent decision, not one made at the last minute. This was also clearly the direction in which various decisions made during the year 2007 were headed, up until the decision of August 30, 2007. Then, suddenly, for unexplained reasons, a change was made to allow a city rabbi control over matters relating to the sabbatical year within his city.... Why? ... We have been told in oral argument of the case that there was a discussion before the decision was made. What were the claims against the existing policy, how was the discussion conducted, who took part, what opinions were expressed and was a record made of the discussion? What were the opinions of the Chief Sephardic Rabbi and of the rabbis of the large cities of Haifa and Beer Sheva [who are members of the Chief Rabbinical Council and were willing to accept the sales permit in their own localities]? ... Did they decide not to participate or did they express any opinion? We asked this question about the Chief Sephardic Rabbi, but did not get an answer. Assuming there was no choice but to make the decision by telephone ... there is no reason this could not have been done in a conference call.

The Substantive Aspect of the Decisions

In examining the decisions themselves, I see two shortcomings: (1) the balancing between opposing considerations was highly inappropriate, and (2) the decision permits determinations related to the sabbatical year to be made on a local basis, although the problem requires a determination on the national level.

Analysis and Balancing of the Opposing Considerations

The Chief Rabbinate changed its policy in order not to impinge on the autonomy of the local city rabbis.... But, against this important interest, it had to weigh the economic, national, and perhaps even constitutional interests of the agricultural sector and of consumers. Other than claiming that the Petitioners' calculations of harm are incorrect, there was no consideration given to the degree of harm to agriculture.... The subject of the sabbatical year is all about agriculture. Even without relations to the constitutional issues such as freedom of occupation ... sensitivity to observance of the commandment of the sabbatical year cannot ignore the needs of agriculture.

The Chief Rabbinate was required to weigh the opposing interests. The decision chosen does not reflect that it did so (nor does the manner in which the decision was made). The prior policy did reflect such a balance and did not harm any interests to a substantial degree.

Local Decision for the National Issue

[Matters related to the sabbatical year have always been determined on the national level.] Could the decision now be made locally and depend on the opinions of the various local rabbis? That is not permissible. A decision to make such a change would require a far more serious and substantive discussion than was presented before us and would have to take into consideration the factors that influenced the Chief Rabbinate over all the years and their implications at the present time. It would require giving a hearing to those in the agricultural sector and in the various ministries who deal with related matters.

Is it appropriate for a matter this important to be decided locally? The answer cannot be affirmative. This is not only because of the unbroken chain of prior decisions, but also for practical reasons. Local decisions will create an impossible level of confusion when, in one city, the use of the sale permit will be forbidden, but on the other side of a street, in another city, which is physically adjacent, the sale permit is accepted.

Conclusion

The decisions of the Chief Rabbinical Council of the dates August 22 and August 30, 2007, are invalid.

The Chief Rabbinate must operate under its prior decisions that in any locality where the chief rabbi will not give a kashruth certificate based on the sale permit, the Chief Rabbinate will use the alternative authority provided to it under statute and will authorize other rabbis to give the certificates.

Comment

The case involved an interpretation of Jewish law. The underlying issue was the same as that underlying matrilineal descent in the Law of Return: whose version of Jewish law shall control? The Chief Rabbinical Council acted in a way that allowed it to avoid handing down a definitive interpretation. Instead, it refused to use its authority in section 2(a)(1) of the Law Prohibiting Fraud as to Kosher Food and allowed city rabbis to give and to enforce their own interpretations of the sabbatical year laws in their own areas. This was different from what the Council had done in previous years. In effect, though, the Chief Rabbinical Council's decision allowed the restrictive interpretation of Jewish law to control in localities where the city rabbi supported this interpretation. The Supreme Court said that its own role was not to interpret Jewish law. Although it hinted that the restrictive interpretation was wrong, it did not include a ruling on the correct interpretation of Jewish law in the holding. Rather, it held that the Council decision was wrong as a matter of administrative law. The Council decision was faulty not for its content, but because it was based on procedural and substantive violations of administrative law rules. The procedural violations were the failure to make a record showing what was considered in reaching the decision; the failure to show that there was a real discussion of issues among Council members; and, perhaps, failure to give a hearing to those in the agricultural and governmental sectors with information on relevant issues. The substantive violations were the failure to consider important economic, national, and perhaps constitutional values that are at stake and the failure to give determinative weight to the need for a uniform national decision on the acceptability of the sale permit. In other words, the Court avoided deciding directly on the proper interpretation of Jewish law but forced the Council to retain the existing, more liberal interpretation. It also protected the interests of those who would be harmed by the restrictive reading.

In discussing whether the Chief Rabbinical Council weighed all the proper values, Justice Rubinstein's opinion suggests that there may be constitutional implications that should have been discussed. Under the principles of constitutional law, if the Council's decision impinged on the freedom of occupation of those who work in the agricultural sector or who sell agricultural products, then the validity of the decision would have to be tested under the limitation clause. It was not necessary to reach the question of constitutionality because the decision was invalidated on administrative law grounds.

The Court is also disturbed by the timing of the decision. By the time the Chief Rabbinical Council came out with its decision, many people had already made plans to comply with the previously-existing rules accepting the sale permit. While Israeli law allows laws that disrupt reasonable reliance interests, it disfavors them.

Questions

5. A bakery applies to the local city rabbi for a certificate of kashruth. It is denied on the grounds that the owner of the bakery is not Jewish and therefore cannot be trusted to maintain the standards of kashruth required by Jewish law. Is the denial legal?

6. The next sabbatical year will be in 2014. Is the Chief Rabbinical Council free to decide that local city rabbis may refuse to issue a kashruth certificate to any establishment that sells produce grown under a sale permit, and to give the local city rabbis the exclusive jurisdiction to decide on the issue within their localities?

Israel does not have the same broad structure of laws designed to facilitate the religious practices of non-Jews. The laws facilitating religious observance of non-Jews are in the areas of marriage, divorce, and other issues of personal status, all of which are considered in the next chapter. In addition, there are a few legal provisions designed not so much to facilitate religious observance of non-Jewish groups as to accommodate such observance. For example, the Population Registry Order (Exemption of Muslim and Druze Women from Providing Photographs) 5714-1954, provides an exception to the law that requires that a person's photograph appear on the official identity card issued to Israeli citizens and residents. These cards are used for proof of identity in both official purposes, such as for tax-related transactions and for voting, and for unofficial purposes, such as in credit transactions. Israelis use their identity numbers and cards in situations in which an American would use a Social Security number or a driver's license. Under the order, which is a regulation issued by the minister of interior, Muslim and Druze women who avoid being photographed "for reasons of religion and tradition" can obtain an identity card without a photograph on it and the card can be used for all purposes for which a regular identity card can be used.

Israel also provides direct funding for religious services. The following case considers the question of the extent to which Israel, as a Jewish state, is obligated to provide financial support for religious services for non-Jews.

Israeli Case

Adalah Legal Center for Arab Minority Rights in Israel v. Minister of Religious Affairs

HCJ 1113/99, 54(2) PD 164 (2000)[36]

[Burials for Israeli citizens and residents in Israel are paid for by the state. For the most part, Jews are buried by Jewish burial societies and Arabs by their Muslim or Christian burial societies. Kibbutzim and moshavim handle their own burials. A new law, discussed in the case, provides for civil, non-religious burials for Jews. In addition, there are a few private cemeteries providing burial for those who pay for their services.]

---

36. The translation is based on that on the website of the Supreme Court at http://elyon1.court.gov.il/files_eng/99/130/011/i13/99011130.i13.htm.

Justice I. Zamir:

The first question ... is whether the Ministry of Religious Affairs is obligated to allocate funds from the Ministry's budget in an equal manner to all segments of the population, without distinction as to religion or nationality.

The Principle of Equality in the State Budget

The principle of equality binds every public entity in the State. First, it binds the State itself. The principle of equality applies to all the areas in which the State operates. It applies first and foremost to the allocation of the State's funds. The resources of the State, whether in land, money, or other resources, belong to all citizens, and all citizens are entitled to benefit from them in accordance with the principle of equality, without discrimination on the basis of religion, race, gender or other illegitimate considerations.

The principle of equality must also guide the legislative authority, which, like any other authority in the state, must act as a fiduciary to the public in accord with the basic values of the State of Israel as a Jewish and democratic state, which include equality. This is the case in each and every law, including the Budget Law.

Furthermore it is not sufficient that the laws of the state are consistent with the principle of equality; it is just as important that the implementation of the laws be consistent with this principle. This is the case for every law, so too the Budget Law. Indeed, since the laws of the State are generally consistent with the principle of equality, the primary threat to equality stems from the implementation of the law. The threat is particularly severe in implementation of the Budget Law. From a practical standpoint, in implementing the Budget Law it is relatively easy for state agencies to discriminate in allocation of funds on the grounds, *inter alia*, of religion or nationality. Such discrimination, particularly if it is methodical, may cause very severe damage not only to a specific person or a specific organization but also to the social fabric and the feeling of cooperation which are pre-conditions for our all living together in a community. Such discrimination is illegitimate at its core from both a moral as well a legal perspective.

Discrimination on the basis of religion or nationality in allocation of state funds, which is prohibited even if it is done indirectly, is clearly prohibited when it is done directly. A marked example is discrimination in allocation of funds from the state budget by a governmental agency.

Indeed, it is standard for budget funds to be insufficient to meet all needs, and therefore it is necessary to allocate funds according to a list of priorities. Such a list necessarily results in differences between those who are high on the list and receive funding and those who are low on the list and do not. The placement on the list must be based on relevant considerations which are consistent with the principle of equality, and not illegitimate considerations such as religion or nationality.

The duty incumbent on all authorities to allocate state funds in an equal manner is expressed in the Budget Principles Law, 5745-1985. Section 3a of this law sets out the mechanism under which governmental agencies provide support from the state budget to public institutions operating for purposes of education, culture, religion, and more. It establishes that such support will be distributed exclusively "according to egalitarian criteria."

The principle of equality in allocation of funds from the state budget applies even in the absence of a law that explicitly requires that the government follow the principle of equality.

In HCJ 240/98 *Adalah Legal Center for Arab Minority Rights in Israel v. Minister of Labor and Social Affairs* 52(5) PD 167 (1998), the petitioners claimed that the Ministry of Labor and Social Affairs was acting in a discriminatory manner in the allocation of funds from the ministry's budget for the support of the needy during the period leading up to the Passover holiday and was not allocating funds for the Arab needy during their holiday times. The Ministry of Labor and Social Affairs acknowledged its duty to act in an equal manner in the provision of support for the needy of different religions. As a result, the parties reached an agreement under which the Ministry of Labor and Social Affairs would amend the criteria relating to support of needy families on the occasion of the Passover holiday such that it would also apply to members of other religions. The Court granted the parties' application and granted the agreement the status of a judgment.

Application to this Case

It is clear that the Ministry of Religious Affairs must act in an egalitarian manner when it allocates funds from the ministry's budget to provide for the religious needs of members of the various religions. In fact, there are differences in the religious needs of members of the different religions: each religious community has its own holidays, traditions, institutions, and needs. It is appropriate to take these differences into consideration in connection with the allocation of funds from the State budget in order to provide for the special religious needs of each and every community. Therefore allocation of funds from the state budget for the satisfaction of religious needs does not have to be equal in the formal sense. It must be equal in the substantive sense. An unequal allocation of funds can still be equal in a substantive sense.

From a substantive perspective, the differences that may justify different treatment of members of different religions are blurred for deceased individuals of those same religions. The dignity of deceased individuals, which is derived from the dignity of living individuals, requires that the cemetery where they are buried be well-kept and well-maintained, and this requirement is the same whether Jews, Muslims, Christians, or Druze are buried there. Therefore substantive equality, relating to allocation of funds from the State budget for the maintenance of cemeteries, approximates formal equality.

Indeed, counsel for the minister of religious affairs wholeheartedly agreed that the requirement of equality also applies to the Ministry of Religious Affairs in the allocation of funds for the maintenance of cemeteries.

The question is, and opinions differ on this, whether the Ministry of Religious Affairs breached the equality imperative in its allocation of funds for the maintenance of cemeteries. In order to answer this question, it must be ascertained first what the directives of the Budget Law are as they pertain to the support of the Ministry of Religious Affairs for the maintenance of cemeteries, and then, how the ministry implemented the law's directives.

The Law's Directives

[The law directs that funds be allocated to cemeteries.]

Implementation of the Law

The Ministry of Religious Affairs claims that it distributes the funds that were allocated in the Budget Law for cemeteries in a manner that complies with the principle of equality and does not discriminate between Jewish cemeteries and other cemeteries.

The rule is that any discrimination is illegitimate, even if it is denied. Camouflage will not salvage discrimination. Substance and not form is determinative.... Implementation of the Budget Law by a government ministry in a way that results in prohibited discrimination is invalid, and the fact that intent to discriminate was not proven or that intent to discriminate was denied is not sufficient to validate the discrimination. Attractive words are not sufficient to validate bad acts. The illegitimacy in discrimination is in the act of discrimination.

The question, therefore, is whether the sections of the Budget Law pertaining to cemeteries have been implemented in a manner that is discriminatory. The primary facts as to the implementation of the sections in the Budget law that pertain to cemeteries are not in dispute. These are the facts:

[The opinion continues with a detailed examination of how funds were actually allocated under each section of the ministry's cemetery budget.]

In conclusion, of the budget of the Ministry of Religious Affairs designated for cemeteries in the year 1999, ... only the amount of NIS 202,000, which is designated for clearing of fatal casualties in times of emergency, and which appears not to be used to maintain cemeteries, may also serve a population that is not Jewish. The remainder of the amount, namely NIS 16,658,000, serves Jewish cemeteries entirely (or almost entirely).

What is the reason that Arab, Muslim and Christian cemeteries, which serve more than one sixth of the total population in Israel, do not receive their portion of budget sections designated to serve cemeteries? We have not heard any reason from the Ministry of Religious Affairs that would explain why it has implemented these sections in a manner that seemingly violates the principle of equality.

The Petitioner has shown that inequality exists in the allocation of funds from the budget of the Ministry of Religious Affairs for Jewish cemeteries on the one hand and Arab cemeteries (excluding Druze cemeteries) on the other.

This picture is in line with that which arises from a letter of the attorney general, dated 1.26.95, to the prime minister and the minister of religious affairs in which he alerted that "the non-Jewish population [receives] a low proportion of the support budget [of the Ministry of Religious Affairs] without any relation to its proportion in the general population in Israel," and raised a proposal for "more balanced budgeting for the religious needs and the religious judicial services of the non-Jewish communities in the State." Similar statements were made in the Report of the State Comptroller, Number 46 from the year 1995: "In the opinion of the office of the State Comptroller, the Ministry of Religious Affairs is to operate to increase the equality among the various segments of the population, and to ensure that the portion the Muslims have in the budget of the Ministry will match their relative proportion in the population."

This being the case, and after the Petitioner has shown that the Ministry of Religious Affairs did not fulfill its duty of acting in accordance with the principle of equality in allocation of funds for cemeteries in the year 1999, the question arises what remedy should be imposed.

The Remedy

Seemingly it would be appropriate for the Court to make a declaration that the Ministry of Religious Affairs is to treat Jewish cemeteries and other cemeteries equally in all that relates to allocation of funds for cemeteries. However, such a declaration is superfluous, not only because the matter is clear and obvious on its own, but also because the Ministry of Religious Affairs takes upon itself, and in its response to the Court even glorifies, the principle of equality.

The problem does not lie with the principle but with the implementation. The question is, first of all, what is the implementation that is dictated by the principle. Therefore in order to remove any obstacles down the road, this Court must set specific requirements for the implementation of the principle.

First, according to the proportionality criterion, the goal for distribution of the money among the cemeteries must be allocation according to the relative proportion of members of each religion in the population, and the result of the distribution of the money must match that proportion closely. What does this mean? In distributing the money significant deviation from the relative proportion must be avoided; with that, it is doubtful whether it is possible to be exacting as in a mathematical formula and whether it is necessary to be accurate to the hair's breath, in dividing the money. A slight deviation from the relative proportion does not necessarily mean discrimination.

Second, the criterion of proportionality is not necessarily the only criterion. It is possible to knowingly deviate from this criterion, *inter alia*, for purposes of affirmative action. Affirmative action for a specific public or specific group, that seemingly violates the principle of equality, in fact advances equality. It is permitted, and may be appropriate, when it is directed at compensating a weak community or group that suffers from unequal treatment, in particular if this situation stems from ongoing deprivation, knowing or unknowing, intentional or unintentional.

We need not go far to show that this is permissible. The Ministry of Religious Affairs adopted a five-year plan for advancing the Druze community, and in the framework of this program allocated [from another portion of its budget] in one budget year the amount of NIS 6,000,000 for Druze cemeteries. That is an amount that is relatively high compared to the amount allocated to Muslim and Christian cemeteries. It turns out that this is affirmative action that was designed to compensate the Druze community for lesser support in the past and to advance the principle of equality. This is not prohibited, as long as such preference is not done at the expense of equality among the other communities. Affirmative action which benefits the Druze community should not come at the expense, for example, of the Muslim community, in a manner that will create inequality or exacerbate inequality, for example, between Muslims and Jews. In other words, affirmative action toward the Druze does not justify inequality between Muslims and Jews.

Third, the proportionality criterion, in the context of cemeteries, is built primarily on religious affiliation, as burial in Israel is primarily religious burial. However, there are exceptions to this. These exceptions have recently been recognized in the Right to Alternative Civilian Burial Law, 5756-1996. Under this law every person has a right to be buried in a civilian cemetery in which the burial is performed according to their worldview, and for this purpose the law determines that there will be cemeteries for alternative civilian burial in various regions of the country with reasonable distances between them. Therefore at the time that money allocated for cemeteries is distributed, the need to allocate money in an appropriate measure for alternative civilian burial cemeteries is also to be taken into account, in accordance with the proportionality criterion.

In accordance with this principle, we order the Ministry of Religious Affairs to allocate the money that was determined in the budget of the Ministry of Religious Affairs for the year 2000, for the purpose of the cemeteries of members of the various religions, in an equal manner.

The Ministry of Religious Affairs will pay the Petitioner court expenses in the total amount of NIS 20,000.

Comment

This case is typical of the legal approach to allegations of inadequate services for Muslims or other non-Jewish groups. The cases are usually decided under principles of equality. As established in the case of *Poraz v. City Council of Tel Aviv-Jaffa*, 42(2) PD 309 [1988], discussed in chapter 9, administrative agencies must consider the principle of equality in all decisions. The fact that Israel is a Jewish state does not diminish her obligation to observe this principle in providing services to non-Jews. The opposite is true; the Declaration of the Establishment of the State of Israel, which declared Israel to be a Jewish state, also declared the principle of equality. As a result, the Court found equality to be a value of Israel as a Jewish and democratic state. Because the minister of religious affairs did not follow the principle of equality when allocating funding for cemeteries, the allocation was invalid.

Nonetheless the problem of unequal funding of religious services for non-Jews remains a serious one. The law on the issue is clear: equality is required. As described in the case, implementation is problematic.

Question

7. The decision states that the principle of equality does not require everyone to be treated the same. What exceptions to equal treatment are permitted in allocating cemetery funds?

Some state practices go beyond facilitating Jewish religious observance and require observance of Jewish law. These practices are not based on statutes, but on a political agreement between the religious and secular Jewish communities, commonly called the *status quo*. This was a commitment by those involved in founding the state that certain existing practices would be preserved. Under the status quo, state institutions are closed on the Jewish Sabbath and their food facilities observe Jewish dietary laws. The following case discusses whether the observance of Jewish dietary laws at a public institution has an impermissible adverse effect on non-Jews.

Israeli Case

Raayk v. Prison Services Authority

Request for Permission to Appeal 4201/09 (March 18, 2010)

[The case deals with special dietary laws that apply during the seven-day holiday of Passover.[37] Jewish law prohibits Jews from eating, owning, handling or benefiting from

---

37. Passover is observed as an eight day holiday by Orthodox and Conservative Jews in the United States, but is only a seven day holiday in Israel. The difference in length is the result of a rule in Jewish law.

the use of bread, bread products, or any food that may have come into improper contact with several forbidden grains. (Altogether, the foods that are prohibited are called *hametz*. In the following case, the term *hametz* is translated as bread or bread products.) In addition, Jews must remove all bread and bread products from their possession during this time.[38]]

Justice E. Rubenstein:

Background

The is a request for permission to appeal the decision of the District Court of Tel Aviv to reject the petition of a Muslim criminal convict, hereinafter called the Appellant, to be supplied with bread in the prison during the holiday of Passover. We decided to consider the appeal. The Appellant is in a mixed portion of the prison, where both Jews and Arabs are incarcerated. He claims that only non-Jewish prisoners are in his cell.

Discussion

Counsel for the Appellant asks that his client receive bread during Passover and claims that no Israeli law requires observance of the Jewish dietary laws of kashruth at state institutions. Even the Kosher Food for Soldiers Ordinance, 5708-1948, which applies in the Israel Defense Forces, only deals with the requirement to supply kosher food to Jews.... It is claimed that denying the Appellant bread, a basic food, infringes on a constitutional right and violates the principles of proportionality and reasonableness. It is possible to have non-Jewish prisoners bring bread in from outside of the prison.

Decision

Section 1.a. of the Directive of the Commissioner of Prison Service No. 01.22.00, entitled "Observance of Kashruth by the Prison Service," provides "all kitchens and dining halls of the Prison Service shall be kosher except for kitchens that serve only non-Jewish security prisoners."[39] Section 11 of the Directive provides that "all units of the Prison Service shall undertake the preparations needed for observing Passover in the kitchens, dining halls, and the prison stores. In addition, they shall arrange for observance of the holiday and shall prevent entry of bread products into the cells during the entire period of Passover."

The Directive of the Commissioner No. 4.55.01, entitled "Religious Rights of Non-Jewish Prisoners," relates to providing the opportunity "to prisoners of all religions to observe the requirements of their religions subject to the security and organizational limitations that exist in the prison." This directive does not impose any requirements as to food, except as to Muslims during the Muslim month of Ramadan. Under section d(2), Muslims who fast are to receive an additional large, hot evening meal and also food and drink before the normal time of breakfast the following day.[40]

---

38. It is common to segregate bread and bread products in one closed cabinet and to sell these products to a non-Jew for the duration of the holiday. The Jewish owner of the home or business where this cabinet is located may not use, handle or move the products during the holiday. Due to the sale, the products do not belong to the Jew during the holiday and the Jew has no rights to do anything with them.

39. Israeli prisoners who violate the state's criminal laws are held in prisons much like those of any other country. All segments of the population are found in such prisons. Security prisoners are usually held in separate facilities. Most, but not all, security prisoners are non-Jews. Many are not Israelis.

40. Muslims who observe the month-long fast of Ramadan do not eat during the daytime. They eat a meal before dawn and a meal after sunset.

I find no fault in these directives.

Counsel for the Appellant points to the Kosher Food for Soldiers Ordinance, 5708-1948, in which section 1 provides "Kosher food shall be provided to all Jewish soldiers in the Israel Defense Forces." [He made the point that this requires kosher food only for Jewish soldiers.] The chief rabbi of the Prison Service, the former chief rabbi of the army, informed us that in fact the rules of kashruth are observed in all army units. This matter is not before us, and the only conclusion we can reach is that, apparently, at the time of the establishment of the state, it was not obvious that kosher food would be supplied, so the matter had to be treated by law.

In a memorandum of the chief rabbi of the Prison Service to the Commission of the Prison Service on March 8, 2010, after analysis of the Jewish law on the matter, said it was his opinion that:

> a. It is prohibited to distribute bread products to prisoners who are not Jewish during Passover.
>
> b. It is permissible before Passover to distribute bread products to prisoners who are not Jewish who are in an area where everyone is non-Jewish, and they can keep these bread products.
>
> c. The provisions of section b. apply only in separate areas where non-Jewish security prisoners are kept.

The recommendation:

> In light of what is said above, the Prison Service may provide to non-Jewish prisoners sliced bread (which keeps better without freezing than pita[41]) wrapped in plastic, with an expiration date several days later. They can eat this bread for at least the first four days of Passover. After that, they can have bread that has been frozen. In this way, bread can be supplied without having to add a large number of freezers in the prisons.

The opinion of the Chief Rabbi of Israel sent to the chief rabbi of the Prison Service, dated March 15, 2010, after an analysis of the Jewish law sources, provides:

> a. As to non-Jewish security prisoners who are in separate units, they may be given bread and bread products before Passover, but only under the following conditions: 1. No one may give them bread and bread products during Passover. 2. All bread and bread products will be given to them before the holiday, whether they are frozen or fresh, and will be kept in the separate unit under care of the prisoners, who will distribute it during the holiday. 3. After the bread and bread products are provided to the prisoners, neither the Prison Service nor its representatives shall have any responsibility for it. 4. No Jewish guard shall be required to handle or do anything with the bread or bread products in any way. 5. If the bread and bread products are consumed, no additional such products may be provided during the holiday. In such a case, the prisoners shall receive matzah.[42]
>
> b. As to non-Jewish criminal prisoners who live in a cell with Jewish prisoners: 1. It is impermissible to provide them with bread or bread products during Passover. 2. Because there is no way of creating a proper separation between

---

41. The normal bread in the diet of many Israelis, Jews and Arabs, is pita and not loaf bread or rolls.

42. *Matzah* is a kind of cracker made from wheat but produced through special methods that prevent the dough from rising. This makes it permissible for Jews to eat it during Passover.

prisoners within the cell, these prisoners cannot be permitted to possess or eat bread or bread products in the same cell with Jews.... In the conditions that are present in prison cells, there is no way to prevent the food of one prisoner from getting accidentally mixed up with that of his cellmates. This will lead to a situation in which a Jewish prisoner cannot eat in the cell, or even that the Jewish prisoner cannot remain in the cell with those who are eating bread or bread products.

For this reason, allowing bread and bread products for a non-Jew into a room in which he lives together with a Jew who follows Jewish dietary laws not only constitutes a denial of the basic rights [of the Jewish prisoner], but is almost certain to create great tension among roommates, and even to cause violence.

Even though no one denies the importance of bread, the state's basic obligation is to supply the prisoners with food, and not with a specific type of food. As long as the supply of some important type of food is interrupted for only a short period and there are good substitutes for that food, there is no harm to the prisoners' rights.

It is a fair assumption that bread is an important component of the usual diet. Nonetheless there is no lack of proportionality in replacing it with reasonable amounts of another food for a short period of time. In a Jewish and democratic state, there is no infringement of constitutional rights in not providing bread during Passover in mixed portions of the prison where both Jews and non-Jews live, as long as other food is appropriately provided. It is not necessary to raise constitutional claims in every case, where matters can be otherwise resolved.

We have noted the statement of the chief rabbi of the Prison Service, who said that no one rummages in the private storage closets of non-Jewish criminal prisoners who live in a cell together with Jews in order to check whether before Passover they put aside bread products for themselves. As long as the conditions allow, privacy is respected and people are left alone.... In the interest of keeping the peace, it is rational not to cause unnecessary tension by searching the closets, but to leave things to be solved in a practical manner, as it appears they have been over the years.

In summary: In prisons housing only non-Jewish security prisoners and in branches of regular prisons in which only non-Jews are housed, bread will be supplied before Passover as indicated by the chief rabbi of the prison service, both for consumption and for freezing, as needed. In mixed branches of the regular prisons, where bread and bread products cannot be supplied in the same manner because it might cause difficulties under Jewish law and in practice, the prisoners will get the same type of food as is supplied to everyone.... On the other hand, it has been indicated that no one searches a prisoner's closet to see whether bread and bread products acquired before Passover are stored there. If a prisoner eats such food during Passover no one will disturb him if he does so privately in a manner that does not disturb the religious and national sensibilities of Jewish inmates in the cell. (We are told that the Appellant is presently in a cell that houses no Jews, even though the wing he is in is mixed, and this makes the entire matter simpler.)

Under these circumstances, the petition should be rejected.

Comment

The law involved in this case is found in the directives of the commissioner. No statute explicitly authorizes these directives. As a matter of administrative law, any decision of an administrative agency must be authorized by statute or be in support of another decision authorized by statute. In this case, the Court was apparently willing to assume that the authorization for the directives came from status quo agreement.

The maintenance of Jewish dietary laws at public institutions has important practical implications. Jews who observe the dietary laws could not otherwise eat in the dining rooms of those institutions. This is obviously a problem for incarcerated observant Jewish prisoners, but it would also be a problem at open institutions. But for observance of the dietary laws in public institutions, Knesset members who are observant could not eat lunch with those who are not, clients who are observant could not meet with their lawyers in the court house over a cup of coffee, and students of different degrees of observance could not study together in school cafeterias over a mid-afternoon snack. While the maintenance of the dietary laws by the state has an important symbolic value, it has an even more important functional value in allowing all Israelis to work together.

The result is that those who want to eat ham or shrimp or a cheeseburger, all of which are forbidden by Jewish dietary laws, cannot do so at public institutions in Israel. These institutions may also prohibit people from bringing in their own food into dining halls, because the presence of non-kosher food in a food establishment is also a violation of Jewish dietary laws. The problem in *Raayk* was even more extensive: Jewish law prohibited bread and bread products from being in the possession of any Jew during Passover. The prison, which was owned by the Jewish state, could not allow delivery of bread to the non-Jewish prisoners during this period. The only way the prisoners could have bread was by delivery of the bread into their separate possession before Passover began.

In *Raayk*, the Court found that that the observance of the Passover Jewish dietary laws at the prisons is permissible, even though it inconveniences non-Jews, because the inconvenience was not great. In practice, the problem of laws based on Jewish law injuring non-Jews is not substantial, either because they create exemptions for non-Jews (such as the law dictating a weekly rest period) or because they cause only an inconvenience (such as the law limiting bread in prisons during Passover). The Court took the same approach, holding that some people have to tolerate an inconvenience, in *Solodkin*, where it was Jews objecting to a state law based on Jewish law. The Court held there that people living within a Jewish community where most residents are observant must tolerate the inconvenience of going to another location to buy pork. Similarly in the case involving the prohibition of traffic on a main thoroughfare on the Sabbath in an Ultra-Orthodox neighborhood, the Court held that non-observant Jews living in a mostly Ultra-Orthodox community must tolerate the inconvenience of having their streets closed during prayer hours on the Sabbath, although they do not have to tolerate a much greater inconvenience of having their streets closed for the entire day. HCJ 5016/96 *Horev v. Minister of Tranportation*, 51(4) PD 1 [1997].[43]

Question

8. Justice Rubenstein was clearly annoyed with the claim of a constitutional right to receive bread to eat at all times. In a dissenting opinion, Justice Rivlin said, "I do not join in dismissing the constitutional question in this case with a wave of the hand." Should the Court have recognized a constitutional right to have bread to eat at all times? Why does it matter?

---

43. *Available in English at* http://elyon1.court.gov.il/files_eng/96/160/050/A01/96050160.a01.htm.

Chapter 14

Family Law

This chapter discusses several aspects of family law. Religious law controls some, but not all, of these aspects.

A. Marriage

Israeli law on marriage and divorce is extremely complex. Only some of the main features are presented here.

Israeli law recognizes four forms of marriage or marriage-like arrangements for Israelis:

1. Marriage by the religious court of one of the recognized religious communities.

2. Spousal covenant.

3. Marriage outside of Israel.

4. Reputed spouses.[1]

Israeli law does not allow civil marriage in Israel.

1. Marriage by the religious court: The only form of standard marriage that can take place in Israel is marriage through the religious courts of one of the recognized religious communities. The Israeli statutes giving the religious courts of the major religious communities' jurisdiction over marriage are set out in chapter 12. Under these provisions, the marriage of two Jews must be through the rabbinical courts and must be in accordance with Jewish law; the marriage of two Muslims must be through the Muslim religious courts, which apply Islamic law, etc. A couple married through a religious court is considered married for all purposes under Israeli law.

Despite the fact that religious law controls marriages, state law sets some basic requirements that the religious courts must observe. As discussed in chapter 12, state law prohibits polygamy and sets a minimum age of seventeen for marriage (although a person under that age can marry with court permission if the person is sixteen years old, is a parent wishing to marry the other parent of the child, is a pregnant female, or is a male wishing to marry the pregnant mother of his child. Marriage Age Law, 5710-1950).

2. Under the Spousal Covenant for Persons Having No Religious Affiliation Law, 5770-2010, a man and a woman, neither of whom is a member of one of the recognized reli-

---

1. The term *reputed spouses* is taken from Zvi H. Triger, *The Gendered Racial Formation: Foreign Men, "Our" Women, and the Law*, 30 Women's L. Rep. 479, 504 (2009). Another source, which provides a good overview of Israeli marriage law, uses the term *non-marital cohabitators*. See Gidi Sapir & Daniel Statman, *Religious Marriage in a Liberal State*, 30 Cardozo L. Rev. 2855 (2009).

gious communities, can enter a spousal covenant before an official called a Spousal Relations Registrar. They must both be at least eighteen years old and not married to anyone else. The statute provides that the parties to a spousal covenant are to be considered as a married couple and to be treated as a married couple for the purpose of all matters except those explicitly listed as exceptions in the statute.[2] Because the statute allowing spousal covenants is new, it is not yet clear how it will function in practice. It applies to only a small number of couples, so its major importance may be in opening the door to broader recognition of civil marriage.

3. If a couple married outside of Israel before they became residents or citizens of Israel, they are considered married under Israeli law. If a couple who are residents or citizens of Israel and are eligible to marry in their religious community in Israel instead married in a ceremony outside of the country, they are also considered a married couple under Israeli law whether the ceremony was religious or civil. The status of other couples, who could not have married in Israel, is less clear. They are registered as married in the population registry; this is a formal registration but does not confer rights or status, as explained in the cases below. Such couples receive most of the rights and benefits available to married couples under a variety of laws. Whether they receive all the rights and benefits is still not clear.

4. Reputed spouses have many of the rights and obligations of married spouses. This is sometimes referred to in the English-language literature as common law marriage, although it is not really a form of marriage. The term for this status in Hebrew does not use the term marriage. The couple are *yedoim b'tzibur*, meaning they are *publicly known* as spouses. This form of a relationship is distinct from the others in that it does not depend on any sort of ceremony; the relationship is established by the actions of the parties. Furthermore, either one can end the relationship without judicial involvement.

Under various statutes, such as those dealing with the jurisdiction of family courts and inheritance, reputed spouses have rights and obligations similar to those of spouses in a "regular" marriage. Different statutes have different definitions of the requirements reputed spouses must meet in order to receive the same treatment as married couples under the statute. Some statutes only require that the reputed spouses run a joint household, without a set time period for their having done so; others also require that they not be married to anyone else or that they have declared that they intend to have the status of reputed spouses. Under a limited number of provisions, reputed spouses do not have the same rights as spouses of a regular marriage.

A number of problems arise under this scheme:

Jews not Recognized by the State Rabbinic Authority: Jewish law treats marriage as a contractual matter. A man and a woman who are competent and who wish to marry can do so. The rabbinical authorities exercise supervision, but do not actually create the marriage bond. As part of the process of supervision, the rabbinical authorities must determine that the man and woman are competent to marry. They check that both are single, of age, and that they are Jewish. The latter is required because, under Jewish law, a Jewish marriage can only be between two Jews. Jewish law does not exercise jurisdiction over non-Jews.

The rabbinical authorities that control marriage for Jews in Israel are Orthodox, and many of the rabbis staffing the rabbinical institutions are Ultra-Orthodox. Therefore peo-

---

2. They do not gain rights as spouses under the Law of Return, 5710-1950, the Law on Entrance to Israel, 5712-1952 (another statute on who can enter Israel), or the Citizenship Law, 5712-1952.

ple applying to marry under the auspices of state rabbinic authority must prove that they are Jewish under strict Orthodox standards. Some people who identify themselves as Jewish are not recognized to be Jews by the Israeli rabbinical authorities. The state rabbinical court authorities recognize as Jews only people born of a Jewish mother or who converted in a process that is acceptable to their standards. They do not recognize Jews who cannot prove that they are Jewish according to their standards. For example, some Jews who came from the countries of the former Soviet Union lack documentation proving that their mothers are Jewish. The state rabbinic authority also does not recognize a person who claims to be Jewish through patrilineal descent; i.e., because their father, but not mother, is Jewish. Many of the immigrants from the former Soviet Union and their children, who identify themselves as part of the Jewish community of Israel, have Jewish fathers but not Jewish mothers. In addition, anyone who converted to Judaism under the auspices of a conversion court not recognized by the state rabbinic authority is not able to marry as a Jew. This includes those converted by Conservative, Reconstructionist, or Reform conversions and some of those who have gone through Orthodox conversions that do not meet the restrictive standards of the Israeli rabbinic authorities.

A person who is not recognized as Jewish by the state rabbinic authority has a number of options. That person may go through a conversion process that the authority will recognize and may then marry another Jew. A person not wanting to undertake the sometimes exacting requirements of the state conversion process can marry outside of the country. Most Israeli couples choosing this option marry in Cyprus, which is near Israel. If a couple chooses this option, they will be treated as married for most purposes, although it is not clear whether the marriage will be fully recognized for all purposes. Alternatively, the person and the intended spouse may choose to live together as reputed spouses. If neither one of the couple is considered a Jew or a member of any other of the recognized religious communities, they can enter a spousal covenant.

Jews Preferring a Conservative, Reconstructionist, or Reform Marriage in Israel: A Jewish wedding in Israel must be supervised by a rabbi who is on an approved list maintained by the rabbinical authorities. All rabbis on the list are Orthodox. Some Jewish couples eligible to marry under the auspices of the Israeli rabbinical courts choose not to do so because they want a non-Orthodox Jewish wedding. The couple may marry in a non-Orthodox ceremony in Israel and they may consider the marriage a religiously binding marriage, but it will not be a valid state marriage. The couple can then have a civil marriage ceremony in another country; if they do, and if they were eligible to marry in a Jewish wedding in Israel, the foreign marriage will be recognized as a valid Israeli marriage. Alternatively the couple may choose to live together as reputed spouses. Because as Jews they are members of a recognized religious community, they cannot enter a spousal covenant.

Jews Preferring a Civil Marriage: Some Jews object to having a religious marriage ceremony even though they are eligible for one. Because Israel has no civil marriage, they have to attain their legal status as a couple in some other way. They may choose to have some sort of civil ceremony within Israel to celebrate their marriage with friends and family, but this does not confer any legal status. They can have a civil ceremony in another country or can live together as reputed spouses in Israel.

Interfaith Marriages: Couples from different religious communities can marry through one of the communities only if it will allow marriages for an interfaith couple. The Jewish rabbinic authorities do not allow interfaith marriages and the Islamic authorities allow it only in limited circumstances. A common interfaith scenario in Israel is that of a couple, one of whom is a Jew and one of whom functions as part of the Jewish community and is not affiliated with any other religion but is not technically Jewish, having come to Israel as a relative of a Jew under the Law of Return, or being the descendant of someone who entered as a relative of a Jew. An interfaith couple can marry in another country or can live together as reputed spouses. If one of the couple is a member of one of the recognized religious communities, the spousal covenant is not an available option.

Same-Sex Couples: None of the recognized religious communities in Israel will marry a same-sex couple. A same-sex couple can marry outside of Israel in a place that recognizes such marriages as valid. The marriage will be registered and will be treated as valid for some, but not necessarily all, purposes. A same-sex couple may also live together and gain the same rights as opposite-sex reputed spouses. They may not enter into a spousal covenant, no matter what their religious affiliation, because the statute creating the covenant provides that it is available only to a couple consisting of a man and a woman.

The first major case to deal with the issues raised by the situations described above was HCJ 143/62 *Funk-Schlesinger v. Minister of Interior* 17 PD 225, decided in 1963. A Jewish Israeli man married a Christian woman born in Belgium. The ceremony was in Cyprus. After the marriage, she was registered in the population registry as a resident of Israel, but the minister of interior refused to register her as a married person and refused to list her by her married name, even though she had produced proper documentation of her Cypriot marriage. The Supreme Court ruled that the law on the maintenance of the population registry did not grant the minister authority to question the validity of the marriage document she had presented. The minister was ordered to register the woman as married. The Court's decision related only to registration and did not determine whether the couple would have other rights and obligations as a married couple in Israel.

Forty-three years later, the following two additional important decisions were issued on the same day:

Israeli Case

Anonymous v. Tel-Aviv-Jaffa Regional Rabbinical Court
HCJ 2232/03, 61(3) PD 496 [2006][3]

[Petitioner and her husband are Jewish Israeli citizens and residents. Although they could have married under the auspices of the rabbinical court in Israel, they chose to marry in a civil ceremony in Cyprus. After several years of marriage, the husband filed for a divorce in a regional rabbinical court in Israel. The regional rabbinical court's decision on the divorce was appealed to the High Rabbinical Court. In order to decide whether and how a rabbinical court could grant a divorce to a Jewish couple married in a civil ceremony, the High Rabbinical Court had to determine the legal status of the marriage. It decided that this marriage was not the same as one entered into through a Jewish marriage ceremony, but that under Israeli law the Jewish court still had exclusive jurisdiction to dissolve the marriage in Israel and make each spouse free to remarry. In this case, the divorce proceeding was not the same as it would be if the two had married in a Jewish law ceremony. The marriage could be dissolved by decree of the religious court without the consent of both parties, something that is not possible in dissolution of a marriage contracted according to the requirements of Jewish law. The Petitioner objected

---

3. This translation is based on that on the website of the Supreme Court, at http://elyon1.court.gov.il/files_eng/03/320/022/a16/03022320.a16.htm.

to the issuance of the divorce decree without her consent and sought review in the Supreme Court. In order to determine the validity of the decision of the High Rabbinical Court, the Supreme Court first considered the status of the couple's marriage under Israeli law.]

Chief Justice Emeritus A. Barak:

"Marriages and divorces of Jews shall take place in Israel in accordance with Torah law," (section 2 of Rabbinical Courts Jurisdiction (Marriage and Divorce) Law, 5713-1953). But what is the law concerning marriages between Jews that take place outside Israel? It is universally agreed that if the marriage outside Israel is in accordance with Jewish law, it is valid in Israel. But what if the marriage that took place outside Israel is not a marriage in accordance with Jewish law? No problem arises, from the viewpoint of civil law and the civil courts, if at the time of the marriage the spouses were not Israeli citizens or residents. In such a case, the validity of the marriage is determined in accordance with the rules of Israeli private international law. According to these rules, if the personal law of the couple at the time the marriage was contracted recognizes the validity of the marriage, Israeli civil law also recognizes the marriage. "The law at the time of the act is what determines the validity or the invalidity of the act." "When the parties have acquired, for example, a status of a married couple under their own national law, any change that subsequently occurs in their personal law as a result of a change in their nationality is incapable of denying them the status of a married couple."

But what is the law if at the time of the civil marriage outside Israel both spouses were Israeli citizens or residents? In this matter it was possible in the past to identify two possible approaches. According to one approach, when examining the validity of a marriage that contains a foreign element we should refer to the rules of private international law. The rules of English private international law, which were absorbed into Israeli law by means of article 46 of the Palestine Order in Council, 1922,[4] distinguish between the formal validity of a marriage, which concerns the propriety of the marriage ceremony, and the essential validity of a marriage, which concerns the competence of the parties to marry. Questions concerning formal validity are governed by the law of the place where the marriage was contracted (*lex loci celebrationis*). The question of the competence of the parties is governed by the law of their domicile at the time of contracting the marriage (*lex domicilii*) or the law of the place where they intend to live as a married couple. When we are dealing with a civil marriage between Jews who are competent to marry one another, the formal validity of the marriage (the civil ceremony) will be examined in accordance with the law of the place where the marriage was contracted. Assuming that the civil marriage ceremony is a valid form of marriage in the place where the marriage was contracted, the marriage is recognized by Israeli law since the couple are competent to marry under their personal law.

---

4. 46. Law to be Applied

The jurisdiction of the civil courts shall be exercised in conformity with the Ottoman law in force in Palestine on November 1, 1914, and such later Ottoman Laws as have been or may be declared to be in force by public notice, and such orders in council, ordinances and regulations as are in force in Palestine at the date of the commencement of this order, or may hereafter be applied or enacted; and subject thereto and so far as the same shall not extend or apply, shall be exercised in conformity with the substance of the common law, and the doctrines of equity in force in England, and with the powers vested in and according to the procedure and practice observed by or before courts of justice and justices of the peace in England, according to their respective jurisdictions and authorities at that date, save in so far as the said powers, procedure and practice may have been or may hereafter be modified, amended or replaced by any other provisions. Provided always that the said common law and doctrines of equity shall be in force in Palestine so far only as the circumstances of Palestine and its inhabitants and the limits of His Majesty's jurisdiction permit.

The *second* approach to examining a civil marriage rejects the application of the rules of English private international law (with their distinction between content and form) in favor of personal law. With regard to Israeli residents and citizens, the validity of the marriage will be determined by applying their personal laws at the time when the marriage was contracted. Those who espouse this approach regard the provisions of article 47 of the Palestine Order in Council[5] as requiring the civil courts to apply the personal law of the parties. With regard to Israeli citizens, this is their religious law, even if a foreign element is involved in the marriage. Those who support this approach add that in so far as Jews are concerned, their personal law, which is Jewish religious law, does not distinguish between the content and the form of the marriage, so there is no basis for the distinction that exists in the rules of English private international law. Under this approach, the validity of the marriage of an Israeli citizen that took place outside Israel will be determined in accordance with the religious law of the Israeli citizen, precisely as if the marriage had taken place in Israel. If the religious law does not recognize the marriage, then it has no validity under Israeli law.

Deciding between these two approaches is difficult, but we cannot avoid adopting a position on this question. The High Rabbinical Court adopted a position when it held that, "from the viewpoint of civil law the parties married in a civil ceremony and they are considered married throughout the world, including in the State of Israel."

I agree with this. The recognition of the validity of the marriage is required under the rules of private international law, which constitute an integral part of Israeli law. They were absorbed in the past from English law. These rules now stand on their own as part of Israeli law, and evolve as part of Israeli law [without being tied to their English origins]. They therefore constitute an integral part of Israeli common law. Under these rules of private international law, when there is a foreign component to a marriage, it should be given effect. The provisions of the Palestine Order in Council, which apply religious law as the personal law of a local citizen, are subject to the rules of private international law. Indeed, "the rules of private international law take precedence in their application to any law that is merely municipal or internal." Article 47 of the Palestine Order in Council, which applies religious law as the personal law of a local citizen, is merely a municipal or internal law. The provisions of the article are subject to the rules of private international law.

It follows that the validity of a marriage that was contracted by a Jewish couple outside Israel, even if the two spouses were at that time residents and citizens of Israel, will be determined by applying the rules of the conflict of laws as practiced in Israel. Under these rules, the marriage has formal validity (under the foreign law) and it has essential validity (under Jewish law), and therefore the marriage is valid in Israel (both in its external aspect and in its internal aspect). This result is also required in view of the reality of life in Israel. Thousands of Jews who are citizens and residents of Israel wish to marry by means of a civil marriage that takes place outside Israel. This is a social phenomenon that the law should take into account. This was discussed by Justices Zussman and Witkin in the past, when they expressed the opin-

---

5. 47. Jurisdiction in Personal Status
The Civil Courts shall further have jurisdiction, subject to the provisions contained in this part of this order, in matters of personal status [including marriage and divorce] of persons in Palestine. Such jurisdiction shall be exercised in conformity with any law, ordinances or regulations that may hereafter be applied or enacted and subject thereto according to the personal law applicable.

ion in *obiter* that with regard to the validity of marriages that take place outside Israel between Israeli citizens or residents, it is sufficient that they are valid according to the law of the place where they were contracted, even if the spouses are not competent to marry under their personal law. In the petition before us, we do not need to make a decision with regard to this proposition; we need only adopt the more moderate position that the marriage is valid if the couple are competent to marry under their personal law and the marriage ceremony took place within the framework of a foreign legal system that recognizes it.

This conclusion is strengthened by our recognition of the human dignity of each of the spouses. Our acknowledgement of the right to marry and to have a family life and our duty to respect the family unit reinforce our view that we should recognize the validity of a status acquired under foreign law by Jews who are Israeli citizens or residents, as long as that law is not contrary to public policy in Israel. "One of the most basic elements of human dignity is the ability of a person to shape his family life in accordance with the autonomy of his free will.... The family unit is a clear expression of a person's self-realization." (HCJ 7052/03 *Adalah Legal Centre for Arab Minority Rights in Israel v. Ministry of Interior* (May 14, 2006))[6]

The rabbinical court recognized a civil marriage between Jewish Israeli citizens or residents that was contracted outside Israel, a civil marriage that is not in accordance with Jewish law, in its external aspect.... The marriage is not null and void *ab initio* even from the viewpoint of Jewish law. From the viewpoint of status vis-à-vis the whole world, the civil marriage has far-reaching ramifications. The spouses are not considered unmarried. Without dissolution of the marriage, the couple are not permitted to remarry. The remarriage of either one without dissolution of the existing marriage would constitute bigamy, which is prohibited by the law.

Israeli Case

Ben-Ari v. Director of Population Administration
HCJ 3045/05, 61(3) PD 537 [2006]

Chief Justice Emeritus A. Barak:

Two men who are Israeli citizens and residents were married in a civil ceremony in another country that recognizes such marriages. When they returned to Israel they each applied to change their registration at the Population Registry from bachelor to married. The registration official refused the applications. Was the refusal lawful? That is the question in each of the petitions before us. It should be noted that the question before us is not whether a marriage between persons of the same-sex that took place outside Israel is valid in Israel. The Petitioners are not applying for their marriage outside Israel to be given validity in Israel. The question before us is whether the registration official, whose authority is prescribed in the Population Registry Law, 5725-1965, as interpreted in HCJ 143/62 *Funk-Schlesinger v. Minister of Interior* 17 PD 225 [1963], acted within the scope of his authority when he refused to register the marriage of the two men in the registry. The petitions before us address the question of the registration official's authority and not the question of the validity of the marriage.

---

6. The case is available in English at the English language website of the Supreme Court, at http://elyon1.court.gov.il/files_eng/03/520/070/a47/03070520.a47.htm.

The Petitioners

There are five petitions of five couples before us. Both members of the couple in each of the petitions are men, and they are Israeli citizens and residents. The Petitioners in each of the petitions live together in Israel as a couple, and they maintain a joint household and conduct their lives as a family. Each couple married in a civil marriage ceremony in Toronto, Canada, and the marriage of each is recognized in accordance with the law in that country. After they returned to Israel, they applied to be registered as married at the Population Registry. They attached to their application documents that authenticated their marriages. Their applications were refused. They were told that "marriages of this kind are not legally recognized in the State of Israel, and therefore it is not possible to register them in the register" (the letter of the director of the Population Administration office in Tel-Aviv dated 24 May 2005). This led to the petitions.

The Legislative Framework

The Population Registry Law, 5725-1965, regulates the activity of the population registry. It provides that certain types of information concerning residents are registered at the population registry. The types of information are set out in section 2 of the Population Registry Law:

2. The Registry and Information to be Registered

(a) The following information about a resident[7] and changes in such information shall be registered in the population registry:

(1) First and last names and prior names;

(2) Parents' names;

(3) Date and place of birth;

(4) Sex;

(5) Ethnicity;

(6) Religion;

(7) Personal status (single, married, divorced, or widowed);[8]

(8) Spouse's name;

(9) Children's names, dates of birth, and sex;

(10) Present and former citizenships;

(11) Address;

(12) Mailing address … ;

(13) Date of entry into Israel;

(14) Date on which a person became a resident … ;

(b) An identity number shall be assigned for the registration of a resident who is registering for the first time.

The Population Registry Law sets out the meaning of the registration in section 3 as follows:

---

7. Throughout the statute, the provisions that apply to residents also apply to citizens.

8. The Spousal Covenant for Persons Having No Religious Affiliation Law, 5770-2010, enacted after this case, adds a fifth category to those included in the parentheses: spouse under spousal covenant.

3. The Registry: Prima Facie Evidence

Registration in the registry ... and the identity card provided under this statute shall be prima facie evidence of the information set out in subsections (1) to (4) and (9) to (13) of section 2.

Paragraphs (5) to (8) were excluded from the rule of *prima facie* evidence. These paragraphs concern ethnicity, religion, personal status, and name of spouse. The matter before us—personal status—was excluded from the framework of *prima facie* evidence.

Chapter 3 of the Population Registry Law addresses the powers of the registration official. It provides that the registration official may require someone who asks to provide information for the registry to give the official any information or document in his possession concerning the registration information.

The Population Registry Law distinguishes between initial registration and the registration of changes. Initial registration is based on a public certificate, and if there is no such certificate, based on the applicant's statement. The registration of changes, which is involved in the petitions before us, shall be made in the following manner:

19C. Registration of Changes

A change in the registered information on a resident shall be recorded in accordance with a document provided under section 15 or 16 or in accordance with a statement under section 17, accompanied by the public certificate that testifies to the change.

In the petitions before us, no documents were produced under section 15, which concerns official actions in Israel, such as a marriage that is recorded under the Marriage and Divorce (Registration) Ordinance. Nor were documents produced under section 16, which deals with documents based on judicial decisions. The petitions before us therefore fall within the scope of section 17 of the Population Registry Law, which provides:

17. Duty to Give Notice of Changes

If a change occurs in the registered information on a resident, other than those treated in sections 15 and 16, the resident is obligated to give notice of the change to the registration official within thirty days.

This notice should be accompanied by a "public certificate that testifies to the change." A statement of the applicant alone is insufficient. Under section 19A of the statute, a "public certificate" for this purpose is "as defined in the Testimony Ordinance." The Testimony Ordinance has now been replaced by the Evidence Ordinance (New Version), 5731-1971 [and all references to the Testimony Ordinance are to be understood as references to the Evidence Ordinance (New Version)]. Under the definition of "public certificate" in section 29 of the Evidence Ordinance (New Version), marriage certificates issued by a competent authority in the place where the marriage ceremony was conducted qualify as public certificates.

The Normative Status of the Registry and the Discretion of the Registration Official

What is the scope of the registration official's discretion? This question has been considered in a host of judgments. The main judgment is *Funk-Schlesinger v. Minister of Interior* 17 PD 225 [1963]. This decision was made more than forty-two years ago. In that case Mrs. Funk-Schlesinger, a Christian resident of Israel, married Mr. Schlesinger, a Jewish resident of Israel. The marriage took place in Cyprus. On the basis of the Cypriot marriage certificate, Mrs. Funk-Schlesinger applied to be registered as "married" at the population registry. The minister of interior refused the application. His refusal was based on the position that under the rules of private international law that apply in Israel, the spouses were not married. By a majority it was decided to order the registration. The opinion of Justice Y. Zussman, which was the main opinion, was based on the position that the Residents' Registry Ordinance, 5709-1949 "did not give registration in the residents' registry the force of evidence or proof for any purpose. The purpose of the ordinance is … to collect statistical material. This material may be correct and it may be incorrect, and no one guarantees its correctness."

Against this background, it was held that "the function of the registration official … is merely a function of collecting statistical material for the purpose of maintaining a register of residents, and no judicial power has been given to him." Therefore,

> when he registers the family status of a resident, it is not part of the job of the registration official to consider the validity of the marriage. The legislature is presumed not to have imposed on a public official a duty that the official is incapable of discharging. The official should be satisfied, for the purpose of carrying out his office and registering the family status, if he is presented with evidence that the resident underwent a marriage ceremony. The question of the validity of the ceremony that took place is a multi-faceted one and examining the validity of the marriage falls outside the scope of the residents' registry.

In a similar vein, Justice Zussman said that when the Supreme Court hears petitions against a refusal of the registration official to register the marriage of a petitioner, it does not make any legal determination with regard to the validity of that marriage. He wrote:

> It is not superfluous to emphasize that we are not dealing with the question whether the marriage is valid or not. The question before us is … whether there was a justification for the refusal of the residents' registry official to register the applicant as a married woman.

Justice Zussman recognized that there may be cases in which the incorrectness of the details that a resident wishes to register in the registry is manifest and is not subject to any reasonable doubt. In such cases the official is not obliged to carry out the registration. The public official is not obliged to be a party to an act of fraud. When a person who clearly seems from his appearance to be an adult stands before the official and applies to be registered as a five year old child, what doubt can there be in such a case that the registration is false and that the act of the person is an act of fraud? In such a case the official will be justified in refusing to register the information, and this Court will certainly not … compel the official to forge the population register.

Since the decision in *Funk-Schlesinger v. Minister of Interior*, this Court has followed it consistently. Over the years its weight as precedent has increased. The repeal of the Residents' Registry Ordinance and its replacement by the Population Registry Law did not change its effect.

Criticism has been levelled against *Funk-Schlesinger v. Minister of Interior*. From the beginning it was said that the statistical nature of the registration does not "exhaust the practical importance of the register." Justice Tal emphasized that "the approach that views the registry as merely 'statistical' ignores reality."

The rule in *Funk-Schlesinger v. Minister of Interior* is correct and appropriate. It would not be appropriate if, in the absence of express authorization in the Population Registry Law, the registration official (the minister of interior) should be given the power to decide questions that are of great importance to Israeli society. It is not proper that whenever there is a change in the leadership of the Ministry of the Interior there should be a change in policy on key public issues. These issues ought to be addressed by the people through their representatives in the Knesset. As long as the Knesset has not spoken it is appropriate, in so far as possible, that decisions related to public values should not be made by the act of registration.

Naturally *Funk-Schlesinger v. Minister of Interior* does not prevent a judicial decision on questions of religion, ethnicity and marriage. It simply places the judicial decision in the proper framework.

In the petitions before us we have not been asked by the State to reconsider *Funk-Schlesinger v. Minister of Interior*. All the parties have relied on *Funk-Schlesinger v. Minister of Interior*. The Petitioners said repeatedly that they are not asking for a decision on the question whether their marriage in Canada is valid in Israel. The State also does not ask us to decide the question of the validity of the marriage. The scope of the dispute between the parties concerns the scope of the rule in *Funk-Schlesinger v. Minister of Interior*. The Petitioners argue that the five cases before us fall within the scope of that rule. In each case, the registration official should register the change in the registry on the basis of the marriage certificate that they presented, without examining the validity of the marriage in Israel. Counsel for the State argues that a marriage between persons of the same sex constitutes a legal framework of marriage that is not recognized in Israel, and therefore the rule in *Funk-Schlesinger v. Minister of Interior* does not apply.

The Rule in Funk-Schlesinger v. Minister of Interior and the "Legal Framework" Argument

All the parties agree that the marriage certificates that were submitted to the registration official are lawful under Canadian law, that a marriage ceremony took place in Canada, and that the details appearing in the marriage certificate are correct. On this basis we are *prima facie* drawn to the conclusion that the registration official should register the couple as married.

In her arguments, counsel for the State said that according to the rule in *Funk-Schlesinger v. Minister of Interior*, the registration official should not register something that is manifestly incorrect and is not subject to any reasonable doubt. According to her, the registration of a homosexual couple as married is a registration that is tainted, from a legal viewpoint, with manifest incorrectness, since Israeli law does not recognize this marriage. This argument is fundamentally unsound for two reasons: first, the incorrectness to which the rule in *Funk-Schlesinger v. Minister of Interior* refers is factual incorrectness, whereas the State is arguing with regard to legal incorrectness.

Second, concerning the existence of a manifest mistake, the question is not whether homosexual marriage is recognized in Israel. The question is whether Israeli law recognizes a homosexual marriage that is valid where it was contracted. The answer to this question is not at all simple. It requires us to undertake a precise and detailed analysis. In any case, the decision on this issue, under the rule of *Funk-Schlesinger v. Minister of Interior*, should not be made in registration proceedings or in judicial review thereof.

The State's arguments are based on the contention that there is no social consensus in Israel on the question of the recognition of marriage between persons of the same-sex, that this Court should not decide these questions, and that recognition of a status of same-sex marriages involves questions of values that ought to be decided by the legislature. I agree with these arguments to the extent that they concern the possibility that this Court should decide the question whether same-sex couples may marry in civil marriages in Israel.... In *Ben-Menasheh v. Minister of Religious Affairs*, 51(3) PD 876 [1997] the Petitioner asked us to order the minister of religious affairs to appoint an official who would conduct civil marriages in special cases.[9] The petition was denied. This is what I wrote in my opinion:

> The question of conducting civil marriages between couples who do not have a religious community, just like the question of conducting civil marriages for couples who belong to different religious communities, is a difficult and complex question. There is no national consensus on this. It concerns the recognition of status, which operates vis-à-vis everyone. In this situation, it appears *prima facie* that the proper institution for dealing with and regulating the matter is the Knesset and not a court.

I accept that the question of conducting civil marriages in Israel, including marriages between persons of the same-sex, should be determined first and foremost by the legislature. This is not the question before us. We are not dealing at all with marriage in Israel. Moreover there is no application before us to recognize a marriage between two persons of the same-sex that took place outside Israel. When this question arises, it will be examined in accordance with accepted rules of private international law. All that is before us, and that *Funk-Schlesinger v. Minister of Interior* seeks to resolve, is the question of registration—registration, not recognition—of a marriage between persons of the same-sex that took place outside Israel. The State's approach that we should deny the petitions because the marriage that the Petitioners contracted is not a "legal framework" recognized in Israel is an approach that seeks to adopt a position on the question of status; it is an approach that asks this Court to rule on a social question that is the subject of dispute. The importance of the rule in *Funk-Schlesinger v. Minister of Interior* is, *inter alia*, that it does not result in a court making a decision on matters of status. It is precisely the approach of the state with regard to a recognized "legal framework" that makes it necessary to make decisions that the state itself believes ought to be left to the legislature.

Before we conclude, let us reemphasize what it is that we are deciding today and what it is that we are not deciding. We are deciding that within the context of the status of the population registry as a record of statistics, and in view of the role of the registration official as a collector of statistical material for the purpose of managing the registry, the registration official should record in the population register what is implied by the public certificate that is presented by the Petitioners, according to which the Petitioners are married. We are not deciding that marriage between persons of the same-sex is recognized in Israel; we are not recognizing a new status of such marriages; we are not adopting any position with regard to recognition in Israel of marriages between persons of the same-sex that take place outside Israel, whether between Israeli residents or between persons who are not Israeli residents. The answer to these questions, to which we are giving no answer today, is difficult and complex. It is to be hoped that the Knesset can direct its attention to these questions or to some of them.

The result is that ... the Respondent shall register the Petitioners as married.

Comment

Funk-Schlesinger v. Minister of Interior, Anonymous v. Tel-Aviv-Jaffa Regional Rabbinical Court, and *Ben-Ari v. Director of Population Administration* all deal with the status of marriages of Israeli residents conducted outside of Israel.

---

9. This case was decided before the enactment of Spousal Covenant for Persons Having No Religious Affiliation Law, 5770-2010.

Funk-Schlesinger held that foreign marriages between two Israelis must be registered in the population registry at the request of the parties to the marriage, but said it was deciding on formal registration only and was not ruling on the substantive status of the marriage under Israeli law. The analysis in *Anonymous v. Tel-Aviv-Jaffa Regional Rabbinical Court* goes beyond *Funk-Schlesinger* and reaches the issue of substantive status. It holds that a foreign marriage between two Israelis eligible to marry in Israel is to be treated under Israeli law as a valid marriage. It holds that the rule of private international law used applied under British law also applies to the case. Under this rule, a marriage is valid in the domicile of a couple if the marriage was valid where contracted and the couple was competent to marry in the place of their domicile.

Anonymous v. Tel-Aviv-Jaffa Regional Rabbinical Court does not reach the question of the status under Israeli law of foreign marriages between two people not eligible to marry in Israel. The rule of private international law it adopts would seem to preclude recognizing such marriages, because it requires that the couple be competent to marry in the place of their domicile. This leaves people in the following situations without recognition as having the status of a married couple:

- Male and female interfaith couple: This was the situation in *Funk-Schlesinger v. Minister of Interior*, where the Court decided that they were to be registered as married, but did not reach the question of whether it is an Israeli marriage for all purposes. The barrier would be that marriage is controlled by the religious communities, and most Israelis belong to religious communities that will not marry interfaith couples.

- Same-sex couple: They cannot marry in Israel under the auspices of any of the recognized religious communities, whether or not they are of the same religion. They also cannot form a spousal covenant because that is limited to a couple consisting of a man and a woman.

- Male and female Jewish couple unable to marry under Jewish law: Judaism divides men into three groups. One group comprises men who are descendants of the ancient priestly class. They are not allowed to marry converts or divorcees. In addition, a man and a woman cannot marry under Jewish law if they were previously married to each other and divorced. Some other restrictions also apply.

Ben-Ari v. Director of Population Administration allows registration of same-sex couples married abroad. It applies the holding of *Funk-Schlesinger* and rejects two arguments that the cases are distinguishable. One argument was that the invalidity of the marriage in Israel was clear on its face. This was not true in *Funk-Schlesinger*. The population registry clerk, looking at an interfaith couple, could not determine their religious status; the clerk could determine that a couple is same-sex. The Court found no significance in this difference. It ruled that as long as someone submits a valid marriage certificate, they are to be listed as married in the population registry. The Court reiterated that it was not ruling that the marriage was being substantively recognized, but only that the parties should be listed as married in the registry.

The Court also rejected the argument that the Court should not decide the issue of the status of same-sex marriage, on which there is no social consensus. The Court recognized that there is a significant social issue as to whether to recognize such marriages, but said that this is the justification for applying the rule in *Funk-Schlesinger* to this case. Allowing the registration clerk to decide not to list the persons as married would effectively and inappropriately give the clerk the power to decide the social issues. If the Court decided that the clerk could refuse the registration, it would effectively and inappropri-

ately take upon itself the power to decide the social issue. The Court ordered the registration but left the issue of the substantive status of the marriage undecided. This issue,
the opinion said, would best be decided by the legislature. No relevant legislation has
been enacted.

Nonetheless in the decision in *Anonymous*, Chief Justice Emeritus Barak left a hint
that there may be room for the court to grant substantive recognition to same-sex and other
foreign marriages in the future. He wrote,

> This conclusion [that the foreign marriage of two Israelis eligible to marry in Is-
> rael is valid under Israeli law] is strengthened by our recognition of the human
> dignity of each of the spouses. Our acknowledgement of the right to marry and
> to have a family life and our duty to respect the family unit reinforce our view
> that we should recognize the validity of a status acquired under foreign law by
> Jews who are Israeli citizens or residents, as long as that law is not contrary to
> public policy in Israel.

This language does two things. First, in applying existing private international law it
shifts from asking whether the parties to the marriage were eligible to marry under Israeli
law to asking whether the marriage is contrary to public policy in Israel. This may allow
the Court in the future to use the rule that a foreign marriage will be recognized in Israel
as long as it does not violate Israeli public policy. Use of this rule does not mean that the
three types of ineligible marriages listed above would automatically be recognized in Israel, but it shifts the question to a more open one. Under *Anonymous*, the Court asked
if the parties were eligible to marry in Israel. Under a public policy approach, the result
might not change because it could be argued that Israeli public policy is delineated by
the laws providing that the religious communities have control over marriage. In that
case, none of the three types of marriages in the list above would be recognized in Israel.
On the other hand, a Court could rule that public policy is defined by the myriad of laws
that give the rights and obligations of married spouses to reputed spouses regardless of
whether they are eligible to marry in Israel. These laws show that there is no public policy of recognizing only couples who could be married in Israel and that the relevant public policy is to treat as married any couple that functions as a married couple. Under this
approach, all of the above three classes of foreign marriages could be recognized. But Israeli law has not yet gotten to this issue.

Second, the quoted language of Chief Justice Emeritus Barak suggests that the approach to the validity of foreign marriages may shift completely to a constitutional rights
approach. It says that the issue of whether a marriage should be recognized is related to
the human dignity of each of the spouses. If a future case takes the analysis in this direction, it may determine that the failure to recognize the substantive status of a marriage of a couple not eligible to marry under Israeli law is an infringement on the human
dignity of the spouses. Human dignity is not tied to a person's religion, sexual preference, or other characteristic related to eligibility to marry under religious law. In that
case, the restriction on substantive recognition of a marriage is valid only if it meets the
limitation clause. It would have to be authorized under law, serve a valid purpose, and
be proportional. Again, it is not clear what the outcome would be under such an analysis, but the use of this analysis, rather than the private international law approach adopted
in *Anonymous*, opens the door to recognition.

If this makes your head swim, be assured that most Israelis do not understand these
legal arrangements. In practice, most Israelis marry in religious ceremonies, although a
significant number do have foreign weddings or live together without a wedding. The

system works because official recognition of the marriage turns out not to be a huge problem in practice. Things can get thorny, however, on divorce.

Same-sex couples: In a portion of the *Ben-Ari* decision not reproduced here, the decision discusses the rights same-sex couples have under Israeli law. These include the right of one member of the couple to register an adoption of the child of the other member of the couple (HCJ 1779/99 *Brenner-Kaddish v. Minister of Interior* 54(2) PD 368 [2000]);[10] the right of one member of a couple to adopt the child of the other member of the couple (CA 10280/01 *Yaros-Hakak v. Attorney-General* 59(5) PD 64 [2005]);[11] the same rights as other couples have under collective agreements (HCJ 721/94 *El-Al Israel Airlines Ltd v. Danielowitz* 48(5) PD 749 [1994]); pension rights under the Permanent Service in the Israel Defence Forces (Pensions) Law (Consolidated Version) (MA (TA) 369/94 *Steiner v. IDF* (Jan. 5, 1996) (unreported)); memorial rights (HCJ 5398/96 *Steiner v. Minister of Defence* (Feb. 27, 1997) (unreported));[12] recognition as a spouse for the purposes of the Prevention of Family Violence Law, 5751-1991 (Fam.Crt (TA) 48260/01 Roe v. Roe (unreported)); recognition as a spouse for the purposes of the Family Court Law (FC (TA) 3140/03 *Re R.A. and L.M.P.* (unreported)); recognition as a co-habitee for the purposes of rights under the Inheritance Law, 5725-1965 (CA (Naz.) 3245/03 *A.M. v. Custodian-General* (unreported)); and rights to a surviving relative's pension under the National Insurance Law (Consolidated Version), 5755-1995 (NI (TA) 3536/04 *Raz v. National Insurance Institute* (unreported)).

The question of recognizing foreign marriages arises not only in Israel; other countries also face the issue. It probably arises most frequently for migrant marriages when a couple marries in one country, lives there, and then migrates to another country. Israel also has many marriages of this type; recognition is not generally a problem. The cases that are difficult in Israel are those involving Israeli residents who travel to another country specifically to marry there in order to avoid Israeli marriage laws and afterwards return to Israel. The rule that the Israeli Court applies in *Anonymous v. Tel-Aviv-Jaffa Regional Rabbinical Court* is the rule many countries follow for the migrant marriage cases. The Israeli Supreme Court does not ask whether it is appropriate to apply the same rule to the two types of cases.

In the United States, marriage recognition depends on the law of the individual states. The general rule is that a state will recognize a marriage that occurred in a foreign country if the marriage was valid in the country where it was contracted and if the marriage does not violate a strong public policy of the state where the couple now resides.[13] Again, the issue usually arises as to migrating couples. The question of intentional foreign marriages arises in the context of destination weddings, which pose no substantial policy questions as to their recognition. These are weddings between two people who can marry

---

10. This case involved two women who were Israeli citizens but residents of California. One gave birth to a son and the other received a decree from a California court that she was the adoptive mother. When the two women and the child returned to Israel, they wanted the minister to register the second woman as the adoptive mother. The Court held the minister must do so.

11. This case reached the substantive issue not considered in *Brenner-Kaddish* and held that under the Child Adoption Law, 5741-1981, a lesbian could adopt the child of her same-sex partner.

12. This refers to rights of a spouse in regard to activities designed to memorialize a fallen soldier.

13. *See, e.g.,* Ghassemi v. Ghassemi, 998 So.2d 731 (La. App. 2008) (marriage in Iran valid in Louisiana even though husband and wife were first cousins and marriage of first cousins is illegal in Louisiana, because marriage of first cousins is legal in Iran and does not violate strong public policy of Louisiana); see generally Lynn D. Wardle, *International Marriage and Divorce Regulation: A Survey*, 29 Fam. L.Q. 497, 502–06 (1995).

in the state where they live but want a more exotic setting for the wedding. They are not trying to avoid domestic marriage laws.

The United States is involved in a substantial debate on a somewhat different question: whether the intentional marriage of a same-sex couple in one state should be recognized in the state of residence when the couple could not have married in the state of residence. This issue arises because some states allow same-sex marriages and others do not. This issue is like the issue that arises in Israel because it involves intentional marriages in a different location and recognition of marriages that are not possible in the state of residence. It is different from the Israeli issue in that it involves issues of the relationships between states, which are arguably more complex than the issues of the relationships between foreign countries.

Questions

1. If two Israelis, a man who is recognized by the rabbinic authorities as Jewish and a woman who lacks sufficient documentation to prove that her mother was Jewish or that she was validly converted, wish to marry, what options do they have?

2. Many Israelis want Israel to allow civil marriages. Given the alternatives to religious marriage presently available to Israelis and the fact that the state provides similar benefits to couples using one of those options, what would be the advantages of a law recognizing such civil marriages?

3. In *Ben-Ari*, the petitioners only asked for what the petitioners in *Funk-Schlesinger* had obtained: registration. If you had been advising the petitioners in the case, what reasons might you have for not asking the Court to decide on the validity of the five same-sex marriages?

4. How can the effective preclusion of same-sex marriages in Israel be reconciled with the long list of rights of same-sex couples recognized by case law and by statute?

B. Divorce

Divorce law in Israel is even more complex than marriage law. Termination of marriage is handled in the religious courts, applying mainly religious law. Generally religious and civil courts both have jurisdiction over property division, custody, and any other payments, although the jurisdiction of the religious courts is exclusive if the case is first filed there. A person seeking a divorce may file first in the civil courts to sort out the property issues and afterwards apply to the religious court for a divorce. Application of the rules of religious law and of civil law on property matters can lead to radically different results, depending on the situation of the couple. Civil law requires division based on equal rights of the man and the woman; religious law divides the property on other grounds, often disadvantageous to the wife. This would lead to a race to the court house in some contested cases, with one spouse preferring that the civil court rules apply and the other spouse preferring the religious court rules. The Supreme Court held in HCJ 1000/92 *Bavli v. High Rabbinical Court* 48(2) PD 221 [1994] that religious courts are to use the civil law rules for division of property, but the religious courts, with an underlying commitment to religious law, do not easily comply. In some cases, the religious courts have been able to find a way to absorb the civil rules on division of property into the religious rules and in this way to act in accordance with the Supreme Court's decision without violating their commitment to religious law.

A Jewish marriage can be terminated only through the rabbinical courts applying Jewish law. Jewish law not only treats marriage as contractual, but also allows divorce on agreement of the husband and wife. Jewish law permitted divorce on consensual grounds long before that was the accepted law of many other authorities. No legal problems in terminating a marriage arise for a Jewish couple wishing to divorce who can agree on property division, child custody issues, etc. Problems do arise when they cannot agree. Jewish law is liberal in recognizing grounds for divorce even in the absence of an agreement, but a Jewish court cannot effect the termination of a marriage even if there are acceptable grounds for termination. The parties themselves must do that. In almost all cases, the only method of divorce allowed under Jewish law is through a writ of divorce called a *get*. The husband must give the wife the writ of divorce of his own free will and she must accept it of her own free will.

One persistent problem for Jews is that of the *anchored woman*.[14] If the husband refuses to give his wife a writ of divorce, no court can terminate the marriage. A court can rule that the husband should give his wife a writ of divorce, but it cannot deliver the writ in his place. The husband may refuse to give the wife a writ of divorce out of a desire to continue the marriage, out of stubbornness, or in order to get her to agree to give up her property rights, other financial claims, or her rights to custody of their children. If the husband does not give his wife a writ of divorce, they remain married under Jewish law, even if they are no longer living together or conducting their lives together. The woman cannot remarry; for this reason, she is considered an anchored woman. The opposite problem is less severe. If a woman refuses to accept a divorce, she is forbidden under Jewish law from having sexual relations with any man and she cannot remarry. The husband is not subject to a similar prohibition on sexual relations if they are with an unmarried woman, and sometimes he can get rabbinic permission to remarry. While the adverse social effects of not having a writ of divorce can be harsh on a man as well as on a woman, the problem seems particularly severe as to woman.

The problem of the anchored woman occurs in Jewish communities outside of Israel as well. Outside of Israel, though, the woman can get a divorce degree from a state court and, as a matter of civil law, will no longer be married. She can then legally enter into another marriage. This solution does not help observant Jewish women, who will not remarry without a religious divorce. On the other hand, the solution works for Jewish women willing to remarry in a civil ceremony. In Israel, where Jews can divorce and marry only through the Jewish religious authorities, no Jewish woman can remarry without the writ of divorce. She cannot get divorced in any other way, and the state rabbinical authorities will not give her permission to remarry without a writ of divorce from her husband. (The type of case like that in *Anonymous v. Tel-Aviv-Jaffa Regional Rabbinical Court* is an exception. If a Jewish Israeli couple married in a civil ceremony outside of Israel, a non-consensual divorce decree may be sufficient to dissolve the marriage.)

In reaction to this problem, the Knesset enacted the following statute:

---

14. The term in Hebrew is *agunah*. Technically the term originally referred to a woman whose husband could not be located. She could not live a married life, but also could not be divorced so she could remarry. Today it is common to use the term for a woman whose husband will not give her a get.

Israeli Statute

Rabbinical Courts Law
(Execution of a Divorce Decree), 5755-1995

1. Execution of a Divorce Decree

(a) If a rabbinical court determines in a decree or decision (hereinafter *decree*), that a man should give a writ of divorce to his wife, and the man did not carry out the decree, in order to bring about the implementation of the decree, the court may issue [in accordance with procedures set out in this statute] a restraining order against him as defined in section 2, an order of restraint by way of delaying or voiding a pension (benefit) or stipend as defined in section 2A, an order of restraint by way of coercive imprisonment as defined in section 3, or an order of restraint by way of solitary confinement under the requirements of section 3A (hereinafter restraining order).

(b) For the purposes of this section, it does not matter if the decree used language of coercion, obligation, commandment,[15] recommendation, or other language.

(c) If a rabbinical court determined in a decree that a woman should accept a get from her husband, and she does not carry out the decree, the court may, with permission from the chief judge of the High Rabbinical court, and in order to bring about the carrying out of the decree, issue a restraining order against her.

(f) If a restraining order was issued against a wife under subsection (c), a request of the husband to obtain a permit to marry shall not be considered until three years after the date of issuance of the order.

2. Content of the Restraining Order

(a) Preserving the authority of the rabbinical court [under another statute on execution of its orders], the rabbinical court may issue a restraining order that infringes on all or some of the following rights, for such period of time and under the conditions as the court shall determine:

(1) to leave the country;

(2) under the Passports Law, 5712-1952, to obtain an Israeli passport or document of passage, to hold them or to extend the period of their validity, with the exception that they shall be effective to allow the person to return to Israel;

(3) to obtain, hold, or renew a driver's license;

(4) to be appointed or elected, or to serve in any post created by law or in a body subject to review in the State Comptroller's Law (Consolidated Version), 5718-1958;

(5) to work in any profession in which law regulates participation in the profession, or to operate a business that requires a license or permit under law;

(6) to open or hold a bank account or to draw checks [under certain circumstances];

(7) if the person against whom the restraining order was issued is a prisoner or is a detained person—

(a) to obtain a special leave ... ;

---

15. A rabbinical court may issue an order saying that, under Jewish law, a person is commanded, or required, to do something. The court itself does not issue an order effectuating the divorce; it only determines what Jewish law requires.

(b) to receive and send letters, except for those regarding legal matters or letters to and from the person's lawyer, rabbinical pleader,[16] or the state comptroller;

(c) to receive visitors, except for the following: a lawyer, a religious figure, a rabbinic pleader, an official visitor, minor children if the rabbinical court decided they could visit; provided that the restraining order shall not prohibit the director of the prison or detention facility from permitting a visit of any person if the director is convinced that it will lead to the fulfillment of the decree.

Comment

The term *divorce decree* as used in this statute does not refer to a judicial statement that ends the marriage. The decree is only that the wife is entitled to a divorce or that the marriage should be ended. As indicated in the discussion preceding the statute, the actual divorce occurs only when the husband delivers a writ of divorce to the wife and she accepts it. The following case describes an extreme example of the result that sometimes occurs in practice.

Israeli Case

K.S. v. K.P.
FamC (Jer) 19270/03 (Dec. 21, 2004)

Judge M. HaCohen:

We have before us a claim for monetary damages for the injury caused to a woman by her husband's refusal to give her a writ of divorce after the rabbinical court ruled that he is obligated to do so.... As a matter of fact, it is clear that the husband refused over a period of more than twelve years to give the woman a writ of divorce and that on January 24, 2002, the rabbinical court decided "to obligate the husband without delay to give a writ of divorce to his wife."

The problem of refusal to provide a writ of divorce is a serious one in Jewish law and in the family law of the State of Israel.

I am ... not deciding ... whether, if the Plaintiff's claim is accepted and as a result the husband decides to give her the long-awaited writ of divorce, this will be considered a valid writ.

Factual Background

The members of the couple, who follow an Ultra-Orthodox lifestyle, were married in a Jewish wedding on June 21, 1982. They have six children, three of whom are minors. Their relationship encountered difficulties, and on May 11, 1992, when their youngest daughter was eight months old, the wife filed a complaint for a divorce in the Regional Rabbinical Court of Jerusalem. From the time of the filing, the husband and wife have not lived together. The legal proceedings continued for many years during which, at the request of the husband, they turned to various rabbis asking them to settle the disputes between them.

---

16. A rabbinic pleader is a person who works in the role similar to that of a lawyer but before a rabbinical court rather than a law court. The rabbinic pleader must go through a special education program that includes knowledge of Jewish law and must pass a special test. Some, but not all, rabbinic pleaders are also lawyers.

In addition to the wife's claim for divorce in the regional rabbinical court, in 1997 the husband turned to the court of the Ultra-Orthodox group called the Edah Haredit, which conducted an arbitration of the dispute.[17] On May 19, 1998, the court issued a decision in which it ruled, "We call on the husband to divorce his wife." In reaction to this, the Defendant notified that court that he wanted to withdraw the matter and have it heard before the [state] rabbinical court.

Over the years, the Plaintiff acceded to the requests of the Defendant and turned with him to various rabbis asking them to rule on the dispute between them. Here is a report on some of the rabbis to whom they turned:

Rabbi Dov Weiss, the rabbi of Kiryat Sanz, determined that the Defendant "does not understand how to behave properly to his esteemed wife."

Rabbi Yehoshua Cohen warned the Defendant against his verbal abuse of his wife, especially in the presence of the children.

Rabbi Menachem Mendel Fox determined that despite his investing many hours in an effort to make peace between the couple, "there is no chance of peace in the home."

Rabbi Shalom Eisenberg determined that the Defendant is "a hooligan and emotionally unstable and the wife ... is educated and devout and responsible in educating her sons and daughters properly...." and the Defendant "slanders her through his evil ways."

[They turned to five more rabbis.]

On December 7, 1998, the wife again filed for divorce in the regional rabbinical court and for support. In the hearing on this petition, the couple was referred, again at the request of the husband, to other rabbis in order for them to try to settle the matters.

On August 16, 1999, the wife appealed to the High Rabbinical Court on the amount of support granted her by the regional rabbinical court, and the dispute between the couple was subject to arbitration in that court. Under the auspices of the court, the couple was again referred to various rabbis, in accordance with the request of the husband. In a hearing on June 3, 2001, the husband undertook that if his wife agreed to go to a certain rabbi, he would accept whatever decision the rabbi made. Again, the Plaintiff agreed to the Defendant's request, and the court issued a decision that provided:

> In light of the declaration of the Respondent before the court that he will accept any decision of the named rabbi, the Appellant agreed to go to him with her husband, the Respondent, so that the rabbi could hear both sides and give his opinion on the dispute between her and her husband.

The two appeared before the rabbi, who also decided "it is indisputable that the parties must divorce." At this point, the husband suggested that they go to another well known rabbi.... When the court said to him that it would issue a decision against him, ordering him jailed for a month, the Respondent said, "Even if you put me in prison, I will not deliver" a writ of divorce.

---

17. The Ultra-Orthodox world is divided into numerous sects. The Edah Haredit is one of them. A number of the sects operate their own system of courts that are not state rabbinical courts. They are, rather, private judicial systems that apply Jewish law, and more particularly the view of Jewish law of the sect. People can turn to them voluntarily, just as disputants in the United States might choose to take a matter to a private arbitrator. The court of the Edah Haredit is one of the better known of the private religious courts. These religious courts operate mainly through arbitration of disputes, but can also issue decisions.

On January 24, 2002, the judge of the High Rabbinical Court issued a decision that provided:

> In light of the Respondent's declaration, the court had earlier decided that he would accept any decision of the last rabbi to whom he turned. Indeed, the rabbi spoke with me personally and told me clearly that the couple must divorce. After examining the file and all the records and after hearing the decision of that rabbi, in light of all the circumstances of the case and in light of the great distance between the two parties, we decide to require the husband to give a bill of divorce to his wife without delay.

It is to be added that one of the judges in the religious court, Rabbi Ezra Bar Shalom, would have held that the fact that the parties live apart does not seem to him a sufficient reason to require the husband to give a writ of divorce, but in light of the fact that the husband declared that he would accept the decision of the rabbi, who recommended divorce, the husband should be required to honor the decision of the rabbi.

A year later, on February 2, 2003, the husband not having given a writ of divorce to his wife, the High Rabbinical Court again considered the dispute between the parties and again issued a ruling requiring the husband to give his wife a writ of divorce. The court imposed on the husband the sanction of excommunication[18] but did not use its authority to impose other sanctions on the husband and did not order his imprisonment. This was against the minority decision of the head of the court, Rabbi Shlomo Dichovsky, who thought that the behavior of the husband amounted to debasement and humiliation of the wife and children and disrespect for authority, that he should be compelled to give her a writ of divorce, and he should be imprisoned if he did not do so.

In light of the decision, the husband was excommunicated. The sanctions imposed on the husband up to the time of filing of the complaint in this court had no effect and the husband still has not given his wife a writ of divorce.

Comment

This case shows how extreme the situation of an anchored woman can be, the laconic attitude to her problem sometimes demonstrated by the rabbinical courts, and the failure to use the sanctions available in the Rabbinical Courts Law (Execution of a Divorce Decree). Even when the sanctions are used, the authorities granted to the rabbinical court in the statute are effective in some but not all cases. Periodically the news reports on a man who sits in jail for a long period of time rather than give his wife a writ of divorce. Probably a greater problem is the lack of use of the law; it is not clear that the rabbinical courts commonly use the full powers granted them by the law.

The case of *K.S. v. K.P.* is from the family court, not the rabbinical court. The woman who had been denied a writ of divorce by her husband brought a tort action against him, claiming that the refusal to grant a divorce is a tortious act. This type of claim and this case are examined further in chapter 16 on tort law.

One reason a woman might bring a tort action for damages against her husband is to put pressure on him to grant the divorce. Judge HaCohen is aware of this possibility. Just before giving the factual background of the case, the judge notes that he is not deciding whether, if the husband accedes to this type of pressure and gives his wife a writ of di-

---

18. Excommunication in Jewish law involves exclusion of the person from certain ritual activities and honors in the synagogue. It does not mean that a person ceases to be a Jew.

vorce, the writ will be valid. He is referring to the fact that under Jewish law, a husband must give the writ of divorce of his own free will. The husband cannot be forced to give the wife the writ. Jewish law authorities differ on what constitutes free will. If the husband delivers a writ of divorce to his wife to save himself money, is he giving the writ from his own free will or does this constitute a writ given under force? The problem for the wife who receives a writ of divorce in such circumstances is that if she later wants to marry, the rabbi who checks that she is single may decide that her divorce was not valid because it was forced, she is still married, and she cannot remarry. It is likely that some of the very conservative Israeli rabbinical authorities would take this position, although the wife may be able to find a more lenient rabbi. Justice HaCohen is clear that he is not deciding any of these issues. They must be left to the rabbinical authorities.

C. The Right to Have Children

Israeli law puts a high value on parenthood. The development of the law on this matter is illustrated by the next two cases. They also show some of the perhaps unexpected effects of the legal recognition of the importance of parenthood.

Israeli Case

Nahmani v. Nahmani
Add'l Civil Hearing 2401/95, 40(4) PD 661 [1996][19]

[Ruth and Daniel Nahmani were a married couple. Due to illness, Ruth had a hysterectomy, but she asked to have her ovaries left in place so she could later have biological children through surrogacy. Ova were taken from Ruth's body, fertilized with Daniel's sperm, frozen and stored at a hospital. Israel did not at that time have a law permitting surrogacy, so the couple entered into a contract with an institute in the United States to find a surrogate who would bear their child. Before implantation of the frozen ova into a surrogate, Daniel left home, established a new family and fathered a daughter. He was still married to Ruth, who refused to be divorced. Ruth contacted the hospital and asked for the fertilized ova in order to continue the surrogacy procedure. In the face of Daniel's opposition to the use of the fertilized ova, the hospital refused to give them to Ruth. She filed suit in the Haifa District Court, which ruled that she should be given the fertilized ova. Daniel appealed and a panel of five justices of the Supreme Court reversed the decision of the district court, Justice Tal dissenting. Ruth petitioned for a rehearing, which was granted and held before a panel of eleven justices.

Upon rehearing, the Supreme Court decided in Ruth's favour by a majority of seven to four. The seven justices in the majority discussed two main reasons for their decision: a comparison of Ruth's rights against Daniel's rights, and Ruth's reliance on Daniel's agreement to have children. Six of the justices agreed to the rights analysis; portions of two of the opinions are presented here.]

---

19. Translation based on that found on the website of the Supreme Court at http://elyon1.court.gov.il/files_eng/95/010/024/Z01/95024010.z01.htm.

Justice Ts. Tal:

Development of the Law

Because of the rate at which life has developed, the legislator has not yet addressed all of the questions in the field of fertilization and genetics, and therefore we must create an appropriate norm to apply to the case before us. In doing so, we must: a) consider the conflicting interests; b) determine the legitimate expectations of both parties; and c) weigh the proper legal policy considerations.

The Conflicting Interests

There are two main rights competing with one another: the right to be a parent and the right not to be a parent. Because there is no provision in the law that applies to the case, it would be more precise to say that there are two conflicting *interests* rather than rights: the interest in being a parent and the interest in not being a parent. What is the nature of these interests? The interest in being a parent is one of the most basic aspirations of man and needs no explanation.

Against this existential interest lies the opposite interest, not to be a parent, or to be more precise, not to be a parent against one's will. When we come to balancing these conflicting interests, we should remember that despite the symmetrical forms of speech, "to be a parent" and "not to be a parent", these interests are not equal. The interest in parenthood constitutes a basic and existential value both for the individual and for the whole of society. On the other hand, there is no inherent value in non-parenthood. The value that is protected in the interest of non-parenthood is the value of privacy, namely the freedom and right of the individual not to suffer interference in his intimate decisions.

Let us turn to our case. First, we are not speaking of forced parenthood. We are speaking of a person who already gave his consent to parenthood, but who wants his consent to be required at all steps of the procedure. The interest of society in non-forced parenthood does not necessarily lead to the conclusion that his consent is required over an extended period. The interest in preventing parenthood against a person's will is satisfied by requiring a one-time irrevocable consent.

Secondly for the woman, it can be assumed that this is her only possibility of becoming a parent.

The cumulative weight of these two factors leads to a clear conclusion that the interest of being a parent takes precedence. We can reach the same conclusion by comparing the damage that is likely to be caused by denying the rights. If you take parenthood away from someone, it is as if you have taken away his life. In the Bible we find the desperate cry of our ancestress Rachel, "Give me children, else I die" (Genesis 30:1). Similarly from the teachings of the Rabbis we learn that "whoever has no children is considered as a dead person" (*Bereishit Rabba* 79, 9 on Genesis[20]). Similarly they interpreted the verse in Jeremiah 22:10: "'Do not weep for the dead, nor bemoan him; weep indeed for him who goes'—Rabbi Yehuda said: for him who goes without children" (Babylonian Talmud, Tractate *Moed Katan* 27b[21]). By contrast, denying the interest of non-parenthood amounts

---

20. Bereishit Rabba is a very old commentary on Genesis, probably written in the second or third century CE in the land of Israel. It is written in Aramaic.

21. This is the usual format for citing the Talmud. The citation states which version, the Babylonian or the Jerusalem, the tractate, and the page. The tractate here is *Moed Katan*, which means "Little Festival." It deals with the laws of the semi-festival days of the two extended Jewish holidays, Passover and Succoth, as well as with laws of mourning. The page number is 27b. In the Talmud, each leaf has

to no more than imposing burdens that may not be desirable to that person. Without belittling the weight of these burdens, they are not equivalent to taking the life of the spouse.

Even in *Davis v. Davis*, 842 S.W. 2d 588 (Tenn. 1992), the court decided in favor of the husband's position only because the wife was not asking for the fertilized genetic material for herself, but for another woman. The court said there that had the wife wanted the fertilized material for herself, and had the situation been such that she had no alternative for realizing her right to motherhood, the court would have been inclined to the opinion that the wife's right to motherhood should take precedence over the husband's right not to become a father.

In summary, I will say that the woman's interest in motherhood is greater and overrides the man's opposite interest.

Justice D. Dorner:

1. In this dispute between Ruth Nahmani (the wife) and her husband Daniel Nahmani (the husband) over the fate of their joint genetic material (fertilized ova), the wife's right, in my opinion, take precedence.

The question that arises before us is whether the husband's right not to be a parent, based on his alleged "ownership" of half of the genetic material of the ova fertilized with his sperm, really takes precedence over the right of Ruth, who also contributed half of the genetic material of these ova, to be a parent.

In the case before us, we need to balance between the right to be a parent and the right not to be a parent. Today in a case where a couple requires a surrogate mother who will carry its embryo in her womb, the balance is achieved within the framework of the Surrogacy Agreements (Approval of Agreement and Status of the Child) Law, 5756-1996 (the Agreements Law). The Agreements Law restricts the couple's autonomy and allows a surrogate to be used only if a written agreement is made between the woman intended to carry the embryo and the prospective parents and the agreement is approved by the Statutory Committee (section 2(1) of the Agreements Law).

A surrogacy agreement is therefore not absolutely binding. An agreement made under the Agreements Law is not an ordinary contract. As long as the fertilized ovum has not been implanted in the body of the woman intended to carry the embryos, she is entitled and the two spouses jointly are entitled to be released from the agreement. Even the statutory committee may stop the fertility procedure as long as the ovum has not been implanted. Nonetheless neither of the spouses, without the consent of the other, has the power to prevent the implantation after the ovum has been fertilized. Stopping the procedure at this stage requires approval of the statutory committee.

The Agreements Law that was enacted recently does not apply to the case before us. The parties also did not make a formal agreement between them. But this is irrelevant since, in my opinion, even under the law as it existed prior to the enactment of the Agreements Law, an agreement with regard to having children is not a contract. Couples are presumed not to be interested in applying the law of contracts to matters of this kind. This presumption has not been rebutted in our case. In any event, even were it proven that the parties had such an intention, they still did not have the power to give the agreement be-

---

a number, and the first side of the leaf is *a* and the second is *b*. Rabbi Yehuda's comment, set out in the Talmud, was an explication of the quoted text. He was saying that the verse in Jeremiah calling on us to "weep for him who goes" means we should weep "for him who goes without children."

tween them the force of a contract, since making a contract to have children is contrary to public policy. Therefore the contract would be void ... the Contracts (General Part) Law, 5733-1973. Note that there is nothing improper in the purpose of the agreement— bringing children into the world—or the means of carrying out the agreement. The impropriety lies in the application of the law of contracts to the agreement, which is contrary to public policy.

In a conflict between the right of the husband and the right of the wife, the two have equal status with regard to their relationship to the fertilized ova, which contains their joint genetic material. I do not think that we should distinguish between a man and a woman with regard to their yearning for parenthood. The proper balance between the rights of the two is therefore unaffected by the sex of the spouse who wants the ova to be implanted or of the spouse opposing this.

There are three main ways of balancing between the rights of the spouses if, after the woman's ovum has been fertilized with the man's sperm, they do not agree upon its implantation in the womb of a surrogate mother. These are as follows:

The first way, which was the majority opinion in the *Nahmani* appeal, is to always prefer the spouse who does not want to be a parent. This absolute preference is based on the principle of the autonomy of the individual, which rejects the coercion of parenthood. Under this principle, an agreement to bring children into the world should be regarded as a weak agreement whose existence, prior to the implantation of the ova, is conditional on the consent of both spouses. Enforcement of such an agreement would violate a basic human right and therefore is contrary to public policy. This position has some support in one of two judgments in the United States that considered the issue before us. In *Davis v. Davis*, 842 S.W. 2d 588 (Tenn., 1992), where the judgment was given by the Supreme Court of the State of Tennessee, it was held that, as a rule, the right not to be a parent should be preferred. Nonetheless it was held that this rule would not apply in a case where giving preference to the right not to be a parent would deprive the other spouse absolutely and finally of the possibility of being a parent. Justice Daughtrey wrote as follows:

> Ordinarily the party wishing to avoid procreation should prevail, assuming that the other party has a reasonable possibility of achieving parenthood by means other than the use of the pre-embryos in question. If no other reasonable alternatives exist, then the argument in favor of using the pre-embryos to achieve pregnancy should be considered ... the rule does not contemplate the creation of an automatic veto. *Id.* at 604.

The second way, which is the approach of my colleague, Justice Kedmi, is to give preference to the right to parenthood in all circumstances. This approach views the point of no-return not as implantation of the ovum in the body of the surrogate but as fertilization of the ovum, which is what creates a new entity. This approach has support in the second American ruling that exists on the question before us, *Kass v. Kass*, No. 19658/93, 1995 WL 110368 (N.Y.Sup. Ct. Jan 18, 1995), which was given by a trial court in the State of New York. In this case, the spouses had entered an agreement which included a stipulation that, if they did not reach agreement on how to deal with the fertilized ova, the ova would be used for research. The court held that this agreement should not be regarded as a waiver by the woman of her right to parenthood. The court disagreed with the ruling in *Davis v. Davis*, and it held that there was no basis for distinguishing between *in-vitro* fertilization of an ovum and fertilization of the ovum in the body of the woman, and in both cases, once fertilization has occurred, the husband cannot impose a veto on the continuation of the procedure. Justice Roncallo wrote as follows:

> In my opinion there is no legal, ethical or logical reason why an in-vitro fertilization should give rise to additional rights on the part of the husband. From a propositional standpoint it matters little whether the ovum/sperm union takes place in the private darkness of a fallopian tube or the public glare of a petri dish. Fertilization is fertilization and fertilization of the ovum is the inception of the reproductive process. Biological life exists from that moment forward ... To deny a husband rights while an embryo develops in the womb and grant a right to destroy while it is in a hospital freezer is to favor situs over substance. *Id.* at 3.

The third way, which my colleague Justice Tal advocates, is to balance the rights of the specific parties. In my opinion, this is the correct way, because balancing rights on an abstract level may lead to unjust results.

Of course, even a balancing of this kind is not an *ad hoc* balancing without any guiding principles, but it is made on the basis of rules that are applied to the special circumstances of each case.

Freedom in its fullest sense is not merely freedom from external interference of the government or others. It also includes a person's freedom to determine one's own lifestyle, to realize one's basic desires, and to choose from a variety of possibilities. In human society, one of the strongest expressions of an aspiration without which many will not regard themselves as free in the fullest sense of the word is the aspiration to parenthood. We are not speaking merely of a natural-biological need. We are speaking of a freedom which, in human society, symbolizes the uniqueness of the individual.... Whether man or woman, most people regard having children as an existential necessity that gives meaning to their lives.

Against this basic right, which constitutes a central element in the definition of humanity, we must consider the right not to be a parent. The basis of the right not to be a parent is the individual's autonomy not to suffer interference of the government in his privacy. This was discussed by Justice Brennan in *Eisenstadt v. Baird*:

> If the right of privacy means anything, it is the right of the *individual*, married or single, to be free from unwarranted governmental intrusion into matters so fundamentally affecting a person as the decision whether to bear or beget a child. 405 U.S. 438, 453 (1972).

In the conflict of rights before us we are not speaking of relations between the individual and the government, but of relations within the framework of the family unit. Although the autonomy of the individual is also recognized within the framework of the family, it seems to me that the right of privacy from the government is in general of greater weight than the right of privacy in the family. In the case before us, the husband does not even insist on his right for reasons of principle that oppose bringing children into the world. After all, he has a daughter from another woman and he wanted that daughter. His argument is against parenthood specifically with regard to an embryo created in the fertility procedure that the parties underwent. Moreover the husband has declared that his objection to parenthood does not derive from a fear of the personal and financial burdens involved. Therefore the interest not to be liable for personal and financial obligations towards a child born against the parent's wishes, which might otherwise be a relevant consideration when balancing the interests, is not relevant in this case.

What then is the importance of the freedom expressed in a person's knowing that he does not have a child that he does not want? It seems to me that for both men and women this freedom is regarded as limited, conditional, and in essence secondary compared to the right to have children and to create the next generation.

In so far as a man is concerned, once a woman has been impregnated by a man, he has no power to force her to have an abortion even when he is not interested in a child. In so far as a woman is concerned, as a rule she is not entitled to have an abortion. Abortion is permitted only on the basis of a permit from a statutory committee given according to a closed list of grounds. The mere fact that the woman does not want a child is not one of the reasons on the list. A fundamental principle, which applies to both women and men, is therefore that once a woman becomes pregnant, neither she nor her spouse has a right not to be parents.

Another basic principle is that the right of a man or a woman to be a parent does not override the right of the spouse to control their body, and it does not impose on them positive duties to participate in a procedure that may lead to parenthood.

Subject to these fundamental principles, the balance between the rights of the spouses will be made in each case by taking into account the current stage of the procedure, the representations made by the spouses, the expectations raised by the representations and any reliance on them, and the alternatives that exist for realizing the right of parenthood. I will discuss these considerations in this order.

The current stage of the procedure: The more advanced the stage of the fertilization procedure, the greater the weight of the right to be a parent. As aforesaid, the right to be a parent and the right not to be a parent are subject to a person's right over his body, and in no case can one spouse be compelled to undergo a physical act to realize the right of the other spouse. The situation is different in circumstances where the realization of the right to be a parent does not involve a violation of the other spouse's control over his body. In our case, it can be said that the right to be a parent has begun the journey from theory to practice and is not merely a yearning. On the other hand, the ovum has not yet been implanted, and there is no absolute obstacle to terminating the procedure.

Representations, expectations and reliance: Estoppel by representation prevents a party from denying a representation that he made to another party, if that party relied on the representation reasonably and in good faith and in consequence adversely changed his position. In Israeli law, the doctrine of estoppel—which we received from English law—can be regarded as a facet of the principle of good faith, which is a basic principle in our legal system. In this regard, the following remarks were written in a review of the judgment in *Davis v. Davis*:

> The doctrine of reliance should be applied to resolve a dispute between the gamete providers. The consistent application of a reliance-based theory of contract law to enforce promises to reproduce through IVF will enable IVF participants to assert control over their reproductive choices by enabling them to anticipate their rights and duties, and to know with reasonable certainty that their expectations will be enforced by the courts. Christi D. Ahnen, Comment, *Disputes Over Frozen Embryos: Who Wins, Who Loses, and How Do We Decide?—An Analysis of Davis v. Davis, York v. Jones and State Statutes Affecting Reproductive Rights*, 24 Creighton L. Rev. 1299, 1302–03 (1991).

Nonetheless in my view, the decision between the rights of the parties is not to be based on estoppel alone. Representations made by one spouse to another (including their making an agreement) may be a factor in the balance between the rights of the parties when they created reliance and sometimes even when they created mere expectations.... In our case, as a result of the husband's consent to the procedure, including his encouraging his wife to undergo the limited surgery that allowed her to retain her ovaries, the wife underwent difficult fertility treatments and had the ova fertilized with his sperm, rather than those of an anonymous sperm donor. This adverse change in the wife's position is a major consideration in the balance of interests between the spouses, even if it has not been proved that the husband wanted to become the father of the wife's child even if they separated.

Possible Alternatives: A case of refusal to continue a fertility procedure when the spouse can perform it with another partner is not the same as a case where refusal will doom the other spouse to childlessness. The fewer the alternatives available to the spouse wishing to become a parent, the greater the need to protect that spouse's right to parenthood, even at the expense of trespassing on the rights of the other spouse.

This consideration in our case has an additional weight of justice, since the spouse who is not interested in continuing the procedure, the husband, has been blessed with a daughter of his own in another family that he has established.

In our case, the basic principles and considerations which I have mentioned therefore lead to a preference of the wife to be a parent over the right of the husband not to be a parent. As stated, I do not believe that women and men attach different degrees of importance to having children. Therefore were the positions reversed and were the man to want to continue the procedure and were the woman to refuse, the result I have reached, allowing the implantation of the frozen ova in the womb of a surrogate mother, would not be different.

My opinion, therefore, is that the petition should be granted, the judgment in the *Nahmani* appeal should be reversed, and the judgment of the district court should be reinstated.

Comment

Justice Tal balances Ruth's interest in being a parent against Daniel's interest in not being a parent. Justice Dorner applies the same sort of balancing, but she addresses the matter in terms of "rights" and not "interests." Justice Dorner's language reflects the tendency of the Supreme Court to elevate many individual and social interests to the level of rights.

The four justices dissenting in the Nahmani decision would have decided in favour of Daniel on various grounds relating to his lack of consent to use the fertilized ova under the circumstances as they developed. Chief Justice A. Barak was among the dissenters. He would have ruled that public policy, founded in justice, required consent at every stage of the procedure, including implantation of the fertilized ova.

Justice Dorner's opinion uses the Israeli law on abortion to show that the freedom to avoid parenthood is limited and secondary to the right to parenthood. Her opinion implies that abortions are strictly limited in Israel. In fact, abortion is readily available in Israel. A woman who wants an abortion must gain approval from a hospital committee, but approvals are freely given. The permitted grounds are that the woman is younger than 17 or older than 40, the pregnancy is the result of rape or incest, the pregnancy is out of wedlock, the fetus may have a physical or mental defect, the pregnancy may endanger the woman's life, or the pregnancy may damage her physically or emotionally. Penal Law 5737-1977 § 316(a). These are broad grounds, and 98 percent of all requests for abortions are approved.[22]

Returning to the issue of disposition of fertilized ova, the Israeli approach can be compared to the three approaches taken by state courts in the United States. American courts

---

22. Mordechai Halperin, Termination of Pregnancy: Legal, Moral and Jewish Aspects, 6 Jewish Medical Ethics 41(2008) *available at* http://www.medethics.org.il/articles/JME/JMEM12/JMEM.12.4.asp.

sometimes relate to the issue of destruction of fertilized ova on the basis of balancing of interests or rights, in the way that the majority of justices in the *Nahmani* decision related to the issue. The Tennessee Supreme Court did this in *Davis v. Davis*, 842 S.W. 2d 588 (Tenn., 1992), cited in Justice Tal's decision. In that case, when the couple who produced the fertilized ova divorced, the wife wanted the eggs donated to an infertile couple so she would not feel that all of the painful procedures she went through for production and extraction of the eggs were in vain. The husband opposed any use of the ova to produce a child. He had been raised separately from his parents and objected to having any child of his raised without two parents. Even if the eggs were donated, he feared that the child might be born to a couple that would later divorce. The court referred to the right of procreational autonomy and held that his right to avoid parenthood was stronger than her interest in donating the eggs. It did not say it would have preferred the wife's right to procreate if she had no other way of becoming a mother. In the statement quoted in Justice Dorner's opinion above, the court only said it would give more serious consideration to the mother's interest in such a case; it did not say this weight would be determinative.

In *Kass v. Kass*, 696 N.E. 2d 174 (N.Y. 1998), the Court of Appeals of New York took a different approach. Justice Dorner discusses this case, but refers to the decision of the trial court, which was overturned after the *Nahmani* decision. The couple in *Kass* had signed an agreement at the time they deposited the fertilized ova for freezing under which the ova could be used for implantation only through their joint agreement at the time of use; absent such agreement, the ova would be used for research. At divorce, the wife wanted to have the ova implanted and the husband refused. The court held that the contract controlled and that the ova should be used for research. It explicitly rejected the wife's right to repudiate the contract unilaterally.

In the case of *In re Marriage of Witten*, 672 N.W. 2d 768, 783 (Iowa, 2003), decided seven years after the *Nahmani* decision, the Iowa Supreme Court rejected both the contract and the balancing approach. Again in this case, the wife wanted to use stored fertilized ova to have a child and the husband objected. His objection was specifically to his wife's using the ova; he was willing to donate them to another couple. In deciding how to handle the matter, the Iowa Supreme Court considered the approaches of courts in other states. It rejected the contract approach, reasoning that members of a couple should be able to change their minds on a matter this intimate. The court also rejected the balancing approach and searched for a better alternative:

> We have already explained the grave public policy concerns we have with the balancing test, which simply substitutes the court as decision maker. A better principle to apply, we think, is the requirement of contemporaneous mutual consent. Under that model, no transfer, release, disposition, or use of the embryos can occur without the signed authorization of both donors. If a stalemate results, the status quo would be maintained. The practical effect will be that the embryos are stored indefinitely unless both parties can agree to destroy the fertilized eggs. Thus, any expense associated with maintaining the status quo should logically be borne by the person opposing destruction. *Id.* at 783.

Question

5. Which approach is most compelling, that of *Davis v. Davis*, *Kass v. Kass*, *In re Marriage of Witten*, or *Nahmani v. Nahmani*?

The following decision further develops the concept of the right to parenthood.

Israeli Case

Dobrin v. Israel Prison Service

HCJ 2245/06 (June 13, 2006)[23]

Justice A. Procaccia:

Yigal Amir, a prisoner serving a life sentence, was convicted of the murder of the late Prime Minister Yitzhak Rabin. He applied to the prison authorities requesting permission to send a sperm sample out of the prison in order to enable artificial insemination of his wife, Larissa Trimbobler. On 5 March 2006, the responsible official at the Israel Prison Service decided to grant the request. This is the decision under review in this case.

The Petitioners, who were both members of the last Knesset, filed a petition against the Israel Prison Service and against the prisoner and his wife asking that the decision be held invalid.

Background

Because of the nature of the risk presented by Amir, he was classified by the prison authorities as a security prisoner. This classification led to the imposition of various restrictions upon him, of which the main ones are that he is held separately from other prisoners, surveillance cameras are installed in his cell, and there are visitation restrictions.... Amir's request to allow him to have meetings with the third respondent, his wife, was approved by this Court; this was because, *inter alia*, no evidence was presented with regard to her activity.

In January 2004, Amir submitted a request to the Israel Prison Service to be allowed to marry Larissa and to have conjugal visits with her.... Israel Prison Service gave notice that it decided to deny the request for conjugal visits and that it had not yet formulated a position on the question of marriage. Upon Amir's appeal, the district court, in reliance on privileged intelligence information, decided to deny Amir's petition with regard to conjugal visits. Amir applied for leave to appeal this decision in the Supreme Court, which denied the application. In its decision the Court ... found that in the circumstances of the case there was a real concern that allowing conjugal visits between the couple would lead to a security risk. It said that ... Amir ... remained committed to the terrorist ideology that he espoused in the past. The Court also found that ... there was concern that unsupervised meetings with his wife would be abused in order to transmit messages in the spirit of his extreme views and that he would thereby influence others to carry out extreme acts of the kind that he committed.... The question of Amir's right to marry his wife was not decided in that case, since the Israel Prison Service had not yet made its decision on this matter. At a later stage Amir and Larissa married by proxy, and on July 10, 2005, the marriage was declared valid by the rabbinical court.

On 27 July 2005, Amir submitted a request to the Israel Prison Service for permission to carry out procedures for the purpose of artificial insemination of his wife in order to allow them "to realize their desire to bring children into the world".... On 5 March 2006, after considering the legal position, the Israel Prison Service decided to approve Amir's request.

---

23. Translation based on that on the website of the Supreme Court at http://elyon1.court.gov.il/files_eng/06/450/022/r02/06022450.r02.htm.

The petition before us is directed against this decision.

Decision

We must examine two issues related to the validity of the commissioner's decision: the issue of authority and the issue of administrative discretion. With regard to the issue of authority, the question is whether the commissioner required express authority under the law to grant permission to a prisoner to transfer a sperm sample to his wife outside the prison. With regard to the issue of discretion, the questions are whether the decision is reasonable and proportionate and whether all the relevant considerations and no others were taken into account.

The Commissioner's Powers—a Normative Outline

Does the commissioner's decision to allow Amir to hand over a sperm sample fall within the scope of his authority under the law? Is special authorization required in the law in order to give this permission, such that without such authorization the permission falls outside the scope of the commissioner's power?

There is currently no express statutory provision on the right of a prisoner to provide a sperm sample to his wife for the purposes of insemination outside the prison. Such express statutory authorization is not required for the following reason: under general constitutional principles of law, a person in Israel has constitutional human rights. These are found, *inter alia*, in the Basic Law: Human Dignity and Freedom, which enshrines some of the human rights and gives them a super-legislative status. These rights include the human right to dignity, from which the right to family and parenthood is derived.

In our case, Amir, like any other prisoner, has a human right to establish a family and to be a parent. He was not deprived of the right to establish a family and to bring children into the world by the sentence that was imposed on him, even if the loss of liberty resulting from the imprisonment deprives the prisoner of the ability to realize family life in full. The Prison Service Commissioner therefore does not need an express authorization in order to give practical expression to the realization of this right, which is one of the supreme constitutional human rights in Israel. Had the commissioner denied the basic right, this would have required him to show that there were good reasons that supported the infringement and the denial would have had to meet the tests of the limitation clause.

Constitutional Human Rights and the Right to Family and Parenthood

The Basic Law: Human Dignity and Liberty enshrines the human rights to dignity and liberty and thereby expresses the values of the State of Israel as a Jewish and democratic state. It provides that the dignity of a person as a human being may not be violated and that every person is entitled to protection of his dignity; it recognizes the possibility of infringing on a person's basic constitutional rights, provided that the infringement satisfies the tests of the limitation clause. The tests in the limitation clause make the constitutional legitimacy of the infringement conditional. The infringement must be allowed by a statute or by virtue of an express statutory authorization for some other body to impose the limitation; it should be consistent with the values of the state; it should be for a proper purpose and it should not be disproportionate.

Within the scope of the right to human dignity lies the right of a person to have a family and to be a parent. The right to family is one of the most basic elements of human existence. It is derived from the protection of human dignity, from the right to privacy and from the principle of the autonomy of the will of the individual, which lies at the very essence of the concept of human dignity. Family and parenthood are the realization of the natural desire for continuity and for the self-realization of the individual in society. Within the scope of the human right to dignity, the right to family and parenthood is a constitutional right that is protected by the Basic Law.

On the scale of constitutional human rights, the constitutional protection of the right to parenthood and family comes after the protection of the right to life and to the integrity of the human body. The right to integrity of the human body is intended to protect life; the right to family is what gives life significance and meaning.

Therefore this right is very high on the scale of constitutional human rights. It is of greater importance than property rights, the freedom of occupation, and even the privacy of the individual. "It reflects the essence of the human experience and the concrete realization of an individual's identity."

An infringement of the right to parenthood and family will be legitimate only if it satisfies the tests in the limitation clause. These tests reflect a balance of the weight of the basic rights against other needs and values that are essential for the existence of proper social life. Basic rights, including the right to family, are not absolute; they derive from the realities of life that make it necessary to give a relative value to human rights and other substantial interests, whether of other individuals or of the public. A harmony between all of these interests is a condition for a proper constitutional system. In order for an infringement of a human right to satisfy the constitutional test, it must fall within the proper margin of balances that weigh the right against the conflicting value. The more elevated the status of the constitutional right, the greater the weight of the conflicting interest that is required in order to derogate from the right.

Restrictions on Prisoners' Rights

According to the prevailing constitutional system, an offender who is sentenced to imprisonment does not automatically lose all of his human rights. The infringement of his rights is limited solely to the degree that it is required in order to achieve the goals of a substantial public interest. These goals include, first and foremost, the purpose of the sentence of imprisonment, which is intended to deprive the prisoner of his personal liberty during the term of imprisonment. By being deprived of his personal liberty, a prisoner suffers an infringement of a basic right, but the infringement is made pursuant to a law that befits the values of the state. It is intended for the proper purpose of isolating the offender from society for a defined period in order to protect the public from the danger that the offender presents and to rehabilitate him. The assumption is that the sentence is proportionate to the severity of the offence that was committed and the other circumstances that are relevant to the sentence. Restricting the liberty of a prisoner is an inevitable consequence of the sentence that was imposed upon him, and therefore the infringement on liberty receives constitutional protection.

The restriction upon personal liberty, which is a consequence of the imprisonment, also gives rise to a necessary infringement on certain other human rights that cannot be realized because a person is imprisoned. Thus, for example, the prisoner suffers an infringement of his right to engage in his occupation, his right to privacy, and to a certain extent also his freedom of expression, with all the liberties that derive from it. The infringement on human rights that accompanies imprisonment is limited solely to infringements arising necessarily from the loss of personal liberty.

Another purpose that may justify an infringement of a human right of a prisoner relates to the need to ensure the proper administration of the prison and to safeguard the welfare of its inmates. The prison authorities have the responsibility to impose various restrictions that are required for managing life in prison in an effective manner, and these include maintaining order, security and discipline in the prison, as well as protecting the security of the inmates, the safety of the warders, and the safety of the public from the dangers that are presented by the prison inmates. For the purpose of assuring the proper administration of the Israel Prison Service, the Commissioner may give comprehensive orders with regard to all the aspects of prisoners' lives, and these may in several respects restrict their personal autonomy in various spheres.

If the prison authorities impose restrictions that violate the human rights of a prisoner, and these restrictions do not arise inherently from the loss of liberty as a result of the imprisonment, the restrictions are constitutional only if they materially satisfy the tests of the limitation clause. They should be consistent with the values of the state, be intended for a proper purpose and satisfy the requirement of proportionality.

It should be emphasized that the restrictions on human rights that are imposed by the prison authorities are not intended to add an additional sanction to the sentence that was handed down. Their inherent purpose is not to increase the severity of the sentence that was imposed on the prisoner. Their purpose is not to punish the prisoner for his crimes, for which he has been sentenced to imprisonment, or to make the conditions of his imprisonment more difficult as recompense for his despicable acts. Where this is the purpose of the restrictions, they are likely to fail the constitutional test, since this is not a proper purpose. A restriction that is not required by the realization of the purposes of imprisonment or that is not required by another legitimate public purpose constitutes, *de facto*, the imposition of an additional sentence on the prisoner for the offence of which he was convicted. A restriction that adds to the sentence imposed on the prisoner falls outside the scope of the power to limit the rights of prisoners that is granted to the Israel Prison Service. It is a departure from the principles of criminal sentencing and especially from the principle of legality that is enshrined in section 1 of the Penal Law, 5737-1977, under which there are no offences or sanctions unless they are prescribed in statute or pursuant thereto. The penal sanction takes the form of the actual loss of freedom of movement in a prison, which is determined by the court that handed down the sentence; in view of this, the Israel Prison Service is not competent to add a punitive measure to the sentence that was handed down.

The Power of the Commissioner to Give Permission to Hand Over a Sperm Sample— Conclusions

The premise on which the petition is based is that express statutory authority is required in statute for the prison officials to allow a prisoner to undergo a procedure of artificial insemination with his wife; without this, granting such permission goes beyond the powers granted to them under the law. This premise is fundamentally unsound, and it effectively turns the law upside down and undermines basic principles of public and constitutional law. When a person has a right, and certainly when he has a constitutional right, a public official does not need authorization in a statute in order to uphold and respect the right. The opposite is true: the official requires an authorization in statute in order to restrict or infringe on the right, and where the infringement restricts or denies the realization of a human right, it must satisfy the tests of the limitation clause as a condition for its validity.

It follows that in our case there is no need to ask whether the Israel Prison Service has authorization to permit a prisoner to realize his right to parenthood by means of artificial insemination; at most, we may need to ask whether there is a power to *restrict* this right and what is the scope of such a possible restriction in the special circumstances of the case.... In the circumstances of this case, the commissioner acted within the limits of his authority when he did not find any administrative or other reasons that justify a restriction on the prisoner's right. His decision relies on recognized basic principles of constitutional law and it gives expression to the right of the prisoner when no basis was found for restricting it.

The Decision of the Public Authority under the Test of Reasonableness

In addition to the Petitioners' argument that the commissioner's decision to allow Amir to give a sperm sample to his wife outside the prison was made *ultra vires*, they also argued that this decision does not satisfy the test of reasonableness. They claim that the unreasonableness is expressed first and foremost in the fact that the permission given to Amir to realize his right to have children conflicts with public morality and the public sensibility because it was given to the murderer of a prime minister. They also claim that granting the permission ignores the interests of the child who will grow up without a father. Finally they claim that in giving the permission the commissioner did not make a comprehensive examination of the significance of the issue for all prisoners, and in the absence of a general procedure in this regard, the commissioner acted in a manner that violates the principle of equality among prisoners.

No one denies that the offence of murder that Amir committed and for which he was sentenced to life imprisonment deserves public condemnation and will be recorded in the history of the state as one of the most terrible offences committed in Israel since its founding. But the seriousness of the offence that was committed, with all of its ramifications, found full and final expression in the criminal sanction that was imposed on Amir. The sentencing considerations that are taken into account lie solely within the sphere of authority of the judiciary, and when the sentence was handed down, the sanctions imposed on the offender were exhausted. The Israel Prison Service does not have authority to add to the punishment of the prisoner, in ways that go beyond the sentence that was imposed on him, by restricting human rights that he has even as a prisoner. The argument that the public has feelings of abhorrence for the base acts that he committed is insufficient. The public's feelings of repulsion for an offender who took human life and murdered the state's leader are also incapable of affecting, in themselves, the scope of his human rights while in prison and the nature of the permitted restrictions upon them. Basic principles of public morality and the public's desire for revenge against one prisoner or another do not constitute a relevant consideration or a proper purpose for preventing a prisoner from realizing his human right to parenthood, as long as this realization does not amount to a significant administrative disruption in the management of the prison or another relevant violation of a significant public interest that justifies its restriction. The human right is also retained by a prisoner who was convicted of the most terrible offences. No matter how great the feeling of abhorrence at his acts, it cannot constitute an objective reason for restricting his rights.

Even the Petitioners' additional argument that Amir should not be given permission because of the damage that can be anticipated to the best interests of the child that will be born to the couple cannot serve as a valid ground for violating the right to parenthood in the circumstances of this case.

The question of when the consideration of the best interests of the child may justify preventing his birth is a profound question in the field of ethics and philosophy. The questions of when the law may intervene in this, and when a public authority has power to interfere with the human right to have a child for reasons of the best interests of the child and for other reasons, are very difficult and complex. The right to have a child and the right to be born are concepts that lie to a large extent in the field of morality and ethics that are outside the law. Whether and in what circumstances the Israel Prison Service has a power to restrict the right to have a child against a background of considerations of the best interests of the child is a difficult and loaded question.... With regard to the best interests of the child, it has only been argued that the child will be born to a single-parent mother because the father has been sentenced to life imprisonment. This argument has no merit in the specific context. No reasons have been brought before us to show, on the merits, any real grounds why the best interests of a child that will be born from artificial insemination to the Amir couple will be harmed. No basis has been established for the argument that Amir's wife lacks the capacity to raise a child. Moreover the raising of a child by a single-parent mother while the father is sentenced to life imprisonment does not in itself indicate that the child's best interests are harmed, nor does it allow the public authorities to restrict the right of his parents to have children. In the modern world, the single-parent family has become a common and accepted phenomenon, and does not in itself indicate harm to the interests of the child on such a scale and to such an extent that it justifies the intervention of the public authority in a way that violates the right of individuals to self-realization by bringing children into the world. The mere fact that one of the parents is in prison does not constitute, *prima facie*, a ground for violating the right of the couple to parenthood and the right of a child to be born, for reasons of his best interests.

In this case, no factual basis was established to show harm to the best interests of the child that may be created as a result of giving the permission to the Amir couple. Therefore the question of balancing the relevant conflicting values to the right to parenthood does not arise, and this argument should be rejected.

This leaves the argument that the prison authorities did not conduct a comprehensive examination of the question of prisoners sending sperm samples to their wives, did not formulate a general procedure for all prisoners in this regard, and did not apply the balance of interests correctly with regard to the case of Amir. In their opinion, Amir has received better treatment than other prisoners.

In this matter also the Petitioners' arguments are general and they do not establish a concrete factual basis for the existence of values that conflict with the prisoner's right and that would justify a restriction or denial of his rights. Indeed, the prison authorities have stated that they will prepare general procedures concerning the transfer of sperm samples of prisoners to their wives for the purpose of artificial insemination outside the prison. But their willingness to do this, which is important in itself, has no bearing on the specific decision in Amir's case, which is reasonable.

Since there is no important value that conflicts with the prisoner's right to parenthood, no proportionate balance is required here between relevant conflicting considerations, nor is there a proper reason to violate the prisoner's human right.

In addition, no concrete information was brought before us to support the Petitioners' claim with regard to a violation of equality among prisoners as a result of granting the permission to Amir. The concept of equality in this context is loaded and complex, and it may justify possible distinctions between types of prisoners as to the possibility of their having children while in prison. For example, it is possible that there will be a distinction between the ability of male prisoners to realize parenthood by sending sperm samples to their wives for the purpose of insemination and raising children outside the prison, which does not involve any responsibility on the part of the public authority for the birth and raising of the child and does not require any special institutional and budgetary arrangements, and the ability of the authority to allow pregnancies and childbirths of female prisoners in the prison on a large scale, which gives rise to difficult questions concerning the manner of raising and caring for the children after birth, as well as questions involving resources and budgets that are required for this purpose. This issue involves difficult moral and practical questions that relate both to the prisoners and to the children who are born to a difficult fate. Logic dictates that in this area of realizing the right to parenthood the constitutional test may allow a legitimate distinction between types of prisoners according to various criteria.

American Law

The premise in American law is that prisoners retain their constitutional rights inside the prison: "Prison walls do not form a barrier separating prison inmates from the protection of the constitution." *Turner v. Safley*, 482 U.S. 78, 84 (1987).

Therefore the prisoner retains constitutional rights such as the right to equal protection before the law, the right to due process in the Fourteenth Amendment of the United States Constitution, and the right to privacy. At the same time, other constitutional rights that are not consistent with the actual imprisonment are not retained by the prisoner: "An inmate does not retain [constitutional] rights inconsistent with proper incarceration." *Overton v. Bazzetta*, 539 U.S. 126, 132 (2003); *Turner* at 96.

In the leading decision in *Turner v. Safley*, it was held that the appropriate standard for scrutinizing an infringement of the constitutional rights of prisoners is the lowest level of scrutiny, the rational connection. The reason for this lies in the complexity of the task of administering the prison and the fact that a court lacks the proper tools to allow it to consider the matter. *Id.* at 85, 89.

The right to have children is recognized in American law as a constitutional right that lies at the very heart of the right to personal freedom. *See Carey v. Population Services International*, 431 U.S. 678, 685 (1977); *Cleveland Board of Education v. LaFleur*, 414 U.S. 632, 639 (1974); *Eisenstadt v. Baird*, 405 U.S. 438, 453 (1972); *Stanley v. Illinois*, 405 U.S. 645, 651 (1972); *Skinner v. Oklahoma*, 316 U.S. 535, 541 (1942).

In view of these principles, the United States Supreme Court has held that the right to marry is retained even during imprisonment. *Turner v. Safley*, 482 U.S. at 97–98. Notwithstanding, the federal courts have consistently refused to recognize a right to conjugal visits and intimacy with a spouse as a constitutional right. *Anderson v. Vasquez*, 28 F.3d 104 (9th Cir. 1994); *Hernandez v. Coughlin*, 18 F.3d 133 (2nd Cir. 1994); *Toussaint v. McCarthy*, 801 F.2d 1080 (9th Cir. 1986). The questions (1) whether allowing a prisoner to provide a sperm sample for the purpose of artificial insemination and realizing his constitutional right to have children is consistent or inconsistent with the actual imprisonment and (2) what conditions restricting that right may be imposed have not yet been brought before the United States Supreme Court, but other courts in the United States have approved administrative decisions that restrict the realization of the right.... In *Goodwin v. Turner*, 908 F.2d 1395 (8th Cir. 1990), the Federal Court of Appeals of the Eighth Circuit approved a policy that denied prisoners the possibility of artificial insemination. It was held that even if the right survived imprisonment, there was a rational connection between this policy and the duty of the prison to treat all prisoners equally. The argument was that the prisons would also be required to allow female prisoners to realize the right to have children, and as a result also to care for their needs during pregnancy and for their infants, and that this would lead to imposing substantial costs on the prisons and make it necessary to divert resources from important programs and the security needs of the prison. For this reason it was permissible not to approve artificial insemination for spouses of male prisoners.

Conclusion

We should remember that a civilized country is not merely judged by how it treats its faithful citizens, but also by how it treats the criminals living in it, including the most despicable criminals who wish to undermine its ethical foundations. In a proper constitutional system, the umbrella of human rights extends over every human being, including the criminal sitting in prison, subject to conditions and restrictions that satisfy constitutional criteria. The public authority acted in this case in accordance with the proper constitutional criteria, and its decision was made according to the law.

On the basis of all of the aforesaid, the petition should be denied.

Justice S. Joubran:

I agree with the opinion of my colleague Justice A. Procaccia and the reasons that appear in her profound and comprehensive opinion. Notwithstanding, in view of the complexity of the question before us, I think it right to add several remarks of my own, if only in order to present the difficulties raised in this case from a different and additional viewpoint.

From time to time the Court is asked to consider petitions concerning the conditions of imprisonment and the various restrictions that are imposed on prisoners who are serving sentences in the prisons. On a theoretical level, these petitions involve complex questions concerning the purpose of the sanction of imprisonment. In this context, it is possible to identify two main approaches that conflict with one another. Under the first approach, the purpose of imprisonment is limited to depriving the prisoner of his personal liberty by restricting his freedom of movement when imprisoning him behind bars for the period of his sentence. Under this approach, restricting any other rights of the prisoner is not a part of the sentencing purpose.

Under the second approach, a restriction of additional basic rights of a prisoner, apart from the right to personal liberty, is possible if this is consistent with the additional legitimate purposes underlying the objective of the sentence, including the removal of the prisoner from society, the suppression of crime, specific or general deterrence, a denunciation of the offender, and punishment. In other words, under this approach, the purpose of the sentence of imprisonment that is imposed on the prisoner is not limited to sending him to prison in itself, and the restriction of the prisoner's freedom of movement, together with the other violations of his rights that accompany it, do not express the full sentence that is imposed on him.

It is not superfluous to point out that the distinction between the two approaches is not merely a matter of semantics but a difference that goes to the heart of the purpose of sentencing. Thus it may be asked most forcefully why sentencing should only take the form of a denial of the prisoner's liberty and freedom of movement and not a restriction of other rights. It should be emphasized that the distinction between the different approaches has major ramifications on the scope of the protection given to the rights of the prisoner.

The difference between the two approaches may easily be clarified by giving several examples: serving a prison sentence within the confines of a prison inherently results in an infringement of the prisoner's right to engage in an occupation, since he is subject to various restrictions that deprive him of the possibility of leaving the prison confines. But consider, for example, a case in which a prisoner, who committed crimes that gave rise to public outrage, wishes to publish, from the prison, a novel that he has written, which is based on the story of his personal life. Assuming that the writing of the book during the prisoner's free time does not interfere with the proper functioning of the prison and does not affect the maintenance of order and discipline in the prison, under the first approach the prisoner should not be prevented from publishing the book, by which means he realizes his right to the freedom of expression and the freedom of occupation. Of course, the need to examine the writings of the prisoner and to ensure that they do not include details that may affect order and discipline in the prison may impose such a significant burden on the prison service that it will be justified in refusing publication of the book. In any case, it should be noted that under the second approach it is possible that the publication of the book may be prevented for very different reasons. It may be argued that the purposes underlying the sentence of imprisonment, including punishment, expressing revulsion at the acts of the prisoner, and isolating him from society, justify not allowing that prisoner while he is in prison to derive an economic benefit from the commission of his despicable acts or achieving public recognition as a result of the publication of the book.

Another interesting example concerns the question of the rights of a prisoner to vote in elections to the Knesset. Whereas under the first approach there is no basis for restricting the right of a prisoner to vote, as long as this does not harm the proper management of the prison, under the second approach it is possible to regard the refusal of the right to vote as a measure that reflects the purpose of isolating the prisoner from society, which derives from the idea that there is no reason to allow a prisoner who has been removed from society for a certain period to influence the shaping of its system of government and other aspects of society. This is the place to point out that, in Israel, the arrangement that allows prisoners to realize their right to vote is enshrined in legislation.

It is the first approach presented above that has established over the years a firm basis in our case law.

Petition denied.

Comment

The *Dobrin* case not only recognizes a constitutional human right to be a parent, but emphasizes that it is a very important right. The decision says it is more important than the right of privacy. If that is so, in cases over control of fertilized ova, the interest of the parent who wants to implant the ova will always prevail if the parent wanting to use the ova has no other way to become a parent. As stated in Justice Dorner's decision in *Nahmani*, the other parent's interest in not having the ova used derives from the right of privacy. It is not clear whether the strength of the right to parenthood would also tip the balance where the parent seeking control of the eggs could become a parent in some other way. Perhaps the degree of hardship involved in effecting the right would be relevant.

Question

6. What explains the difference in the results in Israel and in the United States on the issues of parenthood? Consider the following facts: The average fertility rate in Israel is 2.96 births per woman.[24] The average fertility rate in the United States is 2.06

---

24. CENTRAL BUREAU OF STATISTICS, FERTILITY RATES, BY AGE AND RELIGION, STATISTICAL ABSTRACT OF ISRAEL, 2010 (rate for 2009), *available at* http://www1.cbs.gov.il/reader/shnaton/templ_shnaton_e.html?num_tab=st03_13&CYear=2010. The rate for Jews is 2.90; for Muslims, 3.73; for Christians, 2.15; for Druze, 2.49; and for those not classified by religion, 1.56. *Id.*

births per woman.[25] Israel's national health insurance funds fertility treatments for the first two children for a couple. Coverage for fertility treatment in the United States varies from state to state and policy to policy, but most policies either exclude fertility treatment coverage or impose limits not found in the Israeli insurance. The Israeli National Insurance Institute, the rough equivalent of the Social Security Administration in the United States, pays the hospital expenses associated with delivery; provides a birth grant to cover some of the costs associated with a new baby, such as purchase of baby furniture; and makes salary replacement payments to all working women so they can take maternity leave (or to the father if the mother chooses to return to work and he chooses to remain at home).

D. Surrogacy

Israel was one of the first jurisdictions with a statute on surrogate motherhood. The statute clarifies that surrogate motherhood is allowed but sets detailed requirements for surrogacy arrangements. Surrogacy that does not comply with these arrangements is illegal.

Israeli Statute

Surrogacy Agreements (Approval of Agreement and Status of Child) Law 5756-1996
Part I: Interpretation

1. Definitions

In this statute—

"Surrogate mother" means a woman who carries a pregnancy for the intended parents;

"Intended parents" means a man and a woman who are a couple, who have an arrangement with the surrogate mother for the purpose of giving birth to a child;

"Surrogacy agreement" means an agreement between the intended parents and the surrogate mother under which the surrogate mother agrees to become pregnant through implantation of a fertilized ovum and to carry the pregnancy for the intended parents;

"Recognized department" means a department in a hospital or clinic that the director general of the Ministry of Health has recognized ... for the purpose of medical procedures related to in-vitro fertilization;

"Family member" means a mother, daughter, granddaughter, aunt, or female first cousin, except for a woman who is a family member through adoption;

"Approval committee" means the committee appointed by the minister of health pursuant to section 3;

"Social worker under the Surrogate Motherhood Agreement Law" means a social worker appointed for the purposes of this law ... ;

---

25. Central Intelligence Agency, The World Factbook, United States (2011) (rate estimated for 2011).

"Child" means a child born to a surrogate mother as a result of performance of a surrogacy agreement;

"Parental relations" means the range of obligations, rights, and authorities that exist between a parent and a child under all laws;

"Order of parenthood" means an order as to the guardianship of the intended parents over the child and the establishment of parental relations between them;

"Court" means the family court.

Part II: Approval of a Surrogacy Agreement

2. Surrogacy Agreement

The implantation of a fertilized ovum with the goal of the surrogate mother becoming pregnant with a child who will be delivered to the intended parents shall not be done unless the following requirements are met:

(1) There is a written agreement between the surrogate mother and the intended parents that has been approved by the approval committee in accordance with the provisions of this statute;

(2) The parties to the agreement are adult residents of Israel;

(3) The surrogate mother

(a) is unmarried, providing that the approval committee can approve of an agreement with a married surrogate if it was proven to its satisfaction that the intended parents, through a reasonable effort, could not come to an agreement for surrogacy with an unmarried surrogate mother;

(b) is not a family member of either of the intended parents;

(4) The sperm that are to be used for in-vitro fertilization are from the intended father, and the ovum is not from the surrogate mother;

(5) The surrogate mother is of the same religion as the intended mother, provided that if all the parties to the agreement are not Jewish, the committee can deviate from the requirements of this subsection in accordance with the opinion of the religious authority who is a member of the committee.

3. Approval Committee

(a) The minister of health shall appoint an approval committee of seven members comprised of:

(1) Two doctors with credentials as experts in gynecology;

(2) One doctor with credentials as an expert in internal medicine;

(3) One clinical psychologist;

(4) One social worker;

(5) A pubic representative who is a legal expert;

(6) A cleric from the religion of the parties to the surrogacy agreement.

The minister of health shall appoint a chairperson from among the members of the committee.

(b) Among members of the approval committee, there shall be at least three members of each sex.

4. Request for Approval of the Agreement

(a) A request for approval of a surrogacy agreement shall be submitted to the approval committee along with the following documents:

(1) The proposed surrogacy agreement;

(2) A medical opinion stating that the intended mother cannot become pregnant and carry a pregnancy, or that pregnancy is likely to present substantial danger to her health;

(3) A medical opinion as to the suitability for the process of each party to the agreement;

(4) A psychological evaluation of the suitability for the process of each party to the agreement;

(5) A certification from a psychologist or social worker that the intended parents received appropriate professional advice, including advice on the other possible means of becoming parents;

(6) If the parties entered the agreement through the services of a paid agent, the agency agreement along with information about the agent.

(b) The approval committee shall evaluate the documents submitted ... and can request further information from the parties and can hear claims of any other person, as it deems appropriate.

5. Approval of the Agreement

(a) If the approval committee determines that all the requirements set out in section 2 have been met ... it may approve of the surrogacy agreement, or approve of it conditioned on certain requirements, but only if it is convinced that:

(1) All the parties entered into the surrogacy agreement voluntarily and of their own free will and understand its meaning and its effects;

(2) There is no fear of injury to the health of the surrogate mother or the interests of the child to be born;

(3) The surrogacy agreement contains no conditions that will infringe on the rights of the child or of any of the parties, or that will deprive them of such rights.

(b) After the approval committee has approved a surrogacy agreement, both sides shall sign before the committee; any change in the agreement requires approval of the committee.

(c) The approval committee can renew its discussion of an agreement it has already approved if there is a substantial change in facts, circumstances, or conditions that were the basis of its decision, as long as the fertilized ovum has not been implanted in the surrogate mother in compliance with the surrogacy agreement.

6. Payments

The approval committee may approve of conditions in the agreement relating to monthly payments to the surrogate mother to cover actual costs entailed in carrying out the agreement, including the costs of legal advice and of insurance, and in addition compensation for loss of time, for pain and suffering, for loss of income or temporary loss of ability to earn an income, or any other reasonable compensation.

7. Execution of the Surrogacy Agreement

In-vitro fertilization with implantation of the fertilized ovum shall not be carried out other than in a recognized department and under an approved surrogacy agreement.

Part III: Status of the Child

8. Applicability

This part shall apply to the pregnancy and birth of a child who is born under a surrogacy agreement that was approved under the provisions of Part II.

[Sections 9–12 provide a scheme for turning the child over to the guardianship of the intended parents immediately upon birth and for the intended parents to obtain within seven days a court order of parenthood that makes them parents for all legal purposes, unless a court finds that such an order would not be in the best interests of the child.]

13. Renunciation of the Agreement by the Surrogate Mother

(a) If the surrogate mother asked to renounce the surrogacy agreement and to keep the child, the court shall not allow this unless it is proven after receipt of a report of a social worker under the Surrogacy Agreement Law that a change of circumstances has occurred that justifies renunciation by the surrogate mother and that this will not harm the best interests of the child.

(b) After the court has issued an order of parenthood, it shall not permit renunciation of the agreement.

19. Punishment

[The statute imposes a punishment of imprisonment for a year for violations of the requirements and prohibitions in the statute, including punishment for involvement in surrogacy in Israel in a manner other than that specifically authorized in this statute.]

Comments

In order to qualify as intended parents, two people must be a couple and must be a man and a woman. It does not matter whether they are married, either through a religious marriage in Israel or a civil marriage abroad, or whether they are reputed spouses.

Under section 4(a)(2) of the statute, surrogacy is limited to cases where the intended mother cannot carry the pregnancy for medical reasons. Surrogacy may not be used for convenience of a mother who does not want to be pregnant. This provision may reflect a sense that while surrogacy is permissible, it is not free from ethical issues. Where a woman cannot herself carry a pregnancy, the importance of allowing her to become a mother outweighs other issues, but this counterweight is not present where a woman only chooses to avoid pregnancy. The limitation may also reflect the fact that the surrogate mothers are in short supply, although it is not clear that this shortage was anticipated when the statute was drafted.

By virtue of section 2(4), the statute allows only gestational surrogacy, in which the surrogate mother carries the pregnancy but does not supply the ovum. The ovum can come from the intended mother or from a donor. The prohibition on allowing use of the surrogate's own ovum makes the process medically more difficult because conception must be through egg extraction from someone else and through in-vitro fertilization (IVF), rather than through the simpler process of artificial insemination. This requirement may be intended to make the surrogate mother's separation from the child easier, both for her own sake and in order to avoid prolonged battles over the child that can harm also the intended parents and the child. In addition, the sperm must be from the intended father. The reason for this requirement is not clear. Perhaps this is to assure a genetic connection between the child and at least one parent, but if that is the reason, the law would only need to provide that either the ovum or the sperm must come from one of the intended parents.

The Israeli statute permits commercial surrogacy. Under section 6, the surrogate mother may receive not only reimbursement for her expenses, but also compensation. Furthermore, section 4(a)(6) contemplates the existence of commercial agencies to connect, for a fee, intended parents with women willing to be surrogates. Payments to both the surrogate mother and the agency must be approved by the committee.

After the child is born, the statute requires that, within a week, a court issue an order providing that the intended parents are the parents for all purposes. This provides a high degree of certainty as to the status of the child. For the same reason, the statute strictly limits the conditions under which the surrogate can back out of the agreement or obtain any legal rights to the child.

Some of the provisions of the statute reflect concerns that arise under Jewish law. Some of these provide for exceptions for non-Jews, but it is not clear whether these exceptions matter in practice. A member of the intended couple's clergy must be on the approval committee, and it has been reported that neither Muslim nor Christian authorities in Israel allow surrogacy.[26]

The requirement in section 2(3)(a) that the surrogate be unmarried and not be a relative of the father are both related to the perceived need to remove any suspicion as to the status of the child under Jewish law. Jewish law has a strong prohibition on sexual relations between a married woman and a man not her husband. A child from such a relationship is considered a *mamzer*. The rules of Jewish law impose several limitations on a mamzer, including limitations on marriage. Although it is not clear that a child conceived through IVF and implantation in the uterus of a married surrogate (a process which does not involve sexual intercourse) would have the status of a mamzer, barring married women from serving as surrogates removes all doubt. The surrogate mother may be divorced or widowed; a child born of a woman in either status is not a mamzer.

The requirement in section 2(3)(b) that the surrogate mother not be related to the parents is also related to Jewish law. Sexual relationships between close relatives are strictly prohibited and, again, the child of such a relationship is a mamzer. Even though children born through surrogacy are not conceived by sexual intercourse, the statute reflects a conservative view that removes all doubt as to the propriety of the procedure and the status of the child.

In section 2(5), the statute requires that if the intended parents are Jewish, the surrogate mother must also be Jewish. Under Jewish law, the prevailing opinion is that the birth mother, in this case the surrogate, is the mother of the child, and not the woman who supplied the egg. Therefore the statute imposes this requirement to ensure that the religion of the child matches that of the intended parents.

In HCJ 2458/01 *New Family v. Committee to Approve Surrogacy Agreements* 57(1) PD 419 [2002], the Israel Supreme Court ruled that even though the statute discriminated against single mothers by providing surrogacy services in Israel only to couples, it would not hold the statute invalid. The Court was strongly influenced by the fact that the statute was new and that it was the first national statute of its kind. In light of this, the Court held that the Knesset should be allowed to test the waters of surrogacy regulation with a so-

---

26. Abraham Benshushan & Joseph G. Schenker, *Legitimizing Surrogacy in Israel*, 12 HUMAN REPRODUCTION 1832 (1997).

lution that applied only to couples. In HCJ 625/10 *Anonymous v. Committee to Approve Surrogacy Agreements* (July 26, 2011), the Court reviewed a decision of the approval committee to reject a proposed surrogacy contract presented by a couple with three children on the sole grounds that they had too many children, without providing a hearing to the couple and without considering any other factors. The woman had given birth to three children, but had to undergo an emergency hysterectomy due to a problem at the time of the last birth. The couple, who wanted a large family, found a surrogate and submitted a proposed contract to the committee, which rejected it. The Court held that while the number of children a family wants is a relevant factor for the committee to consider, that factor that alone does not justify rejection of a couple. The Court based its decision on statutory language, finding no reason to consider whether the committee's decision interfered with the intended parents' right of parenthood.

In the United States, surrogacy is controlled by state law. Some states have statutes prohibiting surrogacy, some have statutes permitting and regulating it, some have case law allowing surrogacy, and a large number of states have no law on the matter. Some of the states permitting surrogacy prohibit commercial surrogacy. In general, the matter is subject to less detailed legal control in most US jurisdictions than it is in Israel.

The Israeli surrogacy law reveals two tendencies: one is to enable parenthood, and the other is to accommodate religious law restrictions. While some American jurisdictions do not allow use of this new reproductive method and others leave open questions on how conflicts regarding surrogacy will be resolved, the Israeli statute tries to anticipate and solve all potential conflicts, making the use of surrogacy more certain for everyone involved and thereby encouraging its use. The accommodation of religious law restrictions makes surrogacy as comfortable as possible for many segments of the population. On the other hand, the law makes surrogacy unavailable to some segments of the population, including single parents and same-sex couples, and the religiously-based provisions may seem unnecessarily and unfairly limiting for those who do not care about the religious values at stake.

Question

7. One of the persistent concerns about surrogacy is that women will be exploited by working as surrogates. What provisions in the Israeli statute are designed to protect the surrogate mother from exploitation? Is there a downside to these provisions?

Part Five

Private Law

Chapter 15

Contracts

A. Good Faith in Contract Negotiation

Israeli Statute

The Law of Contracts
(General Provisions), 5733-1973

12. Good Faith in Negotiation

(a) In negotiations leading up to the formation of a contract, a person must act in the customary manner and in good faith.

(b) A party that did not act in the customary manner and not in good faith must pay to the other party damages for the injury caused to the other party due to the negotiations or due to the formation of the contract, and the provisions of sections 10, 13 and 14 of the Law of Contracts (Remedies for Breach of Contract), 5731-1970, apply with the necessary changes.

15. Misrepresentation

A person who enters a contract due to a mistake that is the result of a misrepresentation made by the other party or someone acting on the other party's behalf may revoke the contract. For the purposes of this provision, "misrepresentation" includes the failure to reveal facts that should have been revealed under law, custom, or the circumstances of the case.

39. Good Faith in Performance

A person should act in the customary manner and in good faith in performing the obligations that derive from the contract, and this applies also to effecting rights that derive from the contract.

61. Applicability

(b) The requirements of this law shall apply, to the extent appropriate and with the necessary changes, to all legal transactions that are not contracts and to obligations that do not derive from contracts.

Israeli Statute

The Law of Contracts
(Remedies for Breach of Contract), 5731-1970

10. The Right to Damages

The injured party is entitled to damages for the injury caused to that party due to the breach and the results of the breach that the breaching party foresaw or should have foreseen at the time of formation of the contract as the probable result of the breach.

11. Damages without Proof of Injury

a. If an obligation to provide or receive property or a service is breached, and the contract is therefore revoked, the injured party is entitled to receive, without proving an injury, damages in the amount to be paid under the contract for the property or the service and the value of the property or service on the day that the contract is revoked.

b. If an obligation to pay an amount of money is breached, the injured party is entitled to receive, without proving an injury, damages in the amount of the missed payment from the day of the breach until the day of the payment.

14. Minimization of Damages

a. The party that breached is not liable for damages ... for an injury that the other party could have prevented or minimized through reasonable means.

Israeli Case

Panidar Investment, Development, and Building Co. v. Castro
Rehearing 7/81, 37(4) PD 673 [1983]

[The development company and Castro signed a contract for the company to sell and Castro to buy an apartment. Castro paid the company a large sum of money based on this contract. It turned out that the development company did not own the property that was the subject of the contract. Pre-contract negotiations had been conducted by Joseph Panidar, who was an engineer and building contractor. He and his wife owned the shares in the development company. The development company went through bankruptcy proceedings in which unsecured creditors received only fifteen percent of the amounts due them. Castro claimed he was not covered by this arrangement, and the district court agreed. Castro sued both the company and Joseph Panidar personally for damages based on Joseph Panidar's failure to conduct the negotiations in good faith. The district court ruled for Castro, and the defendants appealed to the Supreme Court. The Court rejected the appeal, and the development company and Joseph Panidar asked for a rehearing on the issue of whether Panidar, who was not personally a party to the contract that resulted from the negotiations, could be held liable for damages for negotiation not in good faith. While some of the judges discussed the issue of agency as relates to Joseph Panidar, much of the discussion centered on the question of whether Panidar could be held personally liable under Section 12, the Law of Contracts (General Provisions), 5733-1973, without regard to his status as an agent of the company.]

Chief Justice M. Shamgar:

The Wording of the Statute

This obligation [to act in good faith in pre-contract negotiations] applies to every person who takes part in such negotiations. Nothing in the language limits the obligation to a person who participated in the negotiations and later became a party to the contract. Rather, under the plain meaning of [Section 12 of the Law of Contracts, 5733-1973], the obligation applies to everyone who takes part in the negotiations, whether that person conducts the negotiations in order to form a contract in his own name or not and even if he is only an agent of others. It does not matter whether the person who participates in the negotiations acts alone or whether he is one of a group that works together as the agent of someone else. It is the participation in the negotiations and not the status of a person as a party to a future contract that matters and that is the basis of the application of subsection (a).

Subsection (b), with which we are especially concerned in this case, provides a right to recover damages from "a party that did not act in the customary manner and not in good faith." We must interpret the meaning of this provision as a subsection of Section 12, which in its first subsection creates an obligation, described above. We should see it as a further elaboration of the same obligation which is created in subsection (a). Subsection (a) defined an obligation and described it as applying to everyone who takes part in negotiations, without regard to the person's formal status, even if no contract results from the negotiation. The application of the sanction, that may include damages, must be parallel to the application of the obligation that gives rise to the right to damages.

The wording of subsection (b) includes two terms to which we should direct our attention. On the one hand, it relates to what happens in negotiations as an independent basis for imposition of damages; on the other hand, it uses the term "party."

Usually this term is used to describe a person who enters into a contract with another person. But we should interpret this term according to its context. When it appears in Section 12, which does not deal at all with the contract that may be formed and that may create obligations but rather deals with the stage of the negotiations, we should interpret the term "party" as it relates to the subject that is treated therein.... The context tells us clearly what the term as used here means that a person is obligated to act in a certain way in negotiations. A party that does not do this, it continues in subsection (b), may be obligated to pay damages. This tells us that "party" in subsection (b) is the person who conducted the negotiations. This definition, though, does not cover the full meaning of the term "party." Subsection (b) uses the term "party" in two different contexts. Based on the term "the injury caused to the other party due to the negotiations," meaning injury caused to the other party, we see that "party" means a party to the negotiations, but the term "the injury caused to the other party ... due to the formation of the contract" tells us that it also means a party to the formation of the contract.

On the Meaning of the Obligation of Good Faith

Violation of the duty to act in the customary manner and with good faith can be a failure to do something or the failure to reveal facts that, under the circumstances, one would expect a person participating in negotiations to reveal to the other side. The duty to reveal information under Section 12 is not just a duty to respond to questions of the other side. There are circumstances under which a person must initiate the revelation of information that is essential to the other side in the pre-contract negotiations.

The rules for appropriate behavior are not rules that just require a person to desist from telling lies, but rather they require honesty and fairness. In some circumstances they require affirmative action in a situation in which an evil person would sit silent. The failure to provide information in a case in which provision of the information is appropriate is a violation of the duty of good faith. Where there are facts that would influence the nature of the agreement reached in the negotiations, the duty to reveal the information is part of the duty of good faith. Sometimes the parties must actively reveal information, especially when it is clear to one side that there is a significant difference between what the other side thinks is being obtained and what is really being obtained in the existing factual and legal situation. The obligation of good faith includes the obligation to reveal and clarify material facts prior to formation of the contract, to the extent this is required by the nature of the deal or the specific circumstances. The obligation to provide information derives from the trust between the sides to the negotiation, which turns into a legal obligation by virtue of Section 12.

Sometimes it is possible that failure to reveal information rises to the level of misrepresentation as that term is used in Section 15. It may be that some action constitutes a lack of good faith and, at the same time, is the basis for another cause of action. The principle of good faith is broad, and nothing prevents the injured party from having an additional claim, based on more limited grounds. The plaintiff can chose between the claims.

Comment (Requirement to Negotiate in Good Faith)

We can distinguish between the requirement of good faith in negotiations prior to formation of the contract and good faith in performance of a contract. Section 12, the Law of Contracts (General Provisions), 5733-1973, the provision discussed in these cases, applies to negotiations. Section 39 requires good faith in contract performance; in addition, it requires good faith in effecting rights derived from the contract.

Pre-contract negotiations are also covered by other sources of law in Israel, as indicated in Chief Justice Shamgar's opinion in *Panidar, Investment, Development and Building Co., Ltd. v. Castro.* These other sources of law include tort claims of fraud and negligence, the theory of unjust enrichment, and claims of estoppel.

American law requires good faith in performance of a contract, but not in pre-contract negotiations. "Every contract imposes upon each party a duty of good faith and fair dealing in its performance and its enforcement." *Restatement (Second) of Contracts* § 205 (2008). Comment c. to the Restatement provision sets out explicitly that it "does not deal with good faith in the formation of a contract." The comment further provides that bad faith in bargaining may be covered by contract rules relating to capacity to contract, mutual assent, consideration, fraud, and duress, and by rules in tort and restitution. Some statutory provisions that apply to specific types of contracts require good faith in negotiation. In addition, when a case is brought for specific performance of a contract, a court may refuse this equitable remedy because of the failure of the party seeking specific performance to reveal relevant information in the bargaining stage.[1]

It is not clear whether these enumerated doctrines of American law have the same kind of broad reach that is found in the language of Israeli Section 12 and recognized by Chief Justice Shamgar's opinion in the *Panidar* case. Each of the doctrines in American law is limited to specific circumstances. Furthermore, the law is less unitary and more confus-

---

1. *See, e.g.,* Schlegel v. Moorhead, 170 Mont. 391, 397, 553 P.2d 1009, 1012 (Mont. 1976).

ing when decided under multiple theories. Whether the arguably more limited approach of American law is preferable has been debated in the literature.[2]

The doctrine of good faith in Israeli contract law is derived from the use of the doctrine in civil law jurisdictions, but the Israeli version has developed its own independent characteristics. The Israeli doctrine found in Section 12 applies whether or not a contract is formed. Liability may be imposed if bad faith in contract negotiations prevents formation of the contract, as it did in *Kal Construction Ltd. v. E.R.M. Raanana for Construction and Leasing Ltd*, set out later in this chapter, or if it does not prevent formation of the contract but otherwise causes damages, as in the *Panidar* case. The former principle is called *culpa in contrahendo*. As originally conceived, it applied where no contract is formed to allow the injured party to collect reliance, but not expectation, damages. The principle is recognized in Germany and some other continental legal systems mainly in this doubly limited format: it applies only to cases where no contract is formed and allows only reliance damages. In some cases though, at least in Germany, the doctrine has been expanded to apply where a contract is formed and even may be applied to allow expectation damages where the terms of the contract that would have been formed without the bad faith bargaining are clear.[3]

Israel probably begins with the German approach because the law professors who worked on development of much of Israeli contract law were trained in Germany before they immigrated to the new State of Israel.[4] This is an interesting feature of the law of Israel as a young country. Many of its early lawyers were trained elsewhere, and they brought their ideas with them. The foreign influence is limited, though, as laws based on those of other countries are interpreted by academic lawyers and applied by judges who were trained in Israel or in countries other than that from which the law originated.[5]

Questions

1. What are the advantages and disadvantages of applying a general requirement of good faith to contract negotiations, as Israeli law does, rather than limit the requirement to contract performance, as in US law?

2. What explains the fact that US law, which rejects the notion of good faith as a general requirement in contract negotiations, nonetheless requires good faith in specific situations, such as in negotiation of labor contracts?

3. Is it appropriate to impose obligations of good faith on a person who negotiates a contract even if that person is not a party to the contract?

Comment (Definition of the Good Faith Obligation)

Chief Justice Shamgar's opinion states that the scope of the good faith obligation is broad. The leading scholar on contract law, Professor Gabriella Shalev, has identified the following as violating the obligation of good faith in negotiations in some circumstances:

---

2. *See* Juliet P. Kostritsky, *Uncertainty, Reliance, Preliminary Negotiations and the Holdup Problem*, 61 SMU L. Rev. 1377 (2008); Alan Schwartz & Robert F. Scott, *Precontractual Liability and Preliminary Agreements*, 120 Harv. L. Rev. 661 (2007).

3. *See* Friedrich Kessler and Edith Fine, *Culpa in Contrahendo, Bargaining in Good Faith, and Freedom of Contract: A Comparative Study*, 77 Harv. L. Rev. 401 (1964).

4. Dr. Moshe Gelbard, Netanya Academic College School of Law, suggested this reason.

5. *See* Ricardo Ben-Oliel, *Foreign Influences in Israeli Banking Law*, 23 Tul. Eur. & Civ. L.F. 167 (2008).

- Conducting parallel negotiations with two different parties after telling one party that there are no parallel negotiations, or perhaps without informing one party that such parallel negotiations are occurring
- Making unreasonable proposals in negotiations
- Rejecting reasonable proposals of the other side
- Deciding not to abide to something already agreed to (before the contract is formed)
- Withdrawing an offer already made (before the contract is formed)
- Taking advantage of the economic, social or mental status of the other side to extract agreement to conditions to which the other side would not otherwise agree
- Leaving the country in the middle of negotiations as a way of putting pressure on the other side[6]
- Failing to reveal information, even if the other side did not ask for it (such as the weak financial condition of the company that would be one side of the contract) and even if the other side could have discovered the information
- Withdrawing from the negotiations without justification
- Negotiating without intent to form a contract (in order to buy time or affect another party not involved in the negotiations)[7]

Both Chief Justice Shamgar and Professor Shalev state that the precise content of the obligation depends on the facts of a specific case. This integration of a doctrine of broad reach and application that varies from case to case gives considerable power to courts to define, after the fact, what behavior was and what was not legally permissible. This leaves parties to contract negotiations without clear rules as to what they may and may not do. The court's orientation, like the orientation explored in chapter 9 on administrative law, seems to be designed to obtain the proper substantive result in the case before it. It is not as oriented to formulating clear legal rules that will guide behavior.

Questions

4. The Israeli doctrine of good faith in contract negotiation applies broadly to all contract negotiations. On the other hand, the case law does not give a precise definition of what good faith requires, but leaves that to be determined on a case-by-case basis. What are the advantages and the disadvantages of case-by-case definition of the precise requirements of good faith in contract negotiations?

5. The power of the courts to define what behavior is impermissible in contract negotiation under the duty of good faith can be compared to the power the courts have taken on themselves to define the scope of basic rights found in Basic Laws or to identify the existence of basic rights outside of Basic Laws. See chapter 8. What is the difference between a broad degree of judicial discretion in constitutional law and in contract law? Consider the nature of the persons or bodies affected by the court decision and which courts make the decisions in each of these types of cases.

---

6. Because Israel is a very small country, any substantial travel involves leaving the country.
7. *See* Gabriella Shalev, The Law of Contracts — General Provisions, 148–52 (2005).

Israeli Case

Kal Construction Ltd. v. E.R.M. Raanana for Construction and Leasing Ltd.
CA 6370/00, 56(3) PD 289 [2002]

[The defendant published a tender inviting proposals for a building project. A tender is a term relating to government contracts. When the government seeks to enter a contract for supply of goods or services, it publishes a tender that includes the terms of the contract. Various parties can submit proposals to enter a contract with the government under the terms of the tender. In Israel, extensive legal doctrine governs how the government may select the winning proposal. After negotiations with several firms that submitted proposals, the defendant agreed on terms of a contract with the appellant, who was the plaintiff in the original action. It was necessary to obtain approval of the defendant's administrative council before the contract went into effect, and the council decided not to give its approval. Instead, it entered into a contract with a firm that had not participated in the tender and that did not meet the requirements set out in the tender. At an earlier stage of the litigation, it was determined that the defendant violated the duty to act in good faith in the negotiations. The Court turned to determining the measure of damages to which the appellant was entitled.]

Chief Justice A. Barak:

To what remedy is the injured party entitled in cases of a breach of the obligation of good faith? Everyone agrees that the obligation of good faith is not just an ethical obligation. It is a legal obligation that is accompanied by sanctions. What are these sanctions? The main provision on good faith, Section 39 of the statute [Law of Contracts (General Provisions), 5733-1973] is silent on the matter. This silence should not be interpreted as meaning that there is no remedy. The general rule is that where there is a right, there is a remedy.... The law's silence is explained by the fact that the effects of violation of the obligation of good faith are diverse and vary from case to case. There is no set framework for dealing with all cases.

So what is the remedy for breach of the obligation to conduct negotiations in good faith? Were the statute silent on this matter, we would say that the remedy is the same as that for the duty to act in good faith in performing obligations that derive from the contract and should be determined on the basis of the type of breach. But Section 12 of the statue is not silent on this matter. Section 12(b) provides that the breaching party—the party that conducts negotiations not in good faith—"must pay to the other party damages for the injury caused due to the negotiations or due to the formation of the contract...." What is the meaning of this provision? Does it allow imposing only negative damages (reliance damages), or does it also allow affirmative damages (expectation damages)? Does it prohibit other remedies (that are not damages, such as specific performance)? These are the questions before us in this appeal. We now turn to finding the answer.

"Damages for the Injury Caused to the Other Party Due to the Negotiations or Due to the Formation of the Contract"

Section 12(b) of the statute provides that the party who conducted negotiations prior to formation of the contract without good faith must pay the other party (the injured party) damages for the injury caused due to the negotiations or due to the formation of the contract. This provision has been interpreted in the case law as granting only negative damages (reliance damages).

Under this approach, the objective of imposing damages under Section 12(b) of the statute is to put the injured party in the same position that he would be in if he had not participated in the negotiations at all. In regard to the damages imposed under Section 12(b) of the statute, Professor Shalev writes:

> These damages are reliance damages—negative damages the goal of which is to restore the situation to what it was; that is, to put the injured party, through a cash payment, in the situation he would have been in had he not participated in the negotiation or if there had been no breach of the obligation to behave in good faith.

This approach has a logical underpinning. Simply put, if the contract was not entered into and we do not know what its provisions would have been had the negotiations been concluded and the contract formed, there is no way to provide compensation for the damages for breach of this contract that exists only in the abstract. There is no way, within the framework of returning the situation to what it was, to put the parties in the situation they would have been in had the contract been formed and properly performed. The only thing possible is to put them in the position they would have been in had they not participated in the negotiations. Of course, the negative compensation is not always lower than the affirmative compensation, but it is certainly different from it. So the question is whether it is possible to get affirmative compensation (expectation damages) for violation of the duty to conduct negotiations in good faith. As we have seen, the answer is generally negative. But is this the law in all cases? Why should the law not put the parties in the position they would be in if the contract had been formed in those cases in which the negotiations had reached such an advanced point that the provisions of the contract are known, and it would have been entered into were it not for the fact that at the last minute this was prevented by behavior that was not in good faith. Is there anything in the language or statutory purpose of Section 12(b) of the statute that prevents granting affirmative damages (expectation damages) in such a case? We turn to the analysis of this issue.

We begin with the language of Section 12(b) of the statute. The obligation of the breaching party is to pay the injured party damages "for the injury caused to the other party due to the negotiations." Nothing in this language requires us to conclude that "the injury caused to the other party due to the negotiations" means only the damages caused by participating in the negotiations. We can just as well say that this provision means that in a case in which the negotiations have been completed, but due to the lack of good faith of one side in the negotiations the contract was not formed, the damage caused by the negotiation not in good faith is the failure to form a contract, including the loss of the profit from the contract. Similarly there is nothing in the concept of "damages" that requires limiting the remedy, within the framework of Section 12(b), to negative damages alone. The opposite is true; Section 12(b) of the statute provides that "the provisions of sections 10, 13 and 14 of the Law of Contracts (Remedies for Breach of Contract), 5731-1970, apply with the necessary changes." The application of these provisions, that of course include affirmative damages (expectation damages), is not limited to cases in which the contract has already been formed. Under the language of Section 12 of the statute, they apply "with the necessary changes" even in the case in which the contract is not formed. Therefore, these provisions authorize compensation for the injury that the [breaching] party "foresaw or should have foreseen" (Section 10 of the Law of Contracts (Remedies for Breach of Contract), 5731-1970). In a case in which the negotiations have reached their final stages and in which a contract would have been entered but for the absence of good faith, this injury may be that which flows from the failure to perform the contract. Nothing requires that this injury should be limited to the actual conduct of the negotiations.

Is there anything substantively in the situation which we are now considering, the stage before the formation of the contract, which requires limiting the remedy of damages to negative damages?

The situation with which we are dealing relates to the period before contract formation. There is as yet no contract. Negotiations are ongoing. The sides are free to design the contract terms. They are generally free to break off negotiations. Considerations of individual autonomy allow each side freedom of action. If this freedom is used for a bad end and the negotiations are conducted not in good faith, we impose on the party who breaches the obligation the requirement to pay compensation that reflects the injury that resulted from conduct of the negotiations. Other compensation is not possible because we do not know the content of the agreement that the parties would come to were the negotiations conducted in good faith. This is certainly true in those cases in which the conduct of the negotiations in good faith would reveal information that would cause the cessation of those negotiations. Even when good faith conduct of the negotiations would have allowed those negotiations to continue, in most cases we do not know whether the negotiations would have culminated in the sides agreeing to a contract. In such a case, considering the underlying assumption that a court will not devise a contract for the sides that they did not themselves devise, there is no place to speculate as to what the content of the contract would have been had a contract been formed. This leads us to reject expectation damages and be satisfied with reliance damages. Certainly in such a case, the appropriate balance between the freedom to design the contents of the contract on the one hand, and the obligation to conduct negotiations in good faith on the other hand, is found in the obligation to pay only negative damages. Such damages effect the principle of returning the situation to what it was. They return the sides to the position they would be in had they not entered into negotiations.

This is the situation in most cases but not in all. There are cases in which the negotiation between the sides reaches such an advanced stage that the contents of the contract to which the sides mean to agree is known. Its conditions have been crystallized, but due only to a lack of good faith, the terms of that agreement were not recorded in a contract. In such a case, returning the situation to what it would have been had there not been any bad faith in the negotiations requires that we allow them to present evidence of what the situation would have been if the contract had been concluded. There is no interference with freedom of contract, or no serious interference, if we give effect to a contract the terms of which the parties had in good faith devised. In such a case, the court is not designing the contract for the parties. The only thing the court is doing is removing the barrier erected by one of the parties, acting without good faith, to consummation of the contract. The appropriate balance between the freedom to design the contract terms on the one hand, and the obligation to conduct negotiations in good faith on the other, is now found in allowing to the injured party to recover affirmative damages. Such damages effect the principle of returning the situation to what it was. Therefore, when negotiations have progressed to the final stage, so that but for the lack of good faith a contract would have been formed, the meaning of returning the situation to what it was means returning them to the position they would be in if there had not been a lack of good faith.

The idea can be expressed in this way: There are cases in which the remedy for violation of the duty to negotiate in good faith is enforcement of the contract which the parties would have entered into had the negotiations been conducted in good faith.... In such circumstances, the party who negotiated not in good faith will not be allowed to deny assurances that were made and that would have been part of the contract but for the bad faith negotiations. Based on this principle, it is but a short step to recognition of affirmative damages (expectation damages). If we begin with the assumption that the contract was formed and then breached, we take the case out of the realm of Section 12 of the statute and put it within the ambit of Section 10 of the Law of Contracts (Remedies for Breach of Contract).

Our approach, that in certain cases in which the negotiations have reached an advanced stage in which the terms of the contract have been determined, and but for the bad faith in negotiations, the contract would have been entered into, the injured party is entitled to affirmative damages (expectation damages), is adopted in other countries [citing three treatises on European contract law].

[The Court went on to impose expectation damages equivalent to about $125,000.]

Questions

6. Chief Justice Barak states in several places that reliance damages, which he calls negative damages, return the *parties* to the position they would have been in had they not entered into negotiations. Is this true? If not, why would he have said it? What is the problem with having said this?

7. Does it make sense to allow expectation damages for breach of the duty to negotiate in good faith?

Comments

The Israeli obligation of good faith found in the Law of Contracts (General Provisions), 5733-1973 applies not only to contracts, but also to all legal actions and obligations. Section 61(b). Aharon Barak, while serving as Chief Justice of the Supreme Court of Israel, termed the general obligation of good faith in private transactions a "principle of substantive democracy."[8] In contrast, another prominent former justice of the Supreme Court objected to the breadth of the good faith doctrine:

> The doctrine of good faith can be very broadly deployed and naturally will create disagreement among experts. The glory of the doctrine of good faith, and of its prevention..., fills the world. It can be said that we can fit into this doctrine the entire scope of the law, and that would not be far from the truth. For precisely this reason, whatever the doctrine of good faith means, it seems to me that we should use it only in those cases in which the regular legal tools we have do not work.[9]

In the proposed Civil Code for Israel, which will include all areas of civil law, the obligation of good faith is presented at the beginning as a general principle applying to all civil law. This change of position does not change the formal content of the law, but it probably would increase the emphasis on good faith as an over-arching legal principle.

---

8. Aharon Barak, *Foreward: A Judge on Judging: The Role of the Supreme Court in a Democracy*, 116 HARV. L. REV. 16, 92 (2002).

9. ACA 1407/94 Mediterranean Shipping Co. S.A. v. Credit Lyonnais (Suise) S.A. 48(5) PD 122, 132 [1994] (opinion of Justice Mishal Cheshin).

Questions

8. How do Justice Barak's and Justice Cheshin's approaches to the general application of good faith differ?

9. Which approach, that of Justice Barak or Justice Cheshin, is closer to American law?

10. Which approach is better, that of Justice Barak, that of Justice Cheshin, or that of American law? Why?

B. Contract Formation: Consideration

Israeli Statute

The Law of Contracts (General Provisions), 5733-1973

1. Formation of a Contract

A contract is formed through offer and acceptance, according to the terms of this chapter.

US Law

Restatement (Second) of Contracts

§ 17. Requirement of a Bargain

(1) .... the formation of a contract requires a bargain in which there is a manifestation of mutual assent to the exchange and a consideration.

Comments

Israeli law does not require consideration for formation of a contract while American law does. Under Israeli law, a contract is formed by an offer and its acceptance. Consideration, an additional requirement imposed under American case law, means "a detriment incurred by the promisee or a benefit received by the promisor at the request of the promisor."[10]

This difference in doctrine leads to the question of why there should be such a difference. Are contract transactions in Israel fundamentally different from those in the United States in some way that requires a different legal framework for their recognition? Probably not. Then what justifies the difference in rules for treating essentially similar types of transactions?

There are several answers to this question. It may not be all that relevant whether the law requires consideration because, in most cases, for economic or other reasons unrelated to formal legal requirements, people generally do not purport to bind themselves to do something unless they get something in return. Of course, even if this is true for most cases, it is not a complete explanation. We know that there are cases where parties

---

10. 3 Williston on Contracts § 7:4 (2010).

apparently bargained for a deal that did not include consideration. American law includes cases where courts refused to enforce purported agreements due to lack of consideration, showing that the requirement is sometimes relevant.[11]

History may play a role in explaining the difference between Israeli and US law. The Israeli contract statutes were originally based largely on the German model. German law does not require consideration.[12] The American requirement of consideration came to us through English common law development, beginning as a flexible requirement but later coalescing as a more defined rule.[13]

It may seem startling to an American law student, well drilled in the requirement of consideration as a necessary part of contract formation, to learn that Israeli law does not have such a requirement. In fact, American cases often enforce contracts absent consideration, using the doctrine of promissory estoppel or some other doctrine.[14] More fundamentally, the literature reveals a lack of clarity as to why consideration should be required and considerable critique of the requirement as unjustified.[15] The underlying question is why courts should not enforce all promises to make gifts. The literature provides no clear answer, but the requirement of consideration remains, making promises to make gifts unenforceable under American law unless an exception such as promissory estoppel applies.

The Israeli approach is different. As the material that follows shows, Israeli law treats gifts as enforceable.

Israeli Statute

The Gift Law, 5728-1968

1. The Nature of a Gift

    a)   A gift is a grant of property without consideration.

    b)   The subject of the gift can be real property, personal property, or rights.

    c)   A gift can consist of the donor's giving up of a right against the donee or the donor's relinquishment of a claim against the donee.

2. Permanency of a Gift

A gift is completed by the donor's granting the subject of the gift to the donee based on an agreement between them that the subject is given as a gift.

---

11. *See, e.g.*, Prendergast v. Snoeberger, 796 N.E.2d 588 (Ohio Ct. App. 2003), Matter of Voight's Estate, 624 P.2d 1022 (N.M. App. 1981), Carli v. Farace, Not Reported in A.2d, 2006 WL 618428 (Conn. Super. Ct. 2006), and Stefano Arts v. Sui, 690 S.E.2d 197 (Ga. Ct. App. 2010). For a discussion of what types of cases require consideration and what types do not, see James D. Gordon III, *Consideration and the Commercial-Gift Dichtomy*, 44 Vand. L. Rev. 283 (1991).

12. Mordecai A. Raavilo, *On Gift and Extortion*, 10 Law Studies (Mechkarei Mishpat) 182 (1993) (in Hebrew).

13. *See* Val D. Ricks, *The Sophisticated Doctrine of Consideration*, 9 Geo. Mason L. Rev. 99 (2000).

14. *E.g.*, Neuhoff v. Marvin Lumber and Cedar Co., 370 F.3d 197 (Mass. 2004), Feinberg v. Pfeiffer Co., 322 S.W.2d 163 (1959).

15. *See, e.g.*, Lon Fuller, *Consideration and Form*, 41 Colum. L. Rev. 799, 800 (1941); James D. Gordon III, *A Dialogue about the Doctrine of Consideration*, 75 Cornell L. Rev. 987 (1990); K.N. Llewellyn, *On the Complexity of Consideration: A Foreword*, 41 Colum. L. Rev. 777, 782 (1941); Richard A. Posner, *Gratuitous Promises in Economics and Law*, 6 J. Legal Stud. 411, 417 (1977); Robert A. Prentice, *"Law" and Gratuitous Promises*, 2007 U. Ill. L. Rev. 881, 906 (2007).

3. Assumption of Agreement

It is assumed that the donee agrees to the gift, unless the donee notifies the donor of his rejection within a reasonable time of being informed of the gift.

4. Conditions and Obligations

A gift may be conditional and it may obligate the donee to do some act with the subject of the gift or to desist from doing something; the donor may require the donee to fulfill such an obligation, where the obligation will benefit him.

5. Undertaking to Make a Gift

a) An undertaking to make a gift in the future must be in a written instrument.

b) As long as the donee has not changed his position in reliance on the undertaking, the donor may change his mind, unless he has given up the right to do so in writing.

c) Except as provided in subsection (b), the donor may change his mind if doing so is justified by the shameful behavior of the donee in relation to the donor or in relation to a member of the donor's family, or by a significant worsening of the donor's economic situation.

6. Means of Making a Grant

Ownership in the subject of the gift passes to the donee upon delivery of the item into the donee's hands, or by delivery of a document that entitles the donee to receive the item, or, if the item was in the possession of the donee, by notice of the donor to the donee of the gift; all as long as no other law has specific provisions on the matter.

Israeli Case

Berkovitz v. Klemar

C.A. 495/80,36(4)PD 57[1982]

Justice A. Barak:

The Appellee lived near her daughter. After the Appellee's husband died, she began frequently her daughter, her daughter's husband, and their son, and would even sleep at their house and help with the housework. At a certain point, the daughter and her husband wanted to sell their apartment and purchase one that was larger. They lacked the funds for such a purchase. The Appellee wanted to help her daughter, and also wanted to assure that she would be able to live with the daughter for the remainder of her life. They came to an agreement. The Appellee sold her apartment, and the daughter and her husband sold their apartment. The Appellee gave the proceeds of her sale to her daughter and her daughter's husband. The daughter and son-in-law bought a new, large apartment and gave the Appellee a room of her own, with the assurance that she could live in the room for the remainder of her life.

On November 20, 1975, the Appellant gave her daughter and son-in-law IL 60,000 [Israeli Lira, the currency in Israel at the time].[16] Late in 1976, after they had purchased a new apartment (for IL 220,000), the Appellee went to live with them. The daughter be-

---

16. The Court referred to the amount as 60,500 IL in this part of the opinion, but gave the amount as 60,000 IL in all other parts of the opinion.

came ill with cancer in 1977 and died early in 1979. All this time Appellee continued to live in the apartment. After the death of the daughter, the relationship between the Appellee and her son-in-law, the Appellant in this case, deteriorated. The court of first instance determined that the Appellant acted so as to make the life of the Appellee in the apartment difficult and to coerce her to leave. He locked the bathroom door. He closed off the kitchen. As a result of the Appellant's behavior, in June 1979 the Appellee was forced to leave the apartment. Her son—the brother of the deceased daughter—rented an apartment for the Appellee that was close to where he lived. After she left the apartment [where her daughter] had lived, she filed a complaint in district court against the Appellant and her daughter's estate. Her complaint alleged that the defendants committed a basic breach of the contract between her and them, and that she was entitled to the return of her investment, measured by its real worth.

The Decision in the Lower Court

The court of first instance determined that there was an agreement between the Appellee and the daughter and Appellant, and that this was an agreement of gift. This gift agreement included a condition under which the daughter and son-in-law were required to allocate to the Appellee a room for her reasonable use. The Appellant substantially breached this condition, and therefore the Appellee is entitled to revoke the gift agreement and to obtain the return of the money that she paid to the Appellant and her daughter, together with linkage[17] and interest from the day on which she made the payment until the repayment to her. The lower court ruled that this amount should be reduced by one-fifth, to account for the Appellee's usage of the new apartment over a period of two and a half years (of the twelve years during which she could have expected to use the apartment, according to the actuarial evaluation of her life expectancy). Both sides appeal.

[The son-in-law, as Appellant, claims that there was no connection between the gift of money to the daughter and the Appellee's residence in their apartment; that he did nothing to pressure her to leave the apartment; that the money was a completed gift and not part of an agreement; that even if it was an agreement, any breach was not substantial; and that if he had to pay money to the Appellee, linkage should run from the day she left the apartment and not from the day she gave the daughter the funds. The Appellee claims that the amount due her should not be reduced because of her use of the apartment.

The Supreme Court decided to accept the facts as determined by the district court.]

The lower court found that a contract was formed between the two parties, and this determination is based on the evidence. This does not address the content of the con-

---

17. Israeli currency was very unstable during the period covered by this case. To account for this instability in transactions that occurred over time, it was common to link the value of Israeli currency to the consumer price index (CPI). The CPI is the price of a basket of consumer goods in one year in comparison to the price of that some basket of goods in another year. Thus, the 1982 linked value of a payment of 60,000 IL in 1975 is the amount of money it would take in 1982 to buy the same amount of consumer goods you could buy for 60,000 IL in 1975. The CPI allows calculation of that amount. Because Israeli currency had been subject to significant inflation in the late 70s and the early 80s, the amount the appellant would have to pay in 1982 would be substantially more than the 60,000 IL originally provided by the appellee.

There were other linkage measures, besides the CPI, used for specific types of transactions. This is discussed in the case.

(As of this writing, Israeli inflation is much lower, comparable to that of the United States and Europe, and linkage has become a less prominent part of Israeli economic life.)

tract, which may be a contract with consideration involving a price and remuneration, or it can be a contract without consideration, with no price or remuneration. In other words, the existence of a legal agreement does not prevent the content from being that of a gift. In this regard, the underlying assumption of the Gift Law, 5728-1968, is that a gift is an agreement. Section 2 of the Gift Law provides: "A gift is completed by the donor's granting the subject of the gift to the donee based on an agreement between them that the subject is given as a gift."

This shows that a gift, like a sale, is a contract. It is perfected by offer and acceptance. It is a two-sided transaction. It is not a one-sided legal action, such as a will or license....

Because a gift is a contract, we must conclude that "to the extent that a matter is not specifically treated in the Gift Law, general contract law applies to a gift, for example as to formation of the contract, its revocation and the right to revoke. Similarly because the gift is a contract, the law of breach of contract in the Law of Contracts (Remedies for Breach of Contract), 5731-1970, applies, unless a matter is treated specifically in the Gift Law itself. Thus, a gift "may obligate the donee to do some act with the subject of the gift or to desist from doing something" (section 4 of the Gift Law). Breach of this obligation is a breach of contract, and the usual remedies for breach apply.... We have determined that the question to be decided is not whether there is a contract or a gift between the parties. Without doubt, the parties have entered into a contract. But what is the content of the contract? This is the question which we must address.

Content of the Contract

What is the contract entered into by the two parties? ... Among the many theoretical possibilities, there are only three in this case: an exchange for consideration, a gift that imposes an obligation, and a gift on condition.... There is no basis in the evidence for seeing this contract as a "regular" gift, without a condition or stipulation, leaving the matter of the Appellant's residence to the good will of the daughter and her husband. We will therefore consider the three types of transactions that the matter before us resembles.

A Contract of Exchange

The first possibility is that the parties entered some sort of contract of exchange (broadly defined) or some sort of partnership agreement. Under this approach, the parties' agreement was that each one would contribute a portion (the Appellee — the proceeds from sale of her apartment; the daughter and her husband — the proceeds of the sale of their apartment), and each would receive something (the Appellee — use of the apartment for life; the daughter and her husband — ownership of the apartment, subject to the Appellee's right of use). It would then be a mutual contract ... that creates mutual obligations. A breach of duty by one party is likely to give the other, under certain conditions, the right to revoke the contract (section 7 of the Law of Contracts (Remedies for Breach of Contract), 5731-1970) and the right to return of the investment in the contract. If the contract in our case is of this type, given that the Appellant breached his duty to the Appellee, if this breach is considered substantial — as it is — then the Appellee is entitled to revoke the contract and to require the return of her investment.

A Gift Contract with an Obligation of the Donee

The second possibility is that the parties entered a contract of gift in which the donee took on an obligation to the donor. The Gift Law recognizes such a possibility.... Under this approach, the Appellee gave a gift to her daughter and the Appellant in the amount of IL 60,000. As part of the gift agreement, an obligation was imposed on the donee to give the Appellee the right of use during her lifetime. Under this interpretation, the contract between the parties is not a mutual contract but a one-sided contract, in which the Appellee gives a gift to the donee. The donee also took upon himself an obligation as to the donor. This obligation does not constitute consideration for the gift.... If the donee of the gift breaches the obligation imposed on him, he is breaching a contract obligation, and the donor of the gift has the regular remedies for breach of an obligation, including specific performance, revocation and damages.... These remedies are for the obligation and not the gift contract. Can the donor revoke the gift contract itself? ...

My opinion is that the donor may not revoke the gift due only to the breach of the obligation that accompanied the gift. The reason is that the obligation is separate, not connected by a mutual relationship ... with the gift itself. The gift was completed, and there was nothing defective about it, and there was no breach. The breach was as to the obligation.

A Conditional Gift Contract

The third possibility, like the second, deals with a gift contract between the parties. The difference between the two possibilities is that under the second we are dealing with a gift with an obligation, that is, a gift that is accompanied by a stipulation. In contrast, under the third possibility, we are dealing with a conditional gift. Under this approach, the Appellee gave her daughter and the Appellant a gift in the amount of IL 60,000 on condition that she would be given the right to use the new apartment for life. Under this possibility, like under the second, the contract between the parties did not involve consideration, but was a gift contract. The gift contract is not subject to a stipulation imposing an obligation, but rather to a condition of termination, under which the existence of the gift will cease if the Appellee is prevented from using the apartment. Indeed, the Gift Law provides that "a gift may be conditional" (Section 4). The Gift Law does not set out the legal rule that applies to such a condition. The Law of Contracts (General Provisions) applies to this issue, distinguishing between a condition of postponement and a condition of termination, and providing that "a contract can be conditioned on the existence of a condition (a condition of postponement) or it can cease to exist if a condition occurs (condition of termination)." (Section 27(a).) When we are dealing with a gift contract with a condition of postponement, the gift contract has no legal effect as long as the condition does not exist. When we are dealing with a gift contract with a condition of termination, the gift contract is fully in effect, but if the condition occurs, the contract ceases to exist. When the condition of termination occurs, the gift contract is not breached, and there arises no right of revocation. When the condition of termination occurs, the existence of the contract ceases.

What are the results of the contract ceasing to exist due to the occurrence of a condition of termination? Neither the Gift Law nor the Law of Contracts (General Provisions) directly addresses the matter, because these laws deal with breach of a contract, that is, "an action or omission that is in violation of the contract," (Section 1). If a condition of termination occurs and as a result, the contract terminates, this is not an action in violation of the contract. In such a circumstance, the question arises of whether the donor is entitled to return of the gift. I think the answer is in the affirmative, for all of the following reasons: First, interpretation of Section 4 of the Gift Law allows one to conclude that if the condition no longer exists, the donor of the gift is entitled to its return.

Second, the obligation to return arises under the general principles of unlawful enrichment, set out now in The Law of Unlawful Enrichment, 5739-1979. If, despite the cessation of the gift contract, the donee could continue in possession of the gift, it would constitute unlawful enrichment. Third, even if we assume that there is not provision that applies directly to our case, then we have a lapse in the law that we must fill by way of analogy. The provisions which should be considered and from which an analogy may be drawn are section 21 of the Law of Contracts (General Provisions), which specifies return of the investment in case of revocation of the contract due to a failure in its formation, and section 9 of the Law of Contracts (Remedies for Breach of Contract), which specifies return of investment if the contract is revoked due to its breach.

From this we can conclude that if the contract before us is a conditional gift contract, because the condition of termination occurred—not allowing the Appellee to live in the apartment—the existence of the contract of gift terminated. Therefore, the Appellee has the right to require the return of her investment.

The court below determined that the contract between the Appellee and her daughter and the Appellant was a gift contract and that "the condition that accompanied it was breached." Based on this, we can assume that the court below sees this as a conditional contract (the third possibility).

It seems to me that the court below was correct in its determination that this was a gift contract. We see this from the evidence given by the Appellee, who was perceived as believable by the lower court:

> I gave it to my son-in-law and daughter so that they could buy a large apartment in Afula [a city in Israel] and so that they would provide me with a room in the apartment in which I could live.... I agreed to sell [my] apartment in order to help my daughter, so she could have a large apartment and I could live with her and help her.... I have the money and I said that I am already old and this was to allow my daughter to work and I wanted to help them, but on condition that they would give me a room where I could live for the time remaining to me. At first I asked that they register a portion of the apartment in my name, but he refused. I wanted assurance that they would give me a room in the apartment. He would not sign anything.

It seems that this testimony is evidence of the Appellee's intention to provide a benefit to her daughter, by which she would assure herself of a place to live. This was not a transaction in which consideration is set against consideration, price against price, compensation against compensation. There was the Appellee's generosity of the heart and desire to provide help, accompanied by a desire to assure that she had a place to live. In such circumstances, it seems to me that we should not regard the contract as a contract upon consideration, but as a gift contract.

[The Court decided that the Appellee, the mother, was entitled to return of her investment, that she should receive the current value of IL 60,000 (which, in light of the intervening inflation would be substantially more than IL 60,000), and that the rental value of her room for the period she occupied it should be deducted from what she received.]

Comments

Justice Barak wrote, "Without doubt, the parties have entered into a contract." In a case in one of the states of the United States, this would mean that the transaction was a contract and not a gift. The meaning under Israeli law is different. Justice Barak does not mean that the transfer of IL 60,000 from the mother to the daughter and son-in-law was not a gift but rather that it was a gift and as a result there was a contract. This is because under Israeli law, a gift, whether unconditional or conditional, is a type of contract.

Consider the reasons the court below saw this as a conditional gift contract and not as a contract of exchange. It was not clear whether the son-in-law had promised to allow the mother to remain in the new apartment for the rest of her life. The son-in-law had refused to sign a document providing the mother with a property right in the new apartment. It would have been difficult to show a mutual exchange of obligations. It was more easily shown that the mother handed over the IL 60,000 on condition that she could live in the apartment for life. Presumably the lower court's interpretation of the transaction as a gift allowed it to avoid the necessity of deciding a difficult issue of proof.

This suggests another problem which neither the lower court nor the Supreme Court addressed explicitly. The donee must agree to a gift. See Section 2 of the Gift Law, above. If it cannot be proven that the son-in-law agreed to allow the mother to remain in the apartment for the rest of her life, how can it be said that he agreed to the condition that she attached to the gift?

There are two possible answers to this question. First, Section 3 of the Gift Law says that agreement of the donee is assumed, unless the donee notifies the donor of rejection. There are apparently two donees in this case: the daughter and the son-in-law. Thus, the son-in-law's acceptance could be assumed as long as there was no proof that he notified the mother of his rejection of the gift with its condition. Second, it may be that while agreement of the donee to the gift is needed, agreement to the condition is not required. This may be why the Supreme Court emphasized that the gift and the condition were separate. If they were, the son-in-law needed only to accept the gift of IL 60,000 and not the condition.

American law might deal with the case as a matter of contract law by saying that even if proof that the husband agreed to allow the mother to stay in the new apartment were lacking, the mother might have a remedy under the theory of promissory estoppel. Having allowed her (and the lower court said, helped her) to sell her apartment, allowed her to move in to the new apartment, and taken her money, the son-in-law would now be estopped from denying that he had agreed to let her live there for life. She reasonably relied on his actions to hand over to him and her daughter all her money from the sale of her apartment. This was reliance, and it was detrimental. Therefore, a court in the United States law might find a contract and allow the mother contract remedies.

Alternatively a court in the United States law might see the transaction as a property transaction and say that the mother made a gift of use of the money for a limited time, that time being as long as she was allowed to live in the apartment, with the qualification that the gift became irrevocable at her death. This type of gift might cause difficulty of interpretation, with the term of the donees' rights to the money being indefinite and not falling into any of the traditional categories of property rights. It might be a fee on a condition subsequent, but it is not clear that it would so be interpreted due to the lack of clarity about the structure of the condition. Furthermore, the stipulation that the donees could keep the money after the mother's death, unlinked to an immediate irrevocable gift, might be interpreted as an invalid type of will because it would violate the Statue of Wills. The mother could transfer a future interest to begin at her death without violating the Statute of Wills, but the linkage to the requirement that she be allowed to live in the apartment all her life would make this conditional and possibly unenforceable.

In American law, it matters greatly whether the transaction is a contract or a gift, because contracts are enforceable and gifts are not. In Israeli law, the distinction is less crucial because both contracts and gifts are enforceable.

The Israeli approach can matter in other cases as well. For example, assume an employer and employee agreed that the employee would work for a year at a set wage. Part of the way through the year, the employee gets a better offer. The employee tells the employer, "I am leaving for a better offer." The employer entreats that employee to stay for the remainder of the year and promises to pay the employee a year-end bonus for doing so. The employee stays, the employer does not pay the year-end bonus, and the employee sues. Some courts will require the employer to pay, but some will not due to failure of consideration. The employee did nothing the employee was not already bound to do under the original contract, so there was no consideration for the employer's promise to pay a year-end bonus. Therefore, that promise is unenforceable. See *Davis & Co. v. Morgan*, 117 Ga. 504, 43 S.E. 732 (1903). The Israeli law avoids any question of whether this promise is enforceable. If it meets the requirement of the Gift Law, it is enforceable without any regard to whether there is consideration.

Question

11. Is it a good idea for courts to enforce promises to make gifts, as is allowed under Israeli law?

C. Remedies for Breach of Contract

Israeli Statute

The Law of Contracts
(Remedies for Breach of Contract), 5731-1970
Chapter 1: General Provisions

1. Definitions

(a) In this statute—

"breach"—an act or omission that violates the contract;

"aggrieved party"—a person entitled to performance of the contract that was breached;

"enforcement"—either in an order requiring payment of an amount of money owed or another affirmative order or an injunction, including an order to remedy the effects of the breach....

2. Remedies of the Aggrieved Party

Upon breach of a contract, the aggrieved party is entitled to sue for its enforcement or to terminate the contract, and he is entitled to damages in addition to or in place of one of these remedies, subject to the provisions of this statute.

Chapter 2: Remedies
Part A: Specific Performance

3. The Right to Enforcement

The aggreived party is entitled to enforcement, except in the following circumstances:

(1) The contract cannot be performed;

(2) Enforcement of the contract would entail coercing someone to perform or accept personal employment or personal service;

(3) Implementation of the order of enforcement would require an unreasonable degree of supervision by the court or by the Office for Execution of Judgments;

(4) Enforcement is unjustified due to the circumstances of the case.

4. Conditions

A court may condition enforcement on the aggrieved party's performance of his duties or assurance of performance of them, or on other conditions that the contract requires, depending on the circumstances of the case.

US Law

Restatement (Second) of Contracts
Chapter 16. Remedies

Topic 3. Enforcement by Specific Performance and Injunction

§ 357. Availability of Specific Performance and Injunction

(1) Subject to the rules stated in §§ 359–69, specific performance of a contract duty will be granted in the discretion of the court against a party who has committed or is threatening to commit a breach of the duty.

§ 359. Effect of Adequacy of Damages

(1) Specific performance or an injunction will not be ordered if damages would be adequate to protect the expectation interest of the injured party.

§ 360. Factors Affecting Adequacy of Damages

In determining whether the remedy in damages would be adequate, the following circumstances are significant:

(a) the difficulty of proving damages with reasonable certainty,

(b) the difficulty of procuring a suitable substitute performance by means of money awarded as damages, and

(c) the likelihood that an award of damages could not be collected.

§ 362. Effect of Uncertainty of Terms

Specific performance or an injunction will not be granted unless the terms of the contract are sufficiently certain to provide a basis for an appropriate order.

§ 363. Effect of Insecurity as to the Agreed Exchange

Specific performance or an injunction may be refused if a substantial part of the agreed exchange for the performance to be compelled is unperformed and its performance is not secured to the satisfaction of the court.

§ 364. Effect of Unfairness

(1) Specific performance or an injunction will be refused if such relief would be unfair because

(a) the contract was induced by mistake or by unfair practices,

(b) the relief would cause unreasonable hardship or loss to the party in breach or to third persons, or

(c) the exchange is grossly inadequate or the terms of the contract are otherwise unfair.

(2) Specific performance or an injunction will be granted in spite of a term of the agreement if denial of such relief would be unfair because it would cause unreasonable hardship or loss to the party seeking relief or to third persons.

§ 365. Effect of Public Policy

Specific performance or an injunction will not be granted if the act or forbearance that would be compelled or the use of compulsion is contrary to public policy.

§ 366. Effect of Difficulty in Enforcement or Supervision

A promise will not be specifically enforced if the character and magnitude of the performance would impose on the court burdens in enforcement or supervision that are disproportionate to the advantages to be gained from enforcement and to the harm to be suffered from its denial.

§ 367. Contracts for Personal Service or Supervision

(1) A promise to render personal service will not be specifically enforced.

Israeli Case

Lindoar v. Ringle
C.A. 2454/98, 65(1)PD 225[2001]

Justice E. Rivlin:

Facts and Proceedings

An agreement was reached on May 19, 1996, between the Appellant, Mr. Eliahu Lindoar, and the Appellee, Mr. Jacob Ringle, under which the Appellee purchased from the Appellant 2,400,000 shares in Mishneal and Sons Investment Co. Ltd. (hereinafter *the company*) for a price of NIS 2,400,000[18] (hereinafter *the agreement*). The agreement provided that the price would be paid in three installments: the first, in the amount of NIS 480,000, on the day of signing the agreement (in return for the transfer of all the shares to the name of the Appellee), and the two remaining payments (in the amount of NIS 960,000 each) to be paid on September 15, 1996 and December 31, 1996.

---

18. The amount of the contract was about $740,000.

The Appellee did not meet his obligation to make the second and third payments. As a result, the Appellant filed a complaint … with the District Court of Tel-Aviv-Jaffa, in which he asked for specific performance of the agreement. The Appellee opposed the request for specific enforcement.

The dispute between the parties revolves around the question of whether the Appellant is entitled to specifically enforce the agreement. Both sides base their claims on the provisions in Section 4 and 5 of the agreement, that provide:

> 4. If Jacob Ringle does not make the payment under Section 3b3 [the section that deals with the second and third payments] he shall return the shares to the ownership of Eliahu Lindoar, and the amount that was paid under Section 3a of the agreement, that is the amount of NIS 480,000, shall not be returned and shall be retained by Eliahu Lindoar.

> 5. The failure of Jacob Ringle to fulfill the requirements of Section 3b3 of the agreement shall not prevent Eliahu Lindoar from filing a complaint for any relief and damages for the injury he sustained.

The Appellant claims that these sections should not be interpreted as to deprive him of the right to the remedy of specific performance. The Appellant claims that these provisions explicitly repudiate the possibility of making a claim for specific performance.

The district court dismissed the complaint and held:

> Sections 4 and 5 of the agreement clearly show the agreement of the sides that in case of a breach, the injured party would be entitled to revoke the agreement, to restitution, to agreed damages, or to any other type of compensation for the injury caused, and from this we see that the [Appellant] is not entitled to require specific enforcement of the agreement.

The appeal is against this determination.

Israeli law sees specific performance as the most important remedy. Justice D. Levin expressed this when he wrote:

> The starting point in contract law is that the best and preferable remedy is an order for specific enforcement of the contract. The judicial policy that stands behind this rule is that courts should do what they can to see that the provisions of contracts are carried out and to honor the obligations undertaken in them. Only in exceptional cases will a court desist from ordering specific performance, mainly in the cases set out in Section 3 of the Law of Contracts (Remedies for Breach of Contract).

This is the view that forms the basis of Section 3 of the Law of Contracts (Remedies for Breach of Contract). As Chief Justice Shamgar wrote:

> It is known and accepted that Section 3 of the Law of Contracts (Remedies for Breach of Contract) had the objective of changing the Anglo-American rule on enforcement in place of damages, which rule was in force until enactment of the statute. The new objective was to provide that the injured party is generally *entitled* to specific enforcement of the contract, unless one of the special circumstances enumerated in subsections (1)–(4) of Section 3 applies.

The right to sue for specific performance is provided to the injured party whenever the contract is breached, and the discretion of a court to deny this remedy is ordinarily limited to the four situations set out in Section 3. Of course, the injured party is not required to choose specific performance as a remedy, but if the injured party does choose it, a court will refuse to honor that choice only in exceptional circumstances.

This approach to the law of remedies in Israeli law is different from the approach in Anglo-American law, in which "the contractual undertaking is understood as imposing the risk of having to pay damages, and generally the party responsible for the breach can redeem itself with a payment of money." Gabriella Shalev, *The Law of Contracts* 524 (2d ed. 1995) [in Hebrew]. The Israeli approach rests on considerations of moral principles, fulfillment of promises, protection of the reasonable interests and expectations of the parties to the contract, and a view of a contract as an expression of the meeting of the minds of those parties. But these considerations also lead to the conclusion that it is appropriate to honor the choice of the parties to limit the use of the remedy of specific performance.

In cases in which the remedy provisions of the Law of Contracts (Remedies for Breach of Contract) do not express the will of the parties, they may design their own remedy provisions. Although specific performance is one of the remedies that may be made available to the injured party under the statute, that party may relinquish that remedy and choose another. This may occur either before or after the breach. Where this choice is made beforehand, its implementation effectuates the agreement of the parties.

There are those who find support for this position in the theories of economic analysis of the law. The theory of *efficient breach* says that the seller in a contract should not be required to meet the requirements of the contract if the benefit to the seller from breaching the contract exceeds the damages the seller must pay to the buyer due to the breach. Therefore, "an order of specific performance that prevents breach of the contract has an adverse effect in that it perpetuates economic stagnation by enforcing inefficient contracts." David Katzir, 1 *Remedies for Breach of Contract* 287–88 (1991).

This economic approach has been critiqued and is not accepted in our contract law. In adopting the approach that sees specific enforcement as the primary remedy, the Israeli law rejected the doctrine of efficient breach. Still where the parties themselves choose ahead of time, in the agreement, a relationship that provides for efficient breach (by repudiating the remedy of specific enforcement) and agree ahead of time to the remedy of revocation, this choice should be honored.

The economic doctrine of contract law calls a contract that includes an agreement on all matters and that relates either explicitly or implicitly to all possible occurrences as an efficient contract a *complete* contract. The provision ahead of time for what will be done in the case of breach makes a contract a more complete one. In the case before us, the choice to revoke the contract in case of breach is the common choice of the two sides. If we enforce this choice, doing so is not the same as forcing one or both of them to forego specific performance for reasons of economic efficiency. The parties may prefer not to determine their rights through property rules (that is, by allowing specific performance), but rather through other means (that is, by the remedy of damages). See Guido Calabresi & A. Douglas Melamed, *Property Rules, Liability Rules and Inalienability: One View of the Cathedral*, 85 Harv. L. Rev. 1089 (1971–72). In this way they prevent inefficient allocation of resources. If we ignore such a provision in the contract, we violate the desire of the parties. Recognition of the ability of the parties to provide for the remedies effectuates the principle of fulfillment of promises and also makes economic sense. (On this matter, see Thomas S. Ulen, *The Efficiency of Specific Performance: Toward a Unified Theory of Contract Remedies*, 83 Mich. L. Rev. 341 (1984–85); Anthony T. Kronman, *Specific*

Performance, 45 U. Chi. L. Rev. 351, 352 (1977–78); A. Mitchell Polinsky, *An Introduction to Law and Economics*, 29–34 (1989); Richard A. Posner, *Economic Analysis of Law* (5th ed. 1998)).

The parties in this case were entitled to determine how the relationship between them should be concluded, and since they did this, their stipulation should be given effect. Therefore, the district court correctly dismissed the Appellant's claim for specific enforcement. I would reject the appeal.

Justice T. Orr:

My opinion differs from that of my colleague Justice Rivlin. Were my opinion accepted, I would grant the appeal, reverse the district court decision to dismiss the Appellant's claim, and return the case to the lower court for further consideration of the claim.

Repudiation of the remedy of specific performance must be explicit or at least, according to the more permissive approach, in a manner that clearly and unequivocally reveals the intention of both sides, as shown by the language of the contract and the circumstances under which it was formed. In our case, we can determine the intention of the parties from the language of the contract.

The contract itself contains no explicit repudiation of the remedy of specific performance. Even under the more permissive approach, I do not think we can conclude that Sections 4 and 5 reveal an intention to repudiate the remedy of specific enforcement. The opposite is true. These provisions show that the parties to the contract agreed to preserve all remedies for the Appellant. Section 4, which provides for agreed damages (and the obligation to make restitution), is followed by Section 5, which also treats the subject of breach by the Appellee by non-payment of the second and third installments, and explicitly provides that such a breach does not rule out any other remedy. Therefore, we cannot say that Section 4, which sets out the remedy of restitution, indicates a repudiation of the remedy of specific performance.

Under my colleague's interpretation of Section 5, that provision provides a right to damages for injury caused to the Appellant when the contract has been breached and there is a right to restitution under Section 4. I cannot accept that interpretation. First, Section 5 provides that if the Appellee does not make the second and third payments, the Appellant has the right to file a complaint for "any relief," as well as a right to damages for the injury that he suffered. Under this language, the Appellant may obtain "any relief," and not just damages. Second, the remedy for injury caused by breach of a contract is payment of damages. If so, the term "any relief" must add something more to the possible remedies in case of the Appellee's breach. Any other relief includes, of course, the remedy of specific enforcement.

I do not need to deal with the question of whether, if Section 4 stood alone, without Section 5, the conclusion of my colleague Justice Rivlin would have been justified.

In this case, we cannot conclude that the Appellant repudiated the remedy of specific enforcement, and I would grant the appeal.

[The third Justice sitting on the case agreed with Justice Orr, so the appeal was granted.]

Comments

The term "enforcement" in the Israeli statute has a meaning similar to that of specific enforcement in US law.

Civil law systems are typically more willing to allow the remedy of specific performance than are common law systems. The Israeli preference for specific performance as a remedy derives from the civil law, as does the Israeli broad requirement of good faith in contract formation.[19]

The rules on specific performance in common law countries originate in the split between law and equity, which still influences the common law. Law courts did not order specific performance; equity courts did. When the two court systems were combined, the new unitary system retained the rule from the courts of equity that equitable remedies would not be given unless legal remedies were inadequate. As a result, specific performance is unavailable unless the legal remedy of damages is inadequate. Damages are generally considered inadequate and specific performance available in contracts for sale of land, for sale of unique items, and for those with long term requirements (such as supply of raw materials).[20] On the other hand, the grant of specific performance, because it is founded in equity, is within the discretion of the court, and may be denied for a variety of reasons, even if damages are inadequate. Reasons for denial include unfairness of the contract or unfairness in the negotiations leading up to its formation, and burdensomeness on the courts of supervision of enforcement. The Israeli statute, although it creates a presumption that specific performance is available as a remedy, also creates exceptions to this presumption.

Of course, the historical reasons why specific performance was originally limited in American law do not by themselves justify maintenance of this limitation today. In discussions about whether the existing law on contract remedies should be changed, the traditional common law approach, as expressed in American contract law, has been both defended and criticized. Those defending the status quo in American law, or advocating only some minor tinkering with it, claim that making specific performance broadly available would lead to economic inefficiency in two ways: (1) Parties, most of whom routinely prefer damages as a remedy, would be forced to undertake costly negotiations over contract clauses limiting the availability of specific performance as a remedy, and the need for this negotiation is obviated by a legal rule imposing the same limitation. (2) Administrative costs of supervising specific performance are high. In both cases, the argument is that these costs exceed the value of the specific performance remedy. Proponents of more freely granting specific performance argue that it would protect the subjective value of the contract to the injured party without unduly increasing costs, advance the moral notion that people should keep their promises, and protect the certainty of property rights.[21]

Israeli law received the common law rule from the British. This rule was discarded by enactment of the Law of Contracts (Remedies for Breach of Contract), 5731-1970. Thus the statute reveals a very deliberate decision to reject the Anglo-American's law's limitations on specific performance.

Justice Rivlin's opinion in the *Lindoar* case, which was not the majority decision, may show his uneasiness with the choice made by the Israeli statute. Had Justice Rivlin seen the matter purely as one of construction of the contract, he would not have needed to launch into the discussion of the economic inefficiency of specific performance. It appears that

---

19. *See* Yehuda Adar and Gabriella Shalev, *The Law of Remedies in a Mixed Jurisdiction: The Israeli Experience*, 23 TUL. EUR. & CIV. L.F. 111, 134 (2008).

20. RESTATEMENT (SECOND) OF CONTRACTS § 360 cmt. b, e (1981).

21. *See* Anthony Kronman, *Specific Performance*, 45 U. CHI. L. REV. 351 (1978) (cited by Justice Rivlin in *Lindoar v. Ringle*); Ugo Mattei, *The Comparative Law and Economics of Penalty Clauses in Contracts*, 43 AM. J. COMP. L. 427, 429 (1995); Timothy J. Muris, *The Costs of Freely Granting Specific Performance*, 1982 DUKE L.J. 1053; Alan Schwartz, *The Case for Specific Performance*, 69 YALE L.J. 271 (1979).

Justice Rivlin was attracted to the rationales for not allowing specific performance as long as damages provide an adequate remedy. Given the clear provision of the Israeli statute on specific performance, he could not adopt the common law preference. But he could construe the contract at hand in a manner that gave effect to that preference in the specific case. Justice Orr, in the majority decision, did not deal at all with the policy issues. He treated this as a case involving only construction of the contract language.

The majority opinion is given second in this case. In cases in the United States Supreme Court, the majority opinion, if there is one, always comes first. This is not always true in Israel.

Questions

12. What are the advantages and disadvantages of the Israeli position on specific performance?

13. Given that specific performance is readily available under Israeli law, would most litigants prefer this remedy?

14. Is there a common thread running through all three topics of Israeli contract law examined in this section, the requirement of good faith, the absence of a requirement of consideration, and the availability of the remedy of specific performance?

Chapter 16

Tort Law

A. Development of Tort Law

Tort law in Israel is based mainly on the common law. In 1944, the British Mandatory authority enacted the Civil Wrongs Ordinance, which was mainly a codification of English tort law as it existed at that time. After establishment of the state, the ordinance remained a part of Israeli law. It has been amended from time to time by the Knesset, although the main characteristics of the current version of the law, called the Torts Ordinance (New Version), remain much as they were under the British. The development of tort law and its adaptation to modern conditions has been mainly through decisions of the Israeli courts. The main features of Israeli tort law would be familiar to American lawyers. The discussion below presents a few features in which the Israeli law differs from American law.

B. Tort Actions Based on Husband's Refusal to Grant a Writ of Divorce

As described in chapters 12 and 14, a Jewish marriage can be terminated in Israel only under the rules of Jewish law. This requires that the husband give the wife a writ of divorce and that the wife accept the writ. Some recalcitrant husbands refuse to give a writ of divorce, sometimes because they want the wife to agree to give up rights she would otherwise have to money, property, or child custody.

In recent years, several women have brought tort actions against their recalcitrant husbands. The following case from the Jerusalem Family Law Court is one of the few decisions that have come down in this area. The excerpt from the case is long because it relates not only to the tort rights of a woman denied a divorce, but also to a number of other features of Israeli tort law which are discussed in later sections of this chapter.

Israeli Case

K.S. v. K.P.

FamC (Jer) 19270/03 (Dec. 21, 2004)

Judge M. HaCohen:

We have before us a claim for monetary damages for the injury cause to a woman by her husband's refusal to give her a writ of divorce after the rabbinical court ruled that he is obligated to do so. The injuries for which she asks to be compensated are

mainly non-monetary injuries, including mental suffering, shame, hardship, loneliness, and grief in the years of waiting for a writ of divorce; loss of enjoyment of life
and of sexual pleasure; invasion of autonomy; and loss of the opportunity to remarry
and have children. In addition, the Plaintiff claims compensation for monetary losses
she suffered as a result of the length of the proceedings in the rabbinical courts and
for the loss of income from not having a husband to support her and her family. During the course of the hearing, the Plaintiff withdrew her claim for compensation for
abuse, cruelty and violent behavior of the husband, claims that he denied. The Plaintiff's counsel declared, "I base the remedy requested ... on the damage caused to the
wife due to her being denied a writ of divorce."

As to the facts, it is clear that the husband refused over a period of more than twelve
years to give his wife a writ of divorce and that on January 24, 2002, the rabbinical court
decided "to obligate the husband without delay to give a writ of divorce to his wife."

The problem of refusal to provide a writ of divorce is a serious one in Jewish law and
in the family law of the State of Israel.

In the case before us, we are not dealing with imposing a sanction for denial of
a writ of divorce, with the objective of getting the husband to give the writ. This
court does not deal with providing for a divorce in the future, but only with the direct ramifications that flow from not having given a writ of divorce and with the
right of the wife to tort damages.

In her documents summarizing her claim, the Plaintiff seeks daily compensation for
various types of injuries she has suffered for the period from the day of filing of the claim
to the day when she gets a writ of divorce. This type of compensation is different from
what was claimed in the original complaint or in the initial affidavits. The remedy requested in those documents was not for the future, but for the past injuries caused the
wife in the period in which she has been waiting for a writ of divorce up to the day of filing of the complaint. The remedy requested, if it is granted, will not be conditional on
whether a writ of divorce is later granted, or even on whether a writ of divorce is given
during these proceedings. Neither event would affect my decision in the case before me.

I am also not deciding whether, if the Plaintiff's claim is accepted and as a result the
husband decides to give her the long-awaited writ of divorce, this will be considered a
valid writ.

Factual Background

[This portion of the decision is set out in chapter 14 on family law. On May 11, 1992,
the Plaintiff left the family home with her six children and filed for divorce in the district
rabbinical court. After numerous attempts at reconciliation with the assistance of well-
known rabbis, all consulted at the insistence of the husband and all of whom determined
that the marriage should end in divorce, on May 19, 1998, the district rabbinical court
issued a decision calling on the husband to give his wife a writ of divorce. The husband
refused repeatedly. On July 24, 2002, the High Rabbinical Court issued a decision stating that the husband was required to give his wife a divorce. The rabbinical courts did not
send the husband to jail or impose on him other statutory sanctions. On September 9,
2003, the wife filed this tort action for damages.

Jurisdiction

Three of my colleagues [have been presented with similar cases and] have had to
decide whether this court has jurisdiction to hear complaints such as the one before
us. In all three cases, it was decided that this court has jurisdiction over a wife's claim

for compensation due to injury caused her by her husband's refusal to grant her a writ of divorce. The honorable Judge Greenberg decided that this court has jurisdiction because,

> This court does not get involved at all in the matter of the granting of a writ of divorce, and the wife is not asking us to get involved in that matter. The complaint is for money damages only, based on a cause of action in torts.... The fact that the injurious behavior is related to not giving a writ of divorce does not move that cause of action in torts into the ambit of "matters of marriage and divorce of Jews in Israel" that is in the exclusive jurisdiction of the rabbinical courts.

The Defendant claims that this court is not the suitable forum to hear this matter. It seems to me that what the Defendant means is that the matter before us is not "justiciable in a civil court," or at least that it is inappropriate for the matter to be considered in a civil court.

In other words, is it appropriate for a civil court to get involved in a dispute that is based on Jewish law? Would it not be better, as the Defendant claims, to allow the rabbinical courts to find a cure for the problems of the couple before us, using measures like those used in other cases?

The Plaintiff claims in response that the rabbinical court cannot be the "suitable forum" to hear this complaint because it lacks jurisdiction to hear a complaint in tort between the parties. The matter of the "suitable forum" arises only when two different courts both have jurisdiction to hear a certain complaint, which is not true in this case.

In addition, in my view of things, the decision on tort compensation in a private dispute involves no inappropriate invasion of the area of expertise of the rabbinical courts. The rabbinical courts deal speedily or otherwise with finding solutions under Jewish law to the phenomenon of denial of writs of divorce and development of tools in accord with Jewish law to put pressure on men who refuse to give a writ of divorce so that they will decide that they want to provide the withheld writ. In contrast, in the present complaint the court is not invading this area, and the goal of the decision, if the requested remedy is granted, is not to motivate the husband to give a divorce. The goal of the requested remedy is to compensate the wife for the substantial injuries caused her as a result of her long years as an anchored woman, her loneliness, and the mental anguish that her husband imposed upon her.

The civil courts no longer see themselves are being unable to enter all areas of family law that relate to the exclusive jurisdiction of the religious courts. This is true even in those cases in which the very nature of the dispute is based on the rules of marriage in some specific religious community. Thus, in Req.CA 345/81 *Sultan v. Sultan* 38(3) PD 169, 172–73 [1984] Justice Netanyahu held:

> The fact that the Shari'a law recognized that a divorced woman has certain monetary rights does not negate the fact that she was harmed and injured by being divorced without cause, even though the divorce was recognized in the court with jurisdiction over the divorce. Based on this fact, she has a cause of action in torts.

Causes of Action in the Complaint

Several possible causes of action were given in the complaint: The first was breach of a statutory duty, relating to a breach of the Basic Law: Human Dignity and Freedom, the Penal Code, the Law on Prevention of Violence in the Family, the Contract Law, and international treaties. In addition, the complaint lists a cause of action in negligence and in unlawful imprisonment. It also claims that anchoring a woman should be seen as a tort cause of action of its own. I shall discuss the causes of action mentioned to see if the grounds for each one exist in the case before us. If they do, I shall have to determine if an injury has been sustained and, if it has, the appropriate amount of compensation.

Breach of Statutory Duty: Generally

The cause of action of breach of statutory duty is defined in the Torts Ordinance (New Version) as follows:

63. Breach of Statutory Duty

(a) A person who breaches a statutory duty is one who does not meet an obligation imposed on him by a statutory provision [a statute or an administrative regulation], except for this ordinance, and the statutory provision is properly interpreted as being intended for the benefit or protection of another person, and the breach caused that other person an injury of the type and nature that the statutory provision was meant to cover; but the other person is not entitled to any remedy set out in this ordinance if the statutory provision as properly interpreted was meant to disallow that remedy.

(b) For the purpose of this section, a statutory provision is seen as being for the benefit or protection of a person if as properly interpreted it is meant to benefit or protect that person or people in general or people of a class or defined group to which the person belongs.

In Section 63 of the Torts Ordinance, the legislature provided that breach of a statutory duty could, under the circumstances delineated in that section, give the injured party a right to the remedies set out in the ordinance.

This cause of action is a "framework cause of action," in which "the court has great room to create obligations." This is a cause of action that is given specific content on a case-by-case basis, in which a court must determine, based on consideration of legal policy, which type of matters fit within the cause.

Section 63 of the Torts Ordinance (New Version), as interpreted in the case law, sets out five requirements, all of which must be present:

a. A duty is imposed by a statutory provision on the one who caused the injury.

b. The statutory provision is designed to benefit the injured party.

c. The one who caused the injury breached the duty imposed on him.

d. The breach caused injury to the injured party.

e. The injury that was caused is of the type which the legislature meant to cover.

When we apply the cause of action of breach of statutory duty, we should give it a narrow interpretation, so that the cause of action does not serve as a general source for imposing almost absolute obligations in a way that violates the original intent of the provision.

Breach of Statutory Duty: Penal Code

The wife claims that in not complying with the instructions of the High Rabbinical Court, which obligated him to give her a writ of divorce, the husband violated section 287(a) of the Penal Code that provides:

A person who violates an order properly issued by a court or an official or any person who works in an official capacity and is authorized to deal with the matter involved shall be subject to punishment of two years of imprisonment.

I am not convinced that we should accept this claim. As described above, one of the conditions for imposing liability for breach of statutory duty is that the statutory provision is designed to benefit or protect the plaintiff.

In the matter before us, it seems that the requirement of section 287(a) of the Penal Code was meant to protect the collective values of public order and observance of the law, not to protect individual interests. Therefore ... I cannot rule that the cause of action for breach of statutory duty can be based on a breach of section 287(a) of the Penal Code.

Breach of Statutory Duty: Law on Prevention of Family Violence

The Plaintiff claims that the violation of the Law on Prevention of Family Violence, 5751-1991, should be seen as a violation of a statutory duty under section 63 of the Torts Ordinance.

Section 3 of the Law on Prevention of Family Violence provides:

3. Request for a Protective Order and Conditions for Giving It

At the request of a member of the family, the attorney general or his representative, a police prosecutor, or a welfare officer appointed under the Youth Law (Care and Supervision), 5720-1960, the court may issue a protective order against a person if it appears that any of the following conditions exist:

(3) Continued mental abuse of a family member or behavior in a manner that does not allow another family member to live his life in a reasonable and appropriate manner.

It can certainly be said that in the case of the Plaintiff, the failure to give a writ of divorce constitutes a serious infringement on her ability to conduct her life in a reasonable and appropriate manner and constitutes mental abuse that has continued for many years.

I accept what has been said by the social worker, Rachel Ackerman, who treated women in the Ultra-Orthodox sector who have been denied writs of divorce in The Family Institute, a clinic for family care in the Ultra-Orthodox sector. Ms. Ackerman described the effect of the denial on the Ultra-Orthodox woman in these words:

Women denied a divorce cannot do anything to change their status. As long as they are tied to their husbands, the social status of the women is largely lacking, and their value in the eyes of the community is low. Therefore they feel social isolation, severe humiliation, shame, and distress.

As a result of the centrality of marriage in Ultra-Orthodox life, the community tries to find a match for a single or divorced woman. The interaction of the community with divorced women is concentrated on finding new husbands for them so that they can improve their status in the society. There is no accepted interaction between women denied a divorce and their community. Their place in the community is not clear. On the one hand, they are not considered to be among those who are married, and with the passage of time, the distance increases between them and their friends who are busy having and raising their children. On the other hand, they do not belong to the group of divorcees, matches cannot be proposed for them, and they do not benefit from the community's attempts to help them.

As distinct from the case with section 287(a) of the Penal Code, there is no doubt that the Law on Prevention of Family Violence was designed first of all to protect women who suffer from abuse or cruelty from their husbands.

Nonetheless even though we have said that the statutory provision in this case is designed to protect the Plaintiff, and even though it has been found that the husband violated the statutory provision, it is still necessary to determine whether this statutory provision is properly interpreted as one intended to provide a civil remedy for its violation by granting compensation for harm caused by breaching the statutory duty.

It seems to me that the statute is not intended to provide such a remedy, and the Plaintiff before us cannot base her claim on a cause of action of breach of statutory duty where the alleged statutory duty is in the Law for Prevention of Family Violence.

Breach of Statutory Duty: Basic Law: Human Dignity and Freedom

Section 2 of the Basic Law: Human Dignity and Freedom provides, "There shall be no violation of the life, body or dignity of any person as such." Section 5 of the Basic Law may also be relevant and provides, "There shall be no deprivation or restriction of the liberty of a person by imprisonment, arrest, extradition or otherwise."

The infringement on the dignity and freedom of a woman is extensive when she asks repeatedly over many years to be freed from the bonds of a relationship she does not want and finds herself stuck in a marriage against her will. There is no doubt that her freedom and free will are critically injured in connection with matters that lie at the heart of private life in which one should expect to be able to act on one's own desire and free choice.... This is true for the entire Israeli society, but it seems that in the case of an Ultra-Orthodox woman it is even more so, given the position of marriage in her private life and the degree to which her marriage affects her status in the community to which she belongs.

There is no doubt that refusal of a writ of divorce constitutes an infringement of the values protected in the Basic Law: Human Dignity and Freedom, including dignity, freedom of choice, the right of self-fulfillment, autonomy, social rights, and the right to marry and have children.

But the determination that the husband's refusal to give his wife a writ of divorce creates a continuing infringement of her dignity and freedom is insufficient to obligate him to pay compensation due to breach of a statutory duty. In order for this to happen, it is necessary to determine whether all the grounds for the cause of action are present ... and whether it is appropriate to use this cause of action in relation to the Basic Law: Human Dignity and Freedom.

In Daphne Barak-Erez, *Constitutional Causes of Action* (1994) there is a discussion of the possibility of finding that a governmental action that infringed on human rights is also a constitutional tort that can be treated as a sort of negligence. The time is still far off for recognizing this type of constitutional tort between two private individuals. I will add, though, that the rights protected in the Basic Law: Human Dignity and Freedom can provide guidance in interpreting other causes of action that are already recognized.

Negligence

In my opinion, the refusal of the Defendant to grant his wife a writ of divorce should be considered within the framework of a claim in negligence, as negligence is understood in tort law, and this cause of action can cover the case before us.

Section 35 of the Torts Ordinance (New Version) 5728-1968 provides:

> If a person does something that a reasonable and prudent person would not do, or fails to do something that under the same circumstances a reasonable and prudent person would do ... then this is a negligent act; if a person commits a negligent act as provided in relation to another person as to whom, under the

circumstances, he is obligated not to act in the way he acted, then this is negligence, and a person who through his negligence causes harm to another person engages in a civil wrong.

The cause of action in negligence is based on three elements: The defendant must have a duty of care, he must breach that duty, and the plaintiff must have an injury that was caused by the breach.

In tort law, as distinguished from criminal law, negligence is determined objectively and relates to a deviation from the standard of conduct that the court identifies as appropriate, without regard to the mental state of the person who causes the injury. In the past, Professor Tedeski expressed doubt on whether liability for negligence could be imposed on an intentional act. His approach has been rejected in both the literature and by the Supreme Court.

[The Supreme Court] has addressed the fundamental principles of interpreting the cause of action in negligence ... :

> It has been ruled in the past that "negligence is an inclusive principle that can be applied to a broad range of situations...." A full answer to a problem cannot always be based on a test of expectations; in interpreting the applicability of the law the social and ethical issues of a specific case should be emphasized. It is the court's job to balance among the various interests that should be protected, such that the court has the job of creating norms. The "categories of negligence are not closed, set, or fixed, but are defined in response to the sense of ethics and social justice and changing needs of society." With changing social attitudes, some interests lose their importance and others become more important.

Under the test of the "reasonable person," the Defendant breached the duty of care he owed to his wife and deviated in a substantial and intentional manner from the standard of appropriate conduct. This is shown in his refusal over many long years to agree to his wife's request that they divorce; in his mocking her for a long time by dragging her from rabbi to rabbi, all of whom thought they must divorce; and especially in breaching the obligation to give his wife a writ of divorce that was imposed on him by the High Rabbinical Court. There is no doubt that any reasonable person would expect such behavior to cause emotional damage to the wife and to harm her dignity.

The husband owed a duty of care to his wife, he behaved in a negligent manner in breaching that duty, and he was able to anticipate the damage that his breach would cause to his wife's dignity, to her status in society, to her freedom, and to her soul.

In concluding that the husband owed a duty of care to his wife, I give substantial weight to the relationship between a husband and a wife, a relationship of dependence and closeness. In such a relationship, one would expect particular sensitivity to the feelings and welfare of the spouse, more than would be expected towards another person.

In conclusion as to the tort causes of action, I join in the position taken by my colleague, the honorable Judge Nili Maimon, who expressed her opinion in another case that it would be appropriate for the Knesset to define a special cause of action in tort that would provide a solution for physical and mental abuse within the family.

Judge Maimon wrote:

> Establishing a special cause of action ... including provisions on injury and on compensation, will provide a better solution in the struggle against the terrible phenomenon and will be, along with the Law on Prevention of Family Violence 5751-1991 and the Anti-Stalking Law 5761-2001, part of the war on this deviant social phenomenon.

The Amount of Damages

Since we have established that there was a tortious action, we have to determine what the damages are and determine the correct compensation.

The Plaintiff claims monetary damages and non-monetary damages. As to the former, she asks for compensation for the attorney costs associated with the drawn-out proceedings in the rabbinical courts, her lost income for days she devoted to the proceedings, her travel costs, and the loss she sustained from being the sole support of her family because the Defendant prevented her from remarrying. As to non-monetary damages, the Plaintiff claims compensation for the period during which she was denied a divorce, beginning May 11, 1994, two years after she first filed for divorce, until the day she filed this complaint. This is based on her claim that a reasonable person could anticipate that the refusal to give a writ of divorce to his wife after two years from the time she requested it is likely to cause suffering and distress on her part. It is also noted that the spouses have not lived together from the day she filed for divorce and that in most western countries a separation that lasts for two years is cause for divorce.

These are the details on the compensation claimed:

1. Infringement of the right to marry: NIS 500,000. She claims that as long as the Defendant refuses to give her a writ of divorce, she is prevented from remarrying. The right to marry is recognized as a legal right of great value, and infringement of the right entitles her to compensation.

2. Infringement of the right to have children: NIS 200,000. As long as the Defendant refuses to give her a writ of divorce, she cannot have children with another man, and the right to have children is a recognized right and its infringement entitles her to compensation.

3. Infringement of the right to sexual enjoyment: NIS 500,000. As long as she does not have a writ of divorce, she cannot have the enjoyment and satisfaction of sexual relations.[1]

4. Social isolation: NIS 350,000. Due to her unclear status in the Ultra-Orthodox community in which she lives, being neither married nor divorced, she has suffered social isolation, pain and suffering, and she cannot have any connection or relationship with men.

5. Infringement on reputation: NIS 100,000. Because she is a woman denied a divorce, her reputation in her community is soiled and her social status and that of her children is adversely affected.

6. Infringement on autonomy: NIS 350,000. Due to her husband's refusal to give her a writ of divorce, she feels a lack of control over her future.

7. Shame, suffering, pain, and humiliation: NIS 300,000. These feelings are caused directly by the Defendant's continued refusal to give her a writ of divorce and cause her great mental damage.

She also asks for additional compensation for each day, beginning the day she filed for divorce and until she gets the writ of divorce, for each of these types of damage except the first.

In addition, the Plaintiff seeks aggravated damages in the amount of NIS 200,000. Thus, altogether, the compensation sought is NIS 3,044,000, in addition to the daily compensation of NIS 2433.

---

1. As explained in chapter 14 in the discussion of surrogacy law, Jewish law imposes a very strong prohibition on sexual relations of a married woman with anyone except her husband. This would be especially meaningful to an Ultra-Orthodox woman who lives according to Jewish law.

The daily compensation was not requested in the original complaint, so I shall not consider it.

The woman cannot obtain compensation for two types of damages she claims, damages for the legal proceeding and damages for lost wages. These matters should be covered in a decree for costs in the rabbinical courts and in her request for support.

As to the remaining types of damages, the husband claims he is not obligated to pay compensation on the following grounds:

Infringement of the ability to marry: The Defendant denies his obligation to pay for this injury. According to him, when she chose to marry him, she exercised the right to marry. The Defendant claims that if he had divorced her on false grounds or infringed on her chances to marry again after divorcing her, then she would have such a claim.

Infringement on the ability to have children with another man: The Defendant claims that the Plaintiff did not want any more children, so the Defendant did not prevent her from having more, and in any case she was the one who decided to separate from him. She cannot make a claim against him because she was the one responsible for her failure to have more children.

Infringement of the ability to enjoy sexual relations: He claims that the restriction on her ability to have sexual relations with any man other than her husband begins from the time of their marriage, which she entered of her own free will. The divorce, if there is one, will remove the prohibition that entered into force upon her marriage. He should not be seen as the one who caused this injury, because he is ready to have sexual relations with his wife and it is she who refuses.

Social isolation: The Defendant claims that his wife does not suffer social isolation due to her free choice to live separately from him because, even when they lived together in a loving relationship, they did not go out to coffee houses and theater the way secular members of society do.

Infringement on autonomy: The Defendant claims that, to the extent that she feels a lack of control over her future, he did not cause that feeling.

Subjective claims (shame, suffering, pain, and humiliation): He claims that he did not cause the Plaintiff to feel any shame, suffering, pain and humiliation. The Plaintiff has not proven her suffering, even though the court gave her a diary.

Aggravated damages: The Defendant claims there is no reason or fairness in penalizing him and in making him pay aggravated damages, in light of the fact that his rights have been breached. The Plaintiff rebelled against him and is not behaving toward him as a wife behaves toward her husband, although he has tried to repair the destruction of his home and family. Therefore he asks that the request for aggravated damages be rejected.

In the present case, all the damages we might allow are non-monetary. The Torts Ordinance recognizes this type of damage as compensable.... In many cases, there is no need for evidence of economic damage or its extent, as long as the non-monetary damage is the result of the breach of duty by the tortfeasor.

In my opinion, this principle should be applied in the case before me. The Plaintiff claims several grounds of damage, and even though none of them can be measured or quantified in terms of money, nonetheless they were damages caused to the Plaintiff. In addition, the Plaintiff sought aggravated damages, in light of the special circumstances under which her rights were violated.

I have no doubt that the woman suffered all the seven types of non-monetary injury she claimed. It seems that the infringement on her right to bear children is marginal, because she had six children and we are not dealing with a childless woman who has been denied a writ of divorce.

In her testimony, the Plaintiff stated:

> The fact that I am an anchored woman affects all aspects of my life and makes my life much more difficult than it would be were I divorced. The fact that I am an anchored woman causes me great shame, hurts my feelings, and causes me great pain and suffering from the sense that I am in a situation with no solution.
>
> I do not have the status of a married woman, but on the other hand, I am also not a divorcee. My uncertain status hurts me both emotionally and in fact.... Every family event is a drawn out nightmare for me. I have had to handle things alone with six small children. I see how every other woman comes with her spouse, and I yearn to be in her position.... I am the only one alone. I have often left an event to cry someplace where I would not be seen.
>
> My husband asked me any number of times to go with him to various advisors and assured me he would follow their instructions. Over and over, I gave in to the temptation to believe that he would really do so.... I was forced to expose myself, the story of my life, and my marital problems to unknown men and rabbis. Through superhuman effort I overcame the shame and unpleasantness involved, but it was all for nothing.

[Other evidence is found in the High Rabbinical Court's determination that the husband caused his wife to endure various forms of suffering. There has been ample proof of the injuries she claims.]

I cannot accept the Plaintiff's claim that the damages apply beginning on May 11, 1994, two years after she filed her first claim for divorce. Because the applicable cause of action is in negligence and is based on the determination that the husband acted negligently when he breached the duty of care owed to his wife, deviating from the standard of behavior of a reasonable person, who would have carried out the order of the rabbinical court to divorce, and he could anticipate the damages caused to his spouse due to his behavior of not complying with the court order, the Plaintiff is entitled to compensation for the period from the time the rabbinical court decision was given requiring the Defendant to give the Plaintiff a writ of divorce until the day she filed the present action.

It cannot be said that the husband engaged in negligent acts before the decision of the rabbinical court, but perhaps some other actor was negligent before that decision.

Punitive Damages and Aggravated Damages

In CA 140/00 *Estate of Ettinger v. Company for Reconstruction and Development of the Jewish Quarter in the Old City of Jerusalem Ltd.*, 68(4) PD 486, 561–65 (2004), Justice A. Rivlin summarized the goals of the tort remedy and those of punitive damages in particular:

> The tort remedy is not declaratory or penal, but remedial, and it is intended to remove the damage and remedy it. Indeed the purpose of compensation is to return the injured person, in so far as this is possible by means of a payment of money, to the same position he would have been in after the tortious act had it not occurred. This purpose is also expressed in the principle that a person is only liable for damages that he caused. Furthermore, the purpose stands behind the requirements that the injured party must have suffered some damage and that there be a causal link between the tortious act and that damage.

Nonetheless there are legal systems that recognize a relief of punitive, exemplary or vindictive damages, namely "damages that the tortfeasor must pay to the injured person in an amount that does not reflect an assessment of the damage that the tortfeasor caused to the injured person by the tort, but that intends to punish the tortfeasor for his dangerous conduct and thereby to express revulsion at it." The punitive damages are distinguished from aggravated damages, which also take into account the seriousness of the tortfeasor's conduct, but express a genuine assessment of the damage caused [to the injured person], when this damage has been aggravated by the tortfeasor's improper conduct.... Punitive damages, therefore, do not rely upon a foundation of remedy or reparation. The rationale behind these is to punish and deter.... It should be noted that an award of punitive damages is found more often for torts involving intent, where the conduct of the tortfeasor deserves condemnation. Various legal systems have recognized the possibility of awarding punitive damages also in claims based on the tort of negligence, but the courts do this, as a rule, in limited and exceptional cases.

In CC (TA) 1056/00 *Heirs of the Davosh Estate v. City of Tel Aviv Fire Department* (Dec. 10, 2003), the following was said about punitive damages:

In our system, we do not impose punitive damages for negligence even if the negligence is serious, as long as the injury was caused without malice. It is possible to impose punitive damages in cases where the culpable acts were done with malice, such as in cases of assault or defamation in order to get the tortfeasor and others in his position to behave in a restrained normal manner. Intentional acts undertaken with malice sometimes justify the use of a deterrent such as punitive damages, not as a general rule but in the exceptional case, and not in the case of regular negligence or any other act not accompanied by malice.

As to the objectives of aggravated damages and their nature, the statements of the honorable Judge Nili Maimon are instructive. She granted aggravated damages to a woman for the injury caused by her husband's attack on her and by his cruelty to her:

Aggravated damages are granted when there is an injury that is not to property, such as injury to reputation or to feelings. In deciding whether to grant this type of compensation, the malicious behavior of the tortfeasor and the terms he used [in his verbal attacks on his wife] should be considered. In this case there is reason to increase the amount of compensation in light of the seriousness of the tortfeasor's behavior.... We consider aggravated damages when the damages suffered are not to property, but rather to a person's reputation or feelings, and therefore the amount of damages set are only "at large," meaning that they are not subject to exact monetary evaluation. When evaluating such injuries it is appropriate to consider the circumstances under which they were inflicted, the maliciousness of the behavior of the tortfeasor, and the terms he used. These circumstances are relevant because they affect the degree of harm caused to the plaintiff. The seriousness of the injury to feelings and reputation are sometimes measured by the seriousness of the acts and words of the tortfeasor. For this reason, in deciding whether to grant aggravated damages, as in deciding whether to grant exemplary damages, the seriousness of the tortfeasor's behavior must be considered and the amount of damages increased.

This analysis was provided in relationship to damage to a person's reputation, but it also applies to the circumstances of the case before us. It applies to the emotional injury and the loss of well-being of the Plaintiff for which she should be compensated. In evaluating the injury she has suffered, it is fitting to consider the inappropriate behavior of the Defendant towards her.

In CA 30/72 *Friedman v. Segal* 27(2) PD 225, Judge Etzioni referred to the position of the scholar Professor Julius Stone in relation to the distinction between punitive damages and aggravated damages:

> Professor Stone, in his article…, suggests that aggravated damages in fact have all the characteristics of damages characterized as punitive or exemplary, especially when, as in the case before us, we mean damages for defamation; he therefore suggests doing away completely with punitive damages…. We do not see it that way. Whether considering punitive damages or aggravated damages, a ruling on damages requires consideration of the same factors. As said above, most of the relevant factors apply to both, especially in cases where the claim is one of injury to a person's reputation.

In light of what is said above, we have before us a case in which it is clearly appropriate to impose aggravated damages on the Defendant.

A strong expression of the negative effect on the life of a woman denied a writ of divorce … is found in the words of one of the great interpreters of Jewish law of the twentieth century, Rabbi Y.A. Henkin…. Rabbi Henkin said as follows, "He who delays delivering a bill of divorce because he demands a payment to which he is not legally entitled is a thief, and worse than that, he is one who spills blood."[2]

Thus we are dealing with an injury so serious, even in the eyes of Jewish law, that it should be seen not only as a spiritual, emotional, and mental injury, but also as the spilling of blood in its essence.

Conclusion

Because of the injury caused to the Plaintiff by the Defendant's refusal to give her a writ of divorce, beginning on January 24, 2002, when the High Rabbinical Court obligated him to give his wife a writ of divorce, up to September 9, 2003, when the present complaint was filed, I grant her NIS 200,000 damages a year, which comes to NIS 325,000 for the entire period.

I also impose on the Defendant the requirement to pay aggravated damages of NIS 100,000.

Altogether, he must compensate her in the amount of NIS 425,000.

This amount shall be paid within 30 days, and after that linkage and interest will occur as required by law, from the day of the decision to the day of payment.

The Defendant shall pay costs of NIS 10,000.

Comment (Clarification of Legal Claims)

In order to understand the plaintiff's claims, it helps to understand some features of the typical way of life in the Ultra-Orthodox community. The community puts a very high religious and social value on marriage and children. Both men and women typically marry in their late teens or early twenties and begin to have children soon after. Family

---

2. There is a play on words, because the Hebrew word for "payment" is the same as the word for "blood."

size is large; it is not unusual for a woman to have more than six children. On the other hand, a married woman cannot have children with anyone except her husband. In this context, the Plaintiff's claim to injury from not being able to have additional children is more credible than it might seem in a typical American context.

Social life in the Ultra-Orthodox community revolves around family events. With large families, there are frequent bar mitzvahs, engagement parties, and weddings. The pain and humiliation the plaintiff claimed to feel at these events would have a major effect on her life.

In general, while marriages are not arranged, contacts between potential spouses are. There is no dating for fun. Single men and women meet each other socially only when they are ready to seek a spouse and only for the purpose of determining whether they want to marry proposed candidates. Typically, friends, relatives or professional matchmakers arrange for a meeting between two people they deem suitable for each other. Potential spouses are checked out before the first date. There is little chance of meeting a person of the opposite sex outside of such arrangements. In most sub-groups in the Ultra-Orthodox community, the man and woman can decide if they want to marry, and they usually make this decision after a few meetings. The entire matchmaking endeavor is serious and extensive. Therefore the Plaintiff's complaint that she lacks a recognized place in the community because she is not married and is left out of the matchmaking activity is understandable.

Jewish law values a woman's sexuality, as long as it is expressed within marriage. In fact, Jewish law requires a husband to provide sexual satisfaction to his wife. Within this context, it is clear that the Plaintiff's claim of infringement of the right to sexual enjoyment is a meaningful claim. Her sexuality would be taken seriously, and a married woman separated from her husband would have no legitimate way of obtaining sexual enjoyment.

The legal risk the Plaintiff took in seeking tort damages indicates that she must have been desperate indeed. The judge recognized this risk when he wrote, "I am also not deciding whether, if the Plaintiff's claim is accepted and as a result the husband decides to give her the long-awaited writ of divorce, this will be considered a valid writ." As indicated in chapter 14 on family law, a divorce is valid in Jewish law only if based on the consent of both parties. If the husband gives the wife a writ of divorce due to the threat of monetary liability, or in exchange for her forbearance from enforcing her rights to tort damages, there is a danger that the divorce will be considered invalid because it was not based on his full free will. Should the Plaintiff seek to remarry, the rabbinical authorities will check to see whether she is single and will find the record of the divorce. If they also find record of the tort litigation, or if they otherwise hear of it (and a case like this is rare and quite notorious), they may rule that the man gave her the writ of divorce because he was forced to do so by the prospect of having to pay tort damages, the divorce was invalid, and she cannot remarry. In fact, the very specter of this happening may reduce her chance of finding a man willing to marry her. This strict interpretation of what constitutes consent of the husband to divorce is not certain, but is more likely to occur in the Ultra-Orthodox community. Other Jews are more likely to be able to find rabbis who will accept the divorce and agree to remarry the woman.

Comment (The Decision)

The opinion states it is not dealing with creating an incentive for the husband to give a divorce. That type of incentive is covered in the Rabbinical Courts Law (Execution of a Divorce Decree) 5755-1995 and is in the exclusive authority of the rabbinical courts.

Nonetheless, as indicated in the prior discussion, the tort damages declared in this case and in cases like it can serve as an incentive. A woman may agree to give up on all or part of the award in return for a divorce. In addition, a woman granted monetary compensation for suffering or losses up to the time of the tort lawsuit could theoretically return to the court for additional damages for the period after the first lawsuit if the husband still refused to give her a writ of divorce. Of course, this threat is realistic only if the husband has income or assets; if he does not, the threat of a future monetary claim is less likely to move him.

The decision of the court is consistent with the way the law of torts works in other cases. Although the court insists that it is only compensating the wife for her injuries, it is in fact creating an incentive for this husband, and for all husbands, to deliver writs of divorce when ordered to do so. Compensation to the wife forces the husband to internalize the costs of his tortious behavior, and this internalization can force him to change how he acts. It is very much like the factory that reduces its pollution when it must pay damages for causing a private nuisance.

The judge granted compensation to the wife only from the date of the appellate rabbinical court order stating that the husband must divorce the wife. It took ten years to get to that order. In stating, "it cannot be said that the husband engaged in negligent acts before the decision of the rabbinical court, but perhaps some other actor was negligent before that decision," Judge HaCohen suggested that during that long period, it was the negligence of the rabbinical court that caused the wife's suffering. The question is what caused the delay in the rabbinical courts. Rabbinical courts often urge a couple to reconcile, although much of the delay in this case cannot be attributed to that cause alone. The fact that under the rule of a case like this one, the husband is immune from damages until there is a final decision in the rabbinical courts reduces the degree to which the threat of a tort action creates an incentive for a husband to provide the required writ. It is interesting that article published several years after this case, it is reported that Judge HaCohen later changed his mind and decided that tort damages may be awarded for injury that occurred even before the divorce order was issued.[3]

Aside from compensation for her direct costs, the compensation the plaintiff sought was NIS 2.5 million, which was about $577,000 at the exchange rate as of the day of the decision. She was willing to have allowed her husband two years from her first filing to grant her a divorce, so that left ten years for which she sought to be compensated. The compensation would thus come to about $58,000 a year. The court granted her NIS 425,000 in compensation, or about NIS 261,500 a year for the period since the final decree obligating the husband to give a divorce. This comes to just over $60,000 a year. In other words, she got more per year than she requested, but for a much shorter time. She got less in compensation than requested and more in aggravated damages (she got one-half of the aggravated damages requested, but it covered only one-fifth of the period of time). The court did not explain how it calculated either figure. The decision includes a long discussion of why each of the types of damages claimed is justified, but nothing about how the amount of compensation was calculated.

How much guidance does this give for the future? Not much, but perhaps not much is expected. In the Israeli system, Supreme Court decisions bind lower courts. Decisions by lower courts guide, but do not bind, courts below them. Basic Law: The Judiciary,

---

3. *See* Rivkah Lubitch, *Damages for Divorce Refusal, for Men Too*, YNET (Feb. 27, 2010, 7:46 AM), http://www.ynetnews.com/articles/0,7340,L-3854366,00.html.

section 20(a). The court that decided this case is at the lowest level, so the decision is formally neither binding precedent nor guidance for any other court.

Nonetheless other trial level courts paid attention to this decision. In one of them, FamC (Kfar-Saba) 19480/05 *Doe v. Estate of Doe* (April 30, 2006), a family law court in another city, citing Judge HaCohen's opinion, imposed damages of NIS 711,000 against the estate of a man who had died almost twenty years after being ordered to give his wife a divorce. He had never complied with the order. The court granted compensation for suffering in the amount of NIS 3,000 per month, or only NIS 36,000 per year, and refused to grant aggravated damages. The judge commented that allowing aggravated damages might lead to a situation in which the man gives a writ of divorce but is not considered to have done so of his own free will. Of course, that would not have been a problem in that case, since the husband was already dead. While the judge in *Doe v. Estate of Doe* used the precedent in *K.S. v. K.P.* to allow a cause of action for injury from refusal to deliver a writ of divorce, it set a much lower rate of compensation for what was probably a similar injury. Without detailed explanation of the basis of the damages award of *K.S. to K.P.*, it can provide little guidance to other courts in setting the amount of damages even if they are willing to consider the case.

It is not only men who refuse to agree to divorces. Although refusal by men has gained more notoriety, sometimes women refuse to accept writs of divorce offered by their husbands. A woman may want financial concessions from the husband or have other motivations. Nothing in the legal analysis of *K.S. v. K.P.* limits its rationale to refusal by the husband, although the damage claims by a man denied a divorce may be somewhat different. Judge HaCohen, who decided the case of *K.S. v. K.P.*, ruled six years later that a man could obtain tort damages from a wife who refused to accept a writ of divorce.[4]

The case of *K.S. v. K.P.* treated the actions of the husband as negligence, even though they were clearly intentional. The court ruled that there is no bar to treating an intentional act as a negligent one as long as the requirements for the tort of negligence are met. The requirements are that there must be a duty, a breach of the duty, and an injury caused by the breach. Israeli law does not draw a sharp distinction between intentional torts and negligent torts, at least in cases like this one.

American law does not deal with issues similar to those that arise in the divorce refusal cases, but most states allow somewhat similar tort suits by one spouse against another for physical or emotional injury. Such claims may be subject to state rules regarding spousal immunity, the now-fading doctrine that one spouse cannot sue the other.

Comment (Aftermath of the Decision)

It was reported in 2011 that the plaintiff in *K.S. v. K.P.* collected the damage award in full. The husband still refused to give her the writ of divorce and she stopped pursuing the matter in the courts.[5] The aftermaths of four similar cases have been reported.[6] In each of two cases, after the court denied the husband's motion to dismiss, the wife dropped her suit and the husband gave her a divorce. It may be significant that in each case, the wife also sued members of the husband's family who she claimed were responsible for

---

4. *See* Lubitch, *supra* note 3.

5. *See* SUSAN WEISS, THE TORT OF GET ABUSE (2011), *available at* https://docs.google.com/viewer?a=v&pid=sites&srcid=ZGVmYXVsdGRvbWFpbnxjZW50ZXJmb3J 3b21lbnNqdXN0aWNlfGd4OjQ5Njk2OTI3YzIwMDZjNTY&pli=1.

6. *Id.*

his intransigence. It might have been their fear of liability that contributed to the husband's agreement to the divorce. One of these cases involved an ultra-Orthodox woman and she has since remarried. The fact that the wife dropped the claim before a final determination in the tort action may have helped protect the voluntariness of the man's consent. In two other cases, the women got damage awards in tort cases, but it is not clear whether they succeeded in collecting their awards. In neither case did the husband capitulate and give his wife a writ of divorce.

Question

1. What are the advantages and disadvantages of the recognition of a tort action under Israeli law for a spouse denied a divorce?

C. Breach of Statutory Duty

The divorce case discusses the tort of breach of statutory duty. This is recognized as a tort under the Torts Ordinance (New Version) and can apply to breach of any statute as long as the five conditions set out in the statute and the case are met. These are:

a)   A duty is imposed by a statutory provision on the one who caused the injury.

b)   The statutory provision is designed to benefit the injured party.

c)   The one who caused the injury breached the duty imposed on him.

d)   The breach caused injury to the injured party.

e)   The injury that was caused is of the type which the legislature meant to cover.

The judge in *K.S. v. K.P.* also ruled that the statute violated had to be designed to provide a civil remedy of compensation for breach. In the case before it, the court found that the statutes under which the plaintiff made her claim could not support the tort. The provision in the Penal Code on Breach of a Legal Order did not apply because it failed condition (b); it was designed to benefit public values of law observance and not to benefit individuals. The provision in the Law for Prevention of Family Violence was designed to protect abused spouses, but it was not intended to be the basis of a civil action for compensation.

The Supreme Court took a broader approach to the issue of whether a law is intended to provide private compensation in CA 345/81 *Sultan v. Sultan* 38(3) PD 169 [1984], cited and discussed in *K.S. v. K.P.* In *Sultan v. Sultan*, a Muslim man divorced his wife against her will without a prior decision of the Shari'a court obligating her to accept the divorce. Under Islamic law, a man can unilaterally divorce his wife without resort to any court, but the Israeli Penal Code provides:

181. Termination of Marriage Against the Will of the Wife

A man who terminates a marriage against the will of the wife, without a final decision of a regular court or another authorized court that obligates the wife to accept the termination, shall be subject to imprisonment of five years.

The Court held that the wife could receive compensation in tort based on his breach of the statutory duty established in section 181 of the Penal Code. The Court determined that the provision was designed to protect women in her situation and that it would serve as a basis of tort liability unless it is shown that the Penal Code provision was intended to preclude imposition of compensation under the Torts Ordinance (New Version). The Court found no such showing and held that a decree of damages was appropriate. The statute was found to support a statutory duty even though it is phrased in negative terms, prohibiting a certain action rather than requiring that action.

In the case of *K.S. v. K.P.*, the court said that it was "necessary to determine whether [the] statutory provision is properly interpreted as one intended to provide a civil remedy for its violation by granting compensation for harm caused by breaching the statute." The Torts Ordinance provides, "[a] person is not entitled to any remedy set out in this ordinance if the statutory provision as properly interpreted was meant to disallow that remedy." And in *Sultan v. Sultan* the Supreme Court held that an action for breach of statutory duty is permitted unless it is shown that the statute was intended to preclude imposition of a tort remedy. Thus, the interpretation in the decision in *K.S. v. K.P.* is stricter and less favorable to the tort plaintiff. Whether this makes any difference in practice is not clear.

What is clear is that a private action based on a statutory duty is available where the legislature enacts a statute explicitly allowing a private remedy for its violation. In most cases, however, statutes that dictate duties or impose prohibitions provide only for an administrative remedy or a criminal penalty. As to these statutes, the question arises as to whether a private person damaged by another's violation of the statute can sue for damages. This question has been troubling in a number of common law jurisdictions, with some allowing such private actions and others not allowing them. On the one hand, it can be argued that persons injured by another's violation of the law should be able to obtain compensation from the violating party. On the other hand, it can be claimed that when the legislature sets out certain consequences for a violation, it does not mean to allow private actions to impose additional consequences. Furthermore, the kind of conditions for imposing a damages remedy, such as those set out in Israeli law, can make the law confusing and its application inconsistent.

The tort of breach of statutory duty is recognized in a number of common law jurisdictions outside of the United States. American law takes a different approach but comes to a result similar to that in *K.S. v. K.P.*

US Law

Restatement (Third) of Torts

§ 14. Statutory Violations as Negligence Per Se

An actor is negligent if, without excuse, the actor violates a statute that is designed to protect against the type of accident the actor's conduct causes, and if the accident victim is within the class of persons the statute is designed to protect.

Comment

Under the American approach, a statute declaring an action unlawful creates a private action if: (1) the statute itself creates the cause of action, either explicitly or implicitly, or (2) a court will imply a negligence action based on violation of the statute. The difference between these two categories is that in the first, the private action is under the statute and typically has the contours defined by the statute; in the second, the private action is under a common law tort theory of negligence. In either set of cases, the violation of the statute is negligence per se, but may be subject to some or all of the common law defenses to negligence. The second theory applies only if the statute in question is designed to protect persons like the plaintiff from the type of accident the defendant caused. These limitations are roughly similar to the conditions that apply to the tort of breach of statutory duty in Israeli law.

D. Constitutional Torts

In the case of *K.S. v. K.P.*, the opinion discusses whether a claim of breach of a statutory duty can be based on a breach of a Basic Law. The plaintiff's argument was that breach of a statutory duty is actionable in tort if certain conditions are met, and this should also be true of breach of a statutory duty founded in a Basic Law. Numerous problems exist. One is the question of whether the Basic Laws impose duties on private parties. In most cases, the Basic Laws on human rights are interpreted as imposing obligations on the government, but there are cases in which private parties have been found to be obligated not to violate these rights. The question is whether this private obligation can be extended to cover cases such as a man who infringes on his wife's human rights by denying her a divorce.

A second question is whether the Basic Laws on human rights should be read as providing private tort remedies. The issue is whether the Knesset meant the Basic Laws to be used only as tools for interpreting or invalidating action, and sometimes for requiring actions, but not as tools for obtaining compensation. A statute that serves as the basis for actions in compensation has a different effect on society and on people in the society. For actions against the government, it could create a substantial drain on the public purse. For actions against individuals, it could expose them to unanticipated liability.

A third question relates to the scope of the rights which could be infringed. In the discussion of constitutional law in chapter 8, it was clear that one of the central issues, especially as to the Basic Law: Human Dignity and Freedom, is determining what rights are protected by the Basic Law. The Supreme Court has read the law expansively, but has not interpreted it to have no limits. If infringement of human rights could be the basis of a tort action, every court hearing tort cases could determine the reach of protected human dignity and freedom.

Judge HaCohen refrains from dealing with these questions, putting them off for another day.

E. Punitive Damages

Israeli Case

Estate of Ettinger v. Company for the Reconstruction and Development of the Jewish Quarter
CA 140/00, 68(4) PD 486[2004][7]

[Michael Ettinger, a twelve year old child, fell into an unfenced pit at an archaeological site in the Old City of Jerusalem and died. One of the issues is whether his estate, the

---

7. This translation is based on that on the website of the Supreme Court, at http://elyon1.court.gov.il/files_eng/00/400/001/P05/00001400.p05.htm.

Plaintiff in this case, is entitled to punitive damages. The trial court denied punitive damages. The estate appealed.]

Justice E. Rivlin

Punitive Damages

Section 76 of the Torts Ordinance provides, with regard to the compensation for carrying out a tortious wrong, as follows:

> Compensation may be awarded on its own, in addition to, or instead of an injunction; but if the plaintiff suffered damage, compensation may be awarded only for that damage that is likely to result naturally in the normal course of things and that resulted directly from the tort of the defendant.

The presence of the word "compensation" in the Torts Ordinance tells us the tort remedy is not declaratory or penal, but remedial, and it is intended to eradicate the damage and remedy it. The purpose of compensation is to return the injured person, in so far as this is possible by means of a payment of money, to the same position the person would have been in at the time of the tortious act had it not occurred. This purpose also underlies the principle that a person is liable only for damages that he caused. It also lies behind the requirements that the injured party must have suffered some damage and that there must be a causal link between the tortious act and that damage.

Some legal systems recognize a remedy of punitive, exemplary or vindictive damages, namely "damages that the tortfeasor must pay to the injured person in an amount that does not reflect an assessment of the damage that the tortfeasor caused to the injured person by the tort, but that is designed to punish the tortfeasor for his dangerous conduct and thereby to express revulsion at it." Punitive damages are distinguished from aggravated damages, which also take into account the seriousness of the tortfeasor's conduct, but express "a genuine assessment of the damage caused [to the injured person], when this damage has been aggravated by the tortfeasor's improper conduct." The distinction between punitive damages and aggravated damages was described by Justice Kennedy as follows: "aggravated damage for conduct that shocks the plaintiff; exemplary (or punitive) damages for conduct which shocks the jury." (*Muir v. Alberta* (1996) 132 D.L.R. 4th 695, 714 (Can.). Punitive damages, therefore, do not rest upon a foundation of remedy or reparation. The rationale behind them is to punish and deter (see *Hill v. Church of Scientology of Toronto* [1995] 2 S.C.R. 1130, 1208 (Can.)). On the essence of punitive damages, and the purpose underlying them, the House of Lords made the following remarks:

> Exemplary damages or punitive damages, the terms are synonymous, stand apart from awards of compensatory damages. They are additional to an award which is intended to compensate a plaintiff fully for the loss he has suffered, both pecuniary and non-pecuniary. They are intended to punish and deter. (*Kuddus v. Chief Constable of Leicestershire Constabulary* [2001] UKHL 29, [2002] A.C. 122 (H.L.) (Eng.).

The non-remedial nature of punitive damages constitutes a challenge for the classical clear-cut distinction between civil law, which focuses on compensation, and criminal law, which focuses on punishment. Civil law has always been regarded as seeking mainly to regulate relationships between individuals, and from this perspective punitive damages are classified as an anomaly. In this vein, concern has been expressed more than once that recognizing a power to award punitive damages introduces into civil law a function that is reserved for criminal law, while "compromising" on the rules of evidence, the burden of proof, and the rules of procedure that apply in criminal proceedings. Moreover it has been claimed that awarding punitive damages imposes on the tortfeasor a risk of a "double sanction," where punitive damages are imposed in addition to criminal sanctions. It has also been said that punitive damages are a windfall for the injured person, since punitive damages are granted on top of the remedial compensation. It can be argued that even if it is justified to fine the tortfeasor, it does not necessarily follow that it is right that the injured person, rather than the state, should receive the sum (see *Cassell & Co. Ltd. v. Broome* [1972] A.C. 1027 (H.L.) (Eng.); Jamie Cassels, *Remedies: The Law of Damages* 258 (2000); Allan Beever, *The Structure of Aggravated and Exemplary Damages*, 23 Oxford J. L. Stud. 87 (2003).

Contrary to all of the aforesaid, there are significant reasons in favor of recognizing a power to award punitive damages in those cases where the conduct of the tortfeasor is especially grave or it involved a serious infringement of constitutional rights. On a theoretical level, it is argued that the distinction between civil law and criminal law is not so clear-cut, that these two branches come close to each other in some cases, and it is possible to identify a grey area of "punitive civil law." On a practical level, it is argued that awards of punitive damages are valuable in providing deterrence and education against acts deserving of censure and in strengthening the protection of rights. This often works in situations that the criminal trial cannot reach. The argument concerning the injured person receiving a windfall has been answered by the claim that "he can only profit from the windfall if the wind was blowing his way." In other words, the injured person who took the trouble to promote the public interest inherent in the awarding of punitive damages is the most appropriate person to receive them. It should also be noted that where there was also a criminal proceeding relating to the same facts, its outcome can be considered in determining the amount of the punitive damages.

The economic analysis of the law of torts sees punitive damages as having an important role in providing an effective deterrent. [I]t is customary to say that one should aim for compensation that reflects the damage that was caused. But an additional parameter affects the calculation, and this is the chance that no liability will be imposed at all for the tortious act. Not every tortious act leads to a claim in tort. Various factors play a part in this, including the costs of pursing a claim and the injured person's uncertainty as to whether the tortious act caused the damage or as to the identity of the tortfeasor. There are therefore some who think that punitive damages ought to be awarded; otherwise, the deterrent inherent in tort liability will be defective due to the possibility that tortfeasors will evade liability. The amount of the punitive damages must, under this approach, reflect the chance that the tortfeasor will not be found liable for his tort. Thus, for example, if there is a 25 percent chance that the tortfeasor will indeed be found liable for the damage that he caused, and the damage is in the amount of NIS 100,000, then the amount of the total compensation should be NIS 400,000, of which NIS 100,000 are 'remedial' damages, and the remainder, NIS 300,000, are 'punitive' damages (see A. Mitchell Polinsky & Steven Shavell, *Punitive Damages: An Economic Analysis*, 111 Harv. L. Rev. 869, 882).

The question of the appropriateness of punitive damages is, therefore, a multifaceted one. In any event, in view of the unique nature of punitive damages, case law has usually treated them with reservations, even though it is possible to find different approaches to the issue in the different legal systems. Case law in England held in the past that the court may award punitive damages in any case of tort (*Loudon v. Ryder* [1953] 2 Q.B. 202 (Eng.)), but in 1964 the House of Lords, *per* Lord Justice Devlin, sought to limit punitive damages to certain cases only, on the grounds that such damages can lead to an overlap of the roles of civil and criminal law. Lord Devlin was of the opinion that punitive damages should not be awarded except in three types of cases: where there is an express provision of statute; where civil servants acted oppressively, arbitrarily or unconstitutionally; and where the tortious act of the tortfeasor was planned by him with the purpose of procuring for himself a benefit in an amount exceeding the amount of the expected compensation. The purpose of the latter category is to deprive the defendant of the fruits of his tort, and to make it clear to him and to others that "tort does not pay" (see *Rookes v. Barnard* [1964] A.C. 1129 (Eng.)).... The Law Commission proposed that punitive damages should continue to be recognized, but their scope should be redefined, so that it would be possible to award them in any case of torts where the defendant deliberately and outrageously ignored the rights of the plaintiff (see The Law Commission of the U.K., *Aggravated, Exemplary and Restitutionary Damages*, L.C. 247 (1997)). The matter has not yet been dealt with in legislation.

The precise restrictions that were delineated in *Rookes v. Barnard* were not adopted *verbatim* in countries such as Canada, Australia and New Zealand. Nonetheless the courts there restricted the awarding of punitive damages to exceptional cases, especially those in which the conduct of the defendant is outrageous or deliberate to a degree that justifies his being penalized by means of finding him liable to pay the plaintiff a kind of "civil fine." The purpose of this is to give expression to the disgust of the court, and to allow the tortfeasor and others may see what has happened and be deterred (see *Hill v. Church of Scientology of Toronto*, at 1208). The approach to punitive damages in the case law in the United States is broader as to the grounds for awarding them, the willingness to make use of them as a deterrent, and the amounts awarded (*see and compare B.M.W. of North America Inc., v. Gore*, 517 U.S. 559 (1996)).

It should be noted that an award of punitive damages is found more often for torts involving intent, where the conduct of the tortfeasor deserves condemnation. Various legal systems have also recognized the possibility of awarding punitive damages in claims based on the tort of negligence, but the courts do this, as a rule, in limited and exceptional cases.

The courts in Israel have recognized the possibility of finding a tortfeasor liable for punitive damages. As early as CA 216/54 *Schneider v. Glick* 9 PD 1331 [1955] it was held that:

> The attack of the Appellant on the Respondent was deliberate, without immediate prior provocation, and it was carried out with a savageness that was intended to shame the Respondent in public. The court may take into account these special factors, such as the evil intent of the attacker and the shame that the victim suffered, in determining punitive damages ... taking into account all of these factors, we find that the circumstances justified imposing a substantial amount as general damages. (*Id.* at 1335).

Case law has repeatedly held that the courts in Israel have the power to award punitive damages, even though this approach has been criticized. There are those who think that we should consider the effect of the Basic Laws on this issue (CC (TA) 1549/96 *Levy v. Hadassah Medical Organization* (Jan. 11, 1998)). In practice, the courts in Israel are not accustomed to awarding punitive damages and they do so infrequently. It should be noted that Israeli law has express statutory provisions that specify, in certain contexts, an express power to award punitive damages (see, for example, section 183 of the Patents Law, 5727-1967).

In our case, the district court was of the opinion that "the omissions for which the Defendants were responsible are very serious omissions," but at the same time it emphasized that there are those who cast doubt upon the actual power to award punitive damages and said that, as a rule, "the courts only award punitive damages for torts that require intent or a deliberate act." It seems to me that we should not intervene in the conclusion of the trial court in this regard. The negligence of the Respondents, as reflected in the judgment convicting them, is indeed shocking and led to a tragic outcome. Notwithstanding, it appears that even if the courts in our legal system have power to award punitive damages, and we are not required to decide this issue today, there is insufficient cause, in this case, to intervene in the decision of the district court not to award the Appellants punitive damages.

Comment

Justice Rivlin's opinion examines the claims for and against punitive damages, but does not explain why the claims against punitive damages should prevail in this case. Furthermore, the opinion indirectly suggests that punitive damages may in fact be prohibited. One of the grounds for the district court's decision not to grant punitive damages was its doubts that they are allowed at all. The Supreme Court affirmed the district court decision without examination of its grounds. If punitive damages really are permitted, the Supreme Court should have inquired as to whether the outcome at the district court was tainted by a misunderstanding of the law. This suggests that Justice Rivlin's opinion should be read as having a negative attitude toward punitive damages, because it affirms their denial without sufficient reason.

The opinion also cites the case of *Levy v. Hadassah Medical Organization*. The judge in that case raised the question of whether punitive damages are prohibited by the Basic Law: Human Dignity and Freedom. The argument is that a defendant who pays punitive damages is deprived of a property interest protected by the Basic Law. The property interest is in the money the defendant must pay to meet the punitive damages award. A person can be deprived of property only by a law that meets the requirements of the limitation clause. One of the requirements of the limitation clause is that the deprivation must be authorized in a statute or in a legal rule made pursuant to a statute. Although a few specific statutes authorize punitive damages in limited circumstances, no general Israeli statute authorizes courts to impose punitive damages. Therefore a court decision imposing punitive damages in a general tort action may violate the limitation clause. Justice Rivlin's decision does not examine the validity of this argument, nor has the matter been decided in other litigation.

In practice, lower Israeli courts award punitive damages in a small number of cases involving extreme circumstances, such as in tort actions for rape. As a general rule, decisions that discuss punitive damages decide that it is inappropriate to award them.

In the United States, the topic of punitive damages is hotly debated, but in a somewhat different framework. The issue is less whether punitive damages should be allowed than what limits should be placed on the amount of punitive damages. In this framework the Supreme Court has suggested the possibility of some limitations.

Questions

2. The law set out in the decisions in this chapter distinguishes between punitive damages and aggravated damages. The term in Hebrew for the latter translates literally as "enhanced compensation," although the convention is to translate it as "aggravated damages." What is the difference between punitive damages and aggravated damages, and is the distinction justified?

3. Has Justice Rivlin's opinion led you to question the appropriateness of punitive damages in American law?

Chapter 17

Property Law

Israeli property law is different from that of either common law or civil law. Some aspects of Israeli property law are drawn from each of these sources, but Israeli law also has many unique characteristics, reflective of the special needs and circumstances of the state. For example, the law on trusts is based on the English model; the law on bailments, on the continental model; the law on unjust enrichment, partially on Jewish law; while the public lands laws are based on none of these sources. Furthermore, Israeli property law is not identical to any of its sources, but has developed a distinctively Israeli character.[1] The topics covered in this chapter show these distinctive characteristics.

A. Public Land Ownership

Public ownership of land in Israel is extensive. About 93 percent of the land, or about 20,000,000 dunams (roughly 5,000,000 acres), is publically owned.[2] (A dunam is a measure of land that was used in the Ottoman Empire and is still used in some parts of the world, including Israel. It is 1,000 square meters, and is approximately equal to a quarter of an acre.) By comparison, in the United States, about 39 percent of the land is publically owned, most of it in the vast, sparsely populated areas of the American west and in Alaska. About 28 percent of the land is owned by the federal government, about 9 percent by state governments, and about 2 percent is Indian trust land.[3]

In Israel, public land is managed by two special agencies: the Israel Lands Council and the Israel Lands Administration.[4] The Council sets policy on land management and the

---

1. Joshua Weisman, The Law of Property, General Provisions 32–40 (1993) (in Hebrew). Much of the material on Israeli lands in this section is based on Professor Weisman's discussion in this book.

2. *See* Israel Land Administration, General Information, http://www.mmi.gov.il/envelope/index-eng.asp?page=/static/eng/f_general.html (last visited May 23, 2011). The English language website gives the amount of public land as 19,508,000 dunams. The Hebrew language website gives the amount as about 22,000,000 dunams. *See* http://www.mmi.gov.il/static/p3.asp (last visited May 23, 2011).

3. Econ. Research Serv., US Dep't Agric., Major Uses of Land in the United States, 2002, at 35 (2006), http://www.ers.usda.gov/publications/EIB14/eib14j.pdf.

4. A 2009 statute transferred the powers of the Israel Lands Administration to a new agency called the Israel Lands Authority. The transfer affects administrative arrangements but not substantive authority. The 2009 statute provided that that transfer would come into effect at a later date, after the government reached agreement on work conditions with the union representing Israel Lands Administration employees. As of this writing, the agreement was just reached and the transfer is still in the process of being implemented. Because the cases refer to the Israel Lands Administration, that term is used in the text.

Administration carries out that policy. The law restricts the sale or other transfer of public land into private ownership. Nonetheless, most public land is not left undeveloped. This section examines the reasons for public ownership of land and how public land ownership works in practice.

Israeli Statute

Basic Law: Israel Lands

1. Prohibition on Transfer of Ownership

Ownership of Israel lands, which are lands within Israel owned by the state, the Development Authority, or the Jewish National Fund, shall not be transferred by sale or by any other means.

2. Legal Permission for Transfer

Section 1 shall not apply to types of land and types of transactions permitted by law.

3. Definitions

In this law, "lands" means land, houses, buildings, and every other thing permanently attached to the land.

Comment (History of Public Ownership)

The Basic Law: Israel Lands prohibits transfer of ownership of "Israel lands" unless a law specifically allows such transfer. The term "Israel lands" includes three categories of land: that owned by the state, that owned by the Development Authority, and that owned by the Jewish National Fund. The largest category is that of land owned by the state, which constitutes about 72 percent of all the land in the country.[5] Most of this land was that held by the British Mandate and became the property of the State of Israel upon the establishment of the state.

The Development Authority is a governmental body that owns a much smaller portion of the land. It holds land to be used for public facilities, such as airports and roads. The Development Authority may obtain land by purchase and by eminent domain. In addition, the Development Authority obtains land from the Custodian for Absentees' Properties. Under the Absentees' Properties Law, 5710-1950, the Custodian was granted control of land owned during Israel's War of Independence by any person who was: (1) a citizen or subject of a country that fought against Israel during the war or that sent troops to fight against Israel (Lebanon, Egypt, Syria, Saudi Arabia, Transjordan,[6] Iraq and Yemen), (2) present in one of these countries during the war, (3) present during the war in a portion of the area of the Mandate that was not included in the State of Israel, (4) a citizen and resident of the British Mandate who left his place of residence during the War of Independence to live outside of the area of the Mandate, or (5) a citizen and resident of the British Mandate who left to live an area formerly included in the Mandate but then held by the countries that fought against establishment of the State of Israel. (After the war, Egypt, Jordan and Syria each took possession of a portion of

---

5. WEISMAN, *supra* note 1, at 198.
6. The country is now called Jordan.

the area of the British Mandate that the United Nations had designated for a separate Arab state.) In other words, this was a law confiscating property of those who associated with enemy countries or who fled during wartime.[7] Another statute, the Absentees' Properties Law (Compensation), 5733-1973, provided for compensation in some cases.

The Jewish National Fund (JNF) was established in 1901 for the purpose of purchasing land for Jewish settlement in the area of Palestine that was then part of the Ottoman Empire. From the beginning, the basic principle of the JNF was that the land would be owned for the benefit of the Jewish community as a whole and would not be sold to private owners. A statute enacted in 1953 turned the JNF into an Israeli company.[8] In 1961, an agreement was signed between the JNF and the state providing that the Israel Lands Administration would administer the JNF lands, specifying that the lands would not be sold, and promising that they would be used only for the purposes of the JNF; i.e., for Jewish settlement.[9]

Comment (Reasons for Public Ownership)

While history explains how land came to be publically owned, it does not explain why the law requires the maintenance of public ownership. Except for the relatively small amount of JNF land, the state could have chosen to sell the land to private owners. For the most part, it has not made this choice. There are many reasons why public ownership has been maintained, and they relate to the history of the state, to its political goals, and to its cultural, social and religious values.

The following diverse reasons are given for maintenance of public ownership:[10]

- Public ownership effectuates the Zionist philosophy of the land belonging to the Jewish people. Zionism is the movement supporting the return of the Jewish people to their historical homeland and the establishment of a Jewish state.

- Zionist philosophy also puts a strong emphasis on promoting agricultural development as a part of settling the land. Public ownership makes it easier to allocate land for agriculture and to prevent diversion of agricultural land to other purposes.

- The public ownership of land is a reiteration of the Biblical provision stipulating that private ownership of land is limited. One element of basic Jewish belief is that the land of Israel belongs to God. This is based on a Leviticus 25:23, "And the land shall not be sold in perpetuity because the land is Mine."

---

7. Israel later signed peace treaties with Egypt (in 1979) and with Jordan (in 1994), but both of these countries were at war with Israel at the time the statute was enacted.

8. Jewish National Fund Law, 5713-1953.

9. The term "settlement" has become a loaded term in the modern press, but for the purposes of this discussion, it means only what it meant at the time of the agreement: providing homes to Jews. In 1961 Israel held no territories, so it then referred only to settlement within the original borders of Israel.

10. The list of reasons is based on Weisman, *supra* note 1, at §3.64; HCJ 6698/95 Kaadan v. Israel Lands Administration 54(1) PD 258 [2000]; Ravit Hananel, *Zionism and Agricultural Land: National Narratives, Environmental Objectives, and Land Policy in Israel*, 27 Land Use Pol'y 1160 (2010); Minutes of the Meeting of the Constitution, Law, and Justice Committee of the Knesset, meeting as the Committee for the Constitution by Broad Consensus, July 12, 2003 and February 4, 2004, available in English at http://www.huka.gov.il/wiki/index.php/Israel_Lands_Authority.

- Public land ownership is an expression of the socialist ideology under which means of production should be publically owned. Many of the founders of the Jewish community in Israel had a socialist outlook, and this is just one of the modern expressions of that outlook in the Israeli legal system.

- It was expected that Israel would have to absorb a large number of immigrants, and public ownership of land makes it easier to allocate the land needed to provide housing and workplaces for immigrants.

- Public ownership makes large land development projects easier. It avoids the transaction costs associated with accumulating many contiguous parcels of privately owned land through purchase or condemnation.

- Before the enactment of the planning laws in Israel, public land ownership allowed for land use control. A public body managing the public lands could dictate how the lands would be used.

- Public ownership controls land prices to keep them from becoming too high as demand outstripped the limited supply of land in a small country. The shortage of land is aggravated by the fact that many regions are not arable and are unattractive for development.

- Public control of the land prevents transfer to foreign individuals who are enemies of the state.

- Public ownership facilitates management of the land in a way that meets the security needs of the state, such as by establishing residential communities in strategically important locations to prevent them from being easily occupied by enemy forces and by retaining state hold on areas necessary for military operations.

- Public land ownership makes it easier to manage the land in a way that encourages dispersal of the population throughout the country. Such dispersal reinforces Israel's hold on all areas of the country.

- Public land ownership makes it easier to hold land in reserve for public projects or for the public good.

Question

1. Which, if any, of these considerations are likely to have influenced US land policy in the past or might influence US land policy today? How do these considerations compare with the considerations that influence Israeli land policy?

B. How Public Land Ownership Works in Practice

While section 2 of the Basic Law allows transfers of ownership of Israel lands to the extent that such transfer is permitted by other laws, until recently other laws allowed transfer of ownership in only tightly restricted circumstances. The following statute is the main law setting out terms for transfer of Israel lands.

Israeli Law

Israel Land Law, 5720-1960

1. Definitions

In this law—

"Israel lands" has the same meaning as in the Basic Law: Israel Lands (hereinafter "the Basic Law");

"Urban land" means land designated for the residential or business purposes under the Building and Planning Law, 5725-1965;

"Business" means industry, manufacturing facilities, offices, commercial endeavors, tourist operations, or hotels, but excluding agricultural operations and animal husbandry.

2. Permission to Transfer Land

Section 1 of the Basic Law shall not apply to the following types of transactions:

(1) Activities of the Development Authority [as authorized by statute];

(2) Transfer of ownership of Israel lands to absentee owners of lands or their heirs who are in Israel in compensation for lands vested in the Custodian of Absentees' Property under the Absentees' Property Law, 5710-1950;

(3) Transfer of ownership of property in fulfillment of legal obligations undertaken or of debts legally created in regard to that property prior to the effective date of the Basic Law;

(4) [Certain land exchanges];

(5) [Transfers of small parcels for the purpose of rectifying boundaries];

(6) Transfers between the state, the Development Authority, and the Jewish National Fund [with certain limitations];

(7) Transfer of urban lands that are either state lands or lands of the Development Authority, provided that the total amount of land transferred shall not exceed 400,000 dunams between September 1, 2009 and August 31, 2014 (the first period), and 400,000 additional dunams during the five years after the end of the first period;

provided that no land owned by the Jewish National Fund shall be transferred without its authorization.

2A. Limitations on Selling or Transferring Rights in Land to Foreign Persons

(a) In this section—

"Rights in Land" means ownership or leasehold rights for a period of more than five years … ;

"Foreign persons" means all of the following:

(1) An individual who is not one of the following:

(a) An Israeli citizen or resident of Israel;

(b) A person entitled to immigrate to Israel under the Law of Return, 5710-1950;

(2) An organization controlled by one or more persons who are not among those listed in subsection (1);

(3) Anyone acting on behalf of an individual or organization described in subsection (1) or (2) …

(b)

(1) A person shall not sell or transfer rights in Israel lands to a foreign person, whether for compensation or not, except in accordance with the requirements of this law;

(2) A person who wishes to sell or transfer rights in Israel lands to a foreign person, shall request approval for the grant or transfer from the chairperson of the Israel Lands Council;

(3) The chairperson of the Israel Lands Council may approve the sale or transfer of rights in Israel land to a foreign person [following specified procedures];

(4) In deciding whether to approve [a sale or transfer of land to a foreign person], the chairperson of the Israel Lands Council shall consider, inter alia, the following matters:

(a) The public good and public security;

(b) The connection of the foreign person to Israel, including personal information about the person, the duration of his residence in Israel, and his family relationship to a person who is not a foreign person;

(c) The purpose for which the foreign person seeks to have the land sold or transferred to him;

(d) The amount and nature of lands sold or transferred to the same foreign person in the past;

(e) The characteristics of the lands in question, including its area, location, and designated purpose.

(5) Notwithstanding the provisions of subsections (1) and (3), a sale or transfer of Israel lands may be approved … to anyone of the following persons:

(a) A foreign person who is not an organization, and who seeks to acquire a single residential unit … ;

(b) A foreign person who [received a grant from an Israel agency intended to encourage investment in Israel];

(c) Another country … for the purpose of conducting its affairs in Israel, as provided in an international agreement with the State of Israel.

3. Observance of the Sabbatical Year

The Basic Law shall not affect actions designed solely to allow observance of the commandments regarding the sabbatical year.

Comment

The difference between public ownership and private ownership in Israel is much smaller in practice than in theory. While the Israel Land Law severely restricts outright transfer of publicly owned land, it does not restrict leasing of that land. In practice, the Israel Lands Administration typically leases land for a period of forty-nine years, and the lessee has the option to renew for an additional forty-nine years. The price of a forty-nine year lease is set at the beginning of the period and for most non-agricultural lands is very close to what the full market value would be if the land were sold outright. The payment is made in two parts. The first payment, at the time of the initial lease, is for most of the lease price. The remainder of the lease price is paid in low annual payments. These are called "capitalized payments" because the amount is based on the remaining lease price at the time of the lease. Thus, if the lessee pays 80 percent of the lease price at the time of the lease, in each of the forty-nine years of the lease it will pay an additional amount of 0.4 percent of the lease price (1/49 x 0.2 of the value), with adjustments for interest.

A person who holds a forty-nine year lease can sell the leasehold interest. In fact, most transactions in land, which are technically only sales of the leasehold rights of the long-term lessees, are treated as outright sales. Most buyers do not know that they are getting only long-term lease rights, and if they knew, they would not care. Prices do not reflect the status of the land as leasehold. Mortgages are available on leasehold interests. Leases are regularly renewed, and it is generally assumed that the government will not allow people to be removed from their homes and businesses when the renewed leases expire. So far, the country is too young for this to have become a problem, but no one seems to anticipate that it will be anything but a technical matter to be fixed in the future. It now appears that the problem may be solved by transfer of significant portions of leased land into private ownership.

Different arrangements apply for leases of agricultural land. Agricultural land is leased for a shorter term to a rural lessee, who makes only a low annual payment to the Israel Lands Administration. Leases are regularly renewed, as are urban leases. Most rural lessees are agricultural communities and not individuals. These communities are described in section D of this chapter.

The Israel Land Law originally provided that 100,000 dunams could be sold to private owners. The limit applied to total sales, and not to each sale. The purpose of this provision was to allow outright sales to foreign investors wishing to buy land to build factories that would employ Israelis. Because these investors would not be familiar with the Israeli system of long term leases, there was concern that they would proceed with their investments only if they could buy the land outright. In 2009, a major reform in the law was enacted, under which section 2 (7) was revised to its present form, allowing sale of 800,000 dunams over ten years. This was a substantial increase in the permitted private sales. Although the new amount represents only 4 percent of the Israel lands, it involves urban land, so the change should affect a large number of landowners.

The change resulted from several factors. Beginning in the last decade of the twentieth century, the Israeli government turned to a policy of privatization of governmental holdings as a way of creating a stronger market-based economy. In the main, this policy involved selling off government-owned companies, but it also affected the policies on administration of Israel lands. In addition, experience showed that some of the reasons for holding land in public hands were not working. Privatization of land was seen as allowing faster response to market conditions. It was also expected to moderate land prices, by allowing the market to allocate land as needed and by eliminating the costs associated with the Israel Lands Administration. Many thought that the failure of the Israel Lands Administration to allocate sufficient land to housing was driving up the price of residential property. Moreover there was widespread concern that the Israel Lands Administration and Council were slow, costly, and inefficient, and that bureaucratic costs were not worth the benefits gained from public ownership. Finally, Israel had enacted a detailed legal regime for land use control, so the country was no longer dependant on the Israel Lands Administration to provide for rational development patterns.

After the reform allowing more extensive sale of land to private individuals, there was concern that foreign elements hostile to the existence of the State of Israel would purchase property in Israel.[11] Section 2A was added to the statute in 2011 to control sales to foreign persons. Such sales are still allowed, but only according to statutory criteria and only after administrative review.

Sales to Israeli citizens and residents are not restricted. Thus, non-citizens who reside in Israel are not considered foreign persons under the law. Many Arabs and Druze living in east Jerusalem or on the Golan Heights, who were offered but did not accept Israeli citizenship after the Six Day War in 1967, are Israeli residents but not citizens, and their rights are not limited by the foreign persons provision. The law also does not restrict sales to anyone entitled to immigrate to Israel under the Law of Return. The Law of Return, discussed in chapter 13, applies to all Jews, children and grandchildren of a Jew, and the spouses of any such persons. Many Jews living outside of Israel want to own a piece of the land for ideological reasons. Others buy land in Israel in contemplation of living there someday.

Restrictions on land sales to foreign persons are also found in the laws of some American states and of other countries. Statutes limiting sales of agricultural lands to those who are not citizens of the United States are found, for example, in Minnesota[12] and Missouri.[13] Other jurisdictions limiting sale of land to foreigners, include Prince Edward Island, Canada;[14] Mexico;[15] and Turkey;[16] and there are reports that sale of land to Jews in the area of the Palestinian Authority is punishable by death.[17]

Section 3 of the statute is designed to accommodate the needs of Jews who sell land during the sabbatical year. Such sales are discussed in chapter 13.

Question

2. As described above, the 2009 amendment to the Israel Lands Law allowed privatization of 800,000 dunams of state land over ten years. If privatization is such a good idea, why doesn't the law allow more extensive privatization?

C. Changes in Land Use to Meet Changing Societal Needs

Almost all agricultural land in Israel is held on long term leases by collective and co-operative communities called kibbutzim (singular: kibbutz) and moshavim (singular:

---

11. *See* Draft Bill Amending Lands Law (Amendment—Limit on Transfer of Lands to Foreigners), 5769-2010.

12. Minn. Stat. § 500.221 (2010).

13. Mo. Stat. Ann. § 442.560 (2011).

14. *Lands Protection Act,* R.S.P.E.I. 1988, c. L-5, sec. 4. The Prince Edward Island Legislative Counsel Office's consolidated act is found at http://www.gov.pe.ca/law/statutes/pdf/l-05.pdf.

15. *See* Angleynn Meya, *Reverse Migration: Americans in Mexico,* 18-Aug. Prob. & Prop. 57, 58 (2004).

16. *See* Colonel Mark Ort, *A Turkish Primer for Legal Assistance Attorneys,* 2004-Feb. Army Law 21, 29 (2004).

17. *See* Corinne Souad Aftimos, *Reconciling the Right of Return with Shari'a in Gaza,* 15 U. Miami Bus. L. Rev. 1, 33 (2006); *Alexander Safian, Can Arabs Buy Land in Israel?,* Middle East Quarterly, Dec. 1997, at 110, *available at* http://www.meforum.org/370/can-arabs-buy-land-in-israel.

moshav). The structure of these agricultural communities is described in the next section. The American ideal of the individual farmer owning the land is not part of the Israeli paradigm. Instead, the Israeli vision is that the land will be worked by collective or co-operative communities.

During the past thirty years, the kibbutz and moshav communities came to depend less on agriculture as a major source of income, creating pressure to use their lands for industrial development. The same rural communities sought means to pay off their debts, which had reached very high levels. They wanted to be able to sell some of the land they had been farming for many years. The restrictions in their agricultural leaseholds prevented them from raising capital through land sales. In addition, membership in these communities decreased as many of the adult children of members chose to move to the cities. The remaining members wanted to be able to bring in new residents who would share the maintenance costs of communal facilities, such as kindergartens, cultural centers, and swimming pools. People interested in moving to the rural areas were not interested in joining the collective enterprise but wanted to buy land on which they could build homes away from the crowded conditions and high costs of Israel's cities. At the same time, the influx of approximately a million Jewish immigrants in the 1990s, mainly from the area of the former Soviet Union, created a huge need for housing and employment. The urban land reserves were insufficient to absorb all the newcomers, so formerly agricultural land had to be devoted to provision of housing.

As a result, the Israel Lands Council developed a scheme for redesignating agricultural land to residential and industrial use. The value of land so redesignated increased substantially, and the scheme allocated a substantial portion of the increased value to the agricultural communities that had been working the land. Some people opposed the redesignation of the lands. Environmentalists were troubled by the decrease in open land. Planners were concerned that the redesignations would encourage urban sprawl. On the other hand, some people did not object to the redesignations, but objected to the way in which the benefit of the increased land value was distributed. A coalition of groups with various objections petitioned for judicial review of the Council's decision. The main petitioner was an organization called the Mizrahi Democratic Rainbow New Discourse, an organization of Mizrahi Jews prominent in the arts and academia.[18] They were concerned that people living in the agricultural settlements, most of whom were Ashkenazi, were getting benefits from the new arrangements not available to other members of society. Another petitioner was the Society for Protection of Nature, Israel's oldest and largest environmental organization.

Israeli Case

Organization for a New Discourse v. Minister of National Infrastructure
(Mizrahi Democratic Rainbow case)
HCJ 244/00, 56(6) PD 25 [2002]

Justice T. Orr:

A. Management of State Lands — The Normative Foundation

A basic rule on Israel lands is that the transfer of title in any such land is prohibited. There are exceptions to this rule in special circumstances, where transfers are allowed for

---

18. Mizrahi Jews are descendants of the Jewish communities that existed for centuries in the countries of the Middle East, North Africa, and the Caucuses. See chapter 2.

certain types of land or under certain types of transactions, and these exceptions are defined in statutes. The general rule is set out in a Basic Law. Section 1 of the Basic Law: Israel Lands provides:

> 1. Prohibition on Transfer of Ownership
>
> Ownership of Israel lands, which are lands within Israel owned by the state, the Development Authority, or the Jewish National Fund, shall not be transferred by sale or by any other means.

Section 2 of the same law provides for the possibility of a statute permitting the transfer of ownership of Israel lands, and the Israel Land Law, 5720-1960 sets out in section 2 a list of the types of transactions to which section 1 of the Basic Law: Israel Lands does not apply.

The institution charged with managing state lands is the Israel Lands Administration. Section 2(a) of the Law on the Israel Lands Administration, 5720-1960 (hereinafter the Lands Administration Law) provides, "The Government shall establish the Israel Lands Administration (hereinafter the Lands Administration) that shall manage the Israel lands."

The Lands Administration is headed by a director who is appointed by the Government and who serves under the minister of construction and housing. The Lands Administration Law provides that the director shall submit, at least once a year, a report to the Government on the activities of the Lands Administration. Under section 4 of the law, the Government is to submit this report to the Knesset.

The Lands Administration has no legal identity that is separate from that of the state. It is an administrative instrument of the state subject to the Government and functions as an agency of the state. The Lands Administration works as an agent of the owner, and its authority is limited to administration of the property. As an agent, it must function in a relationship of trust as to its principal and not act outside of the scope of its authority. In its working as a trustee of the state, the standards of public law apply to it, as well as the standards of private law. Its employees are state employees.

Section 3 of the Lands Administration Law provides for establishment of the Israel Lands Council and sets out its authority:

> 3. Israel Lands Council
>
> The Government shall appoint an Israel Lands Council that shall determine the policies regarding property under which the Lands Administration shall operate, shall supervise the activities of the Lands Administration, and shall approve recommendations of its budget, which shall be determined by law.[19]

Section 4A of the Lands Administration Law provides that the Council shall have 18–24 members who shall be appointed by the Government. Half of them shall be selected by the Government and half by the Jewish National Fund. It also provides limits on the number of Council members who can be employed in the agricultural sector. The fact that there is a need for a limit shows that some portion of the Council members are likely to be from the agricultural sector and that the agricultural representatives have a degree of self-interest in everything related to state lands that are used for agriculture.

The administration of Israel lands is controlled by three statutes; the Lands Administration Law, Basic Law: Israel Lands, and the Israel Lands Law, and also by an agreement between the Jewish National Fund and the State of Israel.

---

19. At the time of writing this book, the government was in the process of eliminating the Israel Lands Council as a separate administrative unit.

The objective of all of these laws and of the agreement was to put an end to the duplication of functions that arose when state lands were administered by the two institutions that owned such lands, the state and the Jewish National Fund, and to unify in one institution the administration of the lands of the state, of the Development Authority, and of the Jewish National Fund. The parties to the agreement consented to the establishment of the Israel Lands Administration to concentrate "in the hands of the state, the administration of state lands, lands of the Development Authority, and lands of the Jewish National Fund, including those acquired in the past and those that may be acquired in the future." It was also agreed that "Israel lands shall be administered according to statutory provisions, under the principle that the land should not be sold but only leased." The terms of this agreement were then included in statutory law.

B. The Land Administration Policy as to Lease of Agricultural Lands

Agricultural lands were leased for agricultural use and for associated uses, such as for housing and other services needed by those who live in the agricultural communities. The lessee is obligated to work the land. The rent amounts were determined based on the assumption that the land would be put to agricultural use.... The annual payments for the rights to use the land were very low; they were about 600 shekel a year (as of 2000) [set at 2 percent of the net income from use of the land]. In the cities, in contrast, annual payments were tied to the real value of the land. Decision 1 of the Lands Council provided that each lease of agricultural land specify that if there is a change in the use of the land, it shall be returned to the Lands Administration, and the lessee shall be entitled to compensation based on rules established by the Council.

A Compensation Committee was established; its job was to determine the amount of compensation that those holding agricultural land would receive if the use of the land were changed and the land returned to the Lands Administration.... [As a result of decisions of the committee, leasehold contracts provided] that if land were returned to the Lands Administration, the amount of compensation would be based on the compensation that would have been received had the land been condemned. Under the laws on condemnation, this would be based on the value of the land in its existing use.

Since the beginning of the 1990s, the Council has made several decisions that deviate from this land policy.

C. The Decisions

Decision 727

The goal of Decision 727 was to create a large inventory of land that would be available for residential development. Land that had been designated as agricultural would be redesignated as residential, and an economic incentive would be provided to the present lessees of the agricultural land to return it to the Lands Administration. The decision deals with "agricultural lands the designation of which had been changed under the Israel Lands Administration Law." Section 2(c) is the key provision:

2.

(c) Upon termination of a leasehold agreement [for agricultural land the designation of which has been changed under this provision], the lessee shall be entitled to monetary compensation as follows:

In the central area, 27 percent of the base amount;

[In more peripheral areas], 28 percent of the base amount;

[In certain other areas], 29 percent of the base amount.

> The base amount shall be what the Lands Administration receives from selling
> the redesignated land in a public tender.

The main benefit included in this provision is in the manner in which compensation is calculated if the land is returned. The calculation is based on the new designated use of the land. This means of calculating the payments has no connection to either the terms of the leasehold contracts that, with a few exceptions, pinned the amount of compensation to the value of the land before the change in use, or to the investment the agricultural lessee had made in the land.

Decision 727 was preceded by several other decisions that dealt with the rights of lessees of agricultural land upon change of the designation of those lands. The change in policy on redesignation of Israel lands from agricultural to residential began in the 1990s, with the large aliyah[20] from the Soviet Union, based on a fear that there would be a shortage of land for building housing. The rationale for the new policy on administering the lands was to provide an incentive for lessees of agricultural land to return their lands swiftly to the Lands Administration.

Decision 717

This decision allows agricultural communities to develop industrial areas on the plots of land that they leased from the Lands Administration. The decision provides:

> 2. Upon the request of a kibbutz [or other agricultural community] to establish an industrial facility [a factory, a filling station, or a guest house] on land leased from the Lands Administration or to be leased from the Lands Administration, and [re]designated for such use, the land in question shall be excluded from the lease.

> 3. A separate leasehold contract shall be signed between the agricultural community and the Lands Administration for the industrial facility area ... that shall include the provisions common in Land Administration leases for industrial facilities of the same type in the same area.

> In this section—

> The term "kibbutz" includes several kibbutzim working together and also includes a corporation of which the kibbutz or several kibbutzim together hold the controlling interest.

> The term "hold the controlling interest" in a corporation means that it holds at least 26 percent of the stock of the corporation, that it holds the right to appoint at least 26 percent of the directors of the corporation, and that it has the right to receive at least 26 percent of the profits of the corporation.

The decision provides in section 4 that the capitalized lease payments would be between 16 and 51 percent of the property value,[21] depending on the region where the prop-

---

20. "Aliyah" is the term used for return, or immigration, of Jews to Israel. See chapter 2.

21. To determine capitalized lease payments, the land is evaluated as of the beginning of the lease. For capitalized lease payments based on 16 percent of the land value, that percentage of the value is calculated and then divided into forty-nine payments. One payment, adjusted for interest, is made each year for the forty-nine years of the lease. Thus, if the land were worth $1,000,000, the base annual payment, before calculation of interest, would be $3265 (0.16 x $1,000,000 = $160,000; $160,000 ÷ 49 = $3,265.) In an area where the capitalized lease payments are based on 51 percent of the property value, the base annual payment would be $10,408. Normally a lessee would pay part of the value of the land at the initiation of the lease, and the remainder of the value would be paid over forty-nine years. Under this scheme, there is no initial payment and only part of the value is paid over the forty-nine year lease period.

erty is located. [The rate is higher for property in the center of the country and lower for property in outlying regions.]

Decision 717 is valid for ten years. In order to give a full picture of things, we also note that the Lands Administration Decision 750 permits agricultural communities to sublease property on which industrial facilities are established to persons who are not part of the agricultural community.

K. Reasonableness of the Decisions—Decision 727

Decision 727 allowed lessees to benefit from the change in the designation of the agricultural lands that they were leasing, even though … the lease contract did not give them this right…. According to the state, this benefit was a policy instrument that the Lands Administration used in order to give the agricultural lessees an incentive to agree to the redesignation of agricultural land to allow it to be used for other purposes, especially for residential use. Therefore the central motivation behind the decision was the situation in the residential market and the fear that without a mechanism for quickly changing the use of agricultural land, there would be a serious housing shortage due to the wave of aliyah that had begun from the Soviet Union. It was feared that prices would rise due to the shortage of housing and the need to find temporary housing for the immigrants, because there was an inadequate amount of land ready for building new residential projects. Even though, according to the state, it could have solved the problem through legal proceedings forcing the lessees of agricultural land to turn their land back to the state for payments unrelated to the redesignation of their land, such proceedings would have taken a long time. It was important that property be made available immediately for residential construction. In order to assure that property would be made available quickly, it was justified to provide the agricultural lessees with a benefit beyond that to which they had a legal-contractual right.

The material brought before us in this case shows several contrary factors that should be considered. Some are planning considerations, among them the need to preserve open areas for various purposes and the need to encourage urban development concentrated in the four metropolitan areas of Tel Aviv, Jerusalem, Haifa, and Beersheva. The Milgrom Commission [appointed to consider the matter] determined that changes in the designation of agricultural land should be minimized and, as professional planners suggested, that new construction should be concentrated on making urban areas denser and stronger. Under this approach to planning, use should first be made of available urban land; lands presently designated as agricultural should be used for residential purposes only when there is no other choice. But the financial benefit to agricultural leaseholders from changing the designation of their land and the difficulty of clearing urban land for development led to selecting the policy of putting new buildings mainly in areas formerly designated as agricultural.

Another factor the Council had to consider was the social values affected by the level of compensation granted in Decision 727. The Milgrom Commission determined that the compensation was inappropriately high, would create social tensions, and would raise questions as to the justification for allocating public property to a small, defined sector of society. The Commission thought the compensation could be substantially reduced. Members of the Commission thought that, even with reduced compensation, there would be sufficient incentive for land to be returned to the Lands Administration.

The benefit granted to lessees by Decision 727 provides monetary compensation much higher than that to which they were entitled under their leasehold contracts. The claim is that Decision 727 is tainted by unequal distribution of state property. On these grounds, various groups have complained about the granting of excessive benefits to the agricultural sector and discrimination against other sectors. They claim that this grant of benefits violates the principle of distributive justice.

Against this background we can ask whether, at the time of the decision and also at the present time, there is a need to solve the housing problem by changing the designated use of agricultural land. If the answer is that there is such a need, we must ask whether the Lands Administration did enough to encourage change of use of agricultural lands through means that did not involve granting of compensation, or that involved more modest amounts of compensation.

We cannot conclude from the material before us that the policy of changing the designation of agricultural land through granting of benefits was not necessary. The matter should be given further consideration, but we cannot say that granting benefits for agreeing to redesignation would be impermissible under any circumstances.... But even if in principle it is permissible to do this, the manner in which it was done in this case is subject to criticism.

First, the decision should have affected only those areas where there was an immediate demand for residential land. Changes in designated use were necessary only at the fringes of the cities, and only when there was no other available land. Why should agricultural lands be redesignated in areas where there was no immediate need for residential property? We have heard the response that in such areas, the land was not designated and has remained designated as agricultural land, so there is no danger of excessive compensation. But reality tells us that the chance of obtaining enhanced compensation encourages agricultural lessees to exert pressure for changing the designation of their lands to residential. On this matter, the Milgrom Commission [found that such pressures could affect planning decisions].

Other issues to be considered are what the appropriate level of compensation is for creating the incentive under discussion and how that level should be determined. Setting the compensation at a percentage of the value of the property after the change in its designation is inappropriate for several reasons. First, it creates a connection between the lessee and the value of the land after the redesignation. This is unrelated to the contractual requirement that the agricultural leaseholder use the land only for agricultural purposes and that, in the event of redesignation, the lessee will receive compensation as set out in the contract. Tying the compensation to the value of the land after redesignation creates some sort of right to derive a benefit from the redesignation. It provides this benefit in order to obtain the cooperation of the lessee in allowing the change in designation to be accomplished quickly.

Second, the use of percentages of value creates ambiguity and uncertainty as to the actual amount of compensation. Various commissions have considered different percentages, but it is difficult to compare the actual monetary effects of these proposals.

Third, setting the compensation based on a percentage of the value of the property as redesignated creates distributive injustice among agricultural lessees in different parts of the country. The position of a lessee in an agricultural community in the center of the country is similar to that of a lessee in a community in the north. They have made similar lease payments, and have similar leasehold contracts. Their lands are not different in terms of their value as agricultural land. The lessees have contributed to the same degree. However, when the need arises to redesignate the use of the land, there will be a big difference in how the two are treated. One will be compensated based on the value of residential land in the center of the country [which is near large population centers and very valuable] and the other will receive compensation based on the value of residential land in the [much less populated] far north. We assume that neither one has a legal right to benefit from the redesignation of the property. Both are entitled to some compensation under their leasehold contracts, but that compensation is not related to the increase in value of the property from its redesignation. It is difficult to accept a system under which people with equal rights receive such differing amounts of compensation. It creates a strong impression of discrimination. It also suggests that the amount of compensation is higher than necessary in the center of the country. The fact that those in outlying areas receive one percent higher rate of compensation (28 percent versus 27 percent) is insufficient to compensate for this difference.

We emphasize in this connection that if one of the factors taken into account was a desire to recognize the historical value of the agricultural communities, the amount of compensation could have been based on the investment and effort that these enterprises put into the land, and not on a function of the value of the land after redesignation of its uses, which is a value tied to the location of the land but not to the historical value of the agricultural work.

Another question is whether it was appropriate to consider the difficult financial straits of the agricultural communities — the kibbutzim and the moshavim — and of their members at the time of making the decision on compensation. The state does not claim that this was a factor that was considered, or that such consideration would be appropriate. Nonetheless there are hints in the material put before us that, in fact, this factor was considered.

Would it be appropriate and relevant for the Israel Lands Council to consider the financial straits of the agricultural communities in determining the amount of compensation that these communities would receive upon change of the designated use of the agricultural lands? I would answer this question in the negative. [Under the statute,] using the reclassification of the lands as an opportunity to benefit the agricultural sector due to its difficult financial situation, without any relation to the compensation needed to accomplish the goals of the reclassification, is consideration of an irrelevant matter. It deviates from the authority granted to the Israel Lands Council to establish land policy. The Israel Lands Council was not authorized to find solutions to the hardships of the communal and cooperative agricultural communities, and its actions in this regard deviate from its statutory authority.

Decision 727 applies to large areas of land. The Lands Administration is obligated to pay compensation for a large number of plots of land. We do not have precise figures on the total amount of compensation that can be expected to be paid as a result of the decision, given that this will depend on the size of the areas that are redesignated as residential, and on a comparison of each plot to the value of other plots in the same area. In any case, it is an enormous sum. The amount is much larger than what the agricultural lessees would have received under their leasehold contracts. This difference is in itself sufficient to show that Decision 727 is unreasonable, even if we are to give the appropriate weight to the historical value of the lessees in agricultural communities. We can give examples of the differences in compensation based on the facts presented in the Milgrom Commission report.

According to that report, the average compensation for un-irrigated agricultural land would have been $1000–$2000 per dunam; for irrigated land, $2000–$3000 per dunam; and for orchards, $4500–$5000 per dunam. In comparison, under Decision 727 the level of compensation is much higher for desirable land in the center of the country. In this region, the value of land in some locations is $200,000 to $400,000 per dunam, and even much more in some specific sites. Compensation at the rate of 27 percent of this value comes out to $54,000 to $108,000 for each dunam(!). If we assume that the tax on the compensation is about 20–25 percent, as estimated by the Milgrom Commission, we can estimate the total compensation a community will receive. On every 100 dunams of land worth, for example, $300,000 per dunam, the net compensation after tax will be more than $6,000,000, or about $60,000 per dunam. Comparing this to a compensation of several thousand dollars provided under the leases shows how much larger the compensation would be under Decision 727.

The Council did not supply reasons for its decision and did not explain why the compensation for land in the center region is based on 27 percent of the land value and not on some other percentage. We know that the compensation exceeds by several multiples the value of the land for agricultural use. On the face of the matter, the compensation appears excessive in relationship to the goal of encouraging lessees to agree to have their property changed to residential use.

This analysis explains the fervor of agricultural lessees in the central region to have their property redesignated so they can obtain the compensation. This was described in the Milgrom Commission report as follows:

> [Decisions such as Decision 727] change the farmers in the area of the greatest demand for apartments into persons very interested in redesignation of agricultural land because, in many cases, the compensation greatly exceeds the return that the farmer could expect from continued agricultural endeavors on the land. In this way, agricultural lessees were changed from those who preserved and protected the agricultural lands to entrepreneurs interested in redesignation of the very land they had worked for many years. This is an undesirable phenomenon from the point of view of planning, impinging on the need to preserve open areas and to sustain agricultural endeavors, especially in a country as crowded as ours.

Therefore we emphasize that even if it is legitimate to provide an incentive to allow redesignation of agricultural land, the amount of the incentive must not exceed what is necessary for creating such an incentive.

In conclusion: Decision 727 is unreasonable in the extreme and is therefore invalid, and it should not be implemented.

Reasonableness of Decision 717

The decision is designed to solve the employment problem in agricultural communities by redesignating land for industrial use and establishing industrial facilities that will serve as a source of employment so people can better support themselves. Such a policy is permissible. The Lands Administration adopted this policy against the background of the water shortage and other problems affecting agriculture that have forced these communities to find additional sources of employment for their members. The Milgrom Commission determined that there is no shortage of areas for commercial and industrial development in the state as a whole, and that therefore the decision of the Council does not advance state interests. On the other hand, this does not negate the importance of the decision's objective for the agricultural communities and does not invalidate the goal of creating additional places of employment within the agricultural communities.

Even if this is a valid goal, it is not clear what the justification is for giving the redesignated land to the lessees in the agricultural communities at substantially discounted leasehold payments. The discount is 49 percent or larger, depending on the area in which the land is found.[22] This discount is not available to those who live in the cities, so the decision creates inequality of opportunity for different sectors; it gives a benefit to one sector in order to provide work places, but denies the same benefit to the other sector, apparently without any justification for the distinction. The provision of such benefits not only violates the principle of equality, but also the principle of equality of opportunity that in turn violates the freedom of occupation [because it creates unequal conditions of competition between individuals in different sectors, and freedom of competition is part of the freedom of occupation].

Furthermore, from the findings of the Milgrom Commission it is clear that there is no need to give the agricultural communities such large areas of industrial land in order to meet their employment needs. The Commission recommended that the areas allocated be substantially reduced [by about two-thirds].

On the basis of the information before us, we conclude that the redesignation of agricultural land in order to allow the agricultural communities to provide employment in industry and in tourist services, without any public tender, does not justify the grant of benefit through such an excessive reduction in the lease payments. In addition, there is no justification for redesignation of an amount of land greater than needed to serve the goal.

For these reasons, Decision 171 does not meet the standard of reasonableness and is invalid.

Comment

The Court opposed the compensation scheme in Decision 727 for several reasons. One is that it over-compensated the agricultural communities near the population centers as compared to the communities on the periphery, farther from the population centers. All agricultural communities would receive compensation based on the value of the land for the redesignated use. The value of the land would increase greatly for lands near the population centers and would increase much less for lands on the periphery. Therefore, the communities near the population centers stood to get a huge windfall; those on the periphery would get a much smaller windfall. The scheme in Decision 727 recognized this by allowing communities on the periphery to get 28 percent of the new land value, while those near population centers would get only 27 percent. The Court saw that this differential was insufficient to come close to equalizing the differentials in windfalls.

The Court had another problem with Decision 727. It suspected that the Lands Administration provided this windfall to the agricultural communities to help them out of the economic bind they were in. The origins of the economic bind were also the basis for the Gal law, described in chapters 5 and 8 in connection with the case of *United Mizrachi Bank v. Migdal Communal Village*. The Gal law had helped the financial situation of the agricultural communities by restructuring their debts, but the problems were not completely solved. The windfall in Decision 727 would help out the economically-strapped communities. Justice Orr's opinion rules that consideration of this factor in designing the compensation scheme would have been illegitimate. It is not that the government could not choose to provide financial assistance for the agricultural communities. There is no reason to think that this would be an impermissible goal. In fact, it was a permis-

---

22. There is a discount because none of the value of the land is paid at the beginning of the lease, and only part of the land value is paid over the forty-nine year lease period.

sible goal of the Gal law. The problem was that providing financial assistance to the agricultural communities was not rationally related to the goal of the land redesignation scheme. The Israel Lands Council was acting under a statute that allowed it to deal only in land policy. It had no statutory authorization to deal with the financial problems of the agricultural communities. In Israel, as in the United States, an administrative agency can do only what it is statutorily authorized to do.

Redesignation of agricultural land would create a windfall, but the Court thought that the windfall should go to the public. Payments to the agricultural community should have been limited to the amount needed to create an incentive to agree to the change in land use. The payments in Decision 727 were far higher than this amount.

The Court's objection to Decision 717 was different. Here the goal was to provide employment to agricultural community members who could not, or did not want, to work in agriculture. That was an appropriate goal, according to the Court. Again, the problem was with the means chosen. Decision 717 provided the communities with a financial bonanza, in the form of reduced leased payments, even if they built industrial facilities larger than needed to employ their own members. This would give industries based in agricultural communities a competitive advantage over industries located in other areas. Industries in agricultural communities would make payments for their land based on only part of the value of the land and would not have to make any up-front payment. There would be no need to obtain financing for the large initial payment. Industries on other land would have to make payments for their land based on the full value of the land, with a substantial up-front payment that would require costly financing.

The problem was exacerbated by the fact that the decision would allow an agricultural community to join together with a private entity to form a corporation, as long as the agricultural community retained at least 26 percent of the control and the profits. In other words, the decision would give the advantage granted to the agricultural communities to private companies as well. This would also lead private entities to encourage, pressure, or pay agricultural communities to develop industrial areas on their lands.

This case illustrates one of the disadvantages of the Israeli public land administration scheme. The Court dealt with the concern that the agency handling the lands gave too much weight to one of the interests affected by land policy and paid too little attention to other interests. From the time of their establishment, the Israel Lands Administration and Council had favored the interests of the agricultural communities. When times changed and agriculture was no longer as important a part of the Israeli economy, agricultural land was redesignated for non-agricultural use. Nonetheless the Council continued to favor the agricultural communities even as they became non-agricultural, allotting to them a large share of the increased land value that resulted from redesignation. The *Mizrahi Democratic Rainbow* case held that a greater share of the benefits had to be retained by the state, to be distributed through the state budget to all beneficiaries of state activities.

An analysis of the protocols of the Council meetings leading up to the decisions litigated in this case shows that, indeed, the Council looked almost exclusively at the interests of the agricultural communities.[23] There were historical reasons for this narrowness of vision, but these reasons were no longer valid. At first, the Lands Administration and the Council both saw themselves as charged with implementing the vision of resettling the land. From the early days of the Jewish return to the area, the agricultural

---

23. *See* Hananel, *supra* note 10.

enterprise had been an important part of the resettlement. As supporters of this vision, the institutions had become patrons of the agricultural communities. Even when
the change in Israeli society forced the redesignation of agricultural land, the focus remained on the interests of these communities and the need to compensate them for
their involvement in effectuating the vision. The land administration institutions missed
the fact that the changes in Israeli society brought not only the need to change the way
land was used, but also the need to reconsider what values and whose interests were important to the state.

It is interesting that one of the petitioners in the case was a prominent environmental organization, but the Court paid scant attention to environmental issues. The Society for Protection of Nature in Israel claimed that the decision to encourage redesignation
was made without any consideration of environmental values or of the importance of
maintaining agricultural lands as open areas from which everyone benefited. The problem of preservation of open land is a severe one in Israel due its small size and dense population. The Council paid no attention to environmental values.[24] Even if redesignation
of some land were inevitable, it matters how and where this is done. Should new residential growth be near the cities, or should it be spread around the country? Should it be
high density, to minimize the reduction in open agricultural land, or should it be low
density, in a way that minimizes the environmental impact of each new residential building but requires more roads and transportation services for the new residents? Apparently none of these issues were considered.

Public land in the United States has been managed in a very different manner. The US
federal government at one time owned much more extensive tracts of land than it owns
today. The land was transferred to private owners in a series of low-cost sales and free
land transfers in the eighteenth and nineteenth century. Perhaps the best known of these
are the Homestead Acts under which a settler who established residence and cultivated a
tract of land for five years could obtain 160 acres of land free of charge.[25] Through these
statutes and associated legislation, about ten percent of the land area of the United States
(more than 270 million acres) was transferred into private ownership.[26]

The land remaining in public hands is managed through four federal agencies, three
of which have rather specific missions of preservation. The National Park Services, in the
Department of Agriculture, manages the National Parks. Three agencies in the Department of Interior manage the balance of federal land holdings: the Forest Service is responsible for the National Forests; the Fish and Wildlife Service, for the National Wildlife
Refuges; and the Bureau of Land Management, for the remainder of public lands, including grazing lands and lands with mineral deposits.[27] The Bureau of Land Management,
like the Israel Lands Administration, deals extensively with leases of public lands.

Question

3. What type of decision by the Israel Lands Council would have satisfied the Court?

---

24. *See id.*

25. Homestead Acts (One-Hundred-and-Sixty Acre Homestead Act), ch. 75, 12 Stat. 392 (1862).

26. Robert Hockett, *A Jeffersonian Republic by Hamiltonian Means: Values, Constraints, and Finance in the Design of a Comprehensive and Contemporary American "Ownership Society"*, 79 S. Cal.
L. Rev. 45, 103 (2005).

27. In some cases, National Monuments are administered by another agency.

D. The Kibbutz, the Moshav and Other Rural Communities

Three types of agricultural communities are widespread in Israel. They are based on special property ownership and social arrangements.

Kibbutz: A *kibbutz* (plural: *kibbutzim*) is a collective community. In its original form, all property in the kibbutz was owned collectively. Members turned over all wealth, except for some personal possessions, to the kibbutz. It, and not its individual members, held the lease to the kibbutz lands.[28] Private ownership was essentially abolished for kibbutz members, who received all goods and services, including housing, health care, clothing, education, transportation, and entertainment from the kibbutz. Members ate at a communal dining hall and all labor on the kibbutz was performed by members. Each member was assigned to a job or worked off of the kibbutz. There were no pay differentials, and members who worked off the kibbutz contributed their pay to the community. Decisions were made by the entire kibbutz membership, usually in open meetings.

Kibbutzim were originally established as agricultural communities. With time, the economic base of the country changed to favor engineering and high tech fields. Most kibbutzim expanded their fields of economic activity to include industry and services, including shopping centers, swimming pools, and vacation accommodations. Today, kibbutz industries are highly varied; they include design and manufacture of agricultural technology products, such as drip irrigation systems, chemical production for the agriculture and the plastics industry, and production of filters, meters, and other equipment for water treatment plants. Furthermore, most kibbutzim have now deviated from the strict collective structure and instituted some degree of privatization of property.

There are both economic and social reasons for the changes. The financial difficulties of the kibbutzim were a big factor. Selling off some of the collective property to private buyers offered a way of raising money, but brought private property owners into the midst of the kibbutz. At the same time, the sheen of the collectivist ideal was wearing off for many of the children or grandchildren of the founding generations. Some of these young people left the kibbutzim, leaving the communities with aging populations to support and fewer workers to support them. Again, the sale of property offered a solution. In other cases, some members became disillusioned with what they perceived to be a lack of fairness of the collective structure. Those who worked hard wanted a greater reward for their efforts. As a result, some kibbutzim instituted differential salary structures. To satisfy members who wanted more freedom of personal choice, many kibbutzim allocated money, rather than goods and services, to members, allowing them to choose how to spend that money.

Other factors also contributed to the changes in kibbutz structure and operation. Efficient running of industry was inconsistent with collective decision-making processes. Kibbutzim introduced more structured hierarchies, and some brought in outside managers. More members desired to work off the kibbutz, often in professions, and more laborers, many of them foreign laborers, were brought in to do manual labor.

---

28. In some cases, the Jewish Agency is the lessee and the kibbutz holds a use permit.

While the kibbutz has always been an important part of the Israeli landscape, and is fairly well known outside of Israel, only 1.7 percent of the population lives today on kibbutzim. Even in earlier periods, the kibbutzim were never home to more than a small part of the total population.[29]

Moshav: A *moshav* (plural: *moshavim*) is a cooperative community. The community holds the lease to the land. There are two types of moshavim. In some, the land is worked collectively and profits are allocated equally, although consumption decisions are made individually by each household. In others, the land is allocated to individual households, which decide what to produce on the land and keep the profits from their own work, so that both production and consumption decisions are made individually by each household. In both types of moshavim, supplies were purchased and produce were marketed collectively, although this is not universally true today. The community is governed collectively and conducts its social life collectively. Moshav members comprise about 3.5 percent of the Israeli population.[30] Recent years have seen an increasing influx of non-agricultural households into the moshavim. The newcomers tend to be young families seeking a more pastoral lifestyle, with the adults commuting to jobs in the cities.

Cooperative Community: A cooperative community (*kfar shitufi*) is similar to a moshav except that each household has a separate lease to its own land and makes all decisions on the use of that land.

Community Settlement: A community settlement (*yishuv kehilati*) is generally a small, non-agricultural rural community in which each household conducts its economic life separately.[31] The members usually share a common outlook on life and work cooperatively on social, cultural and educational matters. People wishing to join a community settlement must be accepted by an acceptance committee.

Acceptance Committees: People wishing to join an agricultural community or a community settlement must be vetted by an acceptance committee. This requirement is based on the fact that the communities are envisioned as cooperative ventures and not just as places where people lead separate lives. The Supreme Court has put limitations on the acceptance committees, holding that an Arab family cannot be excluded from a Jewish community built on land owned by the state.[32]

Until recently, the practice of acceptance committees was not anchored in statute. In March, 2011, the Knesset enacted a law specifically authorizing acceptance committees for communities of no more than four hundred families. The law provides, "The acceptance committee shall not refuse to accept a candidate for reasons of race, religion, sex, nationality, disabilities, personal status, age, parentage, sexual preference, country of origin, political views or political affiliation."[33] Two petitions were filed asking the Supreme Court to hold the law invalid because it constitutes a "license to discriminate." According to the petitioners, the law will be used as an excuse to reject applicants on forbidden

---

29. Israel Ministry of Foreign Affairs, *The Land: Rural Life* (November 28, 2010) http://www.mfa.gov.il/MFA/Facts+About+Israel/Land/THE+LAND-+Rural+Life.htm (last visited June 13, 2011).

30. *Id.*

31. The term "settlement" does not relate to location in the territories; community settlements are found throughout Israel.

32. HCJ 6698/95 Kadaan v. Israel Lands Administration 54(1) PD 258 [2000]. Another case, still in litigation, is considering whether the JNF can exclude non-Jews from communities it builds on land it owns and acquired for the purpose of Jewish settlement.

33. Statute to Amend the Cooperative Societies Ordinance, 5761-2011, § 6c(3).

grounds, while hiding the real reasons for the rejection. In addition, the petitioners claim that the law interferes with the right of people to live anywhere they want.[34] As of this writing, the case has not been decided.

E. Urban Buildings

The vast majority of Israelis, ninety-two percent, live in urban areas.[35] Most live in multi-unit buildings. The American ideal of the separate house on its own plot of land is almost unknown in the cities and their suburbs. Even in kibbutzim, most people live in multi-family structures. Single family residences are found only in the other types of rural communities. Multiple unit residential buildings are not structured along the pattern typical of American apartment buildings, with a long hall and many units coming off of it, with most having only one outside exposure. More common in Israel is a structure with a central stairwell with two or three units on each floor, each unit having two or three exposures. In other words, an American would find an Israeli apartment more "homelike." Furthermore, in many parts of the cities, residential and commercial uses are not as separated as in the American suburbs. Most people live within walking distance of at least a small grocery store and other basic services.

Almost all urban buildings are condominiums. This includes residential, office, and commercial buildings as well as mixed-use buildings. The Property Law, 5729-1969, contains detailed provisions on condominium arrangements.[36]

A residential condominium in Israel is an apartment building in which each family owns an apartment. The stairwell, the walls, and the roof are owned by all apartment owners in common. Common areas may also include a parking area and yards not allocated to specific apartments. A technical difference between condominium ownership in Israel and in the United States is that in Israel, in most cases, the "owner" of an apartment actually owns only the lessee's interest in a long term lease from the Israel Lands Administration. Similar arrangements exist for many office and commercial buildings.

The owners of the individual units belong to a "house committee" that conducts the common business, such as arranging for care of common areas. Each owner has a vote and a dues obligation based on the size of that person's unit. The house committee can agree on rules that will govern the operation of the building. In the absence of such agreed rules, the rules set out in the appendix to the Property Law apply.

Rental apartment buildings of the type known in the United States are rare in Israel. Rental units exist, but the lessor is almost always the owner of an individual condominium unit and not the owner of an apartment building.

---

34. A summary in English of the Petitioners' claims is found at The Association for Civil Rights in Israel, *High Court Issues Order Nisi Regarding Acceptance of Communities Law* (June 20, 2011), http://www.acri.org.il/en/?p=2587.

35. Rachelle Alterman, *Land Use in the Face of a Rapid-Growth Crisis: The Case of Mass Immigration to Israel in the 1990s*, 3 Wash. U.J.L. & Pol. 773, 776 (2000).

36. Sections 52–77.

F. Registration System

Israel does not use a recording system for assuring property titles, as is common in the United States. Instead, Israel has a registration of title, or Torrens system (named after Sir Richard Torrens, who introduced registration of land titles into South Australia). In theory, a title registration system is like an automobile registration system: A person who purchases land registers title to the land and obtains a certificate of ownership. When title is transferred, the transferee registers title and gets a new certificate of ownership. A few US jurisdictions allow use of title registration systems (Hawaii; Massachusetts; Cook County, Illinois; Hennepin and Ramsey Counties, Minnesota; and Hamilton County, Ohio), but they are voluntary even where they are allowed.

In theory, the title registration system provides more certainty as to who owns what rights in property, but in reality, it does not always work that way. Two disadvantages of the registration system are the need to carefully check the title to a parcel before it is first registered and the need to keep up with registration of all subsequent interests affecting the title. Both of these actions are expensive and time consuming. The Israeli title registration system is affected by both of these problems and is seriously overloaded.

G. Land Use Planning

Israel has a comprehensive national law on land use planning. In theory, four levels of plans control all development. A series of national plans cover matters of national scope, such as roads, railroads, airports, and protection of open spaces. The country is divided into regions and each region develops a regional plan that applies the national plans with greater detail within the region and treats matters not covered in the national plans. Each regional plan must be consistent with all national plans. Local plans are even more detailed and must be consistent with the applicable regional plans. Plans for specific development projects are still more detailed and must comply with the "higher" plans. National plans are prepared by the National Planning Council; regional plans, by a regional planning commission; and local and development-specific plans, by a local planning commission.

New buildings cannot be constructed without building permits, and no permit should be granted unless the building will meet the requirements of the applicable plans. If a proposed project will not meet plan requirements, then the project must be changed or the plans must be amended. If an amendment to a local plan will violate the regional plan, either the amendment must be abandoned or the regional plan must be amended. Similarly a regional plan cannot be amended if this would violate a national plan.

Planning in the United States is more local than planning in Israel, with more emphasis on local zoning and less on regional and national coordination. The advantages of local planning are that it allows the people most directly affected to have a stronger say in local arrangements and it limits the amount of bureaucracy involved in planning decisions. The Israeli scheme allows more comprehensive planning and more coordination among localities. This type of highly coordinated planning can be seen as necessary in a small, densely populated country with important natural, religious, and historical resources.

The system in Israel is better in theory than it is in practice. Israel's multi-level planning system and the need to require higher level approval of many changes have created what is often considered an overblown bureaucracy. Operation of the system is slow and is plagued by a degree of uncertainty that interferes with necessary change in a highly dynamic society. In reality, at any point in time, many of the plans are in a state of flux. In addition, the law allows for exceptions, and the exception provisions sometimes allow construction of buildings that do not meet plan requirements. At present, there is a movement to give greater planning responsibility to local governments despite objections that this will lead to excessive and insufficiently-controlled growth and to corruption.

H. Water Rights

The Israeli law on property rights in water eschews private property rights to an extent even more extreme than the law on property rights in land. Israeli law recognizes no inherent private rights in water, neither ownership rights nor use rights.

Israeli Statute

Water Law, 5719-1959

1. Water Sources and Their Use

The water sources of the state are public property. They are under the control of the state and are to be used for meeting the needs of its inhabitants and for developing the country.

2. The Identity of Water Sources

For the purpose of this statute, "water sources" means springs, streams, rivers, lakes and other flowing water and standing water, whether above ground or underground, whether natural or created by installation or arrangement of natural waters, whether the water discharges from them, flows in them, or stands in them at all times or intermittently, and including drainage water and sewage water.

3. The Right of the Individual to Water

Every person is entitled to receive and use water in accordance with the provisions of this law.

4. The Connection between Real Property Rights and Water

A person's right in real property does not grant him any right to a water source located on that property or that passes through that property or that borders on that property, but this provision does not derogate from the rights of any person under section 3.

5. Prohibition on Diminution of a Water Source

The right of a person to receive water from a water source is valid as long as it does not cause its salination or diminution.

6. Connection between a Right and its Goal

Every right to water is connected to one of the goals listed here; the right to the water ceases with the cessation of its use for the goal stated. The goals are:

1) Domestic needs;

2) Agriculture;

3) Industry;

4) Labor, trade and services;

5) Public services;

6) Protection and rehabilitation of natural resources and the landscape, including springs, streams and wetlands.

7. Applicability

For the purposes of this law, it does not matter whether a person's right to water was created by law, including by this statute, or by an agreement or by custom or in another manner, or whether it originated before or after the effective date of this statute.

Comment

Israel has a severe shortage of water. It gets natural water from rainfall and from underground aquifers, but the amount is insufficient to meet the country's needs. No rain falls in the summer, which is about half the year. Additional water is obtained from reuse of treated sewage water and from desalination. About 70 percent of the sewage is treated to the level that it can be reused, mainly for crop irrigation. Several desalination plants supply a significant portion of the country's domestic water needs. These sources of water are costly and desalination drains Israel's already limited electric power generation capacity.

The Water Law declares the nationalization of all water in Israel. Water is owned by the public, but managed by the state. No compensation was ever paid to anyone who lost water rights when the statute was first enacted. The Water Law also establishes the Governmental Authority for Water and Sewage, which is the agency charged with managing the water. A person wanting to use water for agricultural or industrial use, or a municipality supplying water for domestic use, must obtain a water allocation from the authority and may use water only according to the terms of the allocation. There are no natural rights to use water and, as section 4 makes explicit, land ownership does not carry with it any right to water running through or abutting the land. The right to use water can be created only by an allocation from a governmental agency.

Some of the provisions of section 2 of the Israeli Water Law reveal specific conditions that exist in Israel. The reference to intermittent sources of water is important. Many water sources in Israel flow only in the winter, when it rains. Most streams are dry beds in the summer. Such an intermittent stream is called a *wadi* (the widely used Arabic term) or a *nahal* (the Hebrew term). Drainage water is mentioned in section 2 because of the problem of swamps, particularly in the flat areas in the northern part of the country. Extensive drainage systems were constructed and the drainage water is available for other uses. Sewage water gets specific mention because of its importance as a useful water source.

Question

4. Is nationalization of water in the Water Law fair?

———————

The following case considers the extent to which the individual has a right to obtain water and how the planning laws and the right to obtain water relate to each other.

Israeli Case

Abu Masaad v. Water Commissioner

CA 9535/06 (June 5, 2011)

[Many Bedouin live in Israel's southern desert, the *Negev*. A significant number live in unauthorized settlements, which are collections of tents and structures they have built without building permits. These are not in locations authorized as settlements under Israel's Building and Planning Law and typically lack the infrastructure for water, sewage, etc. that is provided in authorized communities. Because of their status, the unauthorized settlements are also called illegal or unrecognized settlements. These terms are used interchangeably in the case. Israel has built Bedouin towns in the Negev for Bedouin who prefer to live together and has tried to encourage Bedouin to move to these towns, or to live in other towns and cities.

This case was brought by Bedouin who prefer to remain living in their unauthorized settlements but who wanted better access to water. The respondent is the Water Commissioner, who, together with the Water Council, was in charge of allocation of water under the Water Law, 5719-1959. After the filing of this suit and before its decision, the statute was amended and the administrative arrangements for water allocation changed, so that allocations are now managed by the Governmental Authority for Water and Sewage, with the manager of the Governmental Authority as its chairperson.]

(Retired) Justice A. Procaccia:

This appeal raises the question of the extent to which Bedouin who live in illegal settlements in the Negev have a legal right to demand that the state install private water connections in their homes. At present, they are supplied with water through two alternative supply mechanisms: One is through central water distribution centers located close to their settlements, from which they can obtain water and haul it to their homes. The second is by applying to the Commission on Drinking Water Allocation (the Water Commission), which has authority to recommend that a private water connection be provided to a resident of an unrecognized community for humanitarian reasons specific to the individual resident's situation.

The Petitioners are six citizens, residents of unrecognized settlements in the Negev, who applied to the Commission on Drinking Water Allocation to grant them a private water connection to their homes.... Each Petitioner submitted the request in their name and in the names of several other families, so that each request was in the name of several dozen people, all of them Bedouin citizens of Israel who live in illegal settlements in the Negev.

The Respondents are the manager of the Governmental Authority for Water and Sewage (the authority manager) and the Israel Lands Administration. These are the administrative bodies involved in authorizing connection of individuals through private water connections in illegal settlements. The process for obtaining a private water connection begins with submission of an application to the Water Commission, which is a special commission that operates on a humanitarian basis with the objective of advancing the Bedouin sector in Israel. After submission of the application, the Commission considers the need for and feasibility of permitting an exception to allow a private water connection in the applicant's home. The Commission makes a recommendation on whether to grant the connection to the authority manager, who is the person authorized under the Water Law to authorize such a connection. [The person making an application can appeal the Commission's recommendation to a court.]

This dispute is to be understood against the background of the state's efforts to deal with the illegal Bedouin settlements in the Negev and its policies on this matter. The Bedouin in Israel are concentrated in the Negev.[37] Nearly half of the population lives in permanent towns established by the government of Israel over the years under a general plan relating to this subject. The other half live in illegal areas, which are also called unrecognized settlements. These are improperly organized and unrecognized settlements, some of them new, which were established without plans and without meeting the requirements of the Building and Planning Law, 5725-1965. As a result, in many cases the area of these settlements trespasses on land owned by the government or by private individuals. This type of settlement creates a number of problems, including difficulties in providing necessary services to their residents. The government's general policy, which has implications on the dispersal of the Bedouin in the Negev, involves a number of complicated issues.

The Appellants submitted individual applications for private connections to the Water Commission. Their requests were considered and the members of the Commission visited their communities to determine whether individual connections were needed. The Commission decided to recommend that five of the applications be denied and one be accepted.... [The authority manager accepted the recommendation.]

The Right to Water

We first examine the normative right of the individual to receive water. There are three alternative ways of looking at the right of a individual to water: It can be a right on the level of a statutory right, which could result from either some statutory arrangement or from the common law; it can be a constitutional right to water derived from some other recognized constitutional right in the Basic Law: Human Dignity or Freedom—in this case, the right to a dignified existence; or it can be a constitutional right to water recognized as an independent right and not derived from another right. Such an independent constitutional right is recognized in other countries, especially those in which there is a serious shortage in water resources. (See, for example, the final clause in section 27(1)(b) of the Constitution of South Africa; section 216(4) of the 1996 Constitution of Gambia; section 14 of the 1995 Constitution of Uganda; section 90(1) of the 1998 Constitution of Ethiopia; section 112 of the 1996 Constitution of Zambia; and section 20 of the 1999 Constitution of Nigeria.) It is also recognized in international documents and treaties. (See, for example, Stephan McCaffrey, *A Human Right to Water: Domestic and International Implications*, 5 Geo. Int'l Envtl. L. Rev. 1 (1992); Peter Gleick, *The Human Right to Water*, 1 Water Pol'y 487 (1999); Henri Smets, *Economics of Water Services and the Right to Water*, in *Fresh Water and International Economic Law* 173–77 (Edith Brown-Weiss et al. eds., 2005).

In Israel the individual's right to water is recognized as a statutory right under the Water Law. The right to water is not recognized as an independent constitutional right in a Basic Law. Nonetheless given that the right to water is necessary for human existence and to a dignified existence, we must consider whether the right to water has the normative status of a constitutional right derived from the constitutional right to a dignified existence. We must also determine whether such a right would impose on the state an obligation to supply a person living in Israel with water to the extent necessary for a minimally dignified existence.

The Constitutional Human Right to Water

"Human dignity" is a complex concept, and it includes various values, some related to the physical requirements for existence and some related to the emotional require-

---

37. There are also a number of legal Bedouin towns in the north, in the lower Galilee.

ments. An infringement on human dignity may be expressed in psychological humiliation and debasement, or it may be expressed in denying the physical requirements without which a person cannot lead a dignified existence. Denying a person a place to live, food, water, or basic medical care, can harm his ability to live in dignity and to function as a human being. The importance of the human right to a minimally dignified existence may in certain extreme cases create a situation in which the state will have a constitutional obligation to assure that a person has what is needed for basic existence, including water. In this way, the nature of the human right to minimally dignified existence may impose an affirmative right on the state to assure its implementation. This right is therefore different from other constitutional rights that are characterized by prohibiting the state from interfering with the individual's own implementation of the right.

The right to a minimally dignified existence includes the right of access to water sources sufficient to meet basic personal need. Water is a necessity, and a person cannot exist without basic access to water of a reasonable quality. Therefore the right to water should be considered to be part of the right to a dignified human existence, a right included in the right to human dignity and anchored in the Basic Law: Human Dignity and Freedom.

Like every other constitutional right, the right to water is not absolute. The protection given to the right is relative and requires consideration of important opposing values. Opposing values can include competing interests of others or of the public as a whole.... To the degree that the need for water in a specific case is essential to existence, it will get a greater weight and competing values will have to give way. On the other hand, to the extent that the most basic claim to a water supply is being met and the claim is to have access provided in a more convenient manner, conflicting interests and values are likely to be given greater weight and even to outweigh the claim to a more convenient water supply.

The Statutory Human Right to Water

Water is a public resource. Section 1 of the Water Law sets out the basic norm for arrangements as to the sources of water and their uses in Israel:

> The water sources of the state are public property. They are under the control of the state and are to be used for meeting the needs of its inhabitants and for developing the country.

The water sources are, therefore, public property, and the state functions as a trustee of the public for the purposes of meeting the water needs of the inhabitants and for effectuating plans for development of the country. We have already ruled that "water sources are public property, and the need to protect them derives not only from the principles of good government, but also from the protection granted to this rare and valuable property resource that is held in common by all citizens of the state."

Section 3 of the Water Law provides, "Every person is entitled to receive and use water in accordance with to the provisions of this law." This provision declares a statutory right of every person in Israel to receive water subject to specific requirements set out in the statute. The right to water, therefore, is subject to the provisions of the Water Law and to the authority given to the authorized agencies to manage the water assets of the state.

In addition to the general limitation in section 3 of the Water Law, the statute includes various substantial limitations on the right to water. For example ... the right to water under the statute is generally dependent on payment.

Another important provision is the Water and Sewage Companies Law, 5761-2001 ... This law declares that the water economy in municipalities will function through city water companies. The objective of setting up water companies is to create a *closed economy* for water and sewage, under which the income from water consumption and sewage usage fees will be invested in maintenance, extension, and improvement of the water and sewage systems.[38]

The Authority to Permit Water Connections

Under the Water Law, the manager of the Governmental Authority for Water and Sewage determines when a person shall be allowed to connect to water.

Evaluation of the Authority Manager's Decisions under Principles of Public Law

The decisions of the authority manager that are the subject of this lawsuit must be considered against the background of the general policy of the Authority on provision of water to unrecognized Bedouin settlements and in light of the individual decisions it made as to each of the Appellants. The Authority agreed that there is an obligation to allow Bedouin access to water sufficient to meet their basic needs. This includes a right of access for those who live in unrecognized settlements. The system of access and the way of supplying the water to the residents is affected by another consideration: the need to have settlements established in a legal manner, consistent with the planning and building laws and with governmental policy. Under this policy, the goal is to create incentives for the scattered Bedouin to settle in permanent legal communities of the various types provided by the government. As long as illegal settlement continues throughout the Negev, as a temporary measure to be in effect until a comprehensive solution is found for Bedouin settlement, the Authority works in two ways to provide the Bedouin with water. First, it has established water distribution centers, from which water can be transported to the illegal settlements. Second, permits are given for individual private water connections in specific cases for humanitarian reasons based on the recommendation of the Water Commission.

This policy is to be evaluated to determine whether it meets the tests of relevancy, reasonableness, and proportionality.

Relevancy

The first question is whether it was appropriate for the Authority, in deciding on applications for individual water connections, to consider the illegality of the applicants' settlements and the governmental policy of providing legal communities in place of the illegal ones. Is this a relevant or an irrelevant consideration? Is it permissible to consider the fact that the applicants are residents of illegal settlements and that most of them have the choice of living in legal permanent communities that the state has put aside for them, where they will have access to necessary services, including a regular supply of water directly to their homes?

The answer is that it is permissible to consider the need to deal with the phenomenon of illegal settlements, in light of the existence of an available alternative of living in legal communities. The illegal settlement of the Bedouin in the Negev has become a national problem of the first order. It has many implications in various aspects of life. The illegal settlements are a serious infringement on the building and planning laws and on property rights. They involve groups of people taking the law into their own hands and deciding where they will live without giving any consideration to the laws of the state and to the basic rules of planning. In some cases, these settlements are built on state land or

---

38. Prior to the enactment of the law, water and sewage fees collected by local governments went into the general treasury of the local government unit. The funds could then be used for parks, education, or other governmental expenses, while deterioration of the water delivery and sewage systems was left uncorrected.

on land privately owned by other people, so they constitute trespasses that infringe on the property rights of others. Illegal settlements also tend to adversely affect the environment and the people living in them do not pay certain taxes, including local property taxes.

Beyond this, the phenomenon of illegal settlements of the Bedouin is a serious infringement on the rule of law and the principles of public order that impose obligations on citizens. A civilized state cannot tolerate the phenomenon of certain groups taking the law into their own hands in a way that infringes on the rules of public order and law and deviates from the general rules of a civilized society.

Reasonableness and Proportionality

The question is whether the scheme of the Authority to solve the problem of access to water for residents of the illegal settlements, through water centers from which they can transport water to their homes, together with the possibility of obtaining permits for private connections on humanitarian grounds in exceptional cases, meets the requirements of reasonableness and proportionality.

The requirement of administrative reasonableness means that various considerations must be weighed in a way that gives the appropriate weight to each of them. Proportionality is a test used to determined the appropriateness of an infringement on a basic human right; it is evaluated under the limitation clause found in section 8 of the Basic Law: Human Dignity and Freedom…. [The proportionality test subsumes the reasonableness test. If a measure is proportional, it is reasonable.][39]

The limitation clause in section 8 of the Basic Law provides:

Infringement of Rights

There shall be no infringement of rights under this Basic Law except by a law befitting the values of the State of Israel, enacted for a proper purpose, and to an extent no greater than is required, or by regulation enacted by virtue of express authorization in such law.

In the matter before us, the way that the government's planning policy affects access to water for residents of unrecognized Bedouin villages constitutes an interference with their human right to water. But as long as this infringement meets the tests of proportionality, it does not violate the values of the State of Israel. Furthermore, it is enacted for a proper purpose: to solve the problem of illegal settlement in the south by providing an incentive for the residents of the illegal settlements to move to the legal population centers that the state has provided for them.

Constitutional proportionality consists first of the test of rationality, or the appropriateness of the means used to accomplishing the goal. Second is the test of need, or of whether the means used causes the minimal interference with the right. The third test is the test of proportionality in the narrow sense, which requires an appropriate relationship between the benefit derived from the action that infringes on the right and the injury that may be caused from the infringement on the individual right.

Applying the tests for proportionality to the matter before us, we can say that there is a rational connection between the means used and the goal. The means is the refusal to connect homes in illegal settlements directly to water sources, and to allow access to regional water distribution centers and provision of individual connection permits on humanitarian grounds. The goal is to encourage those who live in an unrecognized settlement to move to legal communities offered them by the state.

---

39. Other cases treat the reasonableness test separately.

The arrangement also meets the test of necessity, or the minimal infringement test. While individual water connections are not allowed for residents of an unrecognized settlement, the presence of regional water distribution centers from which water can be transported to the settlement, and allowing individual connections in exceptional cases, minimizes the infringement on the right to water.

The narrow test of proportionality, which requires the proper relationship between the benefit and cost of the infringement, is also met here. The benefit is to encourage the residents of illegal settlements with an incentive to move to legal communities that are already available and where they can receive all the necessary services directly, without having to access them from afar. This incentive is necessary to prevent perpetuation of the illegal settlements. It is important to prevent indirect encouragement of illegal settlements, which would happen if services were provided directly to the homes in these settlements. Against this, the infringement in this case is in the inconvenience of the access. The governmental policy does not infringe on the substantive right to obtain water.

The infringement is found in the inconvenience the residents of the unrecognized villages suffer in transporting water from the water distribution centers to the settlements, including the costs of transportation over significant distances. It has not been claimed in this case that this deprives anyone of the right to obtain the minimally necessary amount of water, since water is readily available at the distribution centers.

It is important to emphasize that the scheme meets the test of proportionality because in exceptional cases where access to the water distribution centers is not reasonably sufficient to provide the minimal amount of water needed for daily life, or where a person does not have a real option of moving to a legal community, a person can apply for a permit for an individual connection and these factors will be taken into consideration. The availability of such exceptions for humanitarian reasons is an integral part of the scheme.

[The Court considered how the rule of the case applies to the Appellants. It found that three Appellants had adequate access to water in regional distribution centers and denied the appeal as to these three. The other three Appellants did not have sufficient access to regional water distribution centers. In one case, the Appellant had settled in a military area used as a firing range, and water could not be supplied in such an area. In the second case the regional water distribution center near the Appellant's home did not supply sufficient amounts of water and, for technical reasons, the amounts could not be increased. In the third case, the government was in the process of building a regional distribution center to replace private connections. All of these Appellants could move to legal communities. Nevertheless, the Court said that the Authority had to reexamine their cases to determine whether they qualified for humanitarian exceptions.]

Comment

At the heart of the controversy in the *Abu Masaad* case are the claims of the Bedouin to a right to live where they want in areas of the Negev formerly traversed by their tribes. The once nomadic Bedouin are now sedentary, and Israel does not recognize claims based on former routes of passage as the basis of property rights to live on the land. Israel built Bedouin towns in the Negev and provides subsidized housing to Bedouin in these towns. The subsidies are designed to encourage Bedouin to move into the permanent towns. The Supreme Court has upheld the practice of offering such subsidized housing only to

Bedouin against claims that it constituted impermissible discrimination against non-Bedouins in Israel.[40]

Several reasons have been given for the fact that numerous Bedouin remain outside of the permanent towns: The level of services in the permanent towns, while better than in the unauthorized settlements, remains low. Unemployment is high. The towns, or at least the older ones, are not built in a way that allows residents to easily continue their traditional occupations of livestock grazing. People from different Bedouin tribes that did not get along well had to live in close proximity to each other in the towns. Planning was top-down and did not sufficiently involve the Bedouin residents. Furthermore, life in the unauthorized settlements has its advantages. As indicated in the *Abu Masaad* case, residents of such settlements do not pay for their land, do not have to bother with getting building permits (their buildings are illegal and permits would not be available in any case), and do not pay municipal or national taxes. In addition, many hope that if they hold out, they will receive a higher level of compensation from the government for their eventual agreement to move into recognized towns.[41]

The *Abu Masaad* case holds that there is a constitutional right to water. Every resident of Israel has the right to water. The fact that the petitioners are violating the planning laws does not preclude them from claiming such a right. This is clear. What is less clear is the dimension of the constitutional right to water and the relationship between the constitutional right to water and the Water Law.

The limitation on access to water at stake in the *Abu Masaad* case is derived from the Water Law. The Court considers whether the limitation scheme is a permissible infringement. Is the Court asking the proper question? The first part of the opinion suggests that the constitutional right derives from the right to human dignity and is limited to the right to obtain the minimal amount of water necessary for a dignified existence. If that is the case, the question in the case should be whether the Appellants are receiving this amount of water. If they are, there is no infringement on their constitutional rights and the limitation clause is irrelevant. If they are not receiving the minimal amount needed for a dignified existence, then there is an infringement on their constitutional rights and the Court must ask if the infringement is justified under the limitation clause. It is hard to imagine that any infringement on access to the minimal amount needed for a dignified existence would be allowed, though. So if the right is defined in this minimal way, it is probably inviolate.

Alternatively there is a broad, undefined right to water. If that is the case, the Water Law infringes on the right and the Court is correct in applying the limitation clause to determine whether the infringement is permissible. The problem with this analysis is that it is hard to derive a broad right to water from the right to human dignity. It seems silly to assert that human dignity requires that people get as much water as they want.

If the constitutional right is only to the minimal amount needed for a dignified existence, the Court should ask, first, whether Appellants have access to this amount of water. It seems that some of the Appellants do, but it is not clear whether others also have such access. The Court appropriately remanded the matter as to the Appellants in this latter group for a determination by the Authority of whether they had sufficient access.

As to the Appellants who have minimal access, the question is whether the administrative decision to restrict their access is legal, even though it does not infringe on

---

40. HCJ 528/88 Avitan v. Israel Lands Authority 43(4) PD 297 [1989].

41. *See* Talia Berman-Kishony, *Bedouin Urbanization Legal Policies in Israel and Jordan: Similar Goals, Contrasting Strategies*, 17 TRANSNAT'L L. & CONTEMP. PROBS. 393 (2008).

their constitutional right to water. Administrative actions must meet the test of proportionality even if they do not infringe on constitutional rights. This is a principle of Israeli administrative law. As to these Appellants, the Court would have to determine whether there is a rational relationship between the means used and the goal of the administrative decision. There is. Making access to water difficult will indeed create an incentive for people to move to legal communities where access to all services, including water, is easier. Second, the Court would have to determine whether the means chosen cause the minimal amount of harm. They do. The Court held that the Authority did all it could to minimize the harm while still accomplishing the goals of providing an incentive to move to legal communities and not encouraging or rewarding those who violate the law. Third, the harm and benefit must be in the proper relation to each other. In this case, they are. The harm to the Appellants is minimized by the fact that they can get the water they need for daily life, by the fact that those who cannot do so can get a humanitarian exception, and by the fact that they have a choice to move to a legal community. The benefit to the state is large in discouraging violation of the rule of law.

The right to water is treated as part of the right to dignity and not as part of the right to property. Those who own or possess property in the Negev, where there are few natural water resources, would not have water rights under a property-based theory. Similarly Bedouin living illegally on someone else's land would have no property-based water rights. In fact, the Water Law removes all property-based rights to water. Therefore conceiving of water rights as property based would not have helped the Appellants in *Abu Masaad*.

Question

5. What other problems arise if water rights are conceived of as property rights?

Part Six

Regulated Private Activity

Chapter 18

Environmental Law

Environmental law includes both pollution control law and natural resource preservation. The law on pollution control in Israel is founded on a long series of statutes. Some of the prominent ones are the Clean Air Act, 5768-2008; Law for Prevention of Nuisances, 5721-1961 (noise and odor pollution); Clean Water Act, 5719-1959 (fresh water pollution); Ordinance for the Prevention of Sea Pollution by Oil (New Version), 5740-1980; Law on Prevention of Sea Pollution (Waste Disposal), 5743-1983; Law on Prevention of Sea Pollution from Dry Land Sources, 5748-1988; Maintenance of Cleanliness Act, 5744-1984 (solid waste); Business Licensing Law, 5728-1968 (under which rules on hazardous waste disposal have been promulgated); and the Bottle Deposit Law, 5759-1999. All of these statutes define, at least generally, prohibited acts and set out means of enforcement of the statutory requirements. Some set up licensing schemes. All authorize one or more ministers to promulgate rules setting out requirements more specific than those found in the general terms of the statute.

In addition to the pollution control laws, Israel also has a set of statutes on natural resource protection. The Building and Planning Law, 5725-1965, and the Law on National Parks, Nature Reserves, National Sites and Memorial Sites, 5748-1998, are the most prominent of these.

A. Pollution Control — Regulatory Framework

In one of the earliest environmental law cases, the Supreme Court revealed an understanding of the importance of administrative regulations setting specific environmental standards.

Israeli Case

Oppenheimer v. Ministers of Interior and of Health
HCJ 295/65, 20(1) PD 309 [1966]

[The case arose under the Law for Prevention of Nuisances, 5721-1961. This is a petition for review of the failure of the ministers charged with implementation of the statute to promulgate regulations under the statute. The petitioners claim that the ministers are required to promulgate regulations; the ministers claim they have authority to promulgate regulations but are not required to do so. The facts are described by Justice Cohen, but the majority opinion was written by Justice Silberg.]

Justice C. Cohen:

Eight Petitioners were joined for this petition. Each suffered from violations of the same law. Petitioner number 1 suffers from substantial and unreasonable noise from operations of a bakery in his neighborhood, especially during nighttime hours. Petitioner number 2 suffers from substantial and unreasonable noise from watermelon sellers, who operate from a truck in his neighborhood,[1] and from boisterous dance parties, especially at night. Petitioner number 3 suffers from substantial and unreasonable noise caused by the concentration of a number of bus stops near his house and by card clubs in his neighborhood, especially at nighttime. Petitioner number 4 suffers from substantial and unreasonable odors that drift from a compost facility near his home. Petitioner number 5 suffers from substantial and unreasonable odors that are from an instant coffee factory next to his house. Petitioner number 6 suffers from odors from a cement plant. Petitioner number 7 suffers from substantial and unreasonable odor from a compost facility manufacturing organic fertilizer next to his house. Petitioner number 8 suffers from substantial and unreasonable odors, also from a cement plant near his home.

Acting Chief Justice M. Silberg:

Since ... 1961, Israel has had a statute providing that:

> 2. No person shall cause substantial or unreasonable noise from any source if it harms or is liable to harm a person found in the area or those passing by.
>
> 3. No person shall cause substantial or unreasonable odor from any source if it harms or is liable to harm a person found in the area or those passing by.
>
> 4. (a) No person shall cause substantial or unreasonable air pollution from any source if it harms or is liable to harm a person found in the area or those passing by.

The passage of this law did not end the problems associated with these three types of environmental pollution. The birth of the law was easy, but the suffering and the birth pains began immediately afterwards. Even at the time of the final formulation of the terms of the law, its authors, members of the Knesset, knew that without clear definitions of "substantial or unreasonable noise, odor, and air pollution," this law would be stillborn and worthless.

The term "unreasonable" is a very problematic standard to use for criminal matters. This is especially true when we are measuring the reasonableness of odor, smoke, or pollution, which remain ill-defined terms if there is no indication of the relevant nature and characteristics of the matters to which they relate.

Moreover if these terms are not defined as authorized in section 5 (quoted below), the reasonableness of any given noise will be determined on a case by case basis, for the purpose of the specific case only, by the judge considering the case. The sensitivity of people to problems caused by noise is very much subjective. One person suffers from exposure to the loud, sudden noise such as that of close-by thunder, while another is driven crazy by a faucet dripping one drip every ten seconds. Everyone, not only experts, knows this is true. I can imagine that a man with a wife and ten children between the ages of two and twelve would be much less sensitive to noise than an aged bachelor who spends his days in his quiet library. We find, then, that without rules and definitions under section 5, the fate of the accused will depend on how many children the judge has.

---

1. It is common in the summer in Israel for people to drive through residential neighborhoods in trucks, selling watermelons and announcing their wares on portable loudspeakers.

For this reason, the legislature provided in section 5 of the law:

> 5. The ministers shall promulgate rules containing requirements implementing sections 2–4 and are authorized, among other things, to define substantial or unreasonable noise, odor, or air pollution.

The format of this law is *shatnez*; it begins with one thing and ends with another![2] It begins with strong mandatory language: "the ministers shall promulgate....," and then immediately changes to a still soft voice:[3] "and are authorized, among other things, to define substantial or unreasonable noise, odor, or air pollution." Furthermore, why did the legislature need to provide the ministers with the authorization to define terms in the latter part of section 5?[4] Why was the legislature not satisfied with the general authorization in section 18 of the law? This section provides:

> The ministers are charged with implementation of this law and they are authorized to promulgate rules on all matters relating to its implementation.

There is only one answer to these two questions:

Section 5, as distinct from section 18, imposes on the ministers a mandatory duty to promulgate regulations implementing sections 2–4. They may not ignore this duty, for the provision says "they shall promulgate"—language of a command—and not "they are authorized to promulgate." Then what happened? The legislator had doubts: setting out the definition of substantial or unreasonable noise, odor or air pollution, the causation of which is prohibited, in effect defines a criminal act, and that should only be done by the Knesset itself. Therefore the legislator added, "and among other things" meaning among the other rules that they are mandated to promulgate for implementing sections 2–4, they have authority to set out the definition of substantial or unreasonable noise, odor, and air pollution. But once they have this authority, they must use it, for these are "among other things," meaning among the types of rules that they must promulgate under the first part of the provision. In other words, the words "and among other things, they are authorized...." do not detract from the obligation imposed on them in the first half of the section, but gives content to the obligation, providing them with legal authority to do what appears to be a legislative act of defining a criminal violation.

[This] law entered into force on March 21, 1961, almost five years ago. During this period, the ministers have managed to promulgate five sets of regulations, but all relate to section 4. Sections 2 and 3, which deal with noise and odor, have not been addressed by the ministers. The rules promised by section 5 have not been promulgated, and the ministers have not yet defined substantial or unreasonable noise or odor.

[Each Petitioner] complains of loud noise or odor or both, and they claim that if regulations had been promulgated, then they would be better off for two reasons:

(a) They would have found a more attentive ear from the authorities to whom they complained, because both the authorities and the Petitioners themselves would have known just what is allowed and what is not allowed.

(b) They would have benefited from section 10(1) of the law, which provides that once it has been shown that noise or odor exceeds the level defined in rules as substantial or

---

2. The word *shatnez* derives from Jewish law. It means an unpermitted mixture of substances. The use of the term does not indicate that the judge is borrowing a rule from Jewish law; rather, this term is part of everyday language in Hebrew.

3. This is a term from Jewish liturgy that has also entered non-religious Hebrew language.

4. The court here is assuming that the ministers would have authority to define statutory terms even without explicit authorization in the statute. Such authority stems from other sources of law.

unreasonable, the burden of proof as to harm is transferred from the plaintiffs to the defendants [so that the defendants are liable unless they can prove that the plaintiffs were not harmed].

[The Respondent claims, and the dissenting judge agrees,] "There is no need for promulgation of rules in order for the appellants, or others who are similarly injured, to obtain a full remediation for their injuries."

With all due respect to my learned colleague ... I do not think that the legislature meant simply to multiply the number of laws. If the general tort laws, or local ordinances, or the Law for Prevention of Nuisances itself were sufficient without promulgation of rules, then the legislature would not have imposed the burden set out in section 5 on the ministers. The legislature's position is completely rational. One member of the Knesset, a doctor, was convinced that noise, odor, and air pollution present a considerable danger to public health and that it is necessary to take drastic steps to eliminate this calamity. He therefore proposed this law, which was praised by the public and accepted by the Knesset without any opposition. They perceived ahead of time that without creation of the specific legal instruments that would allow the violator to be apprehended, the law would have no meaning. The specific instruments would have to include formal measurements, technical requirements, and methods of measurement, so that everyone would know what is allowed and what is prohibited, and every policeman would know whom to hold for violating the law. This was the objective of section 5, and this is the basis of its great importance. If we say to the Petitioners and others similarly situated that they should resort to all sorts of other laws, or use this law while it is still abstract and lacks the dressing of the regulations and of implementable rules, we turn the legislative enactment into a fraud.

We come, therefore, to the formulation of the order. [The Petitioners agreed not to ask for odor regulations, because they understood that there was insufficient information to allow setting such regulations.] That leaves the matter of noise.

I propose this formulation for the order:

The two ministers, the minister of interior and the minister of health, must promulgate with all appropriate speed rules for implementation of section 2 of the Law for Prevention of Nuisances, 5921-1961.

In light of the fact that it appears that it will be difficult for them to promulgate all the rules at once, they may promulgate them in parts, according to their discretion, but the work must be done with all appropriate speed.

Comments

Notice the date of this case. It preceded the modern American pollution control laws. The first of the modern American statutes, the National Environmental Policy Act, was enacted in 1969. The Clean Air Act came next, in 1970.

There are several reasons why the ministers did not enact rules until forced to do so by the Court. In Israel, at the time of the decision above, implementation of the Prevention of Nuisances Law was in the hands of the minister of interior and the minister of health. Each minister had other major obligations. The minister of interior was in charge of all local governments. Much of the local governments' budget is supplied by the central government and subject to oversight by the minister of interior. The minister of interior was also in charge of the citizenship laws and the population registry, elections, and planning laws. The minister of health was in charge of traditional health matters: administering the countrywide free clinics for infant and pre-natal care; running hospitals; supervising doctors, nurses, and other health professionals; and dealing with epidemics and other public health matters. In 1989 a Ministry of Environment was established (today the Ministry of Environmental Protection) and powers under the Prevention of Nuisances Law were transferred to the new minister. The Ministry of Environmental Protection now administers a substantial number of environmental statutes, but the statute under discussion in this case is one of the oldest. The air pollution control provisions in the Prevention of Nuisances Law have been replaced with a new Clean Air Act, which took effect in 2011. The new law leaves in effect rules promulgated under the old one and requires promulgation of many new rules.

In addition, environmental matters were not taken as seriously as they are now by members of the public. Therefore, the pressure on the ministers to enact the rules was probably not as strong. In this regard, the types of complaints that led to this case are significant. Noise is a major annoyance in Israel's crowded cities that are built largely of stone and have buildings that are not heavily insulated. At the time of the decision, air conditioning was not as prevalent as it is today, so people lived with their windows open most of the year and heard the noise that was outside.

The inter-ministerial procedures for promulgating regulations have also played a role in impeding promulgation of rules setting environmental standards. As described in chapter 9 on administrative law, all proposed rules must be circulated to all ministries before finalization. Objections of other ministers can force delay of the promulgation of the rule, weakening of the rule's provisions, or abandonment of the rulemaking. This is especially true when the minister who wishes to promulgate a rule is politically weak and the objecting ministers are politically strong. The effect of this system has been that it has been difficult to promulgate tough environmental regulations. In the matter of noise control, for example, regulations that impose strict limits on noise from factories might encounter opposition from the minister responsible for industrial development, who sees it as his or her responsibility to promote such development at low cost, and from the powerful minister of finance, who is interested in the tax revenues that industrial development would produce. Rules limiting noise from construction equipment might be opposed by the minister in charge of housing development.

The case illustrates an interesting feature of Israeli law. The statute makes it a crime to cause "unreasonable" noise, odor and air pollution, and the administrative agency is given authority to define what is unreasonable. In essence, the agency is allowed to define the crime. Furthermore, as just described, the agency is subject to political constraints, but few procedural constraints, in formulating its definition. Under American law, this might be considered an unconstitutional delegation of legislative authority to an administrative agency. See *Whitman v. American Trucking Ass'ns*, 531 U.S. 457 (2001). Such delegations of authority to agencies are common in Israeli law and are rarely subject to judicial scrutiny or objection.[5] Perhaps this is because the American unconstitutional delegation doctrine is founded on separation of powers concerns, and separation of powers between the branches of government is less complete in Israel's parliamentary system than it is in the American presidential system. Perhaps, also, it is because of the fact that the Israeli system derives from the British law, which, at least at the time Britain

---

5. One of the rare exceptions, in a non-environmental case, is HCJ 3267/97 Rubenstein v. Minister of Defense 52(5) PD 481 [1998], discussed in chapter 9 on administrative law.

was ruling via the Mandate, gave greater leeway to agencies than does the American un-constitutional delegation doctrine. See Peter L. Lindseth, *Reconciling with the Past: John Wills and the Question of Judicial Review in Inter-War and Post-War England*, 55 U. Toronto L.J. 657 (2005).

The *Oppenheimer* decision left a number of issues unaddressed. Must the ministers promulgate regulations defining what noise is unreasonable for all types of noises? There are many different types of noise, and the effect on people is different for different types. For example, people react differently to continuous noise and to impulse noise. There-fore, the level of what is reasonable depends on the type of noise involved. If the ministries promulgate rules that address the most common type of noise, is this sufficient? Is it nec-essary to address the two most common types? Three? These questions are left unan-swered by the case.

It is likely that the answer would be found not in the environmental statute, but in the field of administrative law. As a matter of statutory interpretation, the statute re-quired the enactment of some implementing rules. Whether a given set of rules en-acted by the minister was sufficient would be determined under the usual doctrines of administrative law: Did the minister consider the statutorily relevant factors in decid-ing what to regulate? Did the minister avoid considering irrelevant factors? Did the minister balance competing factors in a way that gave the proper weight to each one, thus meeting the test of reasonableness? Are the rules proportional; i.e., are the means chosen to reduce pollution by regulating some sources and not others related to the objectives of the statute, do the rules use the least injurious means to obtain their ob-jective, and does the environmental benefit obtained through the rules outweigh the harm they cause? In other words, the choice to regulate noise from jackhammers and not noise from other bulldozers would be proportional if it would reduce 50 percent of the construction noise that generates complaints; if low-noise jackhammers are available but not low-noise bulldozers, so that reducing the same amount of noise from bulldozers would have much higher economic costs; and if the regulation of jackhammer noise alone would substantially reduce complaints at a minor and bearable economic cost to con-struction firms.

It appears that in *Oppenheimer*, the Court was concerned that the ministers were ig-noring statutory implementation as far as noise was concerned. Once some rules were promulgated, this concern would be reduced and the Court would probably be more def-erential in applying the tests of administrative law to the ministerial decision, allowing the ministry greater leeway to decide what specific problems warrant regulation.

In the nearly fifty years since the *Oppenheimer* case, Israel has enacted more rules on air pollution, but their number is only a small fraction of the number enacted under the Clean Air Act in the United States. The standards found in Israeli regulations tend to be less detailed and to cover fewer types of sources than do their American counterparts. In Israel, the minister of environmental protection also has authority to write air pollution control requirements into business licenses for individual sources even when no rules apply to the type of source seeking the license. Because in many cases, there are only a small number of sources of a specific type (Israel is a much smaller country than the United States), it costs less to regulate these sources on a case-by-case basis than to go through the difficult process of promulgating regulations. Case-by-case regulation may also be less politically charged than rulemaking. As a result, the minister tends to rely more on this method. The new Clean Air Act is designed to force the minister to pro-mulgate more rules.

Questions

1. What explains the failure of the ministers to promulgate regulations defining substantial or unreasonable noise or odor? Think about the nature of Israel, its history, and its society.

2. The procedures for promulgation of rules in Israel, described in chapter 9, section D, gives all ministers a strong say in whether specific environmental regulations should be promulgated. Is this a good arrangement?

3. The Court refers to actions the petitioners could have brought without using the statute. Mainly the petitioners could have brought an action in nuisance. Nuisance law in Israel is similar to American nuisance law. In light of this, what concerns led the Court to order the ministers to act? How did the justices determine that the mixed (shatnez) language should be interpreted as mandatory language?

B. Pollution Control — Enforcement

Violations of most Israeli environmental laws are subject to criminal sanctions: fines and imprisonment. The maximum amount of the permissible fine is substantial. Liability is strict. In addition, the environmental statutes typically impose criminal liability on corporate officers and on responsible employees. The following provisions on enforcing pollution control requirements in the Water Law, 5719-1959, are typical.

Israeli Statute

Water Law, 5719-1959

20.7. Correction of the Violation

(1) If the director of the Governmental Authority for Water and Sewage determines that water pollution has occurred, he is authorized to order the person who caused the pollution to do whatever is needed to stop the water pollution, to restore the environment to its former condition, and to prevent renewal of the pollution, all in accordance with the provisions of the order.

(2) If the requirements of an order under subsection (1) are not fulfilled within a reasonable amount of time, which shall be specified in the order, the director of the Governmental Authority for Water and Sewage may take the steps required in the order. If he does so, the person to whom the order was directed is liable for double the costs incurred by the director....

20.21. Punishment for Violation of [the Provisions on Water Pollution]

(a) The punishment for any person who violates the provisions [on water pollution] is imprisonment for a year or a fine of NIS 350,000 [about $95,000], and if it was a continuing violation, imprisonment of seven days or an additional fine of NIS 23,200 [about $6300] for each day the violation continued after the violator received a written warning from the person authorized to deal with the matter by the minister of environmental protection, and consistent with the period set out in the warning.

(b) Strict liability applies to a violation under this provision.

(c) If a person causes a violation of the type indicated in subsection (a) in a dangerous manner or in dangerous circumstances, and as a result substantial environmental damage was caused or was likely to be caused, the punishment is three years of imprisonment or double the fine that a court could otherwise impose for such a violation under this section. If the violation was that of a corporation, the punishment is four times the fine that a court could otherwise impose under this section.

(d) (1) If a person violated subsections (a) or (c) in a manner that conferred a benefit on the violator or on someone else, the court may impose, in addition to all other sanctions, an additional fine equal to the benefit.

(2) For the purpose of this subsection, a benefit includes any cost savings.

20.22. Liability of Corporate Officials

If a corporation committed a violation of Section 20.21, any person who at the time of the violation was an officer, partner (except a limited partner), or senior employee of the corporation responsible for the violation is also criminally liable, unless it is proven that the violation occurred without that person's knowledge and that the person took all reasonable measures to prevent or to terminate the violation.

20.24. Imposition of Costs and Requirement of Cleanup

A court that convicted a person of a violation under section 20.21 may, as part of the verdict, in addition to any punishment it imposes, require:

(1) payment of the costs expended to clean the water and anything polluted due to the violation of the law … ;

(2) implementing whatever steps are necessary in order to—

    (a) stop, reduce or prevent the continued water pollution;

    (b) clean the water and anything polluted due to the violation of the law;

    (c) restore the environment to its former condition.

20.25. Citizen Complaint

(a) Any of the following persons can bring a private criminal action for a violation of [the provisions of this statute on water pollution]:

    (1) Any person—for a violation that caused him direct injury;

    (2) A local government—for a violation that occurred within its borders;

    (3) Any of the public or professional organizations listed in the first appendix—for violation of the provisions. [The appendix lists seven governmental and non-governmental organizations that deal with environmental protection.]

(b) A private criminal action under subsection (a) shall not be filed unless the private prosecutor gave the minister of environmental protection prior written notice of his intent to file the action and the attorney general did not file an indictment within 60 days of such notice.

Comment (Types of Enforcement Proceedings)

In general, there are three mechanisms for enforcing environmental laws: (1) administrative enforcement, within an administrative agency in an informal or a formal proceeding, (2) civil enforcement, in a court in a civil proceeding, and (3) criminal enforcement, in a court through a criminal proceeding. American environmental law allows all three types of enforcement. This is seen in the general enforcement provision of the US Clean Water Act, which follows; subsections (a) and (g) provide for administrative enforcement, subsections (a), (b) and (d) provide for civil enforcement, and subsection (c) provides for criminal enforcement. In practice, EPA uses all three types of proceedings.[6]

US Statute

Clean Water Act
33 USC § 1319 (2006)

Enforcement

(a) Compliance orders ...

(3) Whenever on the basis of any information available to him the Administrator finds that any person is in violation of [any of the listed sections of this statute], or is in violation of any permit condition or limitation implementing any of such sections in a permit..., he shall issue an order requiring such person to comply with such section or requirement, or he shall bring a civil action in accordance with subsection (b) of this section.

(b) Civil actions

The Administrator is authorized to commence a civil action for appropriate relief, including a permanent or temporary injunction, for any violation for which he is authorized to issue a compliance order under subsection (a) of this section. Any action under this subsection may be brought in the district court of the United States....

(c) Criminal penalties

(1) Negligent violations

Any person who negligently violates [any of the listed sections of this statute] shall be punished by a fine of not less than $2,500 nor more than $25,000 per day of violation, or by imprisonment for not more than 1 year, or by both. If a conviction of a person is for a violation committed after a first conviction of such person under this paragraph, punishment shall be by a fine of not more than $50,000 per day of violation, or by imprisonment of not more than 2 years, or by both.

(2) Knowing violations

Any person who [knowingly violates any of the listed sections of this statute] shall be punished by a fine of not less than $5,000 nor more than $50,000 per day of violation, or by imprisonment for not more than 3 years, or by both. If a conviction of a person is for a violation committed after a first conviction of such person under this paragraph, punishment shall be by a fine of not more than $100,000 per day of violation, or by imprisonment of not more than 6 years, or by both.

(3) Knowing endangerment

(A) General rule

Any person who knowingly violates [any of the listed sections of this statute] and who knows at that time that he thereby places another person in imminent danger of death

---

6. *See, e.g.,* U.S. Environmental Protection Agency, Compliance and Enforcement Annual Results FY 2008: Numbers at a Glance (December 1, 2008), http://www.epa.gov/compliance/resources/reports/endofyear/eoy2008/2008numbers.html.

or serious bodily injury, shall, upon conviction, be subject to a fine of not more than $250,000 or imprisonment of not more than 15 years, or both. A person which is an organization shall, upon conviction of violating this subparagraph, be subject to a fine of not more than $1,000,000. If a conviction of a person is for a violation committed after a first conviction of such person under this paragraph, the maximum punishment shall be doubled with respect to both fine and imprisonment.

(6) Responsible corporate officer as "person"

For the purpose of this subsection, the term "person" means ... any responsible corporate officer.

(d) Civil penalties; factors considered in determining amount

Any person who violates [any of the listed sections of this statute] shall be subject to a civil penalty not to exceed $25,000 per day for each violation. In determining the amount of a civil penalty the court shall consider the seriousness of the violation or violations, the economic benefit (if any) resulting from the violation, any history of such violations, any good-faith efforts to comply with the applicable requirements, the economic impact of the penalty on the violator, and such other matters as justice may require....

(g) Administrative penalties

(1) Violations

Whenever on the basis of any information available ... the Administrator finds that any person has violated [any of the listed sections of this statute], the Administrator ... may ... assess a class I civil penalty or a class II civil penalty under this subsection.

(2) Classes of penalties

(A) Class I

The amount of a class I civil penalty under paragraph (1) may not exceed $10,000 per violation, except that the maximum amount of any class I civil penalty under this subparagraph shall not exceed $25,000. Before issuing an order assessing a civil penalty under this subparagraph, the Administrator ... shall give to the person to be assessed such penalty written notice of the Administrator's ... proposal to issue such order and the opportunity to request, within 30 days of the date the notice is received by such person, a hearing on the proposed order. Such hearing shall not be subject to [the provisions for formal adjudication under the Administrative Procedure Act], but shall provide a reasonable opportunity to be heard and to present evidence.

(B) Class II

The amount of a class II civil penalty under paragraph (1) may not exceed $10,000 per day for each day during which the violation continues; except that the maximum amount of any class II civil penalty under this subparagraph shall not exceed $125,000. Except as otherwise provided in this subsection, a class II civil penalty shall be assessed and collected in the same manner, and subject to the same provisions, as in the case of civil penalties assessed and collected after notice and opportunity for a hearing on the record in accordance with [the provisions for formal adjudication under the Administrative Procedure Act]. The Administrator ... may issue rules for discovery procedures for hearings under this subparagraph.

(3) Determining amount

In determining the amount of any penalty assessed under this subsection, the Administrator ... shall take into account the nature, circumstances, extent and gravity of the violation, or violations, and, with respect to the violator, ability to pay, any prior history of such violations, the degree of culpability, economic benefit or savings (if any) resulting from the violation, and such other matters as justice may require.…

Comment (The Use of the Criminal Sanction as a Means of Enforcing Environmental Laws)

In Israel, the criminal sanction has been the primary enforcement tool. Supporters of this arrangement claim that a person who violates an environmental law deserves punishment because the violator caused harm to the public and that criminal law has the greatest general deterrent effect because it is so powerful. Some judges, on the other hand, are hesitant to impose criminal sanctions because they think them inappropriate. They may see environmental violators less deserving of punishment than those who commit more traditional types of crimes. In addition, the demand for a high level of proof of individual culpability in a criminal proceeding makes imposition of the criminal sanction difficult.

Furthermore, under Section 20.24 of the Israeli Water Law, 5719-1959, a court may order a polluter to cease polluting, clean up the pollution, and fix any environmental damage, but may do so only after a finding of criminal liability. Although these remedies appear to be civil in nature, the fact that they are dependent on a finding of criminal liability means that criminal procedural protections and other concepts of criminal law apply before these remedies may be imposed. This is different from the United States, where not only cleanup orders, but also monetary penalties, can be imposed in civil proceedings.

European countries use the criminal sanction as the preferred tool for enforcing environmental laws.[7] In this way, Israel is following the European pattern.

Criminal Liability of Corporations

Israeli statutes clearly impose criminal liability on corporations, even providing for enhanced fines where the defendant is a corporation. Corporate criminal liability is crucial in Israeli environmental law because so many of the regulated facilities are held by corporations. The conceptual question of whether the law should impose criminal liability on corporations arises due to the nature of the criminal violation. Usually it requires both an act and some sort of state of mind. Arguably, as an artificial entity with neither physical capacity nor a mind, a corporation cannot act and cannot formulate criminal intent. The people who manage the corporation and the corporate employees can do both, so the issue is whether their acts and intent can be ascribed to the corporation.

US law allows the criminal actions of a corporate employee to be ascribed to the corporation. *New York Central & H.R.R. Co. v. U.S.*, 212 U.S. 481 (1909). The ability to ascribe intent is less clear, but the type of intent usually required in environmental criminal statutes—intent to do the act, not intent to violate the law—can also usually be ascribed to a corporation. *U.S. v. LaGrou Distribution Systems*, Inc., 466 F.3d 585 (7th Cir. 2006).

Corporations are not subject to criminal liability in all countries. The trend in European countries is to impose criminal liability on corporations, but not all countries yet do so. *See* Sara Sun Beale and Adam G. Safwat, *What Developments in Western Europe Tell Us About American Critiques of Criminal Corporate Liability*, 8 Buff. Crim. L. Rev. 89 (2002); Michael Faure and Günter Heine, eds., *Criminal Enforcement of Environmental Law in the European Union* (2005).

---

7. Oda F. Essens, *Criminal Enforcement of Environmental Law in the European Union, edited by Michael Faure and Gunter Heine*, 19 J. Envtl. L. 147 (2007) (book review).

Criminal Liability of Officers and High-Ranking Responsible Corporate Employees

Any person who personally causes a violation of an environmental statute can be subject to a criminal sanction if the applicable mens rea requirement is met or without mens rea for a strict liability violation. The question arises whether a person who has not personally engaged in an act that violated the law can be held liable derivatively due to liability of a corporation. In other words, can a criminal sanction be imposed on a person who did not actively violate the law because of that person's association with an organization that did violate the law? In such cases, the violation may have been caused by the act or omission of some other person in the corporation. This question is the reverse of the question of corporate liability. For corporate liability, the action of an individual is ascribed to the corporation. For the issue of liability of officers and employees, the liability of the corporation (which is in turn based on the action of some person in the corporation) is ascribed to individuals who are not those who themselves violated the law.

Israeli law clearly imposes liability on officers and responsible corporate employees. "Responsible" in this context means a person with a certain responsibility within the corporation, who may not be the person who caused (or is "responsible for") the violation. An individual that falls into one of these categories can escape liability only if the person took all reasonable measures to prevent the violation *and* the violation occurred without that person's knowledge. This allows an extremely narrow exception to liability.

In practice, Israeli courts rarely impose liability on officers and senior employees of major corporations. Judges may be reluctant to impose a criminal sanction on a corporate officer unless the state shows that the officer was personally involved in causing the pollution, even though a statute clearly allows imposition of criminal liability without such a showing. As a result, it can be argued that the criminal law is too strong to be effective as the main enforcement tool.

In fact, in most cases, the issue of officer liability or liability of high ranking corporate employees rarely comes before the court. Instead, the government files a criminal action against the corporation and these individuals and then uses the individual liability as a bargaining chip to get the corporation to agree to admit liability and pay a fine, in return for dropping the charges against the individuals. Nonetheless, especially recently, courts have found individuals in corporations culpable based on derivative liability, usually imposing on them the sanction of public service.[8]

Many American environmental statutes impose liability on responsible corporate officers. The Clean Water Act does so in 42 U.S.C. § 1319(c)(6). Imposition of such liability is legally permissible. *United States v. Dotterweich*, 320 U.S. 277 (1943). In practice, though, not many cases involve imposition of such liability because of the prevalence of civil enforcement.

Penalty Amounts

Penalty amounts in Israel are much lower than in the United States. For example, in a notorious case involving a huge discharge of untreated sewage to the Mediterranean Sea close to the beaches of Tel Aviv, Israel's largest city, the responsible local sewage authority agreed to pay a penalty of approximately $188,000. The chairperson of the authority and an engineer involved in the event were assigned community service by the

---

8. *See, e.g.*, CrimC(Beer Sheva) 1239/04 Ministry of Environment, Southern District v. Kitan Textile Industries, (Feb. 1, 2005). In this case, the CEO of the corporation was found culpable and subject to community service without being convicted of a crime. This form of sanction is authorized under the Punishment Law, 5737-1977, Sec. 71a(b).

court, but without imposition of criminal liability. CrimC (TA) 9467/04 *State of Israel v. Sewage Association of Municipalities in the Dan Region* (June 25, 2007). In another case, against a major operator of a petroleum storage facility, the magistrates court in Jerusalem imposed a penalty of $263,644 for violation of the water law and two other laws. CrimC 1994/06 (Jer) *State of Israel v. Pi Glilot Petroleum & Pipelines Ltd.* (Nov. 22, 2009). Penalties as high as these are rare, even for major private corporations. In contrast, the average civil penalty amount in environmental cases in the United States for 2010 was in excess of $400,000, while a total of $41,000,000 in fines was imposed in environmental criminal cases.[9]

There are probably multiple reasons that the penalty amounts in Israel are significantly lower than those in the United States. Israel's population is growing rapidly, and much of the growth is due to high immigration rates. This is seen as a societal good, given the philosophy of ingathering of exiles. As a result, authorities are hesitant to impose penalties that are likely to interfere with the ability of the economy to grow fast enough to support the rate of population growth and the costs of absorbing a relatively large percentage of immigrants. In addition, Israel has not absorbed the western view of the importance of environmental protection. Furthermore, although Israeli environmental enforcement may look weak to American eyes, it is probably much stronger than that in other countries in the Middle East.

The low amount of Israeli penalties is not a result of limits on penalty amounts in the environmental statutes. The Water Act is typical in allowing a penalty for each day of a continuing violation after notice (section 20.21(a)). Considering the fact that most violations continue for a long time after notice and before they are brought to court, it is clear that the courts are imposing penalties far lower than the authorized maximum.

Authority of Private Persons to Prosecute Criminal Actions

Many Israeli environmental statutes authorize private persons to initiate criminal enforcement actions. The general aspects of private criminal enforcement were discussed in chapter 6 as part of the discussion of criminal procedure. In the environmental area, most private criminal actions are brought by NGOs rather than by private individuals. An NGO is more likely to have the expertise and resources needed for criminal enforcement of the environmental laws. Just the filing of a criminal action can exert pressure on the defendant, getting it to do what an environmental NGO wants, which is compliance with environmental laws. Several such actions have been effective against notorious environmental problems. Furthermore, in some cases, government agencies are prevented from strict enforcement of the law by political considerations. In such cases, private actions can provide a substitute for enforcement by the government. Israeli attorney Rachelle Adam gives an excellent example of how political forces can inhibit effective enforcement and why private actions would have an effect in Rachelle Adam, *Government Failure and Public Indifference: A Portrait of Water Pollution in Israel*, 11 Colo. J. Int'l Envtl. L. & Pol'y 257, 257–298 (2000).

Comment (Administrative Enforcement)

Section 20.8 of the Israeli Water Law, 5719-1959, allows issuing an administrative enforcement order to someone who violates the law. The authority to issue such an order

---

9. *See* U.S. Environmental Protection Agency, Enforcement and Compliance Annual Results, Numbers at a Glance, Fiscal Year 2008 (Feb. 3, 2011), http://www.epa.gov/compliance/resources/reports/endofyear/eoy2010/numbers.html.

is not in the hands of the minister of environmental protection, but rather in the hands of the director of the Governmental Authority for Water and Sewage. The Governmental Authority for Water and Sewage is established in another provision of the Water Law (Section 124.11) and is responsible for management of water and sewage in the country. Its main job is allocation of water and not prevention of water pollution. Much of Israel is semi-arid and the inadequacy of the rainfall to meet the needs of the dense population is a perpetual problem. All water is nationalized by the Water Law and allocated by the Governmental Authority for Water and Sewage. Because this task is so large, the enforcement of environmental laws gets less attention.

Some recent Israeli laws have provisions allowing the minister of environmental protection to impose administrative penalties. For example, the new Clean Air Act will allow maximum administrative penalties of between $27,000 and $215,000, depending on the nature of the violation and on whether the violator is an individual or a corporation. Even greater administrative penalties are allowed for continuing violations. While the amounts are typically lower than the maximum amount allowed in judicial enforcement actions for the same law, they are at least as high as the penalties actually imposed by judges. The new laws only add the possibility of obtaining administrative penalties; they do not eliminate criminal liability.

In January 2012, the ministry of environmental protection sent a letter to one of the largest Israeli companies threatening to impose an administrative penalty of more than $4 million for violations of the Law on Prevention of Sea Pollution from Dry Land Sources.[10] The fine would be for unpermitted flows of effluents that continued over 19 months and for numerous violations of reporting requirements. This was only a notice letter and, as of this writing, it has yet to be seen whether the recipient will actually have to pay the proposed penalty. Still, the amount named in this letter has the potential to change the standards for penalty amounts.

In addition, a potentially significant administrative sanction is available in some cases under the Business Licensing Law, 5728-1968. Most businesses that can adversely affect the environment require business licenses, and environmental requirements are commonly inserted in such licenses. If a facility is operated without a license, or violates the conditions of a license, an environmental authority can issue an order requiring the business to close. Although the order is only temporary, it can have a devastating economic effect on a business. This potentially potent enforcement tool is rarely used. In the period from 2000–2006, an average of 5.5 such closure orders were issued each year. Orr Karassin, *Enforcement of Environmental Regulations: Increasing the Effectiveness of Environmental Protection Policies* xii (2009).

Despite these administrative authorities, then, criminal enforcement remains the predominant formal means of enforcement for significant violations of most environmental laws.

Questions

4. As is clear from the comments above, Israeli law differs from US law in two respects: criminal law is the main enforcement tool for major violations, and private criminal en-

---

10. Letter from Yitzhak Ben Dod, Senior Assistant Administrator for Enforcement, Ministry of Environmental Protection, to Tenuva Food Industries, *available at* http://www.sviva.gov.il/Enviroment/Static/Binaries/ModulKvatzim/tnuva_knas_012012_1.pdf (in Hebrew).

forcement actions are allowed. Is it a good idea for the main enforcement tool to be the criminal sanction? Why or why not?

5. How do the answers to the previous question explain the move to administrative penalties in Israel? Will the lower penalty amounts inhibit effective enforcement?

6. Is the Israeli practice of using the charge against high-ranking individuals in a corporation as a mechanism to get the corporation to agree to admit liability and to pay a fine appropriate?

7. What are the advantages of private criminal prosecution for environmental offenses? The disadvantages? Would it add significantly to environmental enforcement if US environmental statutes provided for such actions?

C. Constitutional Right to Environmental Quality

Environmental organizations in Israel, dissatisfied with the pace of implementation and enforcement of environmental statutes, sought to have the Supreme Court recognize a constitutional right to environmental quality. In the following case, the Supreme Court considered whether there is such a right.

Israeli Case

Israel Union for Environmental Defense v. Prime Minister of Israel
HCJ 4128/02, 58(3) PD 503 [2004]

[The Building and Planning Law, 5725-1965, sets out the process for approving plans for various types of construction projects. The statute and regulations promulgated under it require that, for major projects, an environmental impact statement must be prepared by the person proposing the project, reviewed by the proper agency, and made available for public review. The statute also provides that members of the public should have the opportunity to review documents related to a proposed project and to submit written objections, and that these objections must be considered before final project approval.

The Knesset amended the Building and Planning Law as it applies to national infrastructure projects such as airports, power stations, and waste disposal facilities. The amendments, designed to allow more rapid authorization of such projects, provided for shortened time periods for environmental impact review and for public submission of objections. The Israel Union for Environmental Defense (IUED) claimed that the shortened time periods were insufficient to allow full consideration of environmental values and would result in approval of projects that have adverse environmental effects. Such adverse effects, according to the IUED, would constitute an infringement of the constitutionally protected right to environmental quality. Any law infringing on a constitutional right must meet the requirements of the limitation clause. The IUED claimed that the amendment to the Building and Planning Law did not meet the requirement of the limitation clause and is therefore unconstitutional and invalid.]

Chief Justice A. Barak:

The Petitioner claims that the [amendment to] the Building and Planning Law is unconstitutional because it illegally infringes on the human right to a suitable degree of environmental quality that is protected by the Basic Law: Human Dignity and Freedom. According to the Petitioner, even though the right to a suitable environmental quality is not explicitly stated in the Basic Law: Human Dignity and Freedom, this right is included in the scope of human dignity and freedom. The Petitioner claims that it is also protected as part of the right to property.

The question before us is not whether case law recognizes a right to a suitable environmental quality that is not based on a Basic Law. The fact that some rights are implicitly included in the Basic Law: Human Dignity and Freedom should not lead us to include that no other legal rights exist outside of the Basic Law. We can leave to later decision the question of whether there is a case law right to a suitable degree of environmental quality. The question before us is only whether a basic right to a suitable level of environmental quality can be derived from the right to dignity, to freedom, and to property.

Does the amendment to the Building and Planning Law infringe on human dignity? I accept the position that the right to human dignity and freedom includes the right to the minimal conditions necessary for human existence. In one case I wrote:

> Human dignity includes ... protection of the minimal conditions for human existence.... A person who lives out of doors and has no home is a person who has suffered an infringement of human dignity. A person who is hungry is a person who has suffered an infringement of human dignity. A person who has no access to elementary medical care is a person who has suffered an infringement of human dignity. A person who must live in degrading material conditions is a person who has suffered an infringement of human dignity.

Thus, a law that degrades environmental quality in a manner that infringes on minimal human existence constitutes an infringement of human dignity and freedom. The amendment to the Building and Planning law does not create an interference with minimal human existence and the Petitioners do not claim that it does. Their claim is that the amendment infringes on a suitable level of environmental quality. Can the right to a suitable environment be derived from the right to human dignity and freedom?

I think the answer is in the negative. Constitutional interpretation of the right to dignity must identify the constitutional dimensions of the right. It would be inappropriate to interpret the right too narrowly and in this way to demean it by failing to give meaning to the goals behind the recognition of this right. On the other hand, the right should not be interpreted so broadly as to include within its ambit every human right, because doing so would make superfluous other basic laws establishing human rights. The proper interpretation of the right to dignity must take a position between these two extremes. Within this framework, I do not see any interpretative possibility of inserting the right to a suitable environment into the right to dignity. In fact, if the right to a suitable environment were included within the right to human dignity, then all political, civil, social and economic rights would also be included. This would not represent an appropriate means of constitutional interpretation.

The Petitioner claims that the amendment to the Building and Planning Law infringes on life and bodily integrity. Certainly the Basic Law: Human Dignity and Freedom provides protection against infringement of life and bodily integrity (see section 2 of the Basic Law). But the Petitioner has not provided a basis for its claim of an infringement. Many social actions may influence the quality of human life, but that does not mean that they all constitute infringements on life and bodily integrity. An infringement on human life or bodily integrity can take many forms. We need not determine that it is impossible that some action of a planning agency that adversely affects environmental quality could be so dangerous and so destructive that it will rise to the level of an infringement of life and bodily integrity. If this occurred, the Petitioner would have to show that the amendment constitutes a real and concrete danger to human life and bodily integrity. The Petitioner has made no such showing. The amendment establishes a general framework for making planning decisions on national infrastructure projects. Its provisions do not infringe on human life or bodily integrity. We can imagine a broad variety of national infrastructure projects that have no effect at all on such rights. Therefore, this claim of the Petitioner is to be rejected.

The Petitioner claims that the amendment infringes on the individual's property rights. This claim is also to be rejected. The amendment does not have any provision that infringes on anyone's property rights. The amendment establishes an administrative framework for making decisions. It is of course possible that some national infrastructure plan that is approved under the amendment's procedures will infringe on the property rights of some person. There is nothing preventing a claim against such a plan based on an illegal infringement of property rights. But this does not mean that the administrative framework itself infringes on property rights.

The constitutional claims of the Petitioner are rejected.

Comments

The discussion in chapter 8 showed that the Supreme Court has read other rights into the right to human dignity and freedom. These are based on claims of specific injuries to individuals. For example, in HCJ 3071/05 *Louzon v. Government of Israel* (July 28, 2008), the Court has recognized a right to basic health services (set out in chapter 8). The claim of a right to an appropriate level of environmental quality is different. A specific individual who was ill and was turned away from a hospital or clinic without treatment can show an infringement of a right to a basic level of health care. For most environmental parameters, it is much harder for a person to show individualized harm from a decrease in environmental quality. In the case set out above, even if the Petitioner had been able to show that such a decrease in environmental quality would occur, it could not have shown that the decline in environmental quality would harm a specific individual. Data exist in some cases that show a correlation between environmental quality and some adverse health effects, but they do not show that a decrease in environmental quality will cause an identified person to suffer from asthma or to contract cancer. This is not because environmental quality does not affect individuals, but rather because the data only show correlations between environmental quality and overall effects in a population. The data can show an increased risk that an individual will suffer some adverse effect, but cannot show more than that. With noise and odor pollution, it is usually possible to show individualized harm, but not for air, water, groundwater, ocean, or other significant forms of pollution. Furthermore, for these problems, even where the adverse effect on the overall population is relatively large, the increased risk to a specific individual is likely to be small.

The case sets up another barrier to ever showing that a law interferes with a constitutional right to environmental quality. Chief Justice Barak ruled that a law interferes with such a right only if it is shown that the law constitutes a real and concrete danger to human life and bodily integrity. For most environmental problems, evidence sufficient to show such a "real and concrete" danger is unavailable. Even if this term does not require proof of individualized harm, it probably requires a degree of proof of danger to the population that is unobtainable for most environmental problems. Most environmental harms may also be caused by non-environmental factors. Thus, if we think that some environmental pollutant increases the incidence of asthma in the population, it is usually impossible to find proof that no other factor, or combination of factors, to which the population is exposed is the real culprit. Sometimes there is evidence of a correlation between the presence of the environmental pollutant and the incidence of an illness, and such evidence shows a danger, but it is questionable whether it rises to the level of showing a real and concrete danger as required by the opinion.

Chief Justice Barak's opinion states that "if the right to a suitable environment were included with the right to human dignity, then all political, civil and economic rights would also be included." It is not clear why this should be so. The right to participate in cultural life is sometimes considered a social right. Why would the recognition of the right to a suitable environment necessary entail recognition of a right to culture? It seems that a rational society could choose to protect one to a greater degree than it protects the other. The problem may be that it would be difficult for a court to decide which of these rights warrant protection. The real problem is probably a somewhat different one. It would be hard for a court to define what level of environmental protection is "suitable," just as it would be hard to determine what types of activities constitute culture. It would be understandable for a court to shy away from undertaking these tasks, although the difficulties involved are not cited in the decision as the reason for the result.

There is another justification for not recognizing a constitutional right to environmental quality. Environmental protection involves a tradeoff between important and complex societal values, and it may be better to have a representative legislature make and an expert agency implement such tradeoffs, rather than having a court determine what level of environmental protection is constitutionally warranted. The Supreme Court is not in a position to know the extent to which people are willing to give up economic development, or to pay increased costs for goods, in order to gain a greater degree of environmental protection. The Court may have avoided giving this as a reason because in other areas, when applying the balancing part of the proportionality test of constitutional or administrative law, the Court does not shy away from balancing social values to determine whether the benefits of a statute or administrative action outweigh the harms they cause.

What the plaintiffs wanted here was probably two things: The first was to elevate the importance of environmental matters on the national agenda. The second was even more important. They saw the approach of the Knesset and the agencies to environmental matters as unsatisfactory. They wanted to be able to turn to the courts with constitutional environmental claims so they could get the courts to use their broad discretionary powers under Israeli constitutional analysis to strike down statutes and administrative actions that were not, in the eyes of the petitioner, sufficiently protective of the environment.

The constitutions of many countries recognize or provide environmental rights.[11] The meaning of a provision in any country is determined both by the language of the provi-

---

11. Partial surveys are found in several sources, including Adriana F. Aguilar, *Enforcing the Right to a Healthy Environment in Latin America*, 3 REV. EUR. COMMUNITY & INT'L ENVTL. L. 215, 216 (1994); Carl Bruch, Wole Coker, Chris VanArsdale, *Constitutional Environmental Law: Giving Force to Fundamental Principles in Africa*, 26 COLUM. J. ENVTL. L. 131 (2001); Ryan K. Gravelle, Note, *Enforcing the Elusive: Environmental Rights in East European Constitutions*, 16 VA. ENVTL. L.J. 633 (1997); James R. May, *Constituting Fundamental Environmental Rights Worldwide*, 23 PACE ENVTL. L. REV. 113 (2005–2006); Oren Perez, *Zchuyot Chevratiot-Kalkaliot V'eichut Ha'sviva (Social-Economic Rights*

sion and by its interpretation by the courts of the country. In a substantial number of countries, there has been very little litigation involving the environmental provisions, even where the constitution provides an apparently justiciable individual right.[12] This may be due to all sorts of problems of institutional capacity, both of the judicial system and of the public interest bar most likely to litigate such claims. The environmental constitutional provisions in many countries are not operative in the way constitutional rights in Israel or in the United States are operative or enforceable. In some countries, the provisions are only aspirational; they authorize legislation but do not in themselves create any enforceable rights. In other countries, the constitutional rights are read as authorizing administrative action, or as creating private access to courts or to administrative proceedings without defining specific rights.

The United States Constitution has no explicit environmental provision and has not been interpreted to create implicit environmental rights. About two thirds of the states in the United States have environmental provisions in their constitutions, but the form of these provisions varies greatly.[13] A few impose very specific requirements about protection of specific resources through detailed funding or other requirements. Some guarantee public rights to natural resources. Others provide that resources are held in trust for the public. Provisions of either kind may be formulated to cover specific resources or all natural resources. Some state constitutions declare a policy of protecting the environment or natural resources. Some empower the legislature or the state to protect the environment by law; others specifically require that this be done. A small number of state constitutions grant persons a right to some degree of environmental quality. A number of state constitutions give the people a right to preservation of the natural resources of the state.[14] As to enforcement of the interests or rights they create, some state constitutions say they are enforceable by the state or by its people, some say the provisions are self-executing, and most are silent.[15] With a few exceptions, state courts decline to enforce environmental provisions in their state constitutions.[16]

Returning to the opinion: At the beginning, Chief Justice Barak distinguishes between a right to a suitable environment based on case law and a right based on the Basic Law: Human Dignity and Freedom. The opinion seems to be leaving some sort of door open, but it is not clear what precisely it means in this regard. Israel has many environmental statutes that could be interpreted as providing statutory rights to environmental quality as specifically defined in the statutes. These would not be general rights to a suitable environment, but rights to the degree of environmental protection set out in the statutes. In addressing rights based on case law, the opinion seems to mean that the Court could

and the Environment), *in* Zchuyot Kalkaliot, Chevratiot V'tarbutiot B'Yisrael (Economic, Social and Cultural Rights in Israel) 225, 242–253 (Yoram Rabin & Yuval Shani eds. 2004); John C. Tucker, *Constitutional Codification of an Environmental Ethic*, 52 Fla. L. Rev. 299, 312 n. 73 (2000).

12. Michael. R. Anderson *Human Rights Approaches to Environmental Protection: An Overview*, *in* Human Rights Approaches to Environmental Protection 1, 20 (Alan E. Boyle & Michael R. Anderson eds., 1998); Barry E. Hill, Steve Wolfson, & Nicholas Trag, *Human Rights and the Environment: A Synopsis and Some Predictions*, 16 Geo. Int'l Envtl. L. Rev. 359, 382 (2004).

13. See Barton H. Thompson, Jr., *Environmental Policy and State Constitutions: The Potential Role of Substantive Guidance*, 27 Rutgers L.J. 863 (1996)

14. *See* Robert Meltz, Cong. Reearch Serv., Right to a Clean Environment Provisions in State Constitutions, and Arguments as to A Federal Counterpart 2 (1999).

15. *See* Bruce B. Ledewitz, *Establishing a Federal Constitutional Right to a Healthy Environment in Us and in our Posterity*, 68 Miss. L.J. 565 (1998).

16. *See* A.E. Dick Howard, *The Indeterminacy of Constitutions*, 31 Wake Forest L. Rev. 383, 401 (1996).

recognize some sort of general right outside of the framework of the Basic Law, much as it recognized rights prior to the enactment of the two Basic Laws on individual rights. Perhaps these rights would be based on international law concepts or on something else. The Court does not explain what it means.

Question

8. If the Court had accepted the claim of the Petitioner in *Israel Union for Environmental Defense v. Prime Minister of Israel* that there is a basic right to a suitable level of environmental quality, what more would the Court have to find before determining that the amendment to the Building and Planning Law is unconstitutional? How competent would a court be to make these findings?

D. Environmental Land Use Planning

As described in chapter 16a on property law, Israel has an extensive national planning mechanism, with national, regional, and local plans. The plans separate conflicting uses of land and provide for preservation of natural areas. In addition, the planning process incorporates an environmental assessment process and environmental impact statements to examine specifically the adverse environmental impacts of major projects before they are authorized.

While the land use scheme would seem, on its face, to provide good protection for environmental values, in practice the system is extremely complex and riddled with exceptions. Furthermore, planning of major projects takes a significant amount of time. In the many periods of rapid growth in Israel, struggles arose between those who wanted to promote development, who complained that the length and complexity of the planning process inhibited the country's ability to cope with rapid growth and other changes, and the environmental community, that asserted that it was precisely in times of rapid pressing change that the environment was most in need of protection. The case of *Israel Union for Environmental Defense v. Prime Minister of Israel* set out in the previous section was the product of one such dispute.

The planning process is further complicated by a number of other factors. All buildings are supposed to have a building permit before construction, and the law allows for destruction of buildings built without the required permits. The requirement of the permit is meant to ensure that the buildings are in appropriate locations, that the installation of sewage, roads and other infrastructure precedes or accompanies construction, and that buildings are safe. Enforcement of this law has become politically charged. In recent years, destruction of buildings constructed in Arab areas of Jerusalem without permits has engendered international controversy about what is often called "house demolitions," with one side saying that this is oppression of the Arab minority and the other claiming that it is normal enforcement of the law that applies to all illegal construction in all areas.

The difficulty of planning is also exacerbated by the size of the country. Preservation of natural areas is challenging, but very important both to provide recreation for the many people who live in crowded urban areas and also to preserve the considerable ecological diversity found in the country. The following case explores how the land use planning system works, or fails to work, to protect the natural environment.

Israeli Case

Israel Union for Environmental Defense v.
Local Planning Commission of Shomron
Civ. App 8116/99, 58(5) PD 196 [2001]

[The National Plan on Building limits construction in areas designated as rural open areas to structures that would not interfere with the character of the area. Construction of tourist services is allowed. If a regional planning commission wants to authorize construction that exceeds these limitations, it must to provide written reasons for doing so and get the authorization of a standing subcommittee of the National Planning Council.

A plan to build a large service station in a rural area was approved by the local and regional planning commissions. The plan provided for a gas station for cars and for large trucks, a store selling supplies for motor vehicles, a tire repair facility, a car wash, and a restaurant. The project would include a two story building and would entail covering an area of about one and a half acres with asphalt. Authorization of the national subcommittee was neither sought nor obtained. The planning commissions claimed that this type of facility did not exceed the limitations on local and regional approval set out in the law and that approval of the national subcommittee was not required. An environmental NGO brought an action seeking a determination that approval at the local and regional level, without submitting the matter for approval at the national level, was invalid. The issue before the Court was whether the local and regional planning commissions were correct in their determination that this project did not have to be referred for approval at the national level.]

Justice Y. Englard:

Open space is important for a number of reasons. Ecologically, open spaces are needed as the habitats for the variety of animals and plants native to the country. Additionally open spaces serve to provide areas in which water can penetrate the ground and reach the aquifers that provide drinking water. Open areas also make a crucial contribution to the quality of life. They protect those who live nearby from the disturbances of noise and pollution and help provide clean air to breathe. They provide people with the opportunity to take part in leisure activities in the bosom of nature, the demand for which grows as our population grows and free time increases. We must also note the importance of open vistas as part of the way people think about the land of Israel, its culture and its history. These are major components in attracting tourism.

It is an important feature of the system for implementing the planning law that it puts the discretion whether to deviate from the objectives of the national plan, by constructing a service station in a rural open area, in the hands of a national planning body. This matter is of great significance. The open areas are a diminishing national resource, so every decision that harms this asset should be taken at the national level by national planning institutions. Any diminution of land resources should be cautiously undertaken and carefully reviewed. We must remember that land development activities are irreversible. The question of what should be preserved and what need not be preserved must be made after consideration of all the variables: on the one hand, the particular nature of the open areas in question, their value, their sensitivity and how they function, and on the other hand, the needs of development, of the local community, and of its well-being. The balance between infrastructure development and income enhancement for the country's residents, on the one hand, and protection of natural values and open spaces, on the other, is a balance between very substantial opposing interests. Therefore, it is my opinion that such a decision should properly be made at the national level. Local interests are not always in line with the general good. At the local level, it is sometimes logical to maximize the economic return on the property and not its value for the entire population and for future generations. Thus, for example, in the present case, the head of the local authority of Givat Ada [a community close to the site of the proposed facility], who as part of his position serves as a representative of his community and its residents on the local planning commission, supports the construction of the service station. Among the considerations that he has taken into account he mentions the capital improvement levy that his community will receive from the developers, the income from which has already been factored into the annual budget, and also the interest of the residents in the existence of competition between several service stations in the area of the community.

Of course, there are also local interests in protecting green areas, but it appears that this idea has not yet been fully assimilated. In many cases, planners and elected officials in local governments and commissions see preservation of open areas as a negative limitation that they must try to get around, rather than as a positive value.

National planning institutions have a broader and more inclusive view of all interests, considerations, and goals. They are not influenced by locals with a direct interest in the matter, and they have the tools to give more careful consideration to the good of the country and all its inhabitants. Under the law, representatives of public interest groups dedicated to environmental protection serve on the national institutions. The importance of ceding local interests is discussed in Moti Kaplan & Eren Dayan, *Thematic Planning Policy: The Open Space System, in Israel 2020—A Master Plan for Israel for the Twenty-first Century* (1996) (in Hebrew):

> Sustainable development of land resources necessarily involves giving up measures that have a short term benefit in favor of steps that will bear fruit only in the distant future. Planning will require responsibility beyond that which is immediately evident and that involves more than the considerations relevant on a local level.

And further:

> Management of land resources in a manner that takes into consideration the interests of all generations is likely to occur only in the hands of a governmental authority that is responsible for managing all state assets for the overall good and for the good of coming generations, rather than not in the hands of authorities whose interest is in obtaining immediate returns from these assets.

Therefore the appeal should be granted. The result is that the permit to construct the service station is invalidated and the plan is to be submitted for approval to the National Council or to the Subcommittee of the National Council for Fundamental Planning Issues, along with a written justification for approving the plan from the Local Planning Commission of the Shomron.

I would like to add a final comment: Sadly, the awareness of environmental quality and protection of natural resources for the good of all and for the good of future generations is not yet well developed. We are handicapped in the matter of the environment and backwards in comparison to most developed nations. This is especially serious due to the very limited natural areas that are found in Israel, and every erroneous decision on management of these resources deals a fatal and irreversible blow to these assets that we are obligated to protect with vigilance. In my opinion, this Court has an important role in creating the public awareness that the Israeli public so much needs. Therefore, when we interpret terms in the existing laws, we must make every effort to interpret them so as to protect the very limited natural resources we have. We should acknowledge that private organizations have also undertaken this important goal, adding their efforts to those of governmental planning bodies. We should strengthen their ability to protect natural beauty, and it is therefore appropriate that an additional planning institution should examine this service station project.

Comments

The opinion discusses the failure of Israelis to give sufficient weight to preservation of open spaces. In other matters, Israelis are ahead of most of the world in environmental protection. For example, since 1964, Israel has had a law prohibiting the picking of wildflowers. (The current version is the Law on National Parks, Nature Reserves, Nature Sites, and Memorial Sites, 5758-1998 § 33. This statute authorizes the minister of environmental defense to issue a list of protected natural assets and prohibits anyone from harming these assets. The minister has used the authority to declare a long list of wildflowers as protected natural assets. Declaration on National Parks, Nature Reserves, Nature Sites, and Memorial Sites (Protected Natural Assets), 5765-2005.)[17] The law is enormously successful; Israelis go on vacation to see and photograph wildflowers. In the spring, rangers from the Nature Reserve Authority are stationed around the country to advise people where they can see flowers blooming. Wildflowers are a national passion, but Israelis do not pick them.

Israel has well developed environmental technology. Drip irrigation was developed in Israel, the country has succeeded in reversing desertification in its arid south and is increasing the area of arable land. Seventy percent of Israel's sewage water is treated and reused.[18] In contrast, in the United States, Florida, a leader in wastewater reuse, reuses about 42 percent of its wastewater.[19] As described in the next section, Israel also has a law requiring all homes to have solar collectors to supply hot water. Yet there is no doubt that Justice Englard is correct; in sensitivity of the general population to protecting open areas, Israelis are behind most of the developed world.

Questions

9. Justice Englard writes in 2001, well after the dawn of the modern environmental era, that Israelis are backwards in their appreciation of environmental values, especially

---

17. The declaration is found in English at http://www.sviva.gov.il/Enviroment/Static/Binaries/Articals/national_parks_nature_reserves_national_sites_and_memorial_sites_proclamation_protected_natural_assets_2005_1.pdf.

18. Israel Ministry of Environmental Protection, Effluent Disposal and Reuse, Jan. 28, 2010, http://www.sviva.gov.il/bin/en.jsp?enPage=e_BlankPage&enDisplay=view&enDispWhat=Object&enDispWho=Articals^12090&enZone=Wastewater_Treatment. Other countries in the Middle East have much lower reuse rates, even though they face the same arid conditions. Less than 30 percent of treated wastewater is reused in Tunisia. Redouane Choukr-Allah, *Wastewater Treatment and Reuse, in* ARAB ENVIRONMENT: WATER, SUSTAINABLE MANAGEMENT OF A SCARCE RESOURCE 107, 110 (Mohamed El-Ashry et al eds., 2010) available at http://www.afedonline.org/Report2010/main.asp. Jordan reuses virtually all of its treated wastewater and Lebanon reuses half, but most of the wastewater of each country remains untreated. *Id.* At 110–111.

19. WATER REUSE PROGRAM, FLORIDA DEPARTMENT OF ENVIRONMENTAL PROTECTION, WATER REUSE INVENTORY 22 (2011), *available at* http://www.dep.state.fl.us/water/reuse/docs/inventory/2010_reuse-report.pdf.

those connected to the preservation of open space. In light of the history, geography and social structure of Israel, why do you think this might be so?

10. Do you agree with Justice Englard that a court should use its authority to interpret the law in a way that increases public awareness of environmental values? Is this approach consistent with the approach of the Court you saw as to constitutional issues?

E. Alternative Energy

Israel is a leader in using some forms of alternative energy. The following rule is the legal basis for Israeli's intensive use of solar energy. This rule is part of the national building code. The law provides that new buildings cannot be constructed without building permits. In order to get a building permit, a builder must submit plans for a proposed building and these plans must show that the structure will meet the requirement set out in the permit rules. The rule set out here requires that passive solar technology for hot water heating be installed in most residential buildings.

Israeli Law

Planning and Building Rules
(Permit Request: Requirements and Fees), 5930-1970
Second Appendix

1.09 Obligation to Install a Solar System

(a) A solar system for supplying hot water shall be installed in the building.

(b) The storage tanks and the solar collectors shall be installed on the roof of the building in a manner that is satisfactory to the local planning commission, applying the following requirements:

(1) The tank and the collector shall not be visually offensive;

(2) The tanks shall be placed in such a way that they will integrate with the architecture of the building;

(3) The collection tank shall be white, unless the local planning commission makes a different determination.

(c) A backup system shall be installed to provide hot water for times when there is not sufficient sunlight to provide hot water.

(d) These requirements do not apply to buildings taller than 29 meters or to a building or portion thereof which serves entirely, or partially, as an industrial facility, a workshop, or a hospital.

(e) If the local planning commission determines that it is not possible to use the solar energy due to shade falling on a building, or that installation of a solar system on a building will be unreasonably offensive from an architectural point of view, the commission is authorized to excuse the permit applicant from these requirements as to all or part of the building, but only after providing [opportunity to members of the public to submit objections].

Comments

Solar collection panels sit on top of almost all residential buildings in Israel. Each apartment has its own solar panels. These are connected to an insulated hot water tank that sits on or just under the roof. Pipes from the tank run to the apartment. Apartments also have auxiliary systems to heat water by electricity when there is no sun or when the demand for hot water exceeds the capacity of the solar tank. Most days are sunny, so the auxiliary systems are used mainly in the winter and only part of the time even then.

The exception for tall buildings applies to those higher than about ten stories. Until recently, there were few such tall buildings in Israel. The exception is based on the fact that a tall building may not have sufficient roof space for the solar collectors needed to supply hot water to all units within the building. Almost all Israelis live in multiple unit dwellings with two or more units, but with fewer than ten stories, so the application of the law is nearly universal.

The size of the hot water tanks in Israel is smaller than typical hot water tanks in the United States. Israelis use hot water differently than do Americans. It is unusual for an Israeli to leave the water running while washing dishes or to take a long shower. Washing machines and dishwashers are of the type used in Europe; the appliances are connected to cold water lines and water is heated within the appliance when it is needed. In the United States, such appliances typically are connected to the hot water line.

Pictures of solar hot water systems in Israel can be found at http://leadearthblog.blogspot.com/2010/05/sustainable-agriculture-is-big-business.html and http://www.ecofriend.com/entry/almost-the-whole-of-israel-heats-water-with-suns-energy-only/.

The first state statute requiring solar collectors in the United States was enacted in Hawaii in 2008. Haw. Rev. Stat. § 196-6.5 (2008). The requirement in the law went into effect on January 1, 2010. The Hawaii law applies only to new single family residences, so it is less inclusive than the Israeli law.

Questions

11. Why did Israel enact a provision requiring solar water heaters in 1980, while Hawaii got around to it only in 2008 and other US states still do not have such mandates? Consider what Justice Englard said about Israelis being behind most of the world in environmental awareness and the fact that Americans are usually considered to be very environmentally aware. What does this suggest about the factors that drive development of environmental law?

12. What barriers are there to imposition of a similar building code requirement in the United States?

Chapter 19

Labor and Employment Law

A. Labor Courts

Perhaps the most prominent of the systems of courts of limited jurisdiction is the labor court system. Israel has both district labor courts and a National Labor Court, established by the Labor Courts Law, 5729-1969. The labor courts have jurisdiction over a wide variety of labor relations disputes, including actions involving work contracts, collective agreements, work-related torts, labor organizations, certain social security matters, and even work-related criminal matters. The district labor courts generally sit in panels of three, with one judge, one public representative of labor, and one public representative of employers. The public representatives need not be lawyers. The National Labor Court sits with a bench of three (one judge, one public representative of labor, and one public representative of employers), five (three judges, one public representative of labor, and one public representative of employers), or seven (three judges, two public representatives of labor, and two public representatives of employers), depending on the type of matter under consideration.

The usual rules of evidence and procedure do not apply in the labor courts. Instead, labor courts are to act in accordance with the rules of *natural justice*. This is a standard of fairness, roughly similar to the concept of due process in American law. Parties may be represented by lawyers. Decisions of the district labor courts are appealable to the National Labor Court. Decisions of the National Labor Court on criminal matters are appealable to the Supreme Court. All other decisions of the National Labor Court are subject to review by the Supreme Court sitting as the High Court of Justice. The Supreme Court has broad discretion to decide whether to review cases falling into this last group. For cases it agrees to review, the Supreme Court applies the rules of administrative law to determine whether the National Labor Court's decision was acceptable.

B. Unions and Collective Agreements

While American law tends to separate labor law (including the right to unionize and to engage in collective bargaining) from employee rights, the two are treated together in Israeli law. This is at least partly the result of the evolution of labor law in Israel. The major Israeli labor organization is called the Histadrut.[1] Until the early 1980s, virtually

---

1. The name means *federation*. The full name of the organization is the General Federation of Labor in Israel.

all Israeli workers were members of the Histadrut.[2] Founded before the establishment of the state as an association of trade unions, the Histadrut became a powerful force in the Israeli economy. In the early 1980s, about eighty percent of all workers belonged to the Histadrut. Workers paid union dues not to their own unions but to the Histadrut, which in turn funded the unions. The Histadrut negotiated agreements on both union powers and employment rules with the government and with the major employer associations. Individual trade or industrial unions bargained with specific employers within the framework set out by these agreements.

The Histadrut had extensive powers due to the high percentage of unionized workers, the breadth of union membership among various members of Israeli society who were not unionized workers, the Histadrut's involvement in other aspects of the economy, and its connection to the political structure of the state. Membership included not only salaried workers, but also some self-employed workers, managers, homemakers and unemployed former wage-earners. Members were drawn from all sectors of Israeli society. In addition to its work in labor negotiations, the Histadrut provided health care, pensions, and other services to its members. For many years, the Histadrut health care and pension funds were the main such providers in the country. The Histadrut's bargaining power was further increased by its ownership of many industrial enterprises; it was the largest non-governmental employer in the country. It was allied with the Labor Party, which controlled the Israeli government from 1948–1977.

The collective agreements negotiated by the Histadrut and its unions sometimes applied, by the terms of the agreements, to workers for the same employers who were not union members. The following statute further extends the reach of the collective agreements.

Israeli Statute

Collective Agreements Law, 5717-1957

25. Authority to Extend Collective Agreement

The minister of labor is authorized, on his own initiative or in response to a request from a party to a collective agreement, to issue an order extending the application of all provisions in a general collective agreement if, in his opinion, it is appropriate to do so, considering the number of workers and employers subject to the collective agreement and the importance of the agreement in establishing employment relations and in regulating working conditions in the labor market.

Comment

The minister of labor has frequently exercised the power granted under the statute and issued orders extending the application of collective agreements to workers otherwise not directly covered by the terms of the agreement. Therefore the Histadrut's power to determine employment conditions extended, and still extends, not only to union members in a unionized workplace, but also, in many cases, to non-union members in workplaces that are unionized (which is similar to the situation in the United States) as well as workers in work places

---

2. This and other information on the structure and power of the Histadrut is taken from Yitzchak Haberfeld, *Why Do Workers Join Unions? The Case of Israel*, 48 IND. & LAB. REL. REV. 656 (1995) and Yinon Cohen et al., *Unpacking Union Density: Membership and Coverage in the Transformation of the Israel IR System*, 42 INDUS. REL. 692 (2003).

that are not unionized (which is not the case in the United States). Workers did not need to join a union to gain the protections provided by the widely prevalent collective agreements. Why then, did they join the unions in such high numbers? It appears that people joined for a utilitarian reason and for an ideological reason. The utilitarian reason was to get the social benefits provided by union membership, especially to get the health care services in areas where only Histadrut-associated health care was readily available. On an ideological level, union membership was associated with seeing the union as an expression of workers' solidarity. In addition, union membership was boosted by the large number of people working in the public sector, which was completely unionized.[3]

Because of the size of the Histadrut and its extensive influence on the Israeli economy in the early years of the state, there was little need of statutes requiring employers to engage in collective bargaining. The power of the Histadrut was sufficient incentive.

Beginning in the mid-1980s, the structure of the Israeli workplace and workforce changed. Union membership dropped to about half of what it had earlier been. The decline has been ascribed to changes in the economy, with a decline in traditional industries and an increase in high tech, where individual and not collective contracts are the norm, and to changes in social values, with declining emphasis on social solidarity and increasing emphasis on individualism. The enactment of the Government Health Insurance Law, 5754-1994, providing all Israeli residents with access to health care services whether or not they belonged to a union, also contributed to the membership decline. Due to the law, the Histadrut lost its former predominant position in provision of health services. Another law decreased its economic power in the area of pensions by broadening that market.

With these changes, the ability to rely on union-negotiated agreements to protect the workforce declined and the need for the government to protect workers, or at least regulate the conditions of their work, increased. The Knesset reacted by enacting a series of laws defining workers' rights. These statutes covered many, but not all, issues of the employer-employee relationship. The courts, both the labor courts and the regular courts, have also taken an active role in setting out the rules of labor and employment law.

The following case discusses the origins of the right to unionize and the dimensions of the right.

Israeli Case

Horn & Leibowitz v. Histadrut

Collective Dispute Appeal 1008/00, 35 PDL[4] 145 [2000]

Chief Judge S. Adler:

Introduction

This appeal deals with ... effectuation of the workers' right to organize, including protection from dismissal due to an attempt to unionize and to strike.

The Appellant (the employer or the company) is a private firm engaged in providing transportation services and in renting out vehicles. It provides services in all parts of the country. The home office is in the city of Afula. The company has a fleet of dozens of buses and employs 217 drivers.

---

3. *Id.*
4. PDL stands for Labor Cases. It is a reporter for decisions from the labor courts.

The Respondent is a union. At the relevant time, the Histadrut represented 83 of the employer's workers, or about 38 percent of all of the drivers. The Histadrut sought to conduct negotiations with the employer with the goal of entering a collective agreement on the conditions of employment at the company, but the employer refused. As a result a dispute arose between the sides and a strike was declared. In reaction to the strike, the employer fired thirty-three drivers, all of whom participated in the strike.

The Histadrut reacted by filing a request for a hearing on a collective dispute in which it asked for revocation of the dismissals, claiming that they were based on the workers' actions in joining the Histadrut and that the dismissals violated the workers' right to unionize. They also sought an order prohibiting the employers from interfering with the unionization of the workers.

The Right of Workers to Unionize

The freedom to unionize is among the social rights recognized in international labor law. The freedom of association is recognized as a basic constitutional right in Israel in both the case law of both this court and the Supreme Court.

A Basic Law: Social Rights has not yet been enacted, and therefore the right to unionize has not yet obtained the status of a written basic constitutional right in our system. Despite this, several statutes include provisions assuring the right of workers to unionize. For example, sections 3 and 4 of the Collective Agreements Law, 5717-1957, define a representative union and section 25(a)(3b) of Wage Protection Law, 5718-1958, sets out a means of supporting the union through deduction of union's professional and organizational expenses from the workers' wages.

The freedom of association protects the right of a person to advance his own interests through unionization and the right to participate in the democratic process of designing the policies that will govern various aspects of his life. The freedom of association has a special meaning in the area of labor relations and labor law and includes the right to organize, which includes the right of employees to establish unions and the right of employers to establish employers' organizations. In the area of labor relations, the right of employees to organize is treated as having two aspects that are effectuated at both the individual and the collective level. The collective aspect of the right is granted to a workers' union by virtue of its representation of a large number of workers. The right to unionize includes the right of the workers' union to conduct collective negotiations with the employer.

The Principle of Equality in the Workplace

The case law in this court has based the right of workers to organize in unions on two grounds: the constitutional right to organize and the principle of equality. As to the principle of equality, the following was stated:

> Equality is an overarching value in Israeli law that includes the obligation to provide equality of opportunity in employment.... This court was a pioneer in developing the principle of equal opportunity, in prohibiting discrimination against female employees, in prohibiting discrimination based on sexual tendencies, in prohibiting requiring union membership as a condition for hiring, and in prohibiting discrimination based on age.... The principle of equality also prohibits discrimination based on whether a worker belongs to a union.... Discrimination against union membership violates the public good. The union worker is entitled to the same employment opportunities as the non-union worker. An employer is not allowed to fire a worker because of union membership or service on a

workers' committee or membership in a committee that is trying to unionize the workers in a factory.

Discrimination against union workers is prohibited because it infringes on the workers' freedom of association. The freedom of association encompasses the obligation of the employer to desist from behavior that will influence workers to join or not to join a union or that will interfere with a professional association. This is a basic principle in international labor law.

Of course, nothing we have said prevents the dismissal of workers when there is a reason justifying their dismissal that is unrelated to their being unionized or not unionized.

The Israeli legislature granted the worker protection from being fired due to participation in a strike. Section 19 of the Collective Agreements Law, 5717-1957, provides that "participation in a strike shall not be seen as a violation of a personal undertaking."

The right of workers to organize would not be meaningful if the union were not granted the power to take action in order effectuate the goal of representation of workers in the workplace.... In other words, interference with the freedom to strike deprives the union of the main tool that it uses to exert pressure on the employer and makes the union useless in the eyes of the workers. We should remember that the legal status of the freedom to strike is drawn from the value of human dignity.

In the case before us, the dismissal of the drivers constitutes an action designed to interfere with the freedom of the employers' workers to join a union and to conduct collective negotiations. Therefore in reaching a decision we must keep in mind the considerable effect of the employer's behaviour on the constitutional rights of the workers before us and on the rights of all workers in the future.

Returning the Dismissed Workers to their Jobs—Dismissal in Violation of an Agreement

The general rule is that in the case of breach of the employment contract or of a collective agreement, the accepted remedy is to grant an award of damages to the injured party. Still, there are exceptions and the court has discretion to nullify the dismissals and order that the workers be given back their jobs.

Returning the Dismissed Workers to their Jobs—Dismissal in Violation of a Statute

The legislature has provided that in appropriate circumstances the courts have discretion to return dismissed workers to their jobs. For example, section 10(a)(2) of the Equal Employment Opportunities Law, 5748-1988, provides,

10. (a) The labor court shall have exclusive authority to hear civil cases based on violations of this statute and is authorized

(2) to issue an injunction or an affirmative order if, in its opinion, granting of damages alone is not justified. In granting such an injunction or order the court shall consider, among other things, the influence of the order on the working relations in the workplace and the possibility that another worker will be injured. If the dismissal resulted from reductions in force, the court shall consider the provisions in any collective agreement that applies to the sides....

Similar provisions are found in section 3(2) of the Protection of Workers Law (Exposure of Offenses and of Unethical Conduct or Improper Administration), 5757-1997 and section 14(2) of the Law on Equal Rights for Persons with Disabilities, 5758-1998. Section 10(c) of the Law for Prevention of Sexual Harassment, 5758-1998 provides that proceedings under that law shall also be subject to the provisions of section 10 of the

Equal Employment Opportunities Law. Section 45C(b) of the State Comptroller Law (Consolidated Version), 5718-1958, authorizes the ombudsman to order the nullification of dismissals or the granting of special damages to a public employee who exposed corruption and was fired. In addition, there are statutes that prohibit the dismissals in specific circumstances and provide that such dismissals are null *ab initio*. These include, for example, section 9 of the Employment of Women Law, 5714-1954; section 41(b) of the Released Soldiers Law (Return to Work), 5709-1949; and section 5a of the Foreign Workers' Law (Prohibition of Unlawful Employment and Assurance of Fair Conditions), 5751-1991.

Returning the Dismissed Workers to their Jobs—Dismissal in Violation of a Constitutional Right

The protection of union members or representatives from being injured by the employer is an integral part of the workers' freedom of association. Therefore dismissal of workers because they want to unionize and participate in a strike is a violation of their constitutional rights. [Our cases have allowed the remedy of returning the dismissed employees to their jobs in such cases.]

In the case before us, the dismissal of the drivers constituted a violation of their constitutional right and therefore we have authority to order that they may return to their jobs.

Is it Appropriate in this Case to Order that the Workers Return to Their Jobs?

[The court considered several factors and found that they did not provide a reason for not returning the workers to their jobs. It also determined that effective protection of the constitutional rights of the workers required their return to work. If the only remedy were requiring the employer to pay damages, the employer might find it worthwhile to fire the workers and pay the damages. Furthermore, the constitutional rights of the workers should not be sold for money.]

The Property Right of the Employer in a Business and the Property Right of the Workers in the Workplace

In relation to the property right and prerogatives of the employer, this court recently ruled:

> The power of the employer to conduct his business as he chooses derives from his property interest in the business, an interest recognized as a basic right in section 3 of the Basic Law: Human Dignity and Freedom. The prerogative of the employer to select workers who are appropriate to the requirements of the business also stems from the same property interest.... But this prerogative is not absolute and is subject ... to the property rights of the workers in the workplace.

As to the balance between the property rights of the owner of the business and those of the workers, we held:

> The business is the property of the employer and the employer can choose how to operate it. In other words, the employer operates the business: this is his job, his responsibility, and even his right. Therefore the employer can decide on the budget ... and has great flexibility in conduct of the business, in order to allow the business to survive in a competitive market, both domestic and foreign. Beyond this, the employer has an interest in setting out the general framework for operation of the business, including the sale and control of shares.

> As to the property rights of the workers: the business is the place of their employment and it is where they earn a living and everything that flows from that, and they

therefore have a great interest in the destiny of the business and in changes in it. Furthermore the workers also have property rights in the workplace.

In other words, the property right of the employer in the business grants the employer, among other things, the authority to run the business and to select the workers. But this right is not absolute and must be balanced with the rights of the workers, the rights of the union, and the public good. In the matter before us, the question is one of proportionality; that is, to what extent will operation of the company's business be harmed by returning the workers to their jobs? We think that if the parties operate in good faith, the Appellant's business will not be harmed. No weight should be given to the employer's stubborn refusal to take the drivers back because of their having joined the union or because they want to strike.

Comment

Horn & Leibowitz v. Histadrut derives the right to unionize from the constitutional right to freedom of association and from general principles of equality. The freedom of association includes the freedom to organize in unions. As an auxiliary principle, employers are obligated not to interfere with employee efforts to unionize. The principle of equality prohibits the employer from treating the unionized worker differently from the non-unionized worker.

What about unionization in the period before the recognition of constitutional rights? Because the Histadrut had great bargaining power, for many years it was not necessary to establish a right to unionize. Only later, as the power of the Histadrut declined, did courts intervene.

The origin of the right to unionize in the United States is different. Unions in the United States never had the power that the Histadrut had in Israel. The role of labor unions in the United States has been more limited and more controversial. Today, although the percentage of the workforce that belongs to unions, called *union density*, has dropped radically in Israel, it is still higher than in the United States. The union density in the United States in 2010 was about 12 percent.[5] Even in the 1940s and 1950s, when union density peaked in the United States, it reached only about a third of the workforce.[6] The major labor laws were enacted in the United States prior to this time. In other words, the increase in unionization in the United States followed the enactment of the statutes. Law, both statutory and judicial, probably had a greater role in shaping labor power in the United States than it had initially in Israel.

In the United States, the right to unionize is statutory. For employees working for private employers, the right derives from the National Labor Relations Act. The dimensions of the right are defined by an administrative agency, the National Labor Relations Board, acting under authority granted it in the statute. Decisions of the Board are reviewable in the courts, but this judicial review does not change the fact that the right originates in the statute and the primary authority to define the reach of the statute and the scope of the right to unionize resides in the Board. In addition, a variety of federal statutes establish the right to unionize for those who work for the federal government. A number of states have statutes establishing a right to unionize for employees not reached by the federal statutes, mainly state employees. Under the Israeli approach, the courts are more involved in establishing

---

5. Bureau of Labor Statistics, US Dept. of Labor, Economic News Release, Union Members — 2010 (Jan. 21, 2011), *available at* http://www.bls.gov/news.release/union2.nr0.htm.

6. Gerald Mayer, Congressional Research Service, Fed. Publications Paper 174, Union Membership Trends in the United States CRS-11, Figure 1 (2004), *available at* http://digitalcommons.ilr.cornell.edu/key_workplace/174/.

the right to unionize and in defining the dimensions of that right. The constitutional freedom of association, as interpreted in *Horn & Leibowitz*, ran against the private employer, who was prevented from interfering with the workers' freedom of association. In the United States, constitutional rights usually run only against the government.

In substantial portions of *Horn & Leibowitz* not presented here, Judge Adler refers to international law as an added source for finding the constitutional right and for defining its dimensions. Labor and employment law in the United States are more insular in their development; agencies and courts dealing with issues in these fields are less likely to refer to international law in making their decisions.

The power of the unions in Israel is increased by the fact an employer has the duty to bargain with a union representing as little as one-third of the workers who will be subject to the agreement, as long as no other union represents a larger proportion of the workers. Collective Agreements Law, 5717-1957, §§ 3, 33H(1). The effective provision was added to the statute in 2009, after initial recognition of the duty to bargain in case law. Non-union members are likely to be covered by collective agreements. They do not pay union dues, but, under the Wage Protection Law, 5718-1958, section 25(a)(3b), cited in *Horn & Leibowitz*, they may be required to pay professional and organizational expenses of the union. In the United States, the union must be supported by a majority of all employees in order to be the exclusive representative in bargaining with the employer on behalf of all employees, both union members and non-members. National Labor Relations Act, § 9(a), 29 U.S.C. § 159(a).

The opinion in *Horn & Leibowitz* addresses the claim that the recognition of the union's rights to organize limits the employer's property rights, which include the right to chose how to run his or her business. The opinion agrees that there is such a limitation, but finds it justified to protect the conflicting rights of employees and unions, as well as the public interest. On this point, the analysis is characteristic of standard constitutional analysis, which sees all constitutional rights as subject to limitation. The court does not engaged in a detailed application of the limitation clause that defines when infringement of constitutional rights is permissible in Israel, but the underlying conceptual framework is not surprising. What is more interesting is that the opinion bolsters its opinion with a quotation from another case that said that workers have property rights in the workplace. Employees' interests in their jobs thus attain constitutional status under the Basic Law: Human Dignity and Freedom, which explicitly protects property rights.

Question

1. *Horn & Leibowitz* rules that an employer cannot fire an employee because of the employee's membership or activities in a union. That prohibition is now found in section 33j of the Collective Agreements Law, 5717-1957, but the statutory provision is an amendment to an older law and was enacted after the decision in the case. In other words, the court ruled on the matter without specific statutory authority to do so. How does this explain the grounds used by the court to justify the prohibition?

C. Employer-Employee Relations

The Israeli legislature has been active in providing specific protections for workers. Statutes provide for a minimum wage, dictate days off and the length of annual vacations (up to 14 to 28 days for full-time workers, depending on the length of employment for the same employer), allow sick leave for employees, allow leave for employees to care for sick family members, and set out many other conditions for employer-employee relations. Employers are required by statute to provide maternity leave for a minimum of twelve weeks, some of which may be taken by the father. Maternity leave pay is provided by the National Insurance Institute, the Israeli equivalent of the Social Security Administration, and not by the employer. There are restrictions on firing a woman on maternity leave as well as on firing a worker of either sex called to reserve military duty.

The statutes do not cover all matters of the employer-employee relationship, and the courts are sometimes called on to determine the permissible terms of that relationship in the absence of legislation. The following case and the discussion after it deal with the question of the validity of covenants not to compete in the employment contract.

Israeli Case

Frumer v. Radguard

Labor Appeal 164/99, 34 PDL 294 [1999][7]

Chief Judge S. Adler:

The Case

This case deals with the following three matters: First, the right of Mr. Dan Frumer, the first Appellant (the Appellant) to be employed by the second Appellant, Check Point, and the right of Check Point to employ Mr. Frumer, as defined by the freedom of occupation granted to the parties; second, the right of the Respondent Radguard to prevent the employment of Mr. Frumer by Check Point, based on the provision in Mr. Frumer's employment contract with Radguard, which limits employment by a competitor of the company for a period of 22 months and is purportedly designed to prevent Mr. Frumer from revealing trade secrets; and third, the question of whether the prior employer, Radguard, proved that Mr. Frumer had trade secrets that he was likely to use within the context of his employment at Check Point.

The district labor court in Tel Aviv acceded to the request of Radguard to issue a temporary injunction preventing the Appellant and Check Point from entering into an employment relationship for 18 months, rather than the 22 month period set out in the covenant not to compete in the employment contract between the Appellant and Radguard. The appeal challenges the validity of the covenant not to compete.

General Background

The high tech industry is considered one of the central pillars of the world economy in general and the Israeli economy in particular. The development of Israeli high tech in recent years has been especially rapid. As a result of the extensive development in high tech, new branches of the industry have appeared, including in the area of communications security. This is a very important area given the competition in the area of computers and computer networks and the need to prevent unauthorized individuals from gaining access to databases located on both public and private computer networks. The owners of computer networks seek to protect the information they contain.

---

7. A summary of this case in English appears at 20 Int'l Lab. L. Rep. 45 (2002). The translation set out in the text is not based on that summary.

One of the advanced systems for protecting information is called VPN (virtual private network), which allows encoding transmissions on networks that have a great number of users and that are open to the public. In the field of VPN, there are aspects that are software-based and those that are hardware-based. A complete VPN product as sold to a client integrates both software and hardware aspects. Check Point mainly develops software products, while Radguard mainly develops hardware products.

The Business Background of the Appellant

The Appellant is a professional program engineer. In his military service, he worked in systems programming in the Air Force. After the completion of his service, the Appellant worked in several firms. Prior to his employment with Radguard, the last place he worked was at Digital, where he gained experience in developing data security.

The Appellant went to work at Radguard soon after the establishment of the company. He was one of the first four employees. His first position was as a senior development engineer. He later became the director of development and worked in that position until he left the firm. In the capacity of director of development, the Appellant participated in management meetings and was exposed to a great deal of information about the firm. On the other hand, he never dealt with marketing of the firm's products.

On August 4, 1998, the Appellant gave notice of his resignation from Radguard. He actually stopped working on August 1, 1998, and the employment relationship terminated on October 31, 1998.[8] The resignation came after the general manager of Radguard, Eli Hershkovitz, decided to transfer the Appellant from his position as director of development to another position. A dispute erupted as to whether Mr. Hershkovitz meant to transfer the Appellant to a more junior position or just to a different position. In any case, it is clear that the Appellant did not leave Radguard due to a job offer from another firm or in order to seek another job. The Appellant began working at Check Point on November 15, 1998.

The Appellant is now an expert in the field of VPN. His expertise covers software development and integration between software and hardware. In addition, the Appellant has acquired experience in staff management in the field of high tech.

During the period between his resignation and the termination of his employment relationship with Radguard, the Appellant sought other employment. The Appellant was assisted in his search by a human resources company with expertise in the field of high tech. The human resources company suggested several positions, the position at Check Point among them. The Appellant also received a job offer from another firm, which he declined.

Covenant Not to Compete

On May 23, 1994, the Appellant had signed an employment contract with Radguard that provided:

> 14. The employee will protect secrets of the company including all commercial, professional, and technical information that he obtains during his employment at the company, and will not communicate any information about his work at the company, the work of the company, its software, equipment or its business to employees who are not directly involved in implementation of such work or to any other person or organization, unless he received permission from the proper authorities.

---

8. It seems likely that Mr. Frumer's employment terminated after he actually stopped working due to accumulated vacation days, which he could take before the employment ended.

15. The employee's obligations under this section shall continue even after his employment at the firm has ceased.

16. Without derogation of what is stated above, and in recognition of the legitimate interest of the company in defending and protecting the said information, and in recognition of the serious damages that could be caused to the company, I undertake not to deal with and not to work in any employment, whether it is as a salaried employee, an independent contractor, or as an independent business, directly or indirectly, for any business that would make use in any way of the knowledge I acquired or that came into my hands during the period of my employment at the company and that is related to the company, its activities, or its programs, in either direct or indirect competition with the company, both during the time I am employed by the company and also afterwards, and I will not deal with or work, either directly or indirectly, at any firm that competes with one or more areas of business of the company, for the following period:

> a. ...

> b. If the period of my employment at the company exceeds twelve months, but is less than five years, the limitation will continue for all the time I am employed by the company and for 22 months after cessation of my employment at the company.

It is clear that the above provisions limit the employment of the Appellant. We deal with the content and period of the limitations below.

The Main Issues in Contention

The main issues that arise from the claims of the two sides in this case are:

> a) What are the legality and the meaning of the provisions that limit the freedom of occupation in the employment contract between Radguard and the Appellant? In other words, what weight should be given to the obligations that the Appellant undertook in the employment contract? Is there any component of the relationship between the Appellant and Check Point that justifies the limitation on the employment of the Appellant?

> b) Assuming that the Appellant has knowledge of Radguard's trade secrets, is there a reasonable probability that he will make use of such secrets during his employment at Check Point in a way that will injure Radguard?

> c) How should this court strike the proper balance between the legally protected freedoms, rights, and interests of the parties?

The Guiding Principles Derived from Case Law

The matter before us involves a conflict among several basic principles: the Appellant's freedom of occupation and the new employer's (Check Point's) ability to employ him; the freedom of contract of the parties to an employment contract; the property right of the prior employer (Radguard) in its trade secrets; the freedom of contract of Radguard and of Check Point; the power to agree on limiting Check Point's freedom of occupation; and the interest of the public in free competition, in workers being able to change their place of employment, and in the rapid market dissemination of knowledge.

In order to reach a decision on the issues raised in this case, this court must balance various basic principles, rank their importance, and apply the appropriate policy in light of the facts of the case. In this matter, we consider the words of Justice Barak in another case:

The freedom of occupation includes the freedom of the worker to go to work for whomever he wants, including a new employer to whom the worker agreed to bring professional secrets. On the other hand, the law does not give full protection to the freedom of occupation. The scope of the freedom is one thing; the protection given it is another.

There are also values that stand in opposition to the freedom of occupation, and the law also needs to provide some protection to them. The degree of protection given to the freedom of occupation is a result of the balancing between freedom of occupation and other individual freedoms, such as the right to property, freedom of contract (which is part of human dignity and freedom), as well as the balancing between the freedom of occupation and the public interest, such as the public interest in protection of professional secrets.... The freedom of occupation, like all other rights, is relative and not absolute. Therefore in opposition to the freedom of occupation of the worker and of the new employer stand the interests of the original employer that warrant protection, among them its right to property (section 3 of the Basic Law: Human Dignity and Freedom) and perhaps even the right to privacy (section 7). In addition, the freedom of contract of the original employer and the public interest should be considered.

In performing the judicial balancing, the court must employ the tests of reasonableness and proportionality, determining whether the limitation of the freedom of occupation meets the test of reasonableness, taking into consideration all the circumstances of the case. In this connection, it is necessary to consider the reasonableness of the period for which the limitation applies in light of the need to protect the trade secrets of the former employer; the scope of the limitation; and the geographic area to which it applies. In addition, it is necessary to consider the degree of damage caused to the worker and the degree of damage caused to the former employer.

The scholars Finkin et al. summarized the rule followed in most of the states of the United States in this way:

On the one hand, an employee cannot be prohibited from selling his knowledge and skills—including general knowledge learned and skills perfected in prior employment. There is a recognized societal interest in allowing individual freedom to practice a trade or profession and to increase the utilization of knowledge and skill.... On the other hand ... the employer's interest in trade secrets—unique information that gives the prior employer a competitive advantage—is also deemed worthy of protection.

The prevailing view in most jurisdictions is that covenants not to compete are enforceable only if reasonable—and reasonableness turns upon an assessment of whether it is greater in duration, scope of employment, and geographic area than is necessary to protect the employer's legitimate interests; imposes an undue hardship on the former employee's ability to earn a living or practice a profession; and the extent to which the public interest is affected.... In some jurisdictions, a finding of unreasonableness makes the covenant totally unenforceable, on the theory that a judicial narrowing of the covenant will only encourage employers to write broader covenants hoping to trench closer to (or transgress) the line of reasonableness. Others allow the courts to "blue pencil" the covenant, narrowing the duration, geographic scope, and nature of the work, in an effort to achieve a fair balance of competing interests. Matthew W. Finkin, Alvin L. Goldman & Clyde W. Summers, *Legal Protection for the Individual Employee*, 186–187 (1989).

We should add that the reasonableness test is a broad one that protects many and varied interests of the employer, but that in most cases the protected interest is the employer's trade secrets.

Claims involving limitations on the freedom of occupation and trade secrets involve various areas of law. Freedom of occupation and the right to property are constitutional rights. The limitation on the freedom of occupation stems from, among other things, contractual undertakings of the employee. The subject of trade secrets relates to both torts and intellectual property.

Reasons for not Limiting the Freedom of Occupation of the Employee

In this case, the Appellant, in his personal employment contract that he signed with Radguard, undertook not to compete for a period of 22 months. As we have stated, this undertaking is an expression of the freedom of contract of the parties and of the desire of Radguard to protect its intellectual property, mainly its trade secrets. Nonetheless a limitation on the occupational choice of any person runs counter to the public good and to the policy that supports a free and competitive market.

A covenant not to compete in a personal employment contract is not to be given a great deal of weight. Such a covenant is to be treated as relevant only if it is reasonable and in fact protects the interests of both sides, including mainly the interests of the former employer in its trade secrets. In the absence the conditions we set out below, and especially in the absence of trade secrets to be protected, the principle of freedom of occupation outweighs the freedom of contract. The reasons for this are as follows:

First reason: The Basic Law: Freedom of Occupation grants the worker the right to work in any job, profession, or trade. The freedom of occupation is a constitutional value. The human capital of the worker is valuable. The matter is clearly illustrated in the case before us, in which the Appellant's professional skills are his assets and the basis for his employability. The employee's skills are his property and are protected by the Basic Law: Human Dignity and Freedom.

Second reason: Employment law rests on a basic principle that assumes an inequality in the bargaining power of the employee and the employer. Under this principle, no effect is given to a provision in the personal employment contract if it is assumed that a reasonable employee exercising free will would not agree to the provision. This is similar to cases in which, at the time of hiring, the employee signs a document relinquishing rights given to the employee by statute. We emphasize that, generally, an employee signs a covenant not to compete due to lack of choice in the matter; the employee wants to be hired, and it reasonable to assume that an employee who refuses to sign an agreement with such a provision will not be hired.

The knowledge and experience that the employee obtained during the period of employment with the former employer, including the use of software, operating systems, formulations, equipment, etc., becomes part of the employee's set of skills. These qualifications are the property of a person and, in general, a person should not be limited from using them as they please. A reasonable employee will not relinquish the right to use the skills and experience obtained during the period of employment, even if that employee goes to work for another employer.

Third reason: The place where a person works and spends at least a third of the time is not just a place where a person earns a living, but also a place where a person seeks satisfaction and self-realization. Any limitation on a person's ability to change jobs infringes on the right to self-realization. Generally a person changes jobs in order to advance and to find improved work conditions.... In the present case, there is no doubt that the Appellant could get a better position if he could use the expertise he had acquired in the area of VPN than if he had to work in another software area. In addition, an employee is free to leave an employer and, subject to various conditions, open a business.

Fourth reason: The modern economy is based on free enterprise in an open market and a free economy in capital, particularly human capital. Any limitation of a worker's right to change jobs interferes with free competition. Free competition advances the market and brings with it a lowering of consumer prices. A competitive market encourages establishment of new firms, including firms established by workers who are going into competition with their former employers. Workers offer their talents to a variety of employers and compete for jobs. The employers propose better working conditions in order to attract a skilled workforce.

Fifth reason: Society has an interest in the free and rapid dissemination of information in the market. This is important for both economic and social reasons.

Under What Circumstances Should the Freedom of Occupation of the Worker be Limited?

When should a provision in an employment contract that limits the freedom of occupation be enforced? As we stated above, freedom of occupation and free competition are not absolute values. Conflicting interests of society in general and of the former employer may also be deserving of protection. Society should protect an employer's intellectual property, especially from an illegal use by an employee. Of course, the main protection stems from patent registration or from copyright. In addition, the legal system protects the employer's property rights in cases in which an employer seeks to prevent a former employee from passing on the employer's trade secrets. But before imposing a limitation on the employee, the court must consider the following:

1) Trade secret: It is appropriate to limit the freedom of occupation of an employee in order to prevent illegal use of a *trade secret* that belonged to the former employer. Trade secrets are protected by laws that deal with intellectual property [and other law]. Because the matter is subject to legislation, there is no need for a covenant not to compete in order to protect the rights of the former employer.

2) Special training: In cases in which the employer invested special and costly resources in training the employee and has obligated the employee to remain for a specified period, this imposition of a limitation on the freedom of occupation of the employee may be justified as a consideration for the employer's investment. On the other hand, if the employee acquired skills as a result of the regular assigned work, or if the employee paid for special training that occurred during the employee's free time, the former employer may not limit the employee's use of these skills.

3) Special consideration: It is appropriate to determine whether the employee received special compensation for agreeing to the covenant not to compete after termination of the employee-employer relationship.

4) Obligation of good faith and the fiduciary duty: It is necessary to consider the good faith of the employee and of the new employer. A trust relationship exists between the employee and the employer. The fiduciary duty that the employee owes the employer imposes on the employee a stricter standard of behavior that does the obligation of good faith. An employee who, during the period of employment, assists other people in copying the production process of the employer breaches the fiduciary duty.

In this context, it should be said that the fiduciary duty imposed on those who hold senior positions is broader than that imposed on more junior employees. The fiduciary duty is the source of many obligations, most of which exist during the period of the employee-employer relationship. Nonetheless the fiduciary duty continues after the termination of the employment relationship, generally in connection to the employee's competition with the former employer.

As to the second and third considerations, which are not treated in statutes, the court will limit the freedom of occupation of the employee only if the employment contract contains a covenant not to compete. In contrast, the obligation of good faith and the fiduciary duty apply to the employee even without an explicit contract provision.

The four conditions listed above do not constitute a closed list, and the court must consider all the circumstances of each individual case. The guiding principle is that any covenant not to compete in an employment contract shall not be given effect except in the presence of one of the conditions listed above. But the presence of one of the conditions is not sufficient to obligate the court to give effect to the contractual provision, and the decision should be made after considerations of all the principles and interests in play in a specific case and in light of the particular facts involved.

Protection of Trade Secrets and Intellectual Property

The employee's obligation to protect the trade secrets of the employer is drawn from statutory provisions, from the fiduciary duty between the two, and from the covenants not to compete in the personal employment contract.

The court will not issue an injunction that limits the employee's freedom of occupation unless the employee's work at a new employer threatens the very existence of the former employer. The former employer must prove that the use of the trade secret will cause injury to its business.

Whether the Appellant Made Use of Trade Secrets to Assist Check Point

The Appellant explicitly undertook not to use and not to convey to anyone Radguard's trade secrets. This is sufficient to protect Radguard's right if it becomes clear that the Appellant violated or is violating his undertakings, because Radguard will be able to file an action against him.

The catch is that at this point of the proceedings, there is no evidence that the Appellant violated or is violating this undertaking or that there is a great chance that he will do so during his employment at Check Point. Radguard has not proven that the Appellant and Check Point plan to use the Appellant's knowledge of Radguard's trade secrets. The opposite is true. Under the facts before us at this stage of the proceedings, Check Point did not intentionally seek to hire an employee who had recently been working at Radguard. The Appellant did not apply for work at Check Point during the period he was actually working at Radguard. The Appellant's resignation from Radguard was not undertaken in order to move to a position at Check Point, but rather because Radguard did not offer him another senior position.

The Appellant did not receive any special consideration for undertaking to limit his own employment opportunities.

Summary

The employment contract signed by the Appellant and Radguard includes provisions that limit the freedom of occupation of the Appellant. Under these provisions, the Appellant agreed not to work for a competitor of Radguard for 22 months after cessation of his employment. A close examination of the facts shows that Radguard and Check Point compete in the area of data security.

In light of the facts brought before us, the temporary injunction preventing the Appellant's employment at Check Point should not remain in force for these reasons:

The Appellant was an expert in software development in the area of data security even before coming to work at Radguard. During his work there, he deepened his knowledge and acquired experience in this area, which is natural for a professional employee. This expertise can be defined as part of his professional skills. These skills are his property and he can use them in any workplace, including at a competing firm, even if the employment contract includes provisions limiting his right to do so. The Appellant's skills are not trade secrets.

Based on the evidence presented at this stage of the proceedings, the only trade secret in the hands of the Appellant is the development plans of Radguard. By now, after the passage of nine and a half months, these plans are no longer secret, so there is no reason for maintaining the limitation of the Appellant's occupation. The attorney for Radguard did not point out any other trade secret.

The Appellant and Check Point acted in good faith, so the facts of the case do not justify limiting the freedom of occupation of the Appellant.

Agreements should be kept and weight should be given to the freedom of contract. But the public good, the freedom of occupation, and the right of a person to self actualization and to improvement are to be given greater weight in this case.

Comment

The decision in *Frumer v. Radguard* leaves two issues unaddressed. First, although the court finds that a covenant not to compete infringes on the freedom of occupation of the employee, and although the court mentions the proportionality test, it does not apply the limitation clause of the Basic Law: Freedom of Occupation, which includes the proportionality test, to determine whether the infringement is a permissible one. Justice Adler's opinion uses a balancing test to determine whether the infringement is justified, listing relevant factors and balancing them in a general, not structured, manner. Is this the proper means of striking a balance, or should the structured balance of the limitation clause be used to determine whether the infringement on the constitutional right is permissible? Second, if the covenant not to compete is problematic because it violates the freedom of occupation, why does the freedom of occupation apply against a private employer?

All of these issues were further discussed in a later Supreme Court case addressing another covenant not to complete. In CA 6601/96 *AES System Inc. v. Saar*, 54 (3) PD 850 (2000), the Supreme Court cited Judge Adler's opinion in *Frumer* with approval multiple times, clarified the remaining constitutional law issues, and held the covenant not to compete invalid. The case arose as a contract action by a company that sued a former employee for damages the company alleged that it sustained from the defendant's breach of a covenant not to compete. The Supreme Court, hearing the case on appeal from a district court decision, considered the question of the validity of the covenant not to compete. It approached the question, first, as a matter of contract law. Section 30 of the Law of Contracts (General Provisions), 5733-1973, provides, "A contract is invalid if its formation, content, or goal is unlawful, unethical, or contrary to public policy." Chief Justice Barak's opinion for the Court ruled that, although basic constitutional rights lie directly only against the government, these same rights define the public policy that is protected in the language quoted from Law of Contracts (General Provisions). In this way, the constitutional rights also apply indirectly to actions of private parties that would infringe upon them. "Public policy" is defined not only by the need to protect constitutional rights, but also by other values, all of which are balanced to determine where the public policy lies in any given case.

In other words, a balancing test is used for determining the permissibility of the infringement on the freedom of occupation because the issue is not one of constitutional law but of determining public policy, in which constitutional rights play a part but not the only part. The constitutional right is relevant as to the private employer for the same reason.

In determining the content of public policy and what covenants not to compete are valid, the Supreme Court followed a line of reasoning similar to that in the *Frumer* case. The relevant values to be balanced to determine public policy include, on the side of the employer, freedom of contract, the employer's constitutional property interest in its investment in the training it gave the employee, and the public interest in having employers train their employees. On the side of the employee, the relevant interests are freedom of employees to work for whom they choose including for themselves, derived from the constitutional freedom of occupation; the public interest in free competition in order to reduce prices and increase the quality of goods and services, also derived from the freedom of occupation; the employees' interests in their own skills; and the public interest in the employees being able to use their skills freely to bring more knowledge to the marketplace.

The interest of the employer in preventing competition from the employee is not an interest to be considered because it is not a *legitimate* interest. No doubt, employers have a real economic interest in preventing their former employees from entering into competition with them, either on their own or by going to work for a competing firm, but the Court explicitly refused to consider this interest as legally legitimate. On the other hand, the employer's interest in protecting its trade secrets or customer lists is legitimate and would be considered.

The Supreme Court also agreed with the National Labor Court's determination that there is unequal bargaining power between the employer and the employee, although it noted that the degree of inequality depends on the labor market and the power of unions or other professional associations.

Returning to the National Labor Court's decision in the *Frumer* case, we see that Judge Adler wrote under the heading of "Guiding Principles Derived from Case Law" that one of the matters to be considered was "the power to agree on limiting Check Point's freedom of occupation." He was referring to the power of Frumer and Radguard, through the covenant not to compete in the employment contract between them, to limit Check Point's ability to hire Mr. Frumer. The decision refers to Check Point's interest in choosing to hire whomever it pleases as part of its freedom of occupation. In other words, the firm has a constitutional right, and this right includes the right to freely choose its employees. This is another example of the constitutionalization of employment law in Israel.

American law on the validity of employee covenants not to compete rests on a basic principle of common law on contracts that the courts will not enforce a contract that violates public policy. One case explained how an employee's covenant not to compete violates public policy in two ways:

> We have consistently taken a cautious approach to the question whether to permit an employer to enforce a restrictive covenant in an employment contract. Such covenants are looked upon with disfavor because their enforcement de-

creases competition in the marketplace and restricts the covenantor's right to work and his ability to earn a livelihood. *Jim W. Miller Const., Inc. v. Schaefer*, 298 N.W. 2d 455 (Minn., 1980).

The law on the validity of covenants to compete differs from state to state. Some states restrict such covenants by statute; some by common law. Some states place greater restrictions than others and some completely outlaw covenants not to compete. Some jurisdictions will not enforce covenants not to compete unless they serve a legitimate interest of the employer in protecting trade secrets or customer contacts. Others put a greater emphasis on the reasonableness of the duration and geographic application of the covenant and examine the precise employer interest less closely. In general, the cases seem to put less emphasis on the protection of the employee's rights and more on the public interest. They differ from the Israeli cases in that they do not approach the employee's rights in constitutional or quasi-constitutional terms. *See generally* Milton Handler and Daniel Lazaroff, *Restraint of Trade and the Restatement (Second) of Contracts*, 57 N.Y.U. L. Rev. 669, 727–750 (1982). Furthermore, American cases do not completely reject the use of covenants not to compete as a way of protecting trade secrets. Judge Adler's opinion holds that, in Israel, trade secrets are to be protected by the law on trade secrets, and not by covenants not to complete. A covenant not to compete designed to protect trade secrets can be enforced only if the employer can show that the use of the trade secret will cause injury to, or, under other language in the case, threaten the "very existence" of its business.

A study of the law on covenants not to compete in two US states argues that the refusal to enforce such covenants contributes to the success of the high tech industry. The study notes that the high tech industry on Route 128 outside of Boston, Massachusetts has been less successful than that in Silicon Valley in California. The study finds that the law on protection of trade secrets is the same in both states, but that covenants not to compete are more readily enforced in Massachusetts, where the matter is left to the courts, than in California, where a state statute prohibits enforcement of such covenants. The California law allows freer movement of employees between firms and gives employees greater leeway to establish their own firms, leading to freer knowledge transfer and a more successful industry.[9] On the other hand, a lawsuit in the US District Court for the Northern District of California alleged that major Silicon Valley employers had an illegal agreement not to poach each other's employees.[10] If there is such an agreement and it is working, then its function in the market may be similar to that of covenants not to compete. To the extent that this is true, the success of the high tech industry in California may be correlated with the law prohibiting enforcement of covenants not to compete, but it is not caused by the law.

Questions

2. Is the Israeli law on covenants not to compete more similar to that in Massachusetts than that of California?

3. The court in *Frumer v. Radguard* holds that a covenant not to compete is not needed to protect trade secrets. The employee has explicitly undertaken not to use or share the

---

9. *See* Ronald J. Gilson, *The Legal Infrastructure of High Technology Industrial Districts: Silicon Valley, Route 128, and Covenants Not to Compete*, 74 N.Y.U. L. Rev. 575 (1999).

10. Poaching Lawsuit Against Tech Companies Will Proceed — Judge, Thomson Reuters News & Insight, Jan. 26, 2012, http://newsandinsight.thomsonreuters.com/Legal/News/2012/01_-_January/Poaching_lawsuit_against_tech_companies_will_proceed-judge/.

trade secrets of the employer; if the employee breaches this undertaking, the employer has a contractual action against the employee even without the covenant not to compete. Furthermore, statutes in the areas of intellectual property law and tort law protect the employer's right to its trade secrets. If this is so, why would the employer ask the employee to sign a covenant not to compete? How does this relate to the Israeli courts' attitude toward enforcement of such covenants?

D. Employment Discrimination

Israeli Case

El Al Israel Airlines Ltd. v. Danielowitz
HCJ 721/94, 48(5) PD 749 [1994][11]

Associate Chief Justice A. Barak:

A collective agreement and a collective arrangement[12] confer a benefit on a "spouse" (husband or wife) or a "person reputed to be a husband/wife" of an employee. Is this benefit conferred also on an employee's same-sex companion? That is the question before the court in this petition.

The Facts and the Litigation before the Labor Court

The first Respondent (the Respondent) works as a flight attendant for the Petitioner (the El-Al company). Under the collective agreement, every permanent employee is entitled to receive free or discounted airplane tickets for himself and his "spouse (husband/wife)" once a year. Under a collective arrangement (entitled "professional guidelines"), airplane tickets (as of January 1, 1986) are given to "person reputed to be a husband/wife of an employee of the company if the couple live together in a joint household as husband and wife in every respect, but they are unable to marry lawfully."

The Respondent applied on January 21, 1988, to the Petitioner with a request to recognize his male companion for the purpose of receiving an annual free or discounted airplane ticket. In his request, the Respondent explains that he has been in a stable and long-term relationship since 1979 with another man. The relationship involves, *inter alia*, running a joint household and living together in a private apartment purchased jointly. The Respondent's request was refused.

The Respondent applied to the district labor court. [The district labor court found in favour of the Respondent. El-Al appealed to the National Labor Court, which dismissed the appeal. Both courts decided that the collective agreement did not cover a same-sex companion, but that its failure to do so violated section 2 of the Equal Employment Opportunities Law, 5748-1988, as amended in 1992.]

---

11. This translation is based on that at the Supreme Court website, http://elyon1.court.gov.il/files_eng/94/210/007/Z01/94007210.z01.htm.

12. A collective agreement is an agreement between an employer and employees that meets the requirements set out in the Collective Agreements Law, 5717-1957. A collective arrangement is a document setting out employment conditions that does not meet all the requirements of the statute. A collective arrangement, like a collective agreement, may be the source of employee rights. The differences between an agreement and an arrangement are not relevant to this case.

The petition before us addresses the validity of the decision of the National Labor Court. El-Al, the Petitioner, asks for a ruling that its refusal to give the Respondent an airplane ticket for his companion does not constitute improper discrimination under the Equal Employment Opportunities Law as amended in 1992. El-Al's contention is that the 1992 amendment to this law added a prohibition against discrimination based on sexual orientation but did not confer rights to receive benefits that an employee was not previously entitled to receive under an agreement or arrangement that predated the amendment. The Respondent argued before us that there is no reason why we should intervene in the National Labor Court's judgment, which ruled that a cause of action based on discrimination was created by the Equal Employment Opportunities Law, justifying giving airplane tickets for the Respondent's companion as of the date when the law was amended (January 2, 1992).

The Interpretive Construction

The Respondent (the flight attendant, the employee) may base his argument to receive the benefit of a free or discounted ticket for his companion on two approaches to legal construction. Under the first approach, his right is founded on the collective agreement that gives benefits to "a spouse (husband/wife)" and on the collective arrangement provision that gives a benefit to a "person reputed to be the husband/wife of an employee." Under this construction, the term "spouse" in the collective agreement and the term "reputed spouse"[13] in the collective arrangement should be interpreted in light of their purpose, and therefore read to include a spouse of the same sex and a "reputed spouse" of the same sex. The Respondent's right to receive the benefit is contractual, and it is founded on the text of the collective agreement and the collective arrangement, just like the Respondent's right to receive any other benefit. This legal approach is interpretive in nature. It is based on the intrinsic nature of the text.

The interpretive construction was rejected by the labor courts. They held that the (legal) meaning of the term reputed spouse (husband/wife) in the collective agreement does not include same-sex companions. The National Labor Court stated:

> In the case before us, the parties to the collective agreement expressly showed that they did not mean a same-sex companion. The collective agreement says "spouse (husband and wife)." The words "husband and wife" attached to the term spouse show that the parties used the term spouse in its narrow sense. It follows that this expression in the collective agreement does not include reputed spouses and same-sex companions who are indisputably not "husband and wife."

With regard to the term "person reputed to be the husband/wife" in the collective arrangement, the National Labor Court held that this does not include cohabiting persons of the same sex. The National Labor Court pointed out that the term "reputed spouses" does not appear by itself, but is accompanied by the words "as husband/wife." This use of language shows "that the intention of the drafter was not to include persons of the same sex."

The Statutory Construction

A second approach to legal construction is also available to the Respondent. This construction starts with the premise that the contractual right to receive a benefit is conferred only on a companion who is not the same sex as the employee. Under this construction, the contractual arrangement, as interpreted through the interpretive con-

---

13. The collective arrangement does not actually use the term "reputed spouse." It uses the term "reputed to be a husband/wife."

struction, is a discriminatory arrangement that is contrary to the Equal Employment Opportunities Law as amended in 1992. The remedy to be given to the Respondent as a result of this discrimination is not to nullify the contractual arrangement, a remedy that he did not request at all, but to issue an order based on the provisions of the law to correct the discrimination. The Respondent will therefore be entitled to the benefit for his companion by combining the discriminatory contractual provision with the corrective statutory provision. This construction is not interpretative. It is extrinsic to the actual text. Its existence derives from the combination of the contractual right and the statutory mandate to prevent discrimination. The resulting right of the employee arises on the day that the statutory prohibition against discrimination on grounds of sexual orientation came into force; i.e., on January 2, 1992. It may be called a statutory (or extrinsic) construction. The National Labor Court accepted this construction, and this is what El-Al is attacking before us. Analysis of this legal model must proceed in two stages: *first*, it is necessary to determine whether the contractual arrangement, the product of the interpretive construction, constitutes discrimination based on sexual orientation; *second*, it is necessary to determine what remedy should be given to an employee who has been the victim of prohibited discrimination on the basis of sexual orientation.

The Respondent did not reargue the interpretive construction before us.... I therefore presume, without deciding the issue, that the Respondent does not have a contractual right under the collective agreement and the collective arrangement to receive the benefit for his companion. On this basis, I will now examine the statutory construction in relation to two issues: whether discrimination is present and what remedy is proper. I shall begin with the first issue.

The Right to Equality and its Violation

Equality is a fundamental value in Israeli law.... The principle of equality is entrenched in Israel in a number of normative sources. First, it is a principle of case-law, the product of Israeli common law that has been developed by the courts. This principle is treated as part of the objective intent of every piece of legislation and guides its interpretation.

Second, the principle of equality is incorporated in Israeli legislation. It is first found in Israel's Declaration of Independence, which provides that the State of Israel shall treat its citizens equally "irrespective of religion, race or sex." It is also found in legislation that creates equality in specific relationships. Thus, for example, the Women's Equal Rights Law, 5711-1951, provides in section 1 that "women and men shall be subject to the same law for every legal act...." Section 42 of the Employment Service Law, 5719-1959, prohibits discrimination by the Employment Service when referring a person for employment. The Equal Remuneration for Female and Male Employees Law, 5724-1964, aims to ensure equality in employees' salaries. Special legislation is intended to allow corrective preferential treatment for women (see section 18A of the Government Corporations Law, 1975). Another law, the relevant one in this case and which we will discuss separately, is the Equal Employment Opportunities Law. This development of the law culminated in the enactment of the Basic Law: Human Dignity and Liberty, which entrenched equality as a super-legislative constitutional right, within the framework of human dignity.

Equality is not an absolute right. The human right of equality, like every other human right, is relative. Sometimes the right to equality is not completely protected. The right to equality may be lawfully restricted if this is consistent with the values of the State of Israel, is for a proper purpose, and if equality is not restricted more than necessary.

The factual premise is that people are different from one another.... [T]he principle of equality does not presume that one rule applies to everyone. It does not rule out different rules for different people. The principle of equality demands that a rule that treats people differently is justified by the nature and substance of the matter treated by the rule. The principle of equality therefore presumes the existence of objective reasons that justify distinctions in some cases. Discrimination, the opposite of equality, exists where different laws are applied to different people for reasons that are insufficient to justify a distinction between them in a free and democratic society.

Therefore a particular law will create discrimination when two individuals who are different from one another are treated differently by the law, even though the difference between the individuals does not justify different treatment in the circumstances. Discrimination is the result of arbitrariness, injustice and unreasonableness.

As we have seen, the contractual regime at El-Al gives a male or female employee a right to receive the benefit of a free or discounted airplane ticket for a wife or husband or for a reputed spouse, provided that they are of the opposite sex. Does this constitute discrimination against a companion of the same sex? As we have seen, the test for equal and discriminatory treatment is the question whether the difference in the sex of the companion is relevant to the issue. This relevance is examined on the criteria of arbitrariness, fairness and justice. The basis for giving a benefit to an employee for a spouse or a reputed spouse is the assumption that it is appropriate to give a benefit of an airline ticket to the person with whom the employee lives and shares a common household, from whom the employee is separated when the employee leaves on flights and to whom the employee returns. This is the criterion that both a spouse and a reputed spouse have in common. The purpose of the benefit is not to strengthen the institution of marriage. Indeed, El-Al gives the benefit to an employee living with another person, even when that other person is lawfully married to someone else. The grounds for providing the benefit is therefore cohabitation for a certain period, specified in the collective arrangement, which is evidence of a firm social unit based on a shared life. In this context, it seems clear to me that denying a same-sex companion this benefit amounts to discrimination and an infringement of the value of equality. Indeed, the only reason for denying the benefit to a same-sex companion is sexual orientation. There is no other reason. This difference is not at all relevant to the issue before us (supporting a firm social unit, based on a shared life). In the case before us, we are dealing with a distinction that is arbitrary and unfair. Is parting from a same-sex companion easier than parting from a companion of the opposite sex? Is the shared life of persons of the same sex different from the shared life of heterosexual couples with regard to the commonality and harmony of the relationship and the conduct of a social unit?

One might argue that the shared life of persons of opposite sexes, whether as husband and wife or as reputed spouses, is so different in its character from the shared life of persons of the same sex that any legal regime giving a benefit to the former relationship does not discriminate against the latter relationship. Although this argument seems to me problematic, I am prepared to reserve judgment, since the question that we must ask is not whether one relationship is different in any way from the other relationship. As stated, I am prepared to assume that in various social contexts this difference does indeed exist. The question that we must ask is whether the difference in the relationship is relevant to the issue before us. The issue before us is the social unit, the shared life that in El-Al's opinion justifies giving a benefit to an employee in the form of an airplane ticket that will enable him to take with him the person with whom he cohabits. In this respect, distinguishing between a shared life between persons of different sexes and a shared life between persons of the same sex is clear and blatant discrimination.

Discrimination on the Basis of Sexual Orientation

We have seen that giving a benefit to a permanent employee for a spouse or recognized companion of the opposite sex and not giving the same benefit for a same-sex companion amounts to a violation of equality. What is the nature of this discrimination? All discrimination is prohibited, but some types are more serious than others. The severity of the discrimination is determined by the severity of the infringement of the principle of equality. Thus, for example, we consider discrimination on the basis of race, religion, nationality, language, ethnic group and age to be particularly serious. In this framework, the Israeli legal system attaches great importance to the need to guarantee equality between the sexes and to prevent discrimination on the basis of sex. It may be said that the discrimination in the appeal before us is based on improper considerations of sex. Conversely it may be argued that discrimination on the basis of sex does not exist, since the same benefit is conferred on male and female employees. This argument, in itself, does not strike me as convincing. However I do not need to decide the issue, since there can, I think, be no doubt that the discrimination in this case is based on the "sexual orientation" of the employee. Discrimination against homosexuals and lesbians is improper. It is contrary to equality. This emerges clearly from the provisions of the Equal Employment Opportunities Law. This law, as amended in the Equal Employment Opportunities Law (Amendment), states in section 2:

(a) An employer shall not discriminate between his employees, or between candidates for employment on the basis of their sex, sexual orientation, personal status or their being parents with respect to any of the following:

(1) hiring;

(2) work conditions of employment;

(3) advancement;

(4) training or professional studies;

(5) dismissal or severance pay.

(b) For the purposes of subsection (a), imposing irrelevant requirements on an employee shall also be regarded as discrimination.

(c) Discrimination does not exist under this section when it is required by the character or nature of the job or position.

In explaining the provision about the prohibition of discrimination on the basis of sexual orientation, the chairwoman of the Labor and Welfare Committee, Mrs. O. Namir, stated, "I hope that adopting the proposed law will contribute towards treating men and women equally, regardless of their sexual orientation, allowing them to live according to their sexual orientation as equal citizens in every respect, and affording them the legal protection enjoyed by every other group."

This statutory provision does not deny the differences between human beings. These differences are natural. This provision states that the sexual orientation of persons shall not be relevant in employment, unless this is required by the nature of the job. With regard to conditions of employment, the employer must be impartial to employees' sexual orientation. The employer must determine the conditions of employment only in view of the criteria required by the nature of the job.... Consider *A*, a permanent employee of El-Al, who shares his life for several years with a woman *B*. They cohabit and run a common household, as required by El-Al for complying with the conditions of a reputed spouse. *A* is entitled to an airplane ticket for *B*. Now consider *A*, who lives in the same way with a man *C*. They too cohabit and run a common household. *A* is not entitled to an airplane ticket for *C*. How can this difference be explained? Does the one carry out his job as an employee differently from the other? The only explanation lies in *A*'s sexual orientation. This amounts to discrimination in conditions of employment because of sexual orientation. No explanation has been given that might justify this discriminatory treatment. There is nothing characterizing the nature of the job or the position that justifies this unequal treatment (see section 2(c) of the Equal Employment Opportunities Law). To be sure, it is possible that El-Al thinks that an employee who lives with a same-sex companion behaves improperly. It is possible that someone at El-Al thinks that this joint lifestyle should not be encouraged. We need not examine this argument on an ethical level. Whether or not we agree with it, it does not amount to a justification that negates the existence of the discrimination.

The Remedy for a Violation of the Right to Equality

I have therefore reached the conclusion that the legal regime created by the collective agreement and the collective arrangement, with regard to the benefit conferred on an employee to receive a free or discounted airplane tickets for a spouse or reputed spouse of the opposite sex, discriminates against an employee living with a same-sex companion. Now we must turn to the second question requiring a decision, namely the remedy to which an employee who has suffered discrimination is entitled. Case-law has established that a discriminatory contractual regime may support a claim that the provision in the contract is contrary to public policy and is therefore invalid. This invalidity may cause the whole contract to be invalid. In most cases, there is no reason to invalidate the whole contract, and it is sufficient to invalidate the illegal part by severing it from the lawful part (see sections 14 and 31 of the Contracts (General Part) Law, 1973).... This technique is not possible in the case before us. Indeed, had the collective agreement and collective arrangement provided that a permanent employee is entitled to a benefit for a companion, except a companion of the same sex, it would have been possible to strike down the limiting provision, and so re-establish equality. But the contractual text in our case is different. It does not allow operating on the body of the text and severing the healthy part from the unhealthy part. What, then, is the remedy to which the Petitioner is entitled?

As we have seen, a possible remedy is voidance of the contractual arrangement regarding the benefit. The result, from the Respondent's perspective, will be a case of "Let me die with the Philistines" (Judges 16:30):[14] the Respondent will not receive a benefit, but neither will recognized companions of the opposite sex. This outcome is not reasonable in the circumstances. Why should recognized companions of opposite sexes suffer a material loss? What wrong have they done? The National Labor Court rightly pointed out that the Petitioner himself did not seek this remedy.

The appropriate remedy in this situation is to confer the benefit also on same-sex cohabiters.

[The] principle of equality applies, by virtue of the express provisions of the Equal Employment Opportunities Law, also in private law. It is not only a principle of public

---

14. This is reference a statement by Samson. God had endowed Samson with unusual strength, attributed to his having dedicated his life to God, a dedication shown by the fact that Samson never cut his hair. After Delilah cut off his hair, he lost his strength and was captured and imprisoned by the Philistines. While in prison, his hair grew back. The Philistines, unaware of his returned strength, brought him to their temple and placed him between two supporting pillars. He pushed out the pillars, bringing the building down on the Philistines, but also on himself.

law. It obliges every employer not to discriminate against any of his employees in the fields of private law. Indeed, with regard to the prohibition of discrimination because of sexual orientation, just as with regard to other kinds of discrimination, the law establishes a mandate that obliges the employer. By virtue of this normative mandate, which is of supreme status with regard to collective agreements and arrangements, the employer is forbidden to discriminate against any of his employees with regard to conditions of employment. When a contractual arrangement drawn up by the employer involves prohibited discrimination, the contract is tainted with illegality. It may be voided by virtue of the provisions relating to invalid contracts. To prevent it being voided, we may demand, as an alternative remedy, that the employer refrains from the prohibited discrimination. This is achieved by compelling the employer to confer the benefit on the employee who is the victim of the discrimination. This does not change the agreement between the parties. We do not thereby read into the contract what is not there. We thereby merely remove the discrimination and comply with the normative mandate not to discriminate. Indeed, the basic fact is the discriminatory contractual arrangement. The contents of this are determined by the parties to the contract, and they control it and can change it. As long as the discriminatory contractual arrangement remains unchanged, the supreme normative mandate, which derives from law [that creates a non-waiverable right] and compels the employer to act in compliance with the principle of equality.... By virtue of this normative supremacy, the contractual regime must be modified to comply with the principle of equality.... This modification does not require voiding the existing contractual arrangement. This modification is achieved by conferring a benefit, which originates not in the contractual arrangement but in the principle of equality that extends the contractual arrangement to equivalent situations, on the class that is the victim of discrimination. This extension is suitable for the contractual model. It adds a small group of beneficiaries and does not therefore impose a significant budgetary burden. Justice is done, and justice is seen to be done.

The petition is denied. The case is remanded to the district labor court, as stated in the judgment of the National Labor Court. The Petitioner shall pay the costs of the first Respondent in a total amount of NIS 10,000.

Justice Y. Kedmi:

[Justice Kedmi would uphold the contract on the ground that society distinguishes between married couples and reputed spouses on the one hand and same-sex companions on the other, and that it is permissible to follow this distinction in granting contractual benefits.]

Justice D. Dorner:

My colleague, Associate Chief Justice Barak, presumed, in the absence of any contrary argument by the Respondent, that the Respondent's right does not derive from the collective arrangement itself. In Justice Barak's opinion, the Respondent's right derives from the statutory amendment, which embodies the principle of equality and the prohibition on discrimination against employees on the grounds of their sexual orientation.

I agree with the result reached by the Associate Chief Justice. However, in my opinion, the Respondent's right derives not only from the Equal Opportunities Law, but also from the general principle of equality that has, for some time, been a part of our labor law.

The law in Israel regarding homosexuals reflects the social changes that have occurred over the years.

Male homosexual relations were, in the past, included in the offence of deviations from nature, an offence punishable by imprisonment of ten years. This prohibition was never enforced ... and the criminal prohibition was repealed [in 1988].

This formal repeal reflects the current position of Israeli society that the law (as opposed to religion) should be indifferent to the sexual orientation of a person, so long as that person does not harm anyone. There is widespread consensus that homosexuals should not be restricted or subject to discrimination. The amendment to the Equal Opportunities Law reflects this approach.

The proper test is therefore to consider the relevance of the sexual orientation to the benefit conferred on the spouse. The functional test meets this requirement. Under this test, no distinction should be made between homosexual couples and heterosexual couples, if the spousal relationship between the spouses of the same sex meets the criteria that realize the purpose for which the right or benefit is conferred. By contrast, when the sexual orientation is relevant to realizing the purpose of the benefit, for instance if the purpose is to encourage having children, withholding the benefit from a same-sex spouse will not constitute discrimination.

Public authorities are clearly required to act in a manner consistent with the principle of equality. This principle also applies in the field of labor relations in general. The employer's contractual freedom retreats when faced with the employee's right to equality. The legislation prohibiting discrimination in labor relations reflects this principle, but did not create it.

In our case, the airplane ticket was not meant for a spouse who is married to the employee, and in any event the purpose of the benefit was not to encourage a lifestyle within a traditional family framework. The benefit is given to the employee for the spouse with whom he shares his life *de facto*. Indeed, although the Petitioner did not intend the arrangement to apply to same-sex spouses, the sex of the spouse is not relevant to the purpose behind granting the benefit.

In Israel, benefits ... may be so substantial that they lead to the doubling of the salary. A significant part of these benefits, such as pension plans and life insurance, are provided for the spouse, including the reputed spouse, and to deny benefits to a spouse with whom a homosexual lives is tantamount to reducing his salary. Consequently denying these benefits is discrimination against the employee himself.

In the case before us, denying the benefit to the Respondent would lead to a reduction of his salary in the amount of the price of the ticket, and there is no justification for this.

For these reasons, I agree that the petition should be denied.

Comment

The statutory provision that formed the basis of Associate Chief Justice Barak's opinion in the above case was later amended several times. This is the current version of the statute:

Israeli Statute

Equal Employment Opportunities Law, 5748-1988

2. Prohibition on Discrimination

(a) An employer shall not discriminate against its workers or applicants for work for reasons of their sex, sexual orientation, personal status, pregnancy, fertility treatments, in-vitro fertilization treatments, their being parents, age, race, religion, nationality, country of origin, views, political party, or their service in the military reserves, their being called up for reserve military duty, or their expected reserve military duty..., including for reasons of the expected frequency or duration of their reserve military duty, as to any of the following:

(1) hiring;

(2) work conditions;

(3) advancement;

(4) training or professional studies;

(5) dismissal or severance pay;

(6) retirement benefits and payments provided to a worker.

Comment

In *El Al Israel Airlines Ltd. v. Danielowitz* the airline claimed that the contract granting free tickets to opposite-sex spouses could not be held invalid for violation of the Equal Employment Opportunities Law, 5748-1988, because the contract in question was entered before the enactment of the statutory provision prohibiting discrimination on the basis of sexual orientation. Associate Chief Justice Barak's opinion responds to this claim by ruling that the contract violated the overarching norm of equality. It drew this norm from the Basic Law: Human Dignity and Freedom, from Israeli case law, and from a variety of statutes that protect equality. The opinion then looked to the amendment to the Equal Employment Opportunities Law to find that the norm applies to people of different sexual orientation.

Associate Chief Justice Barak's opinion did not rest the principle of equality on the Basic Law alone for three reasons. First, at the time of the decision, the Supreme Court had not yet held that the Basic Law: Human Dignity and Freedom provides protection against discrimination. The Basic Law does not explicitly mention equality as a protected value, nor does it explicitly prohibit discrimination. The cases recognizing equality as a protected right under the Basic Law came more than a decade later. These cases, and the reasons for the slow recognition of equality as a basic right, were discussed in chapter 8. Second, even if it were recognized that the Basic Law: Human Dignity and Freedom protected against discrimination, it would be necessary to make the further finding that it protected against discrimination on the basis of sexual orientation. Third, it would be necessary to find that that Basic Law provided protection against discrimination by a private party, or that the parties to the collective contract and collective agreement were of sufficiently public nature that the Basic Law's protections applied to them. The opinion avoided all of these issues by basing the principle of equality on other grounds.

When it came to the matter of remedies, the opinion returned to the statute, which applies by its terms to private agreements. The collective contract and agreement are reformed to comply with the statute, which prohibits discrimination based on sexual orientation. This begs the question of whether it prohibits discrimination based on sexual orientation in contracts formed before that prohibition was added to the statute. Inherently the opinion seems to mean that the statute prevents the employer right now from acting contrary to its provisions, so that the employer must provide a benefit to the employee even if that benefit is not required under the agreement and arrangement.

Justice Dorner reached the same result as Associate Chief Justice Barak, but expressed an additional reason for doing so.

Justice Dorner directly addressed the issue of whether the principle of equality applies to collective labor agreements or whether it applies only to public authorities. She ruled that the requirement of equality applies in the labor relations field. Given the historical nature of labor relations in Israel, with the Histadrut being such a large union, holding such extensive power over the Israeli economy, and maintaining close ties to the Labor Party, this ruling is not surprising and does not require a broader finding that equality requirements apply to all private activity.

Justice Dorner's opinion suggested that in 1994, discrimination based on sexual orientation was already socially unacceptable in Israel. This is arguably not an accurate picture of Israeli society at the time. Since then, social acceptance of gays and lesbians has increased greatly, but negative attitudes still persist and are influenced by religious values in some segments of both the Jewish and Muslim communities. Nonetheless a vibrant gay life is found in Israel's major city, Tel Aviv, and openly gay people live throughout the country.

Justice Dorner's opinion contains the following statement: "By contrast, when the sexual orientation is relevant to realizing the purpose of the benefit, for instance if the purpose is to encourage having children, withholding the benefit from a same-sex spouse will not constitute discrimination." This statement presumes that same-sex couples will not have children. Almost twenty years later, it is not uncommon in Israel for same-sex couples to have children as well as legally protected rights relating to parenthood.

Several statutes, including the Equal Employment Opportunities Law, prohibit discrimination against women in various contexts. Because Israel allowed women in its military before most other countries did so, and because the country had a female prime minister as early as 1969 when Golda Meir began to lead the Government, people outside of Israel may think that discrimination against women has not been a problem. The perceived need for the statutes in this area, and the cases enforcing them, show that there has been a problem.

Another persistent area of discrimination has been against Arabs. Again, several laws apply to the matter. One debate about legal issues relating to discrimination against Arabs involves the practice of many employers who prefer hiring workers who have served in the Israeli army or who have completed national service. Some argue that this is a patriotic position supporting service for the country. Furthermore, employers benefit from both the skills and discipline which potential employees have learned in their military service. Others argue that such a requirement for hiring discriminates against Arabs, who, for the most part, do not serve. As Ultra-Orthodox Jews, who also do not serve, have begun to enter the workforce, they also claim discrimination by employers who impose a service requirement. The debate is ongoing.

Question

4. Should employers be allowed to give preference in hiring to military veterans?

Chapter 20

Health Care Law

A. Introduction to Components of the Health Care System

Israel by law provides universal health care to all residents of the state, both citizens and non-citizens. The main components of the system are:

1. Health services provided by the state that are available to everyone and that are either free or offered at minimal cost

2. Health services included in the basket of services, provided by one of the four health funds and paid through universal mandatory health insurance

3. Health services not in the basket of services, provided by health funds or private providers and paid through optional supplementary insurance or by the patient

4. Health care in the military provided free to all military personnel on duty

B. Health Services Provided by the State

Under the National Health Insurance Law, 5754-1994, the government provides several types of health services: preventative health care, geriatric care, hospitalization for severely disabled youth, some mental health services, and medical equipment. Most but not all of these services require some copayment from the person receiving treatment.

The most prominent of the state-provided health services is the preventative services provided to children and pregnant women. Public health clinics run by the ministry of health are located throughout the country and are supplemented in Tel Aviv and Jerusalem by clinics run by the municipalities. Called *Tipat Chalav*, meaning *a drop of milk*,[1] the main business of the clinics is to provide preventative health care to all children. Parents pay a fee of about $150 per child that covers all vaccinations, routine checkups as to de-

---

[1]. The name of the clinics derives from the name of the neonatal clinics operated by the Women's International Zionist Organization during the period of the British Mandate. The clinics served many poor women, who were too malnourished to nurse their babies. To provide the infants with adequate nutrition, the clinics distributed clean, pasteurized cows' milk and came to be called by the name Tipat Chalav, which reflected this practice. When the state was established and took over the operation of the clinics, the name was retained, even after nursing again became widespread and safe infant formula became widely available.

velopment, hearing, vision, communications, and growth, and other routine health screenings through completion of high school. The clinics, staffed by nurses and physicians, take care of children until they enter school; after that, the health services are provided in the schools. The clinics serve the entire population, not only the poor and not only those in the national health insurance program. The clinics do not provide care for illness; this is provided through the health funds.

The public health clinics also provide basic prenatal care, although most women choose to have prenatal care through their health funds, with the cost covered by their health insurance.

The state has a constitutional obligation to provide a very basic level of health care. In the case of HCJ 3071/05 *Louzon v. Government of Israel* (July 28, 2008), set out in chapter 8, the Supreme Court ruled that the rights to human dignity and to bodily integrity, both protected by the Basic Law: Human Dignity and Freedom, include the right to provision of basic health services. In HCJ 1104/04 *Solomtin v. Minister of Health* (June 27, 2011), the Supreme Court confirmed that this was a right of everyone in Israel, and not just of citizens or residents.

Israeli Statute

Patients' Rights Law, 5756-1996

2. Definitions

"Medical emergency"—circumstances in which a person is in immediate danger to his life or in which there is an immediate danger that a serious, irreversible disability will be caused if the person does not receive urgent medical care; ...

3. The Right to Medical Treatment

(a) Anyone needing medical treatment is entitled to receive it in accordance with the law and with the conditions and arrangements practiced, from time to time, in the Israeli health system.

(b) In a medical emergency, a person has an unconditional right to receive urgent medical care.

Comment

Section 3(b) of the Patients' Rights Law, along with the National Health Insurance Law specifications on health services provided by the state, probably fulfills the state's constitutional obligation to provide basic medical care.

C. Health Services Included in Basket of Services, Provided by the Health Funds

The following provisions from the National Health Insurance Law set out the basic format of the national health insurance system. The cases set out afterwards refer to many of these provisions. The first case that immediately follows the statute includes a narrative explanation of the philosophy of the system.

Israeli Statue

National Health Insurance Law, 5754-1994

1. National Health Insurance

National health insurance under this law shall be based on the principles of justice, equality, and mutual assistance.

3. The Right to Health Services

(a) Every resident is entitled to health services under this law unless the person is entitled to them under other law.

(b) The state is responsible for funding the basket of health services from the sources set out in section 13.

(c) A health fund is responsible to its members to provide all the health services to which they are entitled under this law.

(d) Health services that are included in the health services basket shall be provided within Israel, as indicated by medical judgment, at a reasonable level of quality, within a reasonable time, and at a reasonable distance from the residence of the insured, all within the framework of the sources of funding available to the health funds under section 13.

(e) Health services shall be provided in a manner that preserves human dignity, protects privacy, and maintains medical confidentiality.

7. Basket of Health Services

(a) In this law—

"Basket of health services" means the list in section 7A [regarding health services that must be provided in the workplace] and in the second and third appendix of health services that shall be provided to the insured ... subject to the limitations in section 8;

"Basic basket of services" means

(1) Services that were provided by the Histadrut health fund to its members as of January 1, 1994, ... as detailed in the second appendix;

(2) Health services that were provided by the state as of January 1, 1994, as detailed in the third appendix, subject to the conditions and payments customary at that time, which shall be published by the minister of health;

(5) Listed medications and payments for them as customary on January 1, 1994, through the Histadrut health fund, which shall be listed in an order;

(b) The basket of basic services is the basket of health services.

8. Changes in Health Services and Payments

(a) The minister of health is authorized by order to make changes in the basket of health services set out in the second and third appendices to this law, provided that the minister shall not make changes that reduce the services provided in the basket or that increase its cost.

(b) The minister of health, with the agreement of the minister of finance and with the approval of the Government, may, by order, add to the basket of services set out in the second and third appendices and, with the approval of the Labor and Welfare Committee of the Knesset, may reduce the services.... Such additions or reductions shall apply to the basket of services and the payments to all health funds.

(c) Any order under subsection (a) or (b) shall set out which health services shall be provided subject to a copayment and the rate of the copayment, and which shall be provided without a copayment.

(d) The minister of health is authorized, with the agreement of the minister of finance and the Labor and Welfare Committee of the Knesset, to change the amount of the co-payments for health services included in the basket of basic health services....

(e) Health services shall not be added to the basket of services without a copayment or without a copayment that is lower than the cost of the service unless a source of funding additional to those listed in section 13 is available, or unless the funds are available due to the termination of some other service or due to some other service becoming less expensive.

9. Cost of the Basket of Health Services

(a) The minister of health and the minister of finance shall determine, at the time this law enters into force, with agreement of the Labor and Welfare Committee of the Knesset, the cost of the basket of health services....

(b)

(1) The cost of the basket to the funds shall be updated each year based on the rate of the increase of the health cost increase indicator published by the Central Bureau of Statistics; the components of the health cost increase indicator shall be as set out in the fifth appendix.

(3) The minister of health and the minister of finance are authorized, upon the recommendation of the Health Council and with the agreement of the Labor and Welfare Committee of the Knesset, to change by order the components of the indicator of health costs, or to update the cost of the basket of health services to the funds due to demographic changes in the population.

13. Sources of Funding

(a) The sources of funding of health services provided under this law shall be:

(1) Health insurance premiums ... and [other funds received under various statutes by the National Insurance Institute];

(3) The annual allocation to the minister of health under [the National Insurance Law];

(5) Additional funds from the state budget as determined each year in the annual budget law and that shall be the amount needed for fully funding the cost of the basket after taking into account the amount that the funds receive under clause (6) ...;

(6) Copayments received by the health funds for health services provided and as allowed [under this law].

[The second appendix to the statute sets out a detailed and extensive list of the services that must be provided and the copayments required for various services.]

Israeli Case

Solomtin v. Minister of Health
HCJ 11044/04 (June 27, 2011)

[The case was brought on behalf of several children who were living in Israel but who had the status of neither citizens nor residents. Their rights and those of their parents to live in Israel was in dispute and was under consideration in the relevant governmental agencies. The parents claimed that the children had a right to all health services provided in the National Health Insurance Law. The children were already receiving basic health services provided by the government that were not restricted to residents and some additional health services through a special arrangement of the government with one of the health funds, but the parents sought the right to the full range of services provided by the health funds.]

Justice (Emeritus) A. Procaccia:

Israel's National Health Insurance Law

The National Health Insurance Law provides the main mechanism for public health insurance in Israel. It [came into effect] in 1995, as a result of the recommendations of the Government Commission of Inquiry on the Functioning and Efficiency of the Israeli Health System, which was headed by Justice S. Netanyahu[2] and which was established against the background of the crisis in the health system and the need to reform it.[3]

The National Health Insurance Law introduced substantial changes in the structure, organization, and operation of the health insurance system in Israel by delineating new provisions on the rights of the insured, the relationship between the health funds and the insured, and the relationship between the health funds and the state. Prior to enactment of the law, health insurance was voluntary. Every resident could register as a member of one of the health funds and receive its services, but the law did not require anyone to carry health insurance. An uninsured person could receive health services, but had to pay for those services. The National Health Insurance Law changed this by establishing the requirement that all residents of Israel carry health insurance and by establishing sources of funding for the public health system.

The National Health Insurance Law is part of the social security system of the state and is based on "principles of justice, equality, and mutual assistance" (section 1 of the statute). The principle of mutual assistance is expressed in part by the fact that the amount of the insurance payment is based on the economic ability of the insured. The rates are progressive, with a ceiling on the maximum payment. In contrast, health services are provided based on need and are divorced from the ability to pay.

The central objective of the National Health Insurance Law is to assure that all residents of Israel obtain comprehensive, publicly funded health services of a reasonable quality. For this purpose, the statute defines a system of relationships between three parties: the public, the health funds, and the state. Residents of the state are entitled to health services under the law, with each resident obtaining those services through the health fund of which the resident is a member. The health funds have the responsibility to provide their members with all the health services listed in the statute. The state is responsible for funding health services from the sources identified in the statute.

Health services are to be provided as indicated by medical judgment, of reasonable quality, and provided within a reasonable time and at a reasonable distance from the insured's home. They are to be provided in a manner that preserves human dignity and protects privacy and medical confidentiality. The medical services that are provided are

---

2. Justice Shoshana Netanyahu served as a Justice of the Supreme Court from 1982 to 1993. She served as head of this commission from 1988 to 1990, while still sitting on the Supreme Court. Benjamin Netanyahu, who was later the prime minister of Israel, is her nephew by marriage.

3. Prior to the National Health Insurance Law, the national labor union, the Histadrut, offered health insurance through its own health fund, which was the largest in the country, and was open only to Histadrut members. Some Israelis joined the Histadrut mainly in order to get health insurance. Some Israelis had access to health care through other sources, but some had no health insurance at all.

circumscribed in the *basket of health services*. The existence of this basket is an expression of the basic understanding that the public health system cannot supply, and is not intended to supply, all medical services that the insured may want at the optimal scope and level.

[The Court held that the Petitioners were not covered by the National Health Insurance Law and that any constitutional rights to basic health care they may have were provided by the health care they were receiving from the government and through the government's special arrangement with one of the health funds.]

Comment

The Israeli health funds, which are similar to American health maintenance organizations, are private, non-profit entities that are heavily regulated. There are four health funds and residents of Israel are free to join the one they choose. A health fund cannot reject a resident as a member due to ill health or for any other reason. The health funds are all required by law to provide a mandated list of services at a mandated cost and to substantially subsidize the cost of all medications in the health basket of medications.

Every person must join a health fund. This requirement is enforced through administrative designation of membership for those who do not join voluntarily. If a person does not sign up with one of the health funds, the minister of health assigns the person membership in one of the funds, with each fund to get a proportion of the assigned individuals equal to the proportion of the population that belongs to that fund. National Health Fund Law, 5754-1994, section 4(b).

Health insurance premiums are paid through a *health tax*, which is deducted from wages and is based on income. The health tax is collected by the National Insurance Institute, the rough equivalent of the US Social Security Administration. Insurance is not through the employer, as is much health insurance in the United States, even though the employer in Israel collects the tax. Just as employers in both Israel and the United States collect income tax from their employees and turn it over to the proper government authority, employers in Israel collect and turn over health taxes. Residents who are independent contractors and those who are not working also pay the health tax. As of January 2011 the minimum health tax stood at about $24 a month. For those who work, whether they are employees or self-employed, the tax as of the same date was 3.1 percent of the salary up to 60 percent of the average annual salary and 5 percent of the salary above that amount. Thus the rates are income related and are slightly progressive. The monthly health tax on an average salary, which is about $2300 a month, is $94. The maximum monthly health tax is $994, paid by those earning $20,400 or more a month, which is a very high salary in Israel. Each individual pays the health tax, so typically two people in a family pay the tax.

Several groups of people are exempt from paying the health tax. These include minor children, who are automatically covered by a parent's payments, enlisted soldiers, most prisoners, and married women who do not work outside the home if their spousces are insured. New immigrants and eighteen-year-olds whose military enlistment has been delayed have a statutory exemption for up to twelve months if they have no or minimal income.

In HCJ 1046/09 *Mani v. National Insurance Institute* (Apr. 29, 2010), the Supreme Court ruled that the provision in the law exempting married women from paying the health tax did not constitute unconstitutional or otherwise impermissible discrimination. The Court found that the provision was based on a similar and long-standing provision as to National Insurance premiums; women not working outside the home are also exempt from paying these premiums. The Court noted that the distinction between men and women might violate the principle of equality. To the extent that that equality is protected by the Basic Law: Human Dignity and Freedom, this might then be a violation of that Basic Law. Because the Basic Law is of constitutional status, the statutory provisions exempting women from paying the health and national insurance premiums might be unconstitutional. This was not so, however, because the Basic Law: Human Dignity and Freedom, section 10, preserves the legality of statutory provisions that pre-existed the Basic Law. The Court ruled that the health tax was such a protected pre-existing provision. Nonetheless the Court called on the Knesset to reconsider the matter. The Knesset has not changed the exemption. Its maintenance is probably due to tradition and to a widespread perception that many women, especially poorer women, do not have good employment opportunities and deserve some extra support in the form of the health tax exemption. Nonetheless, the exemption is not income-dependent.

The size of the health insurance premium, expressed in this health tax, is unrelated to the benefits received. Everyone receives the same coverage for the basic health tax, even though those with high wages pay higher premiums. The petitioners in the next case challenged the legality of this arrangement, and the Court, in response, explored both its justification and its legality.

Israeli Case

Lahav-Association of Independent Contractors and Businesses in Israel v. Attorney General
HCJ 6304/09 (Sept. 2, 2010)

[An amendment to the National Health Law raised the ceiling for payments of the health tax. Prior to the amendment, the health tax was assessed at a set rate on incomes up to five times the national average salary. The amendment provided that the tax would be assessed at the same rate on incomes up to ten times the national average salary. A similar change was made to assessments for National Insurance, the Israeli equivalent of Social Security. No change was made in the benefits under either system. In other words, people with incomes between five and ten times the average salary paid more for health tax and for National Insurance payments, but did not receive any increase in benefits. The petitioners challenged the amendment on several grounds, including on the grounds that it violated the principle of equality. The Court discussed this claim as to the National Insurance payments, but the same discussion would apply to the health tax.]

Justice A. Procaccia:

[It is claimed that] there is discrimination between those with a moderate income, who earn up to five times the national average income, and those with a high income, who earn more than five times the national average. This claim of discrimination does not relate to the fact that there is a ceiling on the income subject to insurance payments, or to the change of the ceiling in the statutory amendment, but rather to the change in the relationship between the amount of the insurance paid and the amount of the benefits received. For those with moderate incomes, both the insurance payments required and the benefits received are calculated on the basis of the person's income. For those with higher incomes, the ceiling for calculating the payments required is ten times the average income while the ceiling for calculating the benefits remains at five times the national average.

The claim of discrimination should be denied. First, this claim is based on the assumption that there must be a correlation between the income ceiling for the purpose of calculating the insurance payments and the income ceiling for the purpose of calculating the benefits paid. This assumption is not among those principles on which the Israeli system of social insurance is founded.... [T]he social insurance system does not require either a full or even partial connection between the level of insurance payments collected by the National Insurance Institute and the level of benefits paid to various types of beneficiaries.[4] National Insurance is mandated by statute. The rates are also based on the statute and are calculated as a percentage of the income of the insured. The various types of benefits covered by the National Insurance system have different types of relationships between the amount of the insurance payments collected from the insured and the amount of benefits paid. In some cases, both the payment and the benefits relate to the income of the insured, but in others this is not so, and the rate of the benefits is not at all related to income of the insured or to the payments made by the insured. Even where the calculation of benefits is related to the income of the insured, there is no necessary connection between the way income is calculated for the purpose of setting the amount of the payment and the way income is calculated for the purpose of setting the amount of the benefit.

The system of basing payments in principle on the ability to pay and benefits on the need, and here we mean basic need and not more than that, is likely to lead to using different ways of calculating the relationship of the payments and the benefits to income, and there need be no correlation between these different ways. Calculation of insurance payments as they relate to income is based, as we have said, on the economic ability of the insured. Calculation of a benefit that is meant to replace income is based partially on the income of the insured, but also takes into account the basic needs of the insured (and not needs beyond those) and the ability of the Institute to support the benefit, based on actuarial measures. This approach separates National Insurance from private voluntary commercial insurance, for which there is a structural relationship between the amount of the premiums, calculated on an actuarial basis of risks and probabilities, and the rate of insurance benefit paid if the event insured for occurs. The National Insurance system is built on the conceptual basis of collection of insurance payments according to the ability to pay, in order to fund benefits designed to provide basic social insurance to meet needs in various areas. The idea of social insurance is based on the idea that, on the one hand, there should be a pool of sources of insurance funds and, on the other hand, the needs and priorities for benefits should be defined, without requiring an individualized connection between the amount of payments and the amount of benefits. Even where there was a connection between payments and benefits in the past, there is no obligation to maintain the same connection. Therefore a change that weakens the relationship between the two is possible, so long as the change serves the broad social objectives of providing social insurance to the entire population and of paying benefits, whether they are benefits meant to replace income or benefits for another purpose.

Even though the amendment to the statute diminishes the link between the amount of the insurance payment by those with high incomes and the amount of income-replacement benefits to which they are entitled, the amendment does not violate the basic system of social insurance but, rather, is consistent with it. This is a system of mutual assistance based on ability on one side and need on the other, without any necessary connection between the two. The fact that the increase in the income ceiling for the purposes

---

4. National Insurance beneficiaries include pensioners, the disabled, soldiers on reserve duty, women on maternity leave, minor orphaned children, and others.

of calculating insurance payments was not accompanied by a parallel increase in the income ceiling for the purpose of calculating the income-replacement benefits does not violate the basic structure of the system; it is in fact consistent with it.

Against this background, we consider whether principles of discrimination require that people of moderate incomes and people of higher incomes be treated the same way. For the former groups, the new amendment maintains the relationship between the income ceiling for the purpose of insurance payments and the income ceiling for the purpose of benefits. For the latter group, the amendment undercuts that relationship. The answer is that there is no requirement that the two groups be treated in the same way. The distinction between the two groups relates to their economic capability. The income of the first group is up to five times the national average, and the income of the second is higher than that. There is a substantial difference in the economic capability of the members of the different groups and in their ability to bear the burden of the insurance payments. The statutory amendment imposes an increased burden of insurance payments on those in the second group by increasing the income ceiling on which the payments are calculated. In contrast, because the income-replacement benefits are not meant to cover all income lost if a covered event occurs, but only to provide for basic needs, and because the objective was to increase the source of funding for national insurance and not to reduce the funding, the income ceiling for calculating the benefits was left as it was. The change in insurance payments, based on the ability to pay, did not require a parallel change in calculation of the benefits. The basic needs of the insured did not change as a result of the increase in insurance payments, but remained as they had been, so that the relationship between insurance payments and the benefits does not require equal treatment in the case before us.

In this case, the distinction between the two groups is based on different income levels of the insured and the objective abilities of those in different social-economic classes to contribute their share to the funding of social insurance for all citizens of the state. In fact, the distinction between insured individuals based on their incomes contributes to achieving substantive equality in the social insurance system, and it is an accepted distinction in every progressive tax system and system of required payments based on the ability of the citizen on one side and on provision of social services on the other. Basing the burden of paying on the ability to pay and the right to receive on the basis of need, as in the social insurance system, is essentially a system of substantive equality, even if the actual payments and benefits differ from group to group.... Therefore there is no discrimination in the system which the Petitioners challenge.

Comment

The Court in *Lahav-Association of Independent Contractors and Business in Israel v. Attorney General* went on to reject a claim of discrimination based on inequality between those with incomes below the ceiling and those with incomes above the ceiling. Those in the former group were obligated to make insurance payments based on all of their income; those in the latter group, only on that portion of the income below the ceiling. The Court held that the inequality in treatment of the two groups was permitted because the amendment to the statute met the requirements of the limitation clause, largely because the difference in harm the law caused to the equality interests of the two groups was not so great as to make the law violate the principle of proportionality. The Court seemed unsympathetic to the claim of the wealthy (those with incomes just below the new ceiling) that they were not treated as well as the very wealthy (those with incomes above the new ceiling).

The analysis of the Court applied to the National Insurance payments, which are like Social Security payments in the United States. The justification for allowing the disconnect between the premium amounts and the benefits applies to the health insurance system as well. In the National Insurance system, everyone makes a payment that is a percentage of income, except that no payments are made on income that exceeds a specified ceiling. The structure of the National Insurance payments is much like the structure of the payments for the health tax, except that the rates for National Insurance payments are different and, for employees (as opposed to independent contractors), the employer bears a portion of the payment. Some benefits are not based on income. Others, like pension payments, are, but there is a ceiling so that the benefits do not reflect the income that exceeds the ceiling. The ceiling for calculating the payment owed and the ceiling for calculating the benefits are different from each other, and the Petitioners in the *Lahav* case were complaining about this difference.

As to health insurance, this situation is similar. The insurance premiums, paid through the health tax, are a percentage of income, and the health tax paid by different individuals can vary a great deal. Everyone receives the same basket of health services. The Court's reasoning that the objective of the payment rate is different from the objective of the benefit rate applies to health insurance as well as to National Insurance.

Each health fund must provide its members with a basket of health services that is set out in the statute and in regulations. This basket functions as an allocation system; everyone gets the services in the basket, but only those who pay an additional amount or have additional insurance get other services. The basket is fairly comprehensive but is not all-inclusive. Furthermore, while each health fund member can choose doctors for office care from among the fund's list of doctors, a person may not be able to choose a surgeon or choose the timing for non-emergency surgery. Thus, health services included in the basic basket are provided based on need and are divorced from the ability to pay, but additional health services may depend on ability to pay.

Questions

1. Under the Court's analysis in the *Lahav* case, could Israel impose a more highly progressive health tax rate, requiring those who earn more than the national average salary to pay one more percent of their income above the average, and those who earn more than twice the national average to pay another percent of their income above this amount, etc.?

2. Are there any situations in the United States in which payment is based on ability to pay and services are based on need?

Comment

The government pays the health funds a set amount for each member, with an adjustment for the age distribution of the members of each fund. The payments come from several sources including the health taxes collected, other National Insurance Institute funds, and the national budget. The National Health Insurance Law has a mechanism for updating the amount paid to the health funds. It provides for an automatic update based on an economic indicator related to the increase in health care costs due to inflation. It also includes a mechanism for adjusting the payments due to other causes, but increases based on these other reasons require agreement of the Government generally and of the ministers of health and of finance in particular. In addition, there is a public committee that meets each year and is responsible for recommending changes in services and medications included in the standard basket. The updating mechanism sometimes fails to cover the full increase in costs of health services. The following case explores the problems that result and the ability of the Court to solve those problems.

Israeli Case

Maccabi Health Service v. Minister of Finance
HCJ 2344/98, 54(5) PD 729 [2000]

[Three health funds petitioned against the refusal of the minister of finance and the Government to increase the amount of support given to the health funds from the national budget. The Health Council had recommended an increase in the payments to the health funds, but the minister of finance rejected the recommendation "for budgetary reasons." The Petitioners asked that the Court to hold invalid the Respondent's refusal to approve the increase.

The Health Council is established by sections 48 and 49 of the National Health Insurance Law and comprises 46 members, including ten representatives of various ministries; ten representatives of the health funds; seven representatives of medical professional organizations; an expert in each of the fields of medicine, administration, economics, medical ethics, and social sciences; and representatives from the medical schools and organizations of social workers, unions, employers, local governments, private hospitals, patients, and psychologists.]

Justice M. Cheshin:

The funds claim that the Health Law [the National Health Insurance Law] obligates them to provide the services in the health basket of service to their members. It also, according to their claims, provides that the state is responsible for funding the cost of the basket of health services ("from the sources set out in section 13"). As to the correlation in the amount of the funding to costs, the statute provides a technical mechanism for automatically updating the cost of the basket. The objective of the automatic technical updating is so that the funding will cover the cost to the health funds of the services in the basket, which is based on the economic indicator identified in the fifth appendix to the statute. In other words, this indicator, the *health cost increase indicator*, was meant from the beginning to match the funding to the increase in costs due to inflation. It was not meant to deal with increases in costs due to any other variable.[5]

In addition to this automatic technical mechanism, the statute provides another mechanism, the substantive complementary mechanism, that from the beginning was meant to match the funding to the increase in cost of the basket of services attributable to other variables that are not included in the health cost increase indicator, such as the increase in the population, the aging of the population, technological developments, and other factors. This complementary system is supposed to operate where the automatic technical mechanism does not; that is, it operates when the state fund provided under the automatic technical mechanism does not keep up with the increase of costs to the health funds. When it is found that the automatic technical mechanism is not sufficient to provide funding that matches the cost so that the fund-

---

5. The fifth appendix provides that the health cost increase indicator shall be based 36 percent on the index of salaries in the health sector, 22 percent on the index salaries in the public sector, 40 percent on the consumer price index, and 2 percent on the index of construction prices.

ing is insufficient to cover the real costs of the health basket, the ministers have an obligation to increase the funding through the complementary mechanism. If this is not done, so it is claimed, the health funds will be put in an impossible position and this will go against the intent of the statute. The funds will be obligated to supply services that have a cost of X, but the state will provide them with funding that is significantly less than X. The situation thus created is impossible ... The funds will have to absorb costs that under section 3(b) of the statute should be borne by the state. The Petitioners claim that the statue created a closed system for provision of services and funding, in which the funds provide the services and the state provides the funding of the same services.

The Petitioners' claims make sense as to the obligation of the state. Everyone agrees that the health cost increase indicator does not cover the real increase in the funds' costs. The real costs of health services have increased by a significant amount since the statute entered into force. The state does not fund the difference between the real costs and the historic costs.... Everyone agrees that the recommendation of the Health Council is based on valid factual determinations.

We do not need at this time to go so far as to hold that the state is obligated to give the health funds the increase in funding that they request. [T]here are two stages in the process. The first stage is that a person who has a statutory authorization to act must undertake to exercise his discretion. He must exercise his discretion; he may not simply ignore a request. The second stage is that the authorized person must reach a decision whether to do what is requested or not. At this time, we reach no decision about the substantive aspects of the exercise of the discretionary authority, as to whether the health funds are entitled to receive the requested funding. Instead it is sufficient for us to direct our attention to the first stage; that is, to the question of whether the ministers fulfilled the obligation imposed on them, and we mean the *obligation*, to exercise their discretion and to consider seriously the recommendation of the Health Council and the request of the health funds.

Our examination of the facts brought us to the conclusion that the ministers, especially the minister of finance, violated the obligation to properly consider the recommendation of the Health Council.... Thus, they never got to the second stage of exercising their discretion. In other words, the authorized authorities stopped at the threshold from examining the recommendation of the Health Council and the request of the health funds; they desisted from considering the substance of the recommendation, and in this they violated the obligation imposed on them to examine the substance of the recommendation of the Council. For this reason alone, and without considering the substance of the claim of the health funds, we have reached the conclusion that the ministers shall be ordered to fulfill their legal obligation and that they shall examine the substance of the recommendation of the Health Council.

In our case, the Health Council set out the rationale for its recommendation in full. It explained that the population of the country had increased and would continue to increase, that technology had undergone substantial development that caused an increase in costs, and that the health funds were required to provide psychiatric health services [formerly provided by the state]. All of these factors increased the costs borne by the funds. According to the Council and its recommendation, the law requires that the state take a part in financing these additional costs. This recommendation is appropriate, in light of the objective of the statute, and should be seriously considered and the ministers should provide their analysis of the issues.

And what have we heard from the ministers? We have not heard anything except one thing, and that is that it is necessary to set priorities in the economy and there is no budget for funds in addition to those that have been provided to the health funds. There is no additional reason, none related to the substantive issues presented by the statute, why they reject the recommendation of the Council.

We do not deny that budgetary considerations are relevant, but they are not the only relevant considerations. Yet we have not heard anything about the substantive aspects of the Council's recommendation.

The statute created a unique mechanism in which the obligation to perform the essentially public functions to provide health services to the entire population was imposed on private bodies that are not among the institutions of government. The health funds have no power to choose their members or to choose what health services to provide or not provide to their members.... The obligation of supplying health services to the population is imposed on the health funds, and that of funding the services from the sources listed in section 13 of the statute is imposed on the state.... The state was supposed to supply the funding for the services in the manner set out in the statute, a manner that includes an automatic technical mechanism for updating the payment levels. It quickly became apparent, as could have been expected from the beginning, that the automatic updating mechanism was insufficient to meet the real increase in the costs of health services.

The health cost increase indicator is designed mainly to correct for the erosion in the value of money, but it does not include variables designed to reflect the real increase in health costs. It does not consider the increase in the population of the state, an increase due to immigration and natural increase, even though such a population increase would increase costs to the funds. The effect of the aging of the population also is not taken into account, even though an increase in the number of elderly naturally increases health costs because, as everyone knows, an old person needs more medical treatment and more medications than a young person. The mechanism for automatic updating of the health cost increase indicator does not include variables that that take into account an increase or aging of the population, so that the health funds are forced to absorb the increase in real costs associated with these phenomena. Our attention is called to section 9(b)(3) of the law, under which the ministers have authority "to update the cost of the basket of health services to the funds due to demographic changes in the population." The legislature was aware of the fact that the health cost increase indicator does not reflect size and age demographic changes in the population and therefore placed in the hands of the ministers the authority to change the cost of the health basket. Now, even though there have been substantial demographic changes in the population, the ministers have refused to exercise their authority and have not given a satisfactory reason for their refusal.

The same analysis applies as to technological changes that also require the health funds to provide services to their members but are not included in the health cost increase indicator. Israel is not alone in experiencing a steady increase in the cost of health services. It occurs in other western countries, where the increase in the standard of living, and with it technological and demographic changes, have brought a real increase in health care costs. We also note the claim of the health funds that, due to an amendment in the law, they are now required to provide psychiatric care that was not in the past within their area of responsibility, and the cost of this obligation is not taken into account at all in the cost of the basket of health services and the health cost increase indicator.

We do not grant the relief requested in the petition and we will not issue the order the Petitioners request.

On the other hand, we do not completely reject the petition. We rest our recognition of the claims on the reasons we have detailed in the opinion, and we grant them in part.

Therefore … we instruct the minister of health and the minister of finance to act as required in relation to the Health Council's decision…, to consider the substance of that decision, to make findings, and to reach conclusions, and only after all these steps to reach a decision and to give proper reasons for the decision.

Comment

The decision in *Maccabi Health Services v. Minister of Finance* distinguishes between the increase in health costs due to the erosion in the value of money and the real increase in health costs due to the increase in population, the aging of the population, changes in technology, and other reasons. The automatic increase based on the health cost increase indicator allows the health funds to continue to offer the same services they did in the prior year, even if inflation has increased the amount it costs them to provide those services. If the market cost to the health fund of a flu shot is NIS 20 one year but NIS 22 the next year, the automatic increase assures that the health fund will be able to continue to supply that flu shot. The automatic increase does not allow the health funds to provide services to more people, as may be necessitated by population growth. Therefore if all the health funds together had 4 million members needing flu shots one year and 4.2 million members needing flu shots the next year, and if the increase in need was due solely to the increase in the population of the state, the automatic increase based on the health cost increase indicator would not cover the cost of the added 200,000 flu shots that the health funds would have to administer. The analysis would be the same if the increase in the demand for flu shots were due to the aging of a population of stable size, assuming flu shots were more strongly advised for older people. Similarly the health funds are not covered for costs associated with technological improvements. Assume that in one year, medical standards called for performing computed tomography (CT) scans only in cases of *highest* need for the information they would reveal, because the benefit of the scan was in all other cases outweighed by the harm that could be caused by the radiation dose the patient would receive. Now assume that a new technology was developed that reduced a patient's exposure to radiation during a CT scan. As a result, the medical cost-benefit ratio of the scans changed and the next year it was deemed medically advisable to perform CT scans even where there was only a *moderate* need for the information that would be obtained. The automatic operation of the health cost increase indicator would not provide payment to the health funds for the increased costs of CT scans they would bear if they followed good medical practices and ordered CT scans in more cases.

In a portion of the *Maccabi* case not included in this excerpt, the state claimed that it had transferred extra payments to the health funds, beyond those made mandatory by the law, and that the health funds could cover more of their costs if they eliminated waste and handled their monies more efficiently. In fact, the 2010 report of the State Comptroller (many years after the case) identified misuse of funds at one of the health funds. Nonetheless it has been reported that the additional allocations from the national budget are lower than the actual increases in costs.[6]

As the *Maccabi* case illustrates, the Court sees the problem of inadequate increases in the payments to the health funds as a real one, but is hesitant to order the Gov-

---

6. *See* Guy I. Seidman, *Regulating Life and Death: The Case of Israel's "Health Basket" Committee,* 23 J. Contemp. Health L. & Policy 9, 22 fn. 62 (2006).

ernment to increase the funding. The Court is aware of the real budgetary limitations under which the Government operates and is hesitant to order the political branches of government to give higher priority to health care. This would necessarily mean giving lower priority to some other programs, or raising more money through higher taxes.

The issue of the increase in the government payment to the health funds returned to the Supreme Court in *Clalit Health Service v. Minister of Finance*, HCJ 8730/03 (June 21, 2012). After the *Maccabi* decision, the minister of finance decided that the health cost indicator should be updated, but could not agree with the minister of health and the health funds on how to determine the amount of the increase. While the matter of the appropriate measure of the increase was still under protracted administrative consideration, the Court decided that the principle of reasonability applied not only to the content of an administrative decision but also to the process of reaching that decision. In this case, the delay in making the decision was so long as to be unreasonable. The Court ordered the ministers of finance and health to agree with the health funds on how to determine the amount of the increase within six months. The Court explicitly avoided deciding what factors could be considered, leaving that to further discussion between the ministers and the health funds. Again, the Court avoided ordering an increase in funding of a specific amount. As of this writing, it is not clear what the Court will do if the ministers and health funds do not reach an agreement within the six month period.

Question

3. The decision notes that "the statute created a unique mechanism in which the obligation to perform the essentially public functions to provide health services to the entire population was imposed on private bodies." The "private bodies" are the health funds. In this language, the decision conceives of the supply of health services as an essentially public function. Do you think that provision of health services to the entire population is properly characterized as a public function? Is it characterized that way in the United States?

Comment

Another economic aspect of the Israeli National Health Law involves copayments. When the patient is required to make a copayment in order to receive health care services, the cost of the service is being allocated between the government, which supports the health fund, and private individuals, the patients. Each person who visits a doctor pays a small fee, which was about $6 in 2011. That fee covers all visits to that doctor in each three month period. In other words, a person who sees the same doctor once a month for a year pays about $24. A separate fee is paid for each doctor a person sees. For medications, a person pays about $4 for a month's supply of each medication in the basic basket of medications. Medications not covered by the basic basket cost more. Most medications needed by most people are in the basic basket, but a significant number of medications are not. Copayents are also required for some medical procedures, including some surgeries.

The following case examines the way copayment amounts are established.

Israeli Case

Yisraeli v. Committee for Expansion of the Health Basket
HCJ 2974/06 (June 11, 2006)

Justice E. Rubenstein:

The petition relates to one item in the National Health Insurance Law, 5754-1994...,
clause 14 in the provision on "copayment by the insured," found in the second appendix
to the statute. This provision lists those health services provided by the health fund of
the Histadrut, such as they were at the time of the enactment of the statute ... on January 1, 1994. The Petitioner asks that the provision be corrected to provide that an adult
who is deaf in both ears, whose deafness cannot be corrected by hearing aids, and who
needs a cochlear transplant to save the sense of hearing, shall be exempt from the copayment presently required by the statute. The present requirement is that the insured pay
70 percent of the cost of the surgery, which at present cost means NIS 70,000 out of a
total cost of NIS 100,000 [about $15,600 out of $22,300].

The Petitioner is a teacher and single mother who receives no support from her former spouse. Her salary is low ... and she claims it is difficult for her to support her family. Unfortunately her hearing has for many years been poor, and she is becoming deaf.
Today her hearing is only 15 percent of that of a healthy person. A cochlear transplant might
save her hearing. She claims that without this surgery, her ability to support her family
and to function normally will be impaired. She has turned to the Respondents and also
tried to obtain contributions to pay for the operation. This operation is more effective if
performed on someone who is becoming deaf than on someone who is already completely deaf, so it is important that the surgery be performed soon. It has been set for
June 25, 2006.

The Normative Framework

The goal of the health insurance law is to provide health services to every resident,
with the responsibility for providing the services falling on the state and specifically on
the health funds for their members, all to be financed by the sources set out in the statute.
The health basket is defined in section 7 and refers, for our purpose, to the second appendix of the statute. At the time the statute was enacted, the basket of services provided
by the Histadrut health fund as of January 1, 1994, was copied into the new health insurance
law; the 70 percent copayment requirement is also a product of that copying process and
was required by the Histadrut in 1994 for such a procedure.

The law also set out a process for altering the health basket, and this process involved
several levels of decision-making. Any change that increases costs, such as the change requested in this case, can be made only by the minister of health, the minister of finance,
and the Government acting together (section 8(b)(1) of the statute), and can be made
only once a source of funding is established (section 8(e)).

The mechanism that operates in such cases is as follows: the Public Committee for Expanding the Basket of Health Services (Basket Committee),[7] comprised of members from
various disciplines, makes recommendations to the Health Council, which derives its authority from the National Health Insurance Law. This council is also authorized to give
advice to the minister of health as to changes in the health basket relating to new tech-

---

7. The Basket Committee was not established by the statute, but rather by the Government in
order to provide broader public input on changes in the health basket.

nologies. The order of consideration is therefore: the Basket Committee, the Health Council, the minister of health, the minister of finance, and the Government.

Provision 14 in the second appendix provides: "Internal ear transplants: Copayment of the insured is 70 percent of the cost of the transplant. Insured individuals up to the age of 18 who have deafness in both ears that cannot be corrected through hearing aids shall not be required to make a copayment for a transplant." This language is different from the original, because in 1999 and 2002, provision 14 was amended, first (in 1999) to include the right to full funding without a copayment for patients aged 2 to 18, and later (in 2002) to include full funding for infants up to age 2. No one questions the fact that the large majority of transplants are for minors.

Therefore the issue before us addresses a matter set out in a statute, and one that is not immutable, given the prior amendments and the continuing discussions in the Basket Committee. That committee regularly discusses new technologies and medications, evidence of which is found in the fact that it already made two changes in the provision under discussion as it relates to minors, and those changes have been accepted and made part of the law. As the State claims in its response, the matter of transplants that is now before us has already been discussed in the National Labor Court, which determined, "The language of the statute on this matter is clear. A member of a health fund who is older than 18 is responsible for a copayment of 70 percent of the cost of the transplant." The court determined that the distinction between minors and adults in that provision does not constitute impermissible discrimination, because it is based on the special clinical needs of minors, on medical reasons, and also on social reasons—the lack of the economic means of minors themselves.

Prioritizing and Copayments

No one questions that, first, the decision-making procedures are proper and, second, that prioritization is necessary for the health basket. It is always true that the bed is too short to stretch out on,[8] and the little that is available is insufficient.[9] In a world in which the technological and medical landscape is rapidly changing, sometimes in unrecognized ways, and in which the cost of technology and medications is high, there is no choice but to prioritize various options. It cannot be said, even in painful cases such as the one before us, that prioritization results in discrimination. It is because of the struggle over limited resources that this case has come before the Court, in addition to the struggle conducted in public forums, both parliamentary and extra-parliamentary. It is hard to stand before the cries of those whose life may be extended if they can get a certain medication, just as one cannot be indifferent to the request of the Petitioner, who wants to continue with her personal and professional life at a time when medicine can provide her what she wants but she lacks the necessary economic resources for the medical treatment.

[Medical opinion supports the position that a person who receives a cochlear transplant is thereafter able to hear.]

Is the decision of the Respondent legally defective in some way? I have been bothered by the matter of ... proportionality of the requirement of such a large copayment. I examined the second appendix to the statute. As stated by the Petitioners, the required copayment for most procedures in 10 percent. A few require a copayment of 25 percent or

---

8. This is an expression found in Isaiah 28:20.
9. The full expression is "The little that is available is insufficient to satisfy the lion," BABYLONIAN TALMUD, B'rachot 3b.

50 percent. One other item requires a copayment of 70 percent; that is for a CPAP machine for sleep apnea. One item requires a copayment of 80 percent; that is for hand or feet prosthetics. The Respondent claims that in the other cases of a 70 percent or 80 percent copayment, that amount is not in fact required. The State did not respond to that specific claim. That leaves just our case with such a high copayment. Whether this is true or not, high copayments are required on only a small number of cases. Can a payment of 70 percent by the patient be called a *copayment?* Must a copayment not be lower? Isn't the meaning of copayment necessarily that the main burden of payment falls on some other party, and the person making the copayment is asked to add something, and not that this person is the one making the main payment? Even if there was a copayment of 70 percent before January 1, 1994, when the provisions that had related to the Histadrut were copied into the law, the questions remain.... [Nevertheless] we are addressing a matter in a statute and a provision that has been in place for a long time. Even though the appendix has been amended through an order, which is an administrative act, the law which gives effect to that order is in the statute itself.[10]

The mechanism established for deciding what services are included within the basket—the Basket Committee—and its work procedures are on their face without defect. The Petitioners do not claim otherwise. Therefore we need not consider the extent to which determinations of the committee are subject to review under the rules of administrative law.

In the post-hearing stage, the attorney for the Petitioners raised a quasi-constitutional claim related to considerations of equality, claiming that the requirement of such a high copayment involved impermissible discrimination. The Petitioners pointed to the requirements for proportionality in section 8 of the Basic Law: Human Dignity and Freedom. As I have stated, the requirement of such a high copayment is problematic. Nonetheless we do not have before us a sufficient basis for examining the constitutional aspects of the question.... There is on one hand, the strength of the claim, and on the other, the facts before us, especially the array of discussions in the Basket Committee, which do not allow us to simply accept the quasi-constitutional claim of a lack of proportionality. On this issue, we need the opinions of a variety of experts from different fields that are on the Basket Committee.

The right to equality has been recognized by this Court, and we need not further consider that matter. Nonetheless we cannot accept the claim of discrimination in this case.... We accept the position of the state that these matters cannot be examined on a case by case basis, but must be considered broadly. A broad examination of the matter is within the expertise of the Basket Committee, and we have no basis for finding fault with its work and with its determination of priorities.

In light of the foregoing, I find that we have no legal cause for issuing the order requested.

The Future

Because the matter of the determinations of the Basket Committee is likely to be brought before us again, it seems appropriate to draw attention to what was stated above and to the claims of the Petitioners. First, attention should be given to the question of whether twelve years after establishment of the health basket, and after a decision to concede on

---

10. Section 8 of the statute allows the ministers and the Government to issue an administrative order amending the provisions in the second appendix of the statute. Israeli law allows the legislature to authorize administrative agencies and authorities to amend statutes, as long as the statutory authorization for this procedure is explicit.

the copayment for minors, the time has come for another change involving not a cancellation of the copayment for an adult but rather a substantial reduction of the copayment. This call for reconsideration is based on the fact that the requirement of a 70 percent copayment is exceptional and on the fact that we cannot completely ignore the claim that such a requirement is not proportional. It is important to consider the social and economic changes that have occurred since 1994, even though we express no specific position on those changes. It may be that the Basket Committee should consider, in addition to the medical and human need associated with this matter, the question of the cost-benefit ratio: whether the improvement in the quality of life of patients receiving transplants would allow them to continue working in a way that will prevent them from becoming a economic burden on the state, thus saving other public expenditures. This is in addition to the benefit of the preservation of their sense of human dignity. Similarly although we express no opinion on the matter, we raise the question of whether a process should be established that would examine granting exceptions on a case-by-case basis. This process could involve a committee empowered to decide whether to waive high copayment requirements based on the economic capacity of the patient. (This matter may require an amendment to the statute.)

As to the health funds, ... we presume that ... there is no legal barrier to the health funds accepting a reduced copayment on equality grounds.

We repeat: we are aware of the need for a broad perspective and that the discretion on this issue is assigned to the Basket Committee, which is suitable to the task due to its broad composition and professionalism. Nonetheless the special situation of the single matter at hand stems from the fact of its being one of the few cases in which an extraordinarily high copayment is required.

Final Comments

We are aware that our decision does not provide immediate relief to the Petitioner seeking surgery that she needs. We are sorry about that, and we wish her a full recovery. Perhaps she and the other Petitioners supporting her will gain public sympathy for raising the issue and her problems will get a hearing in the institutions responsible for the matter.

Subject to that, we cannot grant the petition. We make no order for costs.

Comment

After the Supreme Court decision in *Yisraeli v. Committee for Expansion of the Health Basket*, the Israeli cabinet determined that the Petitioner should not have to make the copayment required by the statute. The statute now provides that a cochlear transplant is available without copayment to adults who are newly deaf or whose hearing is deteriorating.

In the *Yisraeli* decision, the Court avoided determining whether the decision of the Basket Committee not to change the copayment for adult cochlear transplants violated the requirement of proportionality. If the Court had fully tested the proportionality of that decision (which was really a lack of an affirmative decision to ask for an amendment of the statute), it would have had to ask, among other things, whether the harm caused to the Petitioner by the decision was outweighed by the benefit of the decision. The benefit would be the avoidance of problems that would be caused by reducing the copayment. If the copayment were reduced, the health funds would have to spend more on such transplants. If the Government payment to the health funds were not increased, the health funds would have to reduce some other services in order to cover the added cost. It would be hard for the Court to anticipate what these reductions would be and whether the harm from the reductions would outweigh the harm caused by the copayment. Government payment to the health funds would be increased to cover the added cost of cochlear transplants only if the minister of health, the minister of finance, and the Government all agreed to the increase. Such a cost increase would not be covered by the automatic increase mechanism, which covers only cost increases due to inflation. If the Court were to order the minister of finance, the minister of health, and the Government to agree to an added allocation to the health funds to cover the cost of cochlear transplants for adults, it would have to anticipate what the government would do to obtain the necessary funds. The government would have to either cut some other services or raise revenues, possibly by raising taxes. Furthermore, if the Court made such an order, everyone who wanted a lower copayment on some service or who wanted some service not provided by the health funds would sue to get it, and the Court would put itself in the position of deciding what health services are the most important or else what the priority of health care should be in the national budget as a whole. Obviously the Court thought it was not in a good position to make these decisions, and certainly not in a better position than the Basket Committee and the Health Council, which provide a mechanism for broad expert input on the matters. In addition, there is vigorous public debate on the contents of the basket of health service, and particularly of the basket of medications, and it can be presumed that the committee and the council pay attention to this debate. In short, the Court seemed to be of the opinion that it could not do a better job of making the hard choices of setting health care priorities than is made by the existing decision-making mechanism.

The high copayment required in this case is, as the Court indicated, unusual. It does not affect many patients. The requirement of high copayments for medications is problematic for a greater number of people. Even if copayments for medications are not 70 percent, they can be a burden for patients who need to take medications over a long period. Furthermore, some medications are not in the health basket at all, so the patient must pay 100 percent of the cost.

Question

4. If the Court in *Yisraeli* was not ready to hold that the law and the decision not to change the law are invalid, why did it express its opinion that the copayment required was too high?

D. Health Services Not in the Basket of Services

Both the health funds and private providers working outside of the health funds provide health services that are not included in the basket of services. Most Israelis buy supplementary insurance to cover the cost of some of these services. Health funds offer supplementary insurance to their members. Members have a choice of several levels of insurance which provide different coverage and have different costs. Some Israelis purchase supplementary health insurance through private insurance companies. Eighty percent of Israelis carry some form of supplementary insurance, mostly through the health funds. The average cost of supplementary insurance was about $16 per month for each insured individual,[11] although some people pay more for more extensive coverage.

---

11. Dov Chernichovsky, Taub Center for Social Policy Studies in Israel, *Israel's Healthcare System, Policy Paper 2011.13 in* POLICY PAPERS SERIES 295, 317 (2011).

E. Health Care in the Military

Health care is provided through the army to all military personnel on duty. Most health care services are provided at military medical facilities that are staffed by enlisted or career soldiers and by civilian doctors on reserve duty. The Ministry of Defense contracts with civilian medical facilities for provision of additional services. Enlisted soldiers pay no health tax or other health insurance premiums. Other military personnel pay the health tax, but the cost of their health care comes out of the Ministry of Defense's budget. Military personnel do not have to make any copayments for the health care services they receive. Furthermore, they receive dental care, which in the civilian sector is part of the basic service only for young children. Military personnel do not have access to supplementary insurance to cover health care services they may want but that the military health care system does not provide. Families of military personnel do not receive health care through the military system but rather through the national health care system.[12]

F. Successes and Failures

Although this is a book on law, it seems reasonable to include some information on how well the Israeli health care system works, especially in light of the intense interest in health care reform in the United States at the time of the writing of this book. Most prominently, Israel has succeeded in assuring that everyone has health insurance. Furthermore, the health care provided in Israel, overall, is excellent. Life expectancy at birth in Israel, at 81 years, exceeds that in the United States, at 78 years.[13] Furthermore, infant mortality is substantially below that of the United States.[14] The number of doctors relevant to the population size is higher than in the United States.[15]

The system is not without problems. The number of hospital beds is low.[16] Health facilities, including both doctors' offices and hospitals, lack the aesthetic appeal that Americans take for granted. Pay is low for medical professionals compared to that in the United States. Although all sectors of the population have equal rights to health care, various health indicators are lower for the non-Jewish segment of the population.[17] Furthermore, there is growing controversy over whether the individuals are being asked to pay too great a share of the health costs. As the cases indicate, the Government allocation to the health funds has not kept pace with changes in demand for health services. The percentage of health costs that are borne by the government has decreased somewhat, while it has grown in the average of the Organization for Economic Co-operation and Development (OECD) countries and in the United States.[18] The percentage of the health costs paid by the government in Israel is still well above the percentage in the United States, but it has fallen

---

12. Military health care in Israel is described in Racheli Magnezi et al., *Comparison of Health Care Services for Career Soldiers Throughout the World*, 170 MILITARY MEDICINE 995 (2005).

13. US Census Bureau, International Database, *available at* http://www.census.gov/population/international/data/idb/informationGateway.php.

14. *Id.*

15. Chernichovsky, *supra* note 11, Figure 9 at 307.

16. *Id.* at Figure 10 at 308.

17. *Id.*

18. *Id.* at Figure 6 at 303.

well below the OECD average and this is raising public concern.[19] Public health care expenditures measured as a percentage of the GDP are also low in Israel. Israel's expenditure on health care under the system described above was about 7.7 percent of the gross domestic product (GDP) in 2007, as opposed to the 8.8 percent average for the OECD states and 16 percent in the United States.[20] Furthermore, the expenditure in Israel as a percentage of the GDP has been steady over a period of twelve years, while it has grown in OECD countries. More of the burden of increasing health care costs is being borne by individuals through payments for health care services or through payments for supplementary insurance. This private cost burden falls most heavily on poorer members of the society, who must pay a higher share of their disposal income for health care.[21]

Despite these problems, the private health care costs in Israel probably remain substantially lower than in the United States. Primary and preventative care is readily available and the standard of medical care is high. Israeli medical institutions are leaders in medical research. As the next section shows, the Israeli health care system provides everyone with some services that are not universally available in the United States.

Question

5. What are the major differences between the legal structure of the health care system in Israel and the United States? What do you see as the advantages and disadvantage of the Israeli health system?

G. Fertility Treatments

The Israeli health care law guarantees free or very low cost fertility treatments to the entire population.

Israeli Statute

National Health Insurance Law, 5754-1994
Second Appendix
[Health Care Services that All Health Funds Must Provide]

6. Other Diagnostic and Treatment Services:

(d) Diagnosis and Treatment of Infertility, such as

Tests needed to determine infertility and for artificial insemination

Treatment of infertility

Artificial insemination, including treatments for sperm enhancement and hormone treatment

---

19. *Id.*
20. This and other cost data are taken from Guy I. Seidman, *Is a Flat-Line a Good Thing? On the Privatization of Israel's Healthcare System*, 36 Am. J.L. & Med. 452 (2010).
21. *Id.* at 319.

In vitro fertilization, for the purpose of giving birth to the first and second child of a couple that has no children from their present marriage, and for a woman who has no children who seeks to establish a single-parent family.

Comment

This provision is a part of the National Health Insurance Law that lists the treatments that the health funds must provide. Women receive free or low cost fertility treatments. The service is available to both married and single women. Lesbians have the same access to these reproductive services as other women. Access to fertility treatments other than in vitro fertilization (IVF) is unlimited. This includes, for example, stimulation of ovulation in women who do not ovulate normally, but who can conceive without in vitro fertilization after their ovaries are stimulated to produce ova. For IVF, the statute does not limit the number of IVF treatments a woman can have; it limits the insurance rights to production of two children. Many women undergo multiple rounds of IVF treatment before giving birth. For the first two children, all these treatments are covered. For a couple, if one or both members have children with another partner, they do not count toward the two child limit. Even after the two child limit is reached, some of the treatments related to IVF are at least partially funded. Not surprisingly, the use of fertility treatments, including in vitro fertilization, is the highest in the world.[22]

In the United States, some insurance policies provide coverage for all fertility treatments, but it appears that most do not.[23] Thirteen states mandate that policies offered by insurance companies regulated by state insurance laws include some types of fertility treatments and two states mandate companies to offer an option to purchase such coverage. None of these mandates apply to policies offered by employers who self-insure; some exclude insurance provided by small businesses, some exclude in vitro fertilization from coverage, and other laws have various limitations and exclusions.[24] None of the laws mandate coverage for homosexuals.[25] The federal Patient Protection and Affordable Care Act, enacted in 2010, does not include any provisions on insurance for fertility treatments.[26]

Question

6. Given the necessary limits on heavily subsidized health services, what explains Israel's choice to provide such extensive coverage for fertility treatments? In answering this question, consider material presented in prior chapters of this book.

---

22. Daphna Birenbaum-Carmeli & Martha Dirnfeld, *In Vitro Fertilisation Policy in Israel and Women's Perspectives: the More the Better?* 16 REPRODUCTIVE HEALTH MATTERS 182 (2008).

23. *See* Camille M. Davidson, *Octomom and Multi-Fetal Pregnancies: Why Federal Legislation Should Require Insurers to Cover In Vitro Fertilization,* 17 WM. & MARY J. WOMEN & L. 135 (2010).

24. NATIONAL CONFERENCE OF STATE LEGISLATURES, STATE LAWS RELATED TO INSURANCE COVERAGE FOR FERTILITY TREATMENT, http://www.ncsl.org/issues-research/health/insurance-coverage-for-infertility-laws.aspx (April 2011); AMERICAN SOCIETY FOR REPRODUCTIVE MEDICINE, STATE INFERTILITY INSURANCE LAWS, http://www.asrm.org/insurance.aspx (last visited Feb. 15, 2012).

25. Amy B. Monahan, *Value-Based Mandated Health Benefits,* 80 U. COLO. L. REV. 127, 185 (2009).

26. *See* Nizan Geslevich Packin, *The Other Side of Health Care Reform: An Analysis of the Missed Opportunity Regarding Infertility Treatments,* 14 SCHOLAR 1, 3 (2011).

Chapter 21

Financial Institutions

A. Construction Financing

Construction financing in Israel is different from that in the United States. In Israel, almost all residential construction is of apartments that will be individually owned. Purchasers of a new apartment often sign a contract of purchase before construction of the apartment has been completed or, not infrequently, before construction has begun. Sometimes the purchaser signs the contract even before the developer has obtained all necessary permits. Due to the shortage of new housing, purchasers are willing to put down substantial sums of money at such early stages. Both the rapid population growth and the increase in the standard of living have created a significant demand for housing that cannot be met by existing apartments.

The purchaser of a new apartment contracts to make installment payments to the builder periodically during the period of construction. Most of the payments are made before construction is completed. In other words, the builder finances the construction with the purchaser's money. In most cases, the purchaser must take out an acquisition loan, in the form of a mortgage, in order to make the payments. Based on this arrangement alone, the risk that construction will not be completed would fall on the purchasers. If construction is not completed, a purchaser only has rights in a partially completed apartment, which is not of great value. Usually it costs more than what remains to be paid on the agreed purchase price to complete construction. This may be because the builder made off with some of the money that the purchaser already put into the building or diverted the funds to other buildings or enterprises, or because a change in economic conditions made completion of the apartment more costly than anticipated at the time of the sales contract.

Construction financing arrangements are different in the United States. Most residential purchases are of individual homes. The builder of a home or an apartment building takes out a construction loan from a lender, using these funds to put up the building. Once the construction is completed, the builder sells the home or units in the building, using the amounts received to repay the construction loan. If the purchaser agrees to buy a home or apartment before construction is complete, the purchaser puts down a small percentage of the purchase price. Thus, the risk that the construction will not be completed falls mainly on the construction loan lender. The construction lender will take steps to see that its risky loan is protected. For example, the construction lender may disperse payments on the loan only after receiving vouchers for work done, or after receiving reports of work completed. The lender may have an onsite inspector to be sure the construction proceeds as scheduled and that the money dispersed by the lender is being invested in the construction.

Israeli builders also have construction loans from banks, but these do not cover all construction costs. Furthermore, the bank is repaid out of payments by purchasers as the building goes up, and not after completion of construction, as in the United States.

The following provision of Israeli law is designed to protect the apartment purchasers from the risk that construction will not be completed and the purchaser will be left with an unfinished apartment that is worth less than the amount the purchaser has paid.

Israeli Statute

Sale Law (Apartments) (Securing the Investment of Purchasers of Apartments), 5735-1974

2. Financial Assurance for the Purchaser

The seller shall not receive from the purchaser, as an advance on the price of the apartment, an amount in excess of seven percent of the price, unless the seller has done one of the following, without regard to the wording of the contract of sale:

> (1) Provided the purchaser a bank guarantee to assure repayment of the entire advance payment in the event that the seller is unable to transfer title or any other right in the apartment as agreed in the sales agreement, due to the attachment of the apartment or the land on which it is built, or due to issuance of a moratorium order,[1] or due to imposition of a receivership, an order of dissolution, or appointment of a receiver against the seller or owner of the land, or for other reasons that completely prevent transfer of possession of the apartment, provided that for this purpose revocation of the sales contract itself is not a reason that completely prevents transfer. The minister [of building and housing], or the supervisor [of banks] may set out the language of the bank guarantee.

Comment

Other provisions in the statute allow four alternative mechanisms for protecting the purchaser's interest, including the seller's purchase of an insurance policy with the purchaser as beneficiary, but due to inadequacies of the other means or lack of a market to support them, the bank guarantee is the main mechanism used in practice. The statute also provides a mechanism for the purchaser to make payments directly into the builder's construction loan account at the bank. This way, the purchaser gets some degree of assurance that the money paid is not being used to finance the builder's other, unrelated business activities or, worse yet, a vacation for the seller's family. For a full discussion of the Israeli financing arrangements, see Shalom Lerner, *Protection of Home Purchasers in Israel*, 24 Banking & Finance L. Rev. 579 (2009).

The foregoing discussion shows that the apartment purchaser and the bank have an intertwined relationship in Israeli new construction. The purchaser provides much of the funds needed during construction, and this greatly reduces the bank's risk associated with

---

1. A moratorium order is an order to freeze legal proceedings sometimes issued at the beginning of insolvency proceedings. This order prevents courts from reaching decisions on interests of some interested parties that might prejudice later adjudication of interests of other parties.

the construction loan. In the American system, all or almost all of the risk of the construction loan remains with the bank until project completion.

B. The Bank's Fiduciary Duty

Banks in Israel are subject to both a duty of good faith and a fiduciary duty, each applying in different circumstances and requiring different sorts of actions. The underlying relationship of the bank to its customer is one of contract. The bank enters into a contract with the customer to provide certain services. Ricardo ben-Oliel, *Foreign Influences in Israeli Banking Law*, 23 Tul. Eur. & Civ. L.F. 167, 167 (2008). As discussed above in chapter 15, The Law of Contracts (General Provisions), 5733-1973, imposes a duty of good faith in negotiation and performance of all contracts, and this includes banking contracts. Thus the bank has a duty of good faith to its customers.

Statutory law imposes a fiduciary duty on the bank when the bank engages in certain specific kinds of activities. Under Section 11 of the Regulation of Investment Advice, Investment Marketing and Investment Portfolio Management Law, 1995, the bank owes a customer a fiduciary duty when it is providing investment counseling. Under Section 8 of the Agency Law, if the bank is operating as an agent for the customer, the bank has a fiduciary duty to the customer as its principal.

The duty to act in good faith and the fiduciary duty are different in several ways. The duty to act in good faith is a duty to act fairly. This includes a duty to act in a manner that reflects consideration of the justified expectations of another party to a transaction and to reveal information central to a transaction. It allows a party to advance its own interests, but in a manner that is not unfair to others.

The fiduciary duty, as conceived in Israeli law, is different. It requires a party to act in a way that protects the interest of the other party, even at the expense of protecting one's own interests. It requires not just fairness, but advancement of another party's interest. The fiduciary duty is therefore much more extensive than the duty of good faith and imposes a heavier burden on the party subject to the duty. *See* Ruth Plato-Shinar, *The Bank's Fiduciary Duty: The Duty of Loyalty*, 20–21 (2010) (in Hebrew). Given the broad dimension of the fiduciary duty, it seems unsurprising that the statutory law has imposed it only in cases in which the party having the duty is powerful, the party owed the duty is vulnerable, or the duty corresponds with the reasonable expectations of the parties.

The case presented below departs from the statutory arrangements by applying the fiduciary duty to a much broader set of transactions. Chief Justice Shamgar read a fiduciary duty into all dealings between the bank and its customer. The precise content of that duty would depend on the type of transaction and the circumstances under which it occurred. This broad fiduciary duty, because it is generally more demanding of the bank than the duty of good faith, effectively replaces that less stringent obligation.

Before reading the case, it is helpful to understand several aspects of banking in Israel. The case makes reference to the customer's dependence on the bank. A person's bank account is central to everyday life in Israel. Most everyday financial transactions run through a person's personal bank account. It is almost a universal practice that pay is deposited by the employer in the employee's bank account. Public subsidies, including social security, income supplements (welfare payments), child payments, maternity leave pay, and military reserve duty pay, as well as private pension payments are also deposited directly into the beneficiary's bank account. Most people have their utility bills, insurance payments, local taxes, mortgage payments, and credit card payments withdrawn automatically from their bank accounts. While some people have these types of relationships with their banks in the United States, virtually everyone in Israel has such an extensive relationship. In addition, banks give investment advice and run investment funds, although they have competition from private brokers in these fields.

Construction financing is handled in a manner in which the bank as construction lender and the purchaser as borrower are intertwined. This is explained in Section A of this chapter. If the purchaser takes a loan from the bank and uses the proceeds to pay the apartment developer, and the developer uses the purchaser's funds to repay the construction loan to the same bank during the period of construction, the bank is using the purchaser's liability on the loan as a way of protecting its own interest in having the construction loan repaid.

Israel does not have the variety of types of financial institutions that are found in the United States. Israel has no savings and loan associations and no credit unions. Deposit accounts are handled only by banks, and banks are the only commercial sources of loans.

Most Israeli loans are *linked*. Because the Israeli currency is typically considered a soft currency, the principal of the loan may be linked to the relative value of a hard currency, such as the dollar, or to a measure of purchasing power. Linkage to a measure of purchasing power was discussed in chapter 6, in the context of contract terms. A loan can also be linked to a measure of purchasing power, but many loans are linked to an indicator related to the value of some hard currency, such as the pound, the dollar, or the Euro. Loans may be linked to an external interest rate, such as the Libor, the London Interbank Offered Rate, a measure of the interest rates banks in London charge each other on interbank loans.

Here is an example of what happens with a loan linked to the dollar: If a person borrows NIS 6000 and repays 10 percent (NIS 600) (plus interest, of course) in the first year, you might assume that the remaining debt is NIS 5400. That is not true, due to the linkage. Assume the value of the shekel was NIS 3 to the dollar at the start of the loan but has fallen to NIS 4 to the dollar at the end of the first year. In this case, the original debt was $2000 (6000 ÷ 3). The payment of 10 percent reduced the principle of the debt to by only $150, because the payment was made at the end of the year and, by then, the value of the shekel against the dollar had dropped. The payment was 600 shekel, which would have been worth $200 at the beginning of the year, but was worth only $150 at the end of the year when the payment was made. The $150 payment is subtracted from the original $2000, so the amount now due on the principle is $1850. In shekel terms, this is NIS 7400 ($1850 x 4 shekel/dollar). In other words, after payment of a principal of NIS 600 on a loan of NIS 6000, the borrower owes the bank NIS 7400. This illustration, while exaggerated due to the large drop assumed in the value of the shekel, shows how difficult it is for an Israeli borrower to get out of debt when taking a loan linked to hard currency, and how important the issue of linkage is. The problem caused to the borrower by linkage is exacerbated by the fact that wages and other sources of income, such as investments in Israeli companies, are usually not linked and typically do not rise in value at a rate sufficient to keep pace with the effect of linkage.

When an individual borrows money from a bank to finance purchase of either a new or existing apartment, the borrower usually can chose among a variety of types of loans that differ in interest rates, whether the rate is fixed or adjustable, term of the loan, whether the loan is linked, and the measure to which it is linked. (Loans without linkage usually have higher interest rates.) In many cases, the borrower can split a loan into parts, with each part having different characteristics as to some or all of these parameters.

Israeli Case

Tefahot Mortgage Bank of Israel, Ltd. v. Tsabach
CA 5893/91 58(2) PD 573[1994]

[Respondents borrowed money from the bank to acquire apartments being built by a construction company that had itself taken substantial construction loans from the bank. The bank knew that the construction company was in serious financial trouble. As it turned out, the company could not complete the construction of the apartments. When the construction company became bankrupt, a deal was worked out with some of the purchasers that would require them to pay additional sums. The respondents in this case were not part of that deal. They did not think it worthwhile to pay the additional sums and sued the bank, asking that the loan agreement be cancelled and that all sums that they had paid the bank on the loan be returned to them. The district court granted them the requested relief and the bank appealed to the Supreme Court.]

Chief Justice M. Shamgar:

The set of relationships between a customer (and, in my opinion, even a person who is not a customer) and the bank is of a special character, which flows from the trust the general public puts in this institution. The bank and its employees are seen by the public as an institution with professional standing, due in part to the fact the bank has information on matters not transparent to the general public. As a financial institution, the bank has special qualifications and technical means available to it that are not available to the private person. All these factors put the bank in a position where it can prevent injury to its customers in ways the customers cannot do for themselves. Because a private party often puts a special degree of trust in the bank, believing in its qualifications and technical abilities and seeing it as a quasi-public body, the private party tends not to exercise the normal measure of caution in order to prevent being harmed, even if the party has the power to do so.

Due to this special set of relationships, special duties are imposed on the bank, duties that are not imposed on the parties to a regular contract.

At the heart of this case is the analysis of two of the obligations imposed on the bank as to its various customers, the obligation of confidentiality and the obligation of disclosure, and the relationship between them.

The matter will be examined thus:

(1) First, we will determine the components and scope of the obligation of confidentiality imposed on the bank.

(2) Second, we shall examine the nature of the relationship between the bank and its customers, for the purpose of establishing a fiduciary duty, which is greater than the duties imposed on the parties to a regular contract.

(3) Third, we shall show that the business relationship that creates the fiduciary duty sometimes imposes an enhanced duty of disclosure on the bank, a duty that exceeds the duty of disclosure that is imposed on the parties to a routine contract, and that the scope of this duty is not fixed, but can vary with the type of activity in which the bank was engaged.

(4) Fourth, we shall establish the test for balancing between the above obligations in cases in which they conflict. This test must take into account the relative importance of the obligations imposed on the bank and the arrangements the par-

ties would have wanted at the beginning of the transaction. My conclusion is that, under this test, the Appellant in the case before us acted improperly. Therefore we should affirm the result below and deny the appeal.

[On the first question, Chief Justice Shamgar concluded that the bank had a duty of confidentiality based on its contractual relationship with the borrower. In this case, that duty applied to the bank's relationship with the construction company is its role as a borrower from the bank. He added, though, that this duty of confidentiality was limited by other legal duties imposed on the bank by law.]

As to the obligations imposed on a bank, we note the obligations imposed on it under The Banking Law (Customer Service), 5741-1981, which imposes on the bank additional obligations that are unique to this relationship.

Israeli case law interprets the system of relationships between the bank and the customer as a system that imposes fiduciary duties on the bank in relation to the customer. Thus it was decided in CrimA 122/84 *Mantsour v. State of Israel* 38(4) PD 94, 101 [1984] that:

> In all matters relating to the funds of the customers that it is holding, the bank and its officers are to act in the best interests of the customer. The relationship between the bank and the customer is one in which the customer depends on the bank. Furthermore, the conflicting loyalty that is likely to arise in balancing the good of the customer against the earnings of the bank requires a great deal integrity, honesty, and fairness. Because of the wealth of information in the hands of the bank's employees and the dependence of the customer on the advice provided by these employees and on the services they provide, the opportunity for corruption may arise.

A relation of trust exists between the banks and their customers, and customers place the responsibility for managing their financial affairs in the hands of the banks' employees. These employees owe a duty to all customers and to the public in general to carry out their duties with a high level of integrity and without regard to concerns other than the interest of the customers.

The same rule is found in CA1/75 *Mortgage Bank of Israel, Ltd. v. Hershko* 29(2) PD 208, 211[1975]: "While it is indisputably true that a person is obligated under a contract he signs, it is also true that the bank has a special fiduciary duty to its customers."

Dr. Ricardo Ben-Oliel concludes that the bank has a fiduciary duty to its customers:

> The power of the bank over the ordinary customer, who depends on the bank's services (the conditions of which are usually determined by the bank in a contract of adhesion), leads to the formation of a special obligation of the bank to the customer, which is a fiduciary duty. The goal of this obligation is that the bank will perform its job in the best possible manner in light of all circumstances.

> In relation to bank services, the customer is often dependant on the bank, not only for performing the service, but also for determining the legal rules that apply to the relationship. In addition, the relationship of the customer to the bank is based primarily on the customer's trust in the expertise of the bank in providing services. The customer legitimately believes that in providing these services the bank will conduct itself according to the highest standards of professionalism, fairness, and excessive care; that is, the customer believes that the bank will follow work and management practices that are higher than might be followed by a business other than a bank.

Dr. Ariel Porat did a good job of summarizing this point in his essay, where he said:

> Customers and others alike typically place a special degree of trust in a banker with whom they are in contact, as well as in qualifications of the bank and in its technical abilities. Frequently they do not need another opinion before they follow the bank's advice in some matter, nor do they check out any review of the bank's activities. It is true that this trust was undermined over time, as a result of a few events that impacted the public, especially the bank shares crisis of 1983.[2] But this lack of trust relates to the banking system in general, and not to the bank employee with whom a person has dealings on a daily basis. This employee is generally regarded as a trustworthy person who will provide the public with professional, fair services. The public functions that the banks supply only serve to strengthen this impression. The banks, on their part, work diligently to increase the public's trust in them. Thus, it is reasonable to impose obligations on the banks that are meant to realize the reasonable expectations, which they themselves contribute to creating.

On the other hand, we should not conclude that the bank's obligation to the customer is the same in all cases. The scope of the obligation and extra degree of loyalty required of the bank varies from case to case and depends on the nature of the relationships between the customer and the bank, the degree of the bank's involvement in these relationships, and other factors. The relationship between the bank and the customer is found in many different kinds of banking activities, and the extent of the bank's obligation depends on the type of activity. The degree of loyalty required of the bank acting as an investment advisor is different from that required when the bank is providing a loan to the customer. Similarly the standard is different when the bank deals with a loan to a customer for some transaction than when the bank deals with a person who is providing security for the debts of third parties to the bank. Furthermore, it is not clear whether the same standard of behavior applies to the bank's dealings with an account holder as to its dealings with a person who only takes a one-time loan from a bank. The scope of the duty owed by the bank also depends on the degree to which the customer justifiably depends on the bank in a specific case.

I am aware of the fact that under the law of England and the common law rule, the relationship between the bank and the customer is not generally defined as entailing a fiduciary duty as to most matters, but that such a duty may be created in particular cases in light of the actions of the bank. This is set out in E.P. Ellinger, *Modern Banking Law* (1987):

> The reliance on the bank's advice is usually the crucial matter for determining the presence of a fiduciary relationship. It must be shown that the customer placed the required degree of reliance on the bank's advice, and that the bank was aware of his attitude. The bank's mere failure to volunteer advice does not necessarily lead to the creating of a fiduciary relationship.

Thus, in England, it is necessary to show that there was a certain degree of reliance on the bank by the customer, and that the bank knew of this reliance, before a fiduciary duty is imposed.

Similarly the approach in the United States is that the relationship between the bank and the customer is not a relationship of trust, but that such a relationship may be formed

---

2. This is a reference to the events that led up to the case of HCJ 935/89 Ganor v. Attorney General 44(2) PD 485 [1990], discussed in chapters 6 and 9.

in various circumstances. The case law frequently refers to the fiduciary duty in relationship to the bank's duty of disclosure to the customer.

The courts have traditionally viewed the relationship between a bank and a depositor to be one of a debtor-creditor, the bank's obligation being merely to return the sum deposited, upon demand made by a depositor. And this relationship, it has been further recognized, does not ordinarily impose a fiduciary duty of disclosure upon the bank. Annotation, *Existence of Fiduciary Relationship between Bank and Depositor or Customer so as to Impose Special Duty of Disclosure upon a Bank*, 70 A.L.R. 3d 1344, 1347 (1976).

Thus for example, a case regarding the statute that applies in the state of Texas ruled that under Texas law there is not general fiduciary obligation between

> a lender and a borrower or between business parties.... A fiduciary relationship may arise in some circumstances, however, when "moral, social, domestic or purely personal relationships" are shown to exist between the parties.... Similarly the existence of "a professional and close personal friendship" between the parties may also establish a fiduciary relationship. *In re Letterman Bros. Energy Securities Litigation*, 799 F.2d 967, 975 (5th Cir. 1986).

In my opinion, today, in light of economic and industrial development and the important place of the banks in such activity, it would be an error to maintain that the relationships between the bank and its customers, or even between the bank and the person seeking to borrow money, is a relationship that can be characterized as a regular debtor-creditor relationship. In almost all cases, the bank serves as a financial advisor in investment matters and provides advice even as to the type of loan that it is best to take, the best way to spread the payments on such loans, the variable interest rates, etc.

Furthermore, the bank employee is viewed by the customer as a trustworthy person who can be relied upon, and the customer often accepts the employee's advice as to financial matters.... Therefore I think we should separate ourselves from the view of the common law as seen in England and the United States, and rule ... that the relationship between the customer and the bank is based in large measure on trust, and it is only in exceptional circumstances that it is merely a borrower-lender relationship in the traditional sense.

Hints of this approach can be found even in the United States, in the fiduciary duty that applies to the bank in relation to the obligation of disclosure imposed on it:

> Present day commercial transactions are not, as in the past, primarily for cash; rather, modern banking practices involve a highly complicated structure of credit and other complexities which often thrust a bank into the role of an adviser, a role that banks have accepted to the extent that they now frequently advertise [themselves as providing confidential services. And as banking practices] have changed, increasing recognition has been given to the view that certain bank-customer relationships—often characterized in general terms by the courts as relationships going beyond the conventional bank-depositor relationship, or as relationships of trust and confidence—may impose a fiduciary duty upon the bank to disclose facts when dealing with the customer. [Citing the A.L.R. annotation cited above.]

Therefore in Israel, it has been determined that the relationship between the bank and the customer is one involving a fiduciary duty of the bank. The degree to which the customer relies on the bank and its operations has led not only to the creation of this obligation, but also to the determination of its scope and characteristics. As we have said, the scope and characteristics will change depending on the circumstances of specific cases, in light of the nature of the relationship and the type of bank operations involved. So, for example, when a bank advises a customer to invest in a specific mutual fund in which the bank has an interest, the fiduciary obligation imposed on the bank will be broader than in the case in which the bank gives a customer a loan without any knowledge of what the customer intends to do with the borrowed funds.

One of the Obligations is the Duty to Disclose

From what we have said we can see that, based on the fiduciary duty imposed on it, the bank has an obligation to disclose to its customers the essential facts of a transaction, and that this duty is more extensive than that imposed on the sides of a regular contract. Just as the scope of the fiduciary duty changes from case to case, so does the scope of the duty of disclosure.

We should emphasize that the obligation of disclosure applies only as to information that is in the hands of the bank.

In the present case, the question arises whether the bank's obligation of disclosure extends beyond the technical matters of the percent of interest, the term of the loan, etc. and applies also to matters indirectly related to the loan, such us how the borrower will use the loan, the nature of that use, whether the use is economically worthwhile, etc. In the normal case, the bank's obligation of disclosure does not reach such matters. When a person borrows money for a certain financial transaction, the bank does not need to review the borrower's economic calculations.

In such cases, the bank is the one who funds that transaction but does not know its details. Even if in some case the bank knows the nature of the transaction, it cannot serve as a financial advisor to its customers, reviewing their activities and pointing them in the right direction. The American case law, for example, concluded in more than one case that in situations such as these, there is no obligation of disclosure because there arises no fiduciary duty that would require such disclosure. (See, for example, the minority opinion in *Barnett Bank of West Florida v. Hooper*, 498 So.2d 923 (Fla. 1986).) But there are other cases in which the bank's involvement in the borrower's transaction extends far beyond that of the involvement in the regular case, and the bank's position is not just that of the party that finances the transaction. In such cases, where the customer's reliance on the bank is more extensive, the degree of duty which the bank owes the customer is also more extensive, as is the scope of the duty of disclosure. This may be the case, for example, when the bank advises the customer to act in a certain manner or persuades the customer to take a loan for certain purposes, and the customer relies on such advice from the bank. The bank's degree of duty is even higher when the bank has its own interest in having the customer act in a certain manner. This is true, for example, when the bank persuades the customer to invest in the bank's own subsidiary. In such cases, the bank must disclose to the customer its connection to the subsidiary as well as other relevant facts and must allow the customer to check out its advice and to exercise independent judgment on the investment, with full consideration of the bank's interest in the matter. I think that even if the bank does not give the customer advice about the use of the loan but knows what the customer intends to do, and the bank has a clear and substantial interest in giving the loan for this purpose, the bank must disclose that interest. Such an obligation of disclosure assures that the bank will act fairly.

On this subject it may be said that:

> The particular degree of trust that the public in general and the customer in particular has in the bank (or its employees), and the possible conflict of interest be-

tween what is good for the bank and what is good for the customer, requires special care on the part of the bank. It can be assumed that there will even be cases in which the bank will be required to give advice to the customer even if the customer does not ask for that advice, because the customer will not know how essential such advice is.

In my opinion, if there are circumstances in which it is appropriate to impose on the bank a duty to give advice, it is clearer that we should impose a duty of disclosure as to its possible conflict of interests in some transaction. The bank should inform the customer that the bank has a specific interest in the financial transaction the customer is about to undertake. We do not mean cases where the bank's interest is just in collecting a fee for its services, but where the bank has an essential interest in the transaction going through, based on interests beyond those connected to its transaction with the customer.

The Test for Balancing the Different Obligations

What should a bank do when there is a conflict between its various obligations? How should it behave when, on the one hand, there is an obligation of confidentiality to one customer, but at the same time and in connection with the same transaction, there is an obligation of disclosure to another customer?

This question has arisen in several cases in American law, and different judges have different positions on the matter. A good example of such a conflict can be found in *Richfield Bank and Trust Co. v. Sjogren*, 244 N.W. 2d 648 (Minn. 1976). In that case, the bank granted a loan to a customer without prior advice or pressure on the customer to take the loan. Still, despite the absence of such pressure, the court ruled that, due to the circumstances of the case, the bank had a duty of disclosure in light of its positive knowledge of fraud by the company in which the customer was investing his money. The fraud was in the fact that without any doubt the company knew that it would not be able to meet its contractual undertakings to the same customer. On this matter, the court said:

> We hold that under the unique and narrow "special circumstances" of this case, in which the bank had actual knowledge of the fraudulent activities of one of its depositors, it had an affirmative duty to disclose those facts to the Respondents before it engaged in making the loan to Respondents which furthered the fraud.

Despite the determination that an obligation to disclose applied, the court was aware of that this determination was problematic in that it was likely to conflict with the bank's obligation of confidentiality which it owed to a company that had a contract with the bank. Because of this, the court said the following:

> The determination of whether the facts of this case fall within a special category of circumstances which would justify imposing on the bank the duty to disclose the financial condition of its depositor ... is complicated by the principle that the bank is generally under a duty not to disclose the financial condition of its depositors.

The court determined that in this situation, the burden was on the bank and not on the parties, and the bank must take steps to prevent the occurrence of a situation in which there is a conflict between its duties to different customers:

> We recognize, as stated herein, that disclosing facts concerning a depositor may, under some circumstances, constitute a breach of the bank's duty to its depositors not to disclose confidential information. In circumstances to [sic] which that may be the case, the bank should simply refuse to make the loan. A bank should not undertake any duty to a new customer when to do so involves either

furtherance of fraud or breach of its duty to an existing customer. *Id.* at 652, note 2.

That is, in circumstances such as these, the bank should refuse to give a loan. It is notable that in the same matter, the court emphasized the personal connection between the loan officer and the company that perpetrated the fraud—the officer was the only bank employee that dealt with the company's bank account, loaned money to people in the company from his person funds, and received benefits from them in return. It also was clear that this bank officer took an active role in decisions of the company.

Another case in which an American court examined the topic at hand was *Barnett Bank of West Florida v. Hooper*, 498 So. 2d 923 (Fla. 1986). In this case as well the bank did not reveal to one borrower information about another customer that was crucial to the borrower's loan transaction. The bank assumed the borrower was going to use the borrowed funds to invest in the second customer and was to transfer the borrowed funds to the second customer's account. The bank was suspicious that the second customer was using this account for fraudulent activities. In this case, the court also found as a matter of fact that if the loan were not made, the bank would suffer a loss, but that with the loan, the funds of which were deposited in the second customer's account, the amount of the overdraft on the second account would be reduced.

The opinion of the court on the case was divided. The majority held:

> Where a bank becomes involved in a transaction with a customer with whom it has established a relationship of trust and confidence and it is a transaction from which the bank is likely to benefit at the customer's expense, the bank may be found to have assumed a duty to disclose facts material to the transaction that are peculiarly within its knowledge and not otherwise available to the customer. Where the bank defends its breach of duty on the ground that it owes a conflicting duty of confidentiality to a second customer, the jury is entitled to weigh the one duty against the other. *Id.* at 925.

The jury, or in our case the court, will engage in balancing the obligation of the bank to one customer against its obligation to the second customer, and based on this balance, will determine the scope of the obligation of disclosure if one is found.

Against this, the minority opinion would have held that the evidence in the case was insufficient to establish the duty discussed and that the obligation of confidentiality toward one customer should not easily be breached because

> there was nothing in the evidence sufficient to establish that the bank had the relation and duties of a fiduciary with regard to Dr. Hooper and because under the circumstances I do not believe the bank's duty of confidentiality to its other customer can be so lightly swept aside. *Id.* at 926.

The judges in the minority added that there is a closed list of exceptions to the obligation of confidentiality, because adding exceptions would be burdensome for banking operations in reducing the level of certainty that is so necessary in this area.

> Settled case law defines the circumstances under which the duty of confidentiality can be relaxed. Any further "special circumstances" providing exceptions are burdensome for financial institutions because their officers are thereby required to predict what a jury will do. *Id.* at 929.

We have thus seen that American law offers a number of solutions to those situations in which there is a conflict between the bank's duties toward its customers. Judges there, weighing the duty of confidentiality against the obligation to disclose, disagree as to the appropriate balance.

In my opinion, we should not now set out a general rule to govern the proper balance between the different duties imposed on banks in relationships with their customers. This case involves a conflict between the duty of confidentiality to the construction company and the duty of disclosure as to the Respondents, and we will deal with this specific case. Other cases of conflict will be dealt with in the future on the basis of their specific facts, and so that law will develop over time.

In my opinion, when we are dealing with a mortgage loan, a loan which, by its nature, has a vast effect on the future of the borrowers (especially for mortgages given to a specific sector of the population—young couples ...), and the relationship between the borrower, the bank and the contractor is a close one (generally the contractor brings the customer to the bank) and the bank knows what will be done with the funds loaned, and the bank knows that the company to which these funds will be given will not be able to meet its obligations, and the bank has a substantial interest in having the flow of funds to that company continue, the balance between the obligation of confidentiality and the obligation of disclosure requires the bank to inform the customer of the bank's conflict of interests. I think that this is a desirable result, representing the proper balance between the obligation of disclosure that applies to the bank and the obligation of confidentiality. In fact, the latter is not compromised by the obligation of disclosure in that the bank need not reveal substantive details about the company. The burden placed on the bank is not too great. In such cases, it is sufficient if the bank tells the customer taking out the loan that due to the conflict of interests of the bank, and the duty of the bank to the borrower and to the customer to whom the borrowed funds are to be transferred, the bank will not engage in the transaction requested.

Because the Appellant did not conduct itself in this manner, I think it appropriate to adopt the decree of the district court that the mortgage agreements are invalid and that there is no obligation to make payments under those agreements. This is subject to the requirement that the appellees transfer their rights in the apartments to the bank.

The appeal is rejected.

Comments

This case of *Tefahot Mortgage Bank of Israel, Ltd. v. Tsabach* shows clearly the way in which Israeli law is a mixed law system. As we saw in chapter 15, the statutory law on contracts that underlies much of banking law in Israel is derived from the civil law system in general and from German law in particular. The court recognized this law but went beyond it. The opinion quotes extensively from common law sources, English and especially American, in developing the theory of the bank's fiduciary duty, which does not derive from the Israeli statutes. Yet the way the Court applies the fiduciary duty is peculiarly Israeli. The breadth of the application of the duty goes far beyond the application in American law, where the fiduciary duty is usually confined to defined types of transactions and specific circumstances.

The case rules that the bank has a fiduciary duty to its customers. That decision was essential to the outcome of the case. The plaintiff borrowed money in order to make payments on an apartment to the developer. The bank knew that this was the plaintiff's intention and also knew that there was a good chance that the developer could not complete the project. The plaintiff blamed the bank for not telling him about the developer's problems; if the plaintiff had known, the plaintiff would not have taken the loan and would not be stuck having invested money in a now-unfinished apartment. The bank argued that the developer was a borrower and customer and the bank owed it a duty not to harm it by disclosing its business with the bank. This was an obligation of confidentiality that would prevent the bank from telling the plaintiff that the developer was in financial trouble. The duty not to disclose the developer's business is a duty only not to act. The plaintiff argued that the bank had an affirmative duty to disclose information or take affirmative steps to protect the plaintiff's interest. In order to find the duty to disclose, the Court found that the bank owed its customers a fiduciary duty, which could entail the duty to take affirmative steps to protect their interests.

Question

1. What considerations led the Court *in Tefahot Mortgage Bank v. Tsabach* to impose, or recognize, a general fiduciary duty of banks towards their customers?

Having established that the bank owed the plaintiff a fiduciary duty which might include a duty to disclose, the Court turned to the question of how the duties owed to different customers must be balanced against each others. It does not enunciate a definitive rule as to how the bank is to perform this balance. The Court said this must be decided on a case-by-case basis in light of the specific facts of each case. This gives little guidance to bankers who want to know just what they must do and what they may not do. On the other hand, the case-by-case approach is understandable in light of the large number of situations in which a bank may find it has conflicting obligations to different customers.

In the *Tsabach* case, the Court pointed to two factors which influenced it in performing the balance: the bank (1) knew the money would be used for a bad investment and (2) stood to gain from this use. The Court ruled that that result of the balance in this case was that the bank should have refused to give the loan. It is interesting to try to imagine the conversation of the loan officer with the purchaser applying for the loan. The bank officer would inform the purchaser that the bank would not provide the required loan. The purchaser would ask whether the reason the bank refused to give the loan was that the purchaser was not credit-worthy. The bank's loan officer would have to answer in honesty that this was not the reason. The purchaser would then naturally ask what the reason was, and the loan officer would have to say something about a conflict of interest, but refuse to divulge just what that conflict was. The Court was clear that the bank's obligation of confidentiality to the developer would prevent it from disclosing the developer's financial problems. The upshot would be that the sophisticated customer would understand what was happening and realize that the developer was not reliable. According to what the Court said, the bank would have to refuse to give the purchaser a loan due to a conflict of interests only if it knew the developer was in trouble. The customer who knew the case law would understand that the refusal was probably a sign that the customer should not purchase the apartment. The unsophisticated customer—the typical young couple posited by the court—would be confused.

Perhaps the young couple would apply to another lender, who might ask them to reveal that whether they had applied for a loan elsewhere and been refused. They would acknowledge that this had happened, but could not give much detail on the reason for the refusal. The second lender might fear that there was a problem with their creditworthiness and might refuse them. Alternatively, the second lender might sense that it would be worthwhile to check out the project. Perhaps the second lender would smell that something was wrong somewhere and refuse the loan, keeping the naïve borrowers safe but uninformed on why they could not get a loan to purchase the apartment they want. Or the borrowers might get the loan from the second bank and then wind up in trouble due to the developer's failure to complete the project. In this case, they would not have any recourse against the second lender that had neither the knowledge nor the conflict of interest of the first lender.

On a more general level, the duty of the bank as a fiduciary has been described by a leading Israeli scholar on banking law in these terms:

> The bank is obliged to act with integrity and fairness. It must also act with professionalism and skill. Underpinning the fiduciary duty is the bank's duty to exercise the power vested in the bank without abusing it. The key words are loyalty and fidelity. The bank *as a fiduciary* is required to perform its duties solely for the purpose for which the power was vested in it, without ulterior motives and while protecting the interest of the beneficiary—the customer. Moreover the bank must prefer the interest of the customer to the interests of others, including its own self-interest. In fact, the bank may under no circumstances be in a situation of a conflict of interests. The fear is that the bank might not withstand temptation and might not promptly guard the interest of the customer before its own interest.
>
> By virtue of the fiduciary duty, the bank is prohibited from receiving any benefit from a third party; prohibited from competing with a customer's business or taking advantage of a customer's business opportunity; prohibited from making a profit, in any manner, from the performance of its duties; and prohibited from misleading the customer. Moreover the fiduciary duty includes not only prohibitions or negative obligations, but also positive obligations, such as the obligation of broad disclosure to the customer; the obligation to provide explanations, including legal explanations with regard to the nature of the transaction and its results; and, of course, the obligation of maintaining confidentiality. Ruth Plato-Shinar, *An Angel named 'The Bank': The Bank's Fiduciary Duty as the Basic Theory in Israeli Banking Law*, 36 Comm. L. World Rev. 27, 29–30 (2007).

The duty may include a requirement that the bank explain the relevant documents to the customer and even the duty to be sure that the customer understands those documents. Ruth Plato-Shinar, *The Bank's Fiduciary Duty, supra*, at 235–43 (2010) (in Hebrew).

In the case above, the beneficiary of the bank's fiduciary duty was the mortgage loan customer, and, to some extent, also the construction company that had an account with the bank. But note the language that Chief Justice Shamgar added in parentheses at the beginning of the portion of his opinion that is presented here. Attorneys, courts, and the Knesset have latched on to that language to explore the question of whether banks owe a fiduciary duty to those who are not bank customers.

The fiduciary duty of the bank was extended to guarantors by legislation after case law rejected such an extension. Plato-Shinar, *An Angel Named 'The Bank', supra*, at 41–42. A guarantor is a person who provides a legal assurance that if the primary debtor does not pay a debt to the bank, the guarantor will pay.

The following case considers extension of the duty beyond customers and guarantors who deal with the bank.

Israeli Case

A. & G. Advanced Systems for Driving Instructors Ltd. v. Bank Leumi of Israel Ltd. Rehovot Branch

Permission for CA 9374/04 (Sept. 11, 2004)

[The bank refused to honor fourteen checks drawn on the account of the petitioner.[3] The petitioner brought a legal action requesting that the bank be forced to honor the checks because it had a reasonable basis for assuming that the bank would indeed honor them.[4] The petitioner claimed that he had an agreement with the bank under which the petitioner could exceed its overdraft limit. The petitioner also claimed that it had given the security assets in excess of the amount of the overdraft and, further, that the bank had honored even larger overdrafts in the past. Finally the petitioner claimed that the bank's refusal to honor the checks was not in good faith, but rather was based on the bank's desire to disrupt the petitioner's transaction with a third party that would require the petitioner to move its account to another bank. The lower court determined that the bank had lowered the petitioner's overdraft limit, the petitioner knew this, and there was no agreement to allow the larger overdraft. On appeal, the district court affirmed. The petitioner now asks permission for an appeal to the Supreme Court.]

Justice E. Rubenstein:

The attorney for the Petitioner ... did not convince me ... that this is an appropriate case for a further appeal.

We have here a case in which the district court properly noted the facts. Furthermore, we must take note of the fact that this case arises in the framework of a national calamity of uncovered checks and that there is no choice but to do something about this problem. Therefore I join in that point of view.... which derives from the decisions of Chief Justice Shamgar in various cases: obligations of a public nature are imposed on banks as holders of fiduciary duties as to the public, because they provide necessary services and have great power. I think that in order to protect the consumer and the customer, it is necessary to provide ongoing reinforcement to the supervision of the banks through legislation.... Banks operate first of all as commercial entities. But their special status in the economy also imposes on them public obligations, among them, honesty, fairness, proper disclosure, proportionality, etc. Subject to this, they have the normal obligations of commercial entities. What is the proper balance between these different obligations?

In my opinion, at all times and especially in times of economic hardship, in order to protect the interest of the public, the bank must be careful that credit limitations be honored. Of course, there is a need for a balanced approach that takes into account personal needs and social and ethical values, so as not to interfere excessively with the lives of others and so as to allow room to encourage business activity of small and medium-sized

---

3. The term *Petitioner*, rather than *Appellant*, was used by the Court because this was a petition for an additional appeal which is not a matter of right. As explained in chapter 5, Israeli law provides one appeal as a matter of right. After that, a person must petition for leave to appeal. This case began in the municipal court and was appealed to the district court. The losing party then petitioned the Supreme Court for leave to appeal.

4. It is common in Israel for bank customers to sign authorizations for overdrafts on their checking accounts. The bank sets the limit of the permissible overdraft. The customer pays interest on the overdraft amount. In effect, this is a rolling credit agreement and is referred to as a credit arrangement by the Court.

businesses. On the other hand, there is an obligation not to increase the provision of risky credit. Credit arrangements are based on contracts that include the obligation of good faith that falls on both the bank and the customer. In this case ... both the customer and its accountant were told of the overdraft and warned that the situation could not continue as it was.

The interest in protecting the credit limits and in not allowing excessive overdrafts involves not only the borrower alone, but also the entire public that has a need for credit, so that a situation will not be created in which the "doors are locked before borrowers."[5] [P]roper supervision of bank credit is in the public interest, not only in order keep the door from being locked before borrowers, but also to protect the public purse, which is too often called upon to cover uncontrolled losses caused by anarchy in the credit market. Commercial sense and the public interest bring us to the same conclusion. Uncontrolled credit ... can harm the stability of the bank with widespread consequences, so that an obligation is imposed on both the bank branch and the bank management to protect the limits on credit available to a customer. Of course, the internal bank auditors and the system for supervising the banks must also act appropriately on this issue.

[The request to appeal is denied.]

Comment

Justice Rubenstein's referred to the bank's fiduciary duty to the public. In the case of *Bank Tefahot v. Tsabach*, the bank's failure to meet its fiduciary duty to its customer nullified the loan it had given to the apartment purchasers. In the present case, the bank's fiduciary duty to the public justified the bank's action; i.e., its refusal to extend further credit to its customer. Here, as the court noted, the bank's self-interest and its duty to the public coincided. That leaves open the question of what would happen if the bank's self-interest as a commercial entity and its fiduciary duty to the public were in conflict. Under fiduciary theory, the duty to the public would prevail. On the other hand, the very content of the fiduciary duty to the public as envisioned by Justice Rubenstein is to protect the bank's own solvency. It is not clear, then, how this would work out.

Pay attention to the justifications offered by Justice Rubenstein for imposing on the banks a fiduciary duty to the public. He mentions that banks provide necessary services and that they have great power. It is clear that both of these conditions are factually correct. The question is whether this should be sufficient to impose on banks a fiduciary duty to the public.

In contrast to Justice Rubenstein's view, Dr. Ruth Plato-Shinar argues that imposition of such a duty is not justified. She argues that the very strong fiduciary duty should be based only on a personal relationship, which is missing between the bank and the public as a whole; that determining what the duty entails would be difficult because the public is diverse and has conflicting interests; that the burden on the banks in altering their operations to meet the burdens of a fiduciary duty to the public would be excessive; and that the cost to the banks from curtailed activities might endanger their stability, which is also important to the public. *See* Ruth Plato-Shinar, *An Angel Named 'The Bank'*, *supra*, at 46–47. Elsewhere it has been argued that for banks to conduct their business,

---

5. This is a term from Jewish law sources, which refer to the case in which borrowers are so protected by the law and creditors so disadvantaged that creditors simply stop providing loans, leaving borrowers without recourse. During the period in which this law developed, the concern was for poor farmers who needed loans in order to finance the sowing of their crops.

they need rules with a high degree of certainty that they can follow. Marcia Gelpe, Ruth Plato-Shinar, & Amichai Kerner, *Lender Liability for Environmental Harm Caused by Borrowers: The American Experience as a Model for Determining the Proper Israeli Arrangements*, 50 HaPraklit 439, 495–7 (2010) (in Hebrew). Certainty is not provided by a vague concept of a fiduciary duty to the public, the content of which can change from case to case. It could be provided by regulatory oversight that defined the duties of the bank in clear terms.

Both of these cases demonstrate two tendencies in Israeli case law: entering into areas treated by statute and adding judicial requirements to those required in the statute, and leaving open the details of just what is required by the court-announced legal doctrine. This later tendency creates great difficulty for those who plan their activities with legal requirements in mind, such as large commercial entities and governmental agencies.

Question

2. How would you advise a bank that is your client to adjust its activities in reaction to what is said in this case about the bank's fiduciary duty to the public?

American law on the fiduciary duty of banks is substantially different from Israeli law. The bank-customer relationship in itself does not create a fiduciary relationship. Most courts will, however, impose a fiduciary duty where special circumstances of an individual case justify doing so. Factors courts consider in deciding whether to impose on a lender a fiduciary duty to a borrower include the lender's power over the borrower, the borrower's actual reliance on the lender, the duration of the relationship between the lender and the borrower, and whether the lender benefited from the loan in a degree that exceeds the usual profit from placing a loan. Thus, where a borrower has been a customer of a bank for more than twenty years, had a pattern of trusting a bank officer, and that officer acted as a financial advisor, a fiduciary relationship between the bank officer—and possibly the bank—and the customer might be imposed. *Deist v. Wachholtz*, 678 P.2d 188 (Mont. 1984).

Similarly the cases discussed in the *Bank Tefahot v. Tsabach* decision involved special circumstances. In *Barnett Bank of West Florida v. Hooper*, the bank's behavior was especially egregious. The bank officer had advised Hooper, the borrower, that the investment he planned to make with another bank customer was sound. Later, Hooper sought to borrow more money for another investment with the same person. By that time, the bank was already suspicious that the second bank customer was running an illegal check kiting scheme. The loan was nonetheless made to Hooper, who deposited it in the second bank customer's account. The bank benefited directly from this deposit; without it, the second customer's account would have been overdrawn by approximately the same amount. Under these facts, the court held that the bank could be found to have a fiduciary duty to Hooper to disclose information about the problems with the second transaction. The court was quite explicit, though, that it was discussing only whether the bank had a fiduciary duty to disclose and that it was imposing that duty due to the special circumstances of the case.

In *Richfield Bank and Trust Co. v. Sjogren*, also discussed in *Bank Tefahot v. Tsabach*, Sjogren borrowed money from the bank to purchase equipment from National Pollution, another bank customer. The jury found that the bank knew that National Pollution had no reasonable prospect of being able to meet the order for the equipment. In fact, the bank officer involved was deeply enmeshed in National Pollution's affairs and had received travel and other benefits from that company. Under these circumstances, the court found that the bank had a duty to disclose its knowledge that National Pollution could not fulfill the order to Sjogren. It based this duty on the requirement that the bank not further a fraud on the borrower; it did not discuss specifically whether there was a fiduciary duty.

The cases do not impose a general fiduciary duty on a bank as a lender. When examining not only these cited cases, but the full range of American cases on the topic, it becomes apparent that the outcomes are highly fact sensitive, and cases with seemingly similar facts may have different outcomes. Thus, sometimes even in the presences of special circumstances, and certainly in their absence, American courts refuse to treat the lender-borrower relationship as fiduciary in nature. On the American approach, see Niels B. Schaumann, *The Lender as Unconventional Fiduciary*, 23 Seton Hall L. Rev. 21 (1992). Clearly the American position is far different from that of the Israeli courts. Professor Eileen Scallen has argued that the imposition of a fiduciary duty on American banks should be expanded. Eileen A. Scallen, *Promises Broken vs. Promises Betrayed: Metaphor, Analogy, and the New Fiduciary Principle*, 1993 U. Ill. L. Rev. 897, 946–57. Furthermore, in response to the sub-prime loan crisis, it has been argued that a fiduciary duty should be imposed on mortgage brokers. Cassandra Jones Havard, *"Goin Round in Circles" ... and Letting the Bad Loans Win: When Subprime Lending Fails Borrowers: The Need for Uniform Broker Regulation*, 86 Neb. L. Rev. 737 (2008). Nonetheless, the American position remains far different from that found in the Israeli cases.

Professor Schaumann has pointed out a great difficulty in treating a lender as a fiduciary. A fiduciary must prefer the beneficiary's interest to that of the fiduciary. Yet the lender regularly includes in loan documents all kinds of clauses that are beneficial to the lender and harmful to the borrower. In this regard, he points to acceleration clauses, rights to foreclose and the right to repossess the borrower's property. Schaumann, *supra*, at 39. How, he asks, can this work out in practice? The answer of the Israeli Court is that it depends on the case, but if this answer means that the bank as fiduciary is not required to always put the beneficiary's interest before its own, it calls into question whether the bank is really a fiduciary.

Given the reluctance of American courts to impose on lenders a fiduciary duty owed to borrowers, one would expect them to be even more reluctant to impose a fiduciary duty to guarantors, with whom the lender has a more distant relationship. Some court decisions state that a fiduciary relationship may be imposed as to guarantors in certain circumstances, but decline to find such a relationship. One such decision is *deJong v. Leitchfield Deposit Bank*, 254 S.W. 3rd 817 (Ky. App. 2007). American courts do not recognize financial institutions as having a fiduciary duty to the public as a whole.

Questions

3. What are the relative advantages of the Israeli law and of the American law on whether a bank as lender owes a fiduciary duty to a borrower?

4. Does the Israeli approach to liability of banks seem consistent or inconsistent with other areas of Israeli law on commercial transactions?

5. What differences between Israel and the United States might account for the different approaches to the fiduciary duty of banks?

C. The Global Economic Crisis and the Israeli Economy

Israel suffered much less than the United States from the economic crisis that began in 2007–8. This can be attributed to several factors. First, Israeli banks are more conservative than American lenders in requiring mortgage borrowers to prove their ability to repay a loan. Thus, Israel has seen less of the phenomenon of borrowers unable to make payments out of their current income and banks relying on the increase in value of the property as their main security for mortgage financing. In addition, borrowers generally must make significant down payments before receiving a loan, and those borrowing a high percentage of an apartment's valuation must either purchase insurance or provide guarantors. Typically a purchaser can finance up to 70 percent of an apartment purchase price with a mortgage, and in 2010 there was a move to reduce this percentage. This is far from the 95 percent financing so common in the United States. Young first-time apartment purchasers in Israel often get assistance from their parents in making the required substantial down payment. This may seem to require an extravagant contribution from the parents, but it should be considered in the context of the fact that Israelis pay much less for higher education than do Americans, and students, rather than parents, often pay the tuition.

Second, housing prices in Israel did not go through the extreme increase that was seen in the United States preceding the events of 2008. While Israeli housing prices were high in this period, they were less volatile. The Bank of Israel is active in taking steps to prevent the formation of a housing bubble.

Third, Israeli financial institutions did not have heavy investments in the foreign mortgage-backed securities whose value dropped so precipitously.

Index